KV-245-026

BROMLEY LIBRARIES
30128 005308427

THE HISTORY OF CORNWALL

by

Richard Polwhele

Introduction by

A. L. Rowse

KOHLER AND COOMBES LTD
DORKING
1978

First edition published 1803–1808

This edition published Dorking 1978 by Kohler & Coombes Ltd.

The publishers are indebted to Cornwall County Library for all their help in making this project possible and for providing the original copies of Polwhele from which this reprint has been made.

ISBN 0 903967 11 1

Printed and bound in Great Britain by The Scolar Press Ltd.,
59–61 East Parade, Ilkley, Yorkshire

THE HISTORY OF CORNWALL

by

Richard Polwhele

Volume 3

KOHLER AND COOMBES LTD
DORKING
1978

THE

HISTORY

OF

CORNWALL:

CIVIL, MILITARY, RELIGIOUS, ARCHITECTURAL, AGRICULTURAL, COMMERCIAL, BIOGRAPHICAL, AND MISCELLANEOUS.

BY THE REVEREND R. POLWHELE,

Of Polwhele, and Vicar of Manaccan.

"Jam nunc cogita, quæ potissimum tempora aggrediamur. Vetera et scripta aliis? Parata inquisitio; sed onerosa collatio. Intacta et nova? Graves offensæ; levis gratia. Si laudaveris, parcus: Si culpaveris, nimius fuisse dicaris; quamvis illud plenissime, hoc restrictissime feceris. Sed hæc me non retardant."

"Ad quæ noscenda iter ingredi, transmittere mare solemus; ea sub oculis posita negligimus: Seu quia ita natura comparatum, ut proximorum incuriosi, longinqua sectemur; seu quod omnium rerum cupido languescit, quum facilis occasio est: seu quod differimus, tanquam sæpe visuri quod datur videre, quoties velis cernere. Quacunque de causa, permulta in provincia nostra, non oculis modo, sed ne auribus quidem novimus; quæ si tulisset Achaia, Egyptus, aliave quælibet miraculorum ferax commendatrixque terra, audita, perlecta, lustrataque haberemus." *Plin. Epist.*

VOL. III.

FALMOUTH:

PRINTED BY T. FLINDELL,

FOR CADELL AND DAVIES IN THE STRAND, LONDON.

1803.

CORNWALL ERRATA.

Page 4, FOR unproductive, READ unproductive *in wheat*
7, FOR we have many, READ we have *not* many
15, FOR charters to which I have already referred, there is, READ charters, there is
15, FOR privilege that Truro, READ privilege *which* Truro
36, FOR the, READ they
50, FOR this county, READ Cornwall
60, FOR to empty it, READ to empty *the pool*

THE

HISTORY OF CORNWALL.

BOOK THE SECOND.

FROM VORTIGERN TO EDWARD I.

CHAPTER THE FIFTH.

PASTURAGE, AGRICULTURE, GARDENS, PARKS.

I.—1. AGRICULTURE had been long declining for more than a century in this country; when the Saxons, having fixed themselves in their respective principalities, began to turn their attention to the arts of cultivation. That they much improved the uninclosed country, is by no means probable. It was sufficient to restore to its former fertility, the land which had run to waste amidst the disorder of repeated hostilities. Our extensive commons were again covered with flocks and herds: And many of our stone circles, were converted into sheep-folds, to protect the sheep from wolves and other beasts of prey. The Saxon chief is said to have divided his estate into two parts, the inlands and the outlands. The inlands lying contiguous to the mansion-house of the chieftain, were cultivated by his slaves for the provision of his family: The outlands at a distance from the house, were let to the ceorls or farmers at a certain rent, which was generally paid in kind. The rates of these rents were ascertained by law, according to the number of hides or ploughlands of which a farm consisted. By the laws of Ina our West-Saxon king, a farm containing ten hides (for instance) was to pay, ten casks of honey - - - three hundred loaves of bread - - - twelve casks of strong ale - - - thirty casks of small ale - - - two oxen - - - ten wethers - - - ten geese - - - twenty hens - - - ten cheeses - - - one cask of butter - - - twenty pounds of forage - - - five salmon - - - and one hundred eels. In some situations, we find other articles substituted for several of those which I have recounted: This depended on the nature of the farm, or custom of the country. Yet money-rents for farms were not altogether unknown at this time. During the Normans, there was a continual fluctuation between plenty and scarcity: But still agriculture was not neglected or discouraged. Among the legantine canons made at London by the bishop of Winchester, in the reign of Stephen, there is one which says, "that the plough and husbandman in the fields, should enjoy the same peace as if they were in the churchyard." This sanctuary given to the tillers of land in their own grounds, would have been of great benefit to the public, if duly regarded. But the civil war paid little respect either to spiritual or temporal laws.

2. To speak more particularly of the Pasturage and Agriculture of this county.---The "town of trees,"* still indicated the "barton." Here, on the coarser grounds the sheep and kine were depastured; in the meadows were kept the cows; and on the arable land were produced the bread-corn and other provisions for the family. The sheep of Cornwall were from "*auncientie,*" very small; and their fleeces so coarse that the wool was called Cornish hair; under which name, the cloth manufactured from that wool was allowed to be exported without being subject to the customary duty paid for woollen-cloth. This privilege was confirmed to the Cornish, by Edward the Black Prince, as a privilege derived from their ancestors.† The goat,‡ which requires little assistance from human cultivation, was familiar to the

* "To this day in Cornwall, we call a grove near a dwelling-house, a town of trees. Mine has been called so, ever since my remembrance; and the place where it grows, the town-place or town. This looks like the remains of the old British custom mentioned by Cæsar and Strabo." *Moyle's* Works, v. i. p. 257.

† *Carew*, f. 24.

‡ The Rev. Jer. *Trist*, of Behan Park, and vicar of the parish of Veryan, lately shewed me a skull, I think of some non-descript animal. He found it on the beach at no great distance from his house. From its size it might be judged the skull of a kid: Its apparent horns were of one and the same substance with the skull.

Cornish: And our black cattle that live on heath and furze, where exist no better pastures, are some of the aboriginal race. The process of the dairy in Cornwall, is peculiar to this county, and a part of Devon: It was British; not Saxon or Norman.§ We have various names which indicate the places where the little horses of Cornwall were bred, or ran wild.|| As to the arable part of the farm¶ nothing is more erroneous, than the idea, that the Cornish were, during this period, inattentive to tillage.* Our arish-mows† were indisputably British: but whether the appellation *arish* came from *aridus,* or from the Saxon *eddish,* appears doubtful. If we may believe Hals, *potatoes* were cultivated here even as early as the Normans.‡

3. There are parts of Cornwall, and particular spots, that have been remarkable from the earliest times for fruitfulness or sterility. I shall mention some of the most

§ Our scald-cream-butter will hereafter be described.

|| "Karn-margh beacon, or Carn-marigh, signifyinge rocke wher horses shelter them; It is a heade beacon in Gwynop parish." *Norden,* p. 46.

¶ "The word *Barton,* used in Cornwall and Devon only, is probably derived from *Bara Bread*---the place which affords the lord, bread. I prefer this to the Saxon *Bere hordeum Barley,* whence comes our *beer.*" *Tonkin's MSS.*

* "Richard, king of the Romans and earl of Cornwall, made a grant to the Cornishmen to take sand freely out of the sea, and carry it through the whole county, to manure their ground withal; which was confirmed by Henry 3d.* By which it appears (says *Gibson* in his "Additions to Camden") that, ever since Henry the Third, at least, this hath been the chief way of improving their ground.† And no doubt long before; or there had been no occasion to apply for that grant; which was certainly occasioned by the exactions of owners of lands on the sea-coast. The same author mentions one of Saltash, in the next reign, demanding twelve shillings a year for each barge that carried sand up the Tamar. Such exactions now daily occur. There is an ingenious "Discourse on Sea-sand," by Dr. Dan. Cox, in the Phil. Trans. No. 113. p. 293. Abridg. v. 2. p. 729.

† See book I. chap. 5.----The Cornish names of the twelve months, have some reference to agriculture:---MIS-GENVER, *(January)* i. e. Tenaer, *cold air month.*---MIS-HUEVRAL, *(February)* i. e. Hu evral, *the whirling month.*---MIS-MERH, *(March)* i. e. *the horse month, when the Gauls began to set forth with horses to war.*---MIS-EBRALL, *(April)* i. e. Ebrilly, *the primrose month*; or, A brilly, *the mackarel month, when the Gauls and Normans set out to go to sea for catching mackarel.*---MIZ-ME, *(May)* i. e. *the flowery month.*---MIZ-EPHAN, *(June)* i. e. *the Summer month*; or, *head of Summer.*---MIZ-GOREPHAN, *(July)* i. e. *the chief head of the Summer month.*---MIZ-EAST, *(August)* i. e. Eausti, *the month to get in harvest.*---MIZ-GUEDN-GALA, *(September)* i. e. *the white straw month.*---MIZ-HEDRA, *(October) the watry month*; or, *month of courage.*---I prefer the first.---MIZ-DIU, *(November)* i. e. *the black month.*---MIZ-KEVARDHIN, *(December)* i. e. *the month following the black month*; or, *the black month.*—*In Armoric,* Mis-Querdu, *the month also black.*

‡ *Hals's MSS.*

* R. Chart. de An. 45, Hen. III.

† "They still continue the same method (says Gibson) carrying the sand ten miles up into the country; and for a great part of the way, too, upon horses backs."

fertile. --- The hundred of § Pider has been for ages, famous for its corn; Roseland, for rich enclosures, abundantly productive of all the fruits of the earth; and the district of || Meneg for barley. On the Sylleh Isles, the soil is at present unproductive; good as it is said to be for other sorts of grain. Yet wheat was usually sown on these islands, and seems to have repaid the labour of the husbandman, before the time of Henry the III.¶ As to particular spots, some may be noticed for their *wood; some for their † pastures; others for their corn. A part of that ground between Marazion and Penzance, which had lain a waste for ages, has been recently brought back to a state of cultivation.‡

§ "This hundred lieth stretched out on the north sea, very narrow at the western end, but broader and broader towards the eastern, in the shape of a wedge. It is very fruitful for the most part (especially on the sea coast) in all sorts of grain, and chiefly wheat. The western part at the beginning of it, being barren and open downs, as is also much of the middle of it. But then that defect is made up in the western part by very rich mines of tin, lead, and copper; of which there are some likewise, but not so good, scattered up and down in other parts of it. Some parts of it too being much exposed to the N. W. winds, are covered with sand on the sea shore, and most of it destitute of wood, though not quite so in well-sheltered places, and the most eastern parishes off from the sea in the inland part; which in requital, are much of a coarser soil, with large wastrels and downs intermixed, and abound in sheep." *Walker's MSS.*

|| Mawgan, in the hundred of Kerrier, may be called the isthmus over which we pass to go to the chersonesus of *Meneg* --- this chersonesus containing (with Mawgan) twelve parishes.

¶ "Henry III. commands Drew de Barrentine, governor of his Islands of Scilly, or his bailiffs, that they deliver every year to Ralph Burnet seven quarters of wheat, which Robert Legat used to receive, and which is escheated to the king." Rot. Claus. 32. Hen. III. m. 2." *Borlase's* Scilly, p. 68. note.

* *Calstock*, on the Tamar, is plentiful in oaks; whether its name indicate that circumstance or not. --- *Glynn* hath been for ages well wooded: It signifies, indeed, a woody dale or *glen*. All the banks of the Fawey were once covered with trees. --- *Skewys* (the name of a manor) in Cury, is so called from the *shade* of the many trees originally growing there. --- If, as Leland tells us, there were anciently wild boars, in St. Nicholas or the isle of Trescaw, the isles of Sylleh (or this island at least) could not have been deficient in wood." *Leland*, v. vii. p. 108.

† *Boyton* in Stratton, seems to have taken its name from the quality of its soil; as being adapted for pasture; the Cornish word *byuh*, which is pronounced *boy*, signifying a cow, or ox: --- or perhaps it may have been so denominated from the French word *bois*, which signifies a wood, this part of the country abounding in woods. ---- The manor of *Trevenen*, or *Tremenen*, in St. Goran, derives its name from the fruitfulness of its capital place; signifying "the *butter-town*." ---- The manor of *Trigavethan* in Kea, signifies "the dwellers in the meadows:" And whoever sees the place, will be convinced of the truth of the etymology.

‡ The road from Marazion to Penzance is conducted over a bank of sand, which separates the bay from a large tract of marsh-land. The greater part of the latter is a steril, unprofitable bog: but the laudable exertions of an individual* has rescued and preserved thirty-six acres from the inundations of the tide; and, by skilful management

* Dr. Richard Moyle of Marazion, who has received the gold medal of the "Society for the promotion of arts, manufactures, and commerce;" and also a handsome premium from the Board of Agriculture; as rewards for his successful scheme. The whole quantity of ground under improvement is seventy-five acres.

II. With respect to gardens; I can descend to few particulars. 1. The vine was much cultivated by the Saxons. Vineyards are mentioned by Bede, as early as the commencement of the eighth century.* And there were many vineyards about a thousand years ago, throughout England. The Domesday-book expressly says, that before the Norman conquest, wine was made in the county of Essex. But our gardening was much improved by the Normans, who coming from a country

and perseverance, has obtained several crops of corn and potatoes from the renovated land. The singular process by which this was effected, we are induced to particularize, from a persuasion, that it may be equally serviceable to other persons in similar situations. The whole of this district was occasionally covered with water, and always immersed by the sea at spring-tides. To carry off this superfluity, and secure the land from future inundations, were the objects of consideration. This was effected by introducing an aqueduct, or wooden pipe, of nine inches in diameter, through one hundred and seventy-four yards of sand, and thus opening a communication between the sea and a reservoir at the lower part of the marsh. The pipe is in some places twenty-four feet beneath the surface of the bank, and is fixed (on that part of the sand called *Half Ebb)* to a large rock, to preserve it from removal by the turbulent waves. Its mouth towards the sea is secured by a valve, to prevent the intrusion of salt-water, and is always closed by the pressure of the swelling tide. At the opposite end of the pipe is another valve, opening into the reservoir, which is eighteen feet square, by eight feet deep, and properly situated to receive the drainage water from all parts of the inclosed marsh. Several open canals, or trenches, cut at right angles, convey the water from all parts of the inclosure to the reservoir ; and on the retiring of the tide, the collected water rushes through the aqueduct with great velocity. The land having been so long saturated with sea water, was unproductive for the first four years ; but its present appearance promises to reward the adventurer for his expence and perseverance.* The labourers, when cutting the open drains, discovered an earthen pot, containing nearly one thousand Roman copper coins. They were very much corroded by the salt-water ; but many of the impressions were sufficiently legible to identify the emperors, who lived between the years 260 and 350. The urn in question was found erect, just, we may presume, as it was originally placed. This, in the opinion of some people, discredits the traditionary tales of the great change here supposed to have happened : But the ground might have sunk to any supposeable depth, and the urn along with it, still preserving its erect position. A vast number of hazel-boughs with perfect nuts adhering to them, have been found between Marazion and Penzance, below the natural bed of the soil. This (with other facts already stated) must prove a subsidence of the earth, or some change in the strata.--- Hazel-nuts have thus been found in the Sithney stream-works, and many other places; particularly near Newbridge; of which a correspondent thus writes :---" A very singular curiosity hath been brought to me---a hazel-nut upwards of four thousand years old, an antediluvian nut, which indisputably grew and was in being before Noah's flood, by which it was buried, and hath lain close upon the stratum of firm slate-shelf, covered by upwards of twelve feet deep of black mud, which hath never been disturbed or moved from that time to this. It was discovered this week, with some scores of others, in sinking a shaft near a mine called Huel Tamer, just below Newbridge, on the turnpike road leading to Callington. The nut is a very dark brown, but quite perfect. Whether Noah and his predecessors were or were not stouter as well as longer lived, than the present race of mortals, certain it is that this antique vegetable production is not larger nor differently shaped from a common hazel nut of the last year." *Letter from the late Mr. Gullet.*

* *Bede's Eccles. Hist.* l. i. c. 1. The name of vineyard yet affixed to the ruinous scites of our castles and and monasteries, proves, beyond a doubt, the great frequency of vineyards.-----There are many such in Cornwall. See *Richard*, p. 13.

* See the 14th vol. of the Transactions of the Society for the Promotion of Arts, &c, and the 2d vol. of Communications to the Board of Agriculture, for further particulars.

abounding with vineyards and orchards, naturally wished to introduce the same accommodations into their new settlements. The vineyard, however, was soon neglected; from no other cause, perhaps, than the cheapness with which wine was imported, before it was burdened with high duties. There are some of opinion, that orchards were introduced into this county, by the Normans: But *cyder (sicera)* is British. † --- 2. That the kitchen garden was not disregarded, is probable, as Stratton produced abundance of ‡ garlick: And garlick, was scarcely left a solitary plant.

III. Of the seats of gentlemen, uniting in one elegant whole the farm and the garden, and thus blending ornament with utility, I can say little, at this early period. Yet, in the neighbourhood of our castles and monasteries, there were plantations, parks, and fishponds. The parks of the earls and dukes of Cornwall are mentioned, as ancient in the time of Henry the Eighth. In these parks (said to have been nine) were a great number of forest trees, and much luxuriant coppice.§

† Says *Wolridge,* see his *Vinetum Britannicum.* p. 18.-----The orchards on the glebe at Ruan-lanyhorne, suggest some curious observations. " One is *park-apple.* This is a field of more than twenty statute-acres, including the moor. The name bespeaks its application. When that was imposed, the ground was an orchard. Park is a word continually occurring, in the names of our Cornish fields; and is Pairc (I.) a park or field, Parc (C.) a field. Afal also (W.) Avall, Avell (C.), and Abhal, Ubhal (I.) is an apple; and must have been pronounced, as it is now written. Parc-aval, or park-apple, then, signifies exactly the same that apple-garth does in Yorkshire, an inclosure for apples, or in other words an orchard. The rectorial orchard it could never have been. It is too large for that. That too was originally the lower-part of the front-court garden. Mr. Grant was the first, I believe, who enlarged this contracted orchard of the parsonage. He fenced in a hollow and warm part of Culver-close and Great Meadow, and turned it into a second orchard. But what is either of these to the extent of Park-apple? They are as nothing. It could be only the magnificence of a castellated mansion and a baronial houshold, that will account for an orchard of such vast dimensions, As an orchard indeed to such a household and such a mansion, it is in character. It is upon the same scale of greatness, as the rest. And I have always considered, therefore, Park-apple field, to have been the original orchard of the lord, conceded generously by him as a field to the rector." *W. T.* v. 2. p. 117.

‡ Margery, wife of William Whitestan, gives and grants to John Ermyce and Alice and John two gardens, &c. in Stratton, to have and to hold, on certain conditions; two of which are, that they shall dye annually four ells of cloth of a red colour; and shall render yearly at the feast of Easter, a *hundred of* GARLICK, for all services. The deed, in which this passage occurs, bears date 42, Edw. III. But it seems to shew, that long before this point of time, garlick was plentiful in Stratton.

§ They were disparked by Henry the Eighth.--- *Pencarrow* is commonly derived from its deer. *Tonkin* deduces the word from its quarries. " Pencarrow, in Egleshayle, (says he) for wood, water, and stone, may vie with any other part of the kingdom: Nor are the lands inferior to any in the neighbourhood for fruitfulness. *Pencarrow* is *Pencarrig* so softened, " the head quarry of stone." It is of much more ancient date, than the introduction of deer into this county." *Tonkin.* But I take *Carrow (Caer-row)* to mean *Castrum Romanum,*

CHAPTER THE SIXTH.

MINING.

I. FROM the Saxons to the time of Edward the First, we have many documents respecting the Cornish mines. The Saxons* are said to have neglected the mines of Cornwall. In this county, indeed, they had no authority, till it was conquered by Athelstan. Whether the Normans derived any great emolument from the Cornish mines is doubtful; as in the reign of king John, their product was so inconsiderable, that the tin-farm amounted to no more than one hundred marks.† The Jews were now the sole managers of the mines: And memorials of the Jews are still disco-

* The Saxons, says Camden, seem to have employed the Saracens. "That the ancient Britains wrought those tinn-mines, is plain from Diodorus Siculus who lived under Augustus; to omit Timæus the historian in Pliny, who tells us, that the Britains fetched tinn out of the isle Icta,‖ in their little wicker-boats covered with leather. For Diodorus affirms, that the Britains who lived in those parts, digging tinn out of a rocky sort of ground, carried it in carts at low-tide to some of the neighbouring islands; that thence the merchants transported it into Gaule, and then on horse-back in thirty days to the springs of Eridanus, or the city Narbona, as to a common mart. Æthicus too, whoever he was, that unworthily goes under the name of being translated by St. Jerom, intimates the same thing, and adds that he gave directions to those workmen. The Saxons seem not to have medled with them, or at most to have only employed the Saracens: for the inhabitants to this day call a mine that is given over, Attal-Sarisin, that is, the leavings of the Saracens." *Gibson's Camden*, pp. 2, 3.

† "According to which valuation the bishop of Exeter received then in lieu of his tenth part, and still receives from the duke of Cornwall annually the sum of six pounds thirteen shillings and four-pence; so low were the tin-profits then in Cornwall, whereas in Devonshire the tin was then set to farm for one hundred pounds yearly. King John, sensible of the languishing state of this manufacture, granted the county of Cornwall some marks of his favour, disforested what part of it was then subject to the arbitrary forest-law, allowing it equal title to the laws of the kingdom with the other parts of England, and is said to have granted a charter to the tinners (Carew, p. 17), but what it was does not appear." *Borlase*, p. 190.

‖ This hint seems to favour a conjecture, that Bolen (Cæsar's Iccius Portus) might take its name from this island Icta. For Stephen's edition of the Commentaries reads it Ictius, and the Greek version calls it Ἴκτιος λιμην, as in another place Ὄκτιος. And why might not that haven be as well called Ictius from the place with which it had the most considerable trade, as Britannicus, from its being the chief port to and from Britain.

verable in the names of different places in Cornwall.* In the time of Richard, king of the Romans, and earl of Cornwall, the produce of tin-mines is represented as immense: And the Jews were farmed out to the prince by his brother Henry the Third; insomuch that the interest which they possest was at his disposal. The working of tin-mines in Spain was at this time, also, obstructed by the Moors: And none were as yet discovered in Germany, Malabar, or the East-Indies: The earl of Cornwall, therefore, engrossed nearly the whole tin-trade of Europe.‡

* "It is supposed that the Jewes firste endeuored to dyue into theis rocks for this commodious minerall, thowgh they then wanted theys preuayling instruments, which latter times doe afforde. Their pick-axes were of weake mater to comaunde the obdurate rockes; as of holme, which some call holee or huluer, of boxe, hartes horne, and suche like; which kinde of tooles modern tynnmen finde in olde forsaken workes, which to this daye retayn the name of *Attall Sarazin*: the Jewes cast-off workes, in their Hebrew speache." *Norden*, p. 11, 12.---"The Jews are still mentioned in the "*Attal Sarazin*," the offcasts of the *Saracens*; old works supposed to have been wrought by the Saracens, or Jews. "The Cornish tradition is, that the Saxons inhabiting these parts, were the chief workers and searchers for tin, who in those antient days wrought not with spades, and working tools, made with iron, as they now do, but all made of oak; they, as they got their tin, had their blowing-houses, now called smelting-houses, near their works; for proof whereof, divers workers of tin have often found their shovels, spades, and mattocks, made all of oak and holly: but whether those workers were Saxons, or Danes, or any other nation, is not certain; the tinners call the antient works by the name of the working of the Jews; it is most manifest, that there were Jews inhabiting here until the year of our Lord 1291, and this they prove by the names yet enduring, viz. *Attall Sarazin*, in English, The Jews Feast. But whether they had liberty to work and search for tin, does not appear, because they had their dwellings chiefly in great towns and cities; and being great usurers, were in that year banished out of England, to the number of 15,060, by the most noble prince Edward I. It appeareth by some antient records, relating to the customs of the stannaries, that the tinners, before the charter of Edward I. wrought and searched for tin in wastrell ground, and in the prince's several lands only, where any tin might be found, and had liberty to dig, search, and make shafts, and pitch bounds, paying only to the prince, or lord of the soil, the fifteenth boll, to and for toll of their tin, and to work for tin in places of the most advantage, excepting only sanctuary ground, churches, mills, houses, and gardens; provided always, that if the said tinners, in their working, chanced to subvert or work up any man's house, or high way, the tinners so subverting, should, at their own proper cost and charges, make, or cause to be made up, the said houses, or highway, so subverted or undermined." *Pearce's* Pref. pp. 2, 3.

‡ "Olde Robert of Glocester in the time of king Henry III. honoured his countrey with these his best English rimes, which I doubt not but some (although most now are of the new cut) will giue the reading.

England is a well good land; in the stead best
Set in the one end of the world, and reigneth west.
The sea goeth him all about, he stint as an yle,
Of foes it need the lesse doubt: but it be through gile
Of folke of the selfe land, as me hath I sey while
From south to north it is long, eight hundred mile,
And two hundred mile broad from east to west to wende
Amid the land as it might be: and not as in the one ende,
Plentie men may in England: of all good see
But folke it agult, other yeares the worse and worse be,
For England is full enough of fruite and of treene
Of woods and of parkes that ioy it is to seene.

II. With respect to the mode of working for minerals, the ancient *streaming* was still continued. In the mean time, the *shammel-works* must, I think, have been almost superseded by *shafts*.|| And that shafts were sunk to a considerable depth before the close of this period, is plain from the immense riches of the tin-mines, and

Haue patience also to reade that which followeth in him of some cities in this realme:
In the countrey of Canterburys most plentie of fish is,
And most chase of wilde beasts, about Salisbury I wis,
And London ships most, and wine at Winchester.
At Hartford sheepe and oxe: and fruite at Worcester.
Soape about Couentrie: and yron at Glocester.
Metall, lead, and tinne in the countrey of Exeter." *Camden's Remains*, p.
The country of Exeter then included, in the common forms of speech, both Cornwall and Devon.

|| Pryce however thinks differently. "I do not suppose (says he) the present methods for working tin mines, by deep shafts, and by driving and stopeing under the firm ground has been practised more than three hundred years past. Prior to those means for raising of tin, they wrought a vein from the bryle to the depth of eight or ten fathoms, all open to grass, very much like the fosse of an intrenchment. This was performed by meer dint of labour, when men worked for one-third of the wages they now have. By that method they had no use for foreign timber, neither were they acquainted with the use of hemp and gunpowder. This fosse they call a coffin, which they laid open several fathoms in length east and west, and raised the tin-stuff on shammels, plots, or stages, six feet high from each other till it came to grass. Those shammels, in my apprehension, might have been of three kinds, yet all answering the same end. First, they sunk a pit one fathom in depth and two or three fathoms in length, to the east and to the west, of the middle part of the lode discovered; then they squared out another such piece of the lode for one or two fathoms in length as before; at the same time others were sinking the first or deepest ground sunk in like manner; they next went on and opened another piece of ground each way from the top as before, while others again were still sinking in the last and in the deepest part likewise: in this manner they proceeded step after step; from which notion arises the modern method of stoping the bottoms under-ground. Thus they continued sinking from cast to cast, that is as high as a man can conveniently throw up the tin-stuff with a shovel, till they found the lode became either too deep for hand work, too small in size, very poor in quality, or too far inclined from its underlie for their perpendicular working. Secondly, if the lode was bunchy, or richer in one part than another, they only laid open and sunk upon it, perhaps in small pitches not more in length than one of the stopes or shammels before described. The shortness of such a piece of lode would not admit of their sinking stope after stope; it was then natural and easy for them, to square out a shammel on one side or wall of their lode, and so to make a landing-place for their tin-stuff cast after cast. Thirdly, if the lode was wide, and the walls of it, and the adjoining country, very hard solid ground, it was in such case more easy for them to make shammels or stages, with such timber, &c. as was cheapest and nearest at hand. This, with streaming, I take to be the plain simple state of mining in general, three centuries ago; and from hence is derived the custom of shammeling both above and under-ground at this time; for in clearing of attle, (deads) or filling the kibble with ore, the miners prefer a shammel, which is a stage of boards, for the more light and easy use of their shovels. But as this manner of working was irreconcileable with the discovery and raising any tin-stuff below a certain very shallow depth, it became necessary to contrive some other way to follow downwards the inviting rich stones of tin some lodes produced. The method of shammeling, even in those moderate times has been expensive, where a very small lode of tin occurred in a hard country. To remove a dense hard stratum of rocky overburden, must be very fatiguing and perplexing; therefore they found it most adviseable to sink shafts down upon the lode, to cut it at some depth, and then to drive and stope east and west upon the course of the lode: in time, no doubt, such improvements presented, as rendered that the cheapest and most established custom of mining." *Pryce's Minerol.* pp, 141, 142.

the great quantity of silver raised in Cornwall. In the reign of Edward the First there was enough produced to defray the expences of his wars. Yet the remains of mining in the isles of Sylleh, exhibit no other appearances than those of common stone-quarries.||

III. We cannot speak with certainty of any particular stream-works or mines. The Porth-stream-works were situated near the shore of Trewardreth-bay.* The ore was of the purest kind, and contained rather more than two-thirds of metal. The pebbles from which the metal was extracted, were in size from sand-like grains to that of a small egg; they were included in a bluish marle mixed with sand, and containing various marine exuviæ. The depth of the principal bed was nearly twenty feet, and its breadth about six or seven. This appears to have been worked at a very remote period, and before iron tools were employed; as large pickaxes, made of oak, holm, and box, have been found in it. The soil in this vicinity is supposed by Dr. Maton to have been partly formed by a deposit from the sea, and partly by mould and fragments washed from the surrounding mountains. In St. Blazey, St. Austel, St. Stephens in Brannel, and St. Ewe, are many old stream-works; which are commonly attributed to the Jews.† The Carnon-

|| "On the downs in the isle of Trescaw (says Borlase) we saw a large opening made in the ground, and dug about the depth of a common stone quarry, and in the same shape. There are several such in the parish of St. Just, Cornwall, where they are called koffens, and shew that the more antient way of mining was to search for metals in the same way as we at present raise stones out of quarries, which, as the metals bear no proportion to the strata of stone in which they lie, must have been very tedious and expensive. A little further, we found a row of shallow tin-pits, none appearing to be more than four fathom deep, most of them no deeper than what the tinners call costean shafts, which are only six or eight feet perpendicular; to the west end of these pits there is the mouth of the drain, or adit. This course of tin bears east and west nearly, as our loads of tin veins, do in Cornwall. These are the only tin pits which we saw, or are any where to be seen, as we were informed, in these islands." *Borlase's* Isles of Scilly, p. 45. Of this work, see pp. 72, 73, 74, 75, 76, 77, 78. The tin-mines on Dartmoor, that were wrought very anciently, were abandonded for want of machinery on account of their depth; though I own, that depth was shallowness itself when compared with the present depth of the Cornish mines, in general; not to mention that at the time when the Dartmoor tin-mines were worked, the use of gunpowder for blasting rocks, was also unknown.

* These stream-works are classed in Maton's Observations on the Western Counties, with the most considerable of the kind, in Cornwall. They were all washed away by the sea in the year 1801.

† "There are several streams of tin in St. Stephen's Brannel, St. Ewe, St. Blazey, and other places, but the most considerable stream of tin in Cornwall is that of St. Austel moor, which is a narrow valley about a furlong wide, (in some places somewhat wider) running near three miles from the town of St. Austel southward to the sea. On each side, and at the head above St. Austel are many hills, betwixt which there are little valleys which all discharge their

stream-works were probably known before the present æra. They are situated near an arm of Falmouth harbour, called Restronget creek, into which flow a number of rivulets from the hills eastward of Redruth. At present, they occupy a portion of ground nearly one mile in length, and three hundred yards broad, and are by far the most rich and extensive of any stream-works in the county. The pebbles from which the metal is extracted, are embedded in a marle, mixed, like that at Porth, with sand and marine shells. The whole space, indeed, now occupied by the stream-works, appears to have been gained from the sea; the mud and other matter washed down by the streams, having raised a sort of enbankment, which, by its continual extension, and some assistance from art, has gradually contracted the boundaries of the tide. The bed of tin-pebbles is about thirty-six feet below the surface of the ground: its thickness is from four to six feet. Immediately on the bed of tin several stags-horns have been found, one of which measured three feet from the root to the point. Skulls and other bones

waters, and whatever else they receive from the higher grounds, into St. Austel moor: whence it happens that the ground of this moor is all adventitious for about three fathoms deep, the shodes and streams from the hills on each side being here collected and ranged into floors, according to their weight, and the successive dates of their coming thither. The uppermost coat consists of thin layers of earth, clay, and pebbly gravel, about five feet deep; the next *stratum* is about six feet deep, more stony, the stones pebbly-formed, with a gravelly sand intermixed; these two coverings being removed, they find great numbers of tin-stones from the bigness of a goose-egg, and sometimes larger, down to the size of the finest sand. The tin is inserted in a *stratum* of loose smoothed stones, from a foot diameter downwards to the smallest pebble. From the present surface of the ground down to the solid rock or karn, is eighteen feet deep at a medium: in the solid rock there is no tin. This stream-tin is of the purest kind; and great part of it, without any other management than being washed upon the spot, brings thirteen parts for twenty at the melting-house. In one of the workings here were lately found, about eight feet under the surface, two slabs, or small blocks of melted tin, of about twenty-eight pounds weight each, of a shape very different from that which for many years has obtained in Cornwall; and as they have no stamp on them, probably as old as the time when the Jews had engrossed the tin manufacture in the time of king John. They have semicircular handles or loops to them, as if to sling and carry them more conveniently on horseback: they are much corroded by the sharp waters in which they have layn, a kind of rust or scurf-like incrustation inclosing the tin. Probably there were some Jewish melting-houses near the place; and when these houses were plundered and destroyed, some of the blocks remained in the rubbish, and by the floods, which this valley is so subject to, washed downwards, and covered where they were found. In the stream-works in St. Stephen's Brannel, they also find now and then some small lumps of melted tin, two inches square and under. What I have seen of this kind cuts with difficulty, and is more harsh and gritty than the common melted tin, owing to this perhaps, that the ancient melters had not then discovered how to flux their tin into the purity and toughness of the present age. These nodules I look upon also as fragments of melted tin, scattered from the Jewish melting-houses." *Nat. Hist*, pp. 162, 163, 164.---"In St. Blazey Moor, at the depth of twenty feet, they have what they call stream (tin ore) about five feet in thickness in the bottom, great part of which had been anciently wrought before iron tools were known, several wooden pick-axes of oak, holm, and box having been lately found therein. Over this they have a complete stratum of black mud, fit for burning; on this a stratum of gravel, very poor in tin; on this another stratum of mud; and uppermost gravel again." *Pryce*, p. 68.

have likewise been discovered here: and, what renders it apparent that these works were known at a very early period, a wooden shovel, and various picks made of deers horn, have also been found. Almost all the vallies in Cornwall, indeed, were anciently streamed for tin. And many places took their denomination from this circumstance.* Of shammel-works or shafts, I mention the places, with much hesitation. It appears, that a store of tin was raised in former times, on Hengsten down.‡ There were old tin-mines in St. Agnes; in Gwennap; in Wendron; and in Breage.||

IV. Of the methods of stamping and dressing, melting and coining the tin, a circumstantial account will be hereafter given. The art of manufacturing tin, was, doubtless, ancient; but, during the times of the Saxons and the Normans, it seems

* Carew tells us, that Polwhele may be interpreted "the *miry work*." On this Mr. Tonkin remarks. "I take the true etymology of this work to be Polgueul, the top of the field: For the present Mr. Polwhele assures me, that he could never discover the footsteps of any workings or mines in or near this place. But in 1734, an old work was discovered on this barton, in a *very miry place*, which answers to Carew's idea. It is now in working." *Tonkin's MSS.* But "the miry work" certainly refers to the old stream tin-works in a valley, which are still very apparent, and which tradition ascribes to the Jews.

‡ "From Plymmouth hauen, passing farther into the countrie, Hengsten downe, presenteth his waste head and sides to our sight This name it borroweth of Hengst, which in the Saxon signifieth a horse, and to such least daintie beasts it yeeldeth fittest pasture. The countrie people haue a by word, that,

Hengsten downe, well ywrought,
Is worth London towne, deare ybought.

Which grewe from the store of tynne, in former times, there digged vp: but that gainfull plentie is now fallen to a scant-sauing scarcitie. Those workes afford store of the formentioned Cornish diamonds. The neighbouring inhabitants obserue also, that when the top of Hengsten, is capped with a cloud, the same bodeth a showre within short time after. Roger Houeden reporteth, that about ann. 806. a fleete of Danes arriued in West-Wales with whome the Welsh ioyned in insurrection against king Egbright, but hee gloriously discomfited them, at Hengistendune, which I take to be this place (if at least West-Wales may, by interpretation, passe for Cornwall) because the other prouince, of that time, is more commonly diuided into north and south." *Carew,* f. 115. b.

|| "In this parish, stands Godolphin-Ball, i. e. Godolphin Plague, or a place that bringeth death: and this and all other tin-mines are generally under this or like circumstance, whereof in British, many of them are called balls, (as St. Agnes Ball, Ball-dehen, Gwenap, and others.) This is that inexhaustible mountain or tin-work, which for some hundreds of years hath afforded its owners, or lords, the Lamburns, Stephens, Godolphins, and other adventurers, several thousand pounds worth of tin per annum, and which is called a Ball, from the dangerous, wet, deep, and miserable occupation of the labouring tinners therein. For which reason when the Romans ruled here, Tacitus, from the speech of Galgack ap Lienack, king of the Northern Britons, informs us, that none but captives, slaves, and condemned persons were obliged to work under ground in tin mines." *Hals.* p. 139.---"It pays the wages of at least three hundred men yearly." *Tonkin's MSS.*--- *St. Mewan* (Muin) a *mine*; so called, Hals thinks, in reference to the many tin-lodes and works in the parish!!!

to have been very imperfect. At the place of coinage, indeed, the process was nearly the same, as we shall notice at a future period.§

CHAPTER THE SEVENTH.

MANUFACTURES.

I can state few facts respecting our Manufactures. First, for the Woollen. From some scattered memoirs it appears, that the English wool was of a superior quality to any other; and that the Spanish wool owed its celebrity to a present of some sheep from Henry II. to the king of Spain. But the woollen manufacture in England, was almost lost, at the close of the period before us. And unmanufactured fleeces were sent to foreign markets. In the mean time, the Cornish wool had, from its coarseness, the name of Cornish hair; in consideration of which, it was exempted

§ When the tin is brought to the coinage town, the officers appointed by the Duke of Cornwall assay it, by taking off a piece of one of the under corners of the block of about a pound weight, partly by cutting and partly by breaking; and, if well purified, stamp the face of the block with the impression of the seal of the dutchy;* which stamp is a permission for the owner to sell, and at the same time an assurance that the tin so marked, has been purposely examined and found merchantable. The stamping of this impression by a hammer (in like manner as was anciently done to money to make it current) is called coining the tin.

* The arms of Condorus last earl of Cornwall of British blood (temp. W. 1.) were Sab. 15 bezants (5, 4, 3, 2, 1) in pale, Or. See Camden, p. 26. Richard king of the Romans, earl of Cornwall, son to king John, threw these bezants into a bordure round the bearing of the earls of Poictou: he bore, therefore, argent a lyon rampant gul. crowned or within a bordure sable garnished by bezants, (see Camden, p. 27) and this still continues the dutchy seal.

from the duties of exportation. We are told, indeed, that Cornish cloth was exported, free from the customary duty: if so, the fleece seems to have been manufactured in Cornwall.* The manufacture of tin, which was carried to some degree of perfection by the ancient Britons, now greatly declined. Tin cups, basons, and pitchers were originally made by the Cornish: And the Romans taught them to combine two or three of their metals, and form another; I mean the argentarium, or pewter. But with the Romans, we seem to have lost, for a while, our ingenuity. The art of making earthen vessels, so frequent with the Roman-Cornish, was probably continued in the Saxon and the Norman times. The finest clays for porcelain were always at hand: And, the steatite at the Lizard, was not, perhaps, unknown to our forefathers.

* To Bishop Blaze, the reputed inventor of wool-combing, Cornwall hath some claim; if St. Blazey be dedicated to that bishop, and if, as tradition says, St. Blazey was his landing-place. His effigy is preserved in the church; And an annual festival is held in the parish for his commemoration at the same time that it is observed by all the wool-combers in the kingdom. In his "Fleece," *Dyer* celebrates St. Blasius, who,

.... "filled at length
With inspiration, after various thought,
And trials manifold, with well-known voice
Gather'd the poor, and o'er Vulcanian stoves,
With tepid lees of oil, and spiky comb,
Shew'd how the fleece might stretch to greater length,
And cast a glossier whiteness. Wheels went round;
Matrons and maids with songs reliev'd their toils;
And every loom received the softer yarn.
What poor, what widow, BLASIUS, did not bless,
Thy teaching hand? thy bosom, like the morn,
Op'ning its wealth? What nation did not seek,
Of thy new-modell'd wool, the curious webs?
HENCE the glad cities of the loom his name
Honour with yearly festals: through their streets
The pomp, with tuneful sounds, and order just,
Denoting labor's happy progress, moves,
Procession slow and solemn."

Book II. pp. 55, 56.

FAWEY HARBOUR.

Published by R. Polwhele March 25th 1803.

CHAPTER THE EIGHTH.

COMMERCE.

IT might naturally be expected, from the extent of the coasts of Cornwall, and our various ports or harbours, that I might enter into some detail, on the subject of Commerce. But the present period is too early for circumstantial narrative. I possess, however, a few scattered particulars of our ports and shipping, our exports, and our fairs, and markets, and coins.

I. Respecting the Cornish* ports or harbours, the chronicles of these days are, in general, silent.--- *Saltash* had large privileges over the haven appertaining to it, a yearly rent of boats and barges, anchorage of strange shipping, and dragging of oysters, except between Candlemas and Easter. These liberties it derived from the castle of Trematon, the head of that honor.----- As a port, *Fawey* had considerable privileges.†-----In the *Truro* charters, to which I have already referred, there is no intimation of that grand privilege that Truro certainly possessed, and which is thus

* *A port* is a place to which only, the officers of the customs are appropriated, and which includes all the privileges and guidance of all the members and creeks thereto allotted. *A member of a port*, is a place where anciently a custom-house was kept, and officers or their deputies attend: And such are lawful places for importation or exportation. *A creek* is a place where commonly officers are or have been placed, by way of prevention, not out of duty or right of attendance: Such are not lawful places for importation or exportation, without particular licence or sufferance from the port or member under which it is placed. See Acts of Parliament relating to ports; 1. Eliz, c. 13. 14. Charles, 2. c. 14. 6. Anne. c. 26, 18.

† "The townsmen vaunt, that for reskuing certaine ships of Rye from the Normans, in Henrie the Third's time, they beare the armes, and enjoy part of the priviledges appertaining to *the Cinque Ports*; whereof there is some memorie in their chancell window, with the name of Fisart Bagga, their principal commander in that service." *Carew*, f. 135.

referred to in the last visitation of the county. "We find that the mayor of Truro hath always been and still is mayor of Falmouth, as by an ancient grant now in the custody of the mayor and burgesses doth appear." The superiority of Truro over all the harbour of Falmouth is here attested by a record of 1622, and an ancient grant now "in the custody," &c. appealed to by the record. This distinguishing privilege had been ceded to Truro by a grant of a particular nature; but from the manner the visitation refers to it, the grant must have been so early as to be without a date, and was probably, therefore, about the same age as Reginald's and Lucy's charters. Yet the privilege had in all likelihood been transferred from another town, and possibly from Tregoney, as that was the first town on the arm of the harbour.---That *Helston* was once a port, I have before stated as a traditional tale. But the Loe-pool seems to have been a lake, as at the present day, for many generations.‡---It should seem, that there was once a port at the *Mount*, called *Ruminella*.||---On the north coast, *St. Ives*, *Padstow*, and *Bude*, were, doubtless, ports of consequence.---I find

‡ When the waters extend so far, as to obstruct the working of the mills at Helston and Carminow, the millers apply to the lord of the manor, and presenting him with two leather purses, each containing three-halfpence, solicit his permission to open the bar. This is a very ancient usage.

|| "Edward the Confessor, first founder of this monastery, gave to St. Michael the Archangel for the use of the brothers there serving God, St. Michael next the sea, and all the land of Vennefire, as also the port called Ruminella." Here is a port, that is, a place for landing and embarking for import and export for safe ingress and egress of shipping mentioned as early as Edward the Confessor and a particular name given to that port of which there are now no remains any where in the neighbourhood or elsewhere in Cornwall. This Ruminella was a port it seems (i. e. a place for export and import) had mills, and fish-ponds and lands (called territorium) round it, some cultivated, some not, but yielding some revenues. But I find the haven (or port) of Romney in Kent had a name very like it. "The king, (viz. Henry the Third, in the year 1258,) being informed that this haven of Romenale (alias Romney) in Kent, was in danger of being destroyed by stoppage of the river Newenden, had sent into those parts Nicholas de Handco, soon after lord of Barstall," &c. *Dugdale's* History, p. 14. cited in *Kenn.* Par. Ant. p. 254. Whether Romney was the Ruminella mentioned, or the townlet of which the legend of St. Michael speaks, now (as Leland says) under water "is very difficult to ascertain but by the register of this house, still extant, as bishop Tanner says, in the library of the earl of Salisbury." *Price's MS. of the Mount*, pp. 43, 44.----"This mount is comparatively a pyramidal stragg of white and gray cloe rocks, that is to say, a sort of marble, containing about seven acres of land in compass. At the foot whereof, towards the land, is a level piece of ground covered with grass; where there is a wharf or key, for landing goods and merchandizes from the sea; also some dwelling-houses, and fish-cellars, and a cemetery for burying the dead. To this mount the sea daily makes its flux and reflux; and affords safe riding and anchorage to boats, barks, and barges, with some winds. And that which tends more to the convenience and security of this place, at low water it is all a part of the insular continent of Britain, and at full sea an island of itself. To which purpose thus speaks Mr. Carew, out of the Cornish Wonder-gatherer;—

FALMOUTH.

Published by R. Polwhele March 25th 1803.

Hugh de Nevil warden of the sea-ports for *Cornwall, Devon, Dorset,* and *Hants*; and accounting for 170*l.* 11*s.* for casual profits arising out of these ports.§

Who knows not Migell's mount and chair, the pilgrim's holy vaunt,
Both land and island twice a day, both fort and port of haunt." *W. Hals*, p. 37.

----In examining the state of our ports and harbours, I must necessarily speak of the Isles of Sylleh. In these isles, however, great changes must have taken place, since the times of the Saxons and the Normans. "I observed (says Borlase) the Guel hill of Brehar, and the isle of Guel, stretching away towards the little isle of Scilly, and with it making a curve, of which Scilly is the head land; and from the furthermost hill of Brehar a promontory shoots out, at the extreme point of which rises a vast rocky turret called the castle of Brehar: on every side many rocks shew themselves above water, and intimate their former connexion with Brehar, and their being reduced to their present nakedness by the fury of the ocean. From this disposition therefore of the rocks and islets on this side, we may answer a question, which would otherwise be extremely difficult to solve, viz. How came all these islands to have their general name from so small and inconsiderable a spot as the isle of Scilly, whose cliffs hardly any thing but birds can mount, and whose barrenness would never suffer any thing but sea birds to inhabit there? A due observation of the shores will answer this question very satisfactorily, and convince us that what is now a bare rock about a furlong over, and separated from the lands of Guel and Brehar about half a mile, was formerly joined to them by low necks of land, and that Trescaw, St. Martin's, Brehar, Samson, and the rocks and islets adjoining, made formerly but one island; nay, to these, I believe, I may safely add the eastern islands and St. Mary's too, there being great flats reaching from St. Martin's almost to both, all uncovered at low-water, and having but four feet water in the deepest part. This (at that time) great island had several creeks, such as New and Old Grynsey and others, by the sea's incroachment, or by the dipping of the lands, since extended into harbours: It had also several head-lands, of which that now called Scilly was the highest, outermost, and consequently most conspicuous. To pursue this conjecture a little further; when all these islands abovementioned made but one, that one went by the name of Sylle, or some word of like sound and derivation, and having some little islands scattered round it, it imparted its name to its inferiors, whence what were called by the Greeks, Cassiterides, were named by the latin authors Sigdeles, Sillinæ, Silures; and by the English, Sylley, Sulley, and Scilly.* I must go farther still, and observe, that the promontory now called Scilly island, lying the westernmost of all the high lands, was the first land of all these islands discerned by traders from the Mediterranean and Spanish coasts, and as soon as discovered was said to be Scilly, nothing being more usual with sailors upon their first seeing land, than to call the part by the name of the whole, with proofs of which I will not detain you. But when this considerable island was broken to pieces, and the great portions became inhabited, they required distinct appellations, and were called according to the religion of the times, when the monks were settled among them, after the names of particular saints. The chief division was called St. Mary's in honour of the virgin-mother; the next dedicated to St. Nicholas, the general patron-saint of all sea-faring people, the others to St. Martin, St. Samson, and so on, but this remarkable promontory now called Scilly, being no longer fit for habitation was dedicated to no saint, but left to enjoy its ancient name, and notwithstanding the modern Christian dedications, sailors went on still in their own way; this high land was called Scilly still, and the islands in general are still denominated (from what was anciently their principal) the Scilly Isles. These islands being so noted among the ancients, I expected to find among the inhabitants a conscious esteem of their own antiquity, and of the figure they had made in history before the other parts of Britain were at all known, or at least regarded. I was not without some hopes of finding old towns, old castles, perhaps inscriptions, and works of grandeur; but there is nothing of this kind; the inhabitants are all new comers; not one old habitation, nor any remains of Phenician and Grecian art in the ports, castles, towns, temples, or sepulchres. All the antiquities

§ *Mag. Rot.* 15. John. 8. 15. *Madox's Hist. Excheq.* 213, 530, 531. *Baron. Anglican.* 531.

* The natives called these islands "Sulleh"---"flat rocks dedicated to the Sun."

2. For our shipping; Alfred is commonly esteemed the founder of the naval strength of England. But the laws of Athelstan gave peculiar encouragement to

here to be seen, are of the rudest Druid times, and if borrowed in any measure from the oriental traders (superstition being very infectious) were borrowed from their most ancient and simple rites. We are not to think however but that Scilly was really inhabited, and as frequently resorted to anciently, as the old historians relate. All the islands, by the remains of hedges, walls, houses contiguous to each other, and a number of sepulchral burrows shew that they have been fully cultivated and inhabited. What the ancients say of its name, customs, trade and inhabitants, I shall not trouble you with, as affording us few lights; you will find all this collected in the last edition of Camden, (p. 1519) but I should not excuse myself, if I did not lay before you the hints, which things themselves suggested, and which our own records supply us withal. That these islands were inhabited by Britons is past all doubt, not only from their neighbourhood to Britain, but from the Druid monuments; the several rude pillars, circles of erect stones, kistvaens without number, rock-basons, and tolmens, all monuments common in Cornwall and Wales, equal evidences of the antiquity, religion, and original of the old inhabitants; they have also many British names at present for their little islands, tenements, karns, and creeks, and more, doubtless, have been forgot or jostled out by modern ones. How came these ancient inhabitants then, it may be asked, to vanish so, as that the present have no pretensions to any affinity, or connexion of any kind either in blood, language, or customs? How came they to disappear and leave so few traces of trade, plenty, and arts, and no posterity that we can hear of behind them? In answer to which, as this is the most remarkable crisis in the history of these islands, you will excuse me if I enlarge; and if I make use of the same arguments which I had the honour lately to lay before the Royal Society, it is because they have the same weight with me now as they had before, and the course of the present subject will not suffer so momentous a part of natural history to be omitted. Two causes of the extinction of the old inhabitants, their habitations, and works of peace, war, and religion, occur to me; the gradual advances of the sea, and a sudden submersion of the land. The sea is perpetually preying upon these little islands, and leaves nothing where it can reach but the skeleton, the bared rock. It has before been mentioned that many hedges now under water, and flats which stretch from one island to another, are plain evidences of a former union subsisting between these now distinct islands. History speaks the same truth. "The isles of Cassiterides (says *Strabo*) are ten in number, close to one another, one of them is desert and unpeopled, the rest are inhabited." But see how the sea has multiplied these islands, there are now reckoned more than one hundred and forty, into so many fragments are they divided. The continual advances which the sea makes upon the land at present, are plain to all people of observation, and within these last thirty years have been very considerable. I was shewn a passage which the sea has made within these seven years through the sand-bank that fences the Abby-pond, by which breach, upon the first high tide and violent storm at east, or east-south-east, one may venture to prophesy that this still, and now beautiful pool of fresh water, will become a branch of the sea, and consequently exposed to all the rage of tide and storm. What we see happening every day may assure us of what has happened in former times, and from the banks of sand and the low lands giving way to the sea, and the breaches becoming still more open and irremediable, it appears that there has been a gradual declension and diminution of the solids, and as gradually a progressive ascendancy of the fluids for many ages. But farther, ruins and hedges are frequently seen upon the shifting of the sands in the friths between the islands, and the low lands which were formerly cultivated, (particularly those stretching from Samson to Trescaw,) have now ten feet water above the foundations of their hedges, although at a reasonable medium we cannot suppose these foundations formerly to have been less than six feet above high water level, when the lands were dry, arable or pasture grounds; this therefore will make sixteen feet difference at least between their ancient and present level; there are several phænomena of the same nature to be seen on these shores; as particularly a straight-lined ridge like a causeway, running cross the Old-Town creek in St. Mary's, which is now never seen above-water. On the isle of Annet there are large stones now covered by every full tide, which have rock-basons cut into their surface, and which therefore must have been placed in a much higher situation when those basons, in other places generally so high, and probably of superstitious use for receiving the waters of heaven, were worked into them. Again, tin-mines they certainly had in these islands two hundred years before Christ. What is become of these mines? for the mines at present to be seen shew no marks of their being

navigation. The merchant, who had been thrice across the high seas upon his own

ancient. To account for these alterations, the gradual advances and slow depredations of the sea will not suffice; we must therefore either allow that these lands, since they were cultivated, and built upon, have sunk so much lower than they were before, or else we must allow that since these lands were fenced and cultivated, and the houses and other works now under water, the whole ocean has been raised as to its surface, sixteen feet and more perpendicular; which latter supposition will appear to the learned without doubt much the harder of the two. I conclude, therefore, that these islands have undergone some great catastrophe, and besides the apparent diminution of their islets by sea and tempest, must have suffered greatly by a subsidence of the land, (the common consequence of earthquakes) attended by a sudden inundation in those parts where the above-mentioned ruins, fences, mines, and other things of which we have no vestiges now remaining, formerly stood. This inundation probably destroyed many of the ancient inhabitants, and so terrified those who survived, and had wherewithal to support themselves elsewhere, that they forsook these islands, by which means the people who were the aborigines, and corresponded so long with the Phenicians, Greeks, and Romans were reduced to the last gasp. The few poor remains of the desolation might soon lose sight of their ancient prosperity and eminence, by their necessary attention to food and raiment; no easy acquisitions, when their low-lands, ports, and towns were overwhelmed by the sea. Give me leave to observe in the next place, that this inundation may be traced in the traditions we have had for many ages among the Cornish, and stands confirmed by some phænomena on the shores of Cornwall. That there existed formerly such a country as the Lionesse, stretching from the Land's-end to the Scilly Isles is much talked of in our parts. Antoninus places a little island called Lissia here, but whether he means the Wolf ledge of rocks, or any portion of the Scilly Isles is uncertain; however there are no appearances of any island in this channel at present. Mr. Carew, (in his Survey of Cornwall, p. 3.) argues from the plain and level surface of the bottom of the channel, that it must at one time have been a plain extended above the sea. In the family of Trevilian, now resident in Somerset but originally Cornish, they have a story, that one of their ancestors saved himself by the help of his horse, at the time when this Lionesse was destroyed; and the arms of the family were taken, as 'tis said, from this fortunate escape. Some fishermen also have insisted that in the channel betwixt the Land's-end and Scilly, many fathoms under water, there are the tops of houses, and other remains of habitations; but I produce these arguments only as proofs of the tradition and strong persuasion amongst the Cornish, that such a country once existed and is now buried under the sea, not as proofs of the matter of fact, for of that I am very dubious, the Cassiterides, by the most ancient accounts of them, appearing always to have been islands. I rather guess that this tradition of the Lionesse, and a great country between the Land's-End and Scilly being overwhelmed by the sea, might have taken its rise from that subsidence and inundation which not only these islands have certainly undergone, but part of the shores of Cornwall also, for in Mount's-Bay we have several evidences of a like subsidence. The principal anchoring-place is called a lake, but is now an open harbour. St. Michael's Mount, from its Cornish name, must have stood formerly in a wood, but at full tide is now half a mile in the sea, and no tree near it. Leland (Itin. vol. iii. p. 7.) talking of this Mount, says that an "ould legend of St. Michael speaketh of a tounelet in this part, now defaced and under the water;" in confirmation of which alterations I must observe, that on the beach betwixt the Mount and the town of Penzance, when the sands have been dispersed and drawn out into the sea, I have seen the trunks of several large trees in their natural position, (as well as I can recollect) worn smooth just above their roots, upon which at full tide there must be twelve feet of water. Neither is what Mr. Scawen says in his MS. an inconsiderable confirmation that Cornwall has lost much land on the southern coast, that there was "a valley between Ramhead and Loo, and that there is to be seen on a clear day, in the bottom of the sea, a league from the shore, a wood of timber lying on its side uncorrupted, as if formerly grown therein, when it was dry ground thrown down by the violence of the waves. Of this several persons have informed me (says Mr. Scawen) who have, as they said, often seen the same." So that the shores in Scilly, and the neighbouring shores in Cornwall (not forgetting the Wolf ledge of rocks midway between both) are equal evidences that there has been a subsidence of the land in these parts, and the memory of the inundation which followed upon that subsidence is preserved by tradition, though, like other traditions, greatly enlarged and obscured by fable. When this inundation happened we may be willing to know, but must be without hopes of knowing with any certainty. In the time of Strabo and Diodorus Siculus, the commerce of these islands seems to have been in full vigour; "abundance of tin carried in carts," says

account, became entitled to the rank and privileges of a thane.* Yet the royal navy had no existence under the Saxon monarchs, except in the pinnaces or barges for the king's own use. The different sea-ports of the kingdom were bound by their tenure to supply their quota of ships, whenever the public service required it. According to some of our historians, the ships of Edgar amounted to more than three thousand. But these ships, though many in number, must have been insignificant in point of size. That English ships were much valued in the time of Henry II. we may conclude from a law of that king prohibiting the sale of them to foreigners.† And the fleet of Richard the First were much admired at Messina in Sicily, for their number, magnitude, and beauty.‡

the latter; "but ten islands in all, says Strabo, and nine of these inhabited." The destruction therefore of Scilly, must be placed after the time of these authors; that is, after the Augustan age, but at what time after, I find nothing as yet that can determine: Plutarch indeed (of the Cessation of Oracles) hints that the islands round Britain were generally unpeopled in his time; if he includes Scilly among them, and was rightly informed, then this desolation must have happened betwixt the reign of Trajan and that of Augustus. There was a great subsidence in the southern coasts of England, in the time of Edward the First, whereby Winchelsea, near Rye, in Sussex was swallowed up, and its ruins are now three miles within the high sea, and for the unhappy inhabitants who had lost their town, Edward the First bought land and gave it them, and there stands the new Winchelsea. But I must observe that if the subsidence at Scilly and Mount's-Bay were so late, we could not have been without some notice of it, and in the complaints of the monks of Scilly to Edward the First, we must needs have found so great a misfortune particularly mentioned; whereas their petition was only for protection from pirates and foreign sailors. In the year 1014 happened a great inundation, of which the Saxon Chronicle gives this account: "Hoc item anno in vigiliis Sancti Michaelis contigit magna ista maris inundatio per latam hanc terram quæ longius expatiata, quam antea unquam, demersit multa oppida et hominum numerum inenarrabilem." But I think the catastrophe of these islands cannot be placed even so late as this; for the monks being placed here either by Athelstan, in the year 938, or soon after, nothing of this kind could have happened but it would have appeared somewhere or other, in the papers or history of Tavistock-abbey, at least, if the monks of Scilly were united to that abbey at its first foundation in the year 961. I therefore conjecture that this inundation must have happened before Athelstan's time; and by the Irish annals I find an inundation which might probably have affected the south of Ireland, and at the same time reached Scilly and the coast of Cornwall, which are not above fifty leagues distant from it to the east, nor much more than a degree to the south of it. "In the end of March A. D. 830, Hugh Dorndighe being monarch of Ireland, there happened such terrible shocks of thunder and lightning, that above a thousand persons were destroyed between Corca-Bascoin, a part of the county of Cork then so called, and the sea side. At the same time the sea broke through its banks in a violent manner, and overflowed a considerable tract of land. The island then called Innisfadda, on the west coast of this county, was forced asunder and divided into three parts This island, says my author, lies contiguous to two others, viz. Hare Island and Castle Island; which lying in a range, and being low ground, might have been very probably then rent by the ocean." As this inundation in the southern parts of Ireland seems well attested, and might not unlikely have reached Cornwall and Scilly, I should think it most suitable to history, that this was what reduced, divided, and destroyed the Scilly Islands, and over-run the lands on Mount's-Bay." *Borlase's Isles of Scilly*, pp. 57 ...... 61.---84........99.

† *Benedict. Abbas*, p. 368.

‡ *Gauf. Vinesauf.* lib. 2. c. 26 p. 316.----As numerous ships have been wrecked on the coasts of Cornwall, it may be proper to state the following particulars. We find in Sir H. Spelman's code of the ancient statute laws of

3. The principal articles of Cornish exportation, were tin and fish. We may form some idea of the great quantities of tin that were exported, from an article in the accounts of Henry de Casteilan, chamberlain of London in the year 1198. In these accounts, he charges himself with 379*l.* 18*s.* which he had received in fines from the merchants of London, for leave to export tin.‖ The royal revenues arising from the tin-mines of Cornwall and Devonshire, were valued at this time at two thousand marks a year; a sum equivalent to ten thousand pounds of our money. They were granted at that rate to queen Berengaria, widow of Richard the First.¶ In the time of Richard, son of king John, king of the Romans and earl of Cornwall, the Cornish mines were immensely rich; and the Jews being farmed out to him by his brother Henry the Third, their interest was at his disposal. In the mean time, the tin-mines in Spain were stopped from working by the Moors: And no tin was as yet discovered in Germany: So that Devonshire and Cornwall had all the trade of Europe for tin; and the earl almost the sole profit of that trade.* Henry the Third ordered the merchants not to send away the *tin* from his land or the earl of Cornwall's without licence, either by land or sea; and unless signed by the coinage of the king or their earl.† Our *fish* (certainly the pilchard) formed a considerable article of commerce.‡

the kingdom of England, that, by the ancient law or custom of the English, when a ship was wrecked on the coast, if those who escaped from it did not repair to it within a limited time, the ship and all belonging to it, that was driven ashore, became the right and property of the lord of the manor. Henry the First abhorring this custom, made a law to be observed throughout all his dominions, that, if but one man had escaped alive out of the wreck, the ship and its whole cargo should be given to him. This statute remained only in force during the life of the king who enacted it; for, under his successor, the nobles of the kingdom restored the ancient custom, to their own benefit. Henry the Second, however, revived the law of his grandfather, and enforced it with severe penalties against offenders.

‖ *Madox*, p. 531.

¶ *Rymer's Foed.* tom. i. p. 243.

* To Devonshire and Cornwall, the commerce for tin was solely confined till about the middle of the thirteenth century; when one of our tinners being disobliged by Richard earl of Cornwall, king of the Romans, went into Germany, found the same metal, and taught the Saxons how to distinguish, search for, and dress their tin. The quantity of tin, however, which the Saxons raised, was very inconsiderable, and by no means adequate to the expence of raising and carrying it by land. And our tin continued to be superior in quantity and quality, and facility of exportation, to that of all the rest of the world.

† See Patent Rolls.

‡ "The Cornish (says *Camden*) make a gainful trade of those little fish called Pilchards, which are seen upon the sea-coast, as it were in great swarms, from July to November. These they catch, garbage, salt, smoke, barrel,

In his satire against Henry of Avranches, poet-laureat to Henry the Third, Michael the Cornish poet, thus celebrates his native shores:---

Non opus est ut opes numeram quibus est opulenta,
Et per quas inopes sustentat non ope lenta:
Piscibus et stanno nusquam tam fertilis ora!

4. For the more easy disposal of our commodities, fairs and markets were instituted by the Anglo-Saxon kings: And the times and places in which the people were accustomed to assemble, were commonly regarded. Hence the weekly markets, were often held at churches, on Sundays. A little before the conqueror's time, the day was, in general, changed from Sunday to Saturday: But the markets were still kept in the vicinity of churches. The greater commercial meetings or fairs were always held near some cathedral church or monastery, on the anniversary of the dedication of the church, or on the festival of the saint to whom it was dedicated. The bishops and abbots observing that people came from all parts to celebrate the festivals of their patron saints, applied to the crown for charters to hold fairs at these particular times. By this means they consulted the accommodation of strangers; and, what was their chief motive, increased their own revenues by the tolls which their charters authorised them to levy at those fairs.* ----As *Launceston* was a principal residence of the earls of Cornwall for a great number of years, its consequence continually increased, and many liberties and privileges were bestowed on its inhabitants. Soon after the conquest, the market, which, from the time of Edward the Confessor, had been held at Lanstuphadon, or the "town of St. Stephen's church," about a mile distant, was transferred to Launceston; and in the reign of king John, the townsmen paid five marks for the privilege of removing the market-day from Sunday to Thursday; but it has since been changed to Saturday. In the reign of Henry the Third, the town was made a free borough by Richard, earl of Poitiers and

press; and so send them in great numbers to France, Spain, and Italy, where they are a welcome commodity, and are named *Fumados*." Pp. 3, 4.---The *Fumados* were, perhaps, the *Gerres* of Pliny.

* The occupiers of tenements held of the castle and honor of Plymton under certain rents and services constantly paid and observed, enjoy several benefits and immunities, and, in particular, are freed and discharged from paying any custom at *fairs and markets* within the counties of Devon and CORNWALL.

Cornwall, and brother to the king. He also granted the inhabitants some additional immunities, which were confirmed by subsequent charters.* ---- Of *Kellington*, the first mention I have met with, is in the reign of Henry III. when that king granted to Reginald de Ferrers, and his heirs, a market at his manor of Calweton, every Wednesday, and a fair annually, viz. on the eve, day, and morrow of the nativity of the blessed Mary.† --- There was a market at *St. German's*, at the Norman invasion. It was held on the Lord's day. But it was soon reduced to nothing by the rival market of the earl of Moreton at Trematon castle. --- The royalty of the town of *Bodmin* was at the time of the conquest held by this church; which had, as Domesday book informs us, in Bodmin, sixty-eight houses, and a market, valued at thirty-five shillings per annum, to which privilege of a market, with claim of a gallows, pillory, view of frank pledge, and a fair at Bodmin, the prior of this place certified his right in Edward the First's time. --- The bishops had two fairs yearly, within the manor of *Pawton* in *St. Breock*, on the first of May, and on Michaelmas-day.‡ --- The name of *Marazion*, or *Market-Jew*, (as my readers have been already informed) points out its market. And there is a tradition in the town, that there was a market of the Jews formerly there, and that it was held on the western strand of the sea.

5. As to the current coin of the county, it has been suggested, that we had none in gold, till Edward III. Yet in the Saxon and first Norman times, vast sums were paid in gold. The annual tribute exacted from the Cornish and Welsh by Athelstan, was twenty pounds of gold, and three hundred pounds in silver. And in Domesday, we find gold in ingots, contradistinguished from gold coin.§ There "were two coyners established at Exeter by the Saxons," says Camden. "The

* R. Fin. A. 7. Joh. p. 1. m. 12.

† Rex, &c. Sciatis nos concessisse, &c. Reginaldo de Ferrariis, quod ipse et Hæredes sui inperpetuum habeant unum mercatum apud manerium suum de Calweton, in comitatu Cornubiæ, singulis septimanis per diem Mercurii, et unam feriam ibidem singulis annis per tres dies duraturam, viz. in vigiliis, in die, et in crastino nativitatis beate Marie. Nisi mercatum illud et Feria illa sint ad nocumentum vicinorum, mercatorum, et vicinarum feriarum. Dat apud Wintoniam, 10 die Novembris, Cart. anno. 52. Henr. 3. m. 12.

‡ "They are held in Wadebridge-town, on the west side of the bridge, and enjoyed by Sir Wm. Morice, as lord of the manor. The town consists of only one street, in which are about thirty houses." *Tonkin's MSS.*

§ Libras auri ad pensum—libras ad numerum.

Norman kings continued the same form. In king Stephen's time, any earl and baron erected his mint; but Henry the Second suppressed them all; and granted the liberty of coining to certain cities and abbies. "In the time of Richard the First, money coined in the east parts of Germany, began to be in request in England for the purity thereof, and was called *Easterling* money "† The authors of the Magna Britannia‡ tell us, that, some years since, was found near Constantine church, a buff-bag full of silver pieces, some of king Arthur's coin, and some of king Canute's; and that a cross once stood on the spot where it was found. Carew§ mentions *leather-coins* found in the castle-wall at Launceston. They were French. Philip de Comines|| informs us, that for a long time after king John of France was taken prisoner, the current coin of that kingdom, was nothing but bits of leather, with a silver nail in the middle of them. Probably, these were some of the sort.

† *Camden's Remains*, pp. 203, 204. "Neuerthelesse (continues Camden) this easterling good money was in a short time so corrupted and clipped by Jewes, Italian vsurers called then *Corsini*, (who were the first Christians that brought in usury among vs) and Flemings, that the king by proclamation was enforced to call in the old money, make a new stampe and to erect exchanges where the weight of old money was exchanged for new, allowing thirteen-pence for every pound, to the great damage of the people, who beside their trauaile, charge, and long attendance received (as my author saith) of the bankers scant twentie shillings for thirtie, which the earle of Cornewall farmed of the king reserving only the third part for the king." The late Mr. Southgate, in a letter to the author, thus writes:—"The Anglo-Saxon coins bear a peculiar relation to your county. There was a copious mint at Exeter from the time of Athelstan, which is extended to the reign of Edward the First. A great number of silver coins were also struck at that place from the crown to the penny in the time of Charles, and an occasional mint also of the half-crown, shillings, and half-shillings in the reign of William III. These two last coinages have been already engraven in Folkes and Snelling, so that you need only mention them and refer to those authors. But a series of those Anglo-Saxon and English coins to Edward I. inclusive, which relate to the county of Devon, and make a part of its history, should certainly appear in your work, especially as they have never been brought together. And that I may contribute my share, I have already got drawings of several coins, struck not only at Exeter, but at Totnes, Lydford, Tingmouth, and I believe Barnstaple. At least I have procured one, from a private collection, of Ethelred II. the reverse of which reads EVRHSIGEMO. BARO. The duke of Devonshire has one, which reads BERDESI. I should be glad to know your sentiments on this subject, and by what name Barnstaple was called in the Saxon times. The drawings I have mentioned would have been completed long ago, but from the repeated disappointments I have met with from my delineator. I now employ young Basire, a parishioner of mine, and as soon as the series is finished, I will present them to you, together with the descriptions, and send them wherever you think proper. Town pieces and tradesmens tokens, as they are called, have of late years frequently made their appearance in county histories." The death of Mr. Southgate, put an end to this valuable correspondence.

‡ P. 310.

§ *Carew*, f. 116.

|| B. 5. c. 18.

I shall conclude this chapter with one observation. It is an idea at first carelessly adopted, and then repeated by almost all our historical writers, that the manufactures and commerce of this country, were yet in an infant state. But the truth is, manufacture, especially the woollen, had been growing up and flourishing under the Saxons and Normans, and spreading vigorously during the reigns of Henry II. and Richard I. But in the tumultuous reigns of John and Henry III. it languished, and almost sunk into annihilation.---A distinction should always be made between the first dawning of the arts, amidst the ignorance and unskilfulness of a semi-barbarous people, and their casual eclipse in civilized society. That the latter was the case, in the present instance with respect to England, and Cornwall in particular, I have no scruple in asserting.

CHAPTER THE NINTH.

LANGUAGE, LITERATURE, LITERARY CHARACTERS.

I.---1. AS the study of language must be always preparatory to that of the sciences, the state of the Cornu-British tongue at this conjuncture, and the changes which the Saxon and Norman invasions and settlements produced in it, seem to be the first and most obvious subjects for enquiry. The British tongue had several languages ingrafted in it, before the arrival of the Saxons. When the inhabitants of this island, therefore, were dispersed before the Saxon conquerors, they retired into Wales and Cornwall, and thence into Bretagne, after these innovations had made a considerable progress in the British language. Thus they carried with them a language which was not so greatly altered,* as to lose all its original features; though it retained not its oriental purity, as in Ireland and the Highlands.‡ And the Welsh and the

* In the distinct dialects of the British,----the Cornish, the Welsh and the Armoric, the radicals were so much alike, that they were known and admitted by the inhabitants of either country; but the grammatical construction of the language, and the mode of pronunciation so greatly varied in a short time, that those three tribes could, with difficulty, communicate their ideas to each other, in conversation. The Cornish dialect still preserved the more leading features of its original British. It was sonorous and bold; and spoken by the greatest part of present Devon, as well as Cornwall. The names of places and persons in Cornwall and in Bretagne, are very similar, and often the same. The late Mr. *Trevanion* of *Carhayes* in Cornwall, in a tour through Bretagne, was greatly surprized at the echoes of his own *name* and *seat:* It is very remarkable, that he there discovered both a *Trevanion* and a *Carhayes.* And the French emigrants at Bochym near Helston, in 1793, were delighted with the similarity of Cornish names to those of their own country of Bretagne, particularly *Bochym* and *Penquite.* I have heard, that once at Algiers a lady speaking *Welsh* was well understood by the Moors.---This reminds me of *Marchese Maffei,* who, in his Verona Illustrata, describes a small nation at the Lago di Guarde, beyond Roveredo, that spoke a *language of an unknown origin.* Of the *Romansh* spoken in the vicinity of this spot, Mr. Coxe gives us a very short vocabulary, in which, two words are nearly Welsh---*Mellen,* yellow, in Welsh, *Melyn;* and *God,* wood, in Welsh, *Coed* and *Gwydd.* It is the *distance* of these places from Wales, that occasions the wonder. If, however, the *Moorish* be a branch of the Arabic, or derived from the Phenician, we need not be surprized at its affinity with the Welsh. The similitude between the Welsh and the Arabic, may be learnt from *Bruce's* travels. "*Bahar Kolzom* is a name given to that part of the Red Sea where tradition says the Egyptians perished in pursuing the Israelites. A Welshman would write it *Mor y Coll'som;* in English, *the sea where we were lost:* Mr. Bruce translates it, *the sea of perdition.* The great affinity of the Welsh with the Phenicians, appears from a fragment, copied from one of the Bath Guides. It runs thus:---"Zus hu asphirà acrahitha, meni arits chuia; asphira hu chiyl d'alha dilh la strura ula shulma acrahn mydh; vehnia hu rucha d'alha dmchina cul ylma." The same in Welsh:---Sws yw aesffer a groniaetha, mewni arwys chwiwia; aesffer yw chwyl d'allu, dull ei ystraw oleua yshilfa ograwn fydd; i'w chwnu yw rhoch d'allu, dymchwyna cwbl hilfa. Translation of the Welsh;---"*Zws* is a mighty sphere producing a circle; in it the earth revolves; the mighty sphere shews the course of the self-puissant one; the nature of his inherent wisdom illuminates the seat of animation (world), thence made prolific; to make it ascend is the mighty breath of the self-puissant, which sets in motion the whole animated system." From this example it must appear that the Phenician and the Welsh are but one and the same language.

‡ I shall here exhibit the Lord's Prayer first in *British, Erse,* and *Irish,* and secondly in *Cornish, Welsh* and *Armoric;*

BRITISH.

Eyen taad rhuvnwytyn y neo foedodd;
Santeiddier yr hemvu taw:
De vedy dyrnas daw:
Guueler dy wollys arryddayar megis agyn y nefi.
Eyn-bara beunydda vul dyro innihed-divu:
Ammaddew ynny eyn deledion, megis agi maddevu in deledvvir ninaw:
Agna thowys ni in brofedigaeth:
Namyn gvvaredni rhag drug. Amen.

ERSE.

Ar Nathairne ata ar neamh.
Goma beannuigte hainmsa.
Gu deig do Rioghachdsa.
Dentar do Tholsi air dtalmhuin mar ata air neamh
Tabhair dhuinn ar bhfcacha, amhuil mhathmuid dar bhfeicheamhnuibh.
Agas na leig ambuadhread sinn.
Achd sor sinn o olac.
Oir is leatsa an Rioghachd an cumhachd agas an gloir gu scorraidh.
Amen.

IRISH.

Ar nathair ata ar neamh.
Naomhthar hainm.
Tigeadh do rioghachd.
Deuntar do thoil ar an ttalamh, mar do nithear ar neamh.
Ar naran laeathcamhail tabhair dhu. inn a niw.
Agus maith dhninn or bhfiaeha mar mhaitmidne dar bhfeitheamhnuibh fein.
Agus na leig sinn a ccatghuhadh.
Achd faor in o olc.
Oir is leachd fein an riogbachd agus an cumhachd, agus an ghloer go scorruighe. Amen.

Armoricans § were enabled to preserve it, from the remoteness or inaccessibility of their situation. From similar causes, the Cornish, also, upheld their ancient tongue in opposition to the Saxons; whilst the eastern provinces, compelled to adopt the Saxon language in a certain degree, very quickly lost the idiomatic genius of their own, and at length, indeed, every trace of it.

2. In every part of the island, the Saxons were despotic in imposing names. They called the Cornish *Kernow*, and the Roman *Cornubia Cornwealas*;* and our

ANCIENT CORNISH.

Pydzhadou a'n Arluyth.

An Taz ny es yn nef, bethens thy hannow ughelles, gwrenz doz thy gulasker: Bethens thy voth gwreiz yn oar kepare hag yn nef. Ro thyn ny hithow agan peb dyth bara; Gava thyn ny agan cam, kepare ha gava ny neb es cam ma erbyn ny; Nyn hombrek ny en antel, mez gwyth ny the worth drok: Rag gans te yn an mighterneth, an creveder, hag an' worryans, byz a venitha.

An dellna ra bo.

MODERN CORNISH.

Padar a'n Arluth.

Agan Taz leb ez en nev, benigas beth de hanno, gurra de gulasketh deaz, de voth beth gwrez en' oar pokar en nev. Ro dony hithow agan pyb dyth bara; Ha gava do ny agan cabmow, pokara ny gava an gy leb es cam ma war bidn ny: Ha na dege ny en antail, buz gwitha ny dort droge: Rag an mychteyrneth ew chee do honnen, ha an crevder, ha an 'worryans, rag bisqueth ha bisqueth.

An dellna ra bo.

WELSH.

Ein Tad yr hwn wyt yn y nefoedd, sancteiddier dy enw: Deued dy deyrmas; byd dy ewyllys ar yddaiar megis y mac yn y nefoedd dyro i ni heddyw ein bara beunyddiol: a maddeu i ni ein dyledion, fel y maddewn ni i'n dyledwyr: ac nar arwain my brofe digaeth, eithr gwared in rhag drwg.

ARMORIC.

Hon Tat, petung so en eoun, ot'h Hano bezet samtifiet De vet de omp ho Rovantelez Ha volonte bezet gret voar an douar euel en eoun Roit dezomp hinou hor bara bemdezier. Ha pardonnit dezomp hon offancon evelma pardon nomp d'ae re odeus hon offancet. Ua n'hon digacit quel e' tentation. Hoguen hon delivrit a droue.

§ *Camden* tells, that "the Armorican Britons, marying strange women in Armorica, did cut out their tongues, lest their children should corrupt the language with their mother's tongues." *Remaines*, p. 30. The Cornish approaches nearer to the Armoric, than to the Welsh or Irish. Q, though never used by the Welsh and Irish, was yet received by the Cornish, (as bisqueth *never)* though not so much used amongst the Cornish, as the Britons of France. It seems, however, to have been very anciently used in Cornwall, in the same manner as in the Armoric, viz. *Qu* as *K*. For I observed the ancient British name Kynedhav inscribed on the stone at Gulval, QVENETAV.

* "*Wall* in Cornwall comes from the Saxon *Wealh*, foreign or strange----the Saxons calling the inhabitants of this part Cornwealas as being foreigners and strangers to them; and their country *Wesewealas*, West Wales from its situation. Wealas first occurs in the laws of Ina which were made at least a hundred years after the extirpation of the Britons." *T. T.* p. 2.---" In the times of the Saxon wars, when a great many of the Britons retreated into this country, sheltering themselves in the nature of the place, (for, as for the land-roads, they knew they were by reason of mountains and the breaches made by æstuaries, in a manner unpassable; and those by sea were extreme dangerous to persons altogether ignorant of them:) then the Saxon conqueror, who called foreigners and every thing that was strange, *Wealsh*, named the inhabitants of this part *Cornwealas* and *West-wealas*. From hence arose the name Cornwallia, and in later writers Cornubia, as also that of some writers Occidua Wallia, *i. e.* West-Wales. So far is

viæ stratæ, streets: and towns placed on these streets, they named Street-towns, or *Strettons.* But they were not content with these changes. They imposed new names on places, wherever they could, without any reference to the old. It does not appear, indeed, that *Cornwall* was generally known by the name of *Triconshire,* notwithstanding Athelstan. They did not even stop here. They endeavoured to extirpate our language; by instituting Saxon schools, such as at Tavistock, (a reputed though no longer a legitimate town of Cornwall) and by discouraging the use of our vernacular tongue on all public occasions.* The conqueror and his followers, as soon as they were settled in this country, made every effort to substitute the Norman-French for the Anglo-Saxon, which was generally spoken in England. In their attempts, however, to recommend their own language to the attention of the English, both themselves and their successors were for several generations unsuccessful. The Saxon prevailed in every part of England, excepting Devonshire and Cornwall. In Devon, indeed, it became fashionable among the superior orders of the people, though

Cornwall from borrowing its name from the conquering Gauls, as is urged by some out of a compliment to the nation. But if they were as knowing at home as they are medling abroad, they would quickly apprehend that their Bretagne upon their sea-coast, is so called from ours; and that a little tract therein called Cornovaille, where the Cornish language is spoken, was so termed from those of our nation transplanted thither. For as those western Britons of ours were assisting to the Armoricans in France, in their wars against Cæsar, (which was, indeed, his pretence for the invasion of Britain,) and afterwards marching over thither and changing the name, called it Bretagne: so in former ages they sent aids to their countrymen the Britons against the Franks, and in those cruel Danish wars, many of them went over thither, where they left that more modern name of Cornovaille." *Gibson's Camden,* p. 2.---*Hengist's-Hill,* was, in Saxon *Hengestendun*; *Camelford,* was *Galulford*; *St. Michael's Mount, Michael's-Stow*; the *Land's-End, Penwith-Steort.* But the Cornish were very unwilling to adopt the Saxon appellation of places. There is one Saxon word, however, that seems to have crept early into our language, and to have been applied by the Cornish to church-yards in particular. In England, in general, no more is understood by *Hays,* than a small field or inclosure near an house. Fields so situated are so termed on numbers of estates in this country: but in the eastern part of England small fields so situated are named the *Haws,* derived from the Saxon word Hæz. *Ho* seems to signify a mound or boundary. Witness the terrace round the fort of Plymouth called the Ho; but it should be spelt *Hay.*

* According to the ingenious Mr. Britton, "the length of time through which the natives retained their original language," furnishes a presumption against the Roman conquest of Cornwall. P. 312. But Mr. B. should recollect, that the Romans did not wish to introduce their own language into any part of the island---that the latin, however, spontaneously crept into the *British,* and became incorporated with it, in proportion as the Romans mixed with the natives; and that more Roman words are to be found in the Cornu-British, than the British at large. The Saxons acted differently from the Romans. They attempted to substitute their own language for that of the natives; and of course, were not so successful on this side of the Tamar, as in other parts of the island, where they settled in greater numbers. This will sufficiently account for the long continuance of the Cornish tongue.

the inferior classes adhered firmly to their old vernacular tongue. Not that the Cornu-British was abandoned by every Devonian of rank or education: It was certainly spoken in Devonshire by persons of distinction, long after the present period.

II.---1. Whether any relics of our venerable language, now no longer oral, be yet preserved in traditionary proverbs, or songs, or MSS. or printed books, curiosity will naturally enquire. There are several proverbs still remaining in the ancient Cornish, all savouring of truth, some of pointed wit, some of deep wisdom. *Neb na gare y gwayn coll restoua:* "He that heeds not gain, must expect loss." *Neb na gare y gy, an gwra deveeder:* "He that regards not his dog, will make him a choak-sheep." *Guel yw guetha vel goofen:* "It is better to keep than to beg." *Gura da, rag ta honan te yn gura:* "Do good, for thyself thou dost it." Many proverbs relate to caution in speaking, as *Tau tavas:* "Be silent, tongue." *Cows nebas, cows da, ha da veth cowsas arta:* "Speak little, speak well, and well will be spoken again." Of talking of state-affairs, there are some remarkable cautions: *Cows nebas, cows da, nebas an yevern yw an gwella:* "Speak little, speak well, little of public matters is best." The danger of talking against the government is excellently represented in this proverb: *Nyn ges gun heb lagas, na kei heb scovern:* "There is no downs without eye, nor hedge without ears." In the following there is a sententious gravity----*Der taklow minniz ew brez teez gonvethes, avelan tacklow broaz: dreffen en tacklow broaz, ma an gymennow hetha go honnen; bus en tacklow minnis, ema an gye suyah haz go honnen:* "By small things are the minds of men discovered, as well as by great matters: Because in great things, they will stretch themselves; but in small matters, they follow their own nature." *Gwra, O mateyne, a tacklow ma, gen an gwella krevder, el boaz pideeres an marudgyan a go terman; ha an tacklow a vedn gwaynia klos theez rag nevera:* "Do, O king, those things which, with the best strength, may be thought the wonders of their times; and those things will gain glory to thee for ever." *Po rez deberra an bez, vidn heerath a seu; po res dal an vor, na oren pan a tu, thuryan, houl zethas, go gleth, po dihow:* "When thou comest into the world, length of sorrow follows; when thou beginnest the way, 'tis not known which side, east, west, to the north, or south."* We have a Cornish pastoral, not much unlike, I think, the twenty-seventh idyllium of Theocritus---- "Daphnis

* *Colloquies.*

Ese leath luck gen vue?	Is there milk enough with the cow?
Whelas tees tha trehe kesow.	Look men to cut turf.
Whelas poble tha trehe ithen.	Look people to cut furze.
Moas tha an gove tha herniah an verh.	Go to the smith to shoe the horses.
Gora an ohan en arder.	Put the oxen in the plow.
Aras an kensa an todn.	Plow first the lay.
Gora an soch, ha an troher, tha an gove.	Put the shear and coulter, to the smith.
Gora an dens harraw tha an gove tha lebma.	Put the harrow-tines to the smith to sharpen.
Danen rag teese tha trehe gorra.	Send for men to cut hay.
Whelas megouzion tha medge an isse.	Look reapers to reap the corn.
Pan a priz rag hearne?	What price for pilchards?
Priz dah.	A good price.
Deez ubba do gawaz an dega?	Come you here to have the tithe?
Thera ve cara why en colon, betha why lawanneck.	I love you in heart, be you merry.
Bene tu gana.	Farewell.
Hagar awell, ha auel teag.	Bad, or foul weather, and fair weather.
Yein kuer, tarednow, ha golowas, er, reu, gwenz, ha clehe, ha kezer.	Cold weather, thunder, and lightning, snow, frost, wind, and ice, and hail.
Bennen vaz, ha dre-maz.	The good woman, and the good man, i. e. the bride and bridegroom.
Ma hy a humthan.	She is breeding.
Gwag o ve, ra ve gawas haunsell?	I am hungry, shall I have breakfast?
Gora an bara en foarn.	Put the bread in the oven.
En an bara pebes luck?	Is the bread baked enough?
Gora tees en an skeber tha drushen.	Put men in the barn to thresh.
Gora an vose tha shakiah an kala.	Put the maid to shake the straw.
Gora oh tees tha'n fer tha guarr ohan.	Put my men to the fair to sell oxen.
Dry dre an mona, ha perna muy.	Bring home the money, and buy more.
Bargidnia gen dean da mose da whele sten.	Bargain with a man to go to work tin, or to a tin-work.
Ry tha stener deck pens en blethan.	Give to a tinner ten pounds a year.
Coria an stuff stenes tha an stampes.	Carry the tin-stuff to the stamping-mill
Cariah an stean tha an foge.	Carry the tin to the blowing-house.

Proverbial Rhymes.

An lavor goth ewe lavar gwir,	The old saying is a true saying,
Ne vedn nevera doaz vas a tavaz re hir;	Never will come good from a tongue too long;
Bes den heb tavaz a gollas e dir.	But a man without a tongue shall lose his land.
Ez kez? ez, po neg ez; ina sez kez,	Is there cheese? is there, or is there not; if there be cheese,
Dro kez; po negez uez, dro peth ez.	Bring cheese; if there is not cheese, bring what there is.
Sav a man, kebner tha li, ha ker tha'n hal;	Get up, take thy breakfast, and go to the moor;*

* That is, go and work to Tin; they call that especially going to Moor, when they work on the Stream Tin.

and the Shepherdess." They are both equally characterized by flippancy, familiarity, and the rudest rusticity. Our Cornish idyllium has all the simplicity of

Mor-teed a metten travyyth ne dal.	The sea-tide of the morning is nothing worth.

This proverb is spoken in St. Just, in Penwith, where are both fishermen and tinners.

Karendzhia, vendzhia,	Good will (or love) would do it.
Ravaethiaz na vendzhia.	Covetousness will not do it.

These four I had from Mr. Lhuyd, when he was in Cornwall.—Tonkin.

Cusal ha teg, sirra wheage,	Soft and fair, sweet Sir,
Moaz pell.	Goes far.
Re a ydn dra ny dal traveth.	Too much of one thing is good for nothing
Ma leiaz gwreage,	There are many wives,
Lacka vel zeage.	Worse than grains.
Gwell gerrss,	Better left,
Vel kommeres;	Than taken;
Ha ma leiaz, bennen,	And there are many women,
Pokare an guenen,	Like the bees;
Eye vedn gwerraz dege teez	They will help bring men
Dendle peath a'n beaze.	To get the wealth of the world.
Fleaz hep skeeanz,	Children without knowlege,
Vedn guile go sceanz;	Will do (to) their sense;
Buz mor crown gy penderi,	But if they should consider,
Pan del go gwary,	What ought to be their play,
Ha madra ta,	And study well,
Pandrig seera, ha damma?	What did father, and mother?
Na ra henz moaz dan cooz,	They should not go to the wood,
Do kuntle go booz;	To gather their meat;
Buz, gen nebas lavirians,	But, with little labour,
Eye venjah dendle go booz, ha dillaz,	They would get their meat, and cloaths.
Cowzow do ve,	Speak to me,
Che dean mor ffeer,	Thou man so wise,
Do leba ez mear a peath, ha leiaz tir;	To whom is much of wealth, and much land;
Ha me rig clowaz an poble galarou,	And I did hear the people complain,
Ta eth reas do chee eithick gwreag dah:	That there is to thee a huge wife good:
Hye oare gwile padn dah gen tye glan;	She knows to make cloth good with her wool;
Ha et eye ollaz, hye dalveath gowas tane.	And she must hearth it, she ought to have fire.
Na dalle deez perna kinnis war an sawe,	Nor ought men buy fuel by the seame,
Na moaz moaz cuntle an drize dro dan keaw:	Nor go to gather brambles about the hedges;
Rag hedda vedn boz cowzes dro dan pow:	For that will be spoken about the country;
Gwell eye veyha perna nebas glow;	Better she had bought some coal;
He hedna vedn gus tubm a theller e a rag.	And that will warm you behind and before.
Ha why el evah cor gwella, mor seez de brage.	And you may drink best beer, if you have malt.
Na dale dien gwile treven war an treath;	Nor ought men to make houses on the sand;
Buz, mor mennow direvall war bidn an pow yeine,	But, if you will build up against the country cold,
Why dal veya gowas an brossa mine,	You must have the biggest stones,
Ha ryney vedn dirra bidn mor, ha gwenz.	And they will last against sea, and wind.
Na-g-ez drog vyth grez, lebben, na kenz.	There is no hurt at all done, now, nor before."

These I had from Mr. Lhuyd; and since, with some difference, from Mr. Gwavas, whose is the translation.—(Tonkin.)

the ancient Amœbean strain. It resembles the extemporaneous numbers of the Sicilian and the Tuscan shepherds. And the old Cornish had the same readiness in metrical responses, as the Welsh possess at the present day. "Incompositum temere ac rudem alternis jaciebant."† Of MSS. in the Cornish, perhaps, there is one only, of great antiquity. It is emphatically called, the *Cotton MS.*‡ - - - - With respect

" This sort of verse was, for what I can yet find, the oldest, if not the only verse amongst the ancient Britons. for tis the oldest in our Welsh books, and I have heard an old man repeat one of them in the Highlands of Scotland; and had another from the clerk of St. Just, viz.

An lavar koth yw lavar gwir,	The old saying is a true saying,
Na boz nevra doz vaz an tavaz re hir;	A tongue too long never did good:
Bez den heb davaz o gollaz i dir.	But he that had no tongue, lost his land.

† A Cornish Idyll.

Pelea era why moaz moz, fettow, teag,	Pray whither so trippingly, pretty fair maid,
Gen agaz bedgeth gwin, ha agaz blew mellyn?	With your face rosy-white, and your soft yellow hair?
Mi a moaz tha'n venton, sarra wheag,	Sweet sir to the well in the summer-wood shade,
Rag delkiow sevi gwra muzi teag.	For strawberry-leaves* make the young maiden fair.
Pea ve moaz gen a why, moz, fettow, teag,	Shall I go with you, pretty fair maid to the wood,
Gen agaz bedgeth gwin, ha agaz blew mellyn?	With your face rosy-white, and your soft yellow hair?
Greuh mena why, sarra wheag,	Sweet sir, if you please - - - it will do my heart good—
Rag delkiow sevi gwra muzi teag.	For strawberry-leaves make the young maiden fair.
Fatla gura ve agaz gorra why en dowr,	If gently I lay you on strawberries down,
Gen agaz, &c.	With your face rosy-white, and your soft yellow hair?
Me vedn sevel arta, sarra wheag,	I will rise up again, Sir, nor mind a green gown—
Rag, &c.	For strawberry-leaves make the young maiden fair.
Fatla gura ve agaz dry why gen flo,	And, what if I bring you with child in the wood,
Gen agaz, &c.	With your face rosy-white and your soft yellow hair?
Me vedn ethone, sarra wheag,	I will bear it, sweet sir, - - - it will do my heart good—
Rag, &c.	For strawberry-leaves make the young maiden fair.
Pew vedn a why gawas rag seera rag guz flo,	Pray, who to your child shall be father, pray who,
Gen agaz, &c.	With your face rosy-white, and your soft yellow hair?
Why ra boz e seera, sarra wheag,	Be father, sweet sir! Why no other than you!
Rag, &c.	For strawberry-leaves make the young maiden fair.
Pen dre vedd a why geil rag lednow rag 'as flo,	But your child, pretty maid, will want whittles, perdie,
Gen agaz, &c.	With your face rosy-white, and your soft yellow hair?
E seera veath trehez, sarra wheag,	Sweet Sir! his good father a taylor shall be—
Rag delkiow sevi gwra muzi teag.	For strawberry-leaves make the young maiden fair."

‡ "I know not whether I mentioned that I had sent Mr. Moor a copy of an old Cornish glossary in the Cotton library. It is a valuable curiosity; being probably seven or eight hundred years old. If you cannot procure it, you shall have a copy of mine: alphabetically, or in the order of the Cotton MS. which is in continued lines, but with some regard to natural order." *Extract of a letter from Lhuyd to Tonkin.* - - - - " Mr. Anstis found a British vocabulary, hand-written many ages since, in the Cotton Library in London, and, as he did

* In the "Rival Mothers" of Madame de Genlis, Zephyrine was detected in eating the strawberries which were prepared for washing Mademoiselle du Rocher's hands.

to books, so inattentive were the Cornish to printing, that many years after the discovery of this art, they never adverted to the preservation of the MSS. in their language.

always, so according to his good will on the like occasions before and after, he wrote to me about it. When I had looked over the book, I perceived very well that it was not a Welsh vocabulary, according to the Latin name (written at the latter end) vocabularium wallicum; but a Cornish vocabulary, as the thing (according to my thought) must appear to every British reader, that shall consider upon the translations of these Latin words, viz. Angelus, *Ail*; Stella, *Steren*; Membrum, *Ezel*; Supercilium, *Abranz*; Collum, *Conna*; Palatum, *Stefenic*; Mentum, *Elget*; Tibia, *Elesker*; Vitricus, *Altro*; Regina, *Ruivanes*; Vulgus, *Pobel biogo*; Puer, *Floh*; Senex, *Coth*; Mercator, *Guicour*: Prora, *Flurrog*; Umbra, *Scod*; Milvus, *Scoul*; Bufo, *Croinoc*; Rana, *Guilschin*; Passer, *Golvan*; Pullus, *Ydhnunc*; Scomber, *Brethyl*; Lucius, *Denshoc dour*; Vulpes, *Louuern*; Ursus, *Ors*; Scrofa, *Guis*; Echinus, *Sorb*; and many other words, which are not known among us Welshmen. I know full well that I could produce one, and that with more true likeness, than can the small vocabulary of the British Armorick, or British of the country of Lezou in France, be; for that dialect is near thereunto; and in truth there are many words of them to this day still spoken by the people of Lezou, although they are not used now in the county of Cornwall. But this wrong-thinking is put away, without much trouble, when we discover that the author of this vocabulary, when he was in want for British words, did write down Old English words for the same, by giving them sometimes a Cornish termination; and did not bring any of the words from the French, as he would without doubt, if he had been an Armorick Briton. Now these, and the like, are the words thereof, taken out of the Old English; Comes, *Yurl*; Lector, *Redior*; Hamus, *Hye*; Fiald, *Harfel*; Saltator, *Lappier*; Sartor, *Seuyad*; Contentiosus, *Strivor*; Spinther, *Broach*; Fibula, *Streing*; Raptor, *Robbior*; Noctua, *Hule*; Halec, *Herring*; Prahun, *Bidin*; Lagena, *Kanna*; Trutta, *Trud*. Now as it could not be any Armorick Briton, that wrote this vocabulary, so neither could it be written by any Welshman. For had he been a Welshman, he would without further consideration, have written *Darlhennodh, Breyr, Hox, Telyn (or Kruth) Neidiur, Guniadydh, Kynhennys, Guaeg, Aruestr, Yspeiliur, Pylhyan, Pennog, Guerlodh, Ysten (*or *Kynnog Piser,* or *Kostrelh)* and *Brethylh*. In like manner, if it had been done by an Armoric Briton, he would never have named the things called in Latin, *Quercus, Rhamnus, Melis, Lepus, Hœdus*; Glastanen, Eithinen, Broz, Scouarnog, Min: but instead thereof, *Guazen daro, Lan, Lus, Gat,* and *Gavar bian*. Doctor Davies (according to my thought) has named this Cornish Vocabulary in the Cotton Library, 'Liber Landavensis: for there are many words, in this Welsh vocabulary, marked, Lib. Land. which I never saw in another book. But yet, as he had seen the book which is now in the Cotton Library, I wonder that he would not draw all the words from that to his own book. Nevertheless the truth is, I know very well that the words therein marked Lib. Land. are not written in the book called Liber Landavensis: for I have looked over that before written book, in the library of that most learned and most knowing gentleman, the lord of Lanner in the county of Guenez, i. e. North Wales, and likewise a fair transcript in the library of Jesus College, in Oxford. There is some hope in me, that the reader will forgive me, that I do not always write after the language of our time, nor yet keep to the writing retained in this Cornish vocabulary. By perusing the aforesaid written books, I have discovered that there have happened four noted changes (or variations) and remember very much, in the Cornish tongue, within this age, or these last hundred years: and the same being before very little printed in the Latin and Celtic vocabulary, I was very desirous to give them in the Cornish English vocabulary by hand here to you. The first change is, to put the letter *b*, before the letter *m*, and to speak and write *Tybm, Tabm, Kabm, Gybman, Krobman,* and *Kylobman*, &c. in the place of *Tym. Tvm, Kam, Gymman, Kromman,* and *Kylomman*. The second is to put the letter *d*, before the letter *n*; and to speak thus, in the place of *Pen, Pan, Pren*; *Guyn, Guan, Bron, Brynan*: Pedn, Padn, Predn, Guydn, Guadn, Brodn, Brydnan. Neither did I see fit to give a place to these changes in this vocabulary; for neither will they hereafter retain these changes; and likewise their language is thence more hard and rugged, than it was before: and for that many times you must turn the *m*, and *n*, to *b*, and *d*, by saying *tubbi, obba, hodda, hedda,* where you said before *tubmi, obma, hodna,* and *hedna*. And this second novelty hath cast off these

2. As the language§ of the *Saxons* operated, at this period, so little on the Cornish, to wave a distinct consideration of their literature---would scarcely be deemed an omission. With the Normans our connexion was more intimate. The

words so far from the former words *tummi*, omma, *henna*, and *hanna*,—that not any can at all, neither *Armorick Briton*, nor yet *Welshman*, find out their foundation, by seeing from what place they are come. The third change is, to put the letter *d* before *s*, (the which *s* is almost always pronounced as *z)* and to speak the *s* as *sh*, for I have found out in one of the aforesaid written books, which is a book setting forth miracles out of the holy scripture, written, more or less, one hundred and fifty years since, where are these words just as you now speak them, *Kridzhi*, *Pidzhi*, *Bohodzock*, *Pedzhar*, *Bledzhar*, *Lagadzhò*, &c. instead of these, *Cresy*, *Pesy*, *Behosoc*, *Peswar*, *Lagaz*. I know very well that you do not write these words as I write them, with dzh, but only with the single letter *g*, or with an *i* consonant; but this falls in with the manner of the English writing: and since the speaking is from thence, the writing must be put and likewise changed from z, [or s] as was the s before from *d* or *t*. The fourth change is turned very much like the third: and that is, to put *sh* after *t*, or (according to the Armoric writing) of late the letter *t*, for *ch:* and so to change the words *Ty* (or *Tey)* to *Tshey*; *Ti* to *Thi* (or *Chee) Pysgetta*, to *Pysgetsha*, and many more the like. From whence the other speakings, in which you go off very far from us Welshmen, viz. in speaking *a* for *e*; *e* for *o* and *y*; *i* for *e*; *o* for *a*; and *v* consonant for *f*; and likewise *h* for *x*; *th*, *s*, or *h*, for *t* and *d*; and *l* for *lh*; nor will I for any thing take upon me these novelties; in part, for that the speaking from thence is easy enough; and in part, for that few of them are so old (if any of them are very old) as our language, and the language of the people of Lezou. And another is, in naming of late the letter *t*, for *s*; which is not so hugely old, yet may be old enough for the good taking, and keeping it hereafter. But now the reader will ask me without doubt, why I have in this writing, preserved the aforesaid alterations myself, since I knew the deficiencies of them? my answer is, that it was my great desire that they might be taken aright; and that every one might know to speak Cornish (or understand further) according to this letter. But my hope is, that you will not in such a manner suffer any other defects in your future Cornish printings, as you have hitherto done in the forewritten alterations.—Neither can any one make many novelties in any tongue so ever at one time. It is an early work, and therefore too short a licence to take any one thing, before that it be born and bred in the country, to offer it. When any one is willing to know the more late Cornish alterations, that he may the better find them out, let him compare the Cornish words with the like Welsh words of the country of Gunek (or which is much nearer) and the Armorick words; and when you see the agreement and concord, about the consonant letters of these two tongues, then you may see whether the Cornish hath kept to these consonants, or not; if not, you may without any doubt, know, that the Cornish words are changed. For example; when you see that we turn the English words, *to laugh*, *to play*, *to whistle*, *bitter*, *six*, *sister*, in the language of Guenek, *xuerthin*, *xuare*, *xuibany*, *xueru*, *xuex*, *xuaer*; and in the Cornish, *xoasin*, *xoari*, *xuibanat*; *xuero*, *xeux xosr*; but in the Cornish, *huerthin*, *guare*, *huibanat*; *huero*, *hui*, *hor*; we know then very easily that the Cornish is changed. For the like passages are never thus turned by the people of the Welsh Guenez; and the people of Lezou have learned to turn from them" *Lhuyd's Preface to his Cornish Grammar and Vocabulary*.--- Among some old British MSS. which *Pryce* describes, there are two, which he calls *Loegrian-British*. One is entitled Ovidii Nasonis Artis Amatoriæ, Lib Primus. This old fragment is bound with various others, and is preserved in the Bodleian Library, NE. D. 2. 19. The other is a tract of Eutex, the grammarian's *De Discernendis Conjugationibus*, gloss'd with British. They seem to have been the old Loegrian British, in some measure yet retained in Cornwall; which I gather partly from the elegance of the hand, and partly from some terms; as morhaur, *many*, *much*, caiauc, *a book* (probably from the Latin *codice)* guarim, *a play*; guardi, *a scene*, &c. not to insist upon the plural termination of nouns in *ou*; as loimou, *bushes*; runiou, *fillets*; which was constant amongst the Cornish as well as the Armoric Britons, and never used in Wales.

§ A specimen of the Saxon language, from the Saxon chronicle. Brittene Igland is ehta hundmila lang. ed twa hund brad. And her sind on wis Iglande fif getheode. Englisc ed Brittisc ed Wilsc ed Scittisc ed Pihtisc ed

Saxons were, by no means, the patrons of science. Illiterate and fierce, themselves, the looked down with contempt on the noiseless pursuits of the learned.---In divinity, the subtleties of casuistry, every where, usurped the place of truth: And, indeed, the most contemptible quibbling seemed to derive to the disputant the fame of erudition. At this juncture we have only to contemplate mental darkness wherever we turn our eyes. The prospect is, doubtless, dreary: But a few scattered rays from the Scandinavian muse seem to break, at times, through the gloom. Adhelm, a prince of the royal family of Wessex, and a bishop of Sherburne, was the best poet of his age: And the greater number of our kings, after the union of the heptarchy, from Egbert even to Harold, discovered a genius or prepossession for the poetry of the north. Alfred regularly allotted a part of his time amidst all the turbulence of war, to the Saxon poets: And Canute was a distinguished patron of the bards. As these kings, therefore, were more especially conversant with the original inhabitants of East-Cornwall; and as the Saxon and Danish poetry was highly figurative, and in this respect resembled the strains of the Druids; it is probable that the best educated people in this county were not inattentive to the northern muses, both with a view to preferment, and from a disposition to amuse their minds with the fables of Odin. The Normans avowed themselves|| the friends of literature; and endeavoured to enlarge the circle of the sciences; and to introduce a taste for the fine arts. Under their

Bocleden. Erest weron bugend wises landes Brittes wa coman of Armenia, ed gesatan suthewearde Brittene arost-Da Gelamp hir y Pihtis coman of suthean Scithean: mid langum Scippum na manegum. ed wa coman arost on nord hybernan up. ed sar bædon.

|| Most of our proverbs in the English language were in circulation, I believe, before the close of this period. "*To give one a Cornish hug.*" A Cornish hug is a lock in the art of wrestling, peculiar to the Cornish-men, who have always been famous for their skill in that manly exercise, which they still continue to practise.---"*Hengston-down, well ywrought, is worth London-town dear ybought.*" Hengston-down was supposed not only to be extremely rich in tin, but also to have in its bowels Cornish diamonds, vulgarly estimated superior to those of India. In Fuller's time, the tin began to fail here, having fallen, as he terms it, to a scant-saving scarcity. As to the diamonds, no one has yet judged it worth his while to dig for them.---"*He is to be summoned before the mayor of Halgaver.*" This is a jocular and imaginary court, wherein men make merriment to themselves, presenting such persons as go slovenly in their attire, untrussed, wanting a spur, &c. where judgment in formal terms is given against them, and executed, more to the scorn than the hurt of the persons.---"*When Dudman and Ramhead meet.*" These are two headlands, well known to sailors; they are near twenty miles asunder; whence this proverb is meant to express an impossibility. Fuller observes that, nevertheless, these two points have since met together (though not in position) in possession of the same owner, Sir Pierce Edgecombe enjoying one in his own right, and the other in right of his wife.---"*The*

influence, the sciences were cultivated with increasing success; though the Aristotelian logic had spread over them a most unpleasing colour. But theology was deeply tinctured by it: And the school-divinity enjoyed great triumphs in the monasteries that were rising on every side. The canon and the civil law, and even the common law were infected by the subtleties of logic. In the mean time, the study of medicine, which was almost confined to the clergy, and the profession of which had become so lucrative, that it drew even the monks from their cloysters, was subjected to the influence of astrology and magic. That the polite arts should have made any striking progress at this period, is more than we can expect: Yet the Normans were as attentive to poetry, as the Anglo-Saxons; particularly latin poetry.¶

III. I meet with no records of particular schools erected in Cornwall, by the original natives, the Saxons, or the Normans; though, doubtless, in this long space of time, many seminaries must have sprung up and flourished in Exeter and the neighbourhood, under the genial influence of so many kings and great personages, who visited our metropolis, and who favoured literature in every shape. Schools were now attached very commonly to cathedrals and monasteries. And we had conventual schools, in Cornwall. Indeed, our religious houses might be considered as colleges. All the orders of our religious men were employed in literary pursuits--- some in the transcript of manuscripts, and others in writing the annals of their country.

devil will not come into Cornwall for fear of being put into a pie." The people of Cornwall make pies of almost every thing eatable; as squab-pie, herby-pie, pilchard-pie, mugetty-pie, &c. &c.----" *He doth sail into Cornwall without a bark.*" This is an Italian proverb, signifying that a man's wife has made him one of the knights of the bull's feather. The whole jest, if there be any, lying in the similitude of the words Cornwall and cornua, horns. Fuller quotes a prophecy in the Cornish language, the sense of which is, that Truru consists of three streets, but a time will come when it shall be asked where Truru stood. On this he observes, that he trusts the men of that town are too wise to mind this prediction, any more than another of the same kind, presaging evil to the town, because ru, ru, which in English is woe, woe, is twice expressed in the Cornish name thereof. But, says he, " let the men of Truru but practise the first syllable in the name of their town, (meaning truth, i. e. integrity) and they may be safe and secure from all danger arising from the second."

¶ And it is natural to suppose, that the learned Britons of Devonshire and Cornwall, would fix on the latin tongue as better adapted for conveying their ideas even to their own countrymen, than the Cornu-British, which was known within a very small circuit, or than the Saxon, which was as yet in a very fluctuating state, and which was greatly disrelished by their countrymen in general; or than the Norman, which had scarcely gained a footing among the English.

For these purposes particular rooms were assigned in our monasteries, and estates were often granted. If the studious any where enjoyed a pause of stillness, it was in the retirement of the monastery. In this view, religious houses are by no means to be despised; whilst we observe their utility, if not in immediately softening the manners, yet in affording a retreat for the studious. The pursuits of these men, though mostly ill directed, in the dark ages before us, ultimately contributed to the advancement of literature.

IV. Of our literary natives, the *divines* claim the priority.---The first Cornish theologian was HUCARIUS the levite, who (as *Fuller** tells, from Bale and Pits) was born in this county, and lived at St. Germans; was a pious and learned man, and wrote one hundred and ten homilies, besides other books---now, I believe, all lost. He flourished in 1040.----Whether GERALDUS CORNUBIENSIS were a theologican or not, we are not able to say: But he seems to be the second Cornish writer upon record; and to have flourished in the year 1150.†----About the year 1170, JOHN OF CORNWALL, was a student at Rome, and in high favor with pope Alexander the Third. He wrote various books, and one, in particular, De Incarnatione Christi, against Peter Lombard, who affirmed "quod christus secundum quod homo est, aliquid non est." This book he dedicated to his friend the pope.‡---From SIMON

* *Worthies*, p. 202.---"In the abbey of St. Germans, A. D. 1040, in the time of Livignus, bishop of Kirton, lived Hucarius, commonly called the Levite, as Bale and others in their writings of Britain tell us; perhaps for that he assisted the priest at the altar, as the Levites of old did, and was more excellent, or did exceed all others in that particular. Otherwise, by the appellation Levite we must understand him a priest, and that he was universally famous in performing his function of preaching and divine service. Certain it is he was a holy and learned man, as the one hundred and ten homilies or sermons, and many other books, which he wrote, declare; but whether he was a native of this province I know not." *Hals*, p. 140.

† "There are (says bishop *Nicholson*, p. 97. speaking of Caradoc of Lancarvan's History of Wales) "three MSS. of good note mentioned by archbishop Usher, (Hist. Eccles. Brit. pp. 29, 32.) which seem to reach much higher than Caradocus pretends to go, all which I guess to have been written about the same time. The first is in Welsh, in Sir John Cotton's library, reported to be the same that was translated by Geoffry of Monmouth. The second is in old English by one Lazimon; and the third, as I take it, in latin, by Geraldus Cornubiensis." Geraldus, if contemporary with Geoffry of Monmouth, lived about 1150.

‡ "Bali, out of Leland tells vs, centuary three, number six, that there flourished a learned man in Cornwall in 1173, named *John de Cornwall*, who beinge well educated in the latin tongue, trauelled beyond the seas, and studdyed the liberal arts in forreigne vniuersities, but chiefly at Rome, where he grew famous for his learninge, which recommended him to the notice of pope Alexander the Third, about the yeare 1180; at which tyme Peter Lombard, (somtyme bishop of Paris, and master of the sentences) had vented som doctrines in favour of Arianisme; wherevpon as Mathew Paris informs us, pope Alexander III. writt to the archbishops of France to suppress the same, but their

THURNAY, whom we find, also, in the catalogue of our divines, no great honor was derived to his native county. "That knowlege puffeth up" is a position sadly exemplified in Simon Thurnay.§ In *poetry*, I would force into the service, the celebrated JOSEPH OF EXETER; since Exeter was still, in courtesy, the metropolis of Cornwall. But I must send my readers into "Devonshire," for the memoirs of Joseph.|| ---- MICHAEL *Cornubiensis* I believe, must stand forth our solitary

indeavors prouinge ineffectual ---- the said pope gaue orders to our John of Cornwall, to write against Lombard and his doctrine, who therevpon writt a booke called De Homine Assumpto; which booke the master of the sentences indeavoured to refute, by writinge an answer thereto, but his holyness and the Roman clergie thought Lombard's booke to consist of weake and fallacious argvments; wherevpon our John of Cornwall by the said pope, was stiled a Catholique Doctor." *Hals* (No. 6.) *in St. Martin-Meneg.*

§ "A. D. 1201, one *Simon Thurnaius*, a Cornishman, brought up in learning, did, by diligence and study, so prosper therein, that he became excellent in all the liberal sciences, that in his days none was thought to be like unto him. He left Oxenford, where he had been a student, and went to Paris, and there became a priest, and studied divinity, and therein became so excellent, and of so deep a judgment, that he was made chief of the Sorbonists. At length he became so proud of his learning, and did glory so much therein, that he would be singular, and thought himself to be another Aristotle; and so much blinded was he therein, and waxed so in love with Aristotle, that he preferred him before Moses and Christ. But behold God's just judgment! for suddenly his memory failed him, and he waxed so forgetful, that he could neither call to remembrance any thing that he had done, neither could he discern to read, or know a letter in the book." *Hooker's MSS.* ---- *Fuller* says, (Worthies, p. 203.) this *Thurnay* not only turned fool, but was struck with dumbness likewise. *Bale* tells us, that he made an inarticulate sound, like lowing. *Polydore Virgil* observes of him (lib. 15. Angl. Hist.) juvene nil acutius, sene nihil obtusius. This great judgment befel him about the year 1201.

|| "Joseph of Excester followed our king Richard the First, in his warres, in the Holy Land, celebrated his acts in a book called Antiocheides, and turned Dares Phrygius so happily into verse, that it hath bene printed not long since in Germany, vnder the name of Cornelius Nepos. The passing of the pleasant riuer Simois by Troy, and the encounter betweene the waues of the sea, and it, at the disemboging, or inlet thereof, he liuely setteth forth thus;

Proxima rura rigans alio peregrinus ab orbe
Visurus Troiam Simois, longoque meatu
Emeruisse velit, vt per tot regna, tot vrbes
Exeat æquoreas tandem Troianus in vndas.
Dumque indefesso miratur Pergama visu
Lapsurum suspendit iter, fluuiumque moratur,
Tardior & totam complecti destinat vrbem:
Suspensis infensus aquis violentior instat
Nereus, atque amnem cogens proculire minorem;
Proximus accedit vrbi, contendere credas
Quis propior, sic alternis concurritur vndis,
Sic crebas iterant voces, sic iurgia miscent.

You may at one view behold mount Ida with his trees, and the country adjacent to Troy in these few lines, as in a most pleasant prospect presented vnto you thus, by the said Joseph:

Haud procul incumbens intercurrentibus aruis
Idæus consurgit apex, vetus incola montis
Silua viret, vernat abies procera, cupressus

poet:¶ And I by no means think him a contemptible one. He flourished in the

Flebilis, interpres laurus, vaga pinus, oliua
Concilians, cornus venatrix, fraxinus audax,
Stat comitis patiens vlmus, nunquamque senescens
Cantatrix buxui: paulo procliuius aruum
Ebria vitis habet non dedignata latere
Cancricolam poscit Phœbum, vicinus aristas
Prægnantes fæcundat ager, non plura Falernus
Vina bibit, non tot pascu Campania messes.

A right woman and lady like disdaine may be obserued in the same author, where he bringeth in Pallas, mating dame Iuno with modest disdainfulnesse before Paris, in the action of beauty, a matter of greatest importance in that sex, after this manner of reply;

Magna parens superum, nec, enim nego; magna Tonantis
Nupta, nec inuideo; meritum, Paris inclyte, nostrum
Si quod erat carpsit; testor freta, testor Olympum,
Testor humum, non armatas in prælia linguæ
Credideram venisse deas; hac parte loquacem
Erubeo sexum, minus hic quam fæmina possum;
Martem alium didici, victoria fæda vbi victus
Plus laudis victore feret, nostrisque trophæis
Hic haud notus honos. Sed quo regina dearum
Effatu tendit, Dea sit, cedo, imo Dearum
Maxima non dextræ sortiri sceptra potentis,
Partiriue Iouem certatim venimus, illa
Illa habeat, quæ se ostentat.

In the commendation of Britaine, for breeding martiall men, and praise of the famous king Arthur, he sung in his Antiocheidos, these which onely remaine out of that work:

.... Inclita fulsit
Posteritas ducibus tantis, tot diues alumnis,
Tot fæcunda viris, premerent qui viribus orbem,
Et fama veteres. Hinc Constantinus adeptus
Imperium, Romam tenuit, Byzantion auxit.
Hinc Senonum ductor captiva Brennius vrbe,
Romuleas domuit flammis victricibus arces.
Hinc & Scæua satus, pars non obscura tumultus
Ciuilis, Magnum solus qui mole soluta
Obsedit, meliorque stetit pro Cæsare murus.
Hinc celebri fato fælici floruit ortu
Flos regum Arthurus, cuius tamen acta stupori
Non micuere minus, totus quod in aure voluptas
Et populo plaudente favus. Quæcunque priorum
Inspice, Pellæum commendat fama Tyrannum,
Pagina Cæsareos loquitur Romana triumphos,
Alciden domitis attollit gloria monstris.
Sed nec pinetum coryli, nec sydera solem
Æquant, Annales Graios Latiosque reuolue,
Prisca parem nescit, æqualem postera nullum
Exhibitura dies. Reges supereminet omnes
Solus præteritis melior, maiorque futuris." *Camden's Remaines*, pp. 317, 318, 319.

¶ Unless *Llywarqhen*, were a Cornish poet. "I have hitherto met with no very ancient writing that seemed to be Cornish; unless we should suspect for such an elegy on the death of Gereint ab Erbyn, a nobleman of Cornwall

time of Henry the Third; "admirable (as Carew saith) for his variety of latin rhymes." *

or Devon, about the year 540, who is mentioned in the Triades as one of the three greatest admirals of the British seas; the other two being March 'ab Meirchyon, and Gwenwyn 'ab Naw. There is in Cornwall a parish called Gerrans, which is the modern pronunciation of Gereint, (they constantly changing *t* into *s*) and another called Trev Erbin, which might be so denominated from his father. It is said in the elegy that he was of the borders of Devon, and that he was slain at Llongborth The word re, which in the Cornish signifies *too much*, as also *soon* or *quickly*, occurs frequently in this elegy; together with a great many others, such as Eloravr, kymrydh, gwehin, moloch, &c. which are lost in the Welsh. But it is owned, this is not enough to conclude the author to have been of Cornwall or Devon. And my old copy is written among some elegies ascribed to Llywarch hen." *Pryce's Vocabulary.* ---- In 1792, Mr. Owen published a translation of *Llywarq's* heroic elegies; from which I shall extract the elegy on Geraint ab Erbin, together with some observations of the Monthly Reviewer of Mr. Owen's book. These observations are highly flattering to Cornwall. "Mr. Owen tells us that Llywarq was descended from Coel king of Britain, and was a guest of Arthur Yet the very existence of a native resident sovereign of the name of Arthur has been disputed. He tells us with equal confidence that Llywarq lived 150 years. It should seem that the patriarchal religion bestowed a patriarchal length of life. The whole tradition of the poetry also required vouchers: as it is said to have been the practice of the later bards to ascribe their own poems to the celebrated names of elder time. We must acknowlege, however, that the internal evidence from the sentiments in the poems, (for of the language and pedigrees we profess not to judge,) scarcely affords a pretence for questioning their authenticity. Nor can it be doubted that, in the sixth century, Wales, Cornwall, and Britany, were the most favoured seats of civilization in Europe. We shall extract the elegy on Geraint ab Erbin, prince of Devon, who is probably the same knight so celebrated in the romances of Britany by the name of Geron the courteous:

'When Geraint was born the gates of heaven were open,
Christ then granted what was requested,
A countenance beautiful, the glory of Britain.

'Let all celebrate the red-stained Geraint
Their lord; I will also praise Geraint,
The Saxon's foe, the friend of saints.

'Before Geraint, the terrifier of the foe,
I saw the steeds hagged with mutual toil from battle,
Where, after the shout was given, frightful deeds began.

'Before Geraint, that breathed terror on the foe,
I saw the steeds bearing the maimed sharers of their toil;
And after the shout of war a fearful obscurity.

'At Llongborth I saw the noisy tumult,
And biers with the dead drenched in gore,
And ruddy men from the onset of the foe.

'Before Geraint, the molester of the enemy,
I saw the steeds white with foam,
And after the shout of battle a fearful torrent.

At Llongborth I saw the rage of slaughter,
And biers with slain innumerable,
And red-stained men from the assault of Geraint.

'At Llongborth I saw the gushing of blood,
And biers with dead from the rage of weapons,
And red-stained men from the assault of death.

V. In the next literary chapter, our views of philology and science will expand into prospects more agreeable to the contemplative mind.

'In Llongborth I saw the quick-impelling spurs
Of men who would not flinch from the dread of the spear,
And the quaffing of wine out of the bright glass.

'In Llongborth I saw a smoaking pile,
And men enduring the want of sustenance,
Aud defeat, after the excess of feastings.

'In Llongborth I saw the weapons
Of heroes with gore fast dropping,
And after the shout a fearful return to earth.

'In Llongborth I saw the edges of blades in contact,
Men surrounded with terrour, and blood on the brow,
Before Geraint, the great son of his father.

'In Llongborth I saw hard toiling
Amidst the stones, ravens feasting on the entrails,
And on the chieftain's brow a crimson gash.

'At Llongborth I saw a tumultuous running
Of men together, and blood about the feet :—
"Those that are the men of Geraint, make haste!"

'In Llongborth I saw a confused conflict,
Men striving together, and blood to the knees,
From the assault of the great son of Erbin.

'At Llongborth was Geraint slain,
A strenuous warrior from the woodland of Dyvnaint,†
Slaughtering his foes as he fell.

At Llongborth were slain to Arthur
Valiant men who hewed down with steel;
He was the emperor, and conductor of the toil of war.

'Under the thigh of Geraint were swift racers,
With long legs, that fed on the grain of deer,
Their course was like the consuming fire on the wild hills.

'Under the thigh of Geraint were fleet runners,
With long hams, fattened with corn;
They were red ones: their assault was like the bold eagles.

'Under Geraint's thigh were fleet runners,
With long legs, they scattered about the grain;
They were ruddy; their assault was like the white eagles.

'Under Geraint's thigh were fleet runners,
With long legs, high-mettled, fed with grain;
They were ruddy; bold their assault, like the red eagles.

'Under Geraint's thigh were fleet racers,
Long their legs; their food was corn;
Red were they; fierce their course, like the brown eagles.

'Swift racers were under the thigh of Geraint;
Their legs were long; they well deserved the grain;
Red were they; bold their course, as the grey eagles

† Devonshire, and Cornwall; "a country abounding with deep vales."

'Swift racers were under the thigh of Geraint;
Whose legs were long; they were reared up with corn,
They were red ones; their assault was as the black eagles.
'Swift racers were under the thigh of Geraint;
Whose legs were long; wheat their corn;
They red ones were; their assault was as the spotted eagles.
'Swift racers were under the thigh of Geraint;
Whose legs were long; they were satiated with grain;
They were grey, with tails tipt with silver.'

* "Merry Michael, the Cornishman, (says *Camden)* piped this vpon his oten pipe for merry England, but with a mocking compassion of Normandie, when the French vsurped in the time of king John.

Nobilis Anglia, pocula, prandia, donat & æra.
Terra iuuabilis & sociabilis, agmine plena.
Omnibus vtilis Anglia fertilis est, & amena:
Sed miserabilis & lachrimabilis absq caterua,
Neustria debilis, & modo flebilis est, quia serua."

The same Michael begged his exhibition of king Henry the Third, with this distich:

Regie rector, miles vt Hector, dux vt Achilles,
Tequia sector, mellee vector, mel mihi stilles.

And highly offended with Henry of Aurench, the king's poet, for disgracing Cornwall, he thought to draw blood of him with these bobbing rimes:

Est tibi gamba capri, crus passeris, & latus apri,
Os leporis, catuli nasus, dens & gena muli,
Frons vetulæ, tauri caput, & color vndiq; Mauri:
His argumentis quænam est argutia mentis?
Quod non a monstro differs: satis hic tibi monstro." *Remaines*, p. 7.---p. 340.

These last lines are thus translated by *Fuller*, who calls him Michael Blaunpayne:

Gamb'd like a goat, sparrow thigh'd, side as boar,
Hare-mouth'd, dog-nos'd, like mule thy teeth and chin,
Brow'd as old wife, bull-headed, black as Moor;---
If such without, what then are you within?
By these my signs, the wise will easily conster,
How little didst thou differ from a monster.

Camden (in his Britannia) terms this Michael the most eminent poet of his age, and recites other verses of the same poem in praise of his country against the said libeller Henry de Abrincis. Of these verses, I shall here insert Fuller's translation. The original lines have appeared in my account of the commodities of Cornwall.

We need not number up her wealthy store,
Wherewith this helpfull land relieves her poor,
No sea so full of fish, of tin no shore.

And then (says *Camden)* after a long harangue on his countrymen, telling us in his jingling verse how Arthur always set them in the front of the battle, he at last boldly concludes:

Quid nos deterret, &c. &c. &c.

What should us fright, if firmly we do stand?
Bar fraud, and then no force can us command.

He flourished in 1250.† The time and place of his death are unknown.----Browne, in his Britannia's Pastorals, speaks of the Cornish Michael. See p. 90.

† Not 1350, as Fuller hath said by mistake.

CHAPTER THE TENTH.

POPULATION, HEALTH, STRENGTH, DISEASES.

I. THOUGH the Romans retained the possession of this island for a long space of time; yet the English have much more of the Saxon than the Roman blood in their veins.-----But not so the Cornish. The Romans were, strictly speaking, our only conquerors. And with the Romans we mixed, in all relations of life. To the Saxons, the Cornish were always hostile; and though forced to give way to the arms of Athelstan, retained their spirit unsubdued.---Of the disinclination of the Cornish to incorporate with the Normans, we have abundant proof. And, indeed, the greater part of the inhabitants of Cornwall, were, at the close of this period, either aboriginal, or Roman-Cornish.

II. Before the first Roman invasion, Cornwall was more populous than in the times of the Saxon heptarchy. From the small number of houses in Exeter, at the Conquest, we may, by induction, argue, that our inferior towns had been reduced also, to a few habitations.

III. Of the strength, activity, and longevity of the Cornish, we have repeated evidence.* The Cornish Arthur seems to have been as gigantic‡ as Orgar: And

* "The Cornish-men are verie stronge, actiue, and for the moste parte personable men, of good constitution of body, and verie valorous; which made Michael Cornubiensis their countryman to sett them forth in this ostentiue manner, among other his laudatory verses: *Fraus ni nos superet, nihil est quod non superemus.* They liue in this countrye verie longe, 80, 90, some 100 and more yeares." *Norden*, p. 28. "The Western-Saxon kingdom, (says *Fuller*, in his Church History) was famed for the *stoutness of active men*, which some impute to the natural cause of their being hatched under the warm wings of the south-west wind. The Cornish (says he) are masters of the art of wrestling; so that if the Olympic Games were now in fashion, they would come away with the victory. Their hug is a cunning close with their fellow combatants, the fruits whereof is his fair fall or foil at the least." See *Fuller's Worthies* of England in Cornwall, p. 197.

‡ What is said, however, of his structure, is doubtless, a very great exaggeration. The distance between his eye-brows, we are told, was a span, and the rest of his body in proportion. *Girald. Cambr*, l. 2. c. 11. "Nor is Corn-

St. Piran, "(if the legend lye not) after that (like another Johannes temporibus) he had lived *two hundred years* with perfect health, took his last rest in a Cornish parish, which therethrough he endowed with his name."† But, without recurrence to apocryphal heroes or saints, we shall be able, hereafter, to produce numerous instances of strength and longevity: Such instances the present period would unquestionably have afforded, had there existed a Cornish annalist to record them; or had not his annals been wrecked, in their descent to posterity.

wall more happy in the soil, than it's inhabitants; who as they are extremely well bred, and ever have been so, even in those more ancient times, (for, as Diodorus Siculus observes, by conversation with merchants trading thither for tinn, they became more courteous to strangers;) so are they lusty, stout, and tall; their limbs are well set; and at wrastling (not to mention that manly exercise of hurling the ball) they are so eminent, that they go beyond other parts, both in art, and a firmness of body required to it. And the poet Michael, after a long harangue made upon his country-men, telling us in his jingling verse, how Arthur always set them in the front of the battel, at last boldly concludes: ---

Quid nos deterret? si firmiter in pede stemus,
Fraus ni nos superet, nihil est quod non superemus.

What can e'er fright us if we stand our ground?
If fraud confound us not, we'll all confound.

And this perhaps may have given occasion to that tradition, of giants formerly inhabiting those parts. For Hauvillan, a poet who lived four hundred years ago, describing certain British giants, has these verses concerning Britain:

———Titanibus illa
Sed paucis famulosa domus, quibus uda ferarum
Terga dabant vestes, cruor haustus, pocula trunci,
Antra Lares, dumetta thoros, cœnacula rupes,
Præda cibos, raptus Venerem, spectacula cædes, &c. &c. &.

———Of Titan's monstrous race
Only some few disturb'd that happy place.
Raw hides they wore for cloaths, their drink was blood,
Rocks were their dining-rooms, their prey their food.
Their cup some hollow trunk, their bed a grove,
Murder their sport, and rapes their only love.
Their courage frenzy, strength their sole command;
Their arms, what fury offer'd to their hand.
And when at last in brutish fight they dy'd,
Some spacious thicket a vast grave supply'd.
With such vile monsters was the land opprest,
But most, the farther regions of the west;
Of them, thou Cornwall! too wast plagu'd above the rest.

But whether this firmness of constitution (which consists of a due temperature of heat and moisture) be caused in the Danmonii by those fruitful breezes of the west-wind, and their westerly situation, (as we see in Germany the Batavi, in France the Aquitani and Rutheni, which lye farthest toward the west, are most lusty;) or rather to some peculiar happiness in the air and soil; is not my business nicely to consider." *Gibson's Camden*, col. 3, 4.

† *Carew*, f. 58, b.

IV. Of the diseases of the Cornish, we have no particular account. A great plague in the time of Vortigern, is noticed by the venerable Bede.§

CHAPTER THE ELEVENTH.

MANNERS, DIVERSIONS, SUPERSTITIONS.

I.---1. BEFORE I attempt to delineate the character of the Cornish; I shall touch on that of the Saxons and of the Normans. The leading traits of the *Saxon* character were the love of freedom and of arms; ferocity and cruelty.* Nor must their gallantry† be forgotten. The story of the Saxon Edgar, and the beautiful

§ "In the time of king Cadwallo, it rained blood for three days; when happened that sanguinary war between him and the Saxons, and ensued a famine; which forced Cadwallo to fly into Armorica for the supply of men, money and provisions." *Florent.* p. 29.

* As the Saxons were a German nation, we may consult Tacitus for their manners and their policy: and in his discourse on the manners of the Germans we shall find the Saxon character portrayed with truth and elegance.

† The Saxons were fond of displaying the sex to advantage: They tell many stories illustrative of female virtue. "Ina, king of the West-Saxons, had three daughters, of whom upon a time he demanded whether they did love him, and so would do during their lives above all others; the two elder sware deepely they would; the yongest, but the wisest told her father flatly without flattery: 'That albeit shee did love, honour, and reverence him, and so would whilst shee lived, as much as nature and daughterly dutie at the uttermost could expect; yet shee did thinke that one day it would come to passe, that shee should affect another more fervently, meaning her husband, when shee were married: Who being made one flesh with her, as God by commaundement had told, and nature had taught hir, shee was to cleave fast to, forsaking father and mother, kiffe and kinne." *Camden's Remains*, pp. 248, 249.---Yet towards the end of the eighth century, our western ladies, had their dignity and influence somewhat diminished in consequence of the following incident. Eadburgh, the daughter of Offa king of Mercia, and queen of *Bearthric* king of *Wessex*, after having committed many detestable crimes, at length poisoned her husband and a young nobleman his favorite. This excited universal indignation: And Eadburgh could only save her life, by making her escape to the continent. The people of Wessex, finding no other way of testifying their resentment, made a law: "That none of the kings of Wessex should from that moment permit their consorts to be crowned, to sit with them on the throne, or to enjoy the name of queen."

Elfrida, hath been told by the historian‡ and sung by the poet. But whether the scene of their loves were the banks of the Tavy or the Tamar, would be fruitless to enquire. - - - The *Normans*, according to William of Malmesbury excelled the Anglo-

‡ "Elphreda (the only daughter of duke Orgarus) was the paragon of her sex, and wonder of nature, for loveliness and beauty; the fame of which sounded so loud in those western parts, that the echo thereof was heard so far as K. Edgar's court, and reached the king; the touch of which string (that made the most pleasing musick in his breast) from his ear soon resounded to his heart; To try the truth whereof, he secretly sent his favourite, earl Ethelwold of East-Anglia (who could well judge of beauty) with commission, that if the pearl proved so orient, it should be seized for his own wearing, intending to make her a queen, and Orgarus the father-in-law of a king. The young earl soon posted into Devonshire to duke Orgarus's court; where, on sight of the lady, he was so surprized with her charms, that he began to woo her for himself; and proved so successful therein, that he procured hers and her father's good-will, in case he could obtain the king's consent. Earl Ethelwold returning, related to the king, that the lady was fair indeed, but nothing answerable to the report of her; however, he desired his majesty, for his leave to marry her, thereby to raise his fortunes. The king, suspecting no deceit, consented, and the marriage was solemnized. Soon after which, the fame of her beauty sounded much louder than before at court; whereupon, the king, much doubting he had been abused, resolved to try the truth himself. In order to which, he comes to Exeter, and thence sends word to the duke, where the fair Elphreda and her husband were, that he designed to be speedily with him, and hunt in his parks; or rather in the forest of Dartmoor there near adjoyning. The ground of whose coming the guilty Ethelwold suspecting, he acquainted his wife with the wrong he had done both her and the king, in disparaging her beauty to him: And therefore, to prevent the king's displeasure, he entreated her very earnestly, to cloath herself in such attire as might least set forth her lustre, in words to this effect: As the richest diamond, said he, rough and uncut, yields neither sparkle nor esteem; and gold, unburnished, gives no better lustre than base brass; so beauty and feature, clad in mean array, is, or slightly looked at, or wholly unregarded: So true is the adage of old, that cloth is the man, and man is the wretch. To prevent, therefore, the thing I fear, and is like to prove my present ruine, and thy future shame; conceal thy great beauty from K. Edgar's eye, and give him entertainment in thy meanest attire; let them, I pray thee, for a time, be the nightly curtains drawn about our new nuptial bed, and the daily clouds to hide thy splendant sun from his sharp and too piercing look; the rays whereof will soon set his waxen wings on fire, that ready are to melt at a far softer heat. Thus, with a kind kiss, hopeing he had prevailed, he withdrew to receive and entertain the king. The fair Elphreda now left alone, began thus to debate the matter with herself. Hath my beauty, thought she, been courted of a king, and by the mouth of fame compared with Hellen's, and must it now be hid? Must I falsify and belye nature's bounty, mine own value, and all mens reports, only to save his credit, who hath impaired mine, and belyed my worth? And must I needs defoul myself to be his only fair fool, that hath despightfully kept me from the seat and state of a queen? However he may answer it to the king his master, to me the injury is beyond repair; who thus hath bubbled me with a coronet, instead of a crown; and made me a subject, who, e're this, should have been a soveraign. It can be no blame in me, to make the most of nature's largesses and art's accomplishments, when I falsify no trust; only with the sun (to which he is pleased to liken me) shew the beams, which, do what I can, will not be hid; nor at this time shall be, be the event what will. Thus, right woman, desiring nothing more than what is forbidden, and considering, that now was the time to make the most of her beauty, she resolved she would not be accessary to her own injury by failing to set it forth to the best advantage; her body she endulced with the sweetest balms; display'd her hair, and powder'd it with diamonds; bestrew'd her breasts and bosom with pearls and rubies; rich jewels, glittering like stars, depended at her ears; and all her other ornaments every way agreeable. And thus, rather angel than lady-like, she attended the approach and enterance of the king; whom with such fair obeisance and seemly grace she received, that Edgar's greedy eye, presently collecting the rays of her shining beauty, became a burning glass to his heart; and the sparkle of her fair look falling into the train of his love, set all his senses on fire. Struck with astonishment and admiration at first sight, the king was fully resolved to be quits with his perfidious favourite; yet dissembling his passion for the present, until the morning came, they went out a hunting;

Saxons in temperance and fortitude, and urbanity. How far the Saxon or the Norman manners operated on the island in general, is an enquiry which I shall not pursue. The British ladies were certainly fond of imitating the Saxon fashions. But whether they were equally assiduous in the imitation of that modest demeanour which is said to have distinguished the Saxon women, I am not authorized to say. The influence of the Roman manners had long circumscribed the pleasures of the marriage-bed, to which the Britons had permitted so liberal an indulgence: And the chastity of the Saxons, whose women were never so highly adorned as by a numerous offspring, the pledges of unviolated love, must, in some measure, have imprest its character on the British race.----To the Conqueror, this county was indebted for the melioration of its manners. William, whilst he endeavoured to incorporate his own people with the English, was sedulous also to introduce the laws, the language, the learning, and the customs and fashions of Normandy. In these

where carefully watching, he at length found an opportunity, and taking Ethelwold at an advantage, slew him. And at a place in Dartmoor forest, called Wilverley, since Warlwood,* the earl was found slain with an arrow, or, as some will, run through with a javelin. Soon after this, K. Edgar having thus made the fair Elphreda a widow, took her to be his second wife; by whom he had two sons; Edmund, who died in his infancy; and Ethelred, who afterwards came to be king of England, by name of Ethelred the unready. The way to which (what may not be disguised) this his mother Elphreda made through the body of K. Edward, eldest son of Edgar, by his first wife Q. Ethelfled; the manner thus: King Edward hunting in the isle of Purbeck, not far from Corff-Castle, where his mother-in-law queen Elphreda, and her son his brother prince Ethelred, were residing; out of his love to both, would needs himself alone give them a visit. The queen, having long laid wait for an occasion, out of ambition to bring her own son to the crown, took the opportunity; and while the young king was drinking a cup of wine at the gate on horse-back, she caused one to run him into the back with a knife; Who feeling himself hurt, set spurs to his horse, thinking thereby to get to his company; but the wound being mortal, and the king fainting through the loss of blood, fell from his horse, and one foot being entangled in the styrrup, he was ruthfully dragged up and down through woods and lands, and at length left dead at Corffe-Gate. Which happened after he had reigned three years and six months, in the sixteenth year of his age, and of Christ Jesus 979. Having thus related queen Elphreda's vile and horrid fact, it is very fit also we should give account of her deep repentance; for being much grieved hereat, to expiate her bloody crime,† according to the religion of those days, she built the two monasteries of Amesbury and Worwel, in the counties of Wiltshire and Southampton; in which latter she lived with great pennance, until the day of her death; and in the same lieth her body interred." *Prince* pp. 481. 482.----According to a latin poem of Dr. Shebbeare, *Okehampton-castle* was the scene of Edgar's and Elfrida's amours. But I was informed some years ago, that the meeting between the lovers was asserted by the Morice family to have been at Werington. In consequence of which, I made some enquiries there; and found not only the voice of tradition confirming the family-persuasion; but evidence apparently more substantial. There is a spot near Werington called *Ladies-cross*, where the lovers are reputed to have met, and an ancient bed at Werington said to be the very bed in which king Edgar slept.

* Risd. Surv. of Dev. in Tavist. MS.

† Speed's Hist, of Gr. Brit, lib. 7, p. 356.

fashions, indeed, there was much pomp and ostentation. And we are told, that in the times of Henry the II. the whole gentry of England, imitating the fashions of the Normans, affected an extraordinary style of magnificence in their dress and equipage.

2. Amidst these varieties of foreign manners and customs, little of the original British character could be recognized; unless its ancient features were to be traced at the extremities of the island. And here their ancient features were traceable: Here were still Britons, proud to oppose their virtues and their manners, to those of the Saxon or the Norman progeny.§ From their remote and peninsular situation, the Cornish must necessarily have retained their provincial peculiarities.|| In peace they were still generous and hospitable; in war, enthusiastically brave.¶ ---In the time of king Arthur,* the Cornish were accustomed to lead the

§ It is curious to observe the anxious wish of *Risdon* and his commentator *Chapple*, to derive the people of Devonshire from CORNISH rather than SAXON progenitors.---" King Arthur honoured these Britons (says *Risdon*) with the first charge in his battles, who, together with the Cornish and Welshmen, by martial prowess, have challenged the prerogative of that regiment in the English army that should second the main battle:" " and although the present inhabitants (interposes *Chapple*) cannot so much boast of their descent from those ancient Cornish, but rather from their conquerors the Saxons; yet as the former continued in possession of a great part of this county in common with the latter 'till about A. D. 936, and doubtless had frequent intermarriages with them, the present Devonians may consider both as their ancestors, and are no less intitled to their martial honours and privileges." " A bold, hardy, brave and valorous people (continues *Risdon*) having no less an aptitude for instruction in military exercises, or courage to maintain their post in an engagement, than docility and readiness in acquiring the requisite qualifications for civil employments."—" Nor ought our sailors to be forgotten (says *Chapple*) of whom this maritime county produces not a few; who for skill in their profession, valour and conduct in engagements with an enemy, patience in hardships and wants, and unlimited generosity in affluence, are not excelled any where."

|| Yet, if we attend to Cornish traditions, we had frequent and familiar intercourse with the Saxon kings.--- In the parish of St. Just, Penwith, is a large flat stone, on which, tradition saith, seven Saxon kings dined at one time and day, at such time as they came into Cornwall, to see the Land's-end. These kings are said to have been, Ethelbert 5th king of Kent; Cissa, second king of the South-Saxons; Kingills, sixth king of the West-Saxons; Sebert, third king of the East-Saxons; Ethelred, seventh king of the Northumbrians; Penda, fifth king of the Mercians; Sigebert, fifth king of the East-Angles; who all flourished about the year 600, and were all crowned heads, as Daniell, in his chronicle tells us." *Hals's MSS.* in St. Just.

¶ On military expeditions, they generally avoided promiscuous intercourse with the rest of the army. This seems to have been their character, from the days of Arthur, when, as merry Michael sings, they led the van, to the rebellion of 1745, when at Exeter, they " *one-and-all*," fled to arms at an imaginary insult, and secure in their combined force, set the city at defiance.

* Warton, in his " Observations on Spencer's Fairy Queen," has given us a most entertaining criticism on the romance entitled " *Morte Arthur*." See vol. i. pp. 19....46.

van:† And, in Egbert's time, they are said to have challenged the honor of leading the van in the day of battle. In the reign of king Canute, whether the danger was greater in the rear on some remarkable retreat of his army, or whether the Dane piqued himself on inverting all the Saxon order of battle, we find the Cornish bringing up the rear. This is attributed by John of Salisbury to their distinguished valour. In the mean time, (it must not be concealed) the Cornish was choleric;‡ and, in some respect, ferocious.§---To distinguish between the manners of the superior order, and the poorer classes, I have to observe, that the former possessed on arbitrary spirit: In many instances, also, they were grossly indelicate.|| The riding upon the black ram, the cocking-stool,¶ and other usages of a similar nature, prove both tyranny and indecency. But these, I

† —— Rex Arcturus nos primos Cornubienses
Bellum facturus vocat, ut puta Cæsaris enses
Nobis non alijs, reliquis, dat primitus ictum
Per quem pax lisque, &c. &c. &c.

Michael Cornubiensis.

‡ "Hur *Welsh* blood is up," is a proverbial expression. But "hur *Cornish* blood is up," would be equally just. And, I think, *Fuller's* observation, that "the Welsh are like the face of their country, full of ups and downs, elevations and depressions----- prone to anger, but soon appeased," is more applicable to the Cornish than the Welsh. The anger of the Welsh generally settles into a deep resentment; and is only expiated by some revengeful stroke. But that of the Cornish, involves in it no sin; "We are angry, and sin not:" We "let not the sun go down upon our wrath."

§ I am ashamed of our shipwrecks. Yet, I believe, the Normans are more blameable than the Cornish, in the instance of the "wrack." "Lamentable is the case of poor sea-faring men that suffer wrack, which the Normans called *varech*; from whom came that custom not unworthy writing, that in ancient times, if a ship were cast on shore, torn with tempest, and were not repaired by such as were left alive within a certain time, then this was taken for wrack. But king Henry I. disliking the justice of that custom, ordained: That if any one thing came on land alive, then the goods and ship should not be seized. This decree was of force all his reign, and ought of equity to have endured for ever. Howbeit, after his death, the owners of land on the sea-shore shewing themselves more careful of their own gain, than pitiful of other men's calamity, returned to their old manner." *Risdon*, p. 236.

|| "For adultery or a rape, let the man and woman each pay eight shillings and fourpence." *Domesday.* Eight shillings and fourpence was, doubtless, a great sum in the Norman times; But a settled pecuniary composition for a rape, is revolting to our conceptions of moral turpitude.

¶ Among the punishments inflicted in Cornwall was that of the *cocking-stool*, (or *cockaigue*, signifying a base woman) a seat of infamy, where loose women and scolds, with bare feet and head, were exposed to the derision of those that passed by, for such time as the bailiffs of manors who had the privilege of such jurisdiction, thought proper to appoint. This jurisdiction was granted (or rather at the inquisition declared to belong) to the manor of Cotford-Farlo in the parish of St. Wenn: "Maner. de Cotford-Farlo, alias Lancorla in St. Wenn-

conceive, were Norman customs. We have so few memoirs of this county, before the time of Edward I. that we must have recourse to the Welsh annals,* for the history of our county. And, perhaps, for the true lineaments of the Cornish character, we

moor, temp. Henr. 3. Quia per objurgatrices et meretrices multa mala in manerio oriuntur, lites, pugne, diffamationes, et alie multe inquietationes per earum putesias; igitur utimur de eisdem quod cum capte fuerint, habeant judicium de cocking-stool, & ibi stabunt nudis pedibus, et suis crinibus pendentibus dispersis tanto tempore ut aspici possint ab omnibus per viam transeuntibus secundum voluntatem balivorum nostrorum capitalium." *Hals's MSS.*

* "How actiue and seruiceable the Welsh were when king Richard Cuer-de-lion lead an armie of them into France, haue this testimonie of William Britto (who then liued) in his fifth book of Philippeidos.

Protinus extremis Anglorum finibus agmen
Wallorum immensum numero vocat, vt, nemorosa
Per loca discurrant, ferroque ignique furore
Innato, nostri vastent confinia regni.

Gens Wallensis habet hoc naturale per omnes
Indigenas, primis proprium quod seruat ab annis.
Pro domibus syluas, bellum pro pace frequentat,
Irasci facilis, agilis per deuia cursu,
Nec soleis plantas, caligis nec crura grauantur
Frigus docta pati, nulli cessura labori.
Veste breui, corpus nullis oneratur ab armis.
Nec munit thorace latus, nec casside frontem,
Sola gerens, hosti cædem quibus inferat, arma,
Clauam cumiaculo, venabula, gesa, bippennem,
Arcum cum pharetris, nodosaque tela, vel hastam
Assiduis gaudens prædis, fusoque cruore.

How afterward in processe of time they conformed themselues to all ciuilite, and the reason thereof, appeareth by these lines of a poet then flourishing.

Mores antiqui Britonum iam ex couictu Saxonum
Commutantur in melius, vt patet ex his clarius.
Hortos & agros excolunt, ad oppida se conferunt,
Et loricati equitant, & calceati peditant,
Vrbane se reficiunt, & sub tapetis dormiunt
Vt iudicentur Anglici, nunc potius quam Wallici.
Huius si quæratur ratio, quietius quam solito
Cur illi viuant hodie, in causa sunt diuitiæ.
Quas cito gens hæc perderet, si passim nunc confligeret.
Timor damni hos retrahit, nam nil habens nil metuit.
Et vt dixit Satyricus: Cantat portatur vacuus
Coram latrone tutior, quam phalaratus ditior.

And since they were admited to the imperiall crowne of England, they haue, to their iust praise, performed all parts of dutifull loyaltie and allegeance most faithfully thereunto; plentifully yeelding martiall captaines, iudicious ciuillians skilfull common lawyers, learned diuines, complete courtiers, and aduentrous souldiers. In which commendations their cousins the Cornishmen do participate proportionally, although they were sooner brought vnder the English command." *Camden's Remains*, pp. 10, 11.

should do right to consult Giraldus Cambrensis, who has drawn a good outline of the kindred Welsh.‡

II. The diversions of the people form always an interesting subject, at every period of time.

Among the gentry, hunting seems to have been the first and favourite sport. And it equally prevailed among the original Britons,§ and their suc-

‡ Giraldus Cambrensis tells us, that not only the nobility and gentry, but the whole people of Wales were universally addicted to arms----That they were exceedingly active and hardy, and dexterous in the use of their arms. That to fight for their country, and lose their lives in defence of its honor and liberty, was their chief pride. The following particulars, also, we learn from Giraldus. King Henry the Second, in a letter to the Greek emperor Emanuel Comnenus, was pleased to take notice of the extraordinary courage and fierceness of the Welsh, who were not afraid to fight almost unarmed with enemies armed at all points, willingly shedding their blood in the cause of their country, and purchasing glory at the expence of their lives. The same vivacity which animated their hearts, inspired their tongues. They were of quick and sharp wit, naturally eloquent, and ready in speaking without any awe or concern before their superiors, or in public assemblies: But from this fire in their tempers, they were all very passionate, vindictive, and sanguinary in their resentments. For even the lowest amongst them had each by heart his own genealogy, together with which he retained a constant remembrance of every injury, disgrace or loss, his forefathers had suffered, and thought it degeneracy not to resent it as personal to himself. To plunder or rob, was scarcely accounted dishonourable among them, even when committed against their own countrymen, much less against foreigners.' They hardly ever married without a prior co-habitation. Their kings and a few of the principal nobles, had built some castles in imitation of the English; but most of their gentry still continued to dwell in huts made of wattle, and situated in solitudes, by the sides of the woods, as most convenient for hunting and pasture, as for a retreat in time of war. Their furniture was as simple and mean as their houses, such as might answer the mere necessities of gross and uncivilized nature. The only elegance among them was music, which they were so fond of, that in every family there generally were some who played on the harp: and skill in that instrument was valued by them more than all their knowlege. Notwithstanding their poverty, they were so hospitable that every man's house was open to all. When any stranger or traveller came to a house, he used no other ceremony than (at his first entrance) to deliver his arms into the hands of the master, who thereupon offered to wash his feet, which if he accepted, it was understood to signify his intention of staying there all night, and none who did so was refused. It was customary among them, to receive in the mornings large companies of young men, who followed no occupation but arms, whenever they were not in action strolled all over the country, and entered into any house that they found in their way; where they were entertained till the evening, with the music of the harp, and free conversation with the young women of the family. One is surprised in observing how absolutely the Britons, after their retreat into Wales, lost all the culture they had received from the Romans. They retained the profession of the Christian religion, but debased with gross superstitions. Giraldus Cambrensis informs us, that they paid in his days, a more devout reverence to churches, and church-men, to the relics of saints, to crosses, and to bells, than any other nation. Their hermits were celebrated for severer austerities than any others in Europe. Pilgrimages to Rome were their favourite mode of devotion, though they had many saints of their own nation, whose shrines were thus adored with the blindest superstition.

§ "Res-ky-mer, dogg-marsh, or fenn, or a place situate on the decliningе part of a hill, upon a meer marsh; or moorish piece of ground; notable for doggs in generall. But whether it referrs to beagles, hounds, spaniells, wolves, or fox doggs, I know not. *Quere.* Whether in this place there was not some carrion poole for doggs; or what sort of doggs is meant by the conjunctive particle *ky?* For Mr. Carew (in his Survey of Cornwall, p. 55.) tells us, contrary to the etymologie aforesaid, that Reskymer signifies

cessive invaders.|| And hawking obtained among all; though an Asiatic

the greate dogg's race; but then it should have been very differently written. Be it how it will, from this place was denominated an ancient familly of gentlemen, surnamed de Reskymer, or rather Res-ky-maur, *i. e.* the greate or large dogg's vallum. From this place in all probabillitie was denominated Kymarus, *i. e.* greate doggs, or this place from him, a British kinge (mentioned in Galfridus's Chronicle, A. D. 1152,) grandsone of Gwintolinus, by Marcia his lady, author of the Marcian lawe, longe after translated out of the British tongue into the Saxon language by king Alured; who had issue by the said Marcia Ceilius, who governed part of this realme fifteen years, father of this Kymarus or Kimarus, as some say, who is reported to have been a wild younge man, and irregular both in his private life and public government; who, after he had reigned three years, beinge in his disport of huntinge with his doggs was trayterously slayne by his owne servants, about one hundred years before Julius Cæsar invaded this land. And that the reader may knowe of what vse and esteem doggs of game were had amongst our ancestors the Britons in those days, the author of the life of Agricola, thus speaks: The inland Britons and many others of that nation, got their livinge by huntinge with doggs; and lived upon the flesh soe gotten; and cloathed themselves with the skins of those beasts, and also made greate advantage of the flesh and skins caught by that art. Moreover Strabo, (in lib. 3.) tells us of the Cassiterides and Ostiones that they digged up great plenty of lead and tynn there; and that they had also among them good quantities of skinns and furrs, which commodities they bartered or exchanged with merchants for earthen vessels, salt, and brass-work. Againe of these Britons thus speaks Cæsar's commentary 5. most of the inland people sowe noe corne, but live on milk and flesh and are cloathed with skins of beasts; moreover their religion will not suffer them to eate either hare, hen, or goose; notwithstandinge they have of all sorts as well for novelty as variety. And of latter tyme it is evident from the rolls of the Exchequer that diverse tenements of land in this island have been held of the crown and other lords, by the tenure, condition, or covenant of payinge and keepinge doggs; for instance, in the pleas of the crowne at Windsor, tempore Edw. I. roll the 28th, we read thus: Johanes de Baye, tenet. duas hidas terræ de domino rege, in Rookhampton, in Surry; per sergentiam custodiendi unam mentam caniculorum harectorum, ad custam domini regis. &c. *i. e.* for keeping a pack or kennell of hare doggs, for the use of our lord the kinge. Again, in the Fines 6. of kinge John in Norfolk; we reade, Joanna quæ fuit uxor Johannis Kinge, tenet. quandam serjantiam in Stenhow, in Norfolk, per Serjantiam custodiendi, unum brackeltum demeritum, domini regis, &c. *i. e.* by keepinge a brache-lete, a little mastive dogg, that shall deserve or procure the favour of our lord the kinge. Again, in the rolls of the Fines 42. Edw. III. in Northampton in latin may be read to this effect, in English, Thomas Eugayne, held lands in Pightesle, in this county, by the service of findinge, at his own proper cost and charges, certaine doggs for huntinge wolves, foxes, martins, catts, and other vermin in the countys of Rutland, Oxford, Essex, Buckingham, and Northampton; it is likely, from hence, he was for those wicked wild creatures, the king's huntsman, by inheritance; for of his progenitor 14. Edw. I. roll 7th in Huntington, it is thus set down:---Johannes Eugayne, tenet. unam carucatam terræ in magna Gedinge in comitatu predict. per serjantiam, currendi ad lupum vulpem, et cattum, et amovendi omnem verminiam extra forrestum domini regis, in comitatu isto. Again, in the Pleas of the Crowne, 18. Edward I. in Essex, we reade Willelmus de Reynes, aliquando tenuit duas carucatas terræ in Boyton in parochiæ de Finchingfeud, in comitatu Essex, per serjantiam custodiendi domino regi quinque Canes Luporarias. Lastly, in the Pleas of the Crown, in Berkshire, 12. Edward I. may be read Willelmus Lovell, tenet. duas carucatas terræ de domino regis apud Benham, in comitatu predict, per serjantiam, custodiendi, a pack or kennell of couragcous or valiant doggs." *Hals in Mawgan.*

|| "I know not well, whether I may referre to the parish of St. Neot, that which Mat. West. reporteth of king Alfred, namely, how comming into Cornwall on hunting, he turned aside, for doing his deuotion, into a church, where St. Guerijr and St. Neot made their abode; and there found his orisons seconded with a happy effect." *Carew,* f. 129.----The author of the Saxon Chronicle, speaking of the rigorous laws which William the Conqueror enacted for the preservation of game, observes: That he *loved the deer, as if he had been their father.*

sport, and existing in Cornwall, long before the Romans. The fighting of cocks was more the sport of gentlemen than the common people.¶ The sports of wrestling and hurling* were, perhaps, almost entirely confined to the inferior classes of the community. And, in these sports, the agility and skill of the Cornish were more especially displayed, at their parish-feasts,† and on saints days.

¶ William Fitz-Stephen, who wrote the life of archbishop Becket, in the reign of Henry II. describes cocking as the sport of school-boys, on Shrove-Tuesday. The theatre was the school: And the master was the director of the sport.

* "Among the general customs, we must not forget the manly exercises of wrestling and hurling, the former more generally practised in this county than in any part of England, the latter peculiar to it. The Cornish have been remarkable for their expertness in athletic contentions for måny ages, as if they inherited the skill and strength of their fabulous first duke Corinæus, whose fame consists chiefly in the reputation he won by wrestling with, and overcoming the giant Gogmagog: And that fable perhaps was founded five hundred years since upon the then acknowleged and universal reputation of the people of this county for wrestling. But to leave fables; what should have implanted this custom in such a corner of Britain, and preserved it hitherto in its full vigour, when either never affected at all, or with indifference in other parts of the island, we cannot say; certain it is the Grecians, who traded hither for tin, and hither only, had the highest esteem for this exercise. The arts of the Palæstra were chiefly cultivated by the Lacedemonians, and yet Plato himself among the Athenians was so far from disapproving the exercise, that he recommends it to the practise of old as well as young women, and thinks it proper for them oftentimes to wrestle with men, that thereby they might become more patient of labour, and learn to struggle with the difficulties incident to a warlike state. The ardour for this exercise so prevailed at last, that all Greece devoted their time and inclinations to the gymnasia and palæstra, and chose rather to be accounted the most expert wrestlers, than to be celebrated as the most knowing and valiant commanders. Whether the Cornish borrowed this custom from the Grecians, or whatever else was the cause, you shall hardly any where meet with a party of boys who will not readily entertain you with a specimen of their skill in this profession. Hurling is a trial of skill and activity between two parties of twenty, forty, or any indeterminate number; sometimes betwixt two or more parishes, but more usually, and indeed practised in a more friendly manner, betwixt those of the same parish; for the better understanding which distinction, it must be premised, that betwixt those of the same parish there is a natural connexion supposed, from which *(cæteris paribus)* no one member can depart without forfeiting all esteem. As this unites the inhabitants of a parish, each parish looks upon itself as obliged to contend for its own fame, and oppose the pretensions, and superiority of its neighbours. It is so termed from throwing or *hurling* a ball, which is a round piece of timber, (about three inches diameter) covered with plated silver, sometimes gilt. It has usually a motto in the Cornish tongue alluding to the pastime, as *Guare wheag, yw Guare teag*, that is, fair play is good play. Upon catching this ball dexterously when it is dealt, and carrying it off expeditiously notwithstanding all the opposition of the adverse party, success depends. This exercise requires force, and nimbleness of hand, a quick eye, swiftness of foot, skill in wrestling, strength and breath to persevere in running, address to deceive and evade the enemy, and judgment to deliver the ball into proper hands, as occasion shall offer: In short, a pastime that kindles emulation in the youngest breast, and like this requires so general an exertion of all the faculties of the body, cannot but be of great use to supple, strengthen, and particularly tend to prepare it for all the exercises of the camp." *Borlase*, pp. 299, 300, 301.

† The famous festival of *Hockeday* has been the subject of much conjecture. In the Teutonic language, *hockzeit* is particularly applied to a wedding-feast: And to this day the German word for a wedding is *hockzeit* At the celebration of the feast at the wedding of a Danish lord Canute Prudan with lady Githa, the daughter of Osgot

In noticing the parish-feast, we approach the confines of religion.* The primeval feast, indeed, was strictly religious: ‡ And so was the miracle-play. The miracle plays were called *Guaremir*, and the place of acting, *Plaen-an-guare.*

Clape a Saxon nobleman, *Hardicanute* suddenly expired. Our ancestors, therefore, had sufficient grounds for distinguishing the day of so happy an event, by a word denoting the wedding-feast, or the wedding-day. The dominion of the Danes had long been extremely galling and oppressive: And Hardicanute, among other rigorous measures, had rendered himself odious to the Danes, by exacting the Danegelt. Chatterton has mentioned Hokeday in several places. In one, particularly, he says:

The Saxonne warryer that did so entwyne,
Lyke the nesh bryon and the eglantine,
Orre Cornysh wrastlers at a hocktyde game.'

From this passage it seems that the wrestling of Cornishmen was one of the hocktide sports.

* The parish-wake, in celebration of the saint to whom the church was dedicated has been mentioned in the third chapter as a religious rite.

‡ In the first volume, I described the Furry of Helston, as a specimen of *Furry* days or Feiræ observed in other parts of Cornwall. Such scenes in honor of Pagan divinities, were now celebrated in honor of Christian saints, on the days of the dedication of churches, or other sacred days. On the third of May, the *Furry* was once kept at Penryn; and on the first of May we have a similar festival at Padstow. On May the first is a festivity kept here, which is called the hobby-horse, from a man being drest up in a stallion horse's skin, led by crowds of men and women through the streets, and at every dirty pool dipping the head in the pool, and throwing out the water upon them. It is therefore the British festivity of May-day, observed in a manner not British. Even an addition completely English has been very lately made to it; by the men and women singing a song in English of which the burden is: "where are the French? Give them to us, that we may kill them." So the *Furry* Feria, Fure [1], For-y (in Cornish pronunciation), at Helston, is kept on the eighth of May, with a song in English, declaring they bring home the *summer* and the *may*, and inveighing against the French and Spaniards. Some pretend, that the French, in queen Anne's time, attempted to land, and were driven away by a figure thus drest up, &c. A tale too ridiculous for refutation! The addition made at Helston shews the addition made at Padstow; that being evidently a very late one. And the *summer* and the *may*, which are retained equally in the Padstow as in the Helston song, mark the main, the original parts of both. The eighth of May, I doubt not, is the day of the parish-feast; and, being so near to the first, has superseded it, yet borrowed the substance of its song from it. --- "Acarnival, which has been kept for ages upon Halgaver-moor near Bodmin, is said to be as old as the Saxons. The season of its celebration, is the middle of July: And thousands of people used to resort to the spot. "The youthlier sort of Bodmin townsmen vse sometimes to sport themselues, by playing the box with strangers, whome they summon to Halgaver. The name signifieth the goat's moore, and such a place it is, lying a little without the towne, and very full of quagemires. When these mates meet with any rawe seruing-man, or other young master, who may serue and deserue to make pastime, they cause him to be solemnly arrested, for his appearance before the maior of Halgaver, where he is charged with wearing one spurre, or going vntrussed, or wanting a girdle, or some such like felony: and after he hath beene arraygned and tryed with all requisite circumstances, iudgement is giuen in formal termes, and executed in some one vngracious pranke or other, more to the skorne, then hurt of the party condemned. Hence is sprung the prouerb, when we see one slouenly appareled, to say, he shall be presented in Halgaver Court. But now and then, they extend this merriment with the largest, to the preiudice of ouer-credulous people, perswading them to fight with a dragon lurking in Halgaver, or to see some strange matter there: which concludeth at least, with a trayning them into the mire"*

* Carew, f. 126, 126 b. --- "The sports and pastimes here held were so well liked by Charles the Second, when he touched here on his way to Scilly, that he became a brother of the jovial society!" See Heath's Description of the Isles of Scilly, printed in 1750.

---They lasted sometimes more than one day, and were attended not by the vulgar only, but by people of the first rank.§ Carew compares these inter-

§ "Of the *Guare-mir* I have seen some faint remains both in the east and west of Cornwall during the Christmas season, when at the family feasts of gentlemen, the Christmas plays were admitted, and some of the most learned among the vulgar (after leave obtained) entered in disguise, and before the gentry, who were properly seated, personated characters, and carried on miserable dialogues on scripture-subjects. When their memory could go no farther, they filled up the rest of the entertainment with more puerile representations, the combats of puppets, the final victory of the hero of the drama, and death of his antagonist." *Borlase*, p. 299.----In the "Old English Gentleman," I have taken occasion to describe the geese-dance, and other festal celebrations.

"In the gay circle of convivial cheer,
Blithe Christmas came, with chaplets never sear.
How beam'd delight, in every eye, unblam'd,
When at the hallow'd eve for carols fam'd,
The greenwood towering o'er the heapy turves,
First fum'd and crackled in elastic curves;
When brightly blaz'd the sap-besprinkled ash,
And glistening holly danc'd with many a flash,
And, every vulgar fire design'd to mock,
Repos'd in sombrous state the *Christmas-stock.
Alas! uprooted in the tempest's roar,
And hewn in sunder to its hollow core;
Andarton's oldest oak the flame attacks—
For ages yet it 'scap'd the forest-axe!
Rais'd high amid the turf, the kindled sprays,
It bids awhile defiance to the blaze;
And, though it redden deep, preserves its claim
Twelve days and twelve long nights to feed the flame.

The rites now paid, their pipes they clear'd, to chime
The current carols of unletter'd rhyme;
Or told appropriate tales with gamesome glee—
"How once an owlet † from the Christmas-tree
(Such as, perhaps, now glow'd amid the blaze)
Flew with scorcht pinions to the wondering gaze;
Or how a cuckoo † scar'd the circling throng,
As a new warmth reviv'd her April song.

With box and myrtle sprig'd, and leav'd with bay,
The windows were adorn'd to meet the day,
When, as the merry bells announc'd the dawn,
Soft symphonies came wafted o'er the lawn;
And, honour'd by a peal, the parish-feast
Perchance, by its peculiar rites increas'd
The general joy, and round the church-town drew
Alike the thrifty train, the careless crew,—

* Called, in the north of England, the Yule-block.

† † These are actually facts: they both happened not many years ago on this peninsula.

ludes to the old Roman tragedy: And he is peculiarly happy in this mode of illustration.||

From day to day each appetite amus'd,
And o'er the farms its alehouse mirth diffus'd—
Adapted the wild dance to various tunes
From crazy * *crowds* or Jew's-harps, or bassoons,
(When "kiss-her-sweet," the fidlers archly play'd,
And the quaint summons every swain obey'd—)
And rous'd to emulation all the clowns.
Or at the tower, the green, or open downs;
If still the ‡ intense desire of praise attach
Each rival parish to the ringing-match;
Or, (as a less impetuous spirit hails
A band of striplings to the town of kailes)
If ancient ardour in the athletic game
Bid Cornwall pant again for Grecia's fame,
And to the extensive heath the hurlers call
To deal, to bear away the mottoed ball; ||
Till now no more with stomachs to carouse,
Some crown'd with hats, and some, with silver cows, §
Some smarting from the bruise, the broken shin,
Others, perhaps, escaping in whole skin,
The revel with one general yawn they close,
And seek their homes, impatient of repose.

But the new year brought ever to the knight
Its ¶ "happy" hour with festal glory bright.

'Twas on this day, the villagers in flocks
Caught fine effluvia from the roasted ox,
With stomachs haply not inclin'd to dwell
With perfect satisfaction on the smell;
Whilst, open to each voluntary guest,
The laurel'd hall to many a mouth address'd
Productions rich with dextrous art dispos'd,
Among the rest, mince-pyes, how neatly ros'd!

Towering o'er all, the †imperial dish appear'd
On the long-groaning table as it rear'd
(Delicious to polite or vulgar gust)
Its brown magnificence its walls of crust.
Within, what various cates promiscuous lurk,
Geese stuff'd with tongue, and turkeys cram'd with pork,

* Crowd. A fiddle, a violin.

‡ Laudumque immensa cupido.

|| The manner in which the game is played, is pretty generally known: But hurling is almost extinct in Cornwall.

§ Gold-laced hats, silver-cows, &c. proposed as prizes to the wrestlers, &c.

¶ The old wish---"a happy new year"---is almost forgotten.

† The standing Christmas pye.

III. From religious rites to superstitious tenets, the transition is imperceptible and easy: The one was closely connected with the other. The greater part of our

And hares and hams embracing and embrac'd
High-season'd to solicit every taste!
So proud, in each opinion to outvie
The mighty Trojan horse, aspir'd the pye;
And drew from all, or delicate or coarse,
Praise never boasted by the Trojan horse!

Hah! 'mid that monster skulk'd the foes of Troy,
The insidious Greeks in ambush to destroy;
Ere-long descending from its wooden womb
To speed the vengeful torch from dome to dome,
But, darkly-leagued, the citadel surprize
Ere yet the extensive flame involv'd the skies.
So may, perhaps, those cates in ambuscade
The unweeting stomach with like power invade,
To the parcht liver treacherous fire impart,
And steal upon that citadel, the heart!

A massy bowl, to deck the jovial day,
Flash'd from its ample round a sun-like ray,
But, from a deeper gilding wont to beam,
On its worn rim betray'd a silver gleam—
A long-transmitted bowl that high-embost,
And with quaint figures astrologic crost
More prominent the *Andarton* arms display'd,
To throw the inferior symbols into shade.

Full many a century it shone forth, to grace
The festive spirit of the *Andarton*-race,
As, to the sons of sacred union dear,
It welcom'd with lambswool the rising year.

Nor sooner, at its chill and transient close,
Had evening ting'd a dreary waste of snows,
Than from the great plumb-cake whose charms entice
Each melting mouth, was dealt the luscious slice;
As all the painted tapers in array
Flung round the jovial room a mimic day,
To wake to wonted sports the fancy wild,
Where, e'en the greybeard re-assum'd the child.

Yes! all—the gay, the serious—prompt to share
The merry pastime, cried—avaunt to care!
All—while each slip a forfeit would incur,
(A slip that hardly left a lasting slur!)
With the same ardor as when childhood dawns,
Survey'd the accumulating store of pawns;
And all enjoy'd, with eyes that rapture beam'd
The frolic penance that each pawn redeem'd—

Cornish superstitions, in truth, were attached to saints or devils. There scarcely appeared a rock whose shape or position was singular or fantastic, without inspiring the idea of supernatural agency. Not a pool, whose situation was dreary or

Perhaps, self-doom'd to ply the gipsey's trade,
Or thro' the gridiron kiss the kitchen-maid,
Or, by a gentle metaphoric trick,
With cleaner lips salute the candlestick,
Or catch the elusive apple with a bound
As with its taper it flew whizzing round,
Or, with the mouth, half-diving to the neck,
"The splendid shilling" in a meal-tub seek,
Or, into wildness as the spirits work,
Display a visage blacken'd o'er with cork.

Meantime, the † geese-dance gains upon the sight,
In all the pride of mimic splendor bright;
As urchin bands display the pageant show,
In tinsel glitter, and in ribbons glow;
And pigmy kings with carnage stain their path,
Shake their cock-plumes, and lift their swords of lath; ‡
And great St. George struts, valorous, o'er the plain,
Deck'd with the trophies ‖ of the dragon slain,
And in a speech, the stoutest hearts to daunt,
Paints the dread conflict, at the monster's haunt;
And, thick where shiver'd lances strew the ground,
A champion fails, transfixt by many a wound,
But sudden, by the necromantic trump
Awaken'd, sits erect upon his rump;
And little dames their favouring smiles bestow,
And "father Christmas" bows his head of snow!"

‖ "The *Guary-miracle*, is a kind of enterlude, compiled in Cornish out of some scripture-history, with that grossness which accumpanied the Romanes. *Vetus Comedia.* For representing it, they raise an earthen amphitheatre, in some open field, having the diameter of this enclosed playne some forty or fifty foot." *Carew*, f. 71.---- The miracle-play not only resembled the *Vetus Comedia*, but was actually a continuation (as I have intimated in a former chapter) of the Pagan drama----mutatis mutandis----gods and goddesses for saints. And the circle in which it was celebrated, served alike for dances and scenic exhibitions. We have a great number of stone circles, generally supposed to be Druid circles; which the Cornish people call *Dawns-men*, or the *Stone-dance*. And "they called it so, (according to an ingenious writer) on no other account, than that they are placed in a circular order, and so make an area for dancing."* To confirm this opinion, I have to observe, that *dawnse*, in Cornish, signifies a dance; and that in a circular figure in the hundred of Penwith, the very ancient dance of *Tremathieves*, (as they name it) was practised not long since, among the Cornish.

† Geese-dance, i. e. guise, or disguise-dance—for so the Cornish pronounce guise. The geese-dancers of Cornwall answer to the mummers of Devon, and the morrice-dancers of Oxfordshire, &c.

‡ As the verses repeated in the geese-dance contain an allusion to the crusades, the following couplet was first written:

"And pigmy kings, by Paynim sabres gor'd,
"Shake the light plume, and glance the mimic sword."

‖ Spoliis indutus opimis.

* See Moyle's Posthumous Works, vol. 1. p. 239.

uncommon, but shewed marks of the cloven foot on its margin: And, certainly, there were few wells, without their tutelary saints.* - - - - - The duel between St. Just and St. Keverne is one of our traditionary tales: And the three stones of *Tremenheverne* are still pointed out to travellers, as proofs of saintly prowess.‡ The battle of the devil and the saints at Karnbre, is among the popular stories of the neighbourhood. To this battle, is owing that accumulation of enormous rocks, which were flung at random over all the mountain. But amidst all the wonders that work upon a Cornish imagination, the acts of *Tregagle* have surely a right to the pre-eminence. If nature appear in forms that are fantastic, or strike by uncommon occurrences, Tregagle is at once called in, to solve the difficulty: He is the being to create or to conduct the machinery. The pool of Dosmary is, in the vulgar opinion, unfathomable. The idea is preserved in the task

* St. Sancred was famous for curing diseases in swine: And to Sancred parish, swine were formerly driven from all quarters.

‡ St. Just came to pay a visit to St. Keverne, who hospitably entertained him for some days. He then took his leave to return home; and they parted good friends. Soon after St. Just's departure, St Keverne missed a piece of plate. After examining his servants he could hear no tidings of it, and was convinced St. Just must have taken it away. St. Keverne then went in pursuit of his brother saint; and on crossing Crowsaz-down, put three very large stones (weighing 300 pounds weight at least) into his pocket, and overtaking St. Just a little beyond Breage, in the parish of St. Germoe, charged him with the robbery; and a contest ensued. But St. Keverne, well armed with his three stones, soon overcame his adversary, and made him deliver the plate. Not chusing to carry back his ammunition, he left them on the spot; where they are to be seen to this day; sunk triangularly into the ground, in a nook on the right-hand-side of the road, as we go from Breage to Marazion. They are called *Tremen-heverne*. Tradition says, that these stones have been removed, by way of repairing hedges; but that they were always found, in the place where they now stand, the next morning. They are the iron stone of Crowsaz-downs. - - - - None of the sort are found in Breage or Germoe, or the neighbourhood.§ - - - - - I am here tempted to observe, that the ideas of the Arabs at this day, (derived from high antiquity) are very similar to those of the Cornish, respecting rocks and stones, which were grotesque in their appearance, or which retained a situation which could not be accounted for, in spite of human efforts. The author of "A Journal from Cairo," tells us: "We passed the mountain called *Gebel el Scheitan*, that is, "the mountain of the devil; which, as it is entirely of a black colour, gives foundation for the Arabs to report, that the devil sometimes dressed his victuals under it, by the smoke of which it acquired that blackness. They relate also another fabulous history about a head erected on high towards the entrance into the mountains, upon the left hand of the road; being a very large stone, supposed to have been the head of a sea captain, whose name was Baube, which was cut off by the Arabs, and put on the summit of that mountain, where it now remains; and, they say, should any one throw it down from the place where it is fixt, it would by the next day be restored to its situation. But these are only the fables of the Arabs." *See "Journal from Cairo to Mount Sinai,"* p. 48.

§ There is a manor in the parish of St. Keverne, called Lan-heverne.

to which he is condemned ----- to empty it with a limpet-shell,§ with a hole in the bottom of it. That, before the existence of the Loe-bar, Helston was a port, is more than a notion of the lower classes. This persuasion also, is proved and illustrated by the giant Tregagle's dropping his sack of sand between Helston and the sea: His sack of sand was the bar. If the echoes of the Loe hills be heard in the storm, they are the howlings of Tregagle: So extensive, indeed, is his fame or his infamy, that if there be a high wind in Cornwall, it is "Tregagle roars."‖ Amidst a variety of legendary personages crouding around me, I scarcely know where to close my narrative: Still in the rear, are there devils and saints without number. To draw, therefore, the curtain over all, I must conjure up Merlin, the enchanter and the prophet, who seems to have possessed a power over devils and saints. As an enchanter we have seen him in the story of Arthur: We are now to recognize him as a prophet. "In the parish of Paul, on the sea-shore, is a rock called in Cornish *Merlyn-Car*, or Merlin's rock. There, perhaps, he delivered that old prophecy in the Cornish tongue, foretelling the destruction of Paul church, Penzance, and Newlyn, long before they were in existence. It is as follows:

Aga fyth tyer, war an meyne Merlyn,
i. e. *There shall land on the stone Merlin,*
Ara neb fyth Leskey, Paul, Penzance, hag Newlyn.
*Those who shall burn Paul, Penzance, and Newlyn.**

§ On the rising of an easterly wind, the devil used to chase him three times round the pool; when he would make his escape to Roche rock; where putting his head into one of the chapel-windows, he was safe.

‖ The exact crisis of Tregagle's entre into being, is enveloped in darkness. But I think that he is a personage hoary with age; and that he was known to our remote progenitors; notwithstanding the familiarity of "Janny Tregagle," now current amongst us. The story is, that he by some means got within his grasp the heir to a considerable property, murdered the father and mother, and seized the estate of their orphan child.

* This prophecy was fulfilled when the Spaniards landed "*an meyne Merlyn*," in 1595, and burnt those very places: And so great was the conflagration at Paul, that the fire consumed the stone pillars of the church. *Carew*, f. 158. b. 159. ---- *Walker's Hals* in Paul.

A

SUPPLEMENT

TO THE

FIRST and SECOND BOOKS

OF THE

HISTORY OF CORNWALL;

CONTAINING

REMARKS ON ST. MICHAEL's MOUNT,

PENZANCE,

THE LAND's END,

AND THE

SYLLEH ISLES.

By THE HISTORIAN OF MANCHESTER.

PRINTED BY TREWMAN AND SON, HIGH-STREET;
FOR CADELL AND DAVIES, IN THE STRAND, LONDON.

1804.

A SUPPLEMENT, &c.

St. MICHAEL's MOUNT.

THIS Mount ſhooting up conically from a broad baſe to a narrow ſummit, and forming a Peak of Teneriff in miniature, will naturally ſeem to every eye that traces the reſemblance, equally with that the production of a volcano. Standing too within the ſea, when it certainly ſtood once upon the ſhore, and ſurveying from its eminence a large ſcene of deſolation, wrought by the ocean around; it naturally combines this ſcene with that aſpect in the mind of a reflecter, and ſuggeſts the deſolation to have been the effect of the volcano. So reaſoning, however, we ſhould argue with much of probability, but little of truth. Nature has reared her conical hills, as ſhe has ſunk her rounding *craters*, without uſing the aid of a volcano. The caſtle-hill of Launceſton, in our own county, and probably a thouſand hills beſide, in the other counties of the iſland, are exiſting proofs for the truth of the former aſſertion; as what is vulgarly called *the Devil's Punch-bowl*, on Hind-head, in Surry, is an equal proof for the juſtneſs of the latter.* We contract too rigidly the plaſtick powers of nature, in confining their operations to a ſingle mode only. We ſhew a creeping poverty of thought unworthy of Providence, when we ought to expand our ideas, and let looſe our imaginations, in an eagle's flight after God. We ſuffer philoſophy to bind up our wings, and to chain down our feet, rather than take a free range with theology and judiciouſneſs in the air, to catch the diverſified appearances of the working Hand Divine. And, as the Mount has at no period exhibited any ſymptoms of a volcano in itſelf, ſo is its form ſeen in hiſtory, juſt what it appears at preſent, ages *before* the deſolation.

I. Upon the crown of this original pyramid of nature, ſtands proudly eminent a Church, extending from eaſt to weſt, and ſhowing a tower in the middle. It was built by our Edward the Confeſſor, who added habitations adjoining for the clergy attendant upon it, and then endowed it with the whole Mount, &c. " I, Edward, by the grace of God, king of the Engliſh," he ſays in the very original ſtill preſerved, " willing *to give the price* for the redemption of my ſoul, and

 " of

* This *crater* is little known to the reading public, but lies in the road from London to Portſmouth, near the 43d mile-ſtone.

" of the fouls of my parents, with the confent and teftimony of fome good men," the fubfcribers to the charter, " *have* delivered to St. Michael the Archangel, *for the ufe of the brethren ferving* " *God in the fame place*, St. Michael," or the Mount and Church.* He alfo gives them " all the " land of *Vennefire*," a diftrict in Cornwall probably, but certainly a large one, as containing one or more *towns*; it being granted, " with the *towns*, houfes, fields, meadows, lands cultivated and " uncultivated, and with their rents."† But he finally gives them " the port Ruminell," Romney in Kent, " with all things that appertain to it, that is, mills and fifheries," &c.‡ And the Church appears from Domefday Book, to have thus poffeffed two hides of land in Cornwall alone.|| With thefe it muft have alfo poffeffed what it ftill retains, thofe " royalties over the Mount's Bay, as far north as Long Bridge in the manour of Lanefeley," which have *given to the Bay the appellation of the Mount*, " with wrecks, anchorage of fhips, keyage or wharfage of goods," &c.§ At the conqueft comes the falfely reputed founder of this, Robert, earl of Mortaign and Cornwall, not merely to enlarge its endowment a little, but to affociate it as a monaftick church with another of the fame appellation in Normandy. In a new charter, equally with the former undated, he, as " bearing" himfelf " the ftandard of St. Michael in war," fays: " I give and grant St. Mi- " chael's *Mount*, in Cornwall, to God and the monks ferving the church of St. Michael *de periculo* " *maris*, with half a hide of land."¶ But, " as of late I have very certainly found," he adds, " that " *a fon has been granted to me of my own wife*, by God, through the merits of the bleffed " Michael, and the prayers of the monks, I have increafed the donation to this bleffed prince of " the cœleftial army; I have given, and do grant, in Amaneth, three acres of land, namely, " Travelabeth, Lifmanoch, Trequaners, Carmailoc," all evidently lands in Cornwall.*† This very earl, fo devout to the archangel and fo liberal to the church, before Domefday book was compiled, had taken away from the church no lefs than half its whole endowment, even one out of two hides.‡‡ So ftrangely compounded, and of elements fo oppofite, was the mind of this man! He had even done more than this, *after* the book was compiled: as here he transfers this church, " with" its endowment of only " *half a hide* of land," to that in Normandy. Yet he reftored, probably, what he had taken away, in his additional donation of " three acres of land;" three Cornifh acres, of fixty ftatute each, compofing juft one hide and a half."|||| The lands thus given

* Monafticon i. 551. " Ego Edwardus dei Gratia Anglorum rex, dare volens pretium redemptionis animæ meæ vel pa- " rentum meorum, fub confenfu et teftimonio bonorum virorum tradidi Sancto Michaeli Archangelo, in unum fratrum Deo " fervientium in eodem loco, Sanctum Michaelem."

† Ibid, ibid. " Addidi etiam totam terram de Vennefire, cum oppidis, villifagris, pratis, terrifcultis et incultis, et cum " horum redditibus."

‡ Ibid, ibid. " Adjunxi quoque datis, portum addere qui vocatur Ruminella," fee Somner's Roman. Ports and Ports in Kent, p. 47, 54, 55, " cum omnibus quæ adeum pertinent, hoc eft, molendinis et pifcatoriis." &c.

|| " Ecclefia S. Michaelis tenet Trival," the fame region evidently with Vennefire. " Brifmar tenebat T. R. E." before Edward alienated it to the church: " Ibi funt II. hidæ, quæ nunquam geldaverunt." § Hals in MS.

¶ Monafticon i. 551. " Ego Robertus—habens in bello Sancti Michaelis vexillum—do et concedo Montem Sancti Mi- " chaelis de Cornubiâ, Deo et monachis ecclefiæ Sanctæ (Sancti) Michaelis *de periculo maris* fervientibus, cum dimidiâ terræ " hidâ."

*† Ibid, ibid. " Poftea autem, ut certiffimé comperi, Beati Michaelis meritis monachorumque fuffragiis michi a Deo ex " propriâ conjuge meâ filio conceffo, auxi donum ipfi Beato militi celeftis Principi; dedi et dono in Amuneth tres acras " terræ, Travelaboth videlicet, Lifmanock, Trequaners, Carmailoc."

‡‡ Fol. 120. " De his ii hidis Comes Moriton abftulit 1 hidam."

|||| Hals obferves in p. 159 of his manufcript, that " every antient Cornifh acre" is " fixty ftatute acres of land." In Domefday book, fol. 120, indeed, " 1 acra terræ—eft terra 1 caracatæ." So the regifter of bifhop Lacy makes it " a hun- " dred and twenty ftatute-acres." (Borlafe's Nat. Hift. of Cornwall, 319). In this variation of meafures, we may take any of them that fuit our purpofes.

given and re-given to the Mount, were the manor and pariſh of St. Hilary, formerly including thoſe of Peran Uthnoe; the churches of both theſe pariſhes being appropriated to the church on the Mount, before the Valor was made in 1291, tradition averring the union of both formerly; the lands themſelves being characterized as *Triwal* in Domeſday book, and *Triwal* ſtill exiſting as a conſiderable place within them; a charter of Richard, king of the Romans, to the Mount, alſo noticing its fair of *Marhaſgon* (Marhaſ-zon or Market-jew); the Mount ſtill poſſeſſing the right of "keeping annual fairs *on the ſea-ſhore near it*, Sept. 29," St. Michael's own day, with "Monday "after Mid-lent Sunday;" and theſe being *the very fairs of Marazion* at preſent.* In the charter for theſe fairs, granted by the very Richard above, brother to the third Henry, the monks "for "the future, and for ever, may hold" the fairs "upon their own ground at the market-place, "cloſe to their own grange;" that tithe-barn which is ſtill ſtanding in Market-jew, which ſeems to be a building of great antiquity, and on both ſides of which the fairs are ſtill held. But finally comes Leofric, the biſhop of Exeter, in a charter dated expreſſly 1085, to do what appears to have been much deſired, but ought never to have been granted, to free the church from all epiſcopal juriſdiction.‡

Thus erected, thus endowed, and thus freed, the church remained to the days of William of Worceſtre; and he gives us the dimenſions of it: "Memorandum; the length of the church of "St. Michael's Mount contains 40 feet, and is 30 ſteps, the breadth contains about twelve ſteps."§ Carew alſo ſpeaks of it as "a chapel for devotion, builded by Will. (Robert) earle of Morton," Carew ſo ſpeaking with the multitude in giving the church to the earl, when he ought to have united with records in giving it to the confeſſor; and "greatly haunted, while folke endured "(endeared) their merits by farre travailing."|| Carew thus refers obſcurely, perhaps unconſciouſly, to a particular privilege enjoyed by the church, which was given in one decree from Pope Gregory, and confirmed in another from Biſhop Leofric. "Know all men," cries the pope, "that the moſt Holy Father Gregory, in the year from the incarnation of our Lord *one thouſand* "*and ſeventy*," the very year, therefore, in which the earl aſſigned this church to another in Normandy, "bearing an affection of extraordinary devoutneſs to the church of St. Michael's Mount, "in the county of Cornwall, has piouſly granted to the ſaid church," and "to all the faithful "who ſhall ſeek or viſit it with their oblations and alms, "*a remiſſion of a third part of their pe-* "*nances*

* Tanner mentions, among the papers relative to the Mount, "cartam Ricardi regis Romanorum de Feriis in Marhaſgon;" Hals in MS.; Great Map of Cornwall; and Pope Nicholas's Valor. *Venneſire* thus appears the ſecular name for the pariſh of St. Hilary, and its "towns" muſt have been one at the church, a ſecond at Market-jew, with a third at the Mount. Yet *Venneſire* has been ſuppoſed by ſome, from a very partial preſervation of the name, to have been *Trevenna*, a village contiguous to Marazion on the eaſtern ſide. But Domeſday book, which calls it *Triwal*, a name and a place ſtill remaining, refutes the ſuppoſition at once. "That Perran Uthno was formerly taken out of the pariſh of St. Hilary, as you ſuſpect, there "is a tradition preſerved to this day. It is ſaid, that the whole was the property of one gentleman, who gave his younger ſon "ſuch a part as he could walk round in a given time, and which now makes the pariſh of Perran Uthno. Running acroſs a "common in this pariſh is a trench about three feet deep, and at different diſtances in this trench are ſhallow pits, which "were called the *Giant's Steps*. It is ſaid that this trench led from Godolphin and Tregonning hills to St. Michael's Mount, "and was the road the giants travelled. It was lately viſible thro' much incloſed and cultivated land, but I believe 'tis now "to be ſeen on Perran Downs." Rev. Malachy Hitchins.

‡ Monaſticon i. 551.

§ Itineraria Symonis Simeonis et Willelmi de Worceſtre, 1778, p. 103. "Memorandum; longitudo eccleſiæ Montis "Sancti Michaelis continet 40 pedes, et eſt 40 ſteppys; latitudo continet circa 10 ſteppys."

|| F. 154.

" *nances to them.*"* Thus "folke endeared their merits," not merely "by farre travailing," but by an exertion ftill more trying probably to themfelves, and certainly more profitable to the clergy, a demand upon their purfe. On the performance of fuch a vifit, and the payment of fuch a tax, a third of all thofe acts was to be remitted to them, which the penitents had been enjoined to perform, in order to prove the fincerity of their penitence to God and to themfelves. The church, which had enjoined thofe acts, had a right to commute them; and the current of penitential charity in particular, which had been previoufly left at large, perhaps, was only turned now into one prefcribed channel. The fame privilege is confirmed to the church by the Bifhop of Exeter, the bifhop repeating after the Pope in 1805, thus: "to all thofe, who fhall feek and "vifit that church with oblations and alms, we remit a third part of their penances."† Yet, what is very furprizing, the privilege was fo little ufed as to be wholly forgotten, became nearly as much unknown afterwards as it is at prefent, and was therefore announced formally to the public by the clergy of the church, at the beginning of the 15th century. "Thefe words," obferves the reciter of the privilege, "being found in fome antient regifters that have been difco-"vered within this church *of late*," a little before the reciter's vifit to the church about 1440, being then unknown to the very clergy themfelves, and only difcovered by the difcovery of fome regifters equally unknown, "are exhibited to public view upon the folding-doors of the church, "as they are here recited."‡ Yet even fuch a publication was thought too contracted for fuch a privilege. All the clergy of the kingdom were called upon to publifh it in their refpective churches. "*Becaufe this privilege is ftill unknown to many*," fays the call, "therefore we, the "fervants of God, and the minifters of this church in Chrift, do require and requeft all of you "who poffefs the care of fouls, for the fake of mutual accommodation, to publifh thefe words in "your refpective churches; that your parifhioners and fubjects may be more carefully animated "to a greater exhortation of devoutnefs, and may *more glorioufly in pilgrimages frequent this place*, "for the gracious attainment of the gifts and indulgencies aforefaid."§ From this publication of the privilege did undoubtedly commence that numerous refort of pilgrims to the church which Carew intimates; and of which Norden, who generally is the mere copier of Carew, yet is here the enlarger of him, fays, "the Mount hath bene much reforted unto by pylgrims in devotion to "St Michael."‖ Then too was framed affuredly that feat on the tower, which is fo ridiculoufly defcribed by Carew, as "a little *without* the caftle,—a bad feat in a craggy place,—fomewhat "daungerous

* Worceftre, 101. "Noverit univerfitas veftra, quod Sanctiffimus Papa Gregorius, anno ab Incarnatione Domini millef-"imo feptuagefimo, ad ecclefiam Montis Sancti Michaelis—in comitatu Cornubiæ gerens eximiæ devocionis affectum, pié "conceffit ecclefiæ predictæ—et omnibus fidelibus qui illam cum fuis beneficiis et elemofinis exepecierunt (expetierint) feu "vifitaverint, tertiam partem penetenciarum fuarum eis condonari."

† Monafticon i. 551. "Omnibus illis, qui illam ecclefiam fuis cum beneficiis et elemofinis expetierint et vifitaverint, "tertiam partem penitentiarum condonamus."

‡ Worceftre, 101, 102. "Ifta verba, in antiquis regiftris de novo in hâc ecclefiâ repertis inventa, prout hic, in valvis "ecclefiæ publicé ponuntur."

§ Worceftre, 102. "Quia pluribus eft incognitum, ideó nos, in Chrifto dei famuli et miniftri hujus ecclefiæ, univerfi-"tatem veftram qui regimen animarum poffidetis, ob mutuæ viciffitudinis obtentum, requirimus et rogamus, quatenus ifta "publicetis in ecclefiis veftris; ut veftri fubditi et fubjecti ad majorem exortationem devocionis attenciús animentur, et locum "iftum gloriofius perigrinando frequenent, ad dona et indulgencias predicta graciofé confequenda." Dr. Borlafe, in Scilly Ifles, p. 115, 116, produces a commiffion from a Bifhop of Exeter, as a proof "in *what a ftately ftyle* the bifhops of thofe "days penned their commiffions;" when the only note of ftatelinefs is the ufe of *fubditi* for the perfons of his diocefe. But we here fee it ufed with even fubjecti added to it, for the mere parifhioners of a private clergyman. And both the words are completely innocent in themfelves, meaning merely thofe *under* a prieft, or thofe *under* a bifhop; if proteftantifm was not at times a very fenfitive plant, and contracted before the very vapour of an approaching finger.

‖ Norden, 39.

" daungerous for acceſſe ;"* when it is a chair compoſed of ſtones projecting from the two ſides of the tower battlements, and uniting into a kind of baſon for a ſeat juſt at the ſouth-weſtern angle, but elevated above the battlements on each ſide, having its back juſt within, and hanging high over the rocky precipice below. It thus appears " ſomewhat daungerous" indeed, but not merely " for acceſſe," though the climber to it muſt actually turn his whole body at that altitude to take his ſeat in it, but from the altitude itſelf, and from its projection over the precipice. It alſo appears an evident addition to the building. And it was aſſuredly made at this period, not for the ridiculous purpoſe to which alone it profeſſedly miniſters at preſent, that of enabling women who ſit in it to govern their huſbands afterward ;‡ but for ſuch of the pilgrims as had ſtronger heads and bolder ſpirits, to complete their devotions at the Mount, by ſitting in this *St. Michael's Chair* as denominated, and there *ſhowing themſelves as pilgrims to the country round.* Hence in an author, who lends us information without knowing it, as he alludes to cuſtoms without feeling the force of them, we read this tranſient information:

> Who knowes not Mighel's Mount and *Chaire,*
> The *pilgrim's holy vaunt ?*

Norden alſo re-echoes Carew, in ſaying " *St. Michaels Chaire* is fabled to be in the Mount."† We thus find a reaſon for the conſtruction of the chair, that comports with all the uſes of the church on which it is conſtructed, and that miniſtered equally with this to the purpoſes of religion then predominant; a religion, dealing more in exteriours than our own, operating more than our own, through the body, upon the ſoul; and ſo leaving, perhaps, a more ſenſible impreſſion upon the ſpirits. To ſit in the chair then, was not merely as Carew repreſents the act, " ſome- " what daungerous" in the attempt, " and *therefore holy in the adventure* ;"§ but alſo holy in itſelf as on the church tower; more holy in its purpoſes, as the ſeat of the pilgrims; and moſt holy, as the ſeat of a few, in accompliſhment of all their vows; as the chair of a few, in invitation of all the country.

The whole church remains at this day, beaten by the winds or buffeted by the rains, a venerable monument of Saxon architecture, yet unadmired equally by the gaze of the vulgar, and the inſpection of the curious. In Hals's days, however, that Sir John St. Aubyn, " who for melan- " choly retirement dwelleth here ;" who, in a principle probably of religious ſequeſtration from the world, which is ſo proper in itſelf to be occaſionally reduced into practice, but which is always reckoned " melancholy" by thoſe who want it moſt, the irreligious fools of the world, had retired to this Mount as an aſylum from the world and its follies; repaired the church much, and fitted it up once more for divine ſervice. But the church is now waiting for a ſecond reſtoration by the preſent Sir John. Sir John is at once an antiquary and a man of taſte, I underſtand. He therefore intends to exerciſe this taſte, and to gratify his antiquarianiſm, by renewing the church in a high ſtyle of elegance. He has erected a magnificent organ already. He has alſo procured, at a great expence, a quantity of painted glaſs ſufficient for all the windows. I ſaw one great caſe of the glaſs there, ready for the windows. And, in levelling a very high platform for the altar, under the eaſtern window, a low Gothic door was diſcovered to have been cloſed up with ſtone

* Carew, 154. ‡ Yet this is the only uſe aſſigned for it, by Mr. Gough, i. 13. † Carew, 155, Norden, 30. § Carew, ibid.

ſtone in the ſouthern wall, and then concealed with the raiſed platform. The cloſure was now broken through, when ten ſteps appeared deſcending into a vault of ſtone under the church, about nine feet long, ſix or ſeven broad, and nearly as many high. In this room was found *the ſkeleton of a very large man*, without any remains of a coffin. The diſcovery gave riſe to various conjectures. But the thinking minds generally reſted at that natural centre of all thinking on ſuch a point, the ſuppoſition of the man's having been condemned to die by hunger in the dungeon for ſome crime. The cr*i*me, indeed, muſt have been enormous, to provoke ſuch a puniſhment as *immuring*. The bones of the wretched ſinner, ſo buried alive, and ſo concealed ſince, were brought up from the dark room, which muſt originally have ſerved as the repoſitory of the ſacramental plate, and interred in the body of the church.

II. But with the monaſtery was a NUNNERY upon the ſummit of the Mount. This is unconſciouſly noted by Hals: "One Henry de la Pomeray," he tells us, "Lord of Beri-Pomeroye, "in Deavon, and Tregny Pomeray in this county," caballing with John, Earl of Moretaign and Cornwall, to make the latter king during the abſence of Richard in Paleſtine, or in Auſtria, firſt murdered a man ſent by the regent to ſeize him, and was then "prompted, from the ſin of mur-"der, to that of rebellion, reſolving to reduce this Mount of St. Michaell for Earle John's domi-"nion, and to place himſelfe therein for better ſafety. In order to which he found out this ex-"pedient, to goe with his guard of armed men that dayley attended him, in diſguiſe, to that "place, under pretence of viſitinge a SISTER that he had amongſt THE RELIGIOUS PEOPLE "there; who, upon diſcoveringe who he was, and the occaſion of his cominge, had the gates "opened, where he entered accordingly with his followers; who ſoon after diſcovered under "their clothes their weapons of war, and declared their deſigns." The nunnery thus appears to have been diſcovered by Hals, without being ſeen by him. But it was equally diſcovered, yet was equally unſeen, by Carew. "Until Richard the firſt's reigne," Carew cries, "the Mount "ſeemeth to have ſerved only for religion, and (during his impriſonment) to have bene firſt for-"tified by Henry de la Pomeray, who ſurprized it;" for, having ſtabbed to the heart the king's meſſenger ſent to arreſt him, "he abandones his home, *gets to a ſiſter of his abiding in this Mount*," &c.* The nunnery thus appears again in the ſame ſtory, but plain from the pen of Hals, and obſcure from the pen of Carew; the former infinitely ſurpaſſing the latter, in all this portion of the topography. Yet it appears rather more plain, from the contraſt between this ſurprize of the Mount by Pomeroy, and another afterwards by the Earl of Oxford. After the battle of Barnet, in 1741, "John, Earle of Oxford," ſays Carew, "arrived heare by ſhipping, *diſguiſed himſelf* "*with ſome of his followers in pilgrims habits*, there through got entrance, muſtred *the garriſon*, and "ſeized the place;"† or, as Hals more fully informs us, "they diſguiſed themſelves in *pilgrims* "(apparel,) and" what they could not have worn "*friars* apparel, under which all had lodged a "ſmall ſword and a dagger; they went on ſhore, pretending that they were," not friars, but "*pil-*"*grims*, that had come a long pilgrimage from the remoteſt part of this kingdom, to perform the "penance impoſed upon them by their father-confeſſors, and to perform their vows, make ori-"ſons, and (make) oblations to the altar of St. Michael, who preſided there; upon which pious "pretext

* F. 155. † Ant. 390.

" pretext the monks and *inhabitants* opened their gates, and let them into the *caſtle*." This fact ſhews us the frequency of pilgrimages to the Mount, immediately after the publication of the privilege; but ſhews us not any appearance of a nunnery, the nuns being undoubtedly turned out by Pomeroy to provide apartments for his ſoldiery, and for the ſame reaſon kept out as long as a " garriſon" continued here, " inhabitants" of " the caſtle."

The nunnery had been erected probably juſt a little before Pomeroy's ſurprize of the Mount, then ended with it, and ſo exiſts only in that ſingle memorial of hiſtory. There is one circumſtance in the inſtitution of the nunnery, which proves it could not have been erected before the reign immediately preceding, and was actually erected then. The monks of the Mount were Benedictines recently reformed into Ciſtercians, and more recently improved into Gilbertines; but ſo improved by Gilbert, of Sampringham, in Lincolnſhire, only in the year 1148. It was this improvement, which affected to ſhow the ſuperiority of the ſpirit to the fleſh, and the triumph of the mind over the ſenſes, by placing a nunnery contiguous to a monaſtery. That ſuperiority was tried, and that triumph was exhibited, in every monaſtery of the order.* The nunnery, therefore, could not have been erected before 1148, yet muſt have been erected ſoon afterwards, and ended in leſs than fifty years; Richard reigning only nine. " The nunnery," however, as Dr. Borlaſe informs us, " was lately ſtanding on the eaſtern end of this monaſtery, detached a little " from the cells of the monks; and a great deal of carved work both in ſtone and timber (to be " ſeen a few years ſince) ſhewed, that it was the moſt elegantly finiſhed of any part of this houſe."† But the memory of the chapel ſurvived to the days of Worceſtre, he ſpeaking of it as rebuilt in his time, by calling it " the *chapel* newly built," and in giving us the dimenſions of it.‡ The memory of it even ſurvived to the preſent age, Dr. Borlaſe noting it to have been " lately ſtand- " ing" with the nunnery, and " a chapel dedicated to the Virgin Mary, as in all Ciſtercian monaſteries theſe chapels were."§ The chapel is thus ſhown by the Doctor to have been deſtroyed, when Sir John St. Aubyn religiouſly retired to this place, and built himſelf two elegant apartments in it. Theſe are called the new buildings, one opening into the other; but were originally, not the chapel merely of the nunnery, but the very nunnery itſelf. Theſe about fifty years ago were become very ruinous, and even the roofs had fallen in. But Sir John rebuilt them, and in the Gothic ſtyle, to make them correſpond as nearly as poſſible in their aſpect with the other buildings. The eaſtern end has a Gothic window below, and a circular one above; juſt as the church has, to which it ſtands in a parallel direction. And, in erecting theſe rooms, cart loads of human bones were dug up and interred elſewhere, the remains of burials from the nuns firſt, and from the garriſon afterwards, in the chapel.

III. " The way to the churche," adds Leland concerning both theſe buildings, " aſcendeth by " ſteps and grece weſtward, and then returneth eſtward to the utter," or outer, " ward of the " chyrch. *Withyn* the ſaid ward is a cowrt ſtronly (ſtrongly) walled, wheryn on the ſowth-ſide " is *the chapel of St. Michael*," for the monks, " and yn the eaſt-ſyde *a chapel of our lady*," for the nuns, " and the preſtes lodgings," thoſe the *capytaine* of the garriſon lately continued here, and

* Ant. 386. † Ibid. ibid.

‡ Worceſtre, 103. " Longitudo capellæ novæ edificatæ continet 40 pedes, et eſt 20 ſteppys; latitudo continet circa 10 ſteppys." § Ant. 386.

thofe of the clergy lately attached to the church, "be yn the fowth-fyde and the weft of St. "Michael's chapel."* But as Hals remarks, who is here worthy to join with Leland himfelf, becaufe here he equally fees with his own eyes, and equally hears with his own ears, at "the top "of the Mount,—towards the north-weft, is a kind of level plain, about 4 or 5 land-yards; which "gives a full profpect of the Mount's Bay, the Britifh ocean, Penfance town, Newlyn, Moufe-"hole, Gulvall, Maddern, Paul, and other parifhes, over a downright precipice of rocks towards "the fea, at leaft twenty fathoms high. From this little fquare or plain, there is an artificial "kind of afcent alfo, going towards the eaft; which offers you a full fight of the outer walls of "the caftle, and brings you to Porth Hourn, i. e. the Iron Gate, *part of which is yet to be feen.* "This little fortrefs comprehendeth (comprehended) fufficient rooms and lodgings for the cap-"tain or governour and his foldiers to refide in. To which adjoining are feveral other houfes or "cells, heretofore pertaining to the monks that dwelt here; all admirable for their ftrength, "building, or contrivance." One of thefe was the old hall of the monaftery, difcovered acci-dentally by Hals, in his defcription of a ball of fire, that in July, 1676, "ftruck againft the fouth "moorftone wall of this Mount's church," thence, "by a rebound, ftruck the ftrong oak durns "of the dwelling-houfe entry, and broke the fame in two or three pieces; and fo flew into the "HALL, where it fell to the ground, and then brake afunder, by the fide of Mrs. Catherine "Seynt Aubyn." This hall of the monks remains without the name in a long handfome room, that, from the reprefentations in ftucco round the cornice, of men hunting ftags, even fhooting hares, appears to have been fitted up fince the reformation as a dining-room for a hunting party, and is popularly denominated Chevy Chafe.

Together with the nunnery and the monaftery, was a caftle on the fummit of the Mount, and a town at the bafe of it. We have accordingly feen in our enquiries concerning the nunnery, ftrong traces of the caftle; as we have beheld the Earl of Oxford muftering "the garrifon," and feizing "the caftle." We have alfo feen Carew declaring the Mount "to have been firft forti-"fied by Henry de la Pomeray, who furprized it." And, as Dr. Borlafe fubjoins, "Pomeroy "took refuge here, having a fifter in this nunnery," and being (as Leland fays, Itin. vol. VI. p. 54) "at that tyme lorde of the caftelle of the Mount of St. Michael;" where, finding "the hill on "which the monaftery ftands, fteep and rocky, he fortified it."† This account is evidently a mafs of contradictions; Pomeroy being ftated to have been the lord of the caftle at the time, yet to have taken refuge in it, as having a fifter in a nunnery within it; to have been lord of the caftle before, yet to have now "found" its hill "fteep and rocky;" to have "fortified" the hill, when it is expreffly owned to have been fortified with a "caftle" before. But the real fact, as cleared of all contradictions, is this. The whole tenour of the ftory proves of itfelf, that Pomeroy *at the time* was lord of *no* caftle on the Mount, that there was *no* caftle really exifting on the Mount *at the time*, and that he only furprized it by pretending a vifit to his fifter the nun, be-caufe the hill was a fortrefs in itfelf. Yet how fhall we encounter the pofitive authority of Le-land, for the exiftence of a caftle here? "*One* of the Pomereis of Devonfhir," he tells us in a ftyle of obfervable uncertainty, "*long fyns* loft the moft part of his inheritance, by killing a mef-"fenger

* It was once fhewed me for what I enquired after, the nun's chapel, when *this* has been fome time deftroyed, and *that* has no window on the eaft, no niche for a ftatue there, &c.

† Ant. 386

" fenger or herald fent from the King of England, onto hym; *at that tyme* Pomerey was lord of " Tremington, alias Tremerton Caftelle, in Cornewale, and of *the Caftelle of the Monte of S. " Michael* yn Cornewale, and of the lordfhip of Tamarton."* *At the time* of the murder, Pomeroy was *not* lord of the caftle, but *was immediately afterwards*; and this flight interval of time has Leland overlooked. Juft before Richard's return from captivity, we find from Hoveden, the only *hiftorian* who mentions the fact, all the other accounts being merely traditional; " was furren- " dered to the king's arms the Caftle of Marlborough, the Caftle of Lancafter, and *Saint Michael's " Mount* in Cornwall; which laft Henry de la Pomerai, after he had expelled the monks," by whom are meant the nuns, " *had fortified againft the king*; and the fame Henry, hearing of the " king's arrival, died overwhelmed with fear: but thefe three *caftles*, Marlborough, and Lancaf- " ter, and *Saint Michael's Mount*, were furrendered before the king's arrival."† The hill was now firft fortified, by having the fite of the monaftery and nunnery now firft formed into a caftle. Carew accordingly informs us, that " the Mount feemeth to have bene firft fortified by Henry de " la Pomeray, who furprized it; *from which time* forward, this place *continued* rather a fchoole of " Mars, then the temple of peace."‡ Even Dr. Borlafe fubjoins, though with another contradiction to what he had alledged before; that " *from this time* it was looked upon as a place fit for " defence, and made ufe of as fuch upon feveral occafions, and the commander of the garrifon " had a lodging in the monaftery."§ There was confeffedly, therefore, *no* " garrifon," *no* " com- " mander," and *no* " place" ufed " for defence," *before*.

Nor muft we be drawn from our certain conviction of this, by any expreffions in the Confeffor's charter to " the priory of St. Michael in Cornwall," as giving " to St. Michael the Arch- " angel, for the ufe of the brethren ferving God in the fame place, Saint Michael with all its ap- " pendages, namely," among other things, " *the caftles*."‖ Thefe are only thofe three natural wards of this natural caftle, which compofe the whole of it. " From the foot of Mount St. Mi- " chael," Hals tells us very truly, " you afcend the hill or rock through a narrow, crooked, " craggy path, to the *outer* portal or gate; a confiderable height on the one fide, by the way, in " the rock, is a fmall fpring of water, that falls into pits (a pit) made in the ftones (ftone or " rock) to lodge the fame, for the lower or bottom inhabitants ufe; which water never intermits " its current." This is what is now named the Giant's Wall, what Leland denominates " a fair " fpring in the Mount," but Carew more properly calls it " a lye pit, not fo much fatisfying ufe " as relieving neceffitie."¶ And as all the afcent up to the outer gate forms only the open bafe of the hill, fo the fpace between the outer and fecond gates compofes the firft ward. " Above the " fecond gate," adds Hals, " there is another fpring of water iffuing out of the rocks; that makes " a pretty confluence for fix or feven winter months, and then intermits; (the high pofition of) " which

* Itin. VI. 58, 59.

† Hoveden, f. 418, Savile. " Merleberge redditum eft, fimiliter redditum eft, caftellum de Lancafter, et Mons Sancti " Michaelis in Cornubiâ redditus eft ei, quem Henricus de la Pumerai, expulfis inde monachis, contra Regem munierat; " idemveró Henricus, audito adventu regis, obiit timore perterritus. Hæc autem tria caftella, videlicet Merleberge, et Lan- " caftre, et Mons Sancti Michaelis, reddita fuerunt ante adventum Regis." Carew proceeds on this authority, but vitiates it by careleffnefs; fixing the death *before* the furrendery, 154, 155.

‡ F. 154, 155. § Ant. 386.

‖ Monafticon, i. 551. " Pro prioratu Sancti Michaelis de Cornubiâ. Tradidi Sancto Michaeli Archangelo, in ufum Fra- " trum Deo fervientium in eodem loco, Sanctum Michaelem—cum omnibus appendiciis,—fcilicet—caftellis."

¶ Leland Itin. III. 17, and Carew, 154.

" which renders the portage of it upwards, much the eaſier for the inhabitants uſe in that ſeaſon. " After you paſs through this ſecond gate, betwixt," he means *you take*, " a winding and crooked " path artificially cut in the rocks on the north-ſide thereof, and follow the ſame; (thus) you ar- " rive at the top of the Mount." All this compoſes the ſecond ward. On the top " towards the " north-weſt," as Hals proceeds, " is a kind of level plain;—from this little ſquarer plain, there " is an artificial kind of aſcent alſo, going towards the eaſt, which offers you a full ſight *of the* " *outer walls* of the caſtle, and brings you to Porth Hourn, i. e. the Iron Gate" of entrance into it, the only artificial gate as into the only artificial part of the fortreſs, and remembered ſtill by a very old man to have been exiſting in part during his boyhood. The gates in the firſt and ſecond wards are both as natural as the fortreſs itſelf, being merely narrow paſſes in the aſcent, and with the artificial dividing the whole Mount into three parts, three caſtles, or three wards. Two of theſe exiſted from the firſt formation of the hill, the other from the firſt conſtruction of the mo- naſtery, while all induced Pomeroy to convert the hill into a fortreſs; have ſince induced our go- vernment to keep a garriſon upon it to the reformation, and have ſo fixed upon the priory the name of caſtle to the preſent moment. In the 5th of Henry the Fourth, " the priory" is ſaid ex- preſſly by one of our records, " to be in time of war a fortalice to all the country around."* And cannon are even now placed upon the Mount, ſome lighter pieces above, ſome heavier below.

But prior to all the artificial conſtructions upon the Mount, was the town *at* and *upon* the baſe of it. There is *upon* the baſe of it a town, which conſiſts at preſent of three or four ſtreets, riſing in parallel or direct lines up the hill from the landing-place at the pier; and compoſed of dwel- ling-houſes, rooms for ſtoring fiſh, ſtables, a *chaiſe-houſe* for the proprietor, with a cemetery for the inhabitants. Nor is this only a modern erection; tho' out of the ſeventy-four houſes now ex- iſting, there were only two about 65 years ago, and about 75 years ago only one, as tradition ſays. There was plainly a town on the ground before. This appears as early as the monaſtery; the Confeſſor, in his charter to the latter, giving to the former the Mount, " with all its appendages, " namely, THE HOUSES" in the town, " the fields" or paſturable grounds on the ſouth or ſouth- eaſt, that now breed rabbits, " and the other appurtenants."† Thus alſo, in the ſecond charter concerning " *the* priory of Cornwall," Earl Mortaign ſays thus: " I conſtitute that theſe very " monks, by the conceſſion of my Lord the King, may *there* have a MARKET on the fifth day of " the week."‡ This is the very market ſtill kept upon the oppoſite ſhore, being kept ſtill upon the *fifth* day of the week, and having therefore lent the appellation of the day to the town; *Markiu*, *Marcaiew*, *Marghas-jewe*, or *Marhas-gou*, the recorded appellations of the town, all ſignifying *the Thurſday's Market*; while from the other, the more recent appellation of the town, *Markaſion*, that is. Marghas or Marhas-ſion, now *Marazion*, or Sion Market, and from the tra- dition ſtill prevailing of a *Jewiſh Market* held formerly *without* the town, on the *ſtrand*, on the *weſtern* ſtrand too, *Marghas Jeu* has been vitiated by *Engliſh* pronunciation into *Market-Jew*, as the

* Tanner, from Rymer's Fœdera, viii. 102, 340, 341. " Eſſe tempore guerræ Fortalitium toti terræ circumjacenti."

† Monaſticon i. 55. " Cum omnibus appendiciis, villis ſcilicet,—agris et ceteris attinentibus." Leland, in Itin. viii. 118. " The ſowth ſowth-eſt part of the Mont is paſturable, and breedeth conyes. The reſidue hy and rokky."

‡ Monaſticon i. 551.

the Jew's Market.* The name of Market-jew, then, is the original and proper defignation of that town, which had a market conceded to it on a conceffion of one to the Mount; while the name of Mara-zion is the defignation only of a new, a Jewifh, and a weftern part. " In *Marhas-* " *deythyon*," fays Leland, meaning not " to *fpell* it," as Mr. Gough fays he meant, " Markad- " deyth yon," but actually meaning as he writes, *Marhas Deyth Yon*, the Jew's Day Market, " ys but a poore chapel in the middes of the poore town, and *a little chapel* yn the *fand*, nere by " the towne, *toward the Mont*." Accordingly on the fouth-fide of Marazion, between this town and the Mount, is what is denominated the Chapel Rock; on which tradition alfo reports a chapel to have once ftood, dedicated to the Virgin Mary, though no veftige of it has been difcernible within the memory of man. This chapel is confeft by tradition to have been erected for the inhabitants of Marazion; the rock being then contiguous to the main land, when it is about a hundred yards diftant from it at prefent. The rock is about 150 yards in circumference; but the level part of it, on which the chapel muft have ftood, is about 45 feet in length, and 18 or 20 in breadth. The real Marazion, then, is the new part, formed originally by the Jews, and more wefterly in its pofition. Leland fpeaks of Marazion and Market-jew as if they were two towns ftill diftinct; noticing *Marhasdethyon* as above, and mentioning " *Markefin* a great long town, " burnid a Gallis." " And whereas our borough of Marghas-iewe," fays the charter 13 June, 27 Eliz. 1. " is an *ancient borough*, and was once a *trading town*, and of *great note*, until a de- " teftable rebellion having rifen in thofe parts againft the illuftrious Prince, and our dear " brother Edward the Sixth, the faid town was taken and deftroyed by the traitors and ene- " mies of the faid King; ever fince whofe time the faid borough hath fallen to decay, the " public buildings and dwelling-houfes being at this day in ruins and defolation, as we are in- " formed by divers of our trufty fubjects," &c. Even a *pier* was erected near the town, but on the fheltered or northern fide of the Mount, for the commercial ufes of the inhabitants. " In the " north north-eft," as Leland tells us for his time, " is a garden, with *certen howfes* with *fhoppes for* " *fifcher-men*."† And near to this town ftood, within memory, a building, that belonged to the priory, was forty-five feet in length, and was denominated the Banquetting-houfe. But there is, as Leland remarks in another place, " a *pere* by the Mount."‡ This was almoft entirely rebuilt about 70 years ago, by Sir John St. Aubyn, but is remembered to have had its mouth to the weft, as the new pier has it to the north. It lies at the Mount's end of that ridge of gravel, which, in Leland's time, was " the way to the churche," which " entereth at the *north* fyd, *fro half heb to half fludde*,"§ and now entereth on the *fame* fide for only a few hours of ebb. This ridge, which at

* " *Marca-iewe*—fignifying in Englifhe *Market on the Thurfday*," (Norden 39). " *Marcaiew*, of *Marhas Diew*, in " Englifhe, the Thurfdaies Market; for then it ufeth this traffike," (Carew 156). " *Markiu*, 1. Forum Jovis, quod " ibi Mercatus die Jovis habeatur," (Camden 136). *Marghas-jewe*, in charter the 37th of Elizabeth; *Markefion*, *Markafion*, in the endowment of the vicarage A. D. 1261, and in the Bifhop's confirmation of it A. D. 1313; with the tradition concerning the Jewifh Market (Origin of Arianifm, 331, 334). But the oldeft record, which mentions the town, is one of Richard, King of the Romans, referred to before, and fpeaking of it as " Marhafgon," by a mif-reading for " Marhaf- " gou." The name of Market-jew, then, is the original and proper defignation of that town, which had a market conceded to it in a conceffion to the Mount; while the name of Mara-zion is the defignation only of a new, a Jewifh, and a weftern part. Leland, in Itin. vii. 117.

† From the Rev, Mr. Hitchens.

‡ Itin. iii. 17.

§ From Mr. Hitchins.

at the higheſt ſpring tides has about thirteen feet of water upon it, but about ſeven at the top of the neap tides, and ſeven or eight feet more at the ſides, which is accidentally formed by the two currents of the tide, ſweeping round the Mount, meeting in oppoſite directions beyond it, and then depoſiting at the place of conflict the pebbles, gravel, or ſand brought along with them; had a croſs upon it, which about 75 or 80 years ago was broken down by the violence of a ſtorm, notwithſtanding the protection which the Mount gave it. It being fixed at the loweſt part of the ridge, the *cloſing* and *uncloſing* (as the firſt covering and laſt uncovering of the ridge by the tide are denominated) always happened at this point; but have now changed to a point about 70 or 80 yards nearer Marazion, now made the loweſt on the ridge, by carrying off ſtone for the erection of ſome new houſes there. The whole ridge is about forty yards wide, not tending directly to the mouth of the pier, but reaching the Mount about eight yards eaſt of it; compoſed of pebbles, gravel, or ſand, in each of which the predominant quantity is governed by the roughneſs or ſtillneſs of the tides. At neap tides, and in very bad weather, the ridge ſcarcely *uncloſes* at all, and for only two or three hours in mild weather; but in mild weather, and at ſpring tides, upwards of five hours. Formerly, yet within memory, the ridge was paſſable *half an hour* longer than it is at preſent; and is now paſſable only for about two thirds of the time, or *four* hours in the day. So ſeemingly, ſo apparently, is the ſea encroaching here, within theſe later ages.*

IV. The ſea has been ſenſibly encroaching upon the land here, for ages. We ſee its ravages apparent in the period paſt, and we feel its violence at preſent. "The continual advances which "the ſea makes upon the land at preſent," Dr. Borlaſe obſerves concerning the Sylley Iſles, "are "plain to all people of obſervation; and within the laſt thirty years," before this un-dated letter was publiſhed, in 1756, "have been very conſiderable."‡ Indeed, "the ſea is perpetually prey- "ing upon" all "theſe little iſlands, and leaves nothing where it can reach but the ſkeleton, the "bared rock."§ Yet let us ſtep back into former times, and there examine whether the ſea was ſo troubleſome a neighbour then. "In the bay betwyxt the Mont and Penſants," as Leland tells us, "be fownd neere the lowe water marke rootes of trees yn dyvers places, as a token of the "grownde waſted."‖ "There hath bene," as he adds in another place, "much land devoured "of the ſea betwixt Penſandes and Mouſehole."¶ In 1414, Biſhop Stafford of Exeter thus exhorts all the perſons of his dioceſe, to contribute towards the reparation of damages made by the ſea at the latter: "as the chapel of *Moſal*, formerly built in honour of the Bleſſed Virgin, and "ſituated near a port or creek of the ſea, is *now* by *the force of the ſea* entirely *thrown down and* "*demoliſhed*; which, while it ſtood, was a mark to ſeamen, and which, if it was rebuilt, might "ſtill be the means of the preſervation of many ſailing into this port or creek of the ſea, which is "very narrow, and too dangerous to give aſſiſtance, eſpecially in the time of tempeſts or hurri- "canes; and as the revenues of the ſaid chapel are by no means ſufficient to repair, or more "truly

* Mr. Gough, 13, repeats the miſtake of Pomeroy's "driving out the *monks*," ſpeaks of "a capacious pier at the foot of "the rock for the fiſhermen, whoſe *tents* cover its *ſides*;" and adds, "the Mount is joined to the main land by a *large beach*, "over which the tide flows."

‡ Scilly Iſles, 88. § Ibid. 89.

‖ Itin. vii. 118. ¶ Ibid. iii. 18.

Drawn by Cap. Tremenhere.

Monschole, in Mounts Bay, from the Island.

Published Oct. 1. 1804 by Rev. R. Polwhele.

" truly to rebuild the ſame;" &c.* ſo in 1435, we have an indulgence of forty days, a remiſſion of penances (I believe) for this number of days, " to all thoſe who ſhall charitably contribute, or " lend a helping hand, towards maintaining and repairing the *Quay* of *Mouſehole*;"† and another to all, " who ſhall—contribute towards repairing and maintaining a certain *Key* or *Juttey* at *Newlyn*, in the pariſh of Paul," betwixt Mouſehole and Penzance.§ So uſefully did the church diſpenſe her ſpiritual benefits, for the ſupport of ſecular objects! So much was the ſea at that period bearing with violence upon the land, undermining its quays, and demoliſhing its chapels. We have alſo ſeen the ſea before, encroaching ſo much upon the land on the ſouth-eaſt of Marazion, as to inſulate the very rock on which the original chapel of the town was built; even to inſulate it by a ſtraight about a hundred yards in breadth, ſince the very days of Leland. On the eaſt of Marazion, many yards in the breadth of the cliff have been waſhed away within twenty-four years paſt, about half a mile in length; the ſoil of the cliff being of a very ſoft quality, and the ſpring-tides puſhing up with conſiderable force againſt it. About 70 or 80 years ago, a ſpring-tide was driven by a dreadful hurricane with ſuch a violence upon the town itſelf, as to beat down a whole row of houſes within it, and to carry them, with their very foundations, into the ſea. And, in the confirmation of the endowment to the vicar of St. Hilary, A. D. 1313, the dead of Marazion *are for the firſt time allowed*, from the danger of paſſing with them to the Mount, to be buried at St. Hilary; " *becauſe of the danger of the flux of the ſea* near St. Michael's Mount and " Markaſion," the confirmation ſaying, " and for other cauſes, the bodies of the deceaſed at Mar- " kaſion may for the future be conſigned to ſepulture, in the cemetery of the church of St. " Hilary."‖ But a ſhaft was lately ſunk in the beach between Newlyn and Penzance, when whole trees were found at a good depth under the ground. About half-way between Chyendower and Marazion, in the road from Penzance to the eaſt, about three hundred yards below high-water mark, and near to the line of low water, were ſeen a few years ago by Mr. Giddy, an eminent ſurgeon of Penzance, and ſince ſeen by one of his ſons, upon an extraordinary receſſion of the tide, ſeveral ſtumps of trees *in their native ſoil*, with the *roots* ſhooting out from them, and with the *ſtems* apparently cut off. Theſe trees had been felled, in apprehenſion of the coming encroachments; while the whole trees had been either ſurprized or neglected. On the weſtern ſide of Penzance, and in a line with the brook parting Gulval from Ludgvan pariſh, a range of rocks projects about half a mile beyond the beach; to the eaſt of which have ſtumps of trees been ſeen by

* Regiſter, vol. iii. fol. 203. " Mouſehole," ſays Camden, in Mr. Gough's Engliſh, p. 3, " called in the Britiſh language Port Inis, or the Port of the Iſland;" but a note from Mr. Gough adds thus, " from an iſland lying before it G. (Gibſon) *but quere where*." An aſtoniſhing quere, from one who appears to have travelled into the region! Even ſtill more aſtoniſhing, perhaps, from one who republiſhes theſe words of Leland; " wythyn a crow ſhot of the ſayd key or peere lyeth " directly a *lytle low iſland with a chapel yn yt*, and *thys lytle iſlet* bereth greſſe." Theſe words, indeed, are referred by Leland to *Newlyn*, not Mouſehole. But he certainly meant them for Mouſehole, however they have been mis-placed to Newlyn. Theſe words in Itin. vii. 17, all omitted by Mr. Gough, prove the point: " a litle beyond *Mouſehole* an *iſlet*, and *a* " *chapel of St. Clementes* in it." And the very map of the county, in the very Britannia of Mr. Gough, ſhews us " St. Clement's Iſle" expreſſly, much to the ſouth of Newlyn, and oppoſite to the ground of the unſpecified Mouſehole.

† Lacy's Regiſter, fol. 206. The village, thus called *Moſal* and *Mouſehole*, has taken its ridiculous name, in Engliſh, from an act ſtill more ridiculous in the inhabitants, they ſhewing a large opening in the ſide of a hill as an actual mouſe-hole. The ſatyrical Engliſh caught at the circumſtance, held it up in deriſion of the people, and ſo denominated the village from the folly.

§ Ibid. 254.

‖ " Propter periculum fluxûs maris juxta Montem Sancti Michaelis et Markaſion, corpora decedentium apud Markaſion in cæmeterio eccleſiæ Sancti Hillari tradantur de cætero ſepulturæ." From Mr. Hitchins, with the facts immediately preceding.

by the late Dr. Borlafe, as I fhall foon fhow, and to the weft by my very obliging, very ufeful informant, Mr. Giddy. Nor have thefe ravages of the ocean ceafed at prefent. Betwixt Newlyn and Penzance, on the Penzance fide of the brook parting Maddern from Paul parifh, were fome fields within memory that are now covered with the fea. There were alfo at Penzance five or fix houfes upon the beach weft of the pier, which within memory have been undermined and demolifhed by the fea. Gulval too has a manour within it, called Lanfeley, half of which is now buried in the ocean. But I crown all thefe remarks, with this ftriking notice from Leland: "ther "is an old legend of St. Michael," the old leffon that ufed to be read in the church here on St. Michael's day, "(that fpeaketh of) *a Townlet in this part* now *defaced and lying under the water*."* We thus return to the Mount again. "The Cornifhmen," fays Carew, our oldeft reporter of the Cornifh appellation for it, call it "*Cara Cows in Clowze*," that is, the "Hoare Rock in the "Wood."† Carew knew the Cornifh language too imperfectly, to repeat even the Cornifh appellation accurately. The name meant by Carew is "Cara Clowze in Cows," as the real name is "*Carreg Lûg en Kûg*, a hoary rock in a wood."‡ But Worceftre is the oldeft writer, who gives us the Englifh fignification of it; he informing us, that the Mount was "formerly denomi- "nated Le Hore-rok in the Wodd."§ All ferves to fhew us, that this *Dinfol*, as it is equally denominated by the Regifter of Landaff;‖ this *Hill of Profpect*, as it was termed, becaufe of the wonderful loftinefs of it, and the extenfive view from it, once prefented its rocky fides to the eye, all covered with trees, and once reared its grey head in the air, all naked above them. "Ther "be found," notes Leland, in a paffage of which I fupply the defects by words between paren- "thefes, "from the inward," or northern "part of the .... (Mount) yvers (dyvers) .... re "(quarre) ftones;"¶ and, as the quarry is ftill purfued for the excellence of the ftone in building, the labourers have recently found roots of trees in the clefts of the rocks. It even appears decifively from the charter of the Confeffor, to have been in his time *not* furrounded by the fea during all the flood-tide, and not acceffible by land only during fome hours of the ebb. *Then* it was *not* furrounded at all. It was only NIGH the fea, *then*; the charter defcribing it expreffly, as "St. "Michael

* Itin. iii. 18. "Tho' it is uncertain when this awful event happened in Mount's Bay," fays a refpectable correfpondent, "yet I think it plainly demonftrable that it was upwards of 1400 years ago: for in the fummer of 1793 fome labourers, em- "ployed in digging trenches about 100 yards from the fea, difcovered an urn full of Roman coins, erectly buried two or three "feet under the furface. The coins were of the fame kind as thofe found near Godolphin, in April 1779, and at Morva in "June 1789; viz. fome of Gallienus, Tetricus, &c. All the urns were earthen, buried nearly at the fame depth, and the "coins in general were in good prefervation." Thefe difcoveries prove the Romans to have inhabited the moft wefterly parts of Cornwall, equally with the moft eafterly of Britain. But furely they prove nothing concerning the latenefs or earlinefs of the convulfion which drowned the land about Mount's Bay. I fhall inftantly attempt to point out the period. In the mean time I notice this *demonftration*, in order to fet it afide; as I muft equally fet afide my correfpondent's appeal to facts, that are the refult either of local accidents or of the general deluge. Such is his mention of "fubterranean trees, found half a mile *beyond the prefent reach of the fea*," one of them "hard and found enough for any ufe." Such are alfo the trees "at "a very confiderable depth, difcovered a few years fince by perfons fearching for ftream tin on the margin of Hayle river;" fome of which were hazels, that had "many nuts on them, in a ftate of maturity," as have been equally difcovered at Bath and many other places, (Stukeley's Itin. cùr. i. 147). And fuch finally are the "many human bones, fome fculls, and one "fkeleton almoft entire," found equally by the ftream-workers on Hayle river; but "buried too deep to be the bodies of "fhipwrecked mariners interred there, or of perfons drowned by accident in the river." They were the remains of perfons killed in battle, or murdered by thieves, about a century ago. Thus the firft and the laft cafes are the refult of local accidents, and the intermediate cafe is the confequence of the general deluge.

† F. 154.

‡ Borlafe's Scilly Ifles, 94. Carew, in writing what his informant meant for the two firft words, "Cara Clowze," wrote them merely from the pronunciation, without confidering the divifion; the two words intended being *Carac Louze*. So *Caraclouse* in St. Meria, the grey rock.

§ P. 102. "Antea vocata Le Hore-rok in the Wodd." ‖ Camden, 136. ¶ Itin. vii. 118.

" Michael NEAR TO the ſea."* This evidence is ſufficient of itſelf, to mark in ſtrong colours the encroachments of the ſea here; when what is at high water half a mile within the domain of the ſea at preſent,† was at ſome diſtance from the ſea then. What this diſtance was, the charter does not tell us; but two teſtimonies, hitherto unnoticed and unknown, do. There is a marginal annotation in Leland, which he derived aſſuredly from his " old legend of St. Michael," which has been loſt to the public, however, from the breaches in it, but which I preſume to recover by mending the breaches, becauſe it then lends us important information. I repeat it as it ſtands in print, and place to it my own reading, being all applied to the Mount: " ...... (it) was and " (ſtanding) ..... ons (ons) V. miles .... (fro) the ſea."‡ My reading ſpeaks for itſelf, I think, and reſcues from the ſhades of night a circumſtance uncommonly ſtriking in the hiſtory of the Mount, that it was formerly no leſs than FIVE MILES from the ſea. But we can happily confirm the circumſtance, by an evidence which has not an atom of conjecture in its compoſition, is all clear and certain, yet carries the diſtance to a ſtill greater length. " The ſpace of ground upon " St. Michael's Mount," we are informed by Worceſtre himſelf, and from the ſame legend aſſuredly, " is two hundred cubits, *ſurrounded on all ſides by the ocean*," at flood-tide; " the place " aforeſaid WAS ORIGINALLY INCLOSED WITH A VERY THICK WOOD, diſtant from the ocean " SIX miles, AFFORDING THE FINEST SHELTER FOR WILD BEASTS."§ The fact, however aſtoniſhing, is placed beyond all reach of doubt by the concurrent evidences of the name, the charter, and two authors; each varying ſufficiently from each, to ſhew it is not one evidence multiplied into many by a mere echo; yet all combining into one general teſtimony, about the diſtance of the Mount from the ſea originally. And a tradition comes in as an intermediate link in this ſtrong chain of evidence, to mark the progreſs of the ſea's ſubſequent encroachments about their halfway point; an opinion ſtill prevailing very livelily among the inhabitants of Penzance, that " perſons could once walk directly from the Mount to Newlyn," ſo croſſing the body of the Bay on foot in a line obliquely, from north-eaſt to ſouth-weſt.

This grand encroachment of the water upon the land, reſults plainly from a preponderance of the Atlantick upon the ſhores of Britain; occaſioned, perhaps, by a proportional receſſion from the ſhores of America. It is this preponderance which has thrown ſuch a volume of waters upon the Sylley Iſles, as leaves only their mountains to appear for them, ſo has broken the ten iſles of Strabo into a hundred and forty iſlets.‖ It is this preponderance too, which has ſwept away " the Iſland Silura" of Solinus, beginning then, as appears at once from the very name ſtill through ſo many ages attached to the barren rock of *Sylley*, in a promontory now the moſt north-weſterly of all the iſlets, ſtretching thence in a long range through Brehar, Treſcaw, and Samſon; St. Helen's, Theon, St. Martin's, and St. Mary's; Annet, St. Agnes, Guew, and the eaſtern iſlands, towards the ſhore of Britain; even " ſeparated by a *ſtrait*" only, a ſea narrow in itſelf, and " a turbulent" one, becauſe of its narrowneſs, " from the ſhore of the Dumnonii," or the

coaſt

* Monaſticon i. 551. " Sanctum Michaelem qui eſt juxta mare."

† Borlaſe's Scilley Iſles, 94.

‡ Itin. vii. 118.

§ P. 102. " Spacium loci Montis Sancti Michaelis eſt ducentorum cubitorum, undique oceano cinctum: predictus locus " craſſiſſimâ primó claudebatur ſylvâ, ab oceano miliaribus diſtans ſex, aptiſſimam prebens latebram ferarum."

‖ Strabo iii. 265. Amſtel. Αι δε κασσιτεριδες δεκα μεν εισι, κειναι δ' εγγυς αλληλων.

coaſt of Cornwall, a " ſtrait" now expanded into a ſea of twenty-ſeven miles in width.* And it is this preponderance, finally, which has " plunged in the ſea the" many " pariſh-churches," that Worceſtre avers to have previouſly " ſtood betwixt the Mount and Sylly."† Yet the general fact is one of thoſe events in the annals of Cornwall, which ſeem too miraculous for the ſober faith of hiſtorians, and are therefore thrown aſide by the ſceptical inquirer, as the fiction of fabulous, or the foolery of dubious hiſtory. But the evidence here adduced from Worceſtre, Solinus, and Strabo, proves it to be hiſtorically true; and tradition comes in with a powerful voice, liſping perhaps a little at times, yet ſtill powerful in general, to corroborate the verdict of hiſtory. " The " encroaching ſea," cries Carew, " hath ravined from Cornwall THE WHOLE COUNTRIE OF " LIONNESSE;—and that ſuch a *Lionneſſe* there was, theſe proofes are yet remaining. The ſpace " between the Land's End and the Iſles of Scilley, being about thirtie miles, to this day retaineth " that name" of *Lionneſſe*, " in Corniſh" very differently, " *Lethowſow*; and carrieth continually " an equall depth of fortie or ſixtie fathom, (a thing not uſual in the ſea's proper dominion); ſave " that about the midway there lieth a rocke, which at low water diſcovereth his head. They " terme it the Gulfe," a rock actually lying to the *ſouth*-ſouth-weſt of the Land's End, diſtant eight miles and a half.—" Fiſhermen alſo, caſting their hookes *therabouts*, have *drawn up pieces of* " *doores and windowes*."‡ The memory of this extraordinary ſort of fiſhery, ſtill remains impreſſed upon the minds of the Corniſh near it; the inhabitants of the Land's End repeating the ſtory to me, there. Nor can we, whatever weight we may aſſign to Carew's circumſtances and reaſons, for a moment doubt the exiſtence of the tradition itſelf. " That this promontory," notes Camden, for his time concerning the Land's End, but inaccurately ſpeaks of continuance, when he means a re-commencement, " thruſt itſelf out farther to the weſt, *is believed by the inhabitants*," as it is equally believed by them now, " and from remains drawn up," meaning the pieces of windows and doors above, " *is affirmed by the ſailors*; and that *the land there covered with the over-* " *flowing ſea* was from I know not what fable denominated *Lioneſſe*, is *aſſerted by the natives*."§ The exiſtence of the tradition is thus demonſtrated again. " To which opinion of the promontory's reaching further," adds Gibſon from the private information of Dr. Muſgrave of Devonſhire, but with Camden's inaccuracy of language unconſciouſly repeated, " theſe hints may, per- " haps, contribute ſomething of probability: that about the middle way between Land's End and " Scilly

¶ Cap. xxii. " Siluram—inſulam ab orâ, quam gens Britanna Dumnonii tenent, turbidum fretum diſtinguit." For the breadth of the channel now, ſee Borlaſe's Scilly Iſles, p. 126, and for the number of the iſlets, p. 88. Dr. Borlaſe, who, from an aſtoniſhing contractedneſs of reading, knew nothing of this very remarkable paſſage in Solinus, obſerves, in order to account for the name, " that the promontory—now called Scilly Iſland, lying the *weſtermoſt* of all the high lands," when the argument requires it ſhould iie the moſt *ſouth*-weſterly, and the fact is, that it really lies the moſt *north*-weſterly, " was the firſt " of all theſe iſlands diſcerned by traders from the *Mediterranean* and *Spaniſh coaſts*;" when ſuch traders *never ſee the rock of Scilly at all*; when the light-houſe is on St. Agnes, at *a diſtance* from and *almoſt directly* to the *ſouth* of Scilly; when Sir Cloudeſley Shovel, particularly, coming from thoſe very " Spaniſh coaſts" as from that very " Mediterranean," ran upon the rocks to the *ſouth-weſt* of St. Agnes, " and as ſoon as diſcovered was ſaid to be Scilly," when confeſſedly it could have been ſo called only as part of an iſland ſo called before, when *St. Agnes* or *St. Mary's* muſt have been ſo called if this reaſoning was true, and when the reaſoning is all as falſe as the geography, the rock not receiving its name from the accidental traders of the Spaniſh or any other coaſts, but from the iſland of which it was once the terminating prominence to the north-weſt. And from this iſland it is, that all the iſles are called " Inſulæ de Sully," or " Inſulæ Sullie," or " Inſulæ Sulliæ," in records (p. 60, 107, 115, 116); the greater iſland denominating all the leſſer, and the leſſer being conſidered as *ſatellites* to the greater.

† P. 102. " Eccleſiæ parochiales inter iſtum Montem et Sylly ſubmerſæ."

‡ F. 3.

§ Camden 136. " Hoc promontorium ſe in oceanum immiſiſſe, tradunt incolæ, et ex ruderibus extractis affirmant nautæ; terramque ibi, infuſo mari ado pertam Lioneſſe (ex neſcio quâ fabulâ) dictam fuiſſe, accolæ aſſeverant."

" Scilly, there are rocks called in Cornifh *Lethas*," the *Lethowfow* of Carew, " by the Englifh " *Seven Stones*; and the Cornifh *call that place within the ftones*, Treg-va, i. e. a dwelling; *where*," Dr. Mufgrave thus fixing the precife fpot, " it has been reported, that *windows* and *other ftuff*," as pieces of doors, " *have been taken up with hooks* (for that is the *beft* place for fifhing): that from " the Land's End to Scilly is an *equal* depth of water," as Carew alfo obferves there is an *equal* depth of forty *or* fixty fathoms, a ftrange fort of equality! when the argument, if true, would prove nothing, and when in truth the water is about eleven fathoms at the Land's End, eight at the Longfhips, twenty along the north-fide of them, and thirty on the north or fouth fides, with twenty-five, twenty-one, fifteen in the middle, all the way (I believe) up to St. Martin's head directly weft.* The reality of the tradition, however, is thus demonftrated again. To thefe teftimonies, therefore, I fhall only add one more, Dr. Borlafe's. " That there exifted formerly," cries the Doctor, " fuch a country as the Lioneffe, ftretching from the Land's End to Scilly Ifles; " is *much talked of in our parts.*—Mr. Carew argues from the plain and level furface of the bottom " of the channel, that it muft at one time have been a plain extended above the fea;" when Carew only talks of an equality of ground " not ufual in the fea's proper dominion," and when this equality profeffedly leaps from forty to fixty fathoms.† " In the family of Trevilian, now " refident in Somerfet, but originally Cornifh, they have a ftory that one of their anceftors faved " himfelf by the help of his horfe, at the time when this Lioneffe was deftroyed; and the arms of " the family were taken, as 'tis faid, from this fortunate efcape.‡ Some fifhermen alfo have in- " fifted, that in the channel betwixt the Land's End and Scilly, *many fathoms under water*, there " are *the tops of houfes* and *other remains of habitations*."§ *Where* in the channel thefe tops of houfes, and thefe other remains of habitations, are affirmed by the fifhermen to be, Dr. Borlafe has not told us. But they are fixed by them undoubtedly, where Carew fays the *fifhermen* of *his* time drew up pieces of doors and windows; where Mufgrave equally reports the *fifhermen* of *his* time, to fay windows and other ftuff have been taken up; and where, he adds, is the *beft* place for fifhing, though the Cornifh call it Treg-va, or a Dwelling. The fifh now form their beds in the houfes certainly, in a town probably, of the old inhabitants; that is faid by the Cornifh to be at the Land's End; that is equally faid by an eminent antiquary of Cornwall to have been denominated

* Gibfon II. and the charts.

† Yet Mr. Gough, in his ufual fervility to Dr. Borlafe, paging humbly at his heels, and " worfhipping the very fhadow " of his fhoe-tye," fays with him; that " from the Land's End to Scilly, is an equal depth of water, and the bottom of the " fea *a plain level furface*." (1, 11, 12.)

‡ Pryce under *Vulgy* the *fea* remarks thus: " Mr. Gwavas doth from hence (and I think not improperly) derive the name " of Trevylian, *the dwelling of the feamen*; according to the old tradition and arms of the family of Sir John Trevylian." But under *Chuyvyan* he thus transfers the event to a very different family: " from hence the family *Vyvyan* is fuppofed to take " its name," as he interprets *Chuyvyan* to *efcape*, to *flee*, " for fleeing on a *white* horfe from Lionels, when it was overflown, " that perfon being at that time *governour* thereof; in memory whereof this family gives a *lion* for its arms, and a white " horfe ready caparifoned for the creft." This is a tale derived from the arms, while the very arms themfelves pretend to be derived from the tale. It is a mif-application made by antiquaries and etymologifts, of that original ftory concerning Trevilian; which is " a tradition, that at the time of the inundation Trevelyan fwam from thence, and in memory thereof bears " gules an horfe argent iffuing out of the fea proper." (Gibfon II.) All the while Trevilian muft have been a perfonal name *antecedent* to the event, and fignifies merely the Mill-houfe as a local name.

§ Scilly Ifles, 92, 93. As Mr. Carew has confounded the *Seven Stones* with the Gulf-rock, fo has Dr. Borlafe done in one place; placing, p. 90, " the Gulph-rock midway betwixt *Penzance* and Scilly," but, p. 95, fixing " the Wolf ledge of rocks" as " midway between both," between " the fhores in Scilly and the neighbouring fhores in Cornwall."

minated the *City* of *Lions.** Thus do remains, tradition, and pofitive hiftory, all combine their powers together, irrefiftibly to prove an extraordinary preffure of the Atlantick, upon the Ifles of Sylley and the continent of Cornwall."†

But *when* did this commence? Dr. Borlafe engages in the enquiry; yet begins it without hope, and ends it without fatisfaction. "When this inundation happened," he confeffes, "we may be "willing to know, but muft be without hopes of knowing with any certainty." He therefore, after fome hefitation between the time of Plutarch, when he finds the ifles round Britain, not *overflowed* (as his reafoning requires they fhould have been), but *un-peopled*, (a circumftance totally impertinent here); a great inundation of the fea in Britain itfelf, under the year 1014; and another in Suffex, under the reign of Edward the Firft; he pitches upon one in "the Irifh annals," under 830, "which might probably have" *both* "affected the fouth of Ireland, and at the fame "time reached Scilly and the coaft of Cornwall."‡ He thus beats about for the chronology of an event, when the chronology is plain from evidences at his foot. The ravages made by the fea are not, as they are naturally imagined at firft, and as I once fuppofed them to have been,§ merely the filent encroachments and the flow depredations of the water upon the land; but, as tradition unites with hiftory to fhow, a fudden impreffion given to the whole weight of the Atlantick, in fending it with a hafty violence upon our fouth-weftern coafts at one particular period, and in keeping it to bear with a regular violence upon them ever fince. Thus all the low lands of Sylley were overwhelmed, by a burft of the fea at once; and the hills have been gradually corroded by the fea ever fince.|| "Hence as the (fouthern) fhore" of Cornwall "wheels round "to the north," cries Camden, advancing eaftward from the coaft of Burian parifh, "a lunar "haven is formed that is denominated Mount's Bay; *in which,* fays a prevailing tradition, *the "ocean breaking in with a violent courfe, drowned the land.*"¶ Yet St. Michael's Mount appears from the charter of the Confeffor, to have been only "near" the fea then. The inundation *might* then have taken place, and the fea have *begun* the ravages that it has ever fince been making. A portion of the original diftance between the ocean and the Mount, *might* then have been overflowed; and the Mount brought fo "near to" the fea, as to have no longer fix or five, or perhaps four miles interpofing between them. But the fea has ever fince been working fo powerfully

* Mr. Gwavas, in a letter from Penzance, 12th April, 1735, to Mr. Tonkin, now in my poffeffion, writes thus: "Tre-"veilgian, the fea-towne, contracted into Trevilian; this, I think, agrees beft with the hiftorical part, relating to the family, "that at an inundation, when Scilly was cut off," thrown off farther, "from the Land's End, he did fwime on his horfe in "the fea, *from the city of Lyons*, then *in being*, and landed within *Mount's Bay*."

† The name of *Lethas*, or *Lethowfow*, naturally attracts the attention of an antiquary here. Yet it has never been attempted to be explained. Nor is an explanation eafy. But I will venture upon one, to complete the evidence concerning the country of *Lioneffe*. *Lhîd*-ymil (Welfh) is the *coaft* or *border* of a country (Lhuyd under *Ora*,) *Leithe*-meal (Irifh) is the fame, *Llydaw* (Welfh and Cornifh) of or belonging to a *fhore*, *Llydaw* (Welfh) Bretagné in France, and Armuirc—*læthana* in the middle ages (Ufher 429), *Letewicion* (Nunnius xxiii), *Lidwiccium* (Sax. Chron. p. 88, 115), *Leteoc*, *Læti*, *Letavienfes* (Ufher ibid.) the inhabitants of Bretagné. The ifland Silura, therefore, was called by the Cornifh of the Land's End, juft as Bretagne was called by all the Cornifh and the Welfh, *Lhydaw*, *Lethas*, or *Lethowfow*, the *fhore*. Looking upon it as immediately oppofed to their eye, they denominated it *the fhore* in general. Their anceftors had even carried this familiar ufe of the word fo far, as to call the only coaft of France to which they at firft trafficked, that of Bretagné, by the fame name of *Llydaw*, or *the fhore*. So we have *Lethegas* at prefent, the name of fome rocks immediately fouth of St. Agnes' Ifle.

‡ Scilly Ifles, 95, 99.

§ Hift. of Manchefter, ii. 177, octavo.

|| Borlafe's Scilly Ifles, 88.

¶ Camden, 136. "Hinc fenfim in Auftrum circumacto littore," where *Auftrum* is plainly a mif-print for *Boream*, though both Gibfon and Gough take the text as it ftands, and fo make Camden contradict the very geography of the coaft, "finus "lunatus admittitur, Mount's Bay vocant; in quo oceanum, avido meatu irruentem, terras demerfiffe fama obtinet."

erfully upon the land, as to have annihilated the whole of the diftance at prefent, and to have drawn a good way within it's empire, what was previoufly five or fix miles from it. We have even a hint of that irruption in a charter of Henry the Firft. The hint, indeed, is only incidental and flight. But we muft not expect more upon fuch a fubject. And, amidft the darknefs in which we are involved, a fingle ray of light may ferve to fhow us our path. Henry gives to the abbey of Taviftock " all the churches of Sullye, with their appertinances, and the land as ever " the monks or the hermits IN A BETTER STATE held it, during the time of Edward the King, " and of Burgald, the Bifhop of Cornwall."* A reference is thus made to the *better ftate* of the ifles, in the reign of the Confeffor; and an intimation is thereby given of fome incident, that had lately lowered the condition of the ifles fo much, as to leave a ftrong impreffion of its ravages upon the minds of the king's law-officers, and thence to force itfelf in one retrofpective word into the king's charter. What deluge then is recorded upon the pages of our hiftory, that will come near enough to the reign, and yet be important enough to produce † the effect? Two occur, and either of them is competent. One is marked by its ravages in Normandy, and the other by its deftructivenefs in Britain. Robert, Earl of Mortaign, as I have already fhewn, under the year 1070, gave our St. Michael in Cornwall, as a cell to another in Normandy; and denominated the latter in this very fignificant manner, " the monks ferving the holy church of St. Michael OF " THE DANGER OF THE SEA."‡ This very extraordinary note of difcrimination, which has (I believe) adhered to the monaftery ever fince, here appears fo early as to form a fecond line of chronology; to unite with the notices concerning the ifles or the bay before, in pointing out the exiftence of fome grand inundation; and in fhowing this to have happened under the reign of the Confeffor, to have particularly injured the Norman monaftery, to have occafioned probably the adjunction of the Cornifh to it, to have certainly attached that defcriptive appellation to it, " St. " Michael's *of the danger of the fea.*" But we can illuftrate this appellation, by a reference to a record ftill earlier; in the famous tapeftry of Baieux, and during the reign of the Confeffor, our Harold being reprefented as marching with the Norman William to MOUNT SAINT MICHAEL, there croffing the tide-river, and having many of the men in danger *from the quickfands now there* " Hic Wilielmus Dux," fays the infcription, " et exercitus ejus, venerunt ad *Montem Michaelis*, " et hic tranfierunt flumen Cofnonis, hic Haroldus Dux *trahebat eos de arenâ.*" In the tapeftry " *Mount St. Michael*," notes Mr. Lethieullier, " is reprefented by a caftle upon a fmall hillock," rather by a lofty hill, like our own, crowned on the top, with a church within, a kind of caftle wall around it; " the duke and his army appear on horfeback;—being arrived *at St. Michael*, " they were obliged to pafs the river Cofnon, which by the frequent and violent " *tides* is *filled* " *with fand*, from which it is difficult to get free." Two gentlemen of France, lately attempting to crofs thefe fands, and having the ufual guide to conduct them, the latter went juft a little a head of them, exploring the fands with a pole, and trying whether they were *quick* or not. In this

* Monafticon i. 1002. " Omnes ecclefias de Sullye cum pertinentiis fuis, et terram utcunquam Monachi aut Hære- " mite *melius* eam tenuerunt tempore Regis Edwardi et Burgaldi, Epifcopi Cornuallia."

† To my amazement, Dr. Borlafe in his Scilly Ifles, 101, recites the very charter of Henry, but leaves out the word " meliús;" tranflating the claufe thus, " the land as the monks or hermits held it in the time of Edward." To fo little purpofe are records confulted, when words can be omitted. That fingularity of the term, which forms the very ufefulnefs of it, was puzzling to the reader, and fo was filently dropt by the writer.

‡ Monafticon i. 551. " Monachis ecclefiæ Sanctæ (Sancti) Michaelis de periculo maris."

this operation he fell into a quickſand before he was aware, and was inſtantly ſwallowed up before their eyes. " Paſſengers frequently periſh there," alſo, adds Mr. Lethieullier, " when the tide " *returns*, before they are able to extricate themſelves. The horſemen are there repreſented" in the tapeſtry, " paſſing the river, and holding up their legs and their armour above the water," one on horſeback drawing up his legs, two on foot holding up their ſhields, and a third having his ſhield on the margin as loſt in the water; while " others are ſinking in the ſand," the horſe of one falling headlong, and caſting off his rider into the water, a ſecond man ſtruggling to riſe from his fall upon his back; and " Harold, who was very tall and ſtrong, is very buſy in dragging " them out," with his arms round the neck of a third man drawing him out of the ſands, while this third man is holding the ſecond by the wriſt, and enabling him to riſe. And that violence of the tides, which made this paſs over the river at the foot of the Mount ſo dangerous with its quickſands, was productive aſſuredly of that danger to the Mount and its monaſtery, by corroding and undermining the yielding ſides of the former, which gave the latter ſo early the appellation of " St. Michael's of the danger of the ſea."* This carries us up to that inundation, which wears ſuch a formidable appearance, even under the very general deſcriptions of our neareſt hiſtorians.† " This year, on *St. Michael's* maſs-eve," ſays the Saxon Chronicle, in 1014, " came that mickle ſea flood widely through this land; and it ran up ſo far, as never at no time before; and it drowned MANY TOWNS, and MANKIND TOO INNUMERABLE TO BE COMPUTED." " The " ſea," remarks Marianus in Florence under 1014, " on the 3d of the Calends of October," or Michaelmas-day, when the Saxon Chronicle fixes it on the eve before, it beginning on the eve, and proceeding on the feaſt, " *ſwells beyond its ſhores*, and in *England*," a ſpecification that intimates the deluge to have been equally on the coaſt of France, " buried in the waves VERY MANY " TOWNS, and AN INNUMERABLE MULTITUDE OF PEOPLE."† This account is ſtill ſtronger than the preceding. But I ſhall ſubjoin a third, ſtill ſtronger than either. " The ſame year," we hear from Malmeſbury, " that ſea flood which the Greeks call Euripus, and we Ledo, " SWELLED OUT IN SO WONDERFUL A MANNER, that NO MEMORY OF MAN CAN EQUAL " IT; COVERING TOWNS AT THE DISTANCE OF MANY MILES, and DROWNING THE IN- " TERCEPTED INHABITANTS OF THEM."‡ We thus account for the damage done to Normandy. Let us, therefore, now turn to Britain. § " In the twelfth year of the reign of Rufus, notes Malmeſbury concerning another flood, but notes the violence of it in a partial manner only, " A SEA-FLOOD CAME up the river Thames, and BURIED MANY TOWNS with THE MEN OF " THEM."‖ This is ſufficiently deſcriptive of the general violence, but confines it ſeemingly to the

* Ducarel's Anglo-Norman Antiquities, Appendix 10, 11, and plate.

† Florence, 382. " Mare littus egreditur tertio Cal. Octobris, et in Angliâ villas quam plurimas, innumerabilemque po- " puli multitudinem, ſubmerſit." Hoveden, f. 248. Savile uſes exactly the ſame words. So does Simeon Dunelmenſis 17. Twiſden. Huntingdon 207. Savile. " Addidit autem Dominus malis ſolitis malum *inſolitum*; mare namque, aſcendens " ſolito ſuperius, villas cum populo ſubmerſit innumero." Brompton 892. Twiſden repeats the very words.

‡ Malmeſbury, 39. " Eodem anno, fluctus marinus quem Græce Euripum, nos Ledonem vocamus, mirum in modum " excrevit, quantum nulla hominum memoria poteſt attingere; ita ut villas ultra multa milliaria ſubmergeret, et habitatores " interceptos necaret."

§ Spelman ſhews from Bede, that the ſpring-tide was called *Malina* in the middle ages, and the neap-tide *Ledo*. He derives the latter from the Saxon *leid*, now *lithe*, gentle; as June and July were called *lida* by the Saxons, according to Bede, becauſe they were months of gentleneſs. And he therefore wonders at Malmeſbury uſing the term here, for it's oppoſite the ſpring-tide. But all the language of Malmeſbury here is culpable. He uſes the neap for a ſpring-tide, he puts an arm of the ſea for a ſea-tide, and he talks of a neap when he is deſcribing a ſpring of ſingular violence.

‖ Malmeſbury, 70. " Duodecimo anno fluctus marinus per Tameſim fluvium aſcendit, et villas multas cum hominibus " ſubmerſit."

the fouth-eaftern points of the ifland. Let us fee, therefore, how another hiftorian defcribes it, who equally with the former lived at the time, and fpeaks of it in terms as general as we may be fure its violence was. "On the third of the Nones of November," cries Florence of Worcefter concerning the 11th of that month, in 1099, THE SEA COMES OUT UPON THE SHORE, and bu-"ried TOWNS AND MEN VERY MANY, OXEN AND SHEEP INNUMERABLE."* This account is much more circumftantial than the other, and is very comprehenfive in itfelf. Yet let us fee a third, that is ftill more circumftantial and comprehenfive. "This year eke," we hear the Saxon Chronicle relating, under 1099, "on St. Martin's mafs-day," the 11th of November, "SPRANG "UP SO MUCH THE SEA-FLOOD, and SO MYCKLE HARM DID, as NO MAN MINDED THAT "IT EVER AFORE DID; and there was this ylk day A NEW MOON."† This then is fuch an inundation, as anfwers all our expectations; as is competent to overwhelm all the low grounds of Scilly, to burft in at the mouth of the Mount's Bay, and to cover the lands on every fide of it for miles. It bore in a violent courfe up the Britifh Channel, beat back in a violent manner the flood from the German ocean, and compelled it to pufh in a violent tide up the Thames particularly. But one intimation in the Saxon Chronicle carries us ftill further, in faying the "fea-"flood—fo myckle harm did, as no man minded that it ever afore did;" the flood of 1099 being thus exalted in magnificence of mifchief, over that of 1014. At the diftance only of 85 years, fome probably remained to fee the latter inundation, who had beheld the former; and the Chronicle, which fpeaks of both fo diftinctly, fpeaks plainly of the latter as the more formidable of the two. It even affigns a phyfical reafon for the fuperiority of terriblenefs in this to that, the fea-floods coming on the very day of a new moon. The exprefs reference alfo in a charter of the firft Henry, to the "better ftate" of the Scilly Ifles during the reign of the Confeffor; compels us to take this flood in preference to that, as not only more formidable, but as *fince* the reign of the Confeffor, and *juft before* the reign of Henry. We have thus found at laft a caufe adequate to the effect, an hiftorical caufe adequate to the vifible effect, an hiftorical account of what our anceftors fuffered feverely at the moment, to what even a charter juft afterwards tranfiently refers, and what even *we* feel fenfibly at prefent. The charter is dated in 1114, only *fifteen* years after the dreadful calamity.‡

Yet *how*, *how* was this aftonifhing phenomenon produced? Was it by a fubfidence of the land, or by an elevation of the water? Dr. Borlafe refers it to the former. Noting fome ruins and ftone hedges

* Vigornienfis, 469. "Tertio non. Novembris mare littus egreditur, et villas et homines quam plures, boves et oves in-"numeras, demerfit."

† Sax. Chron. p. 207.

‡ Monafticon i. 1002. "Apud Bornam in tranfitu." This appears from Saxon Chronicle, p. 218, to have been in September 1114, as on *the 17th of the calends of October*. September the 15th, the King was at Bourne, intending to embark for France, but was detained there by bad weather. Dr. Borlafe, in his Scilly Ifles, 97, "thinks the cataftrophe of thefe "iflands cannot be placed, even fo late as this," or even fo late as 1014; "for the monks being placed here, *either* by "*Athelftan* in the year 938, or foon after," a point of hiftory never attempted to be *proved* by the Doctor! "nothing of this "kind could have happened, but it would have appeared fomewhere or other *in the papers of Taviftock Abbey*," an abbey inftantly confeft to have not been founded in the days of Athelftan! "*at leaft*, if the monks of Scilly were *united to that* "*abbey* at its firft foundation in the year 961," *twenty years after the death of Athelftan*, and (as the monaftery appears from *its own annals* to have been actually founded in 981, Tanner), *forty* years after that death. But Dr. Borlafe not only does not *prove* what he takes for his main ground-work, the fettlement of Taviftock monks in Scilly by Athelftan, or foon after him. He *doubts the truth of it* above. He doubts it again in 100, 101, thus: "whether Scilly was included in the founda-"tion of the Abbey of Taviftock in the year 961, *is (I think) uncertain*." But, as his judgment ftrengthens and his courage warms, he *difproves* his own affertion, and *tears up* his own ground-work. "Henry the Firft," he then cries, p. 101, "*grants*, does not *confirm* (which was the ufual," and indeed neceffary "expreffion, when houfes or revenues had before "been granted) to Ofbert, abbot of Taviftock, all the churches of Scilly, with," &c.

hedges that have been feen in the Sylley Ifles on the fhifting of the fands, and that " have now " ten feet water above the foundations of their hedges, although at a reafonable medium we can- " not fuppofe thefe foundations formerly to have been lefs than fix feet above high-water level, " when the lands were dry, arable or pafture grounds;" he concludes thus: " we muft therefore " either allow that thefe lands, fince they were cultivated and built upon, *have funk fo much lower* " *than they were before*; or elfe we muft allow, that fince thefe lands were fenced and cultivated, " and the houfes and other works now under water (conftructed upon them), *the whole ocean has* " *been raifed, as to its furface, fixteen feet and more perpendicular*; which *latter* will *appear to the* " *learned, without doubt,* much the *harder of the two.*"* But this conclufion appears loaded with difficulties aftonifhingly great, and at the fame time proves incompetent to the work of folution. That the whole mafs of the Sylley Ifles, of the fhores of Cornwall, and (as we muft add) of the oppofite fhores of Normandy, fhould all be depreffed by any one fhock of an earthquake below the level of the fea adjoining, even fixteen or more feet perpendicular below this level; is a fup-pofition fo ponderous, maffy, and gigantick, as to ftagger the ftouteft faith. The earthquake, that could produce fuch a mighty convulfion, muft have fhaken all Britain to its centre, and been recorded indelibly in the publifhed terrours of the whole nation. Nor is the caufe, how-ever portentous and incredible in itfelf, at all adequate to the effect produced. This effect is not merely a fudden inundation made fome centuries ago, but the gradual encroachments of the fea in confequence of that. For thefe we muft account, as well as for that. A fubfidence, there-fore, that is competent to the generation of both, muft be actually at work in the prefent mo-ments, actually depreffing the ground at this very moment, actually finking it under our very feet now. This argument reduces the fuppofition to the laft extreme of abfurdity; and compels us to feek out another caufe, even the natural, the obvious, and indeed the only remaining caufe, in the violent bearing at one time, and in the filent preffing ever fince, of the ocean upon our fhores. Occafioned, perhaps, by fome flight inclination of the globe, that threw its aqueous parts in a fudden projection to the eaft, and that keeps them tending to the eaft ftill; the Atlan-tic has been for ages withdrawing from the fhore of America, I believe, and for ages encroaching certainly upon the fhores of Europe. We know when it began, from its ravages then made upon the coaft of Cornwall particularly; and we feel it operating in its corrofivenefs upon the coaft of Cornwall, to the prefent period. This hypothefis fatisfactorily accounts both for the prefent and for the paft, for the facts that occur in hiftory, and for the appearances that falute our eyes. We now read too with fuller conviction, what we have heard juft before; that " about halfway " between Chyendower and Marazion, in the road from Penzance to the eaft, about three hun-" dred yards below high-water mark, and near to the line of low-water, were feen a few years " ago by Mr. Giddy, an eminent furgeon of Penzance, and fince feen by one of his fons, upon " an extraordinary receffion of the tide, feveral ftumps of trees in *their native foil*;" a foil confe-quently no more depreffed under the water by an earthquake, than the general beach of the fea is at every tide of ebb; " with *the roots fhooting out from them,* and *the ftems apparently cut off.*" Even Dr. Borlafe himfelf fhall help us, as I have previoufly promifed he fhould, to a fimilar dif-covery; he informing us in the very work which advances this extravagant hypothefis, " that on the

* Scilly Ifles, 89, 91.

" the beach betwixt the Mount and the town and Penzance, when the fands have been difperfed " and drawn out into the fea, *I have feen* the *trunks*," he means the *ftumps*, " of *feveral large* " *trees* in their *natural pofition*;" a pofition not funk into a cavity towards the land, as it muft have been, if torn from it by violence and depreffed under water by an earthquake, but even when cleared of its incumbent fands, and reduced to its original inclination, lying in a flope from the land to the water; " as well as I can recollect, *worn fmooth*," but more probably, like thofe above upon the fame beach, *cut off*, " above their roots; upon which, at full tide, there muft be " *twelve* feet of water," and on the land-fide of which ought confequently to be an elevation of *twelve* feet of foil, with as many more as the foil originally rofe above high-water mark.*—But I pufh not the doctor's hypothefis any farther: I have already fhewn it to be affailable on every fide. The earth, a heavy inert mafs of matter, has plainly been paffive in the convulfion; while the flexible fluid, equally vigorous and infinuating, has been let loofe upon the earth, to break through the oppofed barriers of nature at firft in one fudden ftorm of violence, and to carry on its encroachments in a filent kind of fap afterwards. Accordingly, in the hiftorical account of that ftorm, we have no earthquake mentioned, no fubfidence of the ground noticed, nothing noticed or mentioned but the fea's afcent over all its antient limits, the fea's irruption of many miles into the land, the fea's abforption of men and towns in its waters. †

V. I now come to St. Michael's Mount.—Why this archangel, the certain leader of the good angels againft Lucifer and the bad, the probable fucceffor to Lucifer's pre-eminence of place on the expulfion of the latter from heaven, fhould have been fuppofed in the various parts of Chriftendom, to have fhown himfelf repeatedly to human eyes *on the fummits of hills*; I can attribute only to his known elevation of rank, and to a fuppofed correfpondency of a hill as his ftation with it,——

D A

* Scilly Ifles, 94.

† Dr. Borlafe, in 93, urges, as one argument for the encroachments of the fea here, that " the principal anchoring-place " is called a *Lake*," Gwavas Lake, " but is now an open harbour." The argument is nothing in itfelf. *Lake*, in its native import, fignifies only water. We have the *Shire-lake* at Oxford, for a current dividing Oxfordfhire from Berkfhire, (Wood's Hift. of Oxford City, by Sir John Pefhall, 258, &c.) We have the *Pool*, for a part of the Thames at London, *Pool* the harbour in Dorfetfhire, Helen's *Pool* for a harbour in the doctor's own Scilly Ifles, p. 50, and thofe arms of the fea the *Loughs*, *Locks*, or *Lakes* of Ireland, or the highlands. The doctor alfo argues in 90, to prove a fubfidence of the ground here, that " on the ifle of Annet, there are large ftones now covered by every full-tide, which have *rock-bafons* cut in their furface, and " which, therefore, muft have been placed in a much higher fituation, when thofe bafons, in other places generally fo high, " and probably of fuperftitious ufe for receiving the waters of heaven, were worked into them." I believe the bafons to have been wrought merely by the rains, and the " fuperftitious ufe" of them to have been merely made by antiquarianifm. But, even if the bafons were wrought for fuperftition originally, even if placed in pofitions " generally fo high," yet the elevation of the fea will juft as well account for the water's covering them at prefent, as the fubfidence of the fhore. In *this* view, Mahomet's approach to the mountain is juft as effectual as the mountain's approach to Mahomet. But the Doctor adds from Heath, that " a perfon, taking a furvey of *the Channel* in the year 1742, took one of his ftations at low water upon this" the Gulph " rock; where he obferved a cavity like a brewer's copper, with rubbifh at the bottom, without being able to affign " a caufe for its coming there." A caufe may eafily be affigned. The rock before the inundation was inhabited, and the cavity was the cellar of a houfe, fince worked round " like a brewer's copper" in the bottom, by the fettlement of " rubbifh" in it, and by the fea's agitation of the rubbifh around it; juft as pebbles on the beach are all rounded by the fea, and by each other. But mine is too eafy a folution for Dr. Borlafe. " This could be no other than a rock-bafon," he cries; " and *con-* " *fequently* this rock is *greatly funk*, by being now entirely covered with the fea, at leaft nine hours in twelve." The antiquary thus joins with the play-wright, in ftriving *to elevate and to furprize*, to elevate by extravagance of fancy, and to furprize by extremes of folly. In a *cavern* within St. Mary's, the principal of the Sylley Ifles, which is called Piper's Hole, " a little diftance from the entrance *within*, appear fome *rock-bafons*, continually running over with frefh water, defcending " as it diftils from the fides of the rocky paffage," confequently diftilling from the *earth* above. (Survey of the Scilly Iflands, un-dated, but publifhed about 1795, by Mr. Troutback, chaplain of the ifles.)

> A ſtation, like the herald Mercury's,
> New-lighted on a heaven-kiſſing hill.

Yet ſo the fact is. "The firſt appearance of St. Michael," as Worceſtre informs us, from that beſt of authorities aſſuredly, the old legend, "was on Mount Garganus, in the kingdom of Apulia, "within the year of Chriſt 391."* But "the ſecond appearance," he adds, "was about the "year of our Lord 710, on the TOMB in Cornwall NEAR TO THE SEA."† Yet where in Cornwall was this tomb? It is the preſent Mount of St. Michael there; we having already ſeen this deſcribed in a charter of the Confeſſor, as "near to the ſea;" and Worceſtre in another place ſpeaking expreſſly of "the appearance of St. Michael on the MOUNTAIN TOMB, that was before "called Le Hore-rok in the Wodd."‡ And the French aver a third to have been made, on their St. Michael's Mount in Normandy.§

To that in Cornwall, not as known from any ſources of information viſited by Worceſtre, but merely as notified by Camden from the intelligence of the monks here;‖ are theſe lines of Lycidas pointed by Milton:

> Sleep'ſt by the fable of Belerus old,
> Where THE GREAT VISION of THE GUARDED MOUNT
> Looks tow'rd Numancos and Bayona's hold.

As "the great viſion" alludes to this very viſion of St. Michael, ſo is "the guarded mount" an appoſite deſignation of a mount, ſo caſtellated and ſo garriſoned, as Camden ſhews this to have been.¶ But then Milton, in a poetical inattention to hiſtorical proprieties, has confounded the latter times with the former, and carried up the military uſe of the Mount into the days of the archangel's appearance. What is ſtill more, though equally un-obſerved by the criticks upon this poem, Milton has again confounded St. Michael's Mount with the Land's End; in his hint concerning "the fable of Belerus old," glancing at the *Belerium* or Land's End, yet fixing this "*where* the great viſion of the guarded mount" is, and then giving St. Michael's Mount the very poſition of the Land's End. "The inhabitants" *here*, as Camden informed Milton, "report a "watch-tower to have been formerly built" upon the extremeſt rocks, "and to have pointed out "the courſe to navigators by lighted fires."*‡ This, as Camden equally informed Milton, "was "undoubtedly a watch-tower *over-againſt Spain*, ſince Oroſius has told us "of a very lofty Pharus "erected at Brigantia in Gallicia—as a watch-tower againſt Britain." †§ But Milton takes the notices and confounds them. He transfers the Mount to the Land's End, and makes *it* the "watch-tower over-againſt Spain." The watch-tower, we ſee, *is* ſaid to look towards *Spain*; but the Mount actually looks toward *France*, its deep bay opening *directly* to the *ſouth*. Yet

* P. 102. "Prima apparicio Sancti Michaelis in Monte Gargano, in regno Apuliæ, fuit anno Chriſti 391."

† Ibid. ibid. "Secunda apparicio fuit circa annum Domini 710 in Tumbâ, in Cornubiâ, juxta mare."

‡ Ibid. ibid. "Apparicio Sancti Michaelis in Monte Tumbâ, antea vocatâ Le Hore-rok in the Wodd."

§ Camden 137. "Quod ad ſuum Garganum Itali, et ad ſuum Michaelis montem in Normanniâ Galli, cartatim rapiunt."

‖ Ibid. ibid. "Monacho uni et alteri conſtruxit [eccleſiam Edwardus, not (as Camden ſays) *Gulielmus*" for Robert "Cornwalliæ et Moritonii Comes,"] qui Michaelem eo monte apparuiſſe prodiderunt."

¶ Ibid. ibid.

*‡ Ibid. 136.

†§ Ibid. ibid. "Ad ſpeculam proculdubio Hiſpaniæ, ut Oroſius 'Brigantiæ Galliciæ altiſſimam Pharum—ad ſpeculam "Britanniæ erectam' fuiſſe prodidit."

Milton has made a ftill greater miftake here. The light-houfe at the Land's End was oppofed to one at "Brigantia in Gallicia," to the light-houfe ftill remaining at Corunna, in Spain, to the only point of Spain that can be faid to oppofe the Land's End of Britain, being the *north-weftern* extremity of the whole region; yet Milton, with the rafh hand of ignorance, has transferred it to a point at the *north-eaftern* extremity, to a point not poffible to be defcribed as oppofite to any part of Britain, to a point buried in the bottom of the Bay of Bifcay, to a point *not in Spain*, but in France. So little of an antiquary, fo little even of a geographer, was Milton at the writing of this poem, and in the twenty-ninth year of his age! So very inaccurate could he even then be, in his learned references, though fo fond of them through life, and though betraying his fondnefs for them fo early here! *

In this account of "the great vifion," our Mount appears to have been popularly denominated the TOMB, or the MOUNTAIN TOMB, by the Cornifh. The appearance attracted the name; the mount rifing up like a vaft barrow, *Twmpath* (Welfh) fignifying a hillock, a knap, a *tump*, *Tuma* (Irifh) meaning a fepulchre or *tomb*, and a round mount or barrow near Bala, in Merionethfhire, being called *Tommen* y Bala, or the Barrow of Bala, at this day. †

In confequence of this vifion upon our Barrow Mount, a cell or cells of monks are fure to have been eftablifhed immediately on the ground. "We" accordingly "find" by the light lent us from the torch of Worceftre, "Monks ANTIENTLY ferving the Lord in this place."‡ But, as Worceftre adds, "a religious Monk of the place, whofe name was Aubert, and whofe rank "was afterwards that of an abbot in France, induced the Confeffor to build a church here in ho-"nour of St. Michael."§ And from this notice we learn to read in a fuller fenfe of the words, than we could give to them before; that the Confeffor "delivered to St. Michael the Archangel, "*for the ufe of the brethren*" or friars "*ferving God in the fame place*, St. Michael" the mount and the church "which is near to the fea."‖

I

* The light-houfe of Corunna is plainly the Pharus of Brigantia, fo ftrikingly diftinguifhed by Orofius as over againft the light-houfe of Britain. It is called the Iron Tower at Corunna, 192 feet high, and fuppofed to be Pompey's or Hercules's Tower. The reader will eafily determine between the two claimants. From a drawing now before me, and given me by my very worthy friend the Rev. Mr. Lyne, of Lefkard, the tower appears to be fquare in the Roman part of it, 120 feet high, with a double buttrefs at each angle, and a kind of *bandeau* for the ftair-cafe, croffing each face five times, at regular diftances. There are two doors at the bottom, over either of which is a modern infcription, one in Latin, the other in Spanifh, to witnefs the defign of the building at firft, and its reparation in 1790. The former thus ftates it to have been, what I have ftated it in my text above; "collegium mercator. *Gallaecia.* Navigantium incolumitati reparationem *vetuftiffimæ ad Bri-*"*gantiam Phari*," or (as the Spanifh calls it) "*antiquo faro* de la *Corunna*." On a rock below is this original infcription, barely legible: "Marti 9 Aug. Sacr. C. Sevius Lupus Architectus A. T. injenfis," *Nardiniem*, in Ptolemy II. 6. p. 44, *Nardinium*, "Lufitanus, ex voto." The door with the Latin infcription opens to the ftair-cafe, that with the Spanifh to a guard-room. An oval wall runs round the whole, and inclofes a fmall houfe built over a piece of rock, upon one fide of which is the original infcription. The communication of the emperour's name to Mars, is not very rare in infcriptions. One occurs in Switzerland. (Courfe of Hannibal over the Alps afcertained i. 147). But how loofely muft have fat upon the minds of the heathens, all reverence for their gods, when they could thus place their gods in the fame parity of reverence only with their emperours! And the mention of Auguftus fhews, that Pompey was no more the builder of the tower than Hercules, it being built in the reign *of one of the emperours*, and of the firft of them, probably, that was called Auguftus. As to *Namancos*, all the commentators fhewed their ignorance in their filence. I am content to own mine. But I fuppofe it to be fome town that Milton, *in his great learning*, found near Bayonne, unlefs, *in his great learning*, he meant *Betancos* as the modern name for Brigantia, thus pointed at *all* the *northern coaft of Spain*, and only miffed the right name by his printer's miftake.

† Gibfon's Camden, 793.

‡ Worceftre, 102. "In quo loco olim comperimus monachos Domino fervientes."

§ Ibid. ibid.

‖ Monafticon i. 551. "Tradidi Sancto Michaeli Archangelo, in ufum Fratrum Deo fervientium in eodem loco, Sanctum "Michaelem qui eft juxta mare."

I have thus ſhown a Mount, which was covered with a thick wood from its baſe to its ſummit, which yet ſhowed its gray head above the tops of the trees, which thus ſpired up like a conical but gigantick barrow, and was uſed for a Hill of Proſpect towards the ſea, or towards the land; to have been at the diſtance of five or ſix miles from the ſea, but to have harboured wild beaſts in its ſhades. In this ſtate it was, when St. Michael the Archangel was believed to have made his appearance upon the ſummit of it. Then the wild beaſts began to be diſlodged, as monks came to people its deſert. Theſe were at laſt united into a college, and furniſhed with a church at the top. But the wild beaſts had been extirpated before, as a town had ariſen upon the baſe of the Mount. And to all the evils of ſociety, which were now introduced into this ſolitude, the animoſity of man to man, turning the Mount into a caſtle, and generating battles upon its ſides; was added the dreadful calamity, of the ſea burſting in upon the land, ſwallowing up in time all the ſpace of ground up to the very foot of the Mount, and now daſhing its wild waves in ſtorms againſt the very rocks of it.*

* " *Long* before this," ſays Dr. Borlaſe concerning the erection of a collegiate church upon the top of the Mount, " this " place *ſeems* renowned for its ſanctity, and therefore *muſt* (according to the cuſtom of the firſt ages of chriſtianity) have " been dedicated to religion." Dr. Borlaſe did not know, *why* and *when* this Mount became " renowned for its ſanctity." He knew not of the reported appearance of St. Michael upon it, though Camden knew. He therefore wanders away in the wildneſs of fabulous hiſtory, into a ſtrangely remote period of the paſt. " For St. Kayne or Kayna, a holy virgin of the blood " royal, daughter of Braganus, Prince of Brecknockſhire, is *ſaid* to have gone a pilgrimage to St. Michael's Mount in Corn- " wall. Now this ſaint lived in the *fifth* century, and, it is not at all improbable, that ſhe ſhould come this pilgrimage to " St. Michael's Mount; a fact, farther confirmed by the legend of St. Cadoc, (though disfigured by fable), who, according " to Capgrave, (fol. 418) made a pilgrimage to St. Michael's Mount, there ſaw and converſed with St. Kayne; *from which* " *it appears*, that this place was dedicated to religion, *at leaſt as anciently as the latter end of the fifth century*." p. 385, 386, Antiquities. The erroneouſneſs of all this is apparent already, though Mr. Gough, p. 13, with a " popiſh implicitneſs of " faith," adopts the errours of *his* ſaint for goſpel truths. St. Michael's Mount became renowned for " its ſanctity," only from the believed appearance of St. Michael upon the ſummit of it, in or about the year 710. And any idea of " pilgri- " mages" to it, muſt not only be poſterior to this period of its ſanctity, but even poſteriour to the privilege conceded to " pilgrimages" by Pope Gregory in 1070, even poſteriour to the publication of the privilege in all the churches of the king- dom about the year 1400; when the publication gave birth to " pilgrimages," and when theſe grew ſo popular all over the kingdom, as to make writers ignorant of their late riſe refer them back to diſtant ages.

PENZANCE.

PENZANCE.

THIS town originally rofe from a few fifhermen fettling near the prefent pier, and building themfelves a chapel dedicated to St. Anthony, that univerfal patron of fifhermen. The chapel continued within thefe three years, when it was rebuilt into a fifh cellar. It was only fmall, however, but had the ftatue of its faint in a niche. Tradition preferved the name of the faint, and antiquarianifm has faved the ftatue of him. It is merely a buft, and of alabafter.

So begun, the town by degrees extended up the hill, from the fite of the pier, to the ground of the church, at prefent. Yet when did it thus begin? For afcertaining this, we want dates. But let us apply what we have, and then obferve the refult.

When the town had extended up the fide of the hill, a fort was built by one of the Tieis, whom tradition recognizes as lords of the town, one of whom, Henry, a baron, is known to have been lord of Alwerton, now Alverton, in the manour of which the town now ftands, and to have obtained the right of a market for Moufehole from *the Firft Edward.** The fame baron probably conftructed this fort. Yet the very exiftence of the fort is attefted only, by the name attached to the fite, and by the afpect of the fite itfelf. In Henry's Valor the prefent chapel is thus defcribed, "BURRITON alias Penzance, chapel to Madern." This name tells to every antiquarian ear, the exiftence of a caftle here; *Bury* or *Burg*, *Bury-ton* or *Burg-ton*, in every part of the kingdom, attefting their own rife as towns from caftles as their parents. And the quality of the ground coincides clofely, with the import of the name; the fite of the chapel being a fmall round eminence, rifing feveral feet in height towards the pier, ftanding at the head of the ftreet, and commanding it, with the pier, or St. Anthony's chapel, effectually. It has even communicated its own name to the town, and thus fhows itfelf to have been prior to the town in general; the town being now denominated in its formal title, "the burgh of the town or vill of BURRYTON, alias "Penfance."† Nor was it in exiftence as a chapel to the town, when the Valor of 1291 was compofed; "the church of St. Madern" being noticed as "cvi. S. viii. D." and no chapel noticed, as in Henry's Valor, belonging to it.‡ There was then, probably, no fort conftructed here by Henry, baron de Tieis, and confequently no chapel within it for the garrifon; though Edward the Firft had now reigned nineteen of his thirty-four years. But a chapel and a fort were erected affuredly, in the remaining fifteen; took the *Englifh* appellation of Burryton, from the Englifh baron who erected them; and with a market, now affuredly obtained equally as for Moufehole, ferved

* Camden 136. "Cui jus mercatûs obtinuit ab Edwardo primo Henricus de Tieis, qui baronis dignitate floruit, Dominufque fuit de Alwerton et Tiwernel in hoc comitatu."

† "Communitatem Burgi oppidi five villæ de Burryton, alias Penfance," in a requeft to the bifhop 1680, hereafter fpecified.

‡ "Eccl. Sti. Maderni, cvi. S. viii. D."

ſerved to enlarge the town by the ſecurity provided for the inhabitants, as well as by the proviſions brought in to them.

Leland accordingly ſays thus: "Penſants, ſtanding faſt in the ſhore of Mont Bay, ys the weſtes "*market towne* of all Cornwayle, and no ſoeur for botes or *ſhyppes* but a *forſed pere* or key. Ther "is but a *chapel* yn the ſayd towne, as ys yn Newlyn. For theyr paroches chyrches be more "than a myle of."* The town had now, a market and a pier. But the latter is expreſſly declared by Leland in another place, to be only "a little peere;"† yet was viſited by ſhips as well as boats. And the chapel is deſcribed in a requeſt, with the caſtle-ground about it, to the biſhop for their conſecration, dated 1680; as "all that parcel of land lying within the Burgh town or "vill aforeſaid, *on which a certain chapel has been long ſince erected and conſtructed*, but *never con-* "*ſecrated hitherto*."‡ It had never been conſecrated as the chapel of the fort. But as the town enlarged, and the petty chapel of St. Anthony could no longer contain the inhabitants; ſome, I ſuppoſe, obtained ſeats in the chapel of the fort. As the town ſtill continued to enlarge, and as the fort was deſerted by the garriſon, more obtained, till what belonged only to the garriſon at firſt, became the excluſive poſſeſſion of the inhabitants at laſt. In 1614 the town was incorporated; in 1680 "the mayor and commonalty"§ petition the biſhop to conſecrate the chapel, with a chapel-yard; and he accordingly conſecrated the former as what it was at the time of the ſecond Valor, as a chapel of eaſe to the vicarial church of Madern.

The town has thus riſen, to be much more conſiderable than I had ever ſuppoſed it to be. It is much larger in itſelf, as having many more ſtreets. It is much more populous of courſe, and much more engaged in buſineſs. It has ſhips of three or four hundred tons in burden, and ſends ſome of them direct to Norway. It has a new pier, in a high broad mound of ſtone, running a good way out into the ſea from eaſt to weſt, and then ending in a ſlight curve to the north-eaſt. Cloſe to this, on the ſouth, has been lately erected a little fort with guns, the *Burryton* of modern times. And as the whole town ſtands forth the fair rival of Truro for pre-eminence, in ſize, in ſhops, in neatneſs; ſo does its market much ſurpaſs that of Truro for plenty or for cheapneſs, the latter circumſtance the perpetual concomitant of the former, and both operating ſo powerfully here, that the butchers kill twenty bullocks a week for this market, more than for the market of Redruth, even for the market of Truro itſelf.

Yet, not to loſe ancient things in modern, let us enquire whence the popular name of the town is derived. Camden derives it at once thus: "Penſans,—that is, the head of the ſands."|| But this intermixture of Corniſh and Engliſh in the name of an old town of Cornwall, is too ridiculous for ſuch a man as Camden to ſuggeſt. It is unworthy even of a ſchool-boy. "Penſans," cries Mr. Gough, therefore, after Biſhop Gibſon, "means the head of the ſaint; the baptiſt's head "in a charger being *their* arms. *If this did not put it beyond diſpute*, it might from its ſituation be "interpreted *Penſavas*, the head of the channel."¶ This interpretation ſavours a little of learning judiciouſly applied. But it ſavours only a little. The interpretation of *Penſans* by *Penſavas*, is ſo violent a diſtortion of the name, as to put all criticiſm upon the rack. Nor, even if not ſo violent,

* Itin. vii. 117. † Itin. iii. 17.

‡ "Totam illam parcellam terræ intra Burgum, Oppidum, ſive villam prediƈtam jacentem, in quâ Capella quædam jam "dudum ereƈta et conſtruƈta fuit, ſed hucuſque nunquam conſecrata."

§ "Majorem et Communitatem." || P. 136. "Penſans,—ideſt, Caput Sabuli." ¶ Gough i. 12, from Gibſon 13.

violent, would it comport with the truth. For of what channel is Penzance thus ſuppoſed to be the head? Of the Britiſh, as mention of "*the* channel" implies? How then is Penzance the head of this? Juſt as it is the *tail* of it, and no otherwiſe. The other derivation, indeed, has been univerſally adopted, ever ſince Biſhop Gibſon produced it; was declared by himſelf at the moment, and is re-declared by Mr. Gough now, to be "beyond diſpute" the juſt one. Yet it is as falſe as the former, though not as ridiculous. The ſolitary village on the ſhore had a name, *long before* it was important enough to have any arms. It could not have had any, before it was incorporated in 1614. Nor would it then have had the head of the baptiſt in a charger, if it had not been a part of the pariſh of Maddern, and thus in its tithes appropriated to the priory of *St. John* of Jeruſalem.* Such is this indiſputable etymon! But what then is the true etymon? It is this, I believe. The large compaſs of Mount's Bay has only two points particularly diſtinguiſhed in it, one called *Gwavas Lake*, and ranging along the ſouth-weſtern ſide of the bay; but the other denominated PENZANCE, and comprehending all the northern. "Yn the bay," cries Leland, "be eſt the ſame towne" of Mouſehole, "ys *a good roode for ſhyppes*, cawled *Guaves Lake*." † This is, he adds in another place, "*a bay from Newlin to Mouſehole*, caullid "*Guaverſlak*." ‡ Here is ſtill the greateſt depth of water throughout the whole bay; and the gun-boat, that is now ſtationed to guard the bay, lies here; while the general depth from Penzance to the Mount, upon an ebb-tide, is only ſix fathoms at high water. But the fiſhery in this part of the ſea was given to the church of the pariſh of Paul, a church here ſtanding high upon the hill, and a pariſh extending along the ſea from the north of Newlyn to the ſouth of Mouſehole; went at the appropriation of the rectory to the abbey of Hayles, in Glouceſterſhire; § and was very valuable to the proprietors, while the law of fiſh-tithe ſtood upon that original baſis of common-ſenſe, the payment of the tithe to the church in which the fiſhermen received divine offices, but has been frittered into atoms by a refinement lately introduced, of paying them to the miniſter of the pariſh in which the nets are laid up, the men ſtill reſiding in Paul pariſh, but laying up their nets in Madern, even laying them up (I believe) on the bare ſtrand there. Another part of Mount's Bay had the Corniſh appellation of *Penzance*, not (as Pryce expounds the name ‖) from being "the "head of the bay," when Chendower (or the houſe in the water) is much more ſo; but, agreeably to the genius of the Britiſh language, and conformably to the mode of impoſing appellations in Cornwall, from being "the bay of the head" or hill. Thus Penzance is the ſame in Corniſh, as Mount's Bay is in Engliſh. Thus too the village of fiſhermen on the beach at Penzance, with their petty chapel of St. Anthony behind, naturally (like Falmouth) took the very title of the bay on which it ſtood; ages before it was important enough to be incorporated and have arms, even years, probably, before its pariſh-church was appropriated to the priory of St. John of Jeruſalem.¶ And the proper Mount's Bay extends only over the northern part of the bay, even "as far north "as

* "Madron, alias St. Madern, V. with the chapel of Penzance (St. Mary) and Morva.—*Pri Sti. Johannis Jeruſalem* "*Propr.*" (Henry's Valor).

† Itin. vii. 117. ‡ Itin. iii. 17.

§ Founded by Richard, King of the Romans, and Earl of Cornwall, in 1246. (Monaſticon i. 928.) But the appropriation was later even than the Valor of 1291, Paul being then a rectory.

‖ Under *Zans*.

¶ In the Valor of 1291, we ſee that it was then appropriated; "Eccles. Sti Maderni, cvi. S. viii. D. *Prior Hoſpital. Sti* "*Johannis percipit in eadem* iiii. Marcas."

" as Long Bridge in the manour of Lanefeley ;" * Camden averring, that " a haven pretty broad " opens *a little above the Mount*, which is DENOMINATED MOUNT'S BAY from the Mount, *where* " is a very fafe ftation for fhips when the fouth and fouth-eaft winds," thofe tyrants of the bay in general, " blow with fury, a ftation fix or feven fathoms deep in the middle of the ebb-tide ;" † and Carew fubjoining, that " *under* the Mount extendeth a bay for *leffer* veffels to lie at, and " *betweene it and the wefterne fhoare* is an *indifferent good road for fhipping*, faving upon fome winds, " CALLED THE MOUNT'S BAY." ‡

* Hals.

† Camden 137. " Pauloque fupra Montem finus, fatis latus patet, *Mount's Bay* a Monte dictus, ubi tutiffima navium " ftatio eft fæviente Auftro," &c. &c.

‡ F. 155, 156. In Penzance pier there are 14½ feet of water at fpring-tides, but only 9½ at neap-tides. In the pier at the Mount there is one foot lefs. But about the middle of the bay's mouth there are twenty fathoms at low water, fourteen higher up the bay, and fifteen or fixteen ftill nearer to the Mount. So much deeper, at prefent, is the water here, than it was in the days of Camden ; or fo inaccurate was Camden, in his information about it !

LAND's END.

LAND's END.

ON Auguſt the 1ſt, 1799, the firſt anniverſary of that ever-memorable day, which ruined beyond recovery the un-principled invader of Egypt, I rode from Penzance to the Land's End, a diſtance of ten miles, reflecting on a leader very different in ſoul, heroical in mind, and humane in ſpirit, a CHRISTIAN. I thought of Athelſtan's march to the *laſt* pariſh in Cornwall in the weſt, when he reached the oratory in which St. Burian was buried, and kneeled down at her ſhrine to pray for ſucceſs in his intended expedition againſt the Sylley Iſles. I found the road a cauſey rough and broken, the remains, probably, of the very road on which he marched with his army to St. Burian's. To St. Burian's he alſo came back, on his return from the conqueſt of the Iſles. "King Ethelſtane," cries Leland from the only document that we have of the fact, and a document ſufficient in itſelf, the traditional and the written evidence of the clergy of the church, recorded aſſuredly in the memorials of the church, and recited from them to the people on every return of the church's feaſt, the praiſes of Athelſtan mingling with the merits of Buriana; "*goyng* "*hens*, as *it is ſaid*, *on to* Sylley, and *returning*, made ex voto a college wher the oratorie was."* Leland thus caught the voice of tradition more faithfully, than Camden caught it. Leland takes in the advance from St. Burian's to Sylley, as well as the return from Sylley to St. Burian's; while Camden relates only the return. "A little village is now on the ground," he tells us, "called "Saint Burian's, formerly Eglis Burian's," in Corniſh, "that is, the church of Saint Burien or "Berian, as conſecrated to a religious woman of Ireland: to this church, *as fame tells us*, King "Athelſtan gave the privilege of a ſanctuary, *when he came hither a conquerour from the Sylley Iſles*; "it is *certain*, that he *built a church here*, and that here was a college of canons under William "the Conquerour, and that the adjacent territory belonged to them."† Athelſtan thus advanced with his army by St. Burian's towards the Land's End; to embark his ſoldiers, probably, at *Pordenack*, a cove immediately to the ſouth of the Land's End, ſtill ſhowing its uſe as a port by its name of a Port among the Corniſh; and at a much larger, but more expoſed haven to the north, thence, perhaps, diſtinguiſhed ever ſince by the Engliſh appellation of Whitſand Bay. He had only a narrow arm of the ſea to croſs; but then the very narrowneſs made it more turbulent. He croſſed it ſafely, however, reduced the Iſles, and returned victorious to St. Burian's.

But, before he ſet out on this maritime expedition, he ſeems to have fought a final battle againſt, and to have obtained a concluſive victory over, the Corniſh of the continent at the Land's

End.

* Itin. iii. 18.

† P. 136. "Viculus nunc illi inſidet, *Saint Burian's*, olim *Eglis Buriens*, 1. *Ecclefia Burienæ* vel *Berianæ*, dictus, Bu-"rienæ religioſæ mulieri, Hibernicæ ſacer.—Huic, ut fama perhibet, conceſſit rex Athelſtanus, cum e Syllinis Inſulis "hic victor appuliſſet. Certum, eſt illum eccleſiam hic conſtruxiſſe, et ſub Gulielmo Conqueſtore canonicorum hic fuiſſe "collegium, et territorium adjacens ad eos ſpectâſſe."

End. That he ſo fought and ſo obtained, I infer from a collection of circumſtances, ſingle in themſelves, but uniting into one maſs of evidence. An accumulation of ſands here compoſes a mountain.

The Britiſh name of the Land's End, as given us by the antients, BOLERIUM in Ptolemy, or BELERIUM in Diodorus Siculus, is very naturally derived by Camden, the moſt eaſy of all etymologiſts in general, from the Britiſh word *Pell,* interpreted by him the *remoteſt*, and conſidered as equivalent to the modern name.* This word actually ſignifies the *Farther*, and actually varies into *Bel,* as in Goon Bel the Farther Down of St. Agnes.† We may alſo, with almoſt as much probability, deduce the name from *Pele* a Spire, ſince " on a little iſland ſeparated from the " Land's End, ſo as a boat with oars may paſs between," actually " ſtood *Caren an Pele*," ſo called becauſe " Caren ſignifies a rock, and Pele a ſpire."‡ But we muſt go deeper ſtill, for the root of the name. The whole of the hundred is denominated from the name of this promontory, at preſent; and the court-houſe of the hundred, therefore, was fixed upon ſome eſtate at it. It was ſo from the firſt, I believe, from the very early and quite primitive inſtitution of hundreds among the Britons.§ The radical word, then, is *Bala*, a houſe or a town. This word, indeed, is very contrarily interpreted by Mr. Lhuyd. And ſhall we preſume to oppoſe ſuch a linguiſt in his own language? " The word Bala," he tells us, " though now very ſeldom (if at all) uſed as " an appellative, denotes (as the author of the Latin-Britiſh Dictionary," Thomas Williams, " informs us) the place where any river or brook iſſues out of a lake, as Aber ſignifies the fall of " one river into another, &c. and hence Dr. Davies ſuppoſes this town," Bala in Merionethſhire, " to be denominated. In confirmation whereof I add, that near the *outlet* of the river Seiont, out " of Lhyn Peris, in Caernarvonſhire, there is a place called Bryn y *Bala*."‖ This evidence of Williams, of Davies, and of Lhuyd, all united in one teſtimony concerning a word in their own Welſh, ſeems to form an evidence, to which even boldneſs itſelf muſt be obliged to bow in a Saxon. And, as Mr. Richards, in his late very uſeful Dictionary, repeats the words and re-echoes the ſentiments of Mr. Lhuyd; ſo Mr. Owen, in his ſtill later and much larger, coincides with all without deigning to mention any, and only ſays " *Bala llhyn* the outlet or efflux of a lake; hence " it is the name of many places in Wales, Ireland, and Scotland."¶ Againſt ſuch an embodied hoſt of Lexicographers, all poſted upon their native hills, and all fighting for their native fields; how can I ſtand the encounter for a moment? Yet I riſque the iſſue of one, and I even challenge a victory in it. The linguiſts of Wales, however unanimous in appearance, are divided in reality; and a civil war in a ſtate always promotes the ſucceſs of an attack upon it. " Others contend," Lhuyd himſelf confeſſes, and " H. Perry in Dr. Dav. Dict. whom we find too apt to preſume " Iriſh words to be Britiſh" or Welſh, is ſpecified on the margin, " that *Bala* in the old Britiſh, " as well as Iriſh, ſignifies a village; I incline to the former opinion, and imagine that upon far- " ther enquiry, other inſtances beſides theſe two might be found, which would make it ſtill more " evident." *† I am one of thoſe who are " apt," like Perry, " to preſume Iriſh words to be " Britiſh;" and think nothing but that ſpirit of arrogation, which denominates Welſh excluſively Britiſh,

* Camden, 135. " Ptolemæo Bolerium dicitur, Diodoro Belerium, fortaſſe a *Pell* Britannicâ dictione, quæ remotiſſimum " ſignificat."

† Pryce. ‡ Gibſon 10. § Hiſt. of Manc. i. 370, octavo. ‖ Gibſon, 792, 793.

¶ Richards publiſhed in 1753, Owen in 1793. *† Gibſon, 793.

Britiſh, could pretend to doubt the fact. The Iriſh language is equally Britiſh with the Welſh; and, however what I am going to ſay may grate upon the honeſt pride of a Welſhman's heart, a Britiſh more pure, more genuine than that of the Welſh, as the Britiſh of a race never ſubdued (like the Welſh) by the Romans, never incorporated into their empire, never habituated to their language, for ages. Perry thus ſhowed himſelf more judicious, than even Davies or Lhuyd; and more wiſe than the very oracles themſelves. Bal, Ball, Baile (Iriſh) is a place or ſpot; Gwâl (Welſh) a place whither beaſts reſort to lie; Bal (Corniſh) a parcel of tin-works together; Gwâl (Welſh) a *wall*; Baili, Beili a court before a houſe in Glamorganſhire; Balla (Iriſh) a *wall* or bulwark; Beile (Iriſh) a home, a village, a town, or a city; Bolla (Corniſh) an entrenchment; Bala, a town in Wales; *Bally* Salley, a village in the Iſle of Man; *Balla* Mona, a monaſtery within it; and Luga-*Ballia*, a Britiſh town in the Roman Itineraries, now Carliſle.* So plainly is Bala at once Iriſh, Welſh, Corniſh, and Manks! So apparently is it Britiſh too, derivatively from thoſe languages and poſitively in itſelf! And ſo contracted, ſo ſuperficial a view had thoſe celebrated criticks taken of all! Yet how is Bala lengthened into Bolerium or Belerium? Camden did not ſtoop in his general aſſuredneſs that he was right, to make out the particular likeneſs. But we muſt, and do it thus. Erw (Corniſh) is an acre, a field; Erw (Welſh) is an acre, land, or eſtate; Gwaederew is a place in Wales, ſo called as the field of blood; and Belra, for Bel-erew, is a pariſh or diſtrict in Iriſh. Here then we have *Bolerium* or *Belerium*, as Bala in Welſh is Bolla in Corniſh above, complete in all its parts; ſignifying at once, like the modern Penwith, the court-houſe of the hundred, the eſtate annexed to it, and the hundred ſubjected to both. The houſe ſtill remains, I conjecture, in a houſe ſtill retaining half the name; *Bol*-lait being a conſiderable houſe in this pariſh of Burian at preſent, and appearing conſiderable almoſt as early as the conqueſt;† while the eſtate, a royal one aſſuredly, was commenſurate, probably, with the preſent pariſh, and ſo extended up to the Land's End.

This promontory, adds Camden, "is called by the Britons," Camden meaning only the Welſh, he with others unwarily adopting the excluſive language of Welſh writers, "*Penrhin guard*, that "is, *the Headland of Blood*; but then it is ſo called only by the bards or poets, the Britiſh hiſto-"rians calling it *Penwith*, that is, the headland on the left, and the inhabitants in their own lan-"guage, *Pen Von Las*, that is, the end of the earth, in the ſame ſenſe as the Engliſh call it the "Land's End."‡ The firſt intimation in this paſſage, is as ſingular in itſelf as it has been unnonoticed by antiquaries. "The headland of blood," as the appellation of the Land's End, carries a ſound to our ears, and a ſignification to our minds, full of hiſtorical intelligence. Nor does the name exiſt merely in the rhapſodies of the bards. Lhuyd himſelf recognizes the name in his Corniſh Grammar, as he ſays thus: "Pennrhynn Penward, the Land's End of Cornwall; *that* "*hundred* is *yet* called Penwyth."§ The preſent appellation of *Penwith*, therefore, appears *not* "to have been as Camden interprets it, from Chuith (Welſh) and Chitach (Iriſh) on the left;"‖ and *not* to have been, as Pryce more judiciouſly explains it, "Pen-with, the head of the breach

* Richards, Pryce, &c. Gibſon 1448, Gough iii. 703, &c. † Gibſon 12.

‡ Camden 135, 136. "Britannis Penrhin guard, id eſt, Promontorium Sanguinis, ſed tantum bardis ſive poetis; Hiſtoriis "vero Britannis *Penwith*, id eſt, Promontorium ad Siniſtrum;—accolis ſuâ linguâ *Pen vos las*, id eſt, Finiſterræ, eôdemque "ſenſu Anglis *the Land's End*."

§ Lhuyd's Vocabulary 238. ‖ Ibid. under *Siniſtra*.

" or ſeparation, as the Land's End from Scilly, which ſignifies to cut off."* But it is merely Pen-*waed*, the promontory of *blood*. Nor does the Corniſh appellation of it, ſtill retained by the inhabitants in the days of Camden, *Pen Von Las*, ſignify as Camden interprets it, the end of the earth. It carries a very different ſignification, and one exactly the ſame as the preceding, *the Headland of Slaughter*. Ladh is to kill or ſlay, Lathe is a violent death, Latha, Las is manſlaughter, in Corniſh; while Llâs, in Welſh, means he was ſlain. But Von is the ſame as Mann (Welſh) a place, the ſame as Mona the name equally of Angleſey and of Man iſlands; varied into *Von*, in the name of Caernarvon, as the town oppoſite to Môna,† and varied again into Eu-*Bonia* in Nennius's name for Man.‡ Thus the recent and popular title of *Pen-von-las* for the Land's End, as marking the promontory of the place of ſlaughter, is exactly the ſame in ſignification with the antient, Penrhin-guard, or the headland of blood. And, as we have ſeen Gwaed-erew, or the field of blood, to be a place in Wales, as we have Gwaettir for the land of blood in the Welſh laws, and Guit (Corniſh) blood, all anſwering to the preſent appellation of the Land's End; ſo have we Bol *Laith* or the houſe of ſlaughter again, in that court-houſe of the hundred which has given denomination to the Land's End through all ages to the preſent.

At Bollait then was this ſlaughter made, which has ſo ſtrikingly *memorized* itſelf in theſe appellations. Yet when could ſuch a ſlaughter have been made, to impreſs ſuch laſting characters of blood upon a houſe and upon a promontory; except at Athelſtan's final reduction of Cornwall, near the Land's End, when the Corniſh, who had hitherto retired without a conteſt before him, were here compelled either to yield at once, or to make one active ſtruggle for all? This appeared ſo obvious in general to Camden, that he even doubted whether he ſhould attribute the circle of ſtones at Boſcawen *as a trophy*, to the later Emperours of the Romans, or "to Athelſtan the " Saxon on his reduction of the Damnonii."§ But, as this circle cannot be preſumed to be either Roman or Saxon, ſo from its ſimilitude to other circles muſt it be acknowleged to be Britiſh. We muſt look, therefore, for other monuments of ſtone, if any were ever erected in honour of this victory. Yet what monuments did the Saxons erect of ſtone, as trophies of victory? None that the antiquarian world knows. There is one, however, though unknown. "The ſtout Duke " of the Weſt Saxons, Harold," cries Worceſter the hiſtorian, "by the command of King Ed- " ward" in 1063, "after the nativity of our Lord, taking with him from Glouceſter, where the " king then was, no large body of horſe, marched in much haſte to Rudelan, in order to kill " Griffin, king of the Welſh, for the frequent ravages which he made in the Engliſh border, and " for the affronts which he often put upon his lord King Edward. But Griffin, apprized of his " coming, fled with his attendants, embarked in a ſhip, and with difficulty eſcaped. Then Ha- " rold, finding he had fled, ordered his place to be ſet on fire, and his ſhips to be burnt with all " their ſtores, and ſet off the ſame day on his return. Yet about rogation-week he ſailed with " an army on board a fleet from Briſtol, and circumnavigated almoſt all the land of the Welſh. " Earl

* Under *Hundreds*.

† Camden's Anglica, Normannica, &c. 865. Giraldus Cambrenſis, "Caernarvon, id eſt, Caſtrum de Arvon, dicitur " autem Arvon provincia quod ſita ſit contra Monam inſulam."

‡ Nennius, c. ii. "Secunda ſita eſt in umbilico maris, inter Hiberniam et Britanniam, vocatuſque nomen ejus Eubonia, " Man."

§ Camden's Britannia, 136. "Hoc, ut conjecturâ probabile eſt, trophæum aliquod Romanorum fuit ſub poſterioribus " Imperatoribus, vel Athelſtani Saxonis cum Damnonios in poteſtatem ſuam redegiſſet."

" Earl Tofti (as the king had commanded) met him with an army of horfe; and uniting their " forces together, they began to ravage the region. The Welfh, therefore, fubmitted to give hof- " tages, promifed to pay tribute, depofed their King Griffin from his throne, and outlawed him."* Yet a Welfhman defcribes this memorable invafion of Wales by land and by water, with fome additional notices. Of all the conquerours of Wales, notes Giraldus Cambrenfis, " Harald the " laft, himfelf on foot, with foot-foldiers all light-armed, and with fuch victuals as the country " afforded, marched about and acrofs the whole of Wales with fo much fpirit, that he left but " few alive. *In fign and memorial for ever of his victory*, you may fee *very many ftones* in Wales, " *at the places where he was victorious*, erected *into a heap* after *the antient manner*, and having let- " ters to this purport engraven upon them, HERE WAS HARALD VICTORIOUS."† Such were the extemporaneous trophies of the Saxons, in a country very fimilar to Cornwall, and at a ftill later period of their empire! Such accordingly we have reafon to expect, on the final reduction of Cornwall by the Saxons! Such we actually find, and on that very eftate of Bollait which we have fingled out before for the fcene of the flaughter! I notice firft, however, what Dr. Borlafe calls the " Long Stone in Bofwen's Croft, Sancred" parifh, erect, with " a heap" of ftones at the foot of it; exactly conformable to Harold's monuments, in all but an infcription.‡ But we have alfo, though equally without an infcription, and without " a heap" too, " two ftones erect at " *Bolleit* in St. Beryan, about a furlong afunder."§ One of them is very tall, the other is taller than that in Sancred, and both unite into a record of the victory " after the antient manner" doubly fignificant. Both, however, unite in vain, for want of infcriptions; yet no more in vain, than the very monuments of Harold himfelf. Thefe, with their infcriptions, are juft as much loft to the world, as thofe are to memory. Thefe are even thrown down to the ground, probably, while thofe rear their heads aloft at prefent. Thefe exift only in a flight fentence of an unpub- lifhed writing, feem to have been there feen by one author only, and are hardly known to any; while thofe ftill fhow themfelves vifible to every eye, ftill folicit the notice of every mind, and ftill tell a tale of wonder to every hiftorical antiquary.

II. Having gained this victory at the Land's End, and fo reduced Cornwall completely, Athelftan refolved to crown all with the conqueft of the ifles, that had been always appendent to Cornwall, were now lying clofe on the other fide of a narrow frith, and feemed ftrongly to invite him acrofs it. Full of the meditated expedition, he repaired to a fmall kind of Chriftian temple in the neighbourhood, which had been a few ages before the hermitage of a religious perfon, which

* Florentius 424. " Strenuus Dux Weft Saxonum Haraldus, juffu regis Eadwardi, poft Nativitatem Domini, equitatu " non multo fecum affumpto, de Glawornâ (ubi Rex tunc morabatur) ad Rudelan multâ cum feftinatione profectus eft, ut " regem Walanorum Griffiinum, propter frequentes depopulationes quas in Anglorum finibus agebat, ac verecundias quas " Domino fuo Regi Eadwardo fæpe faciebat, occideret. At ille, ejus adventu præcognito, fugam cum fuis iniit, navem af- " cendit, et vix evafit. Haraldus vero, ut eum fugiffe comperit, palatium incendere et naves ejus cum armamentis combu- " rere juffit, eôdemque die rediit. Sed circa Rogationes de Bricftowe claflicâ manu profectus, magnâ ex parte terram Wa- " lanorum circumnavigabat. Cui frater fuus Comes Toftius, ut Rex mandârat, cum equeftri occurrit exercitu, et, viribus " fimul junctis, regionem illam depopulari cæperunt. Unde Walani coacti datis obfidibus fe dederunt, et fe tributum illi " daturos promifferunt, regemque fe cum Griffinum exlegantes abjecerunt."

† Camden's Britannia, 448. " Haraldus ultimus, ipfe pedes, cumque pedeftri turbâ, eplevibus armis, victuque patriæ " conformi, tam validé totam Walliam circumivit et tranfpenetravit, ut vix paucos vivos reliquerit. In cujus victoriæ fignum " et perpetuam memoriam, lapides in Walliâ more antiquo in tutulum erectos, locis in quibus victor extiterat, literas hujus- " modi infculptas habentes, plurimos invenias, HIC FUIT VICTOR HARALDUS."

‡ Ant. plate x. figure 3.

§ Plate x. figures 1 and 2.

which after her death had been turned into a chapel, and was now held in high veneration assuredly by the region around, from reverence to her memory as a saint, and to her remains as buried there. " S. Buriana an holy woman of Ireland," we are told by Leland, " sumtyme dwelled " in this place, and there made an " hermitage which afterwards became an " *oratory.* King " Ethelstane, goyng hens—onto Sylley made " a vow to build " a college where the *oratorie* " was." * There was a mere oratory or chapel then, at St. Burian's; this female saint having retired into a solitude near the Land's End, not covered with wood, as it was the scene of a battle, and not a desert, as it had the court-house of the hundred upon it, but a lonely part of the parish of Paul, though many miles distant from its church. In this oratory, and at the shrine or tomb of St. Burian probably, did Athelstan now kneel in prayer to God for a blessing on his intended enterprize; and did now prefer his vow, of erecting the little oratory into a collegiate church, if God blest him. God did bless him, he remembered his vow, he returned to the place, and " returning made *ex voto* a college where the oratorie was."†

He probably formed the *Bel-erw* or *Belra*, the estate of the king's court-house, into a parish of itself; he built the present church; and he added the late college. " The remains of the college," Dr. Borlase informs us, " were wantonly demolished by one Shrubsall, governor of Pendinas " castle during the usurpation of Cromwell;" a man, who seems to have united the two extremes of human folly in his soul, an aversion to every historical monument, and an abhorrence for every religious structure, who, therefore, destroyed the equipoise of that famous rocking-stone the Main Amber in Sithney parish, and equally burnt down the college at Burian; who has thus, like another Herostratus, given himself up to the fame of infamy for ever.‡ The parish extends from the borders of Paul on the east, to the Land's End on the west; and comprehends more than two thirds of the peninsula, in which it lies conjointly with Paul parish. From its tall tower, and its high position, the church stands conspicuous to all the country; and from its aspect much, but from its history more, attracted my attention particularly. I entered it with enthusiasm, and examined it with awe. It is handsome, lofty, and large, consisting of a nave with two ailes, and having a fine tower at one end. The inside is still disposed nearly as Athelstan left it, being filled generally with forms for seats, and having the forms carved in a very antique style. Some of the gentry, who have seats near the quire, have turned their antient forms into modern pews, and have so far violated the venerable uniformity of the whole. But the stalls of the dean and prebendaries are as antique as the rest of the church. These, equally as at Manchester college, the church of Ashetin near Manchester, &c. present each a broad plane, when the moveable seat is let down, but a narrow triangle when it is lifted up. The stone also inscribed with the name of Clarice, wife of Geoffrey de Bolleit, said by Hals to have been found by the sexton in sinking a grave, at the depth of four feet in the ground, is still there; and appears, what Gibson describes it to be, " a tomb in the church," an antient shallow tomb, lying near the altar-rails, but on the floor in the northern access to it, and blocking up the access in part. The outside of the church is all uniform, except at the east end; where a new projection has been made, as a recess for the altar. Yet the stones of the church carry such a face of freshness with them, as to lend an aspect of newness to the whole. The freshness, however, is the same in every part, and results merely from

* Itin. iii. 18. † Ibid. ibid. ‡ Borlase's Ant. 181, 384.

from the frequent wafhings, to which its high pofition on a hill, and its pointed expofure to the rains from the Atlantick, continually fubject it. The windows alfo are the fame in every part, each having a fquare entablature over head, and each being divided into long, narrow compartments, that are rounded with a little peak above. And the roof within, which once with pride fhowed its carved timbers to the eye, has lately learnt to conceal them behind a coved cieling. The endowment of the church originally, was an eftate annexed to the college, and thus defcribed in Domefday Book: " the canons of St. Berrione hold Eglofberrie" or the church of Buryan, " which was free in the time of King Edward; " *there is* 1 *hide, a land of eight carucates*; " *there is half a carucate,* vi *villani, and* vi *bordarii, and* xx *acres of pafture*; *it is worth* x *fhillings*; " *when the earl received the land, it was worth* xl *fhillings*."* Thefe with the tithes compofed an income, fufficient in itfelf for the four clergymen fettled here, but very infufficient as unequally partitioned thus; the dean having his proportion eftimated in 1291 at twenty pounds a year, yet the three prebendaries poffeffing only fifty fhillings, forty-fix and eight-pence, or fifteen refpectively.† Thefe were all eftimated in the fecond Valor, at £.48 12 10 for the rectory, being affuredly the amount of the tithes, and £.9 16 0½ for the deanery, being the rent of the eftate annexed to it; £.7 6 8, 7 0 0, and 2 0 0 to the prebendaries refpectively, being equally the rents of their refpective eftates.‡ The vacant prebends were always filled by the dean, I apprehend, as the Bifhop of Exeter, once ufurping the patronage of the church, even fince enjoying the deanery *in Commendam* occafionally,§ has now the patronage of the petty prebend;|| and as the real, the legitimate dean now abforbs the two prebendaries befide, by never nominating to their prebends. Thefe, however, as nominated by the dean, and as equally Englifh with him, therefore, had long ceafed with him to refide.¶ The whole parifh has been thus left to be fpiritually managed by one ftipendiary curate, inftead of a dean and three prebendaries; all the purpofes of Athelftan's donation being thus defeated. The abfence of the prebendaries, indeed, may *perhaps* better be fupplied now by the prefence of two perpetual curates, one fettled at St. Sennan near the Land's End, the other fixed at St. Levan on the fouthern fea, each having his own church there. But then thefe fubftitutes of the prebendaries are not half fo dignified in themfelves, half fo well provided with an income, half fo capable therefore of promoting the interefts of religion; as the prebendaries were or would be themfelves. Nor can ever religion be properly promoted, or the purpofes of Athelftan ever be anfwered, before our kings begin to nominate *Cornifhmen* for the deanery, before they oblige them to refide at the church, before they compel them to nominate prebendaries equally Cornifh and equally obliged to refide, even before they induce them to make a more equal partition of the whole income between the prebendaries and themfelves. The very reduction of the income would readily make way for the nomination of the prebendaries, and for the refidence of all the chapter. It would extinguifh the eager ambition of Englifhmen for the deanery. It would thus throw the deanery into the hands of the Cornifh. It would appoint thofe to be deans, who were ready to refide themfelves, and induce the deans to nominate others equally ready for their affiftants. And the church of Athelftan would then prove

a

* Fol. 121. " Canonici S. Berrione tenent Eglofberrie, quæ fuit libera Tempore Regis Edwardi. Ibi eft 1 hida, vi. villani, " et vi. bordarii, et xx. acræ pafturæ. Valet x. folidos. Quando Comes terram accepit, valebat xl. folidos."

† " Eccles. Stæ. Berianæ xx. Li. Præbenda—l. S. Præbenda—xlvi. S. viii. D. Præbenda—xv. S."

‡ Bacon's Liber Regis. § Hals, 40. || Liber Regis ¶ Leland's Itin. vii. 117.

a bleſſing to this wild extremity of the iſland, a kind of ſpiritual *Specula* in Britain, ſet at the Land's End, yet lending its light to the whole iſland, but eſpecially lending it to this dangerous part of the whole.*

Attending Athelſtan to the Land's End for his embarkation at Pordenack cove and Whitſand bay, we ſee the country now, whatever it was then, all cultivated nearly up to the brim of the ocean. We even ſee Cape Cornwall to the north, ending in a high point, that ſhowed it once reached out (as tradition ſays it reached) to a rock a little diſtant, inſulated, but denominated the Breſan; and, juſt before it joined the point, diſcloſing in a hollow its wheat all yellowing towards harveſt. There being a haze out at ſea, though the ſun ſhone bright, we could not behold the Sylley Iſles but ſtood looking with curious wonder at that nearer and more ſtriking object before us, the Longſhips, ranging in an oblique line before us, and ſhowing the waters all in a foam at their baſe. The rock called the Wolf, and which to my ſurprize I find not noticed by the great map of Cornwall, did (as I was informed at the Land's End) lie to the ſouth of us, under the land, and inviſible to us. It was exactly (as I ſince underſtand) ſouth ſouth-weſt from us, diſtant eight miles and a half. On this rock was lately attempted to be fixed the figure of a wolf in copper, that ſhould paſs the wind through it with a great noiſe, or that ſhould have bells to ring with the wind, in order to apprize the manner of his approach towards it. But the whole was found impracticable in the execution, becauſe of the violent tides there; and perceived to be ſurely ineffectual in the deſign, becauſe the wind that puſhed on to the rock would keep back the ſound. And after two or three attempts to fix the figure, or to hang the bells, in one of which the projector was like to have been drowned, the plan was of neceſſity abandoned. The Land's End projected before us into the weſtern ſea, while the northern was on our right, and the ſouthern on our left. Before we took this ſtation, we came to a new-built houſe on our right, which is called upon its ſign the Land's End Hotel. We ſtopt at the door, to order our dinner againſt our return. The houſe is good in appearance, but could not be expected to be well ſtocked with proviſions. We ordered a couple of boiled fowls, with bacon and greens. The fowls were not only dreſt, but *killed* againſt our return, and *the feathers then lay ſcattered before the door.* A few yards farther to the weſt, in the ſame church-town of Sennan, is the ale-houſe mentioned by Mr. Barrington, as called on its ſign *the laſt in England.*† But it is alſo called, though he has not noticed the circumſtance, on the *other* ſide of its ſign, *the firſt in England.* This village Mr. Barrington ſtrangely calls "*the* Sennan or *moſt weſtern* point;"‡ when the village is ſituated about *a mile and a half* from that "moſt weſtern point" the Land's End, and when it takes its appellation from the ſaint of its petty church, Sennan or Sinnin of Ireland. This church I entered, and found it one aiſle, with a ſide chapel, like St. Helen's in Sylley hereafter, the aiſle being the original church, and the chapel erected for the ſaint's ſepulture; *the latter*, therefore, having the beheaded ſtatue of the ſaint ſtill fixed on its bracket of ſtone. There was nothing elſe to catch my eye. But the church-yard preſented an object of curioſity to it, perſons buried in earth ſhaped like coffins, by edging the grave with ſlate-ſtones, and ſtrewing the ſurface with ſand. The graves thus look

* Camden 136. "In extremis hujus promontorii ſcopulis—Speculam Britanniæ erectam fuiſſe prodidit;—viculus nunc "illi inſidet, *Saint Buriens.*"

† Archæologia iii. 280. ‡ Ibid. ibid.

look like coffins peeping out of the ground, and ſlightly covered with earth. So at St. Martin's, one of the Sylley Iſles, " is the form of a grave, ſurrounded with ſtones " pitched edge-" wiſe, in the ſhape of a coffin, eight feet long, and three feet over the wideſt part." (Troutbeck 108.) So, in the ſame iſle, the ſea " has waſhed away the ſand, where a great many " graves " of all ſizes have lately appeared, and ſtones ſet edgewiſe in the form of coffins, which lie " *eaſt and weſt*," * and conſequently are chriſtian like thoſe at Sennan, the heathen mode of burial in Britain and its iſles being, to lay the body *north and ſouth*, with the head to the north. † As we paſt by a groupe of houſes about a mile beyond, the laſt groupe before we reached the Land's End, and properly " the moſt weſtern point" as a village; the men, the boys, and the girls crouded after us, or ran by our ſides, till we reached a bleak common, and came up to a long ſtone, riſing with a ſharp ridge, about a yard high from the ground. Here, to my ſurprize, the collected company *ſeized our bridles* and *ſtopt our progreſs*, as we were now at the rock denominated the *Whale's Fin* from its form. Then the girls came up with ſaucers held in their hands, ſome open to the eye, others having their aprons drawn tightly over them, but all containing little ſhells, twenty or thirty in a ſaucer, at ſixpence a ſaucer, for ſale. I entered freely into converſation with the men, drew from them all the little which they knew concerning the ſea, or the rocks, or the iſles, and offered ſterling money for *Corniſh words*. They knew no Corniſh however, and my money was offered in vain. They knew enough of Engliſh indeed, to ſolicit my benevolence for their informations. To ſo many, I ſaid, all benevolence was impoſſible. They therefore contracted their petitions cunningly, and requeſted me to ſingle any one or two individuals for my bounty. I did ſo to one, who had attached himſelf to me on the way, and who afterwards took the lead in talking. And as a boy without ſhoes or ſtockings, who attended me on my return, to ſhow how ill my benevolence was beſtowed, aſſured me, that the receiver of it was *a good farmer*; ſo he arrived at the hotel almoſt as ſoon as I reached it, accompanied with a couple of men almoſt equally leaders with himſelf in the converſation, to ſpend my little gratuity in drinking.

Mr. Barrington, let me here obſerve, in 1773, pretendedly ſung the death-ſong of the Corniſh language, and committed it to the grave with Dolly Pentraeth, the fiſhwoman of Mouſehole.‡ But in this he appears to have been as much miſtaken, as Dr. Borlaſe was before him; when the doctor, a native and a reſident, an antiquary and a linguiſt, ſo early as 1758, declared it to have " altogether ceaſed, ſo as not to be ſpoken any where in converſation." At that very time, as Mr. Barrington has obſerved, to the diſgrace of his attention, an old woman was living " within " four miles of him," and talking the language fluently.§ Nor can we convict Mr. Barrington of a ſimilar in-attention. He was merely a ſtranger and a viſitant in the country. But the language ſurvived *its laſt ſpeaker*. In 1790, William Pryce, M. D. of Redruth, Cornwall, publiſhed his " *Archæologia Cornu-Britannica*; or an eſſay to preſerve the antient Corniſh language." In the preface to this publication, he gave us ſuch information, as ſhowed the Corniſh language to have not expired with Mr. Barrington's fiſhwoman, to have been ſtill continuing in exiſtence, and to have had its laſt ſtruggles for life, *if it is even yet dead*, at or about this very prominence of the Land's End. " As for the vulgar Corniſh YET SPOKEN," cries Dr. Pryce, not adverting directly to

* Troutbeck, 112. † Stukeley's Stonehenge, 45. ‡ Archæologia iii. 283. § Ibid. 281, 282.

to the ſuppoſed extinction of the ſpoken Corniſh in Dolly Pentraeth, yet ſpeaking deciſively to the point, " it is SO CONFINED TO," and therefore ſtill ſurviving in, " the *extremeſt* corner of the " county; and THOSE ANCIENT PERSONS, who STILL PRETEND TO JABBER IT, are even " there SO FEW; the SPEECH itſelf is ſo *corrupted*, and THE PEOPLE too, for the *moſt* part, are " ſo *illiterate*, that I cannot but wonder at my patience, and aſſume ſome merit to myſelf, for my " ſingular induſtry in *collecting* the words which I have communicated from ORAL INTELLI- " GENCE; eſpecially, as hardly *any* of THE PERSONS WHOM I HAVE CONSULTED, could give a " tolerable account of the orthography, much leſs of the etymology or derivation of thoſe words " WHICH THEY USE. For they often join, or rather run two or three words together, making " but one of them all; though THEIR PRONUNCIATION IS GENERALLY CORRECT. As, for " inſtance, 'Meraſtadu,' which THEY PRONOUNCE IN ONE BREATH as if they were a ſingle " word; whereas it is a contraction of four, 'Meor 'ras tha Dew,' *many thanks to God,* anciently " written 'Maur gras the Deu;' and 'Meraſtawhy,' *many thanks to you,* a contraction of 'Maur " 'ras tha why.'" This evidence is complete. The Corniſh was ſtill ſpoken, when the voice of Dolly was choked in the grave. She was not, indeed, the ſolitary ſpeaker of a language loſt to all other tongues, the ſingle repreſentative of the purely Corniſh nation, the mournful outliver of all her kindred and ſpeech. Numbers talked it at the very time.

Vixêre fortes ante Agamemnona
Multi; ſed omnes illacrymabiles
Urgentur, ignotique longâ
Nocte, carent quia vate ſacro.

Nor did they talk it, we find, with even any of that viciouſneſs of pronunciation, which has changed the Latin into Italian, and the Saxon into Engliſh. They gave a juſtly Corniſh tone, to the truly Corniſh words that they uſed. They only ſpoke ſome ſhort words, that muſt have occurred frequently in converſation, and that were uſed uniformly as a whole ſentence, with a rapidity which made them ſound like one word. We do the ſame in *prythee* for *I pray thee,* even leaving out the principal word in ſpeaking. The ſpeakers of Cornwall were more exact, we ſee, pronouncing every word, and pronouncing every word with fidelity. So accurately was the Corniſh then ſpoken by *many*, at " the extremeſt corner of the county!" But, what renders the accuracy more ſurprizing, theſe *many* were in general " illiterate" perſons; ſo, like the " illiterate" among ourſelves, unable " to give a tolerable account of the orthography," and ſure, therefore, to be tenfold more unable, as even our very ſcholars generally are, to account for " the etymology " or derivation of thoſe words which they uſe." I even heard in my viſit to the weſt, of two perſons ſtill alive that could ſpeak the Corniſh language. On my offer of Engliſh money for Corniſh words, to the men at the Land's End, they referred me to an old man living about three miles off to the ſouth, at St. Levan (I think), a ſecond chapelry with St. Sennan, in the pariſh of St. Burian; and intimated, that I might there have as many words of Corniſh as I would chuſe to purchaſe. On my return alſo to Penzance, Mr. Broad (captain of a volunteer company of ſeafencibles) additionally aſſured me, that there was a woman then living at Newlyn, who could equally ſpeak Corniſh. I will go ſoon, and ſee both; that I may hear the genius of Cornwall ſtill ſpeaking from his opened grave, as it were, and ſtill greeting an Engliſh ear with the native

tive articulation of the Cornifh. Even when this articulation is all funk in the clofed grave of death, that genius will ftill be talking a mixed Cornifh, by the tongues of his anglicized fons, or his adopted Englifhmen; Cornwall, like Greece, having conquered its conquerors and fubdued its fubduers, by giving to the Englifh language a multiplicity of Cornifh words, blending them intimately with the Cornifh in the common intercourfe of life, in mining, in fifhing, even in domeftick actions, and thus making the Cornifh to triumph filently amid the open triumph of the Englifh over it.

I have one obfervation more to make, concerning the Land's End.—" In the rocks " about " Whitfand Bay," Mr. Gough relates on fome grofs mis-information from others, or from fome grofs mif-conception in himfelf, by confounding the Whitfand Bay, near the Land's End, with another of the fame name near Plymouth, and confounding all with a mixture of mis-information, thus confounding and confounded, " the body of —— Tilly, efq. who died about fifty years ago, remarkable for the freedom of his principles and life, was inclofed by his own order, dreffed in his cloaths, fitting in a chair, his face to the door of a fummer-houfe at Pentilley, the key put under the door; and his figure in wax in the fame drefs and attitude in the room above."* The language of Mr. Gough, in his additions to Camden's account, is the very oppofite of Camden's own; Camden's being juft, grave, and dignified, but his enlarger's low, colloquial, and ungrammatical. We fee this in the prefent paffage; where we find the man " fitting in a chair," *with* " his face to the door of a fummer-houfe," *with* " the key put under the door, and" *with* " his figure *in* wax *in* the fame drefs and attitude *in* the room above." Thefe are evidently the hafty notes of a mere *tourift*, accuftomed to write with an illiterate negligence, and then laying his notes in their rude unfafhioned ftate before the public. But the *matter* here is much worfe than the *manner*. The fact is moft amazingly falfe in *geography*. The very circumftances fhow this. A man buried with " his face to the door of a fummer-houfe at *Pentilly*," could not poffibly be buried " in the rocks" at the Land's End. Thefe two points of Cornwall have nearly the whole very extraordinary length of Cornwall interpofed between them; as Pentilly lies at the *eaftern* end of the county, and on the banks of the *Tamar*. But Mr. Gough was told the fact at or near the Land's End, thus inferted it with a carelefs reference only to Pentilly, and afterwards copied it where he found it, with a ftill more carelefs inattention to his own reference. The real ftory is this; and it is proper to be laid before the public, as well to correct this aftonifhing blunder in Mr. Gough, as to expofe " the freedom of" thofe " principles," or of that " life," which ended in fuch an order for the body's burial. Hals has luckily preferved the moral portrait of the man, and I hang it over his head in his cave of death. " Pentyley," we are told by this gleaner of private hiftories, here ufefully employed, is " a houfe—built and foe named by one Mr. James " Tyley, fon of   in the parifh of St. Keverne, labourer, who, as I am informed, was " placed by him a fervant or horfeman to Sir John Coryton, bart. the elder; who afterwards, by " his affiftance, learninge the inferiour practice of the law, under an attorney, became his fteward. " In which capacities, by his care and induftry he foon grew rich; fo that he marryed Sir Henry " Vane's daughter; by whom he had a good fortune or eftate, but noe iffue. At length, after the " death of his mafter, he became a guardian in truft for his younger children, and fteward to their

F 2   " elder

* V. I. p. 12.

" elder brother Sir John, that marryed Chiverton.*—Whereby he augmented his wealth and " fame to a greater pitch, when, ſoon after King James 2d. came to the crowne, this gentleman, " by a great ſumme of money, and falſe repreſentations of himſelfe, obtained the favour of knight- " hood at his hands. But that king ſom ſhort while after being informed, that Mr. Tyley was at " firſt but a groome or horſeman to Sir John Coryton, that he was noe gentleman of blood or " armes, and yet gave for his coate armour the armes of Count Tillye of Germany; ordered the " heraulds to enquire into this matter. Who, findinge this information trew, by the king's order " entered his chamber at London, tooke downe thoſe armes, tore others in pieces, and faſtned " them all to horſe tayles, and drew them through the ſtreets of London, to his perpetuall diſ- " grace, and degraded him from the dignity of that bearinge, and impos'd a fyne of £.500 upon " him for ſoe doeinge, as I am informed. But alas! maugre all thoſe proceedings, after the death " of his then maſter, Sir John Coryton the younger, not without ſuſpicion of beinge poyſond, he " ſoon marryed (one) with whome common fame ſaid he was too familliar before; ſoe that he " became poſſeſt of her goods and chattalls, and a greate joynture. Whereby he *liveth* in much " pleaſure and content in this place, honour'd of ſom, lov'd of none, admiringe himſelfe for the " bulk of his riches, and the arts and contrivance by which he gott it; ſom of which were all- " together unlawfull. Witneſs his ſteward Mr. Elliot's beinge endicted for a mint, and coyninge " falſe money for his uſe; who on notice therof forſooke this land, and fled beyound the ſeas, " though his other agent and confederate Car alias Popjoye, indicted for the ſame crime of high " treaſon committed at Saltaſh, was taken, tryed, and found guilty, and executed at Launceſton " 1695. At which tyme the writer of theſe lynes was one of the grand jury for the body of this " county, that found thoſe bills; when William Williams, of Treworgye, in Probus, eſq. was " ſheriff, and John Wadden, eſq. foreman of that inqueſt.

" Since the writinge of the above premiſes, about the yeare 1712, Sir James Tyley dyed, and " (as I am inform'd) by his laſt will and teſtament obliged his adopted heire, one Woolley, his " ſiſter's ſon, not only to aſſume his name, haveinge noe legitimate iſſue, but that he ſholde not " interr his body after death in the earth, but faſten it in the chair where he dyed with iron, his " hatte, wigge, rings, gloves, and beſt apparel on, ſhooes and ſtockings, and ſurround the ſame " with an oake cheſt, box, or coffin, in which his bookes and papers ſhold be leyd, with penn " and inke alſo; and *build* for reception thereof, *in a certaine feild of his lands, a wall'd vault or* " *grott to be arched with moorſtone*; in which repoſitory it ſholde be leyed without chriſtian buryall: " for that, as he ſaid but an hower before he dyed, in two years ſpace he wold be at Pentyley " againe. Over this vault his heir likewiſe was obliged *to builde a fine chamber*, and ſet up therin " the picture of him, his lady, and adopted heir for ever; and at the end of this vault or cham- " ber *to erect a ſpire or lofty monument of ſtone*, from thence for ſpectators to overlooke the conti- " guous country, *Plymouth, Sound, and Harbour*. All which, as I am tolde, is accordingly per- " formd by his heir, whoſe ſucceſſors are obliged to repaire the ſame for ever out of his lands and " rents, under penalty of looſinge both. However I heare lately, notwithſtanding this his pro- " miſe of returninge in two years ſpace to Pentiley, that Sir James's body is eaten out with " wormes,

* " Chiverton *aforeſaid*," as in page preceding, Sir John is ſaid to have " marryed one of the heirs of Sir Richard Chi- " verton, knight, bred a ſkinner in London, and *was* lord mayor of that city. 9 Charles 2d, 1657."

"wormes, and his bones or ſkelleton falne downe to the ground from the chaire wherin 'twas "ſeated, about four years after it was ſett up, his bookes and wearinge apparell all rotten in the "box or chayre where it was at firſt layd."* If the character here drawn be a juſt one, this founder of the family of Tilley, of Pentilley, was one of thoſe perſons, whom we frequently ſee riſing up in life; men born in a low ſituation, from their earlieſt years looking up to grandeur with a fooliſh feeling of admiration, and as they grew in manhood aſpiring to procure what they have ſo long envied. Then, unawed by any dread of God for want of religion, and exerting the powers of intellect that God has given them for better purpoſes, they become men of buſineſs, clever, dexterous, cunning, and knaviſh; practiſing every enormity that is ſafe from the ſword of the law, and wading ſucceſsfully through guilt into wealth. Such ſeems James Tilley to have been! He had thus lived, till he feared to die. His fear at laſt operated ſo powerfully, as to ſtupify his underſtanding, and extinguiſh his common ſenſe. He felt he muſt die, but he perſuaded himſelf he ſhould ſoon revive. In *two* years he fancied he ſhould revive, and ordered himſelf to be dreſt ready for the revival, but forgot that in *two* years his dreſs and his fleſh would be equally rotted off from his body. He believed he ſhould riſe and take poſſeſſion of Pentilley again, in a couple of years; yet gave Pentilley away *for ever* to an adopted heir, ordered *him* to build a vault for his own reſidence at preſent, and commanded his *ſucceſſors* to keep the vault in repair *for ever*. Such a fool to fear was this man! Such an idiot in death does perſevering wickedneſs make, even the wiſe of the world! Mr. Gough, however, has heightened the account of this fool in one part, we ſee, and diſtorted the deſcription of his idiotcy in another. He did not order himſelf to be placed "in the rocks" near the Land's End, but in a room on his eſtate at Pentilly. He did not order himſelf to be placed, with "his face to the door of a ſummer-houſe at Pentilly," and with "the key put under the door;" but ordered what is wildly meant by a ſummer-houſe, "a ſpire "or lofty monument of ſtone," to be erected at the end of his vault, for the view that ſpectators might have from it of the country round. "The key" too has been "put under the door" by the ingenuity of the living; the deceaſed having naturally forgotten this little circumſtance, in his forgetfulneſs of that grand point, the ſpeedy corruption of his body. Nor was "his figure in wax "in the ſame dreſs and attitude in the room above," as Mr. Gough relates; becauſe we know of no upper room ordered "in the rocks" near the Land's End, becauſe the upper room ordered was actually "a fine chamber" over the vault, and becauſe in it was ſet up, *not* "his figure in "wax in the ſame—attitude, but merely his *picture*," the picture too of "his lady," with the picture of his "adopted heir." All are, in the ſame futility of infidel folly, commanded to be kept there "for ever;" as an infidel's eternity is merely—a couple of years. Such, however, are the many miſtakes of Mr. Gough, in this ſhort paſſage concerning the Land's End! Yea, ſuch are the tales of indiſtinctneſs, the anecdotes of confuſion, the narratives of ignorance, that all travellers hear, that the injudicious receive with the very ſtamp of folly upon their brow, and that the preſumptuous publiſh,

With all their imperfections on their head,
——— Full-blown as May ———.

III.

* M. S. under St. Mellyn.

III. But let us now advert to the Sylley Isles, and trace their history downwards from the descent of Athelstan, even from the first visits paid them by the Phenicians. We shall thus be able to throw some new light upon a dark subject, to show the true state of Cornwall with its isles originally, and to complete the discoveries which we have made before.

" Dr. Borlace thinks it *highly probable*," as Mr. Gough tells us, and I have made it *certain* before, " that there was a time when" *almost* " all these islands made but one. N. B. In Henry's Valor, even so late, " Silley Insul Chapel."—*Hence* he naturally *infers*," what is surely not inferrible at all, and what the doctor was too wise to infer, " that the antients included under the " name of Cassiterides *the western part of Cornwall*, if it did not *then join to it*."* Mr. Gough here has strangely distorted the sentiments of Dr. Borlase. Wild and illogical as the doctor really is, Mr. Gough has made him ten times more illogical and wild. The doctor actually speaks of " the *Cassiterides*," as, " by *the most ancient accounts* of them, appearing *always* to have been " *islands*;† and therefore *not* joining to Cornwall. The doctor also " infers that the ancients in-" cluded under the name of Cassiterides, the western part of Cornwall," from other and very different premises. " From this hill" of the Giant's Castle in St. Mary's, says the doctor himself, " we were pleased to see our own country, Cornwall, in a shape new to us, but what certainly in-" duced the ancients to reckon it among the isles, generally called by them Cassiterides; for as an " island it appears to every eye from Scilly."‡ Dr. Borlase thus takes for granted what is absolutely false in fact, and then endeavours to account for it by a logick all frivolous in itself. That any of the antients ever spoke of Cornwall as one of the Sylley Isles, I utterly deny; and that they could possibly have so spoken of it because it now appears as an isle from Sylley, I equally deny. If they ever beheld it from the Giant's Castle, if they—beheld it looking like an isle, they could not have considered it as one of the isles *from which they were viewing it*, and they must have considered it as *another* isle. Even if the antients were so absurd, as to denominate the land which they saw, an isle, merely because it carried some appearance of an isle to their eyes; yet the *natives* must have corrected their errour, and made them know the land for a part of Britain. But of the natives Dr. Borlase never thought. Nor did he think much about the antients, to make them view Cornwall only from the Giant's Castle, to make them describe it only from this erroneous view, and to make them *always* viewing, *always* describing from this alone. But, though Dr. Borlase *here* takes it for granted, that the ancients included the west of Cornwall in the isles of Sylley; yet near sixty pages afterward he himself considers it as doubtful, and endeavours to reason his reader into a belief of it. " Whoever sees the land of Cornwall from these islands," he then says, turning his mode of accounting for the averred fact into a proof of the fact itself, " must " be convinced, that the Phenicians and other traders did most *probably*" do what was assumed as *certain* before, " include the western part of Cornwall among the islands, called Cassiterides."§ The doctor is thus, through the whole work, straining up a steep precipice, in his first efforts mounting successfully, but then disabled by the very ardour of his efforts before, and finally beaten by his own struggles down to the bottom. Yet, in want of better hold-fast, he endeavours to stay his descent, and to save his neck, by an appeal to two authors, one of whom, as a modern, could prove only he was as wild as the doctor himself; and the other, who as an antient, proves nothing to

* Gough iii. 758, misprinted 578. † Scilly Isles, 93. ‡ Scilly Isles, 18. § Ibid. 75.

to the point. " Ortelius is plainly of this opinion," cries the doctor, thus grounding his aſſumed certainty before on a mere opinion, now, on the opinion too of a mere foreigner, " and makes " Cornwall a part of the Caſſiterides."* I ſtop not to examine, whether Ortelius is really of this opinion; I haſten to the doctor's next appeal. " Diodorus Siculus," he adds, " does as plainly " *confound*, and in his deſcription *mix*, the weſtern parts of Cornwall and the Caſſiterides, indiſ- " criminately one with the other." Suppoſing he does, how would this prove a part of the main land of Britain to be reckoned for one of the Sylley Iſles? Theſe iſles are an integral part of Cornwall now, have indeed been always a part. Yet does this prove Cornwall to be conſidered as one of them? The queſtion anſwers itſelf. Yet, to purſue this ſhadow of a reaſon, this evaneſcent ghoſt of logick, till it is loſt in the light of day; how does Diodorus " confound and mix" Cornwall with the iſles? Dr. Borlaſe tells us himſelf juſt afterwards, when he ſpeaks of him as " *con-* " *founding*" *not* the *mainland* with the iſles, *but* the *trade* of both, even " the *tin-trade* of thoſe " weſtern parts of Cornwall with that carried on in Scilly."† Thus to ſpeak of the pilchard-fiſhery of Cornwall and Sylley now, is in this mockery of reaſoning a proof, that Cornwall is reckoned a part of Sylley, even the weſt of it one of the Sylley Iſles. Such reaſoning is beſt to be anſwered by ridicule,

As to be grave exceeds all power of face.

The antients knew Cornwall too well, to make ſuch miſtakes as theſe. They knew it early, they knew it late. They knew it in the Phenicians at firſt, in the Greeks afterwards, and in the Romans at laſt. They knew it even in thoſe not merely by views from Sylley, but by voyages along the very coaſt, by landings upon the very beach, and by both *beyond* the *weſt* of Cornwall, *beyond* the *middle* of Cornwall, *beyond* even the very *eaſt* of it. But what is ſtill more, the Romans came with their conquering armies *from* the eaſt of Britain, entered Cornwall as a part of the continent of Britain, and reduced it with the reſt of the continent. How then *could* the ancients, in general, have *poſſibly* conſidered Cornwall as an iſland, as one of the Sylley Iſlands, as what they ſaw, what they felt it not to be? Antiquaries at times take a peep into the cells of Bedlam, imagine they behold the antients there playing their anticks of frenzy, and become deranged themſelves by the imagination.‡

" That the Phenicians accounted their trade to theſe iſlands for tin of great advantage," as Dr. " Borlaſe tells us, " and were very jealous of it; is plain from what Strabo ſays, that the maſter " of a Phenician veſſel bound thither, perceiving that he was *dodged*," dogged, " by a Roman, ran " his ſhip aſhore, riſking his life, ſhip, and cargo (for which he was remunerated out of the pub- " lick

* Scilly Iſles, 75. † Scilly, 76.

‡ Mr. Troutbeck, a very noted ſurveyor of the Sylley Iſles, cited before, ſtrangely ſays the iſles " ſometimes are miſtaken " for the proverbial Scylla, the name of a rock near the Italian ſhore, oppoſite the iſland of Sicily, mentioned by Virgil, lib. " iii. v. 246, &c." p. 1. He then, without any acknowledgement, in p. 3, repeats from Dr. Borlaſe thus: " Scilly, lying " fartheſt to the weſt of all the high lands, was the firſt land of all theſe iſlands, that could be diſcovered by traders from the " Mediterranean and the Spaniſh coaſt, on which account ſailors went on ſtill in their old way, and called them in general " the Scilly Iſlands:" and thus in p. 9, " whoever ſees the land of Cornwall from theſe iſlands, muſt be convinced that the " Phoenicians and other traders did moſt probably include the weſtern part of Cornwall among the iſlands called Caſſiterides; " and Diodorus does plainly confound, and in his deſcription mix, the weſtern parts of Cornwall and the Caſſiterides, indiſ- " criminately one with the other; for talking of the promontory Bolerium, alias Belerium, the tin commerce and courteous " behaviour of the inhabitants, he ſays they carried this tin to an adjoining Britiſh iſle," &c. Theſe are the very abſurdities of Dr. Borlaſe, continued by Mr. Troutbeck, and refuted by me above. A body once ſet in motion, ſay the mathematicians, would continue to move for ever; if it was not checked by the friction of matter, and by the reſiſtance of air.

" lick treaſury of his country) rather than he would admit a partner in this traffick, by ſhewing " him the way to theſe iſlands. The Romans, however, perſiſting in their reſolution to have a " ſhare in this trade, at laſt accompliſhed it."* This is all truly ſaid, but with ſo much indiſcrimination, as might be pardonable in one writing at the time, when every point was well known, but is certainly un-pardonable in others, that live at ſuch a diſtance of time, and that *can* write with a greater diſtinctneſs of language. The full hiſtory is this.

Theſe Phenicians were indeed Phenicians in origin; but were no more Phenicians in reality, than the Engliſh of America are Germans or Gauls at preſent. They were Phenicians tranſplanted to Carthage in Africa, and again tranſplanted to Cadiz in Spain.† From their ſettlement at the latter, inheriting all the nautical genius of their Tyrian anceſtors, and improving it in adventures upon the once dreaded Atlantick before them; with a ſpirit of enterprize, which reflects high honour upon them, they found their way to the Sylley Iſles at the neareſt end of our own Britain. They there diſcovered, in their very curious inquiſition into the products of the countries which they viſited, a metal not unknown to the nations on the Mediterranean, thoſe central tribes of the globe, but very rare among them, and yet of infinite value to them all. None was then diſcovered in Germany,‡ and none then imported from India. It was diſcovered only in Portugal and the adjoining parts of Spain on the north.§ There the Syrians of Carthage previouſly found it, and the Tyrians of Cadiz therefore ranged the ſeas for more of it. The mines of Spain and Portugal appear from the very celebrity of the Sylley mines in all ages of antiquity, to have been as un-productive in themſelves as they muſt have been prior in working; and are now known to have been quite exhauſted for ages. We thus find *tin* expreſſly ſpecified among the metals, with which the Tyrians traded; in that large and ample deſcription of its commerce, which Ezekiel has given us concerning its coming deſtruction; and which exhibits a more circumſtantial account of it, than all antiquity beſides exhibits.‖ I ſhall ſelect only a few touches of the picture. " Now, thou ſon of man," ſays God to the prophet, " take up a lamentation for Tyrus, and ſay " unto Tyrus, O thou that art ſituate at the entry of the ſea, which art a merchant of the people " for many iſles, Thus ſaith the Lord God, O Tyrus, thou haſt ſaid, I am of perfect beauty, " thy borders are in the midſt of the ſeas, thy builders have perfected thy beauty;—fine linen " with broidered work from Egypt, *was that which thou ſpreadeſt forth to be thy ſail*; blue and " purple from the iſles of Eliſha, was that which covered thee; the inhabitants of Zidon and " Arvad were thy mariners; thy wiſe men, O Tyrus, that were in thee, were thy pilots;—*all* " *the ſhips of the ſea, with their mariners, were in thee to occupy thy merchandize;—Tarſhiſh,*" Cadiz, as I ſhall ſoon ſhow, " was thy merchant, by reaſon of the multitude of all kind of riches; with " ſilver, iron, TIN, and lead THEY TRADED IN THY FAIRS." The metal had then been long known to the world. We find it ſpecified among the metals of the eaſt, in the days of Iſaiah, or more than 700 years before the Chriſtian æra, God then ſpeaking of it as the cuſtomary alloy of finer metals, in figuratively promiſing the Jews to free them from their corruptions by his kind puniſhments, and ſo ſaying, " I will turn my hand upon thee, and purely purge away thy droſs, " and

* Scilly Iſles, 72, 73.

† See a note concerning Juſtin, ſoon. ‡ Camden, 136.

§ Pliny xxxiv. 16. " Plumbum candidum, a Græcis appellatum Caſſiteron,—nunc certum eſt in Luſitaniâ gigni et in " Gallıciâ." ‖ Ezekiel xxvii. 2, 4, 7, 9, 12.

" and take away all thy TIN."* But the metal was familiar to Greece, more than four centuries before; Homer maintaining it as one of the metals ufed in the compofition of Achilles' fhield.† Yet the firft mention of tin in the human hiftory is ftill earlier, even fourteen centuries and a half before our æra; Mofes himfelf thus noting it as one of the metals then familiar among the Jews, " the gold and the filver, the brafs, the iron, the TIN, and the lead."‡ Thefe notices are certainly anteriour in fome of them, if not in all, to the exportation of tin from Sylley; and the world muft therefore have been then fupplied with the metal, through the traders of Carthage, from the mines of Portugal or Spain. Eager, probably, to rival their brethren in a commerce, that furnifhed all the world with the metal from a few mines, the Cadizians very fortunately difcovered the ifles of Sylley, all replenifhed with tin. This was as beneficial a difcovery to fuch a maritime and commercial commonwealth, as the difcovery of the Weft-Indies has fince been to the monarchy of Spain; and, what is very furprizing, centered equally with that in the port of Cadiz. They therefore took the one precaution, which the weaknefs of their marine, as calculated only for trade, and the habits of their minds, all bent like the Dutch fince upon the lucre of it, permitted them to take. They brought fuch quantities of tin into the market, from fome diftant ifles in the Atlantick, as gained thofe ifles among the Græcians the general appellation of the TIN ISLES; but they concealed from all the world the exact pofition of the ifles.§ Pliny, plainly reciting fome account much older than himfelf, in a curious but unnoticed paffage, obferves " the tin was called Caffiteron by the Greeks, and fabuloufly narrated to be fought in " iflands of the Atlantick fea, and to be brought to the feekers in wicker boats, fowed round with " leather."‖ We thus catch the very idea that was firft floating in writings, concerning the vifits of the Cadizians to Sylley, and concerning the conveyance of the tin from the fhores to the fhips, in boats of the Britifh fabrick. All this was believed to be fabulous at the time, becaufe of the ftrangenefs of it. But the ifles were known to be in the Atlantick. Yet where in the Atlantick, was not known This ocean, now the great *medium* of paffage betwixt Europe, India, and America; now, therefore, the moft frequented fea in the whole globe, was then a blank, a vacuum, a defert generally to the whole. Nor was concealment all the means ufed by this Dutch kind of republican merchants, for keeping to themfelves the whole trade in Britifh tin. More effectually to preclude all rivals in it, with a truly Dutch fpirit they falfified geography itfelf; by giving fuch lying accounts of their pofition, as impofed upon the world for three or four ages. Even to the days of Pliny, the ifles were believed to " lie oppofite to the coaft of Celtiberia" or Spain.¶

But the Greeks of Marfeilles, with all that fire of activity which they had derived from their anceftors, and with all that fondnefs for maritime enterprizes which had carried them from Phocea

G into

* Ifaiah i. 25.

† Pliny xxxix. 16. " Album habuit autoritatem et Iliacis temporibus, tefte Homero; Caffiteron ab illo dictum." So in Iliad xviii. the metals of Achilles' armour are fpecified thus,

χαλκον δι εν πυρι βαλλεν κασσιτερον τε, κ. τ. λ.

And Achilles' boots are thus faid to have been made,

κνημιδας κασσιτεροιο.

‡ Numbers xxxi. 22.

§ Strabo 265. Προτερον μεν ουν, Φοινικες μονοι την εμποριαν ταυτην εκ των Γαδειρων, κρυπτοντες, &c. &c.

‖ Pliny xxxiv. 16. " A Græcis appellatum Caffiteron, fabuloféque narratum in infulis Atlantici maris peti, ... " . . . . . . navigiis circumfutis corio advehi."

¶ Ibid iv. 22. " Ex adverfo Celtiberiæ complures funt infulæ, Caffiterides dictæ Græcis a fertilitate plumbi."

into Gaul before, reſolved to explore the Atlantick themſelves for theſe iſlands of wealth. They accordingly ſent a navigator, who has rendered his name immortal by the act, PYTHEAS MASSILIENSIS. Yet, with the wonder of ignorance in reciting his diſcoveries, he ſaw a vaſt prodigy (he ſays) in the enormous tides of our ocean; the water riſing no leſs than eighty cubits upon the land.* But he ranged up to the very north of our iſland, as there he beheld another prodigy, and heard of a third "at Thule, the moſt northern of the *Britiſh* iſles," he adds, "where was neither "land, nor ſea, nor air by itſelf, but a ſomething compoſed of all, like the lungs of the ſea; in "which he ſays the land and the ſea, and all things, are ſuſpended on high; and this acts as the "bond of the univerſe, not acceſſible either by land or by ſea: of all which he" ingenuouſly owns "he ſaw nothing himſelf except the likeneſs of lungs, and" merely "relates the reſt from "information."† He had opened a communication with the natives, he had converſed with them by a Gallic interpreter aſſuredly, but had groſſly miſtaken their information. He himſelf, indeed, ſaw only ſuch a thick ſea-fog, as has been frequently miſtaken for land by our own mariners, as would thus be neither land nor ſea, nor air, yet ſomething compoſed of all. And in this, as the natives (we may be ſure) really reported to him, the land and the ſea and all things appeared ſuſpended on high, all nature ſwimming in the fog as it moved ſlowly along the ſhore. He thus puſhed as far (can we conceive it poſſible for navigation then?) as the NINETIETH degree of latitude, or the very north pole itſelf; becauſe he wrote in the journal of his voyage, that at Thule, "ſix days ſail beyond Britain, the days continued for SIX MONTHS together."‡ But from his mention of the iſle as a Britiſh one, as only ſix days ſail to the north of Britain, and from the phyſical impoſſibility of his wintering at the pole, to know perſonally the length of a day for ſix months; we may be ſure he went only as far as the Orkney Iſles, the only iſles on the north aſcribable to Britain, there experienced a day of eighteen hours and a half, ſo went no farther towards the pole than the ſixtieth degree, and related all the reſt from information received there.§ Yet in this amazing voyage of diſcovery, which ſeems to have rivalled all that even the preſent reign has produced, commerce then running an equal race of glory with philoſophy now, and Pytheas ranking in naval action almoſt with a COOKE himſelf; he certainly diſcovered what muſt have been as certainly the firſt object of his expedition, the Sylley Iſles, though he diſcovered not what perhaps, from the extent of his navigation, was equally an object, new Iſlands of Tin. That he reached the former, is plain from what Timæus, the Greek hiſtorian of Sicily, who wrote about the year 300 before Chriſt, and what he could declare only from this the only great voyager of the Greeks in our ſeas; is reported by Pliny to declare, that "the iſland Mictis," the iſland Silura called Mictis, I apprehend, before it was reduced by the Silures, and took their name,‖ "is diſtant from *Britain* weſtward by a navigation of ſix days," that "tin GROWS IN "IT,"

* Ibid. ii. 97. "Octogenis cubitis ſupra Britanniam intumeſcere æſtus, Pythias Maſſilienſis author eſt."

† Strabo 15. ‡ Pliny ii. 75.

§ Borlaſe in Ant. of Cornwall, 33 edit. 2, ſays: Pytheas, "ſailed ſo far north, that he ſaw the ſun diſappear, only for a "moment of time, and immediately to riſe again; which muſt be as far as 68 degrees of north latitude," rather 66, 31. But for the aſſertion itſelf there is no authority. Pliny's is directly againſt it.

‖ Camden 837. "Adjacentem habet *Silly* inſulam exiguam in littore Silurum, *quorum nominis pluſquam umbram retinere* "*videtur*, ut *oppululume regione* in agro Glamorgan." But *Mictis* is from the ſame root in the Britiſh language, that *Vectis* or the Iſle of *Wight* is. We know *this* to be the iſle which "vocatur *With*, quam Britones inſulam *Gueid* vel *Guith* (vocant), "quod Latiné *Divortium* dici poteſt." (Nennius c. ii.) Yet the root is no longer found in any of the branches of the Britiſh language;

"IT," and that "the *Britons* navigate to it in wicker boats sewed round with leather."* Mictis is thus described in the very same terms with which we have just seen Silura and its isles described before; the tin then being "narrated to be sought in islands of the Atlantick sea, and to be "brought to the seekers *in wicker boats sewed round with leather*." And from this voyage it is, that Britain became what Pliny expressly avers it was, what however the industry of learning has toiled in vain to discover whence or how it was, "celebrated in the monuments of the Greeks."‡ The Greeks of Marseilles now visited the Sylley Isles, equally with the Phenicians of Cadiz; and equally exported its tin. Posidonius, who appears to have been cotemporary with Pompey, and to have been visited as a famous orator by Pompey, when the latter was engaged upon the piratical war; in a passage that first notices, and surprizingly for a writer so early notices, the British position of Sylley, says, "tin is generated in the isles the Cassiterides, and is carried from *the British* "*isles* to MARSEILLES."§ But we even know the very name of the first merchant of Marseilles, that exported a cargo of tin from Sylley; MIDACRITUS.‖ These isles received their general and characteristic name of *Cassiterides*, from the Greeks alone. By this name were they known to Herodotus himself, about four centuries and a half before Christ; and probably at a period just posteriour to the very voyage of Pytheas.† By this name did they continue to be known, through all the succeeding ages of antiquity. The Greeks imposed their Greek name upon the isles, when their predecessors and cotemporaries the Phenicians imposed none; because the Greeks gratified their national vanity in imposing them, and could perpetuate the gratification by their writings. They thus appear also to have done, what the Phenicians appear not to have attempted; to have not only prosecuted their voyages of commerce to the isles, but to have taken their stations at them, to have thence directed their voyages of discovery along the main land of Britain, and to have marked their courses by imposing their names as they sailed along. This is a circumstance utterly unnoticed hitherto, yet very obvious in itself.¶

G 2 As

language; though the very name of *Pict* is certainly derived from it, (Hist. of Man. i. ii. 2,) and with a variation similar to that of *Mictis*. Pryce alone, giving a word in his etymons at the end, that he gives not in the body of his work, says thus: "Pen *With* the head of the *breach* or *separation*." "These islands," says Mr. Troutbeck, 189, "were first discovered by "*Hamilco*, a *Carthaginian*, belonging to the *Silures*, a *Phœnician* colony in Spain." Can words be more comprehensive of folly!

* Pliny iv. 16. "Timæus historicus a Britanniâ introrsus sex dierum navigatione abesse dicit insulam Mictim, in quâ "candidum plumbum provenia," &c. &c.

‡ Ibid. ibid. "Britannia insula, clara Græcis monumentis."

§ Strabo 220. Καττίτερον—γενναςθαι—εν ταις Καττιτερισι νησοις, και εκ των Βρεττανικων δε εις την Μεσσαλιαν κομιζεσθαι. See 752, 753, for Pompey.

‖ Pliny vii. 56. "Plumbum ex Cassiteride Insulâ," as one isle principally, "primus apportavit Midacritus." This name however, so plainly Græcian, as being Μιδας Κριτης, is violently distorted by Stukeley after Bochart into *Melcartus*, to make it a *Phenician* name, Stukeley yet acknowledging him as "the first bringing tin into *Greece* from the Cassiterid Islands." (Stonehenge 55.) He certainly meant *Gades* for *Greece*; or why by force does he give the name a Phenician cast of countenance? And the very force is conviction enough, against the user of it. No word, no name peculiarly, should be altered in an antient manuscript, without a *necessity* for the alteration. And to alter this into *Melcartus*, is to new-form the history in the mere impotence of servility to an hypothesis.

† Ουτε νησους οιδα Κασσιτεριδας εξ ων ο κασσιτερος ημιν φοιτα. "Neither do I know any thing of the isles the Cassite- "rides, being those from which the Cassiteros" or tin "comes to us." This Greek name of the isles must have been given by the first Græcian that visited them, Pytheas; his voyage therefore was prior to the history, and only just prior, I apprehend, about a century and a half after the first voyages of the Phenicians from Cadiz to Sylley.

¶ Dr. Borlase in Ant. of Cornwall 28, objects to Bochart concerning the Phenician navigators, that "if the Phenicians "had been near the Straits Mouth about 800 years before the reign of Pharaoh Nechao, viz. in the time of Joshua, it *is not* "*likely*—such enterprizing sailors should make that their ne plus ultra, *for so many ages*;" yet in p. 33 avers himself concerning

As they advanced from the Sylley Iſles to paſs up the Britiſh Channel, they took their departure from the Bolerium Promontorium, our Land's End; but gave it an additional appellation of their own; Ptolemy, a Greek like themſelves, noting expreſſly "ANTI-VESTÆUM Promontory, "which is alſo Bolerium."* But what can be the meaning of ſuch a name? The uſages of the Greeks in impoſing names, ſerve ſufficiently to explain the meaning. We have thus their Rhium and Anti-Rhium in antient Greece, their Bacchium and Anti-Bacchium in the Arabian Gulph, their Barrium and Anti-Barrium in the Adriatick, from the oppoſition of the one to the other.‡ We have alſo from theſe general denominators of half the globe, Libanus and Anti-Libanus, and (to come nearer home) Antipolis or Antibes, ſo named by theſe very merchants of Marſeilles, as ſtanding oppoſite to their previouſly founded Nicæa or Nice, but, to come ſtill cloſer to the caſe of our Anti-Veſtæum, a point on the continent of Phenicia itſelf denominated Antaradus, from its poſition over againſt Aradus, an iſle. We thus ſee the name of Anti-Veſtæum derived, from the name of one of the iſles which it confronted; *Veſt*, like the north and ſouth *Viſt* of the Hebrides. And we thus catch by reflection the original appellation, of another of the ten Caſſiterides. The Greeks then moved along the ſouthern ſhore of Britain, to that grand prominence in it, from or at which our own veſſels take their departure, or mark their return, the Lizard Point; and called it as Ptolemy calls it from them, "the DAMNONIAN which is alſo the Ocrinum "Promontory."§ The latter was the antient name, being the name equally of a long ridge of hills that runs from Bridgwater Bay to the Point,‖ and being the Welſh *Ochr*, the edged rim of any thing, *Ochros* or *Ochren* edged;¶ theſe hills, with this terminating prominence of them, being ſo called as the hills between Yorkſhire and Lancaſhire, are named Blackſtone Edge, ſome hills in Cheſhire are entitled Alderley Edge, or ſome in Warwickſhire are denominated Edge-hill.*† The Greeks afterwards advanced to that promontory near Plymouth, which we now denominate from a fanciful yet new imaginary aſſimilation of the land to an animal, the RAMHEAD in the pariſh of *Rame*; and, as to our agreeable ſurprize we find, in ſo aſſimilating or ſo denominating, we are only echoing the voice of the very Greeks, who called it as they called a point in the Euxine,

cerning the Greeks, navigators *as* enterprizing, that "*about theſe Straits* they *ſtuck and ſettled for ſome ages*." The doctor then fixes the Phenician diſcovery of theſe iſles about 600 years before our æra (p. 27), and the Græcian about 325, (p. 33). He thus overlooks the deciſive teſtimony of Herodotus, for the name of *Caſſiterides* impoſed by the Greeks upon the iſles, and for the conveyance of *Caſſiteros*, or Tin, from them into Greece, *even as early as* "Herodotus, who lived about 440 years "before our Saviour," (p. 29). The *deciſiveneſs* of this teſtimony, however, has been equally overlooked by all; in confining the trade to the Phenicians, when the Greek denomination of the iſles extends it equally to the Greeks.

* Ptolemy ii. 3. *Αντιουεσταιον ακρον το και Βολεριον*. Camden 136, who doubted whether the name was Greek, becauſe he could find no correſpondent name, applied to the Britiſh language for an explanation, but was equally at a loſs there; "cum nihil tale invenerim, ad Britannicam linguam me retuli, nec tamen hic me expedire poſſum." I feel a friendly concern at ſeeing ſuch a man ſo puzzled.

‡ Camden 136. Yet Mr. Gough in i. 3, comes with his "f. Αντιουεσκαιον, ſee Veſci, Veſca in Ortelius, Biſcaian." Half the *actual* uſe of learning is, to puzzle a plain ſubject.

§ Ptolemy ii. 3. *Δαμνονιον το και Οκρινον ακρον*.

‖ Richard 20. "A fluminis Uxellæ finibus continuum procurrit montium jugum, cui nomen Ocrinum; extremumque "ejus ad promuntorium ejuſdem nominis extenditur."

¶ In the Welſh, Awch is the edge of a weapon, Hogi to make a ſharp edge, and Ochri the ſame. I note theſe, becauſe Richards puts a query upon the meaning of Ochren. Analogy, that beſt guide in languages, ſhows determinately what it means.

*† Some doubt may be raiſed, whether *Tol Pedn Penwith* be not the Ocrinum or Damnonium promontorium, rather than the Lizard; as Ptolemy fixes the ſouth-weſtern angle of the iſland at it. But Richard's map ſettles the doubt at once, placing the promontory where it had always been placed, at the Lizard.

Euxine, Κριȣ Μέτωπον, or the Ram's Front.* But the Greeks ftill advanced up the Britifh Channel, and even denominated the Start Point in Devonfhire the HELENUM PROMONTORIUM, or Græcian Cape;† no longer contenting themfelves with giving Greek appellations to our fhores, but fixing upon them the very name of Greece, and fo fixing apparently upon *this* as the boundary of their range along fhore to the eaft. Thus given, the name fhows this expedition of Greeks along our fhore, to be *not* what I have felt inclined, as I proceeded, to confider it, as the very voyage of Pytheas himfelf into the German ocean and the North Sea; but the courfe of fome Greek merchants, exploring our coaft from Sylley, and denominating points in it as if thefe had never been denominated before. *We find no Greek appellations to the eaft of this.* But, what is very extraordinary, we can trace the fame fignatures of their coafting from Sylley, in the *Irifh* as well as the Britifh Channel. Immediately before the mention of Anti-Veftæum, Ptolemy notices what the Greeks had entitled Ηρακλεȣς ακρον, or the Promontory of Hercules, that hero of Greece for peregrinations as wonderful as his deeds; and what proves the familiarity of thefe Greek names among the very natives themfelves, a familiarity which could be introduced only by the Romans, we ftill preferve the Greek title in our Englifh of *Hert-land Point.*‡ The ifle of Lundy near it, fo inconfiderable even now as to have only one family upon it, was then important enough from its cliffs rifing up near eight hundred feet in height, and from its own projection of fourteen or fifteen miles into the fea, to have alfo a fpecifick appellation from the Greeks, to have one correfpondent with the other, and to have the dignified title of HERACLEA or INSULA HERCULEA,§ the Ifle of Hercules. But we crown all with THE PILLARS OF HERCULES, erected upon Hertland Point;‖ the evidently intended fignature of the limits of this coafting navigation to the north, as the Græcian Cape was to the eaft. Thus we actually find "altars erected for the limits of the "Roman empire, and Ulyffes faid after his ftorms on the fea, to have fulfilled his vows upon "them," at the borders of Caledonia.¶ From all we may fairly conclude, that though "the" written "monuments of the Greeks," in which "Britain was celebrated," have not reached us; yet we have enough of notices remaining, to fee how it was celebrated, by feeing the coafting navigation of the Greeks from Sylley in the Irifh as well as Britifh Channel, by marking the courfe of their progrefs along our fhores to the north as well as the eaft, and by obferving them to define the extent of their progrefs with either fignificant names, or fignificant erections. But at the clofe it is amufing to obferve, that thefe navigators of antient times failed along our fhores, and gave appellations to our promontories, with the fame curiofity of mind, with the fame adventuroufnefs of fpirit, with the fame unconfcioufnefs of our future confequence as a nation; with which we ourfelves

* Richard, p. 21. "Promuntoria—Ocrinum et Κριȣ μέτωπον. So Mela ii. 1. for the Euxine.

† Richard's Map "Helenum prom." and p. 20, 21. "tria promuntoria, *Helenis* fcilicet, Ocrinum," &c. Camden had caught fome rumours of this name, but fome that made him affix it to the Land's End. "Quodfi *Helenum* hoc promonto-"rium appellatum fuerit," he writes in 136, "ut Volaterranus et recentiores habent, non ab Heleno Priami filio, fed a *Pen* "*Elin* profluxit, quod cubitum Britannis fonat, ut *Ancon* Græcis." How ingenious, how judicious, yet how wrong!

‡ Ptolemy ii. 3, and Richard's Map "Herculis Prom."

§ Richard's Map, and p. 20, "non procul hinc Infula Herculea."

‖ Richard 20. "Vifuntur hic, antiquis fic dictæ, Herculis Columnæ."

¶ Richard's Map, "Aræ finium Imp. Rom." and p. 32. "Extructas ibi pro limitibus Imperii Romani fuiffe aras, Ulyf-"femque tempeftate fluctibufque jactatum heic vota perfolviffe."

ourfelves have been recently exploring the coafts of New Zealand or New Holland, in the fouthern hemifphere.*

The merchants of Marfeilles thus became fharers with the merchants of Cadiz, in the treafures of the Sylley Ifles. But their intereft equally inftigated them, to conceal the pofition of the ifles from all the reft of mankind. Even their near neighbours and firm friends, the Romans of Narbonne, at that time the greateft emporium of Gaul, and a diftinguifhed colony of Romans,† were not admitted into a fhare of the gainful traffick. In commercial tranfactions of fuch a nature, arrefting all the natural, all the honeft felfifhnefs of the human heart, and even compelling patriotifm itfelf to come in aid of felfifhnefs; there could be no neighbourly kindnefs fhown, and no partiality of friendfhip exerted. Hence the iflands were as much concealed as ever, from the reft of the commercial world. The Romans, however, made a bold effort to difcover the pofition of them, by fending out a veffel to hover about the port of Cadiz, to wait there the ftated outfet of the regular fhip for the ifles, to attend its courfe, and move as it moved to its deftination. The captain of the Cadizian veffel, who was equally the pilot and the proprietor of it, obferved the Roman and perceived his defign. Then, with a mixture of private and publick felfifhnefs, he formed a plan of deceiving him, and he executed it completely, at the rifque of his life, and with the lofs of his property. So valuable was the commerce in itfelf! So much were all the paffions of all the people engaged, in keeping it concealed! And to fuch heights of generofity did even felfifhnefs itfelf exalt the fouls of fome! He had juft left the harbour, he was near the coaft, he knew it well. To miflead the Roman, by carrying him off into the Atlantick, then doubling upon him in the night, and efcaping unfeen to the ifles; would not fatisfy his zeal for this endangered monopoly of the filver metal. He refolved to baffle the prefent, and to preclude a future attack upon the monopoly, by leading the Roman into a deftructive fnare. He accordingly fteered for a point of the coaft, where he knew the water to be fhallow and the bottom foft; where his fhip and cargo would be loft indeed, but the lives of the crew might be faved; and where the purfuing veffel with all her crew would be fure to be loft. Both the fhips *were* loft; but the Cadizian captain got to land with his men, returned to Cadiz, related the adventure, and was immediately indemnified for his loffes out of the publick treafury.‡ Romans however were not then inclined to defpair, under any difappointment. They perfifted in their efforts, and attempted (like the Maffilians) to explore the iflands by themfelves. They made many efforts for the purpofe, but were ftill baffled in their views. The falfified pofition of thefe ifles might well baffle them. They would feek the ifles where they were not to be found, on the north-weftern

* Richard, fo very ufeful in every part of Britain, in this has fallen into two grofs errours. Thus, p. 20, he writes in the following ftrain of folly, once thought to be merely Cornifh; "cum vero defertas propemodum et incultas Britanniæ partes "Romani nunquam falutaverint; minoris omnino momenti urbes eorum fuiffe videntur, et hiftoricis propterea neglectæ." In faying this, however, he is as contradictory as he is erroneous; he having the inftant preceding fpecified two towns, "Mufidum," in the map more properly *Mufidunum*, "et Halangium;" and he fpecifying afterwards thus, "urbes ha-"bebant—Volubam, Ceniam," &c. In p. 20 alfo, and in his map, he fplits one promontory into two; "geographis tamen "memorantur promuntoria Bolerium et Anti-veftæum," and "Bolerium prom." ftanding for one, Cape Cornwall (I fuppofe), but "Anti-veftæum prom." for another, the Land's End (I prefume).

† Diodorus Siculus i. 361. Weffelingius.

‡ Strabo 265. Των δε Ρωμαιων ναυκληρω τινι, &c. &c. How groffly erroneous then is Mr. Troutbeck, in p. 190, when he fays "the Romans, to find out their place of trade, employed *fome* of their veffels to follow a *Carthaginian* or "*Phœnician* in his voyage thither, who perceiving *their* defign, *rather than put into Scilly*, ran his fhip afhore *near the Land's End!*"

weftern coaft of Spain. And our Sylley would appear to them, as loft in clouds and enveloped in fogs. At laft their perfeverance was crowned with fuccefs. Some years before the entry of Cæfar into Britain, a merchant of the name of Publius Craffus, who deferves almoft equally with Pytheas to be recorded for the action, made his way fuccefsfully to thefe objects of defire and doubt. He appears to have been a knowing, thinking, judicious man. He faw their mines of tin, to be very fhallow. He beheld the owners and workers of them, to be living in a peaceable kind of plenty on their little iflands, and never venturing to fea any farther than Cornwall. He ufefully inftructed them therefore, to fink their mines deeper in the earth; and boldly advifed them to pufh over the ocean in order to vifit the ports of the continent.* In all this he feems to have acted a part equally difinterefted and dignified; with all the adventurous turn of a merchant then for gain, to have borne in his breaft the foul of a Roman, that actual conqueror of half the globe, and that afpiring fovereign of it all. But, as merchants are formed for gain and conquerors for glory, he acted affuredly like a merchant, and aimed to divert the golden current from its old channel to a new one. He aimed to begin the exportation of tin from the ifles by the natives, the tranfportation of it to the neighbouring fhores of *France*, and the confequent conveyance of it over land to *Narbonne*. He would thus cut off the envious monopolifts of Cadiz, from all participation in it; and his revenge upon them for their monopoly, would be complete. Having fought for the ifles in vain about Cape Finifterre, he would naturally take his courfe by coafting to the bottom of the Bay of Bifcay, up from it along the weftern fhore of France to Ufhant, and thence to the Sylley Ifles in fight. He muft thus have confidered Narbonne, even Spain itfelf, to be too diftant for fuch a navigation with fuch failors. He could have confidered France alone, the weftern fide of France, and the north-weftern extremity of it, as the only point of the continent acceffible to them, as the only point dividing from them "a fea" juft "wider than the fea "betwixt them and Britain."† The mines of Sylley at the time were merely fuch, as are denominated *Koffens* in Cornwall at prefent; the veins of metal being followed only, as the courfes of ftone are at prefent; and one fuch mine appearing large in one of the ifles at prefent.‡ But Craffus, in order probably to draw them into his meditated plan of diverting the commerce to Narbonne, fuggefted to them the mode of mining that was practifed on the continent, taught them to fink perpendicularly into the earth, and fo *for the firft time* introduced among us the formation of fubterraneous *lodeworks*. Yet thefe, as in the infancy of the practice, were only flight and fhallow; fome ftill appearing in one of the ifles, even near to the very *Koffen* above, none more than four fathoms in depth, but moft only fix or eight feet perpendicular.§ So ufefully did Craffus

* Strabo 265. † Ibid. ibid.

‡ Borlafe's Scilly, 45. "On thefe downs" in Trefcaw "we faw a large opening made in the ground, and dug about the "depth of a common ftone-quarry, and in the fame fhape. There are feveral fuch in the parifh of St. Juft, Cornwall," and there is one near Redruth, "where they are called *Koffens*, and fhew that the more antient way of mining was to fearch for "metals in the fame way, as we at prefent raife ftones out of quarries, which, as the metals bear no proportion to the ftrata "of ftone in which they lie, muft have been very tedious and expenfive."

§ Borlafe's Scilly, 45. "A little further" than the *Koffen* "we found a row of fhallow tin pits, none appearing to be "more than four fathom deep, moft of them no deeper than what the tinners call *Coftean* fhafts, which are only fix or eight "feet perpendicular." *Coftean*, fays Pryce in Mineralogia Cornubienfis 319, "from Cothas to find, ftean tin." This is too devious for admiffion. The word is *Cos ftean* wood-tin, as we have *Stean Coofe*, or Tin-wood, in St. Agnes. It is a term of diftinction, for tin raifed from fhallow works. So *Grain-tin* is the tin of ftream-works, *Mine-tin* that of fubterraneous works, and *Coftean*, ot Wood-tin, that of fuch fubterraneous works as were *the firft to be fupported by timber*, the prior mines needing no timber.

Craſſus adviſe, and ſo readily did the iſlanders adopt his advice! The hiſtorian, indeed, ſays expreſſly, that the iſlanders were "willing" to receive the information of Craſſus.* They readily received it in fact, we ſee from the remains; contraſted as theſe ſtrikingly ſtand, from their very vicinity to each other. And the advice concerning navigation was ſo amply carried into execution, that the very iſlanders of Sylley are celebrated by Feſtus Avienus in the fourth century, for men of high minds, great prudence, as merchants, and for great ſkill as pilots, in ſteering their veſſels of ſkins with dexterity through the vaſt ocean. The Greeks, who had given the iſles the name of Caſſiterides from their produce, gave them alſo the title of *Oeſtromenides* from the appearance of their inhabitants. Theſe, ſays Strabo, "are clad in black, wearing tunicks down to their ancles, girt about the breaſt, walking with ſticks, and *looking like the tragick furies*; they live generally "like Nomades upon their cattle, having metals of tin and lead."‡ This deſcription is very ſtriking. It ſhows us the iſlanders, even with all their aſpect of "Tragick Furies." to have been much more refined in their appearance than the other Britons. The ſkins and the body-paintings of the others are here exchanged, for clothes fabricated of wool, and dyed a black colour. The oppoſition is ſtrongly marked by this circumſtance alone. But the iſlanders had riſen to a ſtill higher degree of refinement. They wore their garments, as our clergy ſtill wear their caſſocks and gowns, as our females (thoſe conſtant leaders in refinement among us) equally wear their gowns and pettycoats, all flowing down to their ancles. They had even mounted to that luxury of refinement in our own faſhions, of walking with canes in their hands, and of wearing girdles about their breaſts. Thus do they juſtify what Diodorus has averred in general concerning the Britons about the Land's End, but what he certainly meant for theſe iſlanders alone; that they were "the moſt civilized of all the Britons.§ Their intercourſe with the Phenicians of Cadiz, and the Greeks of Marſeilles, had produced this improvement in the Britiſh aſpect, as from them they muſt have alſo derived by barter for their tin, the garments and the girdles which they wore. But in this ſtate of civilization, ſo much ſuperior to that of their countrymen, yet ſo totally unnoticed by modern hiſtory, how could they be aſſimilated at all to the Tragick Furies? Only from this caſual combination of ideas, I believe; that the furies upon the Græcian ſtage were attired in this very manner, with long garments of black, with girdles round their breaſts to bind up the garments, and with ſtaffs in their hands to ſupport their perſons; juſt as witches are equipped upon our own ſtage, with broom-ſticks, and clothes that have once been black, and hats that are ſteeple-crowned. The iſlanders, ſays Strabo, "are clad in black, wearing tunicks "down to their ancles, girt about the breaſts, walking with ſticks, and" *ſo* "looking like the "Tragick Furies." From this look the Greeks even proceeded, to give a new name to the iſlands, and to call them the OESTROMINIDES, or the Iſles of the Furies.‖ Accordingly Feſtus Avienus, totally

* Strabo 265.

‡ Ibid. ibid. *Ανθρωποι μελαγχλαινοι, ομοιοι τοις τραγοις.* Inſtead of *τοις τραγοις*, "like goats;" other copies read *ταις τραγικαις*, and the old Scholiaſt accordingly gives us theſe words in his Latin verſion, "Tragicis qui ſimiles Furiis." The juſtneſs of this reading, though the other has been adopted by the beſt editors, ſo much is excellence at times oppoſed to judicioufneſs! is fully evinced by the very appellation of Oeſtromenides for the iſles. Mr. Troutbeck ſays, p. 189, from this paſſage, that "the inhabitants lived by cattle," or rather "upon their cattle, *like the Nomades*," which is all that Strabo ſays; yet, as he adds to Strabo, "and ſtraggled up and down *like them*," he means like the Nomades whom he has omitted to mention, "without any fixed abode or habitation."

§ Diodorus.

‖ Richard 21. "Ultra brachium in oceano ſitæ ſunt inſulæ Syddiles, quæ etiam Oeſtrominides et Caſſiterrides vocabantur, "dictæ." The new name is derived from *οιςρομανια*.

in his defcription of the fea-coafts, fpeaks of thefe ifles by this appellation; and fays they ufed to be vifited for traffick not only by the men of *Tarteffus*, the *Cadiz* evidently of thefe times and the *Tarfhifh* of fcripture, but by thofe alfo who can in no fenfe be faid to have traded with the Sylley Ifles, except as the immediate anceftors of the Cadizians, the men of *Carthage*.

Tartefufque in terminos *Oeftrymnidum*
Negotiandi mos erat, Carthaginis
Etiam colonis.*
At the far-diftant ifles, *Oeftrymnides*
Did the *Tarteffians* ufe to have a trade,
The very colonifts from Carthage.

The authority of fuch a writer as this, confpires with the analogy of hiftory; to beat down the teftimony of Juftin, and to extinguifh the belief of modern hiftorians, concerning the equal origin of the Cadizians with the Carthaginians immediately from Tyre. Here the Cadizians appear, as all their hiftory fhows them to be, Tyrians fucceffively tranfplanted to Carthage and to Cadiz, even "the very colonifts from Carthage" itfelf.‡ And thus that Tarteffus or Tarfhifh, which has been long floating in uncertainty betwixt Carthage and Cadiz, is here fixed firmly for ever at the laft.§ But Feftus tells us what is ftill more important concerning thefe ifles, and fhows us the ready ufe made of Craffus's advice by thefe iflanders.

In quo infulæ fefe exerunt *Oeftrymnides*
Laxé jacentes, et metallo divites
Stanni atque plumbi; multa vis hic gentis eft,
Superbus animus, efficax folertia,
Negotiandi cura jugis omnibus;
Nullifque cymbis turbidum laté fretum,
Et belluofi gurgitem oceani, fecant;
Non hi carinas quippe pinei texere,
Facere remos non abiete, ut ufus eft,
Curvant phafellos; fed, rei admiraculum,
Navigia junctis femper aptant pellibus,
Corioque vaftum fæpe percurrunt falum.†
There raife their heads the ifles *Oeftrymnides*,
Lie loofe together, and in metals rich
Of tin and lead; the men are *very ftrong*,
Proud in their minds, but *in their conduct wife*,

H *Their*

* Camden 857. "Noftri," Pliny iv. 22, "Tarteffon appellant, Poeni Gadir," &c. &c.

‡ Juftin xliv. 5. "Cum Gaditani a Tyro, unde et Carthaginienfibus origo eft, facra Herculis,—in Hifpaniam tranftu-"liffent, urbem que ibi condidiffent," an account too romantick to be true! "invidentibus incrementis novæ urbis finitimis "Hifpaniæ populis, ac propterea Gades bello laceffentibus," the *Tyrians* (we expect) would affift their infant colony, but no! "auxilium confanguineis *Carthaginienfes* mifere. Ibi, felici expeditione, et Gaditanos ab injuriâ vindicaverunt," then "left them as Tyrians and Coufins, we anticipate, but no! confidered them as colonifts, "et majorem partem provinciæ "*imperio fuo adjecerunt*."

§ The voyage of Colæus to Tarteffus, *beyond the pillars of Hercules*, coincides with this. See Herodotus iv. 152.

† Camden 857. The text being corrupt, I have taken the various readings fuggefted by Nonnius or the Parifian editor, to make fenfe and grammar of it.

Their fouls are ever on their traffick bent;
Yet with no boats like ours do they attempt
The wide, the boifterous, monfter-breeding fea;
To form the keel of pine, as others do,
Or fhape the beech for oars, is not the way
They bend their fkiffs; but, wonderful to tell!
They make their veffels with conjoined fkins,
And range in leather o'er the wide-fpread waves.

So much was the genius of thefe iflanders changed, by this vifit of Craffus to them! So very different were they now become, from what they had been! From a life of peace and plenty on their little ifles, knowing nothing of the world about them, confidering the kindred ifle of Britain as a continent, an univerfe to them, and rich in a metal for which they had no ufe, from their want of knowlege in the qualities of the ore, and in the modes of manufacturing it; they were fuddenly vifited by fome ftrangers from a region, then thrown by the general ignorance of the world concerning its own geography, to the feeming diftance of half the globe from them. They were amazed undoubtedly at their drefs, fo fuperior to what they made for themfelves out of the fame materials with their very boats; at their perfons, fo ftrongly attefting the neighbourhood of their country to the fun; and at their fhips, fo ftrongly built, fo largely framed, fo plentifully provided with all kinds of ftores. Yet they would be more amazed, to hear of the vaft diftance from which the ftrangers had come, to find they had a perfon among them, a miner affuredly from Spain or Portugal, whofe eye faftened readily upon their tin ore, whofe hand eagerly picked it up from their brooks, and whofe tongue taught them to collect it carefully for the prefent, to feparate the metal from its adherences by water, and then to fufe it by fire into ingots. So commenced the mining for tin in Britain! It commenced at firft at the fouth-weftern angle, in one of its detached ifles there. It went on there, till the iflanders had been fucceffively taught by the Carthaginians of Spain, by the Greeks of Marfeilles, or by the Romans of Narbonne, to become expert miners, to rife even into bold mariners, and in their fea boats of fkins to explore that very continent, from which they had been now vifited by three different nations of it. Yet, what is perhaps more furprizing than all, this amufing, this inftructive portion of our Britifh hiftory, has never been called out into notice before; though it is fo neceffary to the origin of all our domeftick manufactures, and of all our foreign commerce; fo neceffary even to the hiftory of our commerce and manufactures afterward.*

To

* Dr. Borlafe has totally overlooked this paffage in his Scilly Ifles, important as it is in itfelf, and actually cited by Camden for him. Dr. Pryce, in his Min. Corn. writes thus wildly, for want of knowing the evidence above. " I hope the reader " will not judge it improbable," he cries, in the introduction, " if we fuppofe that the inhabitants of *Cornwall* and *Devon*, " after the flood, *were well acquainted* with tin in its *richeft* mineral ftate; for it requires no uncommon degree of intellectual " examination to comprehend, that, in *the earlieft ages* from that grand epocha, our richeft *fhode* and ftream tin muft have " been found" and fufed and fhipped to other countries; fo " that we fupplied *all the markets of Europe and Afia* with that " commodity, *in early ages*." So eafy is it to fabricate a fyftem, when we know not the facts, of hiftory! " From hence " we would infer," he continues to fay, in p. iii. " that all tin produced in the primitive ages of the poft-diluvian world, " was from ftream or *fhode*," the latter by cutting trenches in the ground in order to difcover veins of metal, " perhaps many " ages before deep mining was at all known." He overlooks the mode of mining by *Koffens*. " We have authority to fay " from Mr. Carew and a M. S. of Serjeant Maynard which we have feen, that the working of lodes was unknown to our an" ceftors *in the firft ten centuries after the Incarnation*; fo that we may reafonably conclude, our lode or mine works are *not* " *700 years ftanding*." They appear above to have begun in Sylley, *about the very period of the Incarnation itfelf*.

To what part of the continent, then, did the iſlanders of Sylley, thoſe earlieſt navigators and firſt merchants of Britain, tranſport their tin? To the region of the Veneti, and to the harbour of Vannes their capital, in Bretagné. We know the fact from the ſubſequent hiſtory. We are ſure that the iſlanders went to the continent, we naturally pitch upon the neareſt part of France as the point to which they went, and we actually behold the natives of this point trafficking afterwards with the iſlanders. "The Veneti," as Strabo obſerves with ſome little deflection from truth in the reaſon aſſigned, but in full accordance with my argument as to the fact alledged, "engaged in a naval war againſt Cæſar, *becauſe* they wiſhed to preclude him from his expedition "into Britain, AS THEY USED THAT EMPORIUM."* "The Veneti," adds Cæſar during this war, "have very many ſhips, with which THEY HAVE BEEN USED TO NAVIGATE INTO "BRITAIN."† But, as he afterwards adds concerning the Veneti, "they ſend for auxiliaries out "of Britain, WHICH LIES CONFRONTING THEIR COUNTRY."‡ And, as he finally ſubjoins with a peculiar reference to auxiliaries ſo ſought, "in almoſt all his Gallick wars he underſtood "auxiliary troops to have been FURNISHED FROM BRITAIN."§ The voyages of the iſlanders to Vannes were not frequent enough in themſelves, or the veſſels of the iſlanders were not roomy enough for ſtowage, or the navigation acroſs the mouth of our channel was not ſafe enough for them. For one or more, or all of theſe reaſons, the Gauls of Vannes, having once acquired an inſight into the traffick from the acceſs of the iſlanders to their port, ſoon ſuperſeded the neceſſity for this by repairing themſelves to the iſles. Then the experience of the Gauls in navigation, the firmneſs of their veſſels, the expeditiouſneſs of their movements, and their habits of commerce, would ſpeedily, without a prohibitory law, throw the whole trade of carrying, into the hands of foreigners again. In both theſe modes of management, however, the tin would certainly form a greater article of commerce than ever, be exported in larger quantities from the iſles, and be lodged almoſt entirely for ſale in the warehouſes at Narbonne.

But the current of commerce is perpetually ſhifting its channel. Some accident intervenes to obſtruct its courſe, or ſome opening is made for dividing its waters. Accordingly the trade for the tin of the iſles took a new courſe ſoon. All Gaul was reduced under the power of the Romans, and the commerce to Britain could be proſecuted upon a larger ſcale. It now became a national object, involved in it the intereſts of half the ſouth of the iſland, and was carried on by a combination of powers that appears gigantick in itſelf, if we compare it with the infantine weakneſs then of the mercantile mind in Britain. Even ſo early as the reign of Auguſtus, as Strabo informs us, "there are four paſſages out of the continent to the iſle familiarly uſed, from the "mouths of the currents of the Rhine, of the Seine, of the Loire, and of the Garonne."‖ The firſt "courſe, or that from the places about the Rhine," as Strabo himſelf explains his own meaning, "is not from the very mouths" of the Rhine, "but from thoſe neighbours of the Me-"napii *the Morini*, with whom is *the Ictium*," or port of Witſand.¶ This is the very courſe which was taken by the merchants of Gaul, near Witſand, in Cæſar's time, in which he meant

 to

* Strabo 297.
† Cæſar De Bell. Gall. iii. 8. "Naves habent Veneti plurimas, quibus in Britanniam navigare conſueverant.
‡ Ibid. 9. "Auxilia ex Britanniâ, quæ contra eas regiones poſita eſt, accerſunt."
§ Ibid. iv. 20. "Omnibus fere Gallicis bellis, hoſtibus noſtris inde ſubminiſtrata auxilia intelligebat."
‖ Strabo 305. ¶ Ibid. ibid.

to move for Britain himſelf, and concerning which he interrogated the merchants when he had convened them.* The ſecond is equally deſcribed by Strabo himſelf thus: " the Rhine upwards " may be navigated a great way, by large veſſels, thence the courſe is up the Arar and the Dubis, " but *there* comes a portage or carrying-place to the river Seine; down this river do they now go " to the ocean, the Lexobii, or the Caleti; and the courſe from them into Britain is leſs than a " day's ſail."† This commenced evidently at the mouth of the Seine, and ended plainly on the oppoſite coaſt of Hampſhire. The third is the very courſe that we have ſeen the iſlanders of Sylley firſt, and the Gauls of Vannes afterward, taking from the iſles to the continent; but on the deſtruction probably of the naval power of theſe primitive Venetians by Cæſar, had been removed from Vannes to Nantz, from the metropolis of the Veneti to the capital of the Monnetes, the building-yard of Cæſar's gallies for their deſtruction, and that harbour at the mouth of the Loire.‡ And the fourth was obviouſly another courſe from France to Sylley, one ſet up to ſhorten the carriage of the Sylley tin from Vannes, or from Nantz to Narbonne, by tranſporting it up the Garonne to Toulouſe probably, and then conveying it by a ſhort portage to Narbonne. So very important did the tin-trade of Sylley ſtill continue. It ſeemingly comprehended one full half of the whole trade of Britain. But it ſeems to have comprehended ſtill more, as another port of paſſage from Gaul into Britain had equally the tin for its commercial object. This is the ſecond of the four, ſo particularly deſcribed by Strabo above, as extending acroſs the whole continent of France from the mouth of the Rhone to the outlet of the Seine, and traverſing the channel to the oppoſite coaſt of Hampſhire. It terminated on this ſide of the channel, at the Iſle of Wight; as we find from a parallel paſſage in another hiſtorian, that relates to the ſame line of commerce, but is more circumſtantial in its narrative, and unites with Strabo's to complete the curious intelligence. Even while the tin of Sylley was tranſported by ſea directly to the Garonne and the Loire, it was equally tranſported, and in more than an equal quantity, I believe, from Sylley, by ſea, into Cornwall, and from Cornwall by land to the Iſle of Wight. There was it ſhipped off for the oppoſite coaſt of France, and gangs of horſes were then employed in conveying it acroſs the continent. Theſe traverſed the country from the channel to the Mediterranean, in thirty days generally; and depoſited their loads at the mouth of the Rhine. They were there put on board the veſſels which waited for them, and carried away to Marſeilles or Narbonne.§ This is a very intereſting account of our tin trade, and arreſts the attention of every hiſtorical mind ſtrongly. It proves the tin of Sylley to have been the grand export from Britain, and the mighty *medium* by which the commerce of Britain was chiefly proſecuted then. The depoſitory at the mouth of the Rhone was the city of *Arles* aſſuredly, which then lay immediately upon the margin of the Mediterranean, though it is now at a conſiderable diſtance from it; becauſe the Mediterranean has been retiring for ages from the ſouthern ſhore of France, as the ocean has equally been from the northern.|| But, in a few years, the active ſpirit of the merchants at Narbonne and Marſeilles, thoſe former contenders for the trade being now the purſuers of it in partnerſhip, improved even

* De Bell. Gall. iv. 20. † Strabo 288. ‡ De Bell. Gall. iii. 9.

§ Diodorus Siculus i. 347 and 361. Weſſelingius.

|| Wraxall's Tour, 121. " Freius, which is ſituated between Toulon and Antibes, where the Emperour Auguſtus laid up " his gallies after the battle of Actium, is now become an inland city." Aigues Mortes alſo, another port once, " is at pre- " ſent half a league from the ſhore." 122. Agde was made a port by Richelieu, in the room of it; but before 1670 Agde was rendered almoſt uſeleſs as a harbour. Then Colbert built Cette, and Cette is now obſtructed greatly by ſand.

even upon this plan of proceeding, and adopted what Strabo has defcribed to us before. They fent out large veffels immediately from their refpective ports, laden with proper commodities for the Britifh market. Thefe entered the mouth of the Rhone, and found in the addrefs of their crews the means of pufhing up that very rapid current, though the French dare not attempt to pufh at prefent, as far as Lyons.* There they left the Rhone for the Saone, advanced eafily up this gentle river, till it receives the Doux; and then took to the channel of the laft, though this is not navigable to the French at prefent.† When thus they had mounted within a few miles from the fource of the Seine, they un-fhipped their cargoes, carried them over-land to the current, and fo fell down with it to the ocean. They advanced therefore by the Rhone, the Saone, and the Doux, as high as Dole or Befancon, both of them the towns of the Romans, yet the only towns that the Romans had on the Doux; then formed a portage of fome miles to Troyes, I fuppofe, another town of the Romans; there embarked upon the Seine, to glide along it by Melun, Paris, and Rouen, to the channel; defcribing a line of inland navigation, which muft appear furprifing even to the prefent age, under all its improvements in managing rivers and conftructing canals for trade, as it interfected the whole kingdom of France from the fouth to the north.‡ But it alfo fixes our eye upon the Sylley Ifles, fhows thefe to be ftill the great fources of tin to the world, and proves them ftill to furnifh the great materials of our very extended commerce with the continent.

So important were the ifles of Cornwall then! Yet the Cornifh writers, in a continued paroxyfm of zeal for the continent, as oppofed to the ifles, have been long affecting either to deny or to difguife this account, to fubftitute Cornwall for Sylley, and to give that a fhare at leaft, even a principal fhare, in all the commercial glory of this. " The veftigia of any ten lodes, " mines, or workings, in the iflands of Scilly," cries the Cornifh Mineralogift, " are infufficient " to convince us, that they only gave this beautiful metal to the world: the remains of any fuch " workings are fcarcely difcernible; for there is but one place, that exhibits even an imperfect " appearance of a mine; and fo neceffary an appendage to a mine, as an adit to unwater the " workings, is not to be feen in all the iflands. If, in thofe days, the metal was produced from " ftream or fhode ftones only, we muft undoubtedly have difcovered in latter times thofe lodes or " veins, from whence they were difmembered by the deluge. Some remains of fuch lodes would " now

* Strabo iv. 175, fhows the *mouth* of the Rhone even then, to be entered with difficulty from the impetuofity of the current. " You cannot poffibly *return* by water" up the Rhone; " for *it is never practifed* on account of the rapidity of the " current, which frequently runs in the Rhone at the rate of feven or eight miles an hour." Gentleman's Guide through France, 149, 150. The boats, that go down laden, muft return un-laden, creeping along the fhore; ufing a fail fome times, as at entering the river, in order to ftem the current; and at other times taking advantage of thofe eddies, which are along fhore in all ftrong currents, and by which a part of the downward current is made to run upwards.

† Breval's firft Travels, i. 202.

‡ The Romans had once formed a plan for uniting the Mofelle with the Saone, fo making an inland navigation betwixt the ocean and the Mediterranean, (Tacitus Ann. xiii. 53.) This was a more circuitous one, than the courfe here. But this very courfe was projected in the prefent century, to be made *without a portage*. " When I was laft at Lyons," fays the knowing Mr. Breval, " an engineer had actually undertaken a junction—between the Rhone and the *Saone*," he means the *Seine*; " which was to be effected by means of the Armenfon and the Ouche." (Second Travels, ii. 116, 117.) In 1784 this junction was began to be made, with two others; one to unite the Rhone and Saone with the Loire, a fecond to unite the Rhone and Saone with the Ill, and the Rhine below Strafburgh, but the third to unite *the Rhone, the Saone, the Youne, and the Seine*. All were hoped to be completed before 1790. But alas! before 1790 arrived, a general fpirit of infanity had feized the whole kingdom, the French were eager to revert into their favage ftate again, and they plunged into Atheifm to reach it the fooner.

"now be visible on the sea-coast or cliffs, if any such had ever been."* I cite this passage only to show in a lively instance, how far the confidence of reasoning will go, in making strong assertions in the very face of facts opposed. The "one place, that exhibits an imperfect appearance "of a mine," is the one appealed to by me before, and thus described by Dr. Borlase himself: "this course of tin bears east and west nearly, as our loads, or tin veins, do in Cornwall; these "are the only tin pits which we saw, or are any where to be seen, as we were informed, in these "islands."† These are said too by Pryce, to exhibit only "an imperfect appearance of a mine;" merely because they are what Dr. Borlase himself calls them, "shallow tin-pits, most of them no "deeper than what *the tinners call Costean shafts*."‡ They are therefore real, perfect mines, and familiar as such to the tinners of Cornwall. Nor is the other assertion true, that "an adit to un-"water the workings is not to be seen in all the islands." At the very place to which he is here alluding, at this "even imperfect appearance of a mine," is actually an adit. The fact may seem astonishing after the averment. But it is mentioned by the very author, to whom Pryce is tacitly referring for an account of these shallow tin-pits. "To the west end of these pits," cries Dr. Borlase, "there is THE MOUTH OF THE DRAIN OR ADIT."§ The islanders of Sylley are thus found to have not only reduced the advice of Crassus into practice, by sinking shafts perpendicularly in the earth, but to have added to their shafts, shallow as they were, what seems to be necessary to deep mines alone, and what is certainly a bold operation of the mining genius, a tunnel under ground for diverting the waters that break in upon the mines. Nor is the insinuation one iota truer, than the assertions before. Lodes or veins of tin are actually "visible on the sea-coast or "cliffs." They are actually noticed as visible, by Dr. Borlase himself. "Nothing surprized me "more," he tells us, "than that there should be *so few* veins in the rocks of these islands."‖ There are *some*, therefore. "I saw one vein," he adds, "at Trescaw," even the very course of tin noticed in the *Costean* shafts before. So exceedingly unfortunate is Dr. Pryce, at that place; falling into the shafts repeatedly, and hazarding his neck at each fall! This vein "might be two "feet wide, on a cliff near a place called the Gun-well." But "there was" also "a very nar-"row one, on the same island," even "under Oliver's Battery."¶ Nor is this all the evidence that we have of the remaining mines in Sylley. "The former," observes Dr. Borlase, "has been "worked for tin, and has several shafts and burrows on the course of it," as indeed we have seen before, "the only ones in all Scilly; the other we could perceive no metal in."*† Such existing remains, however, raise in us a high degree of wonder at the boldness and rashness of Pryce. Yet our wonder still rises as we proceed. "I saw two veins," subjoins the same author, "about "two inches wide, running through the rocks on the back of the pier at St. Mary's." Even "a "gentleman with me," again notes the author, "thought he found one vein in Porth-Mellyn "cove."*‖ Nor is this all the evidence, which his own author was continually holding up to the eye of Pryce, even while he wrote. "There may be also tin-veins," his author ingenuously acknowleges, "in those cliffs which we did not visit, although the inhabitants upon enquiry could "not recollect, that they contained any thing of that kind; as the *Guél* Hill of Brehan, *Guel* Island, the name *Guél* (or *Huêl*) in Cornish, signifying a working for tin."†‡. So Camden argued

* Min. Cornub. Introduction iv. † Scilly Islands, 45. ‡ Ibid. ibid. § Ibid. ibid. ‖ Ibid. 71. ¶ Ibid. 72. *† Ibid. ibid. *‖ Ibid. ibid. †‡ Ibid. 73, 74.

gued to prove the Sylley Iſles the Caſſiterides, (for even this, it ſeems, was doubted very recently by ſome,) "principally from this circumſtance, that they have what no other iſlands in this tract "have, *veins of tin*, and two of the leſſer iſles, *Minan*-witham and *Minuis*-iſand ſeem *to derive* "*their names from mines*."* And, to cloſe all with another teſtimony from Dr. Borlaſe, whom Pryce ſeems as little to have conſulted, as Dr. Borlaſe conſulted Camden, "I have been lately in-"formed," he confeſſes in a note, "that under one of the cliffs of *Annet* there *is a load*, in which "there is *the appearance of tin*; and that *it looks as if it had been worked*."† So very groundleſs is Pryce's aſſertion, of there being little or no ſignatures of mines in Sylley, and abſolutely no remains of adits or of lodes within it! One mine, one adit, and ſeveral lodes, appear ſtill atteſted by names, or ſtill evident to the ſenſes. Even if no mine was to be found, no adit to be ſeen, and no lode to be traced; yet, after ſuch convulſions as the iſles are confeſt to have ſuffered, what would the objection avail? It would avail only to ſhow, that the mines were in the loweſt parts of the iſles, and buried with them in the overflowing ocean. This the Corniſh Mineralogiſt unconſciouſly allows, in alledging that, "unleſs we make great allowances indeed for encroachments "of the ocean ſince thoſe early ages, the iſlands of Scilly are merely in their preſent ſtate a cluſter "of barren rocks."‡ Every one, who knows the hiſtory, and views the ſtate of theſe iſles, *muſt* "make great allowance indeed for" thoſe "encroachments."

Yet, with all allowances, we have ſeen before, and ſhall inſtantly ſee again, many traces of mines in the parts preſerved of the old iſlands. Dr. Borlaſe was a mere viſitor to the iſles, and conſequently could not be expected to collect full information upon the point. But we have another writer, a reſident upon the iſles for years, no antiquary indeed, no ſcholar, but (what is better for our preſent purpoſe) an obſerver of what he ſaw, and a recorder of what he heard. This author has noticed many mines ſtill exiſting in remains upon the iſles, of which Dr. Borlaſe knew nothing. In St. Mary's, he tells us, "at a little diſtance from the entrance of the garriſon, on "the outſide of the lines, is AN OLD TIN PIT, wherein ſome miners were *lately* employed; but, "as they could not raiſe ore of a quality and quantity ſufficient to defray the expence, they were "diſcharged."§ In the very ſame iſland, "on the ſhore of Toll's Porth, cloſe by" a breaſt-work, "are TWO OLD TIN PITS, partly filled up, one of which is now about ſix feet deep, and near "four feet ſquare."|| In St. Martin's Iſle, "a little to the weſt" of Burnt-hill, "is Culver Hole, ſuppoſed to be AN OLD TIN-WORK;" and at Wine Cove, "cloſe to the ſhore, is a round hole, "twelve feet deep, and ſeven feet diameter, ſuppoſed to have been A TIN PIT."¶ In White Iſle, "on the eaſt ſide, a cavern goes in under ground ſo far, that no perſon now living ever ſaw the "farther end of it; I heard a cuſtom-houſe officer ſay, that he went in ſo far in a direct line, in "ſearch of run goods, that he could not ſee the light from the entrance, and that he was afraid "to go further in, leſt he ſhould meet with water or ſome other danger; it is ſuppoſed to have "been AN OLD TIN-WORK, its direction is eaſt and weſt."*† In Treſco Iſle, "on the north "ſide of" Tregarthen-hill, "is AN OLD TIN-WORK, cloſe to which is" what analogy ſhows to be

* P. 857. "Quod caput eſt, cum Stanni venas habeant, ut nullæ aliæ hôc tractu inſulæ, et a fodinis duæ minores, "*Minan-witham* et *Minuis-iſand* nomen duxiſſe videantur." *Menawethan* is one of the eaſtern iſles, but *Minuis-iſand* exiſts no longer under that name. The only names approaching to this, and equally derived from mines perhaps, are Great *Minalto*, Little *Minalto*, *Mincarlo*, and *Menarvorth*.

† Scilly Iſles, 73. ‡ P. iv. § Troutbeck, 53. || Ibid. 102. ¶ Ibid. 110. *† Ibid. 111.

be another, " a ſubterraneous cavern called *Piper's Hole*, which goes in about ſixty fathoms un-" der the hill from the ſea-ſhore; in the middle of this cavern is a pool of freſh water, about " twenty fathoms over and three fathoms deep," a *Koffen* probably, filled up with water; " this " cavern is from ten to twenty feet wide, and about the like in height."* But " on the north-" weſt ſide of Tregarthen-hill is the head of a pond, which is ſuppoſed to have been for WASHING " TIN ORE in ancient times;" while " at the moſt northern extremity of Treſco iſland is a ca-" vern under ground, about twelve feet in height to the roof, and about three feet wide, and " which runs under ground about ſeventy feet; near which is another cavern, about twenty feet " high, which goes under ground about ſixty fathoms, and about ten feet wide; theſe caverns are " ſuppoſed to be OLD TIN-WORKS;" and " at the eaſt-ſide of the entrance of New Grimſby " harbour is a cavern, that goes eaſt north-eaſt under ground about twenty fathoms, ſuppoſed to " have been AN OLD TIN-WORK."† Theſe caverns ſhow us the iſlanders purſuing the inſtruc-tions of Craſſus, not merely in ſhallow *Coſtean* ſhafts ſunk perpendicularly, but improving in con-rage, advancing in ſkill, ſo as to ſink ſhafts to a conſiderable depth; yet in a manner that ſtill marks their half-timidity and half-ignorance, by ſinking their ſhafts half-horizontally, going by a gradual declenſion into the bowels of the earth, and ſo forming a proceſs in mining that was very natural in itſelf, but has never been noticed (I think) as either actual or probable. And theſe ſerve happily to point out to us another cavern, that has all the features of a tin-work, yet has never been ſuppoſed one, " a large ſubterraneous cavern" in St. Mary's, " which is called " *Piper's Hole*," like one in Treſco above;—" going in at the orifice, it is above a man's height, " and of as much ſpace in its breadth, but further in grows narrower and lower;—ſtrange ſtories " have been related of this place, of men going in ſo far that never returned; that dogs have en-" tered here and gone under ground *ſo far as the iſland of Treſco*, where, *at another orifice of the* " *ſame name*, upwards of four miles diſtant, they have come out again with moſt of their hair " off."‡ Upon one ſide of the laſt-mentioned tin-work in Treſco, " about a furlong north from " the old caſtle, is ANOTHER OLD TIN-WORK."§ So pregnant with tin does this ſingle iſle ap-pear to have once been! Yet we have even another relique of its mines to mention. " About " a quarter of a mile weſt ſouth-weſt from the Blockhouſe," continues our uſeful informant, con-cerning theſe ſignificant remains in the Caſſiterides, yet all inſenſible of their ſignificancy, " upon " the top of the hill is a natural rock, about nine inches from the ſurface of the ground, with a " round hole in its centre, eight inches (in) diameter, ſuppoſed for an upright poſt to work round " in; and, at the diſtance of two feet from this hole in the centre, is a gutter cut round in the " rock out of the ſolid ſtone, fourteen inches wide, and near a foot deep, wherein a round-ſtone, " four feet diameter and nine inches thick, did go round upon its edge, like a tanner's bark-mill, " which is worked by a horſe; the round ſtone has a round hole through its centre, about eight " inches diameter: this is ſuppoſed to have been A MILL FOR THE PURPOSE OF PULVERIZING " THE TIN ORE in ancient times, and worked either by men or a horſe, before ſtamping-mills " were known of the preſent conſtruction,"‖ and, as " at the north-eaſt end of Annet Iſland is " an opening, which comes in from the ſea, about forty yards long, near ten feet wide, and " about twenty deep wide, called Lake Anthown, which goes in under ground, and is ſuppoſed " to

* Troutbeck, 124. † Ibid. 125. ‡ Ibid. 58. § Ibid. 125. ‖ Ibid. 133, 134.

"to have been AN OLD MINE," and an "iron" one, "becaufe the rocks here have the appear-"ance of iron ore," when the ifles never in any age produced any iron, and the mine muft certainly be what all the others of thefe ifles are, tin;* fo are there other caverns in the ifles that were tin mines originally, as in St. Mary's "a cave among the rocks, called Tom Butt's Bed, "which is very dangerous and difficult to get at, the ground being fo fteep about it,"† or "a fub-"terraneous cavern called Darraty's Hole, where fmugglers fometimes conceal run goods,"‡ or in St. Martin's "a fubterraneous cavern called the Pope's Hole, about fifty fathoms under the "ground, into which the fea flows, above ninety feet high from the level of the water."§ We thus find the mines of the antient iflanders, in the traditions and in the remains exifting upon the iflands at prefent. We even find a *buddle-pool* and a *ftamping-mill* of the antients, ftill exhibited to the eyes of antiquarian curiofity. We therefore cannot but wonder at the negligence in Borlafe, that could ever fpeak of the fewnefs of the reliques ftill preferved, from the mines of thefe celebrated ifles of tin; and condemn the prefumption in Pryce, that could ever venture to affift either their nothingnefs or their exiftence.

But as to the crowning effort made by Borlafe and Pryce, in conjunction, for diverting Diodorus's account of the tin conveyed to his *Ictis*, or to the *Ifle of Wight*; it is fo full of folly, as reflects infinite difgrace upon the judgments that could make it. By this, avers Dr. Borlafe, Diodorus "means one of the Scilly Ifles, to which they conveyed their tin before exportation from the "other fmaller iflands."‖ But Diodorus expreffly tells us, that the tin was carried to his Ictis in *wains*.¶ This fingle circumftance overfets the whole argument. I need not appeal to the courfe of the navigation for this tin, from the mouth of the Seine to the coaft of Britain oppofite, when there were two courfes more to the weft, from the Loire and from the Garonne; in order to prove the Ictis to be what its name tells us it was, the Ifle of Wight. And as to the fancy which Pryce has borrowed from Hals, of the Ictis being a name ftill preferved in that of "Car-ike road, "the chief part of Falmouth harbour, and Arwyn-ike and Bud-ike lands;"*† it is fuch a ringing of changes upon the name, as is fit only for a cell in St. Luke's Hofpital. I fhall only add therefore, that at this period, when the tin became fuch a valuable article of commerce, was carried by fo many different channels of conveyance into France, and one of thefe a conveyance by land through the whole length of Cornwall; the tin of Cornwall probably came firft to be fought. It was certainly fought by mining at a period juft like this, when the Britons had *not yet* learned the ufe of the mining inftruments of the Romans. "It is fuppofed," cries Norden with a ftrange fubftitution of Jews for Britons, "that the Jewes firft endeavoured to dyve into their rocks," thofe of the Cornifh, "for this commodious minerall; though they then wanted theys prevayling inftruments, "which latter times doe afford. Their pickaxes were of weake mater to comaunde the obdurate "rockes, as of holme, of boxe, hartes horne, and fuch like, which kinde of tooles," obvioufly thofe of the primœval Britons, and anterior to the familiar ufe of iron, "MODERN TYNMEN "FINDE IN OLD FORSAKEN WORKES."*§ So plainly did the Britons work in the mines of the Cornifh continent, *before* the Romans came to conquer them, and fo take them into the great fociety of civilized men! But the argument is enforced, by the appearance of the Romans themfelves

* Troutbeck, 158. † Ibid. 82. ‡ Ibid. 94. § Ibid. 105. ‖ Scilly Ifles, 76. ¶ Αμαξαις.
*† Min. Corn. v. *§ Norden ii. 12.

felves in thefe mines. "The Romans alfo in their time," adds Norden, "tooke their turne to "fearch for this comoditie," tin, "as is fuppofed" and demonftrated "by CERTAYNE OF THEIR "MONIE, which HAVE BENE FOUND IN SOME OLD WORKES revewed."* And, as Leland informs us concerning a difcovery in his own time, "there was found *of late yeres fyns* fpere heddes, "axis for warre, and fwordes" all "OF COPER," all Roman or Roman-Britifh, "wrappid up "in LYNIN," introduced by the Romans, "and perifhid, *nere* the *Mount*, in *St. Hilaries paroch*, "in TYNNE WORKS."† Thefe works would naturally commence at the points neareft to Sylley, and thence advance to the eaftward. They had then proceeded under the Romans, as far as the Mount; proceeded afterwards, but ftill under the Romans probably, to the eaft of the county; and concluded their march at laft, yet probably under the Romans ftill, by vifiting the weft of Devonfhire. The tin mines of Cornwall were affuredly worked with more vigour, as they would certainly be worked with more wifdom, by the Romans; than they ever were before the prefent century. The un-controuled range of our tin throughout their vaft empire, and by their means at times through all the nations around, even to India, in exchange for her jewels;‡ muft have lent fuch an encouragement to the miners, while it alfo opened to them fuch myfteries of mining, theoretical or practical, as no other period of our hiftory could either open or lend. The prefent mode of lining the infide of our copper pans with tin, fo neceffary to our health, fo gratifying to our delicacy, and fo largely multiplying the calls for tin among us; commenced among the Romans, commenced early among them, but was firft practifed by the Gauls under them, even fo ingenioufly practifed, that filver, the ufual lining of fuperior fauce-pans before, could hardly be diftinguifhed from tin now; and thus was one grand caufe probably of fuch large demands from Gaul for the tin of Sylley. §

This ifle ranged *then* all under the eye from the high grounds of the Land's End, much lower than thefe grounds, extending from that prominence on the eaft, to the rock on the fouth-weft, about thirty miles in length. "There is," cries Mr. Troutbeck, fettling what none of our maps, none of our charts, none of our hiftories fettles, "a very bad range of rocks that lies between "Scilly and the Land's End, *about three leagues eaft north-eaft* from St. Martin's Head," which head (as the author fays in another place) "bears due eaft about ten leagues diftant" from the Land's End, and fo feven leagues weft of the Land's End themfelves, "called the SEVEN STONES, very "dangerous to fhipping coming from abroad, as well as for coafting veffels."|| Accordingly we find his Majefty's floop the Lizard was loft upon the *Seven Stones* in February 1747, and all her crew drowned.¶ Others have been equally loft.*† But, as the author adds in direct conformity to

* Norden, 12. "For "revewed" read perhaps "renewed."

† Itin. iii. 17, 18. Norden 37, fays thus: "nere this place," Moufehole, when the difcovery was fome miles from Moufehole, "as Hollinfhed reporteth, certayne tynners in their mineralls founde armour, fpear headdes, fwordes, battle "axes, *and fuche like*, of copper, wrapte up in lynnen clothes, *the weapons* (the cloth) not muche decayde." Camden 137. "Dum ftannum effoderetur, cufpides, fecures, et gladii æenei lino involuta reperta erant."

‡ Pliny xxxiv. 17. "India neque æs neque plumbum habet, gemmifque fuis ac margaritis hæc permutat."

§ Ibid. ibid. "Vix difcerni queat ab argento." The Romans gilt their copper veffels for the kitchen, inftead of tinning them; and gilt them (my author incredibly adds) *without* as well as *within*. (Thickneffe ii. 96, from M. Seguier's collection of Antiques). In the Mufæum at Naples, replenifhed with the fpoils of Herculaneum, are "bronze pots and pans, *fome*," the fauce-pans, "lined with *filver*." (Gentleman's Guide through Italy, 283.) How tenfold more abfurd then does that etymology now appear, to which our Cornifh antiquaries have been for many years reforting, by taking the national name of Damnonii as *Dunmonii*, and explaining it to mean Hills of Tin-mines! It now appears *hiftorically* abfurd, *hiftorically* falfe, *hiftorically* impoffible to be either true or rational.

|| P. 163, 139. ¶ Ibid. 211. *† Ibid. 164.

to what we have heard from Dr. Mufgrave before, "this place is *good for fifhing*, and is *frequented* "by the Scilly *fifhermen* in fummer."* And juft nine furlongs from the Land's End, a little fouth of the weft, is another range of rocks, that is denominated the LONGSHIPS, that extends in a line obliquely abreaft of the Land's End, that in 1786 had a Swedifh veffel ftriking upon them,† that have affuredly had many others before or fince, but have very lately been crowned with a light-houfe upon the largeft of them, a tall, round, big rock in the middle of them. The ifle then appears to have been divided from Cornwall by a channel fomewhat more than ONE mile wide, and ftretching from the Land's End to the Longfhips, but narrowed more than a third of this breadth by a fhoal on the eaft of the Longfhips, that is called *Kettle Bottom* from its form, and has only one fathom of water upon its northern end, with two fathoms on its fouthern. Such *is*, fuch *was* the *Frith* of Solinus, narrow indeed, and therefore *turbulent*, yet deep enough at prefent, to lend a fafe paffage between Cornwall and Sylley to any veffel that draws not more than twelve fathoms. But the ifle was terminated on the fouth-weft by lofty hills, terminated on the north-eaft by hills not fo lofty, yet tall, one in the middle particularly tall, and having a plain extended between both. In this plain, and about two thirds of the diftance from that end of it, appears to have been a town, denominated by the natives of the Land's End, thofe beft repofitories of fuch a tradition concerning fuch an object, the CITY OF LIONS; a *Lugdunum* or *Lyons* probably in Silura as in Gaul, fo named from its pofition on a knoll by the water, and thus giving the popular title of *Lyonois* in Gaul, of *Lioneffe* in Silura, to the region itfelf. The long plain of the ifle was overflowed at once; and nothing remained rifing above the furface of the fea, except the mountains to the fouth-weft, or the hills to the north-eaft. Thefe ftill reared their heads over the deluge around them, thofe in the fhape of ifles, but thefe in the form of rocks. And the fea, which is faid to be forty fathoms in depth at the Longfhips, is only twenty at the very *fide* of this drowned ifle, and not more than eight over the very plain of the ifle itfelf. Even fo, the fea muft have rifen at this extraordinary revolution in the world of waters, not lefs than ten or twelve fathoms in perpendicular height; as we muft allow the land an altitude before of two or four, to refift the violence and to check the overflow of the common tides from the Atlantick. But, what is a very remarkable coincidence in fact, though it has never been remarked before, the half-moon of Mount's Bay was firft formed at the very period, when the plain of Silura was covered with the ocean. A tradition prevailed *in the parifh of Paul* during the days of Camden, that *there* "the "ocean broke in with a violent courfe" into Mount's Bay, "and *drowned the lands in it*."‡ Worceftre alfo has united with Leland before, to affure us, that the Mount once ftood five or fix miles from the fea. The bay was confequently *all dry land* before, a plain of five or fix miles, running down to the margin of the fea, there guarded probably by a ridge of land from it, but opening at the *weftern* end to the violent preffure of the waves, fo fuffering the admitted ocean to exert its violence particularly upon the *weftern* fide of the plain, and thus making *Gwavas Lake* the deepeft part of the bay at prefent. This lake was evidently an houfe and eftate in the parifh of Paul before, as we find one houfe in Sithney denominated *Gwavas*, as we find another near it, denominated

* P. 164. † Ibid. 231.

‡ Camden, 136. "Hinc," from the Land's End and Bofcawen Woon in Burien parifh, "fenfim in Auftrum (Boream) "circumacto littore, finus lunatus admittitur, *Mount's Bay* vocant, *in quo* oceanum, avido meatu irruentem, terras demerfiffe fama obtinet."

nated Tre-wavas, and as we find a rock on the ſhore of this lake, denominated *Carn Gwavas* at preſent; becauſe the lake extends along the ſhore of Paul only, from Newlyn to Mouſehole, and the ſea ſtill pays what the land once paid, tithes to the church of Paul. Worceſtre accordingly aſſures us himſelf, with a comprehenſiveneſs which is very uſeful on the ſubject, that "there was "as well wood-land as meadow-land and tillage-land *between* the ſaid *Mount* and *the Iſles of Syllye*, "and A HUNDRED AND FORTY PARISH CHURCHES were BURIED IN THE WATER *betwixt* "this *Mount* and *Scilly*."* The whole extent of Mount's Bay thus appears to have been before, like the length of Silura, a plain formed into one or more pariſhes, decorated with one or more pariſh churches, and laid out in meadows, corn-fields, or woods. The pariſh-churches *between* the Mount and Sylley, could be only thoſe of Sylley, and thoſe of the Mount; the firm ground at the Land's End being incapable of yielding to the ocean, and leaving only the two extremities of the line to anſwer for the whole. Even thus, the number of pariſh churches loſt is ſo aſtoniſhingly great, as to baffle the power of evidence, to preclude the poſſibility of conviction. I therefore take upon me to reduce the number from 140 to 40, to ſuppoſe a miſtake very eaſy to be committed in numerical figures, to cut off what any daſh of the pen might caſually have created, the firſt figure, and ſo bring the enormous amount of the whole within the compaſs of credibility. Yet however inclined we may be to deduct from the amount, in order to reconcile the general fact to our reaſon; we muſt ſee enough of evidence, and feel enough of conviction, to acknowlege the fact in hiſtory, and to view the bay ſcooped out of the land by that grand inundation, which burſt in upon the body of the iſle. Thus the bay becomes as remarkable now as the iſle has ever been, for the irruption of the ſea into the ſhore, for the ſubverſion of churches by the violence of the uſurping waves, and for the interment of churches, villages, or towns in the very deeps of the dry land. Only, the principal ſcene of deſolation muſt have been within the iſle. An extent of *thirty* miles is *there* buried, while a range of *five or ſix* only is buried *here*. The inundation at Mount's Bay, therefore, is only a miniature copy of that in Sylley. Yet it is a faithful, a lively, a luminous copy. And, as our evidence for the copy is much ſtronger than for the original, the leſſer throws a light upon the greater, illuſtrates the deſolation of this by reflection from that, even unites with this to exhibit the deſolation in all its full ſcope of horribleneſs.†

Such was the grand blow given to the iſland! But it has received an un-interrupted ſucceſſion of blows ſince. The continued ravages of the ſea are equally apparent here, as at the Mount; but are much more diſtinctly traceable here, than there. When Athelſtan made his deſcent upon the iſle, this was in all its magnitude of ſize, and in all its multiplicity of mines. He found hermits, he found monks upon it aſſuredly, and combined the latter (as the former were not combinable) into a ſociety or college, at a place, that was then a part of Silura undoubtedly, denominated

* Worceſtre, 102. "Fuerunt tam boſcus quam prata et terra arabilis inter dictum Montem et inſulas Syllye, et fuerunt "140 eccleſiæ parochiales inter iſtum Montem et Sylly ſubmerſæ."

† Dr. Borlaſe, p. 90, mentions, "particularly a *ſtraight lined* ridge *like* a cauſeway, running *croſs* the *Old Town creek* in "the *ſouthern* ſhore of St. Mary's, which is now never ſeen above water." "In the *middle* of *Crow Sound*," on the *north* of St. Mary's, Mr. Troutbeck tells us in p. 165, "a fine regular pavement of large flat ſtones is ſeen, about eight feet under "low water at ſpring-tides." Are theſe one and the ſame, or are they as different as their poſitions? Either way, the Romans appear to have carried their roads with their conqueſt, over the iſles, as well as the continent of Cornwall.

minated Trefcaw (like our own Bofcawen) from the elder trees around it;* *Tre*-fcaw, becaufe it was a part of the great ifland then, and *Inis*-fcaw fince, becaufe it has fince become an ifland itfelf; yet with only an occafional ufe of the latter name, becaufe the former had been fo long in poffeffion before. The elder is ftill called the *fcew*, in the mixt language of Cornwall at prefent. In this part of Silura did *Athelftan* affuredly fix a college of clergy, with a church, as at Burian on the other fide of the channel; an abbey remaining here to the reformation.† The church and college are expreffly averred by Edward the Third, to have been "founded by our progenitors, "formerly kings of England."‡ Thofe took to themfelves, and even imparted to the whole ifland at times, the name of St. Nicholas; a hermit or monk undoubtedly, who had lived at the place in great devoutnefs, but whofe fame kept up continually before the reformation by the leffon in the church upon his feftival, has fince, from the lofs of that leffon "melted into air, into "thin air." All the iflands derive their original or prefent names, from fainted men, who had lived equally upon them.§ But the abbey had a kind of *royal* jurifdiction, over feveral of the ifles; a jurifdiction, that could have been conceded only by the *royal* proprietor of all. Thus "Reginald, the fon of the king," Henry the Firft, gives "to the monks of Sully," every *wreck* except whale and whale-fhip, made "at the iflands which they *poffefs wholly*;—that is, in *Rente-* "*men*," the original appellation of Trefcaw, or St. Nicholas's Ifle, "and *Nurcho*, and the ifle of "St. Elidius, of St. Sampfon, and of St. Teona."‖ Pope Celeftin alfo in 1193, confirming the adjunction of this abbey to the abbey of Taviftock, confirms the donation of "the ifle of St. "Nicholas, the ifle of St. Sampfon, the ifle of *St. Elidius*, the ifle of St. Theon, and the ifle which "is called *Nutho*."¶ Thefe then were all of them the property of the abbey at Trefcaw, being at prefent Trefcaw ifle, Samfon ifle to the fouth-weft of it, *Nut* Rock, then an ifle, but now a rock merely, to the fouth, *St. Helen's* and Tean ifles to the north-eaft. The four laft mark the extent of the firft, being parts undoubtedly of the fame ifle when they were given by Athelftan, and even with it parts of the great ifle Silura.*†

Thus endowed, the collegiate church of St. Nicholas, in Trefcaw, was the mother or prefiding church to *all* the ifles; the charter of Pope Celeftin granting with the five ifles above, "*all* the "churches

* Leland's Itin, vii. 116. "Ther is a nother cauled *Iniffchawe*, that is to fay, *the Ifle of Elder*, by cawfe yt bereth "ftynkyng elders." Hals 41. Bofcawen "antiently, it feems, produced no other trees than *Scawen* (i. e. elder) proper to "thofe parts of the country; neither, I think, is (are) there any other trees at prefent, that grow there." *Bofcawen* is *Bod Scawen*, the Houfe of Elders.

† Borlafe's Scilly Ifles, 44.

‡ Monafticon i. 1002. "Prioratus Sancti Nicholai in infulâ de Sully, qui per progenitores noftros quondam Regis Angliæ, "fundatus et de patronatu noftro exiftit." This record is ftated by Borlafe 103, to be that "of Edward the Firft," becaufe the king is amply ftyled "Edwardus" in it, not "Edwardus tertius." But the date is a much more decifive circumftance; and the writ is dated "anno regni noftri quadragefimo primo." The firft Edward reigned only 34 years, but the third 50. And, as what the doctor fays in 104, 105, concerning Blankminfter, is founded upon this falfe date, it falls with it.

§ "It is handed down by tradition among the iflanders" of St. Agnes, "that St. Warna came over from *Ireland* in a little "*wicker boat*, covered on the outfide with *raw hides*, and landed here in this" Sancta Warna "bay." (Troutbeck 149.)

‖ Monafticon i. 1002. "Reginaldus Regis filius.—Sciatis me pro animâ Henrici Regis patris mei et meâ, et *pro cartâ* "*ipfius quam vidi*, conceffiffe et confirmaffe—omne *wrec* quod in infulis quas ipfi totas tenent advenerit præter cetum et "navem integram, hoc eft, in Rentemen, et Nurcho, et infula Sancti Elidii, et Sancti Sampfonis, et Sanctæ Teonæ."

¶ Ibid. 998. "Infra infulas etiam de Sully infulam Sancti Nicholai, infulam Sancti Sampfonis, infulam Sancti Elidii, "infulam Sanctæ Theonæ Virginis, et infulam quæ Nutho vocatur."

*† "The chief divifion," fays Dr. Borlafe 61, concerning thefe parts, "was called St. Mary's, in honour of the Virgin "Mother," when it was fo called undoubtedly from the faint of the church, and when this was *not* "the chief divifion," but Trefcaw was; "the next dedicated to St. Nicholas, the general patron-faint to all feafaring people, the other to St. "Martin, St. Sampfon, and fo on." The ideas of the doctor were not fufficiently Cornifh, here. He refers names to the faints of other countries, when they are all local; and attributes them to characters, when they belong merely to churches or oratories.

" churches and oratories conftructed through *all* the ifles of Sully, with the tithes and obventions, " and other their appertinances."* There were even then feveral oratories, and feveral churches, in the ifles; churches and oratories, which had efcaped the grand inundation, like the abbey-church, and, like it, were ftill ufed as the temples of the God of Chriftianity. But the metropolitical church had alfo poffeffions then, in the other ifles; the confirming charter above fpecifying equally with the other eftates of the abbey, " two *bofcates* of land in the ifle of *Aganas*, " and three *bofcates* of land in the ifle of *Ennor*."† The ifle of *Aganas* is obvioufly that of St. Agnes, fo diftinguifhed at prefent by what is denominated the Sylley Light-houfe; and *Ennor* ifle, or *Enmor*, as more properly called in a charter of the Third Edward, appears from the charter's mention of the King's Caftle and the King's Conftable within it, to be St. Mary's at prefent, with its Old-town Caftle, formerly the refidence of the king's governour of the ifles."‡ But the pofitions of thefe two eftates concur with all the evidence before, to fhow us St. Mary's and St. Agnes's ifles as parts of the ifle in which the abbey was placed originally, the *En Mor* or *Great Ifle*; as the ifle Silura, from its fuperiour largenefs to the nine ifles near it, here appears to have been called by the Britons, while all the ifles were denominated Siluræ or Silley. A fpecifick appellation was thus wanted peculiarly for the greater, and this was naturally given it in that of the Great Ifle. Yet fo prevalent was the old language ftill, concerning all thefe ifles; that even as late as 1367, almoft three centuries after the grand inundation, Edward the Third, in a writ of protection, fpeaks of " the *ifle* of *Enmour* in *Sully*," and of " *the priory of St. Nicholas* in the ifle," not ifles, " of *Sully*."§ All was one ifle at firft, guarded on the fouth-eaftern end by what is named the Giant's Caftle at prefent; a caftle placed on a high turret of rocks, that runs down fharply to the fea, but declines lefs fharply towards the land, that has on the fummit of the rocks a wall of ftone at the only acceffible fide, beyond this a tall rampart and a foffe ftill further fecuring this fide, as ranging acrofs the narrow neck of land from fea to fea, and beyond all another rampart with another foffe.‖ This is plainly a *Britifh* fortrefs, one built by the Britons in the firft ages of their wars, and exactly fimilar to fortreffes ufed by them againft the Romans. It was therefore formed by the firft inhabitants of Silura, and the only fortrefs probably oppofed to the Romans. But the Romans affuredly built another, and fo began a Roman town at the foot of it. " *Old Town*," fays Dr. Borlafe, " lies in the eaftern corner of a fmall cove or creek, fronting the " fouth, and was formerly the principal place of dwelling in all this ifland; but the houfes are " now poor cots with rope-thatch coverings: *behind them ftands an eminence, called the Old-Town* " *Caftle*, and part of the walls ftill remains."¶ This was entire in the days of Leland, and it is thus defcribed with the town by his pen, as the only town, with the only caftle in the ifle; " a " poore *town* and a *meately* ftrong pile."*† Such was the ifland then! Such, or nearly fuch, did it continue to the conqueft; when was built, I apprehend, what exifts only at prefent in " the " remains

* Monafticon i. 999. " Et omnes ecclefias et oratoria per omnes infulas de Sully conftructa, cum decimis et obven- " tionibus et aliis pertinentiis fuis."

† Ibid. ibid. " Et duas bofcatas terræ in infulâ de Aganas, et tres bofcatas, terræ in infulâ de Ennor."

‡ Ibid. 1002. " Conftabulario Caftri in infulâ de Enmour in Sully." Leland's Itin. iii. 19, and Borlafe 6. " This caftle," cries Mr. Troutbeck in a carelefs reference to Leland, " has *been a long time in ruins*, for Leland calls it a moderately ftrong " pile, *but difmantled*." How *could* even negligence mount up into interpolations?

§ Monafticon i. 1002. " Infula de Enmour in Sully," and " Prioratus Sancti Nicholai in infulâ de Sully."

‖ Borlafe 16, 17. ¶ Borlafe 6. *† Leland's Itin. iii. 19.

" remains of an old fort; it is a round hillock, and feems to have had a *keep* on the top of it, *in* " *the fame manner as*" thofe Norman conftructions, " *Trematon and Launcefton Caftles in Cornwall,* " but fmaller; 'tis called Mount Holles."* It ftands juft below the prefent lines, and " the walls " of it have been ftripped to build the lines."† It lies at the diftance of a mile from the *Old Town*, and fhews the Normans had then meditated what the Godolphins have recently executed, to fix the principal town where it is now fixed, having not any longer a cove " little, rocky, and " expofed to the fouthern feas," but " a large fandy pool, the neighbourhood of a peninfula " formed by nature for a fortification," and a hill for a caftle to protect the inhabitants.‡ On the fame hill, but higher up, even at the very fummit, did Sir Francis Godolphin, in 1593, erect *his* caftle with lines; and the town below is now, " the moft populous place in thefe iflands," for " here is the cuftom-houfe, and the principal inhabitants and tradefmen live here;" *that* and *this* taking from their Englifh fettlers, their Englifh titles of *Heugh* and *Heugh-town* at prefent.§

Giant's Caftle alfo fhews us the breadth of the Great Ifle, from north to fouth here; which was much greater however on the weft, from the north of St. Helen's to the fouth of St. Agnes. The whole, therefore, feems to have gone broad to the weft, and narrow to the eaft; about twenty miles perhaps broad at the weftern extremity, about ten perhaps in the middle, and contracting perhaps to five at the eaftern end. Such a configuration of the whole feems to be pointed out, by that of the parts at prefent; and plainly accounts with what I have faid before, for the fubmerfion of all the eaftern parts, as well as for the appearance of the weftern, at prefent. And an extent of thirty miles in length with ten at a *medium* in breadth, or a fpace of three hundred fquare miles, will admit *forty* churches, though it will *not* admit *a hundred and* forty, to have been conftructed upon it, to have been with it overflowed by the inundation, and to be now buried with it in the ocean.

Of all the ifles, St. Mary's is confidered now and was formerly confidered, as the principal; being formerly denominated Enmor or Great Ifle, and being now known as the largeft, the moft populous, the moft cultivated of them all. It has always with other ifles belonged to the crown, for the fame reafon that Trefcaw with its ifles belonged to the abbey, becaufe *that* was the eftate of the one as *this* was of the other. In the eftate of the abbey, however, was one portion of St. Mary's, the " three bofcates of land" mentioned before, and the *Holy Vale* plainly of the prefent times. This " is moft pleafantly fituated," as Dr. Borlafe informs us, " it lies warm, well ex- " pofed towards a little fouthern cove, called Porthelik, and fo well fheltered from the north, " that trees grow very well, of which a few tall trees now ftanding are a fufficient proof; and I " am perfuaded, that every kind of fruit-tree common in England might be propagated here with " great fuccefs: the houfe was formerly large and commodious, but was unhappily burnt down, " the

* Borlafe 12. † Ibid. ibid.

‡ Ibid. 10, 9, 10. The doctor intimates in p. iii. that " the lines were defigned to go quite round this *peninfula*, and are " well nigh completed, the whole circuit near two miles."

§ Ibid. 10, 12, 13. " A high ridge or tongue of land running out into the water," notes Dr. Borlafe 12, concerning the name of this hill and town, " is upon the fhores of the Tamar, near Saltafh, called Hue, otherwife Heugh; and among the " fifhermen, he who looks out from the high gronnd into the fea to difcover fifh, is faid to Heugh, and is called a Heugher. " Whether fuch ridges of land have the name from the ufe they are generally applied to in looking out for fifh, and the ufe " its name from *huer* or *heufe* (in French fignifying to fhout or make a noife) or from *hue*, colour and fhew; I muft leave " to etymologifts to determine. Certain it is, that fuch high lands as this in Scilly, are called in Scotland Heughs." They may well be fo called in both, the term being the Saxon *hoga* or *how* a hill. See Spelman under *Haga*.

" the ſpring before I ſaw it: the lands and gardens are much out of order at preſent, but ſeem all " to have had better times, the governors of the garriſon retiring hither formerly from Star-caſtle," Sir Francis Godolphin's fort, " as to their country ſeat. From the name I ſhould judge, that the " monks belonging to the abbey in the iſland of Treſcaw had a houſe and chapel here; but this is " only my conjecture."* In this conjecture the judgment was good, but the memory was bad. When he came, as in a ſubſequent page he comes, to refer to the very record which I have cited before, and to ſpeak of " two *pieces* of *digged ground* in the iſle of Aganas, and three in the iſle of " Ennor,"† as belonging to the abbey, he forgot the word in the original *boſcata*; for *boſcata* is plainly a meaſure of land, and that he was in want of ſuch an evidence before, for appropriating *Holy Vale* in accordance with its name to the abbey. Theſe three *boſcates* of land appear from the very term, to have been *woods* at the time of the grant; and therefore to have been cleared by the monks to whom they were granted.‡ On that ground alſo the monks appear to have erected, as Dr. Borlaſe well conjectures, " a houſe and chapel;" a houſe for the clergyman, and a chapel for the people, in this *remote* part of the Great Iſle *before* the inundation, and in this *inſulated* part *after* it. In ſuch a manner were the intereſts of religion provided for, I believe, till the reformation; when the houſe was ſeized by *the* ſacrilegious ſovereign princes, was then appropriated to the uſe of *his* governor of the iſles, and the chapel was turned into a dining-room perhaps. But what confirms my belief into aſſurance upon the point, no church appears in the whole iſland before; the preſent church being " not ſo old as the reformation," ſays Dr. Borlaſe himſelf,§ being alſo placed, as I add, not at Old Town, not at Heugh Town, but on the weſtern ſide of Old Town creek; too early for the removal of the town to the Heugh, yet with ſome meditated removal of it probably to a point lower down, and on the weſtern ſide, of its own creek.||

With the three boſcates of land belonging to the collegiate church of Treſcaw in St. Mary's, are mentioned two belonging equally to the church, but ſituate in St. Agnes. Here then, as well as there, would the college build a houſe for the clergyman and a chapel for the people. A chapel accordingly appears there, noticed by the pen of Leland. " St. Agnes iſle," he remarks in his brief and paſſing notes of things, " ſo caullid of a *chapel* theryn."|| But this chapel has been long gone, either buried in the ſtill encroaching waves of the ſea, or ſuffered to ſink into ruins from irreligion and diſtreſs united; this, with all the churches, except one in the off iſles, and except the one at St. Mary's which is built in the form of a croſs, being " all built by the family " of Godolphin," notes Dr. Borlaſe, " and I do not think any of them older than the reſtora- " tion;" being alſo plain, low buildings, of a nave without an aile, " from twenty-four to thirty- " two

* Borlaſe 14, 15.

† P. 102. Dr. Borlaſe ſhews us by his ſtrange language of " two pieces of digged ground," that he did not underſtand the original, that he ſaw not it meant a meaſure of land, and that he fancied " boſcata" was derived from *beſcher* in Norman, or *becher* in modern French, to dig. The word is plainly *boſquet*, a thicket, in French, yet plainly uſed for a meaſure of ground, as " three boſquets *of land*" can mean nothing elſe.

‡ P. 8.

§ " The original chapel of this iſland," ſays Mr. Troutbeck 59, 60, " is ſuppoſed to have been in Heugh Town, which is " now converted into a dwelling-houſe, where a great quantity of human bones were dug up, in conſequence of the great " overflowing of the ſea in the year 1744.—What ſeems to ſtrengthen this ſuppoſition, is a ſquare hewn ſtone which now " ſtands near by upon the quay, in the top of which is a ſquare hole, which ſeems as if it had formerly an iron cover, like " the poor man's box in the church. This is ſuppoſed to have been the poor man's box, when this chapel was in uſe. " The walls of the houſe, which was formerly the chapel, appear to be ancient and well built, and ſome of its windows are " caſed with hewn ſtone, like the old windows of the church; and the burial-ground, where the bones were dug up, is on " the ſouth ſide of the dwelling-houſe." The chapel cannot be older than the town, as it was plainly the chapel and burying-place of the town.

|| Itin. iii. 19.

" two feet long by fourteen wide," with a door in the middle of the ſhort length, a window on each ſide of it, and a chimney-like turret for a bell at the weſtern end.* The college thus erected a chapel and a chaplain's houſe, whenever it obtained an eſtate, in any of the *off-iſles*, as even St. Mary's itſelf muſt have been then called. We may therefore be ſure, that it would equally at leaſt erect them, if equally wanted, on *its own* iſles, Nutho, St. Elidius, St. Sampſon, and St. Teona. That on the firſt has been buried with all the iſle in the waves. One on St. Elidius or St. Helen's iſle appears to have been not wanted, as there was one built long before. " St. Lyda's iſle," Worceſtre informs us, is ſo named from one " who was the ſon of a king of ......"† and who lived here (we may be ſure) in great devoutneſs of ſpirit. But he was not (as we may ſuppoſe he was) one of thoſe hermits whom we have ſeen the firſt Henry noticing in his charter, as inhabiting the iſles of Sylley in the reign of the Confeſſor.‡ He was no hermit originally, and he lived long before the Confeſſor. He was a biſhop of Cornwall, before the very days of Athelſtan; and retired into this iſle, to ſpend the cloſe of his days in ſolitary devoutneſs. " The feſtival-day of St. Elidius, the biſhop," ſays Worceſtre from the very calendar of *Taviſtock* abbey, and conſequently from the very calendar of the college at Treſcaw, " is on the eighth of " Auguſt: HE LIES IN THE ISLAND SYLLYS."§ He was buried in the church of the iſle, within a chapel annexed to it; as is plain from a hint in Leland's account of the iſles, and from Dr. Borlaſe's deſcription of the church. " Saynct Lide's iſle," notes the former, " wher yn tymes " paſt at her (his) SEPULCHRE was *gret ſuperſtitioun*."‖ And, as the latter tells us, " the church " of this iſland is *the moſt ancient* chriſtian building in all the iſlands: it conſiſts of a ſouth-iſle," the real nave or body of the church, " thirty-one feet ſix inches long, by fourteen feet three " inches wide; *from* which two arches, low and of uncouth ſtyle, open into a north iſle," really a lateral chapel, in which St. Elid was buried, " twelve feet wide by nineteen feet ſix inches long; " two windows in each iſle," two in the nave, and two in the chapel; " near the eaſtern window " in the north iſle" or chapel, " projects a flat ſtone to ſupport, I ſuppoſe, the image of the ſaint " to whom the church was dedicated," or rather, the ſaint who was buried in the chapel and to whom *it* was dedicated.¶ And *in* this chapel, *to* this image, but *at* the " ſepulchre" beneath it, was undoubtedly ſhown the " gret ſuperſtitioun" noticed by Leland. We thus find a church exiſting in one of the Sylley Iſles, of the moſt remote antiquity in the eſtabliſhment of the goſpel upon the land of Britain. It is more antient than the ſaint, who was firſt revered at his " ſepul-" chre" in the chapel, then communicated his name to the church, and afterwards extended it over all the iſland. The ſize of the church too, about ten yards long and five wide, with only two windows in it; even the " two arches" from it into the chapel, though later in time, yet " low and of uncouth ſtyle;" and the form, ſo exactly correſpondent with that of our old churches in Cornwall, in having a nave and a chapel at its ſide; all unite with this attributed antiquity, and carry up the erection of the church probably to the very eſtabliſhment of the goſpel in Britain. As to the churches of St. Sampſon's and St. Teona, what ſhall we ſay? They had each a chapel upon them, we may be ſure from their bearing the names of ſaints, and from their being the pro-

K perty

* Borlaſe 39. † P. 98. " Inſula Seynt Lyda, fuit filius Regis ......"
‡ Monaſticon i. 1002. " Terram ſicut unquam monachi aut hæremitæ—eam tenuerunt tempore Regis Edwardi."
§ P. 115. " Sancti Elidii epiſcopi, 8 die Auguſti, jacet in inſulâ Syllys."
‖ Itin. iii. 19. ¶ P. 51.

perty of the college. St. Sampſon's has no chapel and no inhabitants, at preſent;* nor has St. Teona any inhabitants, or any thing more than ruins, though it has fields of corn and graſs upon it.† Who theſe ſaints are, I know not. But I know the ſecond *not* to be what Dr. Borlaſe conjectures, when he ſays "Theonus, biſhop of Glouceſter, was elected *archbiſhop* of London A. D. "545, Uſher's Primordia, pag. 525, 526, and was probably the ſaint who gave name to the "iſland;"‡ becauſe I acknowledge no ſuch biſhop in *real* hiſtory, becauſe Dr. Borlaſe himſelf diſclaims any *male* ſaint whatever in reciting the name twice afterwards *Saint Theona*,§ and becauſe the name is actually recited in the charter of Reginald "Sanctæ Teonæ," even more fully in that of Pope Celeſtin "Sanctæ Theonæ Virginis."‖

The metropolitical church to all theſe, as I have noticed before, was at Treſcaw. This had an abbey or college adjoining to it, and a proportionable number of clergy in the college or abbey. The clergy are noticed by Henry the Firſt; he in his charter of 1114 granting "to Oſbert abbot "and the church of Taviſtock, and to *Turold their monk*" then prior of Treſcaw evidently, "all "the churches of Sullye;" and ordering that "*Turold himſelf* and *all* the monks of Sully, as *my* "*proper prebendaries*, have firm peace together with all things which appertain to them."¶ Reginald alſo ſays in his grant of wreck to them on their own iſles, that he grants it "to the monks "of Sully as *the proper prebendaries of my father*."*† Edward the Third too, in his writ of protection to them, mentions "the *prior* of the priory of St. Nicholas in the iſle of Sully, which was "founded by our progenitors, formerly kings of England, and *is of our patronage*, and has been "endowed with poſſeſſions for *his* maintenance, and that of the *monks*, and that of the *ſecular* "*chaplains* there ſerving God;" and provides for the protection of "the *prior*, priory, *monks*, "*chaplains*, and *ſerving-men*."‡‖ How very falſely, then, has Tanner deſcribed the abbey as "a "poor cell of TWO Benedictine monks!" It certainly conſiſted of more, as we ſee "the prior" and his "monks" mentioned, "the prior" and "*all* his monks." The number could not be leſs than four or five, and was probably more. But to theſe were added "ſecular chaplains," clergymen not monaſtick, and intended to officiate (as I ſhall ſoon prove) in the church of the abbey. All theſe muſt have been ſupported by the rents of the five appropriated iſles, by the eſtates in two others, and by the tithes of all. "The abby pond" is "a moſt beautiful piece of "freſh water," as Dr. Borlaſe tells us, "edged round with camomel turf, on which neither briar, "thiſtle, nor flag appears. I judge it to be half a mile long, and a furlong wide. An evergreen "bank, without rock or weed, riſes high enough to keep out the ſea; ſerving at once to preſerve "the pond, and ſhelter the abby. The water is clear, and contains the fineſt eels that can be "taſted.

* P. 62, 65. † Ibid. 52. ‡ Ibid. ibid. § Ibid. 101, 102.

‖ Monaſticon i. 1002. "Inſulæ Sanctæ Teonæ," 998, "inſulam Sanctæ Theonæ Virginis."—Dr. Borlaſe, in citing Uſher 525, 526, for Theonus, cites only the *Index* of Uſher. This ſays "Theonus, Gloceſtrenſis epiſcopus, ad Londinenſem archi- "epiſcopatum tranſlatus fuiſſe *dicitur*, p. 37," by *Geoffrey of Monmouth*, "183" by *Geoffrey of Monmouth* again, "274" by *Geoffrey of Monmouth* once more. Such are Dr. Borlaſe's authors, and ſuch is his reference to Uſher!

¶ Monaſticon i. 1002. "Oſberto abbati et eccleſiæ de Taviſtok, et Turoldo monacho ſuo omnes eccleſias de Sullye," and "quod ipſe Turoldus, et omnes monachi de Sully, ſicut proprii prebendarii mei, habeant firmam pacem cum omnibus quæ "ad eos pertinent."

*† Ibid. ibid. "Monachis de Sully, ſicut propriis prebendariis patris mei."

‡‖ Ibid. ibid. "Prior Prioratûs Sancti Nicholai in inſulâ de Sully, qui per progenitores noſtros, quondam reges Angliæ, "fundatus de patronatû noſtro exiſtit, ac de poſſeſſionibus pro ſuſtentatione ſuâ et monachorum ac capellanorum ſecularium "ibidem Deo deſervientium—dotatus fuiſſet;—nos-gratioſé ſuſcepimus ipſos Priorem, Prioratum, monachos, capellanos, ac "homines ſervientes."

" tafted. The land quite round is cultivated, and by its gentle declivity, even to the brim of the " water, adds much to the beauty of this place. The abby church ftood on a fmall rifing, front-" ing the fouthern end of this pond; and though, higher up on the hill behind the abby, you fee " the bare bones, that is, the rocks and craggs of Scilly, yet here at the monaftery you fee but " little indeed, but it is altogether tender and delicate, compared to what the other profpects in " thefe iflands afford you. The monks, 'tis generally allowed, were very judicious in chufing " fituations the moft pleafant and retired of the country where their lot fell; and were you to fee " the ifles of Scilly, you would think their feating themfelves here was a ftrong proof of that ob-" fervation."* The compliment, here paid to the *monks*, is due only to their *patrons*; and the *judicioufnefs* attributed to thofe, is only the *piety* exerted by thefe. The monks had not, as the compliment implies they had, a power of ranging over a county or an ifland, and a right of fe-lecting the fineft parts in either. The whole was fettled property before. Nor could this pro-perty be transferred to the monks, unlefs it was offered by the owners. Then the owners, acting under the awe of that high principle of delicacy in the law of Mofes concerning facrifices, " if " there be any blemifh therein, as if it be lame or blind, or have any ill blemifh, thou fhalt not " facrifice it unto the Lord thy God;" † looked out for donations worthy of being tendered to God, or pofitions proper for the fequeftration of a monaftery. Thus Athelftan, when he fixed his abbey at Trefcaw, gave it lands that belonged to himfelf by right of conqueft, the lands probably of the Cornifh crown before; and fingled out a pofition for it, the moft rich, the moft retired of all the ifland. And thus Holy Vale in St. Mary's, as we have feen already, is " the moft plea-" fantly fituated" of any there; as " it lies warm, well expofed towards a little fouthern cove, " and fo well fheltered from the north, that trees grow very well." Yet fome of the richnefs of the land, it muft be acknowledged, refults from the agricultural fpirit of the monks. Bred up in habits of literature, refined in their taftes by reading, and poffeffing in many that flame from heaven, genius; they became good architects, good limners, and good fculptors; good fabrica-tors of organs, good dreffers of vines, and good managers of farms. The monks of Trefcaw, ac-cordingly, cleared Holy Vale of its woods, and modelled it into what it is. " Holy Vale," adds Dr. Borlafe, " is indeed capable of every kind of improvement," and received every kind from its monaftical proprietors; " but it has not the happinefs of any" at prefent, from its laical though lordly owners.‡ The very pond in Trefcaw feems to have been equally formed by the monks, and ftocked with eels for their fifh-meals; by raifing " an evergreen bank without rock or weed," as a head to the pond within land, and as a fhelter to their abbey from the fea without. And, as " the land quite round is cultivated," it is fo from their improving fpirit originally. They even feem to have built and maintained a houfe of entertainment for all fea-faring ftrangers that landed on the ifle; as " near the pier," Mr. Troutbeck tells us without any application of the fact, " is " a dwelling called *Trefco Palace*," a name, that marks the magnificence of the building in the eyes of the iflanders, and intimates its relation to the palace of the clergy the college, " which " *formerly* ufed to be much reforted to by mafters of fhips and ftrangers coming to this ifland; but " the cuftom has fome time been altered, to houfes of better accommodation further up the " ifland."§ Juft fuch alfo was affuredly the banquetting-houfe, that I have fhown to have ex-

K 2 ifted

* P. 43. † Deuteronomy xv. 21. ‡ Borlafe 71. § Troutbeck 128.

iſted within memory on the mount, cloſe to the town, and one long room for entertainments. Both were the ſame as the *Almonries* of all our monaſteries, rooms of gratuitous entertainments; but, from the maritime ſituation of our own, placed at the ports of acceſs to them, and in all appearance ſupported by a more expenſive hoſpitality than at monaſteries more inland. But, as Dr. Borlaſe proceeds with his account of the abbey, "the church is for the moſt part carried off," in the ſpirit alas! introduced by the reformation! a ſpirit at once groveling, barbarized, and antichriſtian, "to patch up ſome poor cots, which ſtand below it, on the ſpot where I imagine the "monaſtery ſtood; but the door, two handſome large arched openings, and ſeveral windows, "are ſtill to be ſeen, caſed with very good freeſtone, which ('tis thought) the monks got from "Normandy."* But, in addition to this account, let us peruſe Mr. Troutbeck's, which repeats juſt as Dr. Borlaſe has ſpoken, but adds uſefully to his ſpeech. "No veſtiges of the monaſtery," he tells us from the doctor, "are now to be ſeen; but part of the church belonging to it, is ſtill "ſtanding, and is uſed as a burying-place, the inhabitants eſteeming it more ſacred than any other "ſpot in the iſland.—A great part of the walls of the church is carried off, to patch up ſome poor "houſes which ſtand below it, on the ſpot where, probably, the monaſtery ſtood. This church "is ninety feet in length, and thirty feet in breadth, and ſtands due eaſt and weſt. In the ſouth "ſide wall is a fine arch of good workmanſhip, and on the north ſide has been another arch directly oppoſite to it, and of the ſame breadth, which is now fallen down, and only ſix feet in "height ſtanding. The church appears, from theſe two arches fronting each other, to have been "built in the form of a croſs." But where are the pillars requiſite to compoſe the croſs? "The "arch, that is ſtanding on the ſouth ſide, is twelve feet wide at the bottom, and runs up to a "ſharp point at the top, which is ſixteen feet high from the rubbiſh at the bottom; which is "three or four feet thick upon the floor of the church, where the dead are now buried. And, "on the weſt ſide of the ſtanding arch, is an arched door," much lower in its pitch than the other. "Both arches are raiſed with ſtone of a very fine grit. Several windows as well as doors "have been caſed with the ſame ſort of red ſtone, which it is thought the monks got from Normandy. This fine red ſtone is not ſo ponderous as Portland, or any other ſort of ſtone that is "to be met with either here or in England, i. e. if a piece of the ſame ſize ſhould be weighed. "This church is ſuppoſed to have been burnt down. A man, about thirteen years ago, was employed to remove ſome ſtones and rubbiſh at the weſt end of the ancient building, to make "room for burying the dead, who found a large piece of a bomb ſhell, and ſeveral pieces of "coked timber, among the ſtones and rubbiſh that he cleared away. There is earth ſufficient "carried within the walls of the church, from time to time, upon the old flagged floor, in depth "to dig a reaſonable grave."† And, as Leland uſefully ſubjoins, it was "a paroch chyrche" indeed

* Borlaſe 44.

† Troutbeck 134, 135. "In a little meadow adjoining to it," ſays Borlaſe 48, 49, concerning the *preſent* church, "the "tenant told us he had offered leave to his brother iſlanders, to bury their dead; but they have, continued he, ſuch a notion "of the ſanctity of the abby, that they carry the dead body there, and interr it in that church, though at near two miles "diſtance." They thus prefer the conſiderations of religion, for ages impreſſed upon their minds, to any trifling eaſe for themſelves! They bury where their fathers have been always uſed to bury, rather than bury in a ground *not* ſet a part for burial by any forms of dedication, *not* ſanctified by the reverence of ages, and liable without any reluctance from either religion or from feeling in general, to be tilled next year for corn. Mr. Troutbeck in p. 15, 18, notes many cuſtoms as peculiar to the iſlands, which are common to them and the continent of Cornwall. So in p. 108, he notes what I have noted above at

as well as a collegiate one;* fo could with propriety be feparated from the college, could not indeed without much impropriety be included within it. The church ftill remains in the *fhell* of its lower half, but feems not to have ever had any fide-ailes, and ftill lefs to have had a crofs-aile. The abfence of all pillars, even of fragments of pillars, proves this. The area of the church is all fenced round with walls ftill lofty, ftill fhowing their original ufe, ftill crying to heaven for vengeance upon thofe who caufed them thus to appear in ruins. Who then were thofe? They were affuredly the prefbyterians of the laft century, who with the zeal of heathenifm in their heads, as the "large piece of a bomb fhell" fhows, actually *bombarded the church*, fo beat down the loftier part of the walls, and burnt all the beams into mere "pieces of coked timber." This evidence alone is fufficient to convict them. But let me adduce another of another church. "It is "handed down by tradition," Mr. Troutbeck tells us many ages afterward concerning St. Agnes, "that the old church" noticed by Leland "was *beaten down* by *the parliament forces* in the laft "century, and that it lay in *ruins* many years."†

We thus behold the ifland Silura reduced by one great inundation into feveral parts, thofe parts again diminifhed continually by the triumphant waters, and the ifland Nutho, particularly, wafted away into that mere *Os Sacrum* of an ifland, a rock. But we fhall fee the wafting power of the fea more diftinctly and more comprehenfively, by taking our ftation upon the pages of Leland, and comparing the condition of the iflands *then* with their ftate *before* or *now*. Trefcaw, he tells us, "is the *biggeft* of the iflettes, in cumpace a 6 miles or more," while "S. Mary ifle is a 5 "miles or more in cumpace."‡ In another place he fpeaks of "the *biggeft* ifle (cawled S. Ni-"cholas ifle) of the Scylleys."§ "Ther be yn that paroch," he adds concerning the ifle, "about "a lx. houfeholders."|| Yet it now contains only about *forty* families, and is little more than *half* as large as St. Mary's, which is three miles long and two broad.¶ So much has Trefcaw loft of its extent, in the period only of two centuries and a half! "I was fhewn," Dr. Borlafe remarks, "a paffage which the fea has made within thefe feven years, through the fand-bank that "fences the abby-pond; by which breach, upon the firft high tide and violent ftorm at eaft or "eaft-fouth-eaft, one may venture to prophefy, that this ftill and now beautiful pool of frefh "water will become a branch of the fea, and confequently expofed to all the rage of tide and "ftorm."*|| But let us catch another circumftance in the ftate of this ifland, that has never hitherto been appropriated to it, yet forms a ftriking feature in the difcrimination of its prefent afpect from its paft. In the year 1200, King John "gives, grants, and confirms to the abby of "Scilly the tythe of three acres of *affart* land, in *the foreft of Guffaer*: and commands his fheriffs "and bailiffs that they do not fuffer the *canons* of Scilly to be impleaded for any tenement they "hold, except before him or his fteward of Normandy."*† Where then was this foreft, part of which had lately been *affarted* or cleared for cultivation, and the tythes of which would not have been due without a fpecial grant, as rifing from the foil of a royal foreft? As no one ifle is fpecified

at St. Sennan, in Cornwall: In St. Martin's ifle "the form of a grave, furrounded with ftones pitched edgewife, in the fhape "of a coffin, eight feet long, and three feet over the wideft part." See alfo p. 104 and 155 for other graves in this form, on a part of St. Agnes, called the Guew.

* Itin. vii. 16. † Troutbeck 151. ‡ Itin. iii. 19. § Ibid. vii. 116. || Ibid. ibid. ¶ Borlafe 49, 50.

*|| Borlafe 88, 89.

*† Borlafe 102, 103, from "Cart. i. Joann. pag. 1, n. 155 and 219. Tanner Notit. p. 69." Thus Tanner only *refers* to the record, while Dr. Borlafe *cites* it. There is in Monafticon i. 516, a record very like this in the latter half, but very different from it, as not having the former half, and being marked as "Cart i. Jo. part. 2, num. 65."

fied in the grant, how ſhall we confine it to any one? *From this very circumſtance.* Had the foreſt been in an iſle different from that of the abbey, the iſle *would* have been ſpecified expreſſly. Being both in the ſame iſle, this iſle is not expreſſed either for the abbey or for the foreſt. The foreſt then was in Treſcaw, and was (we may be ſure from the very appellation of the iſle) a foreſt of elder-trees. " There," notes Leland concerning the whole iſle, but evidently means this particular point the foreſt, " be wild bores ſwyne."* But *now* the elder-trees are all rooted up, the foreſt is vaniſhed, and the wild boars are extinct. Such changes have been made in a ſingle iſle, by the continual inroads of the ſea upon it! And ſuch or ſimilar muſt have been the changes that the ſea has made in the others!†

Yet to the violence of the ſea was added another enemy, in the middle ages; one, ſtill more violent for the time, and proceeding nearly to the total deſolation of the iſles. In 1367 Edward the Third ſent a writ of protection to the prior, on his complaint to him. Then, as the complaint alledges, " the priory is ſo much injured and impoveriſhed by the frequent acceſs of mari- " ners, paſſing through the iſland itſelf from the ſhips of all nations, for want of defence to it; " that the prior is not able to ſupport the reaſonable burdens lying on the priory; and the prayers " and devotions, and other works of piety, which uſed to be done there, are much ſubſtracted, " and muſt (it is feared) be ſubſtracted more, unleſs a remedy be provided." The king, therefore, endeavours to provide a remedy againſt theſe " malefactors," as he calls them, by ordering the conſtable at his caſtle, in the iſle of Enmour, to guard and defend the priory.‡ So the king ordered, but ordered in vain. The conſtable could not protect the iſle of the priory, from his caſtle at Old Town in St. Mary's. And the injuries from " mariners of all nations" having " fre- " quent acceſs" to the iſland, then " paſſing through" it, ranging and roaming over it with ſuch a miſchievous ſpirit, as made them " malefactors;" not being actually pirates themſelves, but with the real licentiouſneſs of ſailors on ſhore doing piratical actions; muſt have been continued. The king accordingly provided another remedy, as we have reaſon to believe, in conſtructing another caſtle upon the very iſle of Treſcaw. In Leland's time, we find, there was " a lytle pyle or " fortres" upon it.§ It is now called the Old Caſtle, and ſtood upon a point of land commanding

* Itin. vii. 116.

† *Gaſſaer* is probably from *Gavar* (C), a goat, Hyvr (W), a he-goat, Gauvrſa (A), a ſhe-goat. " Moſt of theſe iſlands " have ſuch paſture and rocky common, as would maintain a number of goats to great advantage, and afford the inhabitants " their kids, milk, and veniſon, at a much cheaper rate than the ſheep does her mutton and lamb, at leaſt without interfe- " ring; and in places where the ſheep will not live without more care than the goat requires." Borlaſe 82. From our etymology (if juſt) it appears, that formerly the iſlanders had anticipated this leſſon, and had ſtocked a foreſt in Treſcaw with goats.

‡ Monaſticon i. 1003. 1003. " Prioratus—per frequentes acceſſus marinariorum navium univerſarum regionum, per ipſam " inſulam tranſeuntium defectu tuitionis, in tantum deſtructus et depauperatus exiſtat; quod dictus prior rationabilia onera " eidem prioratui incumbentia ſupportare non ſufficit; et ſuas preces et devotiones, ac alia pietatis opera, quæ—ibidem fieri " ſolebant, in multum ſubtrahuntur, et plus ſubtrahi formidatur, niſi ſibi de alio remedio per nos provideatur. Unde a nobis " ſupplicavit, ut dictum prioratum contra hujuſmodi malefactores tueri velimus et defendere.—Et tu, prefate conſtabularie, " eidem—poſſe tuo auxilians ſis et intendens," &c. Borlaſe 103, ſtates the ſubſtance of the record thus: " that by the fre- " quent *reſort* of mariners of all nations to that place, the priory for want of proper defence was ſo damaged and impoveriſhed, " that the prior was not able to *repair* it, nor to perform the requiſite duties of church ſervice." Here many miſtakes are committed. To *repair*, a ſpecifick burden, is put for all the burdens, which are general, as " rationabilia onera eidem pri- " oratui incumbentia." Nor is the *priory* ſaid to be damaged " for want of proper defence," but the mariners are averred *to range over the iſland* " for want of proper defence" to it. Nor had " the mariners of all nations" a " frequent *reſort*" to the iſle, which (if true in fact) would be an argument of its trade; but " the mariners *of the ſhips* of all nations" had " fre- " quent *acceſs*" to the iſle, and, by " *paſſing through the iſland itſelf.*" And that expreſſive ſtroke, of the works of piety " there being " much ſubſtracted" already, is wholly omitted.

§ Itin. vii. 116.

ing the prefent harbour of New Grynfey;* a harbour fo denominated, to diftinguifh it from another denominated Old Grynfey, and feemingly by the name formed *within one or two centuries paft*, from the plunder of the ifles about it. And this would undoubtedly prove fome protection to the priory. Yet it was not fufficient even for this ifle, and was no protection at all to the others. The piratical acts therefore went on, till in the reign of the Eighth Henry they had nearly reduced all the ifles to a ftate of folitude. "Few men be glad," fays Leland, "to inhabite thefe "iflettes for al the plenty" in them, "for robbers by the fea, that take their catail of force."† Yet thefe were not pirates, any more than the others before. "Thefe robbers," adds Leland himfelf, "be French men and Spaniardes," then engaged in a war againft each other, and mutually agreeing to plunder thefe un-defended ifles.‡ We even find the ifles expofed long before, in one of our national wars with France, to plundering defcents from the enemy. "By an inqui-"fition in the firft of Richard the Third, A. D. 1484," obferves Dr. Borlafe, "I find the faid "iflands were yearly worth 'in peaceable times,'" when there was an interval of ceffation to the wars, fo long continued with France in the reigns of Edward and the two Henries preceding, "forty fhillings, IN TIMES OF WAR NOTHING."§ But we fee the defolation marked again, in another way. We have found the monks of Sylly to have been feveral in number, when the Firft Henry annexed Sylly as a cell to Taviftock abbey; yet we foon find the number reduced by the reduced confequence of the ifles, into *two*. "The abbot and convent of Taviftock lords of the "ifle of Scilly inhabited within the fea," fays a writ from the Third Edward in the year 1335, "have fupplicated us; that whereas the aforefaid abbey, to which the aforefaid ifle belongs, and "the fame abbot, and the other abbots for the time being, are bound for war to find TWO chap-"lains their *fellow-monks* within the ifle aforefaid, by reafon of their lands and tenements there "being, to celebrate divine fervice *every day*; and the fame monks, as well BECAUSE OF "THE WAR MOVED BETWEEN US AND THE MEN OF FRANCE, as for *various other caufes*, dare "NOT ABIDE THERE IN THESE DAYS; we would pleafe to concede, that the fame abbot fhall "find TWO fecular chaplains to celebrate divine fervice every day within the ifland aforefaid in "the room of the monks DURING THE AFORESAID WAR: we liftening favourably to their fup-"plication, have granted" it.|| Monks, confined to a cloifter, and converfing little with the world, were very fufceptible of fear, and "dared not to abide there in thofe days" of war; but the fecular clergy dared. The fufpenfion, however, was only for the war, and with peace returned the prefcribed obfervances of the abbey. Two monks refided in the ifle, and officiated in the church, as before. Yet the number was again reduced in the reign of Henry the Eighth. Then the piratical defcents of French and Spaniards on the ifles, as we have already feen, were very frequent and very haraffing. Nor did the two forts, that were begun at St. Mary's and at Trefcaw; one called Harry's Wall, but injudicioufly pofited, and never completed;¶ another, which

* Borlafe 46, 47. † Itin. iii. 19. ‡ Ibid. ibid. § Borlafe 109.

|| Monafticon i. 516. "Supplicarunt nobis—abbas et conventus de Taveftoke, domini infulæ de Sully infra mare inha-"bitatæ, ut cum abbatia prædicta, ad quam infula prædicta pertinet,—et idem abbas, et cœteri abbates abbatiæ prædictæ "qui pro tempore fuerint, duos Capellanos Commonachos fuos infra infulam prædictam, ratione terrarum et tenementorum "fuorum ibidem exiftentium,—fingulis diebus celebraturos in perpetuum invenire teneantur; iidemque monachi, tam propter "gueriam inter nos et homines de Franciâ motam, quam aliis variis ex caufis, hiis diebus ibidem non audeant immorari, "velimus eis concedere, quod idem abbas duos Capellanos Seculares, loco monachorum prædictorum, fingulis diebus infra "infulam prædictam celebraturos invenire poffit, durante guerrâ fupradictâ: nos eorum fupplicationi favorabiliter annuentes, "conceffimus."

¶ Borlafe 15, 16.

which is Old Caſtle enlarged a little after Leland's writing, and from the aſpect of the enlargements plainly not older than Henry the Eighth;* either prevent the viſits of theſe plunderers, or preclude the deſertions of inhabitants from the iſland. And, at laſt, the very monks of the abbey, now reduced to one, relinquiſhed the abbey, relinquiſhed the iſle, and retired to Taviſtock. "In—S. Nicholas iſle," cries Leland, "—ys—a paroch chyrche, that *a* monke of Taveſtoke YN "PEACE doth ſerve, as a membre to Taveſtoke abbay."† The monks of the priory were thus dwindled down into one, and that one had now fled away with the inhabitants to the continent of Cornwall. The iſle, the church became ſcenes of ſolitude and ſilence. Both would accordingly ſuffer much in the general diſtreſs. The church was probably left to be ſo delapidated, as to totter at the firſt aſſault of that giant-ſinner Henry the Eighth, even to fall "with the" very "whiff and wind of his fell ſword." And as Leland informs us concerning Old Town in St. Mary's iſle, that "the roues of the buildinges in it be SORE DEFACID AND WOREN;" ſo he equally aſſures us, that "there appere tokens in *diverſe of the iſlettes*, of habitations NOW CLENE "DOWN."‡ Here then was the annihilation nearly of the old Britiſh race, the correſpondents of the Phenicians at Gades, of the Greeks at Marſeilles, of the Romans at Narbonne, and the firſt miners for tin, the firſt exporters into foreign parts, the firſt navigators for commerce to the continent. They had been ſwept away in numbers, by one grand inundation during the tenth century. They had been gradually diminiſhed ſince, by the abſorption of their lands in the waves. They had been even invaded by mariners of all nations at firſt, who plundered them in want or in wantonneſs; and by French or Spaniards afterwards, who in a war with each other made a common war upon neutrals, in landing upon the iſles and carrying off their cattle. The few inhabitants remaining on them, the one only clergyman remaining at the abbey, could no longer be induced by the plenty of productions on the iſles to continue amidſt ſuch diſtreſſes, and deſerted the iſles for poſſeſſions more ſecure upon the continent of Britain. The iſles, once ſo celebrated for their ſubterraneous wealth, for the perſonal appearance of their inhabitants, and for the efforts made from the continent to find theſe concealed *Indies of the North*, became more and more deſerted; till in the reign of Elizabeth, the crown, which by ſacrilege had got poſſeſſion of *all* the iſles again, conſigned them all over to a ſubject for the petty rent of 10l. a year § This ſubject, though a Corniſhman himſelf, yet bred up in England and at the court, brought over a colony of Engliſh to re-people the iſles, and ſecured his colony by a new fort at St. Mary's with another new one at Treſcaw.‖ So ſecured, yet ſecured ſtill more by the growing power of the Britiſh navy, that is continually ſcouring the ſeas and keeping "the mariners of the ſhips of all "nations" in order, the ſlight reliques of the Aborigines united in friendſhip with the colony of Engliſh, had power enough to keep up many of the old or Corniſh names of places, but had not power to prevent the ſuperſedence of many by names new or Engliſh.¶ Thus were they ſoon mingled with the Engliſh, like their countrymen on the continent; like them, half-learned the language,

* Borlaſe 46, 47. † Itin. vii. 116. ‡ Itin. iii. 19. § Borlaſe 112.

‖ Borlaſe 111, 47. "As ſoon as people knew the nature of fortifying better," ſays that author concerning the Eighth Henry's fort at Treſcaw, ſcarcely appropriating any thing, yet obviouſly referring without knowing he refers it to the time of the new colony, "it was neglected, and another more ſerviceable one, which lies below, built out of its ruins, and called "Oliver's Caſtle."

¶ Borlaſe 86, for the Corniſh; the Engliſh are theſe, Eaſtern Iſlands, St. Martin's, White Iſland, Maiden Bower, Broad Sound, Crow Sound, St. Mary's Sound, Old Town, Heugh Town, Holy Vale, &c.

language, the cuftoms of England, and fo became as much Englifhmen in appearance or in reality, as their brethren or their countrymen were. And, as with common concern they all behold their ifles fenfibly fhrinking in their dimenfions ftill, before the waves of the fea; fo with common joy they equally behold a good provifion made for their beft interefts, the facrilege of the crown in feizing the abbey-lands almoft wholly corrected, and, inftead of a fingle clergyman for all the ifles, as in the days even of Dr. Borlafe,* one fettled at Trefcaw, one at St. Mary's, with a third at St. Agnes, each receiving an income of £.100 a year, with a houfe for his refidence, without any of our Englifh taxes, yet with all the original plenty of the ifles.†

* P. 135.

† "You will eafily imagine, that it would be more comfortable as well as more plentiful living here, for people of com-"merce or fortune, and might therefore promote their fettling here, if they had a fmall fhip of forty ton paffing and re-"paffing, as the weather would permit." (Borlafe 134.) Here behold the ufefulnefs of authors. The hint has been taken. A packet goes every week, if wind and weather permit, from Penzance to Scilly, maintained by the general poft-office, and carrying either letters, or packages, or paffengers.

"The foil is very good for grain of every kind *except wheat,*" Dr. Borlafe tells us in 68, "*fome* of which, however, *they* "*have on St. Mary's,* but *not much,* neither *will it make good bread.*" A note adds thus: "wheat however feems to have "been more ufually fown on thefe iflands, in former ages; for 'Henry III. commands Drew de Barrentine, governor of his "iflands of Scilly, or his bailiffs, that they deliver every year to Ralph Burnet, feven quarters of wheat, which Robert Legat "ufed to receive, and which is efcheated to the king.'" Rot. Claus. 32, Hen. III. m. 2. "Mr. Heath, of Scilly, p. 180." The author has overlooked that ftriking declaration in Leland's Itin. iii. 19, concerning St. Mary's: "the ground of this ifle "bereth *exceeding good* corn; infomuch, that, if a man *do but caft corn wher hogges have rotid* (rooted), it *wyl cum up.*" The difference in the produce muft arife from the difference in the cultivation. Thus Agnes is in the doctor's own account, "a well cultivated little ifland, fruitful of corn and grafs," p. 36. Even Tean, though uninhabited, has on it "fields of "corn and pafture," p. 52. And, on the principal tenement in Trefcaw, "its foil is fo very fruitful, that one field of feven "acres has been in tillage *every* year *fince the remembrance of man,* and carries *exceeding plentiful crops,*" p. 48.

Sat. Sept. 28th, 1799.

On the ROMAN ARCHITECTURE and CASTRAMETATION,

By Bishop BENNET.

SUPPLEMENT to the FOURTH CHAPTER of the FIRST BOOK.

ON the subject of Roman Architecture and Castrametation in the west of England, I have been honored with the following letter from * Bishop Bennet: And, in justice to that excellent antiquary, I shall print it entire.

Dublin Castle, 7th March, 1793.

"The wish you have so publicly manifested for information relative to Devonshire, must lay you open to much impertinent intrusion, and I fear you will have too much reason to include this letter under the same censure. I cannot, however, refrain from sending you a few remarks on the Roman antiquities in the west of England; which you have my free consent to work into your own plan, making me a slight acknowlegement in your preface, or if you think them not worth notice, to throw them into the fire, and excuse the liberty I take in troubling you with them. They consist of three heads:

I. *An additional Argument for Moridunum being Seaton.*

In 1778 the present Bishop of Cork (Dr. Bennet), and the Rev. Mr. Leman, travelled the fosse from Ludbrough N. E. of Lincoln, (probably a station), to the borders of Devonshire, where, after trying two days, they gave it up in despair like all their predecessors. Among many other remarks they observed during the whole course of the road, (and it has been confirmed by observations on all the other Roman roads they have travelled) that when the fosse mounted a hill there was generally a distinguished object, either a camp or barrow to be seen on the next rising ground, tho' at many miles distance, towards which the road pointed; as among a thousand instances the barrows at Segsbury, and the beacon barrow near Shepton-Mallet on the fosse; those between Old Sarum and Woodyeats Inn on what Hutchins calls the Skenild-street; those on Gogmagog Hills, near Cambridge, on the Roman road from Colchester to Chester; Celsfield Common on the Stare-street, in Sussex; and the camps themselves at Old Sarum; Bedbury, and many others. Now, upon mounting the hill between Chard and Crewkerne, just by the house called Windwhistle,

* Now Bishop of Cloyne, 1804.

Windwhiftle, at which our travellers loft the foffe (and to a clump of trees near that houfe the road had evidently pointed for fome miles) on mounting this hill one little bay of the fea was directly in the line of the road, making the only diftinguifhed object in the horizon, and the only vifible part of the fea itfelf, and upon enquiring the name of this bay, they found it to be the bay of Seaton. This is an argument which ftrikes more upon infpection than in a narrative; but if there is any force in the remark, that the ancients either pointed their road to fuch objects, or (as in the cafe of barrows) perhaps conftructed them to direct the line of their roads, which Appian fays was actually done in the great road acrofs the fands of Africa, to the Temple of Jupiter Ammon, the hypothefis adopted by Stukeley of Moridunum, being near Seaton, will receive fome additional countenance.

II. *Examination of Horfeley's idea that Ifca Dumnoniorum is Chifelborough.*

Mr. Horfeley's character as an antiquary ftands high, and with great reafon, for in the places where he has been himfelf, he is more to be depended upon than any other writer in his line; but he feems to have known nothing of the weft of England more than what he faw in his map, and this has led him into fome unfortunate miftakes. His arguments for removing Ifca from Exeter are thefe; that he knew of no Roman road to or from it; that it does not fuit the latitude affigned to Ifca by Ptolemy; that it does not agree with the number of miles in the 12th iter of Antonine. To all this it is eafy to anfwer, that a Roman road from Honiton to Exeter has been fince difcovered, and according to Richard of Circencefter, another road went through it, bearing to the weft, traces of which have been alfo feen; that Ptolemy, from his general inaccuracy, and in this cafe his particular and enormous error of miftaking Ifca Dumnoniorum for Ifca Silurum cannot be looked upon as any authority; and that the number of miles in Antonine from Moridunum, not agreeing to Exeter, can be no argument againft the pofition of Exeter, till we know for certain where Moridunum itfelf is; befides that the places in that iter are remarkably confufed, and the miles undoubtedly erroneous: but even if there had been any force in thofe arguments, to remove Ifca from Exeter, why fhould it be fixed at Chefelborough? On looking at Horfeley to difcover his reafon, I find a page filled with arguments to prove it *not to be at Chefelborough*, but at *Ilchefter*; at the clofe of which he is in great doubt whether, inftead of Ilchefter, it might not be at *Hamden Hill*, after which follows this very extraordinary fentence. "Befides "the camp at Hambden Hill, *Ifce* a place called Chefelboro', which founds like antiquity, and "*not very unlike Ifca* as to the former part of the name. Chefelboro' ftands *upon the Parret*; but "Ifca feems to have been a common name for moft of the rivers hereabouts, and one bearing the "name of Ax, is not far off; and I make no doubt but, as I hinted before, this part of Somerfet, "fo near the borders, antiently belonged to the country of the Damnonii. I have, therefore, "*on the whole*, given the preference to this rather than Ilchefter." Thefe then are the reafons for Chifelborough being the Ifca of the Romans, and let us examine the claims of the two places. Exeter has been from the earlieft time the chief city of the Damnonii; Exeter ftands on the Ifca; Exeter has roads leading to it, and many Roman antiquities found at it: What has Chefelborough to urge againft this? Does it agree with the number of miles at which Ifca Damnoniorum is placed in the itinerary? By no means. Have any Roman antiquities been found in it? None at all. Have any roads been traced to or from it? No. Does it ftand upon the river Ifca? Nothing like it. Was it even within the diftrict of the Damnonii? It is not certain it was. Are there any foundations or remains of any kind to lead us to conjecture it ever was a city at all? No fuch have ever been found. What then is its claim? A Roman road which croffes all England happens to pafs half a mile from it, and the name *Chefelboro'* founded to Horfeley's ear not unlike *Ifca* Damnoniorum. And is this really all?—All that ever has been or can be produced upon the fubject. Upon no better foundation than this did Mr. Horfeley (tho' often a judicious and cautious writer) remove Ifca from Exeter, where it had been placed by antiquaries before his time, and publifh what he calls a *corrected* map of Roman Britain, in which Ifca Damnoniorum is boldly placed at Chefelborough. I vifited Chefelborough myfelf, examined it with great care, could fee no mark of Roman antiquity, nor hear of any thing being found but a little diadem or fillet of gold many years ago, which was moft probably a Saxon or Danifh ornament. I was, therefore, from this infpection, and the general weaknefs of the reafons produced by Mr. Horfeley in the paffage before quoted from him, convinced of the abfurdity of the whole hypothefis, and fhould have remained quiet under this conviction, if Dr. Henry, in a Hiftory of England not many years ago publifhed, had not declared himfelf as thoroughly fatisfied on the other fide by the arguments of Horfeley, that Ifca Damnoniorum ought to be placed at Chefelborough; and Mr. Strutt, of Malden, in his late works, adopted the fame idea as an acknowleged truth. Fearful, therefore, that Mr. Horfeley's authority (of whofe general character no one can think higher than myfelf) may lead other authors, prevented from examining the fpot, into the fame miftake, I have thrown my opinion on this fubject upon paper, and fubmitted it to the hiftorian of Devonfhire, to vindicate to the public, if he thinks fit, the antiquity of the chief city in his county.

III. *On the Camps in England.*

The camps in England are in general reducible to three kinds; oblong or fquare, with a fingle ditch; circular, with a fingle ditch; of any figure, with two or more very deep ditches. Modern antiqnaries have made great confufion, by attributing all thefe kinds to the Romans, as the Ancients ufed to do to the Giants, particularly if the camp was large and ftrong. I am inclined to think the firft fort only are certainly Roman; the fecond and third belong equally to the Saxons, Danes, and Britons, with fome little diftinction to be mentioned prefently. This, like all general rules, muft admit of exceptions: but the following obfervations will explain my reafons for adopting this idea. Almoft every camp known certainly to be Roman is of a regular figure; as the camps for inftance at Haerfounds, Battledykes, and Aairdoch in Scotland, and all the camps on Severus's Wall, without one exception: and on the other hand in Ireland, where the Romans did not penetrate, *tho' the northern nations did*, a camp of a regular figure is almoft unknown. I know the authority of Vegetius will be produced againft me, that the Romans made their camps fquare, triangular, oval, or oblong, prout loci qualitas aut neceffitas poftulaverit; but all I mean to affert, is, that when the Romans were not preffed loci neceffitate, they preferred a fquare or oblong, an affertion which this paffage of Vegetius neither confirms nor contradicts, and which no one, I think, can contradict, who has feen the innumerable camps in thefe forms in the Roman roads and walls in the north. A ftronger argument againft my hypothefis at firft fight, is the irregular

regular camps which are acknowleged to be Roman from their poſition agreeing with the itinerary diſtances, or from the Roman coins and antiquities found in them, as Old Sarum, Maiden Caſtle and Badbury in Dorſetſhire, the camp at Gogmagog Hills near Cambridge, and many others. I might get rid of theſe however at once, by allowing them, as they are very few in number, to be exceptions to the rule; but I am rather inclined to think that theſe places have been ſince altered by Danes or Saxons encamping in them, enlarging or diminiſhing them, according to their own numbers, (as General Roy obſerved to be the caſe with the Roman camps in Scotland, and as every eye may ſee in Maiden Caſtle), and fortifying them with double or triple ditches after their own manner; for it is obſervable, that Vegetius ſays the Romans made their ditch "latem "novem, undecim, tredecim, vel (ubi major adverſariorum vis metuitur) pedibus ſeptemdecim;" but never mentions a word of double or triple ditches 50 yards broad. To recur, therefore, to my original idea, I am inclined to look upon every camp of a ſquare or oblong figure to be Roman, and to regard with a very ſuſpicious eye all irregular camps whatever, tho' by this hypotheſis I remove from the honor of being Roman fortifications, many an old Cæſar's camp, as it is vulgarly called; Julius Cæſar being by ſome odd fatality in poſſeſſion of all our old camps, as King John is of all our old palaces. Whenever, therefore, I find a camp of the figure before ſpecified, ſingle ditched, and ſituated conveniently for water, by whatever name it may be diſtinguiſhed, Ceſter Bury or Caſtle, tho' the former is a ſtrong additional argument, I always would aſſign it to the Romans.

Of the irregular camps there is from the nature of them much leſs certainty: The Danes and Saxons being both northern people, and even the Belgæ, who invaded the iſland much earlier, being I believe a Gothic tribe, it is not probable there could be much difference in their mode of encamping; but it is reaſonable to ſuppoſe the Celts, or original inhabitants, both from their antiquity and their low ſtate of civilization, would uſe a leſs artificial way of fortifying themſelves. I would therefore attribute thoſe camps of an awkward figure approaching to a circle with one ditch, eſpecially if in the receſſes of our foreſts, ſuch as Ambreſbury, near Epping, in Eſſex, to the old Britons. The camps better choſen on high ground, and with outlines better defined, and large ditches, may belong perhaps to the Saxons. There is a very extraordinary line of camps of this ſort in ſight of each other, ſo as evidently to have been conſtructed at the ſame period, reaching along the great range of chalk hills from Vandleburg or Gogmagog Hills, in Cambridgeſhire, to the Wiltſhire Downs, as if drawn for the purpoſe of defending that range of country from a northern enemy, a poſition which (the form of the camps putting the Romans out of the queſtion) anſwers to the Belgic or Saxon ſettlers, and to no other people in the iſland. I therefore look upon theſe fortifications as ſpecimens of the Saxon ſtyle, and I diſtinguiſh the Daniſh camps from theſe by a form more *romanized* by more numerous and deeper ditches, and perhaps by the peculiar mode of defending the gateway, as in Yaneſbury camp, Wiltſhire, (ſee Gough, vol. I. plate 8,) the burgh of Moray, (ſee Cordiner's Antiquities, plate X. page 58,) and Maiden Caſtle, in Dorſetſhire, (ſee Hutchins's Hiſtory,) which is evidently the improvement of a late and military age. By theſe conſiderations, if well founded, ſome light may be thrown upon our hiſtory, as well as more accuracy in the antiquities of our counties: For inſtance, it would lead one in your own county to reject Woodbury, Muſbury, and moſt of your other Bury's, from the

the rank of Roman camps; to look upon Hembury from its figure, as having a better claim, and to place in the fame rank, without hefitation, a fmall and regular camp on Exmoor, near Linmouth, formed undoubtedly for the purpofe of guarding the fea coaft in that expofed quarter from the Irifh or northern pirates. On the other hand, Clovelly Dikes which Mr. Gough, in his additions to Camden, calls a Roman camp, tho' no Roman road can be traced to or from it) does not appear to me, from its figure and triple ditch, to have the leaft pretenfions to the name: I fhould from my hypothefis pronounce it Danifh; and it is curious enough, that in this inftance we can go very near to point out the makers of it, for in the year 876 Inquer and Halfdun's brother, two Danifh leaders came from South Wales, where they had wintered with 23 fhips, landed on the coaft of Devonfhire and befieging the E. of Devon, in Appledore-caftle, received a compleat defeat, and loft their celebrated ftandard of the raven. Now a fleet coming with a fair wind at north, from Carmarthenfhire, could make no part of England with fo much eafe as Clovelly Point; it was directly in their courfe, and as was their ufual cuftom, they fortified ftrongly the firft ground on which they landed, then marching along the coaft, Appledore-caftle, then ten miles off, would be the natural object of their attack; and thus the poffibility appears to me very ftrong, that Clovelly dikes was made at this time, and was in fact (as according to my hypothefis it ought to be) a Danifh, not a Roman fortification.

ADDITIONAL PROOFS.

Saxon Camps known.

Tong Caftle, in Kent, was the work of Hengift, or his fon: It is a large hill, flat at top, furrounded with a broad ditch 50 yards, which is again incircled with a ftrong bank or vallum; its figure is nearly circular. Withem, in Effex, was built by Edward the Elder in 913, fimilar in all refpects to the latter. Alfred's camp, near Millon, in Kent, made in 892, in order to check Haftings, the Dane, is certainly of this conftruction, a fmall hill, a broad ditch, and an external vallum inclofing all, the form an irregular oval.

Danifh Camps known.

Haftings' camp, near the laft, is a long fquare, with the corners rounded off, and a ditch and vallum like Alfred's. The breadth of the ditch is the great diftinction between this and a Roman camp.

Bretton Caftle, in Wiltfhire, to which the Danes retired and were forced to furrender by Alfred, is of a fimilar form, the angles rounded, and the gateways defended by additional works. (See Gough's plate, Camden, vol. I. plate 8.)

Burgh Caftle, in Moray, a celebrated Danifh encampment, has the entrance defended by triple ditches, each with a vallum.

At Whitehawk Hill, in Shoreham, is a ftrong camp, triple trenched, and open to the fea. Quere, Danifh? Near it a large fingle circle. Perhaps Saxon againft it.

The keep at Thetford, an enormous work, fortified by three great and deep ditches, is known to be Danifh.

In

In the Isle of Anglesey, near the Ford, by which the Romans passed the Menai, is a square camp, and opposite to it a round one, allowed to be that of the inhabitants (Britons) against it.

I fear, sir, I have tired your patience by this long and perhaps uninteresting memoir, and I can only say, you are at liberty to vent your indignation upon it, by throwing it into the fire, for disturbing you in the midst of your important pursuits: If, on the other hand, there is any thing in it worth your notice, you are at liberty to insert it in your history in any shape you please. You are acquainted with a gentleman who is the best judge now living upon these matters, and whom I sincerely respect, tho' I have not the honor of being personally known to him, I mean Mr. Whitaker, to whose History of Manchester I owe my first love for antiquarian pursuits, and in consequence, some of the most pleasant hours of my life: To his judgment and to your's I cheerfully submit; and am,

SIR,

Your very obedient servant,

WM. CORK."

An ACCOUNT of FOUR ROMAN URNS,

The firſt three deſcribed by the Rev. MALACHY HITCHINS; in a Letter to the Author, dated St. Hilary, Dec. 1803.

SUPPLEMENT to the FOURTH CHAPTER of the FIRST BOOK.

"THE firſt Urn was found on the barton of Godolphin, the property of the Duke of Leeds, in the pariſh of Breage, about five miles weſt of Helſton, in the month of April, 1779, by one Nicholas Pearce, as he was narrowing a bank, which formed the boundary of his field, who ſold the greater part of the coins, which it contained, to a Jew, ſoon after he had diſcovered them, and before he had informed any gentleman of the circumſtance; for which imprudent conduct his neighbours having cenſured and ridiculed him, it had ſuch an unhappy effect on him, as to cauſe a temporary derangement, and danger of ſuicide. The Jew purchaſed 8lb. avoirdupois weight, for which he gave the finder only eight-pence a pound; but as his brother and others found a great number, ſcattered by the violent ſtroke of the mattock, which broke the urn in pieces, I ſuppoſe the whole coin to have weighed about 10lb. and as ten of theſe coins weighed an ounce, the whole number muſt have been about ſixteen hundred. The urn was thick and curiouſly molded, having many furrows and involutions, but I could not get a ſight of the fragments, which might enable me to give a more particular deſcription of it. The ſpot on which it was found lies little more than half a mile from the Roman fort at Boſenſe, in which were diſcovered many curious articles of antiquity, as related by Dr. Borlaſe, p. 316, &c. 2d edit. of Antiq. of Cornwall, many of which are depoſited in the Muſeum at Oxford. The urn lay under the north edge of a bank, which is about ſix feet high, and near ten feet wide, compoſed of earth and ſtones, and running nearly in the arch of a circle for 170 yards, which would be about one-third of the circumference if completed; but, as it appears to have had no foſs on either ſide, it was probably thrown up in haſte to reſiſt a ſudden and unexpected attack of an enemy coming from the oppoſite hill, and the danger of the ſituation and preſſure of circumſtances might occaſion the concealment of the coins; for the ground has none of thoſe recommendations which might induce the Romans to make it a fortified ſtation, as they did the fort at Boſenſe. The urn was covered by a curious ſtone, of bluiſh elvan, about four feet long. two feet broad, and uniformly one foot thick, between which and the urn was a thin ſtratum of earth, and the ſtone itſelf was covered by the ſhelving of the bank.

The next urn was diſcovered by one William Harry, in June, 1789, in the pariſh of Morva, about five miles nearly north of Penzance, and within a few yards of the road between thoſe two places.

places. It was near the N. W. corner of a fmall enclofure, furrounded by a thick uncemented wall, or hedge, which feems to have ftood ever fince the interment of the urn; for it was found at the foot of a very long and large ftone inferted in the wall, which might ferve as a memento, about a foot under the furface of the earth, and covered by a flat ftone of granite. The foil in this enclofure being rather deep, the farmer carried off the furface, even to the fubftratum of clay, to manure other lands, and juftly thinking that potatoes would thrive well in clay, and that the dung in which they were tilled would fertilize the mold, and prepare it for a crop of corn, a method of agriculture very prevalent in Cornwall, in digging up this clay he threw his pickaxe into the urn, and broke it into many pieces. Thefe coins, as well as thofe found at Godolphin, were almoft all of them copper, but a few were of the ancient lead, a coin much more rare than the former, a very perfect one of which fell into my hands. A Jew likewife got poffeffion of thofe coins, and retailed them round the country for about a penny a piece, tho' moftly in a high ftate of prefervation. If this urn had been found in Dr. Borlafe's time, as it lay within three quarters of a mile of Caftle Chûn, between which two fpots there are many walls of a conftruction fimilar to that where the coins were dug up, it would probably have changed his opinion refpecting the builders of that fortification, which he fuppofes to be of Danifh erection; and indeed he feemed to have fome doubts on this fubject, for he fays, page 316, " Some " of our round intrenchments on the tops of round hills in Cornwall, may be Roman works, if " either way pafs near or through them, or coins be found in them." It is difficult to conceive why the doctor did not determine Caftle Chûn to be a Roman fortification; for in his defcription of an intrenchment in the parifh of St. Agnes, he fays, page 314, that it was formed with too much art and military fcience for either Britons, Saxons, or Danes; and yet in fpeaking of Caftle Chûn, which he pronounces to be Danifh, he fays, page 347, " The whole of this work, the " neatnefs and regularity of the walls, providing fuch fecurity for their entrance, flanking, and di- " viding their fofs, fhews a military knowledge fuperior to that of any other works of this kind " which I have feen in Cornwall."*

* " If this Caftle Chûn (fays Mr. Hitchins) was a ftation of the Romans, which feems extremely probable, not only from the great military fkill employed in erecting it, but alfo from the coins lately found near it, anterior to their fettlement there, it was a favourite hill of the Druids, if they were, as is generally fuppofed, the builders of Cromlêhs; for, about five hundred yards from the caftle there is one on the north fide; at little more than a mile there are two on the eaft fide; and two more in the north-eaft, diftant four miles and three quarters. Thefe cromlêhs, except one of them lately found, have been well defcribed and delineated by the learned and accurate Dr. Borlafe; but the great *defideratum* he lived not to fee, i. e. a human body inhumed under one of thofe erections, which has been recently difcovered in the parifh of Madron, and within a half mile of the famous Lanyon Cromlêh, vulgarly called the Giant's Quoit. This Cromlêh was found a few years fince by the following incident. The gentleman, who is leafeholder of the eftate of Lanyon, under Mr. Rafhleigh, happening, in walking through his fields, to be overtaken by a fhower of rain, took fhelter behind a large bank of earth and ftones, and obferving that the earth was rich, it occurred to him that it might be ufeful for a compoft. Accordingly he fent his fervants foon after to carry it off, when, having removed a very large quantity, they difcovered the fupporters of a Cromlêh, from which the cover-ftone was flipped off on the fouth-weft fide, but ftill leaning againft them. Thefe fupporters include a rectangular fpace, open only at the north end, and their dimenfions are of a very extraordinary fize, viz. that forming the eaftern fide being about ten feet and half long; that on the weft nine feet, with a fmall fupplementary one to complete the length; and the ftone fhutting up the fouth end being about five feet wide. The cover-ftone is about thirteen feet and half, by ten feet and half; but its exact length, and the height of the fupporters, cannot be readily afcertained, as they are partly inferted in the ground. The prefent height is about five feet above the furface of the field, and the cover-ftone contains many more folid feet than that of the other Cromlêh ftanding on this eftate. Except the fmall Cromlêh near Caftle Chûn, this is diffimilar to all others found in this county, which have fmall fupporters, and the area under the cover-ftone open on all fides; whereas this, when the cover was on, was fhut up almoft quite clofe, except at the entrance on the north fide, and appears to refemble Kitt's Cotty Houfe, in Kent, though the dimenfions of that are much fmaller. As foon as the gentleman

The third Roman urn was difcovered in June 1793, by fome labourers, in digging a trench about a hundred yards from the fea, in the parifh of Ludgvan, and little more than half a mile N.W. of St. Michael's Mount. It was buried in the fand two or three feet under the furface, and was nearly of the fame fize with thofe found at Godolphin and Morva, but the coins, owing to the dampnefs of the fituation, were more corroded. I faw none of them, but was informed that, like thofe found in the two other urns, they were chiefly coins of Gallienus, Victorinus, Tetricus fenior, &c." *

The fourth urn was found about May 1804, in the neighbourhood of Chiverton, the feat of John † Thomas, efq. about a quarter of a mile from Venton-gymps. Mr. Thomas informed me, that the perfons who difcovered it, were employed in digging a ditch—that they found it about two feet under the foil—that, on their ftriking their tools againft it, and perceiving fomething extraordinary, they immediately broke it into pieces from the fame principle of cupidity which has been noticed as actuating others in fimilar circumftances;—but that their exertions ended in difappointment, as it was filled with earth, and nothing elfe. At the bottom of the urn, the earth was black, but not unctuous. As well as he could judge from the fragments put together, this urn, Mr. Thomas fuppofes, was no lefs than five feet high—its wideft part about four feet in diameter; its mouth about a foot. Its thicknefs was about an inch—the outfide and infide, reddifh; and the inner, much mixed with fmall blue killas. From ‡ its figured work, fomewhat refembling that of the Morvah urn, (fee Hift. of Cornwall, vol. I. p. 139) I place this, without much hefitation, among the urns of the Romans—not to infift on its vicinity to other remains of that people, which I have defcribed in Piran and St. Agnes.

man obferved it to be a Cromlêh, he ordered his men to dig under it, where they foon found broken pieces of an urn, with much afhes; and going deeper they took up about half of a fkull, together with the thigh bones, and moft of the other bones of a human body. Thefe lay in a promifcuous ftate, and in fuch a difordered manner as fully proved that the grave had been opened before; which is alfo further evident, becaufe the flat ftones which formed the grave, or what Dr. Borlafe calls the Kift-vaen, i. e. little cheft, and a flat ftone about fix feet long, which probably lay at the bottom, had all been deranged and removed out of their proper places. The fkull and fome other bones were carried into the gentleman's houfe, and fhewn for fome time as curiofities, but were afterwards inclofed in a box and re-interred in the fpot from whence they had been taken. Thefe bones I have been affured were above the common fize of the prefent race of men; but I was not fortunate enough to hear of this event fufficiently early to get a view of them."

* "About two miles and half N. E. of this laft fpot, in the fame parifh, is fituated the Well of Collurion, very famous for time immemorial for its opthalmic virtues; and it feems a very extraordinary circumftance that it never occurred to any of the hiftorians of Cornwall, who have recorded its wonderful efficacy, not even Dr. Borlafe, who was rector of this parifh, that the name of this well is pure Greek, κολλυριον, i. e. a medicine for the eyes. How it acquired this name is a fubject of curious inveftigation and refearch. It could not be given by the Phenicians who traded here for tin; for though they had much intercourfe with the Greeks, they are known to have fpoken a dialect of the Hebrew, differing very little from the original. Neither is it quite certain that the Greeks had any traffic in Mount's Bay; and the great number of Greek words adopted in our language are well known to have been conveyed through indirect channels. May we not venture to conjecture that the name Collurion might be given to this celebrated well by fome Greek foldiers, who might have been cured by its waters, many of whom were incorporated in the Roman armies during their poffeffion of this ifland?"

† Vice-warden of the Stannaries of Cornwall.

‡ See the impreffion on the oppofite page.

CURSORY

CURSORY REMARKS ON THE ROMANCE OF MORTE ARTHUR.

SUPPLEMENT to the ELEVENTH CHAPTER of the SECOND BOOK.

THE laſt chapter of the ſecond book of this hiſtory, was cloſed with ſome alluſions to the exploits of MERLIN: And in the romance of *Morte Arthur*, Merlin was no inconſiderable perſonage. "Morte Arthur, or the lyf of Kyng Arthur, of the noble knyghtes of the round table, and in "thende the dolorous deth of them all," was tranſlated into Engliſh from the * French, by Sir Thomas Maleory, knight, and printed by Will. Caxton, in 1484. It has been twice or thrice re-printed. The laſt edition is dated 1634. In this romance we are told: "There was a knight, "Meliodas; and he was lord and king of the country of Lyones; and he wedded King Macke's "ſiſter of Cornewale." The iſſue of this marriage, it appears, was Sir Triſtram. We have then, an account of Sir Triſtram's baniſhment from Lyones to a diſtant country, by the advice and under the conduct of a wiſe and learned counſellor, named Governale. (Book II. chap. 1.) After Sir Triſtram had become ſkilled in the language, the courtly behaviour, and the chivalry of France, we are informed, that, "as he growed in might and ſtrength, he laboured ever in hunt- "ing and hawking; ſo that we never read of no gentleman, more, that ſo uſed himſelfe therein. "And he began good meaſures of blowing of blaſts of venery (hunting) chaſe, and of all manner "vermeins: And all theſe termes have we yet of hawking and hunting; and therefore the booke "of venery, of hawking and hunting, is called THE BOOK OF SIR TRISTRAM." (Book II. chap. 3.) In another place King Arthur thus addreſſes Sir Triſtram. "For of all manner of "hunting thou beareſt the priſe; and of all meaſures of blowing thou art the beginner; and of "all the termes of hunting and hawking ye are the beginner." (B. II. c. 91.) I muſt here obſerve, that from "*Morte Arthur*," our Spenſer has borrowed many of his names in the Faery Queen; ſuch as Sir Triſtram, Placidas, Pelleas, Pellenore, Percivall. And Spenſer informs us, that Sir Triſtram was born in Cornwall:

"And Triſtram is my name, the only heire
Of good old Meliogras, which did raigne
In Cornewaile."——6. 2. 28.

And afterwards:

—— "The countrie wherein I was bred
The which the fertile Lioneſſe is hight."——St. 30.

Of

* Arthur was the theme of France and of Italy, when his native Cornwall could boaſt no poet to celebrate his fame. Arioſto has done credit to the ſubject: The XXXIII. Canto of his Orlando Furioſo, is a very ingenious fiction. There Pharamond, king of France, reſolved to conquer Italy, deſires the friendſhip of Arthur, king of Britain. Arthur ſends Merlin, the magician, to aſſiſt him with advice. Merlin, by his ſupernatural art, raiſes a ſumptuous hall; on the ſides of which all the future wars, unfortunate to the French in their invaſions of Italy, are painted in colors exceeding the pencils of the greateſt maſters. A deſcription of theſe pictures, is given to the heroine Bradamant, by the knight who kept the caſtle of Sir Triſtram where the enchanted hall was placed.

Of his fondnefs for field fports, Sir T. fays:

—— " My moft delight has always beene
To hunt the favage chace among my peres
Of all that raungeth in the foreft greene,
Of which none is to me unknown that e'er was feene.——St. 31.
Ne is there hawke that mantleth her on pearch,
Whether high tow'ring, or accoafting lowe,
But I the meafure of her flight do fearch,
And all her pray, and all her dyet knowe.——St. 32.

In Tuberville's Treatife of *Falconrie*, &c. Sir Triftram is often introduced as the patron of field-fports. A huntfman thus fpeaks:

Before the king I come report to make,
Then hufh and peace for noble TRISTRAM's fake.——Edit. 4to. 1611, p. 96.

And in another place:

" Wherefore thou lyft to learn the perfect trade
Of venerie, &c.——
Let him give ear to fkilfull TRISTRAM's lore.

P. 40. See alfo *Mort. Arth.* b. ii. c. 138.

In the romance before us, we meet with the moft extravagant ideas—among which is that of the mantle made of the beards of kings! " Came a meffenger—faying, that King Ryence had " difcomfited, and overcomen eleaven knights, and everiche of them did him homage; and that " was this, they gave him their beards cleane flayne of as much as there was: Wherefore the " meffenger came for King Arthur's berd: For King Ryence had had *purfeled a mantell with king's* " *beards*, and there lacked for one place of the mantell. Wherefore he fent for his berd; or elfe " he would enter into his lands, and brenn and fley, and never leave, till he have thy head and " beard." B. i. c. 24.—Spencer has improved on the idea: His mantle is " with *berds* of knights, " and lockes of ladies lynd." 6. 3. 15.—Drayton, in his Polyolbion, fpeaks of a coat compofed of the beards of kings. He is celebrating King Arthur.

" As how great Rithout's felf, he flew in his repair,
And ravifht Howel's niece, young Helena the fair.
And for a trophie brought the giant's coat away,
Made of the beards of kings."——(Song 4.)

But Drayton, in thefe lines, manifeftly alludes to a paffage in Geoffrey of Monmouth; who informs us, that a Spanifh giant, named Ritho, having forcibly conveyed away from her guard, Helena the niece of Duke Hoel, poffeffed himfelf of St. Michael's Mount in Cornwall, whence he made frequent fallies, and committed various outrages; that, at laft, King Arthur conquered this giant, and took from him a certain *coat*, which he had been compofing *of the beards of kings*, a vacant place being left for King Arthur's beard. *(Orig. et geft. Reft. Brit.* b. x. 13.*)*—It appears, from a paffage in *Morte Arthur*, that knights ufed to wear the fleeves of their miftreffes upon their arms. " When Queen Genever wift that Sir Launcelot beare the red fleeve of the " faire maide of Aftolat, fhe was nigh out of her minde for anger." B. iii. c. 119.—I have elfewhere adverted to the fuperftitious notions of our Cornifh anceftors, refpecting the genii, or the fpirits ſpirits of fountains and rivers. “ The Lady of the Lake,” in Morte Arthur, is one of this claſs of beings. “ The Lady of the Lake and Merlin departed: And by the way as they went, MERLIN “ ſhewed to her many wonders, and came into Cornwaile. And alwaies Merlin lay about the “ ladie to have her favour; and ſhe was ever paſſing wery of him, and faine would have been de- “ livered of him; for ſhe was afraid of him, becauſe he was a divell's ſon, and ſhe could not put “ him away by no meanes. And ſo upon a time it hapned that Merlin ſhewed to her in a roche “ (rock) whereas was a great wonder, and wrought by enchcantment, which went under a ſtone, “ ſo by her ſubtile craft and working ſhe made Merlin to go under that ſtone, to let him wit of “ the marvailes there. But ſhe wrought ſo there for him, that he came never out, for all the “ craft that he could doe.” B. i. c. 60.—The Lady of the Lake was a very popular character in Elizabeth's days: ſhe was introduced to make part of the queen's entertainment at Kenelworth. This romance ſeems to have extended its reputation beyond the reign of Queen Elizabeth. *Ben Jonſon* alludes more than once to Morte Arthur. *Camden*, in his remains, ſpeaking of the name *Triſtram*, obſerves: “ I know not whether the firſt of his name was chriſtened by King Arthur's “ fables.” He ſpeaks, alſo, of *Launcelot* and of *Gawen*. Thus too *Milton*:

—— “ Damſels met in foreſts wide
By knights of Logris, or of LYONES,
Lancelot, *Pelleas*, or *Pellenore*.” Par. Reg. b. ii. v. 359.

———— “ What reſounds
In fable or romance, of Uther's ſon,
Begirt with Britiſh or Armoric knights.” Par. Loſt, b. i. v. 579.*

This much for Morte Arthur: which, we have ſeen, was tranſlated from the French into Engliſh, in the fifteenth century. But of what date is the French original? or, whence was it derived?

* Milton's fondneſs for the old Britiſh ſtory, is no where more pleaſingly diſplayed than in his Latin poems. Thus, in his “ Liber Sylvarum:”

“ Ipſe ego Dardanias Rutupina per æquora puppes *
Dicam, et Pandraſidos regnum vetus Inogeniæ,
Brennumque Arviragumque duces, priſcumque Belinum,
Et tandem Armoricos Britonum ſub lege colonos;†
Tum gravidam Arturo, fatali fraude, Iögernen,‡
Mendaces vultus, aſſumptaque Gorlöis arma,
Merlini dolus. O mihi tum ſi vita ſuperſit,§
Tu procul annoſa pendebis fiſtula pinu,
Multum oblita mihi; aut patriis mutata Camœnis
Britonicum ſtrides, quid enim? omnia non licet uni
Non ſperaſſe uni licet omnia, mi ſatis ampla

Merces.

* *Ipſe ego Dardanias*, &c.] The landing of the Trojans in England under Brutus. Rhutupium is a part of the Kentiſh coaſt. Brutus married Inogen, the eldeſt daughter of Pandraſus a Grecian king; from whoſe bondage Brutus had delivered his countrymen the Trojans. Brennus and Belinus were the ſons of Molutius Dunwallo, by ſome writers called the firſt king of Britain. The two ſons carried their victorious arms into Gaul and Italy. Arviragus, or Arvirage, the ſon of Cunobelin, conquered the Roman general Claudius. He is ſaid to have founded Dover-caſtle.

† *Et tandem Armoricos Britonum ſub lege colonos.*] Armorica, or Britany, peopled, according to the poet, by the Britons when they fled from the Saxons.

‡ *Tum gravidam Arturo*, &c.] Iogerne was the wife of Gorlois, Prince of Cornwall. Merlin transformed Uther Pendragon into Gorlois; by which artifice Uther had acceſs to the bed of Iogerne, and begat King Arthur. This was in Tintagel-caſtle in Cornwall. See Geffr. Monm. viii. 19. The ſtory is told by Selden on the POLYOLBION, S. i. vol. ii. 674.—But ſee HIST. of CORNW. book ii. chap. I.

§ “ And O, if I ſhould have long life to execute theſe deſigns, you, my rural pipe, ſhall be hung up forgotten on yonder ancient “ pine: you are now employed in Latin ſtrains, but you ſhall ſoon be exchanged for Engliſh poetry. Will you then found in rude Bri- “ tiſh tones?—Yes—We cannot excell in all things. I ſhall be ſufficiently contented to be celebrated at home for Engliſh verſe.” Milton ſays in the Preface to CH. GOV. b. ii. “ Not caring to be once named abroad, though perhaps I could attain to that: but con- “ tent with theſe Britiſh ilands as my world.” PROSE-WORKS, vol. i. 60.

derived? In theſe queſtions I feel peculiarly intereſted; as Morte Arthur, in ſome ſhape or other, ſeems to have been perverted into an inſtrument of ſcandal againſt the ancient Corniſh.

I now approach the object which I have, all along, had in view; while I proceed to ſtate, that of the Morte Arthur, Gibbon has made a very curious uſe. The hiſtorian inſinuates, from ſome expreſſions, it ſeems, in the romance, that the Corniſh were cowards!!! "Cornwall (ſays he "in a note) was finally ſubdued by Athelſtan, (A.D. 927, 941,) who planted an Engliſh colony "at Exeter, and confined the Britons beyond the river Tamar. See Malmeſbury, l. ii. in the "Scriptores poſt Bedam, p. 50. The ſpirit of the Corniſh knights was degraded by ſervitude: "And it ſhould ſeem, from the *Romance of Sir Triſtram*, that their COWARDICE was almoſt pro-"verbial." (Vol. iii. p. 617, quarto). Gibbon is doubtleſs right in his notice of the final reduction of Cornwall by Athelſtan. But in this circumſtance I perceive not the ſlighteſt ſhadow of cowardice. Gibbon was a mere coxcomb in hiſtory. He read much; he fancied more: And he erred ſplendidly in both. What an hiſtorian muſt that be, who founds a cenſure of cowardice againſt a whole nation, upon *what he thinks* a feeble reſiſtance, without once weighing the comparative ſtrength of the aſſailants and the aſſailed? In a fair eſtimate of the comparative ſtrength of a county againſt a kingdom, Cornwall behaved with exemplary courage in oppoſing Athelſtan at firſt, and in not yielding at laſt without another battle. It is true, the hiſtorian, to enforce his cenſure, refers us to the authority of Morte Arthur. But can a ſarcaſm in a mere romance be admitted as ſufficient evidence in the caſe before us?—The wiſh to ſee the origin of the French Romance in ſome meaſure illuſtrated, muſt be natural to every true Corniſhman of liberal education.§

Merces, et mihi grande decus (ſim ignotus in ævum
Tum licet, externo penituſque inglorius orbi)
Si me flava comas legat Uſa, et potor Alauni,*
Vorticibuſque frequens Abra,† et nemus omne Treantæ,
Et Thameſis meus ante omnes, et fuſca metallis ‡
Tamara, et extremis me diſcant Orcades undis."

§ I have little doubt that the French Romance was borrowed from the Sir Triſtram of Scotland; a poem, of which, till this very hour, I never heard; and which, by as remarkable a coincidence as ever happened in literature, was announced to me, as I was writing the above paragraph, in a letter from a friend at Edinburgh. This letter is dated Sept. 1ſt, 1803:

"Mr. Scott, of Edinburgh, (ſays my friend) is preparing to republiſh an old metrical romance, entitled Sir Triſtram. The edition in queſtion will be made from an unique copy in the advocate's library in Edinburgh, not for the intrinſic merit of the romance as a poetical production, which certainly would never have cauſed its being reſcued from confinement, but as a genuine record too valuable to remain hanging by a ſingle thread. This ſole relic of Thomas, the rhymer's muſe, is the oldeſt

* Alaunus is Alain in Dorſetſhire, Alonde in Northumberland, and Camlan in Cornwall; and is alſo a Latin name for other rivers.

† *Vorticibuſque frequens Abra.*—] So Ovid, of the river Evenus. METAM. ix. 106.

VORTICIBUSQUE frequens erat, atque impervius amnis.

And Tyber is "denſus vorticibus," FAST. vi 502.—ABRA has been uſed as a Latin name for the Tweed, the Humber, and the Severn, from the Britiſh *Abren*, or *Aber*, a river's-mouth. Of the three, I think the Humber, *vorticibus frequens*, is intended. Leland proves from ſome old monkiſh lines, that the Severn was originally called *Abren*; a name, which afterwards the Welſh bards pretended to be derived from King Locrine's daughter *Abrine*, not *Sabrine*, drowned in that river. COMM. CYGN. CANT. vol. ix. p. 67. edit. 1744. In the tragedy of LOCRINE, written about 1594, this lady is called *Sabren*. SUPPL. SHAKESP. vol. ii. p. 262. A. iv. S. v.

Yes, damſels, yes, *Sabren* ſhall ſurely die, &c.

And it is added, that the river (Severn) into which ſhe is thrown, was thence called *Sabren*. *Sabren*, through *Safren*, eaſily comes to *Severn* See COMUS, v. 826, ſeq. In the ſame play, Humber the Scythian king exclaims, p. 246. A. iv. S iv.

And gentle *Aby* take my troubled corſe.

That is, the river *Aby*, which juſt before is called *Abis*. Ptolemy, enumerating our rivers that fall into the eaſtern ſea, mentions *Abi*; but probably the true reading is *Abri*, which came from *Aber*. *Aber* might ſoon be corrupted into *Humber*. The derivation of the Humber from Humber, king of the Huns, is as fabulous, as that the name Severn was from *Abrine* or *Sabrine*. But if Humber, a king of the Huns, has any concern in this name, the beſt way is to reconcile matters, and aſſociate both etymologies in *Hun Aber*, or HUMBER.

‡ ——*Fuſca metallis—Tamara*] The river Tamar in Cornwall, tinctured with tin-mines.

SANDYS.

ndys, Knight of the Garter and Lord Chamberlain, created andys of the Vine, by writ, 15th of Henry VIII. 1524, died

ord Sandys .... = Elizabeth, daughter of George Manners, Lord Ross.

dys, died in his father's .... = Elizabeth, sister of Edward, Lord Windsore.

ord Sandys .... = Catherine, daughter of Edmond, Lord Chandos.

Sandys, son of Miles, nephew of Edwin San- hbishop of York .... = Elizabeth, daughter and sole heiress of William, Baron Sandys of the Vine, in Hampshire.

Henry Sandys slain ex parte Regis, Car. I. April 6, 1644.

oldeft fpecimen we poffefs of compofitions of the kind, and one of the few that can be proved decidedly of Britifh origin. It is referred to by Robert de Brune in his metrical annals of England, (publifhed by Hearne), and was tranflated into French verfe early in the 13th century, after which probably it was dilated into a profe romance, in French, of confiderable length, in which Sir Triftram figures as a knight of the round table; whereas no mention is made of King Arthur, either by Thomas of Erceldowne, or his French tranflator. The principal dramatis perfonæ are Mark, king of Cornwall, Yfonde his queen, and his nephew Sir Triftram. Of courfe the ftory abounds in wondrous exploits, but from the frequent references that have been made to it, and the veneration that attaches ftill to the memory of the author, the fiction perhaps is more clofely interwoven with truth than ufually happens. The topography may for the moft part be afcertained at the prefent day, and the few exceptions, fairly referable to the ftroke of time, may confequently be looked upon as no inaccurate guide towards afcertaining the former exiftence of places now withdrawn from view. Mention is more than once made of a Cornifh port of the name of Carlioun. If the circumftance of the exiftence of the romance intereft you at all in the developement of your hiftory, it will fufficiently gratify me; I need hardly add, that I fhall readily profecute any enquiries refpecting it, that may fuggeft themfelves to you as of any importance; and I am happy in my friend Mr. Scott's permiffion to fay, that the refpect which he entertains for you as an hiftorian, and the fympathies by which the mufes have in a peculiar degree connected you, make him anxious to affift you, fhould it lie in his power, in your literary purfuits. If his "Minftrelry of the Borders" has fallen into your hands, of which I can hardly allow myfelf to doubt, 'tis fuperfluous for me to fay more of him; if otherwife, I certainly do not incur the rifk of future apologies, in pointing out to you a very elegant and interefting fpecimen of the fruits of "Local Attachment.".—Mr. S. is defirous that our worthy hiftorian of Manchefter fhould be acquainted likewife with the high efteem in which he is held on this fide of the Tweed; nor does any one, I am fenfible, efteem him more highly than Mr. Scott himfelf, which I fhould have been lefs forward in adding, had he been lefs capable of appreciating Mr. Whitaker's merit.—As my fheet admits of it, I fhall fubjoin the firft ftanza of the romance—the reft are equally devoid of poetical merit:

I was at Erceldoune
With Tomas fpak y thare;
Thir Lord y rede in roune,
Who Triftrem gat & bare,
Who was king with crown;
And who him fofter'd yare;
And who was bold baroun,
As their elders ware,
Bi yere;
Tomas telles in town,
This aventours as thai ware."

Jan. 16, 1804. My curiofity refts not here. I have this day written to Mr. Scott, and will report his anfwer.

I am favoured with Mr. Scott's anfwer, dated Caftle-ftreet, Edinburgh, 27th Jan. 1804. It is as follows:

"Sir,—I am honored with your letter of the 16th January, and lofe no time in communicating fuch information about Sir Triftrem as I think may intereft you.

Triftrem (of whofe real exiftence I cannot perfuade myfelf to doubt) was nephew to Mark, king of Cornwall. He is faid to have flain in fingle combat Morough of Ireland, and by his fuccefs in that duel, to have delivered Cornwall from a tribute which that kingdom paid to Angus, king of Leinfter. Triftrem was defperately wounded by the Irifh warrior's poifoned fword, and was obliged to go to Dublin to be cured, in the country where the venom had been confected. Yfonde or Yfondi, daughter of Angus, accomplifhed his cure, but had nearly put him to death upon difcovering that he was the perfon who had flain her uncle. Triftrem returned to Cornwall, and fpoke fo highly in praife of the beautiful Yfounde, that Mark fent him to demand her in marriage. This was a perilous adventure for Sir Triftrem, but by conquering a dragon, or, as other authorities bear, by affifting King Angus in battle, his embaffy became fuccefsful, and Yfonde was delivered into his hands to be conveyed to Cornwall. But the Queen of Ireland had given an attendant damfel a philtre or a phrodifiac to be prefented to Mark and Yfonde on their bridal night. Unfortunately the young couple while at fea, drank this beverage without being aware of its effects. The confequence was the intrigue betwixt Triftrem and Yfonde, which was very famous in the middle ages. The romance is occupied in defcribing the artifices of the lovers to efcape the obfervation of Mark, the counter-plots of the courtier's jealoufy of Triftrem's favour, and the uxorious credulity of the King of Cornwall, who is always impofed upon, and always fluctuating betwixt doubt and confidence. At length he banifhes Triftrem from his court, who retires to Brittanye (Bretagne), where he marries another Yfonde, daughter to the duke of that Britifh fettlement. From a vivid recollection of his firft attachment, he neglects his bride, and returning to Cornwall in various difguifes, renews his intrigue with the wife of his uncle. At length, while in Brittanye, he is engaged in a perilous adventure, in which he receives an arrow in his old wound. No one can cure the gangrene but the Queen of Cornwall, and Triftrem difpatches a meffenger, entreating her to come to his relief. The confident of his paffion is directed, if his embaffy be fuccefsful, to hoift a white fail upon his return, and if otherwife, a black one. Yfonde, of Brittanye, the wife of Triftrem, overhears thefe inftructions, and on the return of the veffel, with her rival on board, fired with jealoufy, fhe tells her hufband falfely, that the fails are *black*. Triftrem concluding himfelf abandoned by Yfonde, of Cornwall, throws himfelf back and dies. Meantime the queen lands and haftens to the fuccour of her lover—finding him dead, fhe throws herfelf on the body and dies alfo.

This is the outline of the ftory of Triftrem, fo much celebrated in ancient times. As early as the eleventh century his famous fword is faid to have been found in the grave of a king of the Lombards. The loves of Triftrem and Yfonde are alluded to in the fongs of the king of Navarre, who flourifhed about 1226, and alfo in Chretien de Troyes, who died about 1200. During the 13th century, Tomas of Erceldowne, Earlftown in Berwickfhire, called the Rhymer, compofed a metrical hiftory of their amours. He certainly died previous to 1299. His work is quoted by Robert de Brunne, with very high encomium. For fome account of this extraordinary perfonage, I venture to refer you to a compilation of ballads, entitled the Minftrelry of the Scottifh Border, v. 2d, p. 262, where I have endeavoured to trace his hiftory. It is his metrical romance

mance which I am publifhing, not from a Scottifh MS. of coeval date, but from an Englifh MS. apparently written during the minority of Edward 3d. The tranfcriber quotes Tomas as his authority and profeffes to tell the tale of Sir Triftrem, as it was told to him by the author. The ftanza is very peculiar, and the language concife to obfcurity, in fhort, what Robert de Brunne called, in fpeaking of Sir Triftrem " queinte Inglis" not to be generally underftood even at the time when it was written. The names are all of Britifh, or if you pleafe, Cornifh derivation, as Morgan Riis, Brengwain, Urgan Meriadoc, &c.

It happens by a moft fortunate coincidence, that Mr. Douce, with whofe literary fame and antiquarian refearches you are probably acquainted, poffeffes two fragments of a metrical hiftory of Sir Triftrem, in the French, or I fhould rather fay, in the romance language. One of them refers expreffly to Tomas, as the beft authority upon the hiftory of Triftrem, though he informs us, that other minftrels told the ftory fomewhat differently. All the incidents of thefe fragments occur in my MS. though much more concifely narrated in the latter. The language refembles that of Mad. Marie. Tintagel-caftle is mentioned as Mark's refidence, a fairy caftle which was not always vifible. In Tomas's romance the capital of Cornwall is called *Carlioun*, as I apprehend *Caftrum Leonenfe*, the chief town of the inundated diftrict of Lioneffe, from which Sir Triftrem took his furname. The Englifh and French poems throw great light upon each other.

When the art of reading became more common, the books of chivalry were reduced into profe, the art of the minftrel being lefs frequently exercifed. Triftrem fhared this fate, and his fhort ftory was fwelled into a large folio now before me, beautifully printed at Paris in 1514. In this work the ftory of Triftrem is engrafted upon that of King Arthur, the romance of the Round Table being then at the height of popularity. Many circumftances are added which do not occur in the metrical copies. It is here that the herefy concerning the cowardice of the Cornifh nation firft appears: there is not the leaft allufion to it in the ancient poems, and it is merely introduced to give effect to fome comic adventures, in which Mark (le roy coux) is very roughly handled; and to others, in which certain knights prefuming upon the univerfal poltronery of the Cornifh, attack Triftrem, and according to the vulgar phrafe, " catch a tartar." This volume is ftated to be compiled by Luce, lord of the caftle of Gaft, near Salifbury, a name perhaps fictitious. But Luce, if that *was* his real name, is not fingular in chufing the hiftory of Triftrem for the ground-work of his folio. There are two immenfe MSS. on the fame fubject in the Duke of Roxburgh's Library, and one in the National Library at Paris, and probably many others. The Morte Arthur which you mention is a book of ftill lefs authority than the Paris folio. It is not a hiftory of the Cornifh hero in particular, but a bundle of extracts made by Sir T. Mallory from the French romances of the Table Round, as Sir Lancelot du Lac and the other folio's printed on that fubject at Paris, in the beginning of the 16th century. It is therefore of no authority *whatever*, being merely the fhadow of a fhade, an awkward abridgment of profe romances, themfelves founded on the more ancient metrical *lais* and *gefts*; I fuppofe, however, Gibbon had not Mallory's authority for his obfervation, which he probably derived from the elegant abridgment of Sir Triftrem (I mean of the profe folio) publifhed by Treffan, in Extracts des Romans de la Chevalerie.

I would willingly add to this fcrambling letter, a fpecimen of the romance of Tomas of Erceldoune, but for the hope of foon having it in my power to fend the book itfelf, which is in the prefs.

I fear that in wifhing fully to gratify your curiofity, I have been guilty of conferring much tedioufnefs upon you; but as it is poffible I may have omitted fome of the very particulars you wifhed to know, I have only to add, that it will give me the higheft pleafure to fatisfy, as far as I am able, any of Mr. Polwhele's enquiries, to whofe literary and poetical fame our northern capital is no ftranger. On my part I am curious to know if any recollection of Sir Triftrem (fo memorable elfewhere) fubfifts in his native country, whether by tradition, or in the names of places. Alfo, whether tradition or hiftory points at the exiftence of fuch a place as * Carlioun, which Tomas thus defcribes:

Triftrems fchep was yare
He afked his benefoun
The haven he gan out furr
It hight Carlioun
Nujen woukes & marr
He hobled up & down
A winde to wil him barr
To a flide ther him was boun
Neighe hand
Deivelin hight the toun
An haven in Ireland.

I may juft add, that Triftrem is defcribed as a celebrated mufician and chefs player, and as the firft who laid down regular rules for hunting. I beg to be kindly remembered to Mr. C. to whom I am much obliged for giving me an opportunity to fubfcribe myfelf,

Sir,
Your moft obedient humble fervant,
WALTER SCOTT."

Mr. Scott calls this " a fcrambling letter:" But, in my opinion, it is an admirable fpecimen of the true epiftolary ftyle; equal, in point of compofition, to Pope's Letters, though they were written for the public; and infinitely fuperior to thofe Letters of Pope to Fortefcue, *which are now firft publifhed*, (from the original MSS.) in the firft volume of the Hiftory of Devonfhire.

* Hence, probably, *Carlyon*, the name of a very refpectable Cornifh family.

TREWMAN AND SON, PRINTERS, HIGH-STREET, EXETER.

THE HISTORY OF CORNWALL

by

Richard Polwhele

Volume 4

KOHLER AND COOMBES LTD
DORKING
1978

Engraved by H^y Meyer.

To

Ralph Allen Daniel Esqr.

this print of his relation

Ralph Allen of Bath Esqr.

is inscribed by R. POLWHELE.

THE

CIVIL and MILITARY

HISTORY OF CORNWALL;

WITH

ILLUSTRATIONS from DEVONSHIRE.

BY THE REVEREND R. POLWHELE,

Of Polwhele, and Vicar of Manaccan.

PRINTED BY TREWMAN AND SON,

FOR CADELL AND DAVIES IN THE STRAND, LONDON.

1806.

THE

CIVIL and MILITARY

HISTORY *of* CORNWALL.

HISTORY ſeldom exhibits a more intereſting, or, perhaps, a more varied proſpect than is now opening before us. Tho' limited by the Tamar, or rather by the boundaries of* ancient Cornwall, in reſpect to other parts of England; yet our views into diſtant countries, will be of very conſiderable extent. And we may have opportunities of viſiting Europe, or even Aſia, which the more general Engliſh Hiſtorian would vainly wiſh to ſeize; occupied as he muſt be by a multiplicity of objects at home, and precluded, therefore, from expatiating abroad. From the connexion of the Corniſh with the Danes and the Normans, the Welſh and the Armoricans, we ſhould reſort, perhaps with advantage, to the memoirs of theſe people, for illuſtrations of the hiſtory of Cornwall. With Denmark, our intercourſe was neither ſo early nor ſo frequent as moſt writers have ſtated.† And our commerce with Normandy, was not more intimate than

* *Robert of Gloceſter*, in his character of different counties and towns, ſays,

"Sope about Coventrie; iron at Gloceſtere;
"Metals, lead and tin, in the countrie of Exceſtere."

Even in the 13th century, Cornwall and Devon were deemed alike "the countrie of Exceſtere."

† From "*Turner's* Hiſtory of the Anglo-Saxons," I ſhall quote a few paſſages, where he ſpeaks of Alfred and the Danes; occaſionally rectifying his miſtakes. "Alfred's love for knowlege made him neither effeminate nor ſlothful. The robuſt labours of the chace ingroſſed a large portion of his leiſure; and he is panegyrized for his incomparable ſkill and felicity in this rural art.§ To Alfred, whoſe life was indiſpenſibly a life of great warlike exertion, the exerciſe of hunting may have been ſalutary and even needful. Perhaps his commercial and poliſhed poſterity may wiſely permit amuſements more philanthropic, to diminiſh their attachment to this dubious purſuit.

"He followed the labours of the chace, as far as CORNWALL. His fondneſs for this practice is a ſtriking proof of his activity of diſpoſition; becauſe he appears to have been afflicted with a diſeaſe which would have ſanctioned indolence in a perſon leſs alert. But his life and actions ſhew, that though a dreary malady haunted him inceſſantly with tormenting agony, nothing eould ſuppreſs his unwearied and inextinguiſhable genius. Though environed with difficulties which would have ſhipwrecked any other man, he ſpurned at the oppoſing ſtorm; he even maſtered the raging whirlwind, and made it waft him to virtues and fame.

"For a while we muſt leave Alfred aſpiring to become the ſtudent," in order "to comptemplate and depict the clouds of deſolation and" the ſtorms of "ferocious war, which were collecting from the north, to intercept the progreſs and diſturb the happineſs of the future king; and to lay waſte the whole iſland, with havock the moſt ſanguinary, and ruin the moſt permanent."

§ *Aſſer* 16.

Mr. Turner now purſues his hiſtory of the Daniſh ravages in England, as connected with events in the annals of Denmark. "Ragnar Lodbrog, whoſe reputed death§ ſong has been long venerated for its antiquity, and celebrated for its genius," after ſome ſucceſsful invaſions of France was thrown by ſhipwreck upon Northumbria, was there ſeized, "and doomed to periſh—with lingering pains in a dungeon, ſtung by venomous ſnakes." In conſequence of this cruelty was executed, what would certainly have been executed without it though perhaps not ſo immediately, a deſcent upon England with a view to conquer it and with a reſolution to ſettlement in the country. "The ſons of Ragnar" landed in Eaſt-Anglia, but marched into Northumbria, and this "appeared no more as an Anglo-Saxon kingdom." The Danes afterwards "paſſed the Humber into Mercia, and eſtabliſhed themſelves at Nottingham" for the winter. The king of Mercia was joined with the forces of Weſt Saxony, theſe commanded by Ethelred and Alfred. Yet a truce was made, Ethelred retired with his brother, and the Danes returned into Northumbria. "Man delights to purchaſe the enjoyment of the preſent," ſays Mr. Turner, "by the ſacrifice of his future good. What other principle has been ſo active, in perpetuating moral evil? By this pacific arrangement, Mercia and Weſſex procured a momentary tranquillity. They embraced the immediate benefit, and forgot that it muſt be tranſient." In a few months the Danes began their incurſions again, entered Lincolnſhire, and beat the forces of the country in battle.

The Danes afterwards ravaged, unoppoſed, Northamptonſhire, Cambridgeſhire, and Eaſt Anglia. Edmund the king of Eaſt Anglia was murdered in cool blood and with a ſportiveneſs of barbarity, by the Danes.

In 871 Alfred ſucceeded to the throne, and "began a new life of anxiety, ſhaded for ſome time with the deepeſt gloom of misfortunes." Within a month after his acceſſion, his army was attacked in his abſence and defeated. Alfred made peace with them, and they quitted his dominions. But in 876 they returned, Alfred again negotiated with them to leave his dominions, and now "had the impolicy to uſe money as his peace-maker. They pledged themſelves by their bracelets,—but Alfred exacted alſo an oath on chriſtian relics. We may ſmile at the logic of the king, who thought that a Chriſtian oath would impoſe a ſtronger obligation on Pagan minds or that the crime of perjury was aggravated by the formalities of the adjuration." Here Mr. Turner has made two ſlight miſtakes. The Danes did not ſwear upon their bracelets, as if all wore and all ſwore upon them. They ſwore only upon one bracelet, and this was the general's aſſuredly, the only one he wore, one upon his right hand wriſt. The oath was taken, ſays Aſſer, "ſuper armill*am*, ſuper *quam* nec alicui gratiâ priûs jûrare voluit [Alfredus];" or, as Ethelward writes with a little variation of words but to the ſame purport in ſignification, "ſtatuunt jusjuramentum in eorum *armillâ ſacrâ*, quod [Dani] cæterarum regignum fecêre nunqam!"* This therefore was one only, and the ſame undoubtedly with the *dextrocherium* of that Roman emperor the younger Maximin: Nor did Alfred exact the additional obligation from them, thinking a Chriſtian oath would bind "ſtronger—on Pagan minds" than a Pagan one. Alfred was not weak enough to admit the moſt diſtant approximation of ſuch a thought. Nor did he even believe the "crime of perjury was aggravated by the formalities of the adjuration." He required ſuch an oath as *they* thought binding, and then ſuch as he thought binding. And the latter he required in a proper confidence of religion, that Providence would avenge upon the Danes the violation of an actual oath, an oath ſworn at once upon *their* bracelet and *his* relicks. "Necnon et ſacramentum," adds Aſſer, "in omnibus, quibus ille rex maximé *poſt Dominum* confidebat, juravit; in quibus *et ſuper armillam*," &c.

"To puniſh Northmen by the impoſitions of oaths, or by hoſtages which appear to have been reciprocal, was to encourage their depredations by the importunity which attended them. It was binding a giant with a ruſh, an eagle with a cobweb." That the hoſtages were reciprocal "I infer —, becauſe in mentioning Alfred's complete and final conqueſt of Guthrum, Aſſer ſays, he exacted hoſtages but gave none.—He adds, that this was unuſual." We cite this to note a miſtake. Oaths would certainly be thought binding even upon Northmen, if they were ſuch oaths as their religion had ſanctified. Accordingly we find in the preſent oath, that it was taken "in — armillâ *ſacrâ*," upon the bracelet which had always been ſanctified by their religion for the reception of oaths. Nor were the hoſtages reciprocal. "Ille exercitus" cries Aſſer, "electos obſides quantos ſolus [Alfredus] nominavit ſine ullâ controverſiâ dedit." Alfred alone elected the perſons and nominated the number. Had there been any reciprocity then, the Daniſh chief muſt have been mentioned as equally nominating and equally electing out of Alfred's army. But the very omiſſion proves there was none. At a later period indeed the Danes "pacem ea conditione *petierunt* ut rex nominatos obſides *(quantos vellet)* ab eis acciperet, *et ipſe nullum eis daret*, ita tamen *qualiter nunquam cum aliquo pacem ante pepicerunt*." They had *before* ſubmitted to theſe terms. They *now* propoſed theſe terms themſelves. And *this* conſtitutes the ſuperiority of the one ſucceſs to the other.

"Alfred is one of thoſe diſtinguiſhed characters, who emblazon the page of hiſtory, and give dignity even to the meaneſt writer, who makes their actions the ſubject of his compoſition. As conſpicuous in the annals of time as the comet in the paths of heaven, a luminous ſtream of praiſe has always accompanied his name. Dazzled by the proud magnificence, the recording mortal has been unable to number the clouds, which may have occaſionally dimmed its orb in a part of its progreſs.

"It is deemed a truth which the experience of ages has demonſtrated, that Alfred's merit was of that rare and beneficent ſpecies which no praiſe can exaggerate. Yet as it is eſſential to uſeful hiſtory to be impartial and diſcriminating, if there be any circumſtances in his life which ſeem reprehenſible, they ought not to be concealed. The faults of Alfred are like the ſhadows, which glide over the ſummer graſs. It is the ſurrounding radiance which occaſions us to perceive them, and the momentary obſcuration laſts only while we gaze. To denote them can no more tarniſh Alfred's well-earned fame, than to mention the flitting vapours of the ſpring can deſtroy the luſtre of the glowing parent of the ſeaſons.

"The policy of Alfred, in the firſt years of his reign, is inexplicably ſtrange. The exertions of Weſt Saxony had preſented an Alpine chain of obſtacles to the ambition of the north. Its unaſſiſted power had proved itſelf moſt formidable, and it was therefore the natural bulwark of the iſland. Yet the Northmen were ſuffered for three years, to moleſt Mercia till they ſubdued it; and Alfred made no effort to prevent them. It is true, that the ingratitude of Burrhed had provoked the deſertion; but we do not expect from a lion the petty paſſions of a mule. Great ſouls ſhould riſe above the degrading humours,

§ Finely tranſlated by Dr. Downman, of Exeter.

* "Savile's Quinque Scriptores, c. 480."
"Hiſt. Auguſt. 632. Lug. Bat. 1661."

mours, which level them to the vulgar meannefs [that] they defpife. The Chriftian fhould moralize the world, by the exalted example of difdaining revenge. Nothing could fave Weft Saxony, unlefs Mercia were protected, and, if the fword of Alfred and his brother had fmitten fo heavy without allies, how triumphant might it have defcended on the fpoilers, if the ftrength of Mercia had multiplied its vigour.

"His conduct to the enemy in his defence of Weffex, feems to have been equally unreflecting; and even if compared with that of his brother Ethelred, a man greatly his inferior in intellect, was injudicious and difgraceful. Ethelred had the weaknefs to permit them to deftroy Northumbria and Eaft Anglia, and to enter his own dominions unoppofed. But when the hour of calamity preffed upon him, Ethelred was active, and determined, and battle after battle was the confequence of his refolution. When Alfred affumed the helm, he fought one more conflict, and then, as if weary of the exertion, he pleafed his indolence with his peace; a peace, which may fairly be characterized as unwife and ignominious, becaufe it gave no fecurity, and was indeed the pacification of defeat, and of an impatience of war."

In this incident the author has made fome miftakes. He had faid before, that "within a month after Alfred's fucceffion the Danes attacked his troops at Wilton in his abfence, with fuch fuperiority of force, that all the valour of patriotifm could not prevent defeat."* Yet Affer fays very differently, that "uno menfe impleto" *he* fought "contra univerfum Paganorum exercitum," not by proxy but in perfon, "in monte qui dicitur Wilton —," and even "cum paucis et nimium inæquali numero acerrime belligeravit." The "fuperiority of force" therefore was not fo great, but Alfred maintained the conteft with much vigour. The armies actually continued the battle very fharply, for a confiderable part of the day; "cum hinc inde utrique hoftiliter et animofé non parvâ diei parte pugnarent." Then fo little were the Danes fuperior in force, fo little was "the valour of patriotifm" unable to "prevent a defeat," that the patriots were victorious and the Danes defeated. "Pagani ad integrum fuum periculum propriis fuis confpectibus cernentes," therefore not pretending merely to fly, but actually flying, becaufe "et hoftium infeftationem diutiús non ferentes, terga in fugam verterunt." But, feeing the Saxons thrown into confufion by the heat of the purfuit, they artfully contrived to rally, and renewed the fight; "fed proh dolor! peraudacitatem perfequentium decipientes, iterum in prœlium prodeunt." They thus wrefted the victory out of the hands of the Saxons, and took poft triumphantly on the field of battle; "et victoriam capientes, loca funeris dominati funt." But the fharpnefs of the engagement at firft, the fadnefs of the reverfe at laft, and the flaughter made between both, had fo humbled the Danes as well as the Saxons, that the former were equally willing with the latter to make a treaty of peace. The former were to abandon the country of the latter, and actually abandoned it; "Saxones cum eifdem Paganis, eâ conditione ut ab eis difcederent, pacem pepicerunt; quod et impleverunt." So unjuftly has Mr. Turner reprobated this peace, and defcribed this war! The battle was not fought "in Alfred's abfence." He fought it himfelf. He had once gained the victory, but loft it again from the diforderlinefs of purfuit in his men. Yet under the defeat he did not grow "weary of the exertion." He negotiated with them upon *equal* terms: he made a peace with them that could *not* be "characterized" as either "unwife" or as "ignominious," becaufe it actually gave him the very "fecurity" that he wanted at prefent, becaufe it did all that another battle could have done, becaufe it freed his dominions completely from the invading and victorious hoft.

This peace "procured to the Danes an interval of repofe from the valour of Weffex, which they made ufe of to deftroy its beft fortrefs, the kingdom of Mercia; and to call over new bands of adventurers, who haftened to recruit their loffes, and to give wings to their ambition." Here is a continuation of the error before, and an addition to it. "The valour of Weffex" had been much lowered by the late reverfe of fortune. The people had been engaged this very year, in no lefs than eight battles; and were actually *worn down* almoft all, by the accumulated weight of them: "erant enim Saxones maximâ ex parte, in eôdem uno, anno octo contra Paganos prœliis *populariter attriti*." The wifdom of Alfred faw the fact, and the genius of Alfred fubmitted to the neceffity. He faw the fact in the fmallnefs of the only army that he could raife; when he was compelled to rifk a battle, "cum paucis et nimium inæquali numero." But he muft have feen it ten times more ftrongly, when this fmall army was almoft annihilated, and the Danes were additionally flufhed with victory. Yet even then he negotiated upon equal terms, and he diflodged them from his country. He could not think of Mercia, when the very exiftence of Weffex was at ftake: He faved Weffex, and he did wonders in faving it. Nor did the Danes attack Mercia, as Mr. Turner intimates they did, in confequence of Alfred's peace with them. In the year of the peace, 871, they retired from Weffex; in 872 marched to London, there wintered, and there made peace with Mercia; in 873 marched into Lincolnfhire, as then a party of Northumbria, wintered in Lincolnfhire, and again made peace with Mercia; in 874 took poffeffion of all Mercia without a fingle battle: fo little could Mercia claim any peculiar exertions from Alfred! in 875 marched to the Tyne with one divifion of their army, ranged up to Cambridge with the other, reduced all Northumbria, and wintered at Cambridge; therefore did not invade Weffex again, till 876.*

"The Northmen in the interval obtained numerous fupplies; but Alfred had not been as alert.—When the fall of Mercia difclofed to Alfred the gulf of his deftruction; when, by failing directly to his dominions, they approached to hurl him into it, they found him fleeping on his arms. They furprized the ftrong caftle of Wareham, near the heart of his dominions. Such a prophetic aggreffion fhould have roufed the moft torpid into activity; it only ftimulated Alfred to buy *another* peace. They gave him oaths and hoftages, as the warrantry of their fecurity; they infulted him with *new* attacks, and he was content with *new* hoftages and *new* oaths.—The policy of Alfred feems to have been a hope, of converting their aggreffions into the guilt of *facrilege*," of *perjury*, as Mr. Turner means; "or what could have been the ufe of treaties which they *never* kept, or of oaths *augmented* in their religious formalities, which they only fwore" in order "to violate."

We have here many miftakes. That the Danes had "obtained numerous fupplies" in the interval between Alfred's peace in 871 and the reinvafion of Weffex in 876, is faid upon the credit of a paffage cited from Affer, which actually refers only to a year later than both, even to 877.† Nor does Alfred *appear* to have been "found fleeping on his arms," when in 876 the Danes reinvaded Weffex and "furprized the ftrong caftle of Wareham." Nor did the Danes invade "by failing directly to his dominions." They actually marched by land, marched from Cambridge into Weffex, and marched acrofs Weffex to Wareham in Dorfetfhire. "Sæpe memoratus Paganorum *exercitus, noctu* de *Grantebryege* exiens, caftellum quod dicitur Wærham intravit." Even afterwards, when they left Wareham, they again went by land and reached Exeter; "nocte quâdam—omnes *equites* quos Rex habebat, occidit, verfufque inde *Domnaniam* altum locum qui dicitur Saxonice EXAN-

CESTRE

* "Affer, 25—27. † P. 29.

that of the reſt of the iſland.‡ It was with our relations the Welſh,¶ and the ||Armoricans, (particularly the latter) that we maintained a regular correſpondence for ages. It was with the kindred

CESTRE, *inopinatè direxit*, et *ibi hyemavit*." This however was only a diviſion of the Daniſh army. The reſt ſtaid in Wareham till the year following, and then puſhed out after the others at Exeter. Some of them were actually embarked in ſhips, while others *are expreſſly mounted on horſes*; " exercitus Paganorum Werham deſerens, partim *equitando* partim navigando," &c. " *equeſtrem* veró exercitum rex Ælfredus *inſequebatur* tunc, quouſque venit ad EXANCESTRIAM." So very " alert" indeed had Alfred been at firſt, and ſo very " alert" did he remain to the laſt! He covenanted with the Danes indeed at Wareham, but he covenanted only for their immediate evacuation of his kingdom; " foedus firmiter *ut ab eo diſcederent* pepicit." Even an Alfred is tied down to the conſiderations of circumſtances, and bound by his very poſſibilities of power. He purſued the Danes to Wareham. He blocked them up in it. He agreed to releaſe them from the blockade, on the condition ratified by a Pagan oath, by a Chriſtian oath, and by as many hoſtages as he choſe to name, of their abandoning his kingdom immediately. Yet that " ſurprize" of Wareham caſtle, notes Mr. Turner, " only ſtimulated Alfred to buy another peace." How was it another, and what preceded it? In fact,

It was itſelf its own great parallel.

The peace made at Wareham was the only peace made by Alfred at this period. Nor did Alfred " buy" this. Ethelwerd indeed ſays he did, and Mr. Turner grounds his aſſertion upon Ethelwerd's authority.* But Aſſer and every other hiſtorian omit the circumſtance. Nor can the feeble evidence of Ethelwerd authenticate a point, ſo totally omitted by Aſſer particularly, and ſo impoſſible in the preſent penury of Alfred's exchequer. To *buy off* the Danes was a practice, much poſterior in its date, and ignorantly anticipated by Ethelwerd here. Yet what are theſe " new attacks," theſe " new hoſtages," and theſe " new oaths," that Mr. Turner notices and reprobates? They are only one attack, one convention, one exaction of an oath, and one requiſition of hoſtages. In 877 " Ipſe Exanceaſtre ubi Pagani hyemabant properans, illis incluſis civitatem obſedit." The Danes then attempted to draw their remaining forces from Wareham, by land and by water; one diviſion was deſtroyed by Alfred's navy, or by ocean's ſtorms; the other was chaſed into Exeter by Alfred's army, and there, unwilling to brave them in poſſeſſion of the *town*, not (as Mr. Turner calls it) the *caſtle*,† yet unable from the exhauſted ſtate of the kingdom to diſlodge them from it, he took the courſe that his fortune compelled, and agreed with them for the ſurrender of the town, the county, and the kingdom to him. This indeed makes not ſuch a magnificent relation in hiſtory, as the ſtorming of the town and the annihilation of the army. Yet it was plainly all he could do, with ſuch inſtruments as he had to wield, and with ſuch reſources as he had for wielding them. And it actually anſwered with all the efficacy of a ſtorm or of an annihilation; as " ipſo anno, menſe Auguſto, ille exercitus perrexit in Merciam."

" It was in this manner that Burrhed was deſtroyed" by *Burrhed's own pacification with the Danes*; " he complained and appeaſed their rapacity," to whom did he complain and with what did he appeaſe their rapacity? All that Aſſer ſays is only, that peace was made between them, " pace inter Mercios et Paganos factâ," &c. " and they ſoothed him with the gewgaw of a nominal peace." It was a real one, and laſted from 868 till 874, no leſs than ſix years. " In the next year they repeated their outrages," on whom? on Burrhed, as the context tells. Yet on Burrhed or on Mercia were no outrages repeated " in the next year." They were however the year following, 870, yet not otherwiſe than by marching through their country; when " memoratus Paganorum exercitus *per Merciam* in orientales Anglos tranſivit." Nor for this reaſon, did " the ſame toy again ſatisfie the weak ſovereign" Burrhed. The toy was not offered, therefore could not be accepted, and conſequently could not ſatisfy. " In the following ſeaſon," that is, no leſs than four years afterwards or in 874, " they made a deciſive attack, and Burrhed fled to Rome, to ſhelter his incapacity within the more fitting walls of a convent."

" The conduct of Alfred was as imprudent," when Burrhed only defended himſelf againſt the Danes in 868, and invoked the aid of the Weſt Saxons to reſcue all Mercia north of Nottingham from the Danes; and when the Weſt Saxons, under Alfred or his elder brother Ethelred, had confeſſedly fought no leſs than eight battles with the Danes in the one year 871. " Inſtead of a ſyſtem of vigilance and vigour, we find nothing but inert quietude, temporizing pacifications, and tranſient armaments;" although he had actually fought ſo many battles, as colleague to his brother, within the compaſs of a ſingle year; though he had actually fought one as king himſelf in 871 at Wilton, with a ſmall army againſt a large one; and though he even diſlodged the Danes from Wareham in 876, diſlodged them again from Exeter in 877, and thus ejected them completely out of Weſſex. " The only plan diſcernible in the firſt ſeven years of his reign, was to gain momentary repoſe;" though he had confeſſedly made ſo many or ſo great exertions, and was in 877 only twenty-nine years of age.

The following is an extract from Shune's Hiſtory of Denmark. " Knut the Great, made Living, Abbot of Taviſtock, and afterwards Biſhop of Crydyntone, (Crediton) 1036. Biſhop Living had great influence over the king, and could make very free with him. He lived a long time with him in Denmark, followed him to Rome, and returned thence to England with the king's letter, where he ſettled every thing to the ſatisfaction of his majeſty. He prevailed on Knut to unite the ſee of Cornwall, with that of Crydyntone; but he abuſed this addition of power, for he was ambitious, proud, and imperious. He died in the time of Edward the Confeſſor, and was buried in Taviſtock."

‡ See Dr. Ducarel's Anglo-Norman Antiquities.

¶ For the ſake of " the fourteen privileges of *the men of Arvon*;" in one or two of which we recognize old Corniſh cuſtoms, I ſhall print the greater part of a letter which appeared in the Gentleman's Magazine, for May 1795. " The moſt likely places to find any records reſpecting the antiquity of Caernarvon, are among the manuſcripts collected by thoſe indefatigable antiquaries Mr. Robert Vaughan, of *Hengwrt*, Mr. John Jones, of *Gelli Lyfdy*, Mr. William Morris, of *Ceſn-y-Braich*, &c. Copies of the above manuſcripts may moſt probably be met with among the collections of the ingenious Mr. Lewis Morris, and the learned antiquary the Rev. Evan Evans. Some of the Morriſian MSS are in the poſſeſſion of

* P. 165, † P. 168.

kindred Welſh and Bretons, that we joined our forces in warlike enterprize; and the ſoldiers of Cornwall, of Wales, and of Britany, were alike regarded for conduct and valour; whether they led the van in Europe, or conquered on the plains of Aſia. There was one event, of all others the moſt effectual in ſtrengthening the alliance of the Corniſh with their ancient friends; I mean the war againſt the infidels of the eaſt. This was a common bond of union. And carrying our forefathers

of Mr. William Morris, *Aberyſtwith, Cardiganſhire*, ſon of the above named Mr. Lewis Morris; others, if I am rightly informed, in the library of the Welſh ſchool, London. The manuſcripts of the late Mr. Evans, are in the poſſeſſion of that great patron of genius, Paul Panton, of Plas Gwyn, Angleſey, Eſq. a gentleman well known for his liberal encouragement of Welſh literature, and whoſe name will be recorded with honour while the Welſh language is ſpoken in the land.

To aſcertain the exact time in which the churches in Wales were built, may, indeed, be a difficult taſk. In the firſt place, the antiquary will find it neceſſary to diſcover in what centuries the patron ſaints lived, and thence to draw proper inferences: but yet this rule is not always infallible, becauſe many of the churches were not built under the immediate inſpection of the ſaints whoſe names they bear, but were dedicated to them at a later period. The antiquary ought always to keep this in view; otherwiſe he will be liable to make palpable miſtakes and bold anachroniſms.

From what has been above-mentioned the following queſtion will occur; viz. Where are we to find any authentic account of the Britiſh ſaints? Anſwer: In a manuſcript intituled *Boneddy Saint*; i. e. *The Pedigrees, or, the noble Deſcent of the Britiſh Saints.* In this manuſcript we have a table of the lineal deſcent of theſe devotees, where they reſided, and what churches were to them dedicated.

Your correſpondent informs us, that the voice of Tradition repreſents Clynog, in this county, to be the burial-place of St. Beuno. It is much doubted whether Beuno was buried at Clynog, or at Enlli (Bardſey); moſt probably the latter. This ſainted iſle is often ſtyled, by the Bards, the Sanctuary of the Saints. In early ages it was much reſorted to; and, for that reaſon, was called The Repoſitory and Depoſitory of the Saints. Here they retired from the world, and ſpent their days in meditation and prayer; in this holy ſpot the Saint's venerable aſhes were permitted to lie undiſturbed. Men of leſs celebrity than St. Beuno were brought from diſtant places to be interred in Enlli.

As to *Bedd Beuno* (Beuno's Grave) in Clynog church, it may be ſuppoſed that it was only a monument erected to his memory; or, perhaps, his ſkull, or ſome other relick, was once depoſited there, as it is ſaid of St. Mechell (St. Mecurus or Mechellus), that his ſkull is depoſited at *Penrhos Lligwy*, the remaining part of the body at *Llan Fechell*, in the county of Angleſey.

The firſt abbot of Bardſey was Lleuddad, or Lleudad (Latinized Laudatus), who was the ſon of Nudd the generous; his mother was Theodori, daughter of Lotho (Llewddyn luddog), of the city of Edinburgh; St. Beuno, and Kentigern (Cyndervn) biſhop of St. Aſaph in Wales, and Glaſgow in Scotland, were his couſin-germans, their mothers being two ſiſters.

St. Dubricius (Dyfrig), archbiſhop of Caerleon, reſigning his biſhoprick of St. David's, retired to Bardſey from the ſynod of Brevi, which was held againſt the Pelagians, about the year 522. Moſt of the clergy of that ſynod retired along with him there, where they ſpent the remainder of their days in a monaſtery.

As I am on the ſubject of the antiquity of Caernarvonſhire, may I be permitted to rectify an error in Mr. Pennant's Tour in Wales, wherein it is ſaid that Caernarvon caſtle was built in the ſpace of three years; whereas it appears, from a certain record formerly belonging to the Exchequer, that it took up twelve years in building?

Some materials towards forming a Hiſtory of Caernarvonſhire may be found in the Triades of the Iſle of Britain, which Mr. Lewis Morris proves, beyond contradiction, to be above a thouſand years old.

The reign of Rhun ap Maelgwyn ſtands as a memorable era in the annals of our country. An expedition was undertaken by him againſt *Elidir Mwynfawr*, which produced the fourteen privileges of the men of *Arvon*. I hope my fair countrywomen will excuſe me for touching upon this part of our hiſtory, though it reflects no great honour on our Arvonian grandmothers.

When the ſaid Rhun had ſpent ſome time near the Caledonian borders in ſettling the affairs of the North, he returned to Cambria. In the mean time the men of Arvon's wives concluding, from their huſbands' long abſence, that they were all ſlain, lay with their ſervants. At Rhun's return, the ſoldiers diſcovered their wives had proved unfaithful. As ſoon, therefore, as this circumſtance was divulged, thoſe, who were before obliged to yield priority to the men of Arvon, and deteſted their pride, had now a good opportunity to ridicule and expoſe them: wherefore King Rhun, in order to palliate the diſgrace, and to recompenſe their good ſervices, honoured them with fourteen privileges above their fellow-ſoldiers. Unfortunately, two of the ſaid privileges were obliterated in an antient law-book, of which that great antiquary Mr. Robert Vaughan took a copy; the other twelve ſtill remain upon record. Leſt poſterity ſhould be ignorant of an antique ſo rare, a copy of the original, with Mr. Vaughan's tranſlation, is here annexed.

1. Rackwys rhac Gwreic, a ſef eu rhachor e Meyrch dôf, a Moch a hwyadheu, a Kar; a dau hechen a venho ar y Gwartheg; a Cloneyt e Kar o'r dohedreſn a venho; *i. e.* A priority over the wife; that is, their choice of their tame horſes, ſwine and geeſe, a cart, and their choice of two oxen of the cattle, and a cartful of their choice houſehold ſtuff.—2. Blaen Gwynedd en c uulteu; *i. e.* To lead the van-guard of the army of North Wales.—3. Na toll anifail; *i. e.* That they toll not their beaſts.—4. Eu terven ar e Gulatoedd ac cauaruont ac Arfon; *i. e.* To ſettle the boundaries of the counties which join upon Arvon.—5. O bit amreſon e rwc dwy vaenawl o'r naw maynawl ſit en Arfon eu diamryſoni o'r faith e dwy heb neb o le arall; *i. e.* If variance happen between two manors of the nine manors in Arvon, the other ſeven, without the interference of others, ſhall end the ſtrife between them.—6. Na bo Righill endhi; *i. e.* That there be no beadle or bailiff in it.—7. Bit ennid (cenad) Peſcodha ar e teyr Afon e ſit endhi yn gyffredin; *i. e.* That they have the liberty of fiſhing in the three principal

forefathers into the midſt of nations before unknown almoſt by name, every expedition had a ſalutary effect, inaſmuch as it improved the manners, and opened new ſources of intelligence. In my former notice of the Cruſades, I could not but regret the circumſtance, that both the exploits and the names of our Corniſh religioniſts were, for the moſt part, buried in oblivion. Yet, if imagination were to connect the counts of Edeſſa, or the emperors of Conſtantinople, with

principal rivers which are in it.—8. Deficient.—9. Na boet freuan hechwg; *i. e.* That they be not ſtrait-milled, or tied to the hand-mill.—10. Luſen tlawdcaut. (Not tranſlated.)—11. Na ddala ar eu cengheuſef; *i. e.* That there ſhould be no delay in their pleadings at law.—12. Na thaler Meirch Gweſteyon, no Gwr ar gylch; *i. e.* That they be not obliged to pay for the horſes of ſtrangers, or men (minſtrels) on their (annual) circuits.—13. Na deleant venet y lety arall o'r Neuat; *i. e.* That they ought not to go out of the court (hall) for their lodging.—14. Pwy bennac a eſtedho endhi un dut a Blwytyn, o bit Gwr alltuthawg e vot en un vry (fri) a Gwr o'r Wlad; *i. e.* That whoever ſettleth in it (Arvon) for a year and a day, though he be an alien, ſhall have the liberty of an inborn or denizen.

Beſides princes and warriors, our county has produced ſome eminent men of genius. Being a warm admirer of the primitive Bards, I cannot refrain from mentioning a few of them. That great Corypheus of the Bards, *Talieſin*, lived, as tradition ſays, in the pariſh of Llanrhychwyn; the ruins of his houſe are to be ſeen at this day. *Gwilym Ddu o Arfon* lived in the pariſh of Llandwrog; the ruins of his houſe are ſhewn on a tenement called Tyddyn Tudur, a little to the South of *Glyn Civon*, the ſeat of the Right Honourable Lord Newborough. *Rhobin Ddu*, another Bard of great celebrity, was born in the pariſh of Llanddeiniolen, near a houſe now called Pant yr Afallen, a little above Moel y don."

The Corniſh and the Welſh were equalled ſkilled in the uſe of the bow. I ſhall relate a few exploits performed by the Welſh Archers, as they are reported by *Giraldus Cambrenſis*.—There is a particular tribe in Wales, ſays this ancient writer, named the Venta; a people brave and warlike, and who far excel the other inhabitants of that country in the practice of Archery. In ſupport of this laſt aſſertion, the following inſtance is recorded. During a ſiege, it happened, that two ſoldiers running in haſte towards a tower, ſituated at a little diſtance from them, were attacked with a number of arrows from the Welſh; which being ſhot with prodigious violence, ſome penetrated through the oak doors of a portal, although they were the breadth of four fingers in thickneſs. The heads of theſe arrows were afterwards driven out, and preſerved, in order to continue the remembrance of ſuch extraordinary force in ſhooting with the bow. It happened alſo in a battle, at the time of William de Breuſa, (as he himſelf relates) that a Welſhman having directed an arrow at an horſe-ſoldier of his, who was clad in armour and had his leather coat under it; the arrow, beſides piercing the man through the hip, ſtruck alſo through the ſaddle and mortally wounded the horſe on which he ſat. Another Welſh ſoldier, having ſhot an arrow at one of his horſemen, who was covered with ſtrong armour in the ſame manner as the before mentioned perſon, the ſhaft penetrated through his hip and fixed in the ſaddle: but what is moſt remarkable, is, that as the horſeman drew his bridle aſide in order to turn round, he received another arrow in his hip on the oppoſite ſide, which paſſing through it, he was firmly faſtened to the ſaddle on both ſides." *Itin. Camb.* Gir. Camb. p. 835.

‖ The Bretons emigrated to Armorica from Cornwall and Wales, from ann. 450 to 500. They carried with them their Biſhops and Prieſts. One colony were Danmonii. And a diſtrict in Armorica, was called Danmonium. See *Lobineau's* Hiſt. of Britany.

I have already pointed out many Corniſh names in Britany, ſuch as *Trevanion*, *Caerhayes*, &c. The late Mr. *Grylls*, of London, found a Grylls at Grylls-Caſtle, in Britany, and his own arms over the gateway of the caſtle. Lobineau mentions a family in Britany bearing the arms of the Corniſh Scobels.

In the hiſtory of France the Armonican's made a diſtinguiſhed figure. In 493, Clovis is repreſented as extending his arms into Britany. In 1167, Geoffrey, ſon of Henry II. King of England, married Conſtantia, daughter of Conan, Count of Britany, who brought him the whole province for her dower, which Henry ſeized in the name of his ſon. Hiſtorians ſpeak of the war in Britany in 1364. when the young Count de Montfort defeated Charles de Blois in the battle of Auray, in which Charles fell. In 1365, the Count de Montfort, concluded a treaty with the widow of Charles de Blois; by which he was acknowleged Duke of Britany, and as ſuch performed homage to the king. On an expedition into Britany, in 1392, Charles the ſixth, who had before diſcovered ſymptoms of madneſs, was ſeized with a ſudden frenzy. The Bretons, diſplayed on every emergency the ſpirit of their anceſtors the Corniſh: and they only acquieſced for ſhort intervals in the ſovereignty of the French kings. The intercourſe between the Corniſh and the Bretons, was carried on to a late age. But, at length, the feelings of affinity were loſt in the urbanities of more extenſive commerce. Not that, even at firſt, the Corniſh confined their viſits to Britany. They had, in early times, a college at Paris.

with the earls of Devon, or the lords of Boconnoc, the tale of the wars of Paleſtine, would be deemed no unwarrantable epiſode in a hiſtory of Cornwall.*

B

At

* A Genealogical Table of the FAMILY of *Joſceline de Courtenay*, Count of *Edeſſa*.

ATHON, who fortified the Town *COURTENAY*, and gave that Name to his Family.

1ſt Wife, *Hildegarde*, Daughter of *Jeofry Ferrole*, Count of *Gaſtinois*, } *Joſceline de Courtenay* { 2d Wife, *Iſabel*, Daughter of *Guy*, Seigneur *de Montlehery*.

1 Daughter, named *Hodierne* = *Jeofry* Count *de Joigny*.

1. *Miles* Seigneur *de Courtenay*. — 1ſt Wife, a Daughter of a Prince of *Armenia*. } 2. *Joſceline*, 1ſt Count of *Edeſſa*. { 2d Wife, a Daughter of *Roger*, Prince of *Antioch*. — 3. *Jeofry de Courtenay*.

Joſceline, 2d Count of *Edeſſa* = *Beatrix*, Widow of *William de Saona*. — *Stephania de Courtenay*, Abbeſs of St. *Mary-Major* in *Jeruſalem*.

1. *Joſceline*, 3d Count of *Edeſſa* = *Agnes* Daughter of *Henry de Buſſle*. — 2. *Elizabeth*, who died young — 3. *Agnes* = *Almerick* King of *Jeruſalem*. She had 3 other Huſbands.

1. *Beatrix* = Count *Alimond*. — 2. *Agnes* = *William de Mandalee*.

1. *Baldwin* 4 King of *Jeruſalem*. — 2. *Sibylla*, Queen of *Jeruſalem* = { 1. *William* Marqueſs of *Montferrat*. 2. *Guy* of *Luſignan*, King of *Jeruſalem*.

Baldwin 5. King of *Jeruſalem*, died an Infant.

The FIRST Branch of the FAMILY of *Peter de Courtenay*, Son of King *Lewis le Groſſe*.

LEWIS le GROS, 6th of that Name, King of *France*.

Philip, crowned King. — *Lewis* 7, King of *France*. — *Henry*, Arch-Biſhop of *Rheimes*. — *Hugh* — *Robert*, Count *de Dreux*. — *Philip*, Religious at *Clairvaux*. — *Peter*, Seigneur *de Courtenay*. — *Conſtance*, Queen of *England*, and Counteſs *de Tholouſe*.

Peter de Courtenay, 1ſt Emperor of *Conſtantinople*, = 1ſt *Agnes de Nevers*, — *Robert de Courtenay*, Seigneur *de Champignelles*. — *Philip de Courtenay*. — *William de Courtenay*, Seigneur *de Tanlay*. — *John de Courtenay*. — *Alice*, Counteſs *de Joigny*, and *de Angouleſme*. — *N.... de Courtenay*. — *Clemence* Viſcounteſs *de Thiern*. — *N.... de Courtenay* Dame *de Charros*. — *Conſtance de Courtenay*, Dame *de Chaſteaufort*, and *de la Ferte Arnaud*. — *Euſtache de Courtenay*, Counteſs *de Sancerre*.

By his 2d Wife, *Yoland de Hanault**

Mahud de Courtenay, Counteſs *de Nevers*. — **Philip de Courtenay*, Count *de Namur*. — *Robert de Courtenay*, Emperor of *Conſtantinople*, = a Daughter of *Baldwin de Neufuille*. — *Henry de Courtenay*, Count *de Namur*. — *Baldwin de Courtenay*, Emp. of *Conſtantinople*, = *Mary* Daughter of *John de Brenne*, titular King of *Jeruſalem*. — *Margaret de Courtenay*, Dame *de Iſſoudun*, and Counteſs of *Viane*. — *Elizabeth*, Counteſs of *Bar-ſur-ſeine*, and Dame *de Montagu*. — *Yoland*, Queen of *Hungary*. — *Mary*, Empreſs of *Nice*. — *Agnes*, Princeſs of *Achaia*. — *Eleanor*, Dame *de Caſtres*. — *Sibylle*, Religious.

Philip, Emperor of *Conſtantinople*, = *Beatrix*, Daughter of *Charles* King of *Sicily*.

Catherine, Empreſs of *Conſtantinople*, — *Charles* Count *de Valois*.

One Son who died young. — *Catherine* = *Philip* of *Sicily*, Prince of *Tarentum*. — *Joan* = *Robert* of *Artois*, Count *de Beaumont-le-Roger*. — *Iſabel*, Abbeſs of *Font-Evrard*.

The

At a very early period, however, our attention is drawn to the Crufaders, anticipating the glory of conqueft on European ground. And the incident to which I allude, will difplay our martial fpirit in a new and ftriking light, and almoft give credit to the tales of Cornifh heroifm, before received as fabulous or apocryphal. But it is an occurrence which authors have coldly and cafually mentioned, or obfcurely reprefented; which our own annalifts have overlooked; and of which Cornifh tradition has loft every trace. With pride, then, I haften to throw a fplendour over Cornwall, which muft Eclipfe even the luftre of her Arthur's fame; confcious that I am the firft to diffipate from an atchievement unparallelled in war, the mifts that have fo long inveloped it, and to bring it to the view in all its radiance. That Lifbon was wrefted from the Moors, by a fleet of European Crufaders, which arrived at the mouth of the Tagus, when that city was befieged by the Chriftians, has been told without intereft, and repeated without curiofity. *Puffendorf* flightly mentions the affiftance of the Netherland fleet, in expelling the Moors from Lifbon in 1147.‡

From

The family of *Paleologus* fucceeded that of *Courtenay*, in the Empire of Conftantinople. We have a record of Paleologus in Cornwall. In the chancel of the church at the village of *Landulph*, a few miles from Kellington, is a mural monument, with the following infcription, on a large brafs plate. The letters are in Roman characters. "Here lyethe the body of *Theodoro* PALEOLOGUS of Pefaro in Itayle, defcended from the imperyall lyne of the laft chriftian emperors of Greece, being the fonne of *Camilio*, the fonne of *Profper*, the fonne of *Theodoro*, the fonne of *John*, the fonne of *Thomas*, fecond Brother to *Conftantine Paleologus*, the 8th of that name, and laft of that lyne, that raygned in Conftantinople untill fubdewed by the Turkes: who married with Mary the daughter of William * Balls of Hadlye in Souffolke, gent. and had iffue 5 children, Theodoro, John, Ferdinando, Maria and Dorothy, and dep'ted this life at Clyfton,† the 21ft of January 1636." Above the infcription is the Imperial Eagle; and in the regifter of Landulph, (which is very imperfect about this time,) is an entry of one of the family of Paleologus, buried in the year 1674.

* In the regifter of Hadleigh, the Balls at that period appear to have been very numerous.

† Clyfton was the feat of Sir Nicholas Lower, in the parifh of Landulph. Sir Nicholas, it is faid, being of the Roman Catholic perfuafion, Paleologus paid him a vifit, was taken ill, and died there. Sir Nicholas caufed this monument to be erected to his memory. The houfe is an old Gothic ftructure, and the kitchen was occupied fome years fince, by the parifh clerk. Whether any defcendants of the royal line of Paleologus are now living, I have vainly enquired.

‡ Thus Puffendorf: "Portugal, which comprehends the greateft part of that Province that the Romans called Lufitania, fell with the reft of Spain, under the laft Gothick King Roderick, into the hands of the Moors, who were in poffeffion of it for a long time; but in the year 1093 Alfonfus VI. King of Caftile and Leon, arming with all his power to attack the Moors, and calling for, and craving the affiftance of foreign Princes; among others, came one Henry, to fignalize himfelf in this war, whofe pedigree is varioufly related by the hiftorians. For fome will have him defcended from the houfe of Burgundy, and a younger fon of Robert Duke of Burgundy, whofe father was Robert King of France, fon of Hugh Capet. Others derive his pedigree from the houfe of Lorain, alledging, that the reafon of his being called a Burgundian was, becaufe he was born at Befanzon. To this Henry, King Alfonfus VI. gave in marriage his natural daughter Therefia, as a reward of his valour, affigning him for a Dowry, under the title of an Earldom, all that part of Portugal which was then in the poffeffion of the Chriftians; which comprehended that part of the country, where are the cities of Braga, Coimbra, Vifeo, Lamego, and Porto; as alfo that tract of ground which is now called Tralos Montes; granting to him withal, a power to conquer the reft of that country, as far as to the river of Guadiana, and to keep it under his jurifdiction; but upon thefe conditions, that he fhould be a vaffal of Spain, repair to the Dyets of that kingdom, and in cafe of a war, be obliged to ferve with 300 horfe. Henry died in the year 1112, leaving a fon whofe name was Alfonfus, being then very young: his inheritance was, during his minority, ufurped by Ferdinand Paiz, Count of Traftamara, his father in-law, he having married his mother. But as foon as he was grown up, he took up arms againft his father-in-law, and beat him out of Portugal, but his mother he put in prifon · and fhe calling to her aid Alfonfus VII. promifed to dif-inherit her fon, and to give him all Portugal. But Alfonfus of Portugal defeated the Caftilians in a battel, by which victory he pretended to have freed himfelf from the Spanifh fubjection. This Alfonfus undertook an expedition againft King Ifmar, who had his kingdom on the other fide of the river Tajo, and being joined by the forces of four other petty Moorifh Kings, drew out againft him. Alfonfus was then in his camp near Cabecas des Reyes proclaimed king, in order to animate his foldiers; and got a moft fignal victory, taking the five ftandards of thofe kings, whence he put five fhields in the arms of Portugal, and retained ever after the title of king. He took afterwards a great many cities from the Moors; and among the reft, *with the affiftance of the Netherland fleet, the city of Lifbon in the year* 1147. This Alfonfus was taken prifoner near Badajoz, by Ferdinand king of Egypt, who gave him his freedom without any other ranfom, than that he was to reftore to him fome cities, which he had taken from him in Gallicia. After he had reigned very glorioufly, and greatly enlarged the limits of his kingdom, he died in the 80th year of his age.

To

To him fucceeded his fon Sanctius, who built a great many cities, and filled them with inhabitants. He took from the Moors the city of Selva, being affifted in the expedition, by a fleet fent out of the Netherlands to the Holy Land. He was, during his whole reign, always in action with the Moors, and died in the year 1212. After him reigned his fon Alfonfus, firnamed Craffus, who did nothing worth mentioning, but that, with the help of the Netherlanders, who went to the Holy Land, he took from the Moors the city of Alcaffar. He died in the year 1223. His fon Sanctius, firnamed Capellus, fucceeded him; who being very carelefs, and ruled by his wife, was excluded from the adminiftration of the government by the Portuguefe, who conferred it on Alfonfus his brother, and Sanctius died an exile in Toledo; and married Beatrice, daughter to Alfonfus X. king of Caftile, with whom he had for a Dowry the kingdom of Algarbia. He reigned very laudably, and united a great many cities to his kingdom, and died in the year 1279. The extraordinary virtues of his fon Dionyfius, efpecially his juftice, liberality and conftancy, are highly extolled by the Portuguefe. He having alfo adorned the kingdom with a great many public buildings, among which is the academy of Coimbra, firft founded by him. There is an old proverb relating to him, ufed among the Portuguefe. *El Rey D. Denys, qui fiz quanto quin:* King Dionyfius, who did whatfoever he pleafed. He died in the year 1325. His fon Alfonfus IV. firnamed the Brave, was very glorious for his atchievements both in peace and war; but he banifhed his baftard brother, who was greatly beloved both by his father and the people; and caufed D. Agnas de Caftro, a very beautiful lady, who was without his confent married to his fon Pieter, barbaroufly to be murdered; which fo exafperated Pieter, that he taking up arms againft the father, did confiderable mifchief, till at laft the bufinefs was compofed. He died in the year 1357. His fon Pieter was commonly called The Cruel, tho' fome will have this rather to have been fpoken to his praife, as having been an exact obferver of juftice, never fparing any offender. He died in the year 1368. His fon Ferdinand contended for the kingdom of Caftile with Henry the baftard, who had murthered his brother Pieter, firnamed The Cruel, king of Caftile. But he being too ftrong for him, he could not maintain his pretenfions, but was obliged to make peace. However, the war broke out afrefh again betwixt them. Henry made an inrode into Portugal; and finding no refiftance, over-ran the greateft part of the country. After the death of Henry, Ferdinand made a peace with his fon John, but it was foon violated again by the Portuguefe, who encouraged *the duke of Lancafter, that marry'd Conftantia daughter of Pieter king of Caftile, to pretend to the crown of Caftile. This duke came with a good army into Portugal*; but the *Englifh growing quickly weary of the war in Spain*, and *living very diforderly in Portugal*, a peace was concluded on both fides. At laft Ferdinand marry'd his daughter Beatrice to John of Caftile, under condition, that fuch children as were born of their bodies, fhould fucceed to the kingdom of Portugal; which was afterwards the occafion of bloody wars. This Ferdinand died in the year 1383, being the laft of the true race of the kings of Portugal.

After the death of Ferdinand, great troubles arofe in Portugal, moft of the Portuguefe being unwilling to live under the fubjection of the Caftilians, whom they mortally hated. 'Tis true, 'twas agreed on in the articles of marriage made betwixt the king of Caftile and Beatrice daughter of Ferdinand, that her mother Eleonora fhould have the adminiftration of the government in Portugal, till fuch children as fhould be born of this marriage fhould be of age. But this Eleonora leaving all to the management of the count of Andeira, her much fufpected favourite, fhe drew upon herfelf the hatred of the Portuguefe. Thereupon John natural fon of Pieter king of Portugal, privately murther'd him, whereby he got both the favour of the people, and encreaf'd the hatred againft the queen Dowager: but fome of the Portuguefe being much diffatisfy'd at thefe proceedings, begg'd the king of Caftile, to take upon him the crown of Portugal; which he might in all likelihood have obtain'd; but he being uncertain in his refolutions, gave by his delays, time and opportunity to the adverfe party to ftrengthen itfelf. In fhort, coming without an army into Portugal, his mother-in-law refign'd to him the government, but he found but an indifferent reception among the Portuguefe, who were very averfe to him, becaufe he uf'd very rarely to fpeak or converfe with them. 'Tis true, a great many of the nobility and fome cities fided with him; but moft out of a hatred to the Caftilians, chofe for their leader John the baftard, a wife and brave man, and much belov'd by the people. The Caftilians thereupon befieged Lifbon, but their army being for the moft part deftroyed by the plague, they were obliged to leave it, without having got any advantage. In the next enfuing year, the Portuguefe declared this John their king, who very courageoufly attack'd thofe places which had declared for the Caftilians, and fubdu'd the greateft part of them. The Caftilians then entered with an army into Portugal, but were entirely routed by this new king near Aliubarotta, which victory is annually celebrated to this day among the Portuguefe. After this battle, all the reft of the cities did furrender themfelves to the new king. *The Portuguefe calling to their aid the duke of Lancafter, to whom they had promis'd the crown of Caftile*, entered into that kingdom with an army: *but the Englifh having fuffered extreamly by ficknefs, the duke of Lancafter thought it moft convenient* to conclude a peace with the *Caftilians*; whereupon it was agreed, that the fon of the king of Caftile fhould marry *his only daughter Catharine, which he had by Conftantia, daughter to Pieter king of Caftile.* At the fame time a truce was made betwixt Portugal and Caftile; but the war foon breaking out again, at laft an everlafting peace was concluded betwixt both kingdoms: fo that John had the good fortune to maintain himfelf in the poffeffion of the crown of Portugal, and reigned with great applaufe. After he was quietly fettled in the throne, he undertook an expedition into Africa, and took the city Ceuta: and his fon firft found out the ifle of Madeira. This king died in the year 1433, and left a memory that is to this day dear to the Portuguefe." *Puffendorf's* Introduction, &c. p. 70, 71, 72, 73, 74. Edit. 1711.

Thus* too, Mickle: " Count Henry, after a fuccefsful reign, was fucceeded by his infant fon Don Alonzo-Henry, who having furmounted feveral dangers which threatened his youth, became the firft of the Portuguefe kings. In 1139 the Moors of Spain and Barbary united their forces to recover the dominions from which they had been driven by the Chriftians. According to the loweft accounts of the Portuguefe writers, the army of the Moors amounted to 400,000; nor is this number incredible, when we confider what great armies they at other times brought to the field; and that at this time they came to take poffeffion of the lands which they expected to conquer. Don Alonzo, however, with a very fmall army, gave them battle on the plains of Ourique, and after a ftruggle of fix hours, obtained a moft glorious and complete victory, and which was crowned with an event of the utmoft importance. On the field of battle Don Alonzo was proclaimed King of Portugal by

* See his Differtation on the difcovery of India, prefixed to his admirable tranflation of the Lufiad.

by his victorious foldiers, and he in return conferred the rank of nobility on the whole army. But the conftitution of the monarchy was not fettled, nor was Alonzo invefted with the Regalia till fix years after the memorable day. The government the Portuguefe had experienced under the Spaniards and Moors, and the advantages which they faw were derived from their own valour, had taught them a love of liberty, which was not to be complimented away in the joy of victory, or by the fhouts of tumult. Alonzo himfelf underftood their fpirit too well to venture the leaft attempt to make himfelf a defpotic Monarch; nor did he difcover the leaft inclination to deftroy that bold confcioufnefs of freedom which had enabled his army to conquer, and to elect him their Sovereign. After fix years fpent in farther victories, in extending and fecuring his dominions, he called an affembly of the prelates, nobility and commons, to meet at Lamego. When the affembly opened, Alonzo appeared feated on the throne, but without any other mark of regal dignity. And ere he was crowned, the conftitution of the ftate was fettled, and eighteen ftatutes were folemnly confirmed by oath, as the charter of king and people; ftatutes diametrically oppofite to the *jus divinum* of kings, to the principles which inculcate and demand the unlimited paffive obedience of the fubject.

Confcious of what they owed to their own valour, the founders of the Portuguefe monarchy tranfmitted to their heirs thofe generous principles of liberty which complete and adorn the martial character. The ardour of the volunteer, an ardour unknown to the flave and the mercenary, added to the moft romantic ideas of military glory, characterifed the Portuguefe under the reigns of their firft monarchs. In almoft continual wars with the Moors, this fpirit, on which the exiftence of their kingdom depended, rofe higher and higher; and the defire to extirpate Mohammedifm, the principle which animated the wifh of victory in every battle, feemed to take deeper root in every age. Such were the manners, and fuch the principles of the people who were governed by the fucceffor of Alonzo the Firft; a fucceffion of great men, who proved themfelves worthy to reign over fo military and enterprifing a nation.

By a continued train of victories Portugal increafed confiderably in ftrength, and the Portuguefe had the honour to drive the Moors from Europe. The invafions of thefe people were now requited by fuccefsful expeditions into Africa. And fuch was the manly fpirit of thefe ages, that the ftatutes of Lamego received additional articles in favour of liberty; a convincing proof that the general heroifm of a people depends upon the principles of freedom. Alonzo IV. though not an amiable character, was perhaps the greateft warrior, politician, and monarch of his age. After a reign of military fplendor he left his throne to his fon Pedro, who from his inflexible juftice was furnamed the Juft, or, the Lover of Juftice. The ideas of equity and literature were now diffufed by this great prince, who was himfelf a polite fcholar, and moft accomplifhed gentleman. And Portugal began to perceive the advantages of cultivated talents, and to feel its fuperiority over the barbarous politics of the ignorant Moors. The great Pedro, however, was fucceeded by a weak prince, and the heroic fpirit of the Portuguefe feemed to exift no more under his fon Fernando, furnamed the Carelefs.

But the general character of the people was too deeply impreffed to be obliterated by one inglorious reign; and under John I. all the virtues of the Portuguefe fhone forth with redoubled luftre. Happy for Portugal, his father beftowed a moft excellent education upon this prince, which added to, and improving his great natural talents, rendered him one of the greateft of monarchs. Confcious of the fuperiority which his own liberal education gave him, he was affiduous to beftow the fame advantages upon his children; and he himfelf often became their preceptor in the branches of fcience and ufeful knowlege. Fortunate in all his affairs, he was moft of all fortunate in his family. He had many fons, and he lived to fee them men, men of parts and action, whofe only emulation was to fhew affection to his perfon, and to fupport his adminiftration by their great abilities.

There is fomething exceedingly pleafing in the hiftory of a family which fhews human nature in its moft exalted virtues and moft amiable colours; and the tribute of veneration is fpontaneoufly paid to the father who diftinguifhes the different talents of his children, and places them in the proper lines of action. All the fons of John excelled in military exercifes, and in the literature of their age; Don Edward and Don Pedro were particularly educated for the cabinet: And the mathematical genius of Don Henry, one of the youngeft fons, received every encouragement which a king and a father could give, to ripen it into perfection and public utility.

Hiftory was well known to Prince Henry, and his turn of mind particularly enabled him to make political obfervations upon it. The wealth and power of antient Tyre and Carthage fhewed him what a maritime nation might hope; and the flourifhing colonies of the Greeks were the frequent topic of his converfation. Where the Grecian commerce, confined as it was, extended its influence, the defarts became cultivated fields, cities rofe, and men were drawn from the woods and caverns to unite in fociety. The Romans, on the other hand, when they deftroyed Carthage, buried, in her ruins, the fountain of civilization, of improvement and opulence. They extinguifhed the fpirit of commerce; the agriculture of the conquered nations, (Britain alone, perhaps, excepted,) was totally neglected. And thus, while the luxury of Rome confumed the wealth of her provinces, her uncommercial policy dried up the fources of its continuance. The egregious errors of the Romans, who perceived not the true ufe of their diftant conquefts, and the inexhauftible fountains of opulence which Phœnicia had eftablifhed in her colonies, inftructed Prince Henry what gifts to beftow upon his country, and, in the refult, upon the whole world. Nor were the ineftimable advantages of commerce the fole motives of Henry. All the ardour which the love of his country could awake, confpired to ftimulate the natural turn of his genius for the improvement of navigation.

As the kingdom of Portugal had been wrefted from the Moors and eftablifhed by conqueft, fo its exiftence ftill depended on the fuperiority of the force of arms; and ere the birth of Henry, the fuperiority of the Portuguefe navies had been of the utmoft confequence to the protection of the ftate. Such were the circumftances which united to infpire the defigns of Henry, all which were powerfully enforced and invigorated by the religion of that prince. The defire to extirpate Mohammedifm was patriotifm in Portugal. It was the principle which gave birth to, and fupported their monarchy: their kings avowed it, and Prince Henry, the piety of whofe heart cannot be queftioned, always profeffed, that to propagate the gofpel was the great purpofe of his defigns and enterprizes. And however this, in the event, was neglected, certain it is, that the fame principles infpired, and were always profeffed by king Emmanuel, under whom the Eaftern World was difcovered by Gama.

The

From the Lufiad, however, it appears, that the reduction of that city, was too memorable an event to be tranfiently noticed: Camoens has been diffufe on the fubject. Thus his elegant and melodious tranflator:

" Nor long his faulchion in the fcabbard flept,
" Alonzo's arm increafing laurels reapt:
" From Leyra's walls the baffled Ifmar flies,
" And ftrong Arroncha falls his conquer'd prize;
" That honour'd town, through whofe Elyfian groves
" Thy fmooth and limpid wave, O Tagus, roves.
" The illuftrious Santarene confeft his power
" And vanquifh'd Mafra yields her proudeft tower.
" The Lunar mountains faw his troops difplay
" Their marching banners and their brave array;
" To him fubmits fair Cintra's cold domain,
" The foothing refuge of the Nayad train,
" When Love's fweet fnares the pining Nymphs would fhun:
" Alas, in vain from warmer climes they run:
" The cooling fhades awake the young defires,
" And the cold fountains cherifh love's foft fires.
" And thou, famed Lifboa, whofe embattled wall
" Rofe by the hand that wrought proud Ilion's fall;
" Thou queen of Cities, whom the feas obey,
" Thy dreaded ramparts own'd the Hero's fway.
" *Far from the north a warlike navy bore*
" From Elbe, from Rhine, and ALBION's mifty fhore,
" To refcue Salem's long-polluted fhrine;
" Their force to great Alonzo's force they join:
" Before Ulyffes' walls the navy rides,
" The joyful Tagus laves their pitchy fides.
" Five times the moon her empty horns conceal'd,
" Five times her broad effulgence fhone reveal'd,

When,

The Crufades, to refcue the Holy Land from the infidels, which had already been, however unregarded by hiftorians, of the greateft political fervice in Spain and Portugal, began now to have fome effect upon the commerce of Europe. The Hans Towns had received charters of liberty, and had united together for the protection of their trade againft the numerous pyrates of the Baltic. A people of Italy, known by the name of the Lombards, had opened a lucrative traffic with the ports of Egypt, from whence they imported into Europe the riches of the Eaft; and Bruges in Flanders, the mart between them and the Hans Towns, was, in confequence, furrounded with the beft agriculture of thefe ages:* A certain proof of the dependance of agriculture upon the extent of commerce. Yet though thefe gleams of light, as morning ftars, began to appear; it was not the grofs multitude, it was only the eye of a Henry which could perceive what they prognofticated, and it was only a genius like his which could prevent them from again fetting in the depths of night."

* Flanders has been the fchool-miftrefs of hufbandry to Europe. Sir Charles Lifle, a Royalift, refided in this country feveral years during the ufurpation of the Regicides; and after the reftoration, rendered England the greateft fervice, by introducing the prefent fyftem of agriculture. Where trade increafes, men's thoughts are fet in action; hence the increafe of food which is wanted, is fupplied by a redoubled attention to hufbandry; and hence it was that agriculture was of old improved and diffufed by the Phœnician colonies. Some Theorifts complain of the number of lives which are loft by navigation, but totally forget that commerce is the parent of population.

" When, wrapt in clouds of duſt, her mural pride
" Falls thundering,—black the ſmoaking breach yawns wide.
" As when th' impriſon'd waters burſt the mounds,
" And roar, wide ſweeping, o'er the cultured grounds;
" Nor cot nor fold withſtand their furious courſe;
" So headlong ruſh'd along the Hero's force.
" The thirſt of vengeance the aſſailants fires,
" The madneſs of deſpair the Moors inſpires;
" Each lane, each ſtreet reſounds the conflict's roar,
" And every threſhold reeks with tepid gore.

" Thus fell the city, whoſe unconquer'd towers
" Defy'd of old the banded Gothic powers,
" Whoſe harden'd nerves in rigorous climates train'd
" The ſavage courage of their ſouls ſuſtain'd;
" Before whoſe ſword the ſons of Ebro fled,
" And Tagus trembled in his oozy bed;
" Aw'd by whoſe arms the lawns of Betis' ſhore
" The name Vandalia from the Vandals bore.

" When Liſboa's towers before the Luſian fell,
" What fort, what rampart might his arms repell!
" Eſtremadura's region owns him Lord,
" And Torres-vedras bends beneath his ſword;
" Obidos humbles, and Alamquer yields,
" Alamquer famous for her verdant fields,
" Whoſe murmuring rivulets cheer the traveller's way,
" As the chill waters o'er the pebbles ſtray.
" Elva the green, and Moura's fertile dales,
" Fair Serpa's tillage, and Alcazar's vales
" Not for himſelf the Mooriſh peaſant ſows;
" For Luſian hands the yellow harveſt glows:
" And you, fair lawns, beyond the Tago's wave,
" Your golden burdens for Alonzo ſave;
" Soon ſhall his thundering might your wealth reclaim,
" And your glad valleys hail their monarch's name."*

It

* See Mickle's Luſiad, Book III.

It ſeems, that the greater part of the Cruſading fleet were Engliſh; whoſe ſucceſsful interpoſition, at ſuch a criſis, muſt have raiſed gratitude and admiration in the minds of the Portugueſe: and the applauſe of a foreign poet ſhould be deemed of ſterling value. In another place, Camoens recurs to his heroes from the Britiſh ſhore:

" There, by the ſtream, a town beſieged behold,
" The Mooriſh tents the ſhatter'd walls infold.
" Fierce as the lion from the covert ſprings,
" When hunger gives his rage the whirlwind's wings;
" From ambuſh, lo, the valiant Fuaz pours,
" And whelms in ſudden rout th' aſtoniſh'd Moors.
" The Mooriſh king in captive chains he ſends;
" And low at Liſboa's throne the royal captive bends.
" Fuaz again the artiſt's ſkill diſplays;
" Far o'er the ocean ſhine his enſign's rays:
" In crackling flames the Mooriſh galleys fly,
" And the red blaze aſcends the bluſhing ſky:
" O'er Avila's high ſteep the flames aſpire,
" And wrap the foreſts in a ſheet of fire:
" There ſeem the waves beneath the prows to boil;
" And diſtant far around for many a mile
" The glaſſy deep reflects the ruddy blaze;
" Far on the edge the yellow light decays,
" And blends with hovering blackneſs. Great and dread
" Thus ſhone the day when firſt the combat bled,
" The firſt our heroes battled on the main,
" The glorious prelude of our naval reign,
" Which now the waves beyond the burning zone,
" And northern Greenland's froſt-bound billows own.
" Again behold brave Fuaz dares the fight!
" O'erpower'd he ſinks beneath the Mooriſh might;
" Smiling in death the martyr hero lies,
" And lo, his ſoul triumphant mounts the ſkies.
" Here now behold, in warlike pomp pourtray'd,
" *A foreign navy brings the pious aid.*
" Lo, marching from the decks the ſquadron ſpread,
" STRANGE THEIR ATTIRE, THEIR ASPECT FIRM AND DREAD.
" The holy Croſs their enſigns bold diſplay,
" To Salem's aid they plough'd the watery way;
" Yet firſt, the cauſe the ſame, on Tago's ſhore
" They dye their maiden ſwords in Pagan gore.

" Proud

" Proud ftood the Moor on Lifboa's warlike towers;
" From Lifboa's walls they drive the Moorifh powers;
" Amid the thickeft of of the glorious fight,
" Lo, Henry falls, a gallant German knight,
" A martyr falls: That holy tomb behold,
" There waves the bloffom'd palm the boughs of gold:
" O'er Henry's grave the facred plant arofe,
" And from the leaves, heaven's gift, gay health redundant† flows.

" Aloft, unfurl; the valiant Paulus cries;
" Inftant new wars on new-fpread enfigns rife.
" In robes of white behold a prieft advance!
" His fword in fplinters fmites the Moorifh lance:
" Arronchez won revenges Lira's fall:
" And lo, on fair Savilia's batter'd wall,
" How boldly calm amid the crafhing fpears,
" That hero-form the Lufian ftandard rears.
" There bleeds the war on fair Vandalia's plain:
" Lo, rufhing through the Moors o'er hills of flain
" The hero rides, and proves by genuine claim
" The fon of Egas and his worth the fame.
" Pierced by his dart the ftandard-bearer dies;
" Beneath his feet the Moorifh ftandard lies:
" High o'er the field, behold the glorious blaze!
" The victor-youth the Lufian flag difplays.
" Lo, while the moon through midnight azure rides,
" From the high wall adown his fpear ftaff glides
" The dauntlefs *Gerrald*: in his left he‡ bears
" Two watchmen's heads, his right the faulchion rears:
" The gate he opens; fwift from ambufh rife
" His ready bands, the city falls his prize:
" Evora ftill the grateful honour pays,
" Her banner'd flag the mighty deed difplays:

" There

† *And from the leaves*——This Legend is mentioned by fome ancient Portuguefe chronicles. Homer would have availed himfelf, as Camoens has done, of a tradition fo enthufiaftical, and characteriftic of the age. Henry was a native of Bonneville near Cologn. His tomb, fays Caftera, is ftill to be feen in the Monaftery of St. Vincent, but without the palm.

‡ *The dauntlefs Gerrald.*—" He was a man of rank, who, in order to avoid the legal punifhment to which feveral crimes rendered him obnoxious, put himfelf at the head of a party of Freebooters. Tiring however, of that life, he refolved to reconcile himfelf to his fovereign by fome noble action. Full of this idea, one evening he entered Evora, which then belonged to the Moors. In the night he killed the centinels of one of the gates, which he opened to his companions, who foon became mafters of the place. This exploit had its defired effect. The king pardoned Gerrald, and made him governor *of Evora. A knight with a fword in one hand, and two heads in the other, from that time became the armorial bearing of the city.*" *Cafteras.*

"There frowns the hero; in his left he bears
"The two cold heads, his right the faulchion rears.
"Wrong'd by his king, and burning for* revenge,
"Behold his arms that proud Caftilian change;
"The Moorifh buckler on his breaft he bears,
"And leads the fierceft of the Pagan fpears."‡

The atchievement which is here fo finely blazoned, was of the utmoft importance to the infant monarchy of Portugal. Lifbon, one of the fineft ports in Europe, was, before the invention of cannon, of great ftrength. The old Moorifh wall, flanked by feventy-feven towers, was about fix miles in length, and fourteen in circumference. And befieged by Don Alonzo, it is faid to have been garrifoned by an army of 200,000 men. That Don Alonzo, then, would have taken the city, without the affiftance of the bold adventurers before us, is extremely improbable. Who thefe adventurers were, or from what part of England they came, feems a natural enquiry. But to our national chronicles, we look to no purpofe for information. In the hiftoric records at Paris, however, we find that the Englifh armament was from *Cornwall* and *Devon*!†

But ftill more happily we bring our refearches to a point, from the evidence of a Welfh Traveller *Udal-ap-Rhys*. This writer, in his tour thro' Portugal, informs us, that Alonzo gave his Englifh friends, *Almada* on this fide of the Tagus, oppofite to Lifbon—that *Villa Franca* was *peopled* by the Englifh; and that they called it CORNUALLA! And they called it Cornualla, unqueftionably, in honour of their native Cornwall! Thus, conquerors of Lifbon, the heroes of of Camoens, were Cornifhmen! And thus, in one of the moft beautiful and fertile fpots in the world, and in the fineft climate, was eftablifhed by *Cornifh* intrepidity the fovereignty of Portugal;—a fovereignty, which, in time fpread its influence moft extenfively, and gave a new afpect to the manners of nations!§

In the Crufade of 1188, our firft Richard was attended by Philip Auguftus King of France, and Frederick Barbaroffa to the Holy Land. His conduct there, and his captivity|| are well

known

* *Wrong'd by his king.*—Don Pedro Fernando de Caftro, injured by the family of *Lara*, and denied redrefs by the king of Caftile, took the infamous revenge of bearing arms againft his native country. At the head of a Moorifh army he committed feveral outrages in Spain; but was totally defeated in Portugal.

‡ Book VIII.

† See in Durand's "Collect. vet. Monument." [Paris, 1724] a Latin letter from a perfon of diftinction on board the combined fleet. It appears, that this fleet was commanded by William Longefpeé.

§ "*The Olive-Branch of Peace*, borne by a *Moor*," is one of Crefts to the Polwhele Arms. Its origin, perhaps, may be referred to the Moors humbled by the Cornifh, and in confequence fueing for peace.

|| "King Richard fetting fail from Syria, the fea and wind favoured him till he came into the Adriatick; and on the coafts of Iftria he fuffered fhipwreck; wherefore he intended to pierce through Germanie by land, the next way home. But the nearneffe of the way is to be meafured not by the fhortneffe but the fafeneffe of it.

He difguifed himfelf to be one Hugo a merchant, whofe onely commodity was himfelf, whereof he made but a bad bargain. For he was difcovered in an inne in Auftria, becaufe he difguifed his perfon not his expenfes; fo that the very policy of an hofteffe, finding his purfe fo farre above his clothes, did detect him: yea, faith mine authour, *Facies orbi terrarum nota, ignorari non potuit.* The rude people flocking together ufed him with infolences unworthy him, worthy themfelves: and they who would fhake at the tail of this loofe Lion, durft laugh at his face now they faw him in a grate. Yet all the weight of their cruelty did not bow him beneath a princely carriage.

Leopoldus Duke of Auftria hearing hereof, as being Lord of the foil, feifed on this Royall ftray; meaning now to get his peny-worths out of him, for the affront done unto him in Paleftine.

Not long after the Duke fold him to Henry the Emperour, for his harfh nature furnamed Afper; and it might have been Sævus, being but one degree from a tyrant. He kept King Richard in bands, charging him with a thoufand faults committed

known. But his cruelty and treachery, after his enlargement, are perfectly new to the English hiftorian: they little accord with the Englifh character.* The exploits of Richard Earl of Cornwall in‡ the Holy Land, were attended with little advantage to the caufe.|| The Crufade of

mitted by him in Sicily, Cyprus, and Paleftine. The proofs were as flender as the crimes groffe; and Richard having an eloquent tongue, innocent heart, and bold fpirit, acquitted himfelf in the judgement of all the hearers. At laft he was ranfomed for an hundred and forty thoufand marks, Cullen weight. A fumme fo vaft in that age, before the Indies had overflowed all Europe with their gold and filver, that to raife it in England they were forced to fell their church-plate to their chalices. Whereupon out of moft deep divinity it was concluded, that they fhould not celebrate the facrament in glaffe, for the brittleneffe of it: nor in wood, for the fpongineffe of it, which would fuck up the bloud; nor in alchymie, becaufe it was fubject to rufting; nor in copper, becaufe that would provoke vomiting; but in chalices of latten, which belike was a metall without exception. And fuch were ufed in England for fome years after: untill at laft John Stafford Archbifhop of Canterbury, when the lands was more replenifhed with filver, inknotteth that Prieft in the greater excommunication that fhould confecrate *Poculum ftanneum*. After this money Peter of Bloys (who had drunk as deep of Helicon as any of that age) tendeth this good prayer; making an apoftrophe to the Emperour, or to the Duke of Auftria, or to both together.

Bibe nunc, avaritia,
Dum puteos argenteos
Larga diffundit Anglia.
Tua tecum pecunia
Sit in perditionem.

And now, thou bafeft avarice,
Drink till thy belly burft,
Whil'ft England poures large filver fhowres
To fatiate thy thirft.
And this we pray, thy money may
And thou be like accurft.

The ranfome partly payed, the reft fecured by hoftages, King Richard much befriended by the Dutch Prelacie, after eighteen moneths imprifonment returned into England. The Archbifhop of Cullen in the prefence of King Richard, as he paffed by, brought in thefe words in faying maffe, *Now I know that God hath fent his angel, and hath delivered thee out of the hand of Herod, and from the expectation of the people*, &c. But his foul was more healthfull for the bitter phyfick, and he amended his manners; better loving his Queen Beringaria, whom he flighted before; as fouldiers too often love women better then wives."—*Fuller's* Hiftory of the Holy War, pp. 130, 131.

* We doubt very much the truth of the following anecdote from "*Ranken's* Hiftory of France." "When Richard at laft obtained his liberty, 'Take care of yourfelf,' faid Philip, writing to John, 'the devil is unchained.' He took care of himfelf, and made peace with his brother, but deferted Philip. The war was renewed. As foon as Richard could leave England, he embarked at Portfmouth, and landed at Barfleur. He raifed the fiege of Verneüil, and took the caftle of Lochis. The war was conducted on both fides with much refentment, and with circumftances of peculiar barbarity. At Evreux, the principal officers of the French garrifon, being invited to an entertainment by the Englifh, were maffacred in a ftate of intoxication. All incapable of refiftance were flain without apprehenfion of their danger, and their heads, reeking with blood, fixed on the walls."—See Hiftory of France, Cadell and Davies, 1804.

‡ "The Chriftians being in deep diftreffe (fays *Fuller*) refolved on a dangerous courfe, but (as their cafe ftood) thought neceffary; for they made peace with the Sultans of Damafcus and Cracci; and fwearing them to be faithfull, borrowed an armie of their forces, with them joyntly to refift the Corafines; feeking, faith Frederick the Emperour, (in his letter to Richard of Cornwall,) to find *fidem in perfidia*, truft in treachery. Many fufpected thefe auxiliary forces; thinking, though the forreft wolves fell out with the mountain ones, they would both agree againft the fheep.

Robert Patriarch of Jerufalem was a moft active commander over all. S. Luke's day was the time agreed upon for the fatall battel; near Tiberias was the place. As the Chriftians were ordering themfelves in array, it was queftioned in what part of their armie their new Turkifh affiftants fhould be difpofed, and concluded that they fhould be placed in the front, where if they did no other good, they would dull the appetite of their enemies fword.

The battel being joyned, the Turks ranne over to the other fide; though fome brand them onely with cowardlineffe not treachery and that they fled from the battel but not fell to the enemies. The Chriftians manfully ftood to it, and though over-powered in number, made a great flaughter of their enemies, till at laft they were quite overthrown. Of the Teutonick Order efcaped but three; of three hundred Templars, but eighteen; of two hundred Hofpitallers, but nineteen: the Patriarch (to ufe his own words) whom God reputed unworthy of martyrdome, faved himfelf by flight, with a few others. And this great overthrow, to omit leffe partner-caufes, is chiefly imputed to the Templars fo often breaking the truce with the Sultan of Babylon." pp. 185, 186.

|| *Matthew Paris* has given us fome entertaining anecdotes of our Cornifh Richard. Ann. Dom. 1240, Rex Baldwinum de Ripariis, juvenem elegantem, balteo cinxit militari, et Comitatu Vectæ inveftivit prefente et ad id procurante Comite Ricardo, *in cujus cuftodia* idem Baldwinus pluribus annis extiterat, et filiaftram fuam, fcilicet Amitiam filiam uxoris fuæ Ifabellæ, Glovernice quandoque Comitiffæ, fibi matrimonialiter copulaverat. Circa idem tempus, Ifabella Comitiffa Gloverniæ et Cornubiæ, uxor fcilicet comitis Ricardi *ictericia* ufque ad mortem periclitans infirmabatur. Cujus cum impletum fuiffet tempus

of Prince Edward was one of the moſt romantic of all.* Among the ſoldiers who accompanied

C 2

Edward

tempus pariendi; erat enim gravida, et partui proxima, exanimata eſt, *præſciſis* copioſarum *comarum* ſuarum *tricis cærulcis*, et facta plenarie peccatorum ſuorum confeſſione, ſimul cum puerulo adhuc vivo, ſed non vivido, et idcirco ſtatim baptizato, cui nomen Nicolaus aptatum eſt, migravit ad Dominum. Quod cum comes Ricardus, qui tunc apud Cornubiam greſſus direxerat, audivit, prorumpens in gemitus lachrimabiles, doluit inconſolabiliter; et feſtinanter reverſus, corpus venerabile uxoris ſuæ veneranter apud Bellum locum Dom. Scilicet quam Rex Johannes a fundamentis conſtruxerat, et Ciſtercienſium ordini addixerat, fecit in preſentia ſua Sepelire." pp. 700, 701.

"Ann. Mill. Ducent quad Secundo, redeunte comiti Richardo de Terra Sancta, ipſe Rex et Regina cum infinita nobilium multitudine occurrit lætabundus. Rex igiter et Magnates fere univerſi eidem diverſa munera *largiendo cumularunt*. Venit idem comes Londinum; in cujus adventu civitas *auleis et pallis adornata* reſplenduit feſtivalis, et epulabantur fratres gaudenter cum *multitudine* Soleanium, quos rex convocaverat, *Convivarum*." pp. 777, 778.

"Ann. Mill. Ducent. quadrag. tertio, comes Richardus deſponſavit uxorem ſuam Cinciam, filiam Reimundi comitis Provinciæ, ſororem videlicet Reginæ, apud Weſtmonaſterium. In cujus nuptiis, tanta convivii nuptialis, totque convivarum Nobilium reſplenduit ſerenitas feſtivalis, ut ille incomparabilis apparátus diffuſos exigeret tractatus et tædioſos. In coquinali miniſterio, pluræ quam triginta millia ferculorum a prandentibus parabantur. Prodigioſaque commenta in præſentia regis, comitiſque novi ſponſi, Reginæ quoque et ſororis ſuæ dictæ *Unciæ* novæ ſponſæ (cujus mutatum nomen eſt, et vocata *Scientia*) Comitiſſæque Provinciæ Beatricis, aliorumque innumerabilium Magnatum exhibita, oculos et cogitatus intuentium in admirationem inauditam rapiebant. Sæculariſque Pompæ, inanis quoque gloriæ, in joculatorum diverſitate, in veſtium varietate, cibariorium numeroſitate, et epulantium populoſitate, delicias tranſitorias, contemptibiles, et umbratilem, præſtigiatorem, mundum manifeſte comprobarunt, cum tanti paratus varietates craſtina dies quaſi nebulam exſufflavit." p. 815.

This dinner, we obſerve, conſiſted of more *than thirty thouſand* diſhes, in celebration of the ſecond marriage of Richard Earl of Cornwall. The Earl had buried his firſt wife, had waged war with the Infidels in Paleſtine, was returned to England, and now married again.

* "Prince Edward (according to *Fuller*) gave evident teſtimonies of his perſonall valour: yea, in cold bloud he would boldly challenge any Infidel to a duell. To ſpeak truth, this his conceived perfection was his greateſt imperfection: for the world was abudantly ſatisfied in the point of his valour; yet ſuch was his confidence of his ſtrength, and eagerneſſe of honour, that having merited the eſteem of a moſt ſtout man, he would ſtill ſupererogate: yea, he would profer to fight with any mean perſon, if cried up by the *volge* for a tall man: this daring being a generall fault in great ſpirits, and a great fault in a Generall, who ſtaketh a pearl againſt a piece of glaſſe. The beſt was, in that age a man fighting with ſword and buckler, had in a manner many lives to loſe; and duells were not dangerous.

Whileſt he ſtayed at Ptolemais, Elenor his lady was delivered of a fair daughter, called from her birth-place Joan of Acres: But fear of her huſbands death abated her joy at her daughters birth. The Turks not matching him in valour, thought to maſter him with treachery, which was thus contrived: The Admirall of Joppa, a Turk, pretended he would turn Chriſtian, and imployed one Anzazim an Aſſaſine in the buſineſſe betwixt him and Prince Edward; who carried himſelf ſo cunningly, that by often repairing to our Prince he got much credit and eſteem with him.

Some write, this Anzazim was before always bred under ground (as men keep hawks and warre-horſes in the dark to make them more fierce) that ſo coming abroad he ſhould fear to venture on no man. But ſure, ſo cunning a companion had long converſed with light, and been acquainted with men, yea, Chriſtians and Princes, as appeareth by his complying carriage; elſe, if he had not been well read in their company, he could not have been ſo perfect in his leſſon. But let him be bred anywhere, or in hell itſelf: for this was his religion, to kill any he was commanded, or on the non-performance willing to forfeit his life.

The fifth time of his coming he brought Prince Edward letters from his Maſter, which whilſt he was reading alone and lying on his bed, he ſtruck him into the arm with an invenomed knife. Being about to fetch another ſtroke, the Prince with his foot gave him ſuch a blow that he felled him to the ground; and wreſting the knife from him, ranne the Turk into the belly and ſlew him; yet ſo, that in ſtruggling he hurt himſelf therewith in the forehead. At this noiſe in ſprang his ſervants, and one of them with a ſtool beat the brains out of the dead Turks head, ſhewing little wit in his own; and the Prince was highly diſpleaſed, that the monument of his valour ſhould be ſtained with anothers cruelties.

It is ſtoried, how Elenor his lady ſucked all the poiſon out of his wounds, without doing any harm to herſelf: So ſovereigne a medicine is a womans tongue, anointed with the vertue of loving affection. Pity it is ſo pretty a ſtory ſhould not be true (with all the miracles in Loves Legends) and ſure he ſhall get himſelf no credit, who undertaketh to confute a paſſage ſo ſounding to the honour of the ſex: Yet can it not ſtand with what others have written; how the Phyſician who was to dreſſe his wounds, ſpake to the Lord Edmund and the Lord John Voyſie to take away Lady Elenor out of the Princes preſence, leſt her pity ſhould be cruel towards him, in not ſuffering his ſores to be ſearched to the quick. And though ſhe cried out and wrung her hands, Madame, ſaid they, be contented; it is better that one woman ſhould weep a little while, then that all the realm of England ſhould lament a great ſeaſon: and ſo they conducted her out of the place. And the Prince, by the benefit of Phyſick, good attendance, and an antidote the Maſter of the Templars gave him, ſhewed himſelf on horſe-back whole and well within fifteen dayes after.

The Admirall of Joppa hearing of his recovery, utterly diſavowed that he had any hand in the treachery; as none will willingly father unſucceeding villany. True it is, he was truly ſorrowfull; whether becauſe Edward was ſo bad, or no worſe wounded, he knoweth that knoweth hearts. Some wholly acquit him herein, and conceive this miſchief proceeded from Guy Earl of Montforts hatred to our Prince, who bearing him and all his kindred an old grudge for doing ſome conceived wrong to his father (in very deed, nothing but juſtice to a rebell) hired, as they think, this Aſſaſine to murder him; as a little before for the ſame quarrel he had ſerved Henry ſonne to Richard King of the Romanes, and our Edwards couſin-germane, at

Viterbo

Edward to the Holy Land, were WALTER DE MOLLESWORTH, and Sir WILLIAM DE FULFORD.† Their exploits were, doubtlefs, heroic:§ but the death of Henry III. was an incident to remind the

Viterbo in Italy. It is much this Guy living in France fhould contrive this Princes death in Paleftine: but malice hath long arms, and can take men off at great diftance. Yea, this addeth to the cunning of the engineer, to work unfeen; and the further from him the blow is given, the leffe is he himfelf fufpected.

Whofoever plotted, God prevented it, and the Chriftians there would have revenged it, but Edward would not fuffer them. In all hafte they would have marched and fallen on the Turks, had not he diffwaded them, becaufe then many Chriftians unarmed, and in fmall companies, were gone to vifit the Sepulchre, all whofe throats had then probably been cut before their return." pp. 219, 220.

† *Walter de Molefworth*, Knt. was of eminent note in the reign of Edward I. To his warfare in the Holy Land, his coat-armour alludes. From this Sir Walter, the Molefworths of Pencarrow are lineally defcended. [Certif. de Camden, et ex Stemmate hujus famil. fub manu Tho. et Hen. St. Geor. Mil.] Several of the *Fulfords* of Fulford, attended the expeditions to Paleftine. Sir *Baldwin Fulford*, Knight and Knight of the Sepulchre accompanied Richard the firft to the Holy War. Sir *William de Fulford*, his Son, Knight and Knight of the Sepulchre, went to the Holy War. So alfo did Sir *Amias de Fulford* knight of the Sepulchre, attending Edward I. in his Crufade. Sir Baldwin Fulford, knight and knight of the Sepulchre, fon or grandfon* to the famous judge Fulford, is faid, alfo, to have gone to the Holy Land: but this will admit of a donbt. According to our Devonian antiquaries, he was a great foldier and traveller of fo undaunted a refolution, that for the honor and liberty of a royal lady in a caftle befieged by the Infidels, he fought in fingle combat a Saracen of gigantic ftature; vanquifhed the Saracen and refcued the lady. The figures of the Chieftain and the Giant, are cut in the wainfcot of the great hall at Fulford-Houfe.—See Sir *William Pole*, and *Prince*; particularly Sir William, who in his famous men, has given us at one view, many of the diftinguifhed characters that occur in this chapter.

§ In memory of thofe heroic exploits, the coat-armour of many families remains to this day. There is no doubt the arms of many houfes were granted to the firft poffeffors of them, in confequence of fome fignal act of victory. We may argue therefore, by induction, where fuch arms are borne, and yet no record of the caufe exifts, that they were the reward alfo, of military merit. We have hinted at the arms of *Molefworth*, "Gules *an inefcutcheon vaire, between eight crofs croflets in orle, or.*" The arms of the *Cheineys* of Bodanan, in St. Teath, were "*Gules on a fefs of four lozenges, argent, as many fcallops fable,*" in memory, as tradition fays, that one of this family going into the Holy Land with Richard or Edward, carried fuch fhells with him for taking up water to drink in the hotter clime of Afia. *Hals*, in St. Teath.

Johnfon tells us in his life of Nicholas Rowe, the Poet, that "the anceftor from whom he defcended in a direct line, received the family coat-armour for his bravery in the Holy War."—Vol. II. p. 323. The arms of Rowe of Bodillyveor and Treganion in St. Michael Penkivel, are *gules, three holy lambs, ftaff, crofs and banner, argent.*

Fuller's remarks on this topic coincide exactly with my ideas. "Chap. 24. Of the honourable arms in fcutcheons of nobilitie occafioned by their fervice in the Holy Warre. Now for a corollarie to this ftorie, if we furvey the fcutcheons of the chriftian princes and nobilitie at this day, we fhall find the arms of many of them pointing at the atchievements of their predeceffours in the Holy Warre. Thus the Dukes of Auftria bear gules a feffe argent, in memory of the valour of Leopoldus at the fiege of Ptolemais. The Duke of Savoy beareth gules a croffe argent, being the croffe of St. John of Jerufalem; becaufe his predeceffours were fpeciall benefactours to that order, and affifted them in defending of Rhodes. Queens Colledge in Cambridge (to which I ow my education for my firft feven years in that Univerfitie) giveth for parcel of her arms, amongft many other rich coats, the croffe of Jerufalem; as being founded by Queen Margaret, wife to King Henry the fixth, and daughter of Renate Earl of Angiers and titular King of Sicilie and Jerufalem. The noble and numerous familie of the Douglaffes in Scotland (whereof at this day are one Marqueffe, two Earls, and a Vice-count) give in their arms a man's heart, ever fince Robert Brufe King of Scotland bequeathed his heart to James Douglaffe, to carry it to Jerufalem; which he accordingly performed. To inftance in particulars were endleffe: we will onely fumme them up in generals. Emblemes of honour born in coats occafioned by the Holy Warre, are reducible to thefe heads: 1. Scallop-fhells; which may fitly for the workmanfhip thereof be called *artificium naturæ*. It feemeth Pilgrimes carried them conftantly with them, as Diogenes did his difh, to drink in. I find an order of Knights called *Equites Cochleares*, wearing belike cockle or fcallop-fhells, belonging to them who had done good fea-fervice, efpecially in the Holy Warre: and many Hollanders (faith my authour) for their good fervice at the fiege of Damiata were admitted into that order.—2. Saracens Heads: it being a maxime in Heraldrie, that it is more honourable to bear the head then any other part of the bodie. They are commonly born either black or bloudie. But if Saracens in their arms fhould ufe Chriftians heads, I doubt not but they would fhew ten to one.—3. Pilgrimes or Palmers Scrips or Bags; the arms of the worfhipfull family of the Palmers in Kent.—4. Pilgrimes Staves, and fuch like other implements and accoutrements belonging unto them.—5. But the chiefeft of all is the croffe: which though

* "It is a doubt with *Dean Miles* whether it was the next defcendant from Judge Fulford, or his grandfon. A copy of whofe letter now before me I will tranfcribe. Of that ftory of the Saracen told by our Devon antiquarian, he makes him one and the fame perfon, with Sir Baldwin, who was beheaded, which differs from that in the family, which ftates him to have been a great warrior and traveller, and to have married Wilmot, daughter and heir of Philip Bryan. But be that as it will, I think Sir Baldwin the grandfon might have performed an exploit of that kind either in Spain or Italy, at that time much occupied by the Saracens, efpecially as his office of under admiral to the Duke of Exeter, might carry him abroad; and tho' he was a knight of the Sepulchre, yet it is not probable he was in the Holy Land. The wainfcot in the great hall, certainly continues the memorial of fuch a fact; and it appears by the ftile of carving to have been erected about that time. Exeter, September 29, 1779, *Jerem. Milles.*" Letter from the late Mrs. Fulford, to the Author.

the Prince of his country and his kingdom. In this manner, the ſpirit of religiouſneſs was kindled into action, and diſplayed in chivalrous adventure. To reſcue Salem from the infidel armies, was to add diſtinction to royalty; and the knights of the ſepulchre were more than human heroes. It was the paſſion of the times, and in this paſſion Cornwall had her ſhare. We have now to contract our views; adverting more cloſely to the annals of the county; ſtill, however, as connected with our iſland hiſtory.

I obſerved, that at the deceaſe of his father Henry III. EDWARD was engaged in the Cruſades. On his return to his kingdom, he had little reaſon to rejoice in the proſpect of affairs either civil or military. In the adminiſtration of juſtice, he ſaw nothing but venality:* even to the graveſt perſonages, the gratification of the ſenſes was avowedly the leading object. Of Corniſh plenty and hoſpitality, the luxurious judges of England, had, certainly, formed no very flattering opinion; ſince in 1272, we find them thus excuſing themſelves to the Lord Chancellor from holding a court of Eyre in Cornwall. "If (ſaid they) we go thither, we ſhall bring back lanthorn jaws"† In his people, the King perceived a turbulent and a diſloyal ſpirit. But wiſe and politic, as well as religious and brave, he had an inſight into the character of his ſubjects, and knew how to adapt meaſures to emergencies: whilſt perſonal civilities availed in conciliating ſome, a ſeverer proceſs was neceſſary for the correction of others. In our weſtern metropolis,‡ where "he kept his Chriſtmas with his Queen," he acquired popularity by ſuggeſting architectural improvements, and affording the means of carrying his plans into execution.§ And the diſaffection of Wales, ſoon awakened into uſeful exertion that valour which had only won romantic laurels. *Merlin* the common ſeer of Cornwall and of Wales, had propheſied, that "Lewellyn ſhould wear the diadem of Brute." And in 1281, the Welſh commenced hoſtilities by the ſurprize of Lord Clifford, the king's juſticiary, whom they wounded and ſent priſoner to the mountains of Snowdon. But Merlin proved a lying prophet‖ though the Corniſh, perhaps,

though born in arms before, yet was moſt commonly and generally uſed ſince the Holy Warre. The plain croſſe, or S. Georges croſſe, I take to be the mother of all the reſt; as plain-ſong is much ſenior to any running of diviſion. Now as by tranſpoſition of a few letters, a world of words are made; ſo by the varying of this croſſe in form, colour, and metall (ringing as it were the changes) are made infinite ſeverall coats: the croſſe of Jeruſalem, or five croſſes, moſt frequently uſed in this warre; croſſe *Patée*, becauſe the ends thereof are broad; *Wavée*, which thoſe may juſtly wear who failed thither through the miſeries of the ſea, or ſea of miſeries: *Molinée*, becauſe like to the rind of a mill: *Saltyrée, or S. Andrews croſſe: Florid*, or garlanded with flowers: the croſſe *croſſed:* Beſides the divers tricking or dreſſing; as piercing, voiding, fimbriating, ingrailing, couping: and in fanſie and devices there is ſtill a *plus ultrà*; inſomuch that croſſes alone as they are variouſly diſguiſed, are enough to diſtinguiſh all the ſeverall families of gentlemen in England."

* Twelve of the king's juſticiaries were found guilty of corruption: one of this number was Adam de Stratton, who was forced to pay a fine of no leſs than three hundred and twenty thouſand marks. See *Weſtminſter, Trivet, Walſingham,* and *Madox.*

† "Si veniamus ibidem, macras genas reportabimus." MSS, apud *Barrington.*

‡ "That King Edward I. frequented Helſton for delight or pleaſure, or, deſigned ſo to do, after the death of his uncle Richard, Earl of Cornwall King of the Romans, when the Earldom of Cornwall reverted to himſelf in right of his crown of England, A. D. 1272; is evident from his granting land by the tenure of grand ſerjeantry, to *William de Trevelle*, on condition of bringing a fiſhhook and a boat and nets at his own proper coſt and charges, for the king's fiſhing in the lake of Helſton, whenſoever the King ſhould come to Helſton, and as long as he ſhould tarry there." *W. Hals, in Helſton.*

§ "By his letter patent, dated 10th March, 1275, the king granted to the city of Exeter an yearly tribute or collection, of all manner of wears brought thither to be ſold, towards paving the ſtreets, repairing the walls, &c. which in old Engliſh is called *Bagavel, Bethugavel,* and *Chippengavel.*" *Hiſt. of Exeter.*

‖ See *Weſtminſter, Walſingham, Powel.* Deluded by Merlin's prophecy, Leolin (ſays Baker) had "no ear for peace, and ſhortly no head." *Chron.* p. 96. [Fol. edit. 1696.]

perhaps, reluctantly followed their earl, to oppofe in arms their kindred Britons.* After the reduction of Wales, Edward very early turned his attention to Scotland; the conqueft of which appears to have been the favourite object of his ambition. Among the military men, whofe fervices were required beyond the Tweed, we have the names of *Richard de Greynvile*, *Richard of Cornwall*, *De Prideaux*, and Sir *Walter Mollefworth*.† It was in the laft year of his reign, that Edward fummoned *Sir Walter*‡ with all the other vaffals of his crown; determined to march into the heart of Scotland, and "deftroy it (as he expreffed himfelf) from fea to fea." But, at the head of one of the fineft armies that England ever faw, he was feized with a fatal difeafe, which fruftrated all his projects; tho' with his dying breath, he enjoined his fon to profecute the war with the Scots. There were two other injunctions he laid on the young prince, to fend his heart to the Holy Sepulchre, and not to recall *Gaveftone* from banifhment: yet Gaveftone, we fhall find, was recalled from banifhment, and even created *Earl of Cornwall.*

Little regard had EDWARD II. to the dying admonitions of his father: no fooner was he invefted with the|| regal power, than he abandoned the war with Scotland, and welcomed home his favourite Gaveftone. To the voluptuous foreigner he devoted his time with a folly only to be equalled by his depravity.‡‡ With Gaveftone he purfued his pleafures; and on Gaveftone he heaped

* In 14 Edward I. Lord Berkley§ was fummoned to be at Glocefter on Midfummer-day; thence with Edmund Earl of Cornwall, the king's uncle, to march againft the Welfh. Ann. 1287. Edmundus Comes Cornubiæ, cuftos Angliæ in regis abfentia, verfus Walliam cum magno exercitu properavit, volens fed non valens cervicofitatem Wallenfium reprimere. Wallenfes dolofitate vulpina fe in fuis latibulis receperant, *frades* et dolos fecundum illorum *Antiquam confuetudinem machinantes.*" *Matt. Weftmin.* f. 179.

† In 25 Edward I. *Sir Richard de Greynvile*, Knight, was one of the principal perfons of Devon fummoned to be at London, on Sunday after the Octave of St. John Baptift, to go with the king beyond the feas for their honour, and the prefervation and profit of the kingdom; being ftiled Dominus Richardus de Grenevyle. MS. Not. B. 5. in Bibl. *John Anftis*, Arm. —In 25 Edward I. at the taking of Berwick upon Tweed, a Javelin from a ftrong tower which the Flemifh merchants had occupied, flew *Richard of Cornwall*, a gallant gentleman, brother to the Earl of Cornwall. *Speed's* England, p. 637.—In the 26th of King Edward Firft, 1298, at the battle of Salkirk, where according to fome authors 60,000 Scots were flain, Staplehill and *De Prideaux*, being two of the Englifh commanders, and by the Enfigns perceiving that each bore the fame coate of armour, they refolved to trye by combate to whome the arms belonged. But the king being unwilling to hazard the loffe of two fuch valiant foldiers, commanded them to caft lots, who fhould have the addition of the Sable in chief gules. At length, the lot fell to Prideaux, which have been worn in the family ever fince. The *Prideaux* Carew, [MS.] at f. 145, b. —In 29 Edward I. *Sir Richard de Greynvile*, had fummons to be at Berwick upon Tweed, with horfe and arms to march againft the Scots. *Clauf.* 29. Ed. I. m. 14.

‡ In 34 Edward I. on a grand feftival at Whitfuntide, when the King, to adorn the fplendor of his court and augment the glory of his intended expedition into Scotland, knighted Edward Earl of Caernarvon, his eldeft fon; the young Prince, immediately at the high altar, in Weftminfter-Abbey, conferred the fame honor on nearly 300 gentlemen's fons of earls, barons, and knights; and among them, Sir *Walter Molefworth*, anceftor of the Molefworths, of Pencarrow. See *Afhmole* on Knighthood, p. 38.

|| On his afcending the throne, a charter of fummons was directed to Sir Walter Mollefworth and his lady, to attend in perfon, at his ¶coronation: and in that year the King appointed Sir Walter with Gilbert de Holme, fheriff for the counties of Bedford and Bucks: and, in the 5th year of that King, he and Gerard de Braybrooke, had their writs of expence iffued out for their fervice, as knights of the fhire for Bedford, in the firft Parliament held at Weftminfter. He alfo ferved again in Parliament for the fame county the eighth of that reign.

‡‡ *Chriftopher Marlowe*, a contemporary of Shakfpeare, was author of a long-forgotten tragedy, intituled "Edward the Second." In this tragedy are fome fine paffages; among which the following is not the leaft poetical. Here, the higheft entertainments

§ For his former fervices againft the Welfh, he had had a fpecial grant of liberty to hunt the fox, hare, badger and wild cat, with his own dogs, within the king's forefts of Mendip, and chace of Kingfwood.

¶ "Rex dilecto et fideli fuo Waltero de Mullefworth et conforti, falutem. Quia hac inftanti die Dominica poft feftum Sti. Valentini, proponimus coronari vobis mandamus quatenus, vos et confor veftra, hujufmodi coronationis noftræ folenniis dictis, die et loco celebrand. Ad Cometivam nobis et cariffimæ conforti noftræ Ifabellæ, reginæ Angliæ ob noftr. et ipfius confortis noftræ honorem faciend. perfonaliter modis omnibus interfitis, et hoc ficut nos diligeris, nullatenus omittatis." Tefte 8 Febii. Rot. Claus. 1 Ed. II. m. 12.

heaped favours and honours. This his fubjects faw with a refentment which they could not fupprefs. To the effeminate companion of the monarch—to the *Earl of Cornwall*, every day more infolent, the proud barons of England were forced to bow: but, whilft they bowed, they threatned. With their vaffals, they were quickly in arms: the Earl of Cornwall was feized: and with a ferocity that fpurned at the forms of a trial, he was hurried to the fcaffold, and beheaded. Still was Edward irreclaimable. The daily intelligence of difaffection and rebellion;* the triumph of the Scots to whom the Englifh were no longer formidable, and the menaces of France,§ might have occafioned fome fleeting apprehenfions of danger, but were not powerful enough to interrupt his pleafures. Yet, when the ftorm was ready to burft upon his head, he was full of terror: and his very fears operated to his deftruction. Such muft ever be the cafe, where guilt is combined with weaknefs.† That in thefe unhappy difputes the Cornifh had their fhare, and that they were fuccefsful in fupporting their ancient military character, would appear, if the hiftoric voice were filent, from the ftrains of the poet *Drayton.* Thus are our forefathers celebrated in "the *Barons Warres*:"

For courage no whit fecond to the beft,
The *Cornifhmen*, MOST ACTIVE, BOLD and LIGHT !‡

The

entertainments then in fafhion, are contrived for the gratification of Edward by his minion Gaveftone.

"I muft have wanton poets, pleafant wits,
Muficians, that with touching of a ftring
May drawe the plyant king which way I pleafe.
Mufic and poetry are his delight;
Therefore I'll have Italian mafques by night,
Sweet fpeeches, comedies, and pleafing fhewes.
And in day, when he fhall walke abroad,
Like fylvan Nymphs my pages fhall be clad,
My men like Satyrs, grazing on the lawnes,
Shall with their goat-feet dance the antick hay.
Sometimes a lovely Boy, in Dian's fhape,
With haire that gildes the water as it glides,
Crownets of pearle about his naked armes,
And in his fportfull handes an oliue-tree,
* * * * * * * *
Shall bathe him in a fpring: and there hard by,
One, lyke Acteon, peeping through the groue,
Shall by the angry goddefs be transform'd.——
Such thinges as thefe beft pleafe his majeftie."

* In 1319, "a fanatic, *John Powdras*, a Tanner's fon of Exeter, gave out that himfelf was the true Edward, eldeft fon of the late King Edward the firft and by falfe nurfe changed in his cradle; and that the now King Edward was a Carter's fon, and laid in his place. But at his death, (being drawn and hanged) he confeffed he had a familiar fpirit in his houfe in the likenefs of a cat, that affured him he fhould be king of England; and that he had ferved the faid fpirit three years before to bring his purpofe about." *Fabian, Baker.*

§ *Ann.* 1322. Edward defirous of avoiding a rupture with the French, fent his queen Ifabella to her brother the French king to effect a reconciliation between England and France. With her went the bifhop of Exeter. This prelate, perceiving her fecret defigns, and the countenance which fhe gave to Roger Mortimer (who two years before had efcaped out of the tower, where with his uncle he had been imprifoned and had been twice pardoned) returned, and acquainted the king with the whole intrigue.

† According to Sir Thomas More, the king had thoughts of retiring for fafety to the ifle of *Lundy*; whither *Morifco*, (a confpirator againft Henry the third) had retired before. Lundy would not have fheltered him from the rage of the barons. Even there he would have fuffered a worfe fate than Morifco, tho' a pirate and a traitor

‡ JOHN, fon of THOMAS ARCHDEACON, was among the military characters of this reign. "Azure, three Chevronels Sable; by the name of Archdeacon of Cornwall. We find, Thomas Archdeacon, governor of Tintagel-Caftle, fummoned by writ

The moft ftriking incident to the hiftorian of the Cornifh, in the reign of EDWARD III. was the inveftiture of the Black Prince with ducal honours: in 1337, the Prince was created Duke of Cornwall.† But he was no fooner Duke, than his Duchy was invaded by the French.‡ The Duke of Cornwall, however, amply revenged the infult. On the 4th of June 1346, the king put to fea, intending to land in Guienne; but driven back by a ftorm on the coaft of Cornwall, he changed his defign, and made for Normandy. Arriving off La Hogue, he landed there; and after having reduced the ftrongeft cities in that neighbourhood, fpread fire and fword on every fide, even to the gates of Paris.‖ The battle of Creffy¶ foon followed: the Duke of Cornwall commanded

writ to the Houfe of Peers, from 14th to 18th Edward II. His fon John was in the wars of France and Scotland, temp. Edward II. and had the like fummons, 16th Edward III. but never after." *Guillim's Heraldry*, abridged by Samuel Kent, vol. 1. p 143. 8vo. London. 1755.—"OLIVERUS de CARMINOW, was one of the men at arms in the 17th year of Edward II,; as was alfo his father Sir JOHN DE CARMINOW, in the faid year: and each of them had 40l. per ann. in land and rents. *Carew.* f. 51.—"Sir Oliver Carminow, of Carminow, knight, was Lord Chamberlain to Edward the fecond." *Tonkin's* MS.—Sir *Henry Willington*, 17 Edward II. took arms againft that king.§

† See *Selden's* Titles of Honour.

‡ In 1338, whilft Edward was profecuting the war by land, the French, with their allies the Scots, greatly annoyed the Englifh coaft. Spreading an alarm over all the weftern coaft, they burnt Plymouth, and infulted Briftol. See *Holinfhed*, vol. 2. p. 357. *H. Knighton*, p. 2573. *Fabian's* Chron. p. 206. *Stowe's* Chron. p. 235. *Froifart.* c. xxxvii. f. 21, 23.—To the laft authority, *Carew* refers us for many of his hiftorical ancedotes. "When *Edward* the third auerred his right to the Crowne of Fraunce, by the euidence of armes, the French for a counterplea, made an vnlawfull entry into *Devon* and *Cornwall*; but *Hugh Courtney* Earle of *Deuon*, remooued it with *poffe Comitatus*, and recommitted them to the wooden prifon that brought them thither. Yet would not the Scots take fo much warning by their fucceffe, as example by their precedent, if at leaft, *Froiffarts* ignorance of our Englifh names, bred not his miftaking in the place. By his relation, alfo, *Cornwalls* neere neighbourhead gaue oportunity of acceffe, both to the Earle *Montford*, when he appealed to Edward III. for aid to recouer his right in Brittaine (albeit I cannot bring home *Cepfee* the defigned port of his landing) and after his captiuitie, to the meffengers of his heroicall Counteffe, employed in the like errand. And from *Cornwall*, the Earle of *Sarum*, *Wil. de Mefuile* and *Philip de Courtney*, fet to fea, with 40 fhips, befides Barks, and 2000 men at armes, befides archers, in fupport of that quarrell. Laftly, his authoritie enformeth me, that thofe fouldiers of *Cornwall*, who vnder their captaines *Iohn Apport* and *Iohn Cornwall*, had defended the fort of Bercherel in Brittaine, againft the power of Fraunce, aboue a years fpace, in the end, for want of due fuccours, upon an honourable compofition furrendred the fame." *Carew*, f. 97, 97, b.

‖ A lift of the fhips which fome of the fea ports furnifhed, in confequence of Edward the third's Naval Parliament in 1344, and which fhips were ufed at the fiege of Calais. From Hackluyt, page 118, vol. 1. All from Cornwall were included in "*the South Fleet.*"

Towns or Ports.	*Shippes.*	*Mariners.*
Loo,	20	315
Fowey or Foy,	47	770
Patricfteftow or Padftow,	2	27
Polerwan, (Polruan)	1	60
Mulbrooke, (Milbrook)	1	12
	71	1184
Plimouth,	26	606
Portfmouth,	5	96
Dartmouth,	31	757
The King,	25	419
London,	25	662
Yermouth or Yernmouth,	43	1075

¶ In the reign of Edward the third, the long-bow is fuppofed to have been much in ufe. Mr. Barrington entertains this opinion very reafonably, from circumftances which occurred at the battle of Creffy. The Arbalefts in the hands of the Genoefe, were

§ "GIDDESHAM, (fuppofed to have been derived from *Gwith ys Ham*, i. e. the place of wood and water) was held by *Gotceline*, in elder ages, and *Combe* by *Odo*: fince it was the inheritance of an ancient family, called *de Lumen* or *Lomen*; of which race were divers knights. Sir *Richard Lumen*, was the laft that lived in this place in the time of King *Henry* III. from whom it came unto the family of *Willington*, and was conveyed unto Sir *Henry Willington*, who dwelt here in the days of King *Edward* II. and made one among the barons that took arms againft the faid king, and was flain in the 17th year of his reign, who is named to be a baron by *Holinfhed*." *Chapple's Rifdon.*

commanded the firſt line of the Engliſh army: the ſecond was led on, by the Earls of Northamton and Arundel.* The victory of the Engliſh at Creſſy, as well as† at the battle of

D

Poictiers,

were all expoſed to a violent ſtorm, which happened juſt before the battle commenced. This ſtorm falling on the ſtrings of their bows, relaxed them ſo far, as to render them incapable of proper ſervice; while on the other hand, the Engliſh bows were kept in their caſes during the rain and were not injured. Hence Mr. Barrington concludes, the Engliſh uſed the long-bow, as that inſtrument was commonly provided with a caſe, but the croſs-bow, being of ſo inconvenient a ſhape, could not be provided with ſuch covering. Indeed this latter kind of bow, is not ſaid to have been even furniſhed with a cover, as far as I have been able to find. The battle of Creſſy, as well as that of Poictiers, (where the archers poured forth their quivers in ſuch bloody victories,) intimates the bow to have been highly cultivated by the Engliſh at thoſe times; but it was found neceſſary by Edward to enforce the practice of archery during the peace which followed, as the ſoldiers rather attended to other amuſements, than archery.

* After the battle of Creſſy, the town of Calais ſurrendered to the Engliſh. There is in the catalogue of the MSS. in the church library at Canterbury, a very curious volume in folio; containing "The names, and armes (emblazoned) of the principall captains as well of noblemen as of knights that were with the victorious Prince King Edward the third, at the ſiege of Callys, 1346. An account of how many ſhips and mariners every port ſent throughout England to that ſiege. Alſo the ſupply of ſhips and mariners from Bayon, Spayne, Ireland, Flaunders, and Gelderland. An account of all the princes and noblemen foreigners that ſerved at that ſiege with their pay and of the whole charge of that ſiege.

The Prince of Wales had by the day for his diet	xx *ſhill.*	
A Duke, not of the Blood Royal	viii *ſh.* iiii*d.*	
An Earle	vi *ſh.* viii*d.*	
A Viſcount	v *ſh.*	
A Baron	iiii *ſh.*	
A Knight	ii *ſh.*	
An Eſquier		xviii*d.*
A Gentleman for him and his ſervant	ii *ſh.*	
Archers on foot		iii*d.*
on horſe		iiii*d.*
A Welſhman on foot		ii*d.*
A Mariner		iii*d.*"

† John Maynard of Axminſter, ſerved under Edward Duke of Cornwall, in his victorious expeditions in France; and, 28th July, 1352, 26 Edward III. was conſtituted governor of Breſt-Caſtle, in Britany.‡ In theſe military expeditions, *Cruwys* and *Carew* are alſo ſignal names.¶

‡ The Maynards had conſiderable property in Devonſhire, and intermarried with ſeveral families in the Weſt of England; among whom were the Bullers of Shillingham, in Cornwall.

¶ "*Cruwys, Sir Robert*, Kt. was born at the antient ſeat of the name and family, in the pariſh, now called *Morchard*, in the hundred of *Witheridge*,, about five miles to the weſt of *Tiverton* in this county. It was heretofore called *Morceſter*; which word *Ceſter*, is often uſed in the old Saxon tongue, for *Caſtle*, or *Fortreſs*; tho' its original be Latin, as derived from *Caſtrum:* but an ingenious gentleman, the preſent heir of this family, *John Cruwys*, Eſq. thinks, that it doth often ſignify a ſeat, or ſeated; and then *Morceſter*, will be the place, or pariſh, ſeated by, or near the *Moor*. But, for what I know, it may do as well, to interpret it a caſtle or place of defence; the ſame, or the ruins whereof, might be there, tho' now not apparent, as the firſt denomination of the place, in, or near the *Moor*; unto which it well agrees, as adjoyning to the foreſt of *Exmoor*.

But then at length it obtained the adjunct of *Cruwys*, from this antient and knightly family; that even from the conqueſt, if not before, were lords thereof, and was called *Morceſter-cruwys*, and now generally *Cruwys-morchard*; the reaſon of which laſt termination, I muſt own myſelf ignorant of,

As to the Etymon or Derivation of the name *Cruwys*, the laſt mentioned gentleman apprehends it to be *de Cruce*, the High-Dutch and Germans calling this family *Croſs* and *Cruce*; and their ſtile in Latin was *Dominus de Cruce*, the lord of the croſs. Which induces me to believe, they derive this name from ſome notable croſs, or place ſo called heretofore, near their houſes or habitation. Which was a practice much in uſe among our Saxon anceſtors, as *Veſtegan* obſerves; whoſe words, for confirmation of this ſurmize, I ſhall crave leave here to inſert: *Divers of our anceſtors took their ſirnames, by reaſon of their abode, in or near ſome place of note, where they ſettled themſelves, and planted their enſuing families, as at a wood, a hill, a field, a brook, a ford, a green, and the like*; as Robert of the Green, *came to be called*, Robert a Green, *and at laſt*, Robert Green. So *Robert de Cruce*, might come at length to be *Robert Cruwys*. But of this enough.

How long this name and family have poſſeſſed this antient inheritance, is not certainly known; but 'tis ſuppoſed, from before the Norman conqueſt. There is a tradition in this country, of three families, ſtill flouriſhing herein, that were here before that time; according to that old *Saw* often uſed among us in diſcourſe,

Crocker, Cruwys, *and* Copleſtone,
When the Conqueror came, were at Home.

There was antiently a vaſt eſtate in this name and family, here in this county; which came to be much impaired by the heat and violence of Sir *Alex. Cruwys*, Kt. who in the days of *K. E.* 3. unhappily quarrelling with *Carew* on *Bicklegh* Bridge, ran him thorow and the rails breaking, threw him into the river. Whoſe pardon, yet to be ſeen, according to a tradition in the family, coſt him two and twenty mannors of land. Notwithſtanding which, there remained a noble eſtate to the heir;

heir; and a very fair one ftill doth: altho' the prefent gentleman's grand father, *Lewis Cruwys*, Efq. lopped off from him, near a thoufand pound a year more; upon what occafion, feeing I am not informed, I lift not to enquire. Only this I fhall add, as very remarkable, that they have lived ever fince Sir *Alexander Cruwys's* time, in K. H. 3. reign, now near upon five hundred years together, in the fame houfe at *Cruwys-Morchard*, with an handfom eftate, without the leaft help of a gown, a petticoat, or an apron; *i. e.* without any augmentation from a lawyer, an heirefs, or a trade in the family.

Which was firft in the poffeffion of this family, *Morchard*, or *Nether-Ex*, I cannot fay: *Olnel de Cruwys* held *Nether-Ex* in K. *H.* 2 days; and *A.* 1233, being the 18th of K. *H.* 3. Sir *Richard Cruwys* held it; whofe fon *William* leaving five daughters and heirs, this mannor was parted among them; who brought their purparties to their hufbands, *de Lucy*, *de Luccombe*, a knightly tribe in this fhire heretofore; *Saint-clere le Reis*, *or Keis* and *de Whitefeild.* Another family of this name flourifhed long at *Anfty-cruwys*, in the north-eaft parts of this county, near the confines of *Somerfetfhire*; which was a younger branch of *Morchard* houfe, planted there in the reign of K. *Edw.*1. which, after four generations, expired in two daughters and heirs, married to *Norton* and *Pollard.* But this land, notwithftanding all their endeavours to the contrary, reverted to *Morchard* houfe; being, after a tedious fuit at law, removed by judgment.

There was yet another family of this name, which did fometime profper well, at their feat called *Denvale*, in the parifh of *Bampton* in this fhire; and continued there, from K. *Edw.* 1. unto Q. *Eliz.* days; when by the heir general, it was fold unto a gentleman firnamed *Triftram.* But as we may guefs by the arms, this was a different family from that of *Morchard*; for they gave *In a Feild Gold, a chevron Gul. between* 3 *Mullets.*

There were feveral knights of this family before Sir *Robert Cruwys's* time, of whom we are treating, who was the eldeft fon of Sir *Alexander Cruwys*, that was unhappily engaged in a duel with *Carew*: of which before. Whofe father having greatly exhaufted and incumbred his eftate, this young gentleman betook himfelf to the wars; which he chofe rather to do, as became a man of honour; when by ferving his king and country, he might get profit and renown abroad, than to lie rufting at home in floth and luxury: and like a true bred Englifh gentleman, however fome effeminate *Beaus* ridicule them by the names of *grinning honours, and honourable fcars*, he rather fought danger than declined it: and having acquitted himfelf well, returned back to his native country with great reputation.

The fcene on which he acted his part was *France*; and the general under which he ferved was that famous captain, the Lord *Walter de Manny*; who, tho' a foreigner by birth, had a great eftate in *England*, and fome in *Devonfhire.* For we are told, *South-Huifh*, near *Kingfbridge*, was his, in the reign of *K. Edw.* 3. If we would then know what particular exploits our Sir *Roger Cruwys* was engaged in, we muft enquire into the actions of that great commander; in moft, if not all which, we may fuppofe him to have a fhare.

In the 14th of *Edw.* 3. this lord made great fpoil in the north parts of *France*, flew more than a thoufand foldiers, and burnt three hundred villages. In the 15th of *Edw.* 3. he came to the caftle of Conqueft, which the French had won the day before; faying, *he would not go thence, 'till he faw who were in the caftle, and how it had been won:* and at length, finding a breach in the wall, entered thereat. About that time alfo, he attended on *K. Edw.* 3. to the fiege of *Nants*; when the *King* made him feveral grants of privileges and emoluments, for the fupport of himfelf and 50 men at arms, with 50 archers on horfe back, in that expedition then made into *France.* His own wages as a Banneret was 4s. *per diem*, the *Knights* (which were twelve) 2s. a piece; the Efquires, 1s. and the Archers 6d.

In the 18th of *E.* 3. being one of the Marefchals of the hoft to the Earl of *Derby*, he went with him to the affault of *Bergerath* (fays Dugd. which I take to be *Bergerac* a city of *Perigord*) in *France*, which being made by fea and land, the town foon yielded. After this in the 19th of the fame *King*, he was at the relief of *Auberoche*; where falling on the *French* in their tents, he utterly vanquifhed their whole hoft. Shortly after, he was at the taking of *Mauleon*, where he did great fervice.

In the 20th of *Edw.* 3. he was, and moft likely Sir *Robert Cruwys* alfo, in the famous battel of *Creffi*, being an eminent commander in the van of the Englifh army; a little before the battel began, what is fomewhat remarkable, 'tis faid, that fhoals and clouds of baleful Ravens, and other birds of prey and ravin (as fore-fhewing the harveft of carcaffes at hand) came flying over the French hoft. Here the Englifh obtained a glorious victory; which the hiftorian makes a controverfy of, whether 'twas owing to the exemplary manhood of the Englifh, or their fingular piety. *Great was the victory*, fays he, *great was the prowefs, and great the glory: but they, like Chriftian Knights and foldiers, forbore all boaft*; *referring the whole thanks and honour to God.* Soon after the battel, *K. Edward* went and fate down before the ftrong town of *Calais*; which the Lord *Manny* knowing (being now, as I fuppofe, with the Duke of *Lancafter* in *Guien*) among his prifoners at *Creffi*, having taken a French *Kt.* who offered three thoufand crowns for his ranfom, he remitted the whole fum for a pafs, which he obtained from the *K.* of *France*, that he might ride through part of his country, with twenty of his company, to *Calais*, then befieged by the Englifh.

Whether Sir *Robert* was one of this twenty that accompanied the Lord *Manny* is uncertain; moft likely he was not, but rather ftayed behind with thofe forces he had left, with *Henry* of *Lancefter*, Earl of *Derby*; who (the Duke of *Normandy* being fent for by the *King* of *France*, to come to the relief of *Calais*, which yet they were not able to effect) was left mafter of the field in *Guyenne.* And having a confiderable army there, of 1200 men at arms, 2000 archers, and 3000 other foot, he took in moft of the towns of *Xantoigne* and *Poictou*; and in the end, befieged and facked *Poictiers*: and then returned to *Burdeaux*, with more pillage than his people could well bear. So Sir *R. Baker* exprefly tells us.

That Sir *Robert Cruwys* was in this action, and a great contributor to the fuccefs thereof, is more than probable; in that I find it recorded of him, *that he gave his acquittance for his wages at* Burdeaux, A. 20 Edw. 3. which was the fame year the victory was obtained at *Creffi*, with the flaughter of 11 princes, 80 barons, 1200 knights, aud 30,000 common foldiers of the French.

That Sir *Robert Cruwys* fhould fight under the command of the Lord *Manny*, let none efteem it as a difparagement to his honour; when *K. Edward* himfelf, and the *Black Prince* his fon, either in the taking (as *Dugdale*) or defending (as *Baker*) of the town of *Calais*, fought both under his banner. In all, or moft of whofe exploits, this our countryman was fo fignally affifting, that he received the honour of *Knighthood* upon that account; tho' whether from the General or the *King's* hand immediately, is not mentioned. For fo we are expreffly told, *that Sir* Robert Crews, *of* Crews-Morchard, *as they are vulgarly called*

called, was knighted for his valiant ſervice done in France, *under the leading of the Lord* Walter Manny, *in the age of King* Edw. 3. Sometime after this he quitted the wars; and being paid off, we may well ſuppoſe, Sir *Robert Cruwys* returned into his own country; loaden with trophies of honour, and the military ſpoils of the declared enemies thereof: whoſe rents alſo being carefully improved in his abſence, at home, and his purſe well filled by his ſervices abroad, he became able to take off the incumbrances on his eſtate, and to pay his juſt and honeſt debts, under which he lay. And this he did, as I am told by the preſent heir of the family, in the church, or rather, the church-porch, belonging to his pariſh, ſoon after his arrival home. Wherein he ſhewed no leſs chriſtian policy, than integrity; in that no one can juſtly expect, that that eſtate ſhould continue long in his poſterity, or that God ſhould ever bleſs it, which he poſſeſt by fraud or violence; and with the cries and curſes of miſerable orphans and widows, undone and ruined by his non-payment of his juſt and honeſt dues. But 'tis not ſo here; for the eſtate of *Cruwys-Morchard* hath continued ever ſince in his name and poſterity, now twelve generations following: which we look upon as an argument of God's particular favour, and that juſtice and honeſty, which hath been ſo conſpicuous in this family.

How long after this Sir *Robert* ſurvived, I do not find; nor where he lieth interred: altho' moſt probably, it is in an old chappel belonging to the houſe, now wholly demoliſhed. In which, that there were ſome funeral Monuments heretofore, may appear from ſome broken pieces of Alabaſter, that have heretofore been digged up there. As for the church, the old being wholly deſtroyed, and the preſent built but about the 20th *K. Hen.* 8. there are no *veſtigia* or tracts found, of any antient Monuments. And before the late flagration by lightning (which hapned *A.* 1689, ſo dreadful, that it wrent the Steeple, melted the bells, lead, and glaſs, nothing eſcaping but the Communion plate) there were only *Orates* for ſome of the family, wth coats of arms inting'n, or painted on the glaſs.

Some of this family, very likely, were the founders of the antient pariſh church, which they endowed well with Glebe-lands, which, with the tythes thereunto belonging, makes the rectory amount to an hundred and ſixty pounds *per Ann.* clear.

Sir *Robert de Cruwys, de Morceſter-cruwys, Kt.* left iſſue *Alexander Cruwys*, of *Cruwys-morchard*; who had iſſue *John*; who had iſſue *John*; who had iſſue *Thomas*; who had iſſue *John*; who had iſſue *John*; who had iſſue *John*; who had iſſue *Humphry*; who had iſſue *Lewis*; who had iſſue *Henry*; who had iſſue *John Cruwys*, of *Cruwys-Morchard*, Eſq. who hath iſſue; which God bleſs to all future generations.

I ſhall here only add a few remarks on the coat-armor of this family, which is, *A Bend between ſix Eſcalopes*; which Eſcalopes, we are informed, are an emblem of that ſteadfaſt amity, and conſtant fidelity, that ought to be, between brethren and companions of one ſociety. For take one of thoſe fiſhes and divide the ſhells, and endeavour to ſort them, not with hundreds, but millions of the ſame kind, you ſhall never match them throughout. The conſideration whereof, moved the firſt founders of the order of S. *Mich.* in *France*, to ſort the Eſcalope ſhells in the collar of this order by couples. And then the number ſix, ſome Armoriſts hold it to be the beſt of even and articulate numbers, that can be borne in one Eſcotcheon. And the bearing the Eſcalope in arms, ſignifies the firſt bearer of ſuch arms, to have been a commander, who by his valor had gained the hearts of his ſoldiers, and made a reciprocation of trueſt love between them." *Prince*, pp. 145, 147.

" *Carew, Sir John*, Kt. Baron of *Carew* and *Mulsford*, was born at *Mohuns-Ottery*, an antient houſe in this county: ſo called from its Lords, the *Mohuns*, who inhabited there: but before that, it had the denomination of *Ottery-Flemming*, from its more antient Lords, the *Flemmings*. Which name was ſometime owner of a great eſtate in theſe parts, as the places to which it ſtill adheres, viz. *Stoke-Flemming*, *Bratton-Flemming*, &c. may declare. This houſe ſtandeth in *Luppit*, quaſi *Low-pit*, a ſmall pariſh, near the town of *Honiton*; where ſome monks at firſt inhabiting in a low ground or pit, gave occaſion to the name: which monks were afterward removed thence, by Sir *William de Mohun*, brother to the Lord *Reginald de Mohun* unto the abby of *Newham*, or *Newenham*, then lately erected by them, in the pariſh of *Axminſter*.

Here, before I proceed to the perſon, I ſhall crave leave to ſpeak ſomething, as to the antiquity and genealogy of this right noble family.

Some there are, who would fetch its original from the Dukes or Kings of *Swevia*, a certain region in *Higher Germany*; and that upon a double account.

Firſt, from that brave and martial temper of mind, both thoſe families obſerved to be of: the Swevians are reported to have been a bold and warlike nation, ſurpaſſing all the reſt of the Germans; *Gens populoſa, fortis, audax, & bellicoſa*; *& Germanorum præſtantiſſima.* So the moſt of this family have been, in all ages, martial men, and worthily deſerving of their Prince and Country.

Secondly, my author would infer this farther, *from that agreement between them in their* coat-armour; the Swevian Dukes or Kings giving, *Sol three Lions paſſant Saturn*; which is the ſame with *Carew's* coat, ſave only, that the former hath the *Lions gardant.* And ſo it is ſuppoſed, that ſome younger brother of that royal houſe, coming hither in queſt of honour, either with the Saxons, Danes, or Normans, ſeated himſelf in this *Kingdom*; in which his poſterity hath flouriſhed unto this day.

But I ſhall diſmiſs this, as little more than conjecture, and proceed to a more certain and ſubſtantial account of the matter. A worthy gentleman of the name and family, owns their original to have been from *France*, in his ingenious *Survey of* Cornwall; whoſe words are theſe,

> Carew, *of antient* Carru *was:*
> *And* Carru *is a Plow:*
> *Romans the Trade, Frenchmen the Word;*
> *I do the Name avow.*

The name being thus owned to be French, we may conclude, the family came into *England* with the Conqueror, *William of Normandy*. So that I ſhall trace it ſo far back as that conqueſt; authenticating what I have to ſay hereof, from the unqueſtionable teſtimony of Sir *William Pole*; who ſpeaking of the ſame, aſſures us, *that he goes no farther in theſe matters, than records and deeds will give him certain warrant.*

The firſt of this line in *England*, was *Walter de Windſor*, ſo called from his being made *Caſtellan de Windſor*, or governour of the caſtle of *Windſor*, ſon of *Otho*; which *Walter* had iſſue two ſons, *William*, from whom the Lords *Windſors* are deſcended; and *Gerald*, from whom the *Carews* and *Fitzgeralds.*

 This

This *Gerald*, was Caftellan, or fteward of the caftle of *Pembroke*, in *Wales*, ; and was an expert man, both in war and peace; and in great favour with K. *Hen.* 1. who beftowed upon him the lordfhip of *Mulsford*, in the county of *Berks*. He married *Nefta*, the daughter of *Rees*. Prince of *South Wales*, a fair lady; whofe dowry was the caftle of *Carew*, in thofe parts: from whence a certain author tells us, notwithftanding the fore-mentioned derivation of it from *Carru*, this antient family derives its name of *Carew*, *a Carew Caftro in agro Pembrochienfi Bognomen fortitus eft:* tho' he doth not fay from whence that caftle fetches its name.

This *Gerald de Windfor*, by this lady *Nefta* his wife, had iffue three fons, *William*, *Maurice*, and *David*. *David*, the youngeft, was bifhop of St. *David's*, in *Wales*, of whom nothing elfe is recorded remarkable. From *Maurice Fitz-Gerald*, the fecond fon, are iffued the noble families of *Kildare* and *Defmond*, in the kingdom of *Ireland*.

William, the eldeft fon of *Gerald*, Lord of *Carrio*, had iffue *Raymond*, *Otho*, and others; *Raymond* married *Bafilia*, daughter of *Gilbert*, and fifter of *Richard Strongbow*, Earls of *Pembroke*, but died without iffue. *Otho de Carrio* had iffue *William*, unto whom K. *John*, in the 14th year of his reign, made a grant of *Mullesford*, reciting the deed, formerly made, unto *Gerald*, by K. *Henry* the firft. This was the firft who took to him, the name of *de Carrio* or *Carru*. This *William* had iffue *William*; which had iffue *Nicholas*; which had iffue *William*, Baron of *Carru* and *Mullesford*, for fo is he ftiled; who had iffue Sir *Nicholas*, the father of Sir *Nicholas* Baron of *Carru* and *Mullesford*; fo fummoned to Parliament by writ in the days of K. *Edw.* 1. for thofe baronages then were not, as now, hereditary; but only during life. Nor did they always give a place in Parliament, without the King's fpecial writ, by which he might advance thither whom he pleas'd; after the expiration whereof, they could challenge no right of voting there.

This Sir *Nicholas*, Baron *Carru* and *Mullesford*, married the fifter and heir of Sir *John Peverel* of *Wefton-Peverel*, near *Plymouth*, in this county, Kt. in the reign of K. *Edw.* 1. by whom he had a great eftate in thefe parts, as this *Wefton-Peverel*, *Afhford-Peverel*, *Mamhead*, and other places. At which time, this honourable ftock took fuch deep rooting in this country, and liked the foyl fo well, that it hath flourifhed well herein ever fince, unto this day, now above four hundred years. By this his lady, fifter of Sir *John Peverel*, Sir *Nicholas*, Baron *Carew*, had iffue four fons viz. Sir *John*, *Thomas*, *Nicholas*, and *William*. From *Nicholas* defcended the honourable family of *Carew*, of *Beddington*, in *Surrey*, in the eaftern parts of *England*.

Sir *John*, the eldeft fon, fucceffively married two wives; his firft *Elenor*, daughter and heir of Sir *William Mohun*, of *Mohuns-Ottery*, Kt. a younger brother to the Lord *Reginald de Mohun*, of *Dunftar*, in Com. *Somerfet*, by whom he had iffue *Nicholas*: his fecond wife was *Joan*, daughter of *Gilbert* Lord *Talbot*, by whom he had iffue Sir *John Carew*, the perfon of whom we are about to fpeak. *Nicholas*, the eldeft fon, married the fifter of his father's fecond wife, a daughter of the Lord *Talbot's*, and died without iffue. But before his death, being in right of his mother, feiz'd of all her inheritance, he convey'd his lands unto the iffue of his father; by means whereof, *Mohuns-Ottery*, and the reft, defcended in this honourable name, and the fucceeding family there, quartered the arms of *Mohun* with their own, altho' they iffued not from that blood. This they made the place of their refidence, in which they flourifhed in great honour for many fucceeding generations, even down to the days of Q. *Elizabeth*, of never dying memory. When *Cicely*, fifter and heir unto Sir *Peter Carew*, the laft of this line, married unto *Thomas Kirkham*, of *Blagdon*, Efq. left it to her daughter *Thomafin*; who brought it to her hufband, *Thomas Southcot*, of *Indeho*, in the parifh of *Bovey-Tracy*, Efq. In which antient and gentile name it having continued about three defcents, the heir thereof, was pleafed to alienate it unto Sir *Walter Young*, Baronet, the father (if I miftake not) of the prefent honourable Sir *Walter Young*, of *Efcot*, Baronet, in whom it now remains.

Having thus given a large account of this noble family in general, I fhall now proceed unto the moft memorable occurrences in the life of Sir *John Carew* in particular; the hiftory whereof, comes very fhort and imperfect to our hands; yet we have him tranfmitted to us under a double very honourable character, of a foldier and a ftatefman.

Firft: he was a great foldier; and is faid, valiantly to have ferved K. *Edw.* 3. againft the rebels in *Ireland*; and its farther added, that his fon Sir *John Carew* was flain there. But I fear, by fome mifhap or other, this will prove a miftake, for I find not any contention that King had with the Irifh all his reign: that account therefore given by a later author, feems more agreeable to the truth, who tells us, that it was in his wars in *France*, that he ferved that puiffant Prince. And very probable it is, that our Sir *John Carew* was prefent at the battle of *Creffy* there, fought between *Edw* 3. of *England*, and K. *Philip* of *France*; at what time the Englifh, under the aufpicious conduct of that fon of *Mars*, called the *Black Prince* (a wonderful general, but of fifteen or fixteen years of age), got an entire victory, with the flaughter of no lefs than thirty thoufand of the enemy: in which engagement, likely enough it is, Sir *John Carew* loft his valiant fon, called by his own name; whofe courage and conduct had prefer'd him alfo to the honour of Knighthood.

How great a ftatefman he was, we may beft infer from hence, that K. *Edw.* 3. (as well a wife as valiant Prince) in the 24th year of his reign, was pleafed to make him Lord Deputy of *Ireland*; how long he continued in that moft honourable poft, and what the memorable actions were he did there, I no where find: only this I do, that he lived after this feveral years. So that likely enough it is, he came back into *England*, and lieth inter'd, either in the church of *Luppit* aforefaid, or fome other in this county. He died *Anno* 36, of K. *Edw.* 3. and of our Lord 1363, on the 16th day of *May*.

This Sir *John Carew*, by *Margaret* his wife, daughter of *John* Lord *Mohun*, of *Dunftar*, had iffue Sir *John Carru*, who (as was faid) died in his father's lifetime without iffue and *Leonard*; (*Leonard de Carru*) married *Alice*, daughter of Sir *Edmund Fitz-Alan*, of *Arondel*. fecond fon of *Edmund* Earl of *Arondel*, and had iffue Sir *Thomas de Carru*, of *Ottery-Mohun*, Knight.

This Sir *Thomas* was alfo a great foldier; he had the truft of the navy, and three thoufand Englifh foldiers committed to him, for the fecuring of the Emperor *Sigifmund*, during his ftay and abode here in *England*, in the beginning of the reign of K. *Henry* 5. He valiantly ferved alfo that heroic Prince in his wars in *France*; and was undoubtedly, at the battle of *Agincourt* in that kingdom, when the victory was fo great, that the Englifh had taken more prifoners, than there were foldiers in their army.

Sir *Thomas de Carru* was appointed to keep and defend the paffage over the river *Seine*, *Anno* 6 K. *Hen.* 5. and was made captain of *Harflew*. He died the 25th of *January*, in the 9th year of K. *Hen.* 6. and by *Elizabeth* his wife, daughter of Sir *William Bonvile*, of *Shute*, Kt. left iffue Sir *Nicholas* Baron *Carew*; who by *Joan* his wife, daughter of Sir *Hugh Courtenay*, of

Poictiers, on a fubfequent expedition, was attributed chiefly to the valour of the Duke. It was in 1355, that* the Duke of Cornwall fet fail from Plymouth, with 300 fhips, for France. He was attended by the Earls of Warwick, Suffolk, Salifbury, and Oxford, the Lord Chandos, and others.† This much it was neceffary to ftate. But I fhould not deem it neceffary to attend our hero to the field of Poictiers, more than I had done to that of Creffy, (minutely defcribed as they both are in the hiftories of England,) but for the pretenfions of a Cornifh houfe to honours that appear doubtful or equivocal. It is afferted in the memoirs of the *Trefry* family, that Sir JOHN TREFRY was the very perfon, to whom King John of France furrendered himfelf a prifoner.‡ That, immediately after the battle, the Duke of Cornwall created Sir John, a Knight-Banneret, and gave him liberty to quarter the arms of France with his own, and for fupporters a wild man with a bow, and a wild woman with an arrow in her hands, is likewife told. And I believe the ftory; becaufe thefe were the arms of Trefry: and they not long fince exifted in feveral of the old houfes of Fawey,§ painted on glafs and carved in wood or ftone. But

of *Haccombe*, Kt. by *Philippa* his wife, daughter and one of the heirs of Sir *Warren Ercedecon*, of that place, Kt. had iffue Sir *Thomas*, and many others.

Sir *Thomas Carew* Kt. Baron of *Carew* and *Mullesford*, and Lord of *Mohuns-Ottery*, married *Joan*, daughter and one of the heirs of *Thomas Carmino*; and had iffue Sir *Nicholas Carew*, which married *Margaret* the eldeft daughter of Sir *John Dinham*, fifter and one of the heirs of *John* Lord *Dinham*, of *Nutwel*, in this county, Lord High-Treafurer of *England*; and left iffue Sir *Edmund Carew*, Kt.

This Sir *Nicholas Carew* was a very eminent perfon, and great at court, where he died on the 16th of *November*, in the 11th year of K. *Edw.* 4. He and his lady lie inter'd in the abby church of *Weftminfter*, among the Kings and Queens of *England* To whofe memory an antient plain tomb of gray marble is there ftill feen erected, with an infcription in brafs round the ledge, and fome coats of arms on the pedeftal, whereby may be gather'd, faith my author, that *Nicholas* Baron *Carew*, and his wife the Lady *Margaret*, who was the daughter of Sir *John Dinham*, Kt. were here intomb'd. He died on the 6th day of *December*, (fo the Epitaph) in the year 1470, and fhe on the 13th day of the fame month, and year following.

The Epitaph here follows:

" *Orate pro animabus* Nicolai *Baronis. Quondam de* Carew, *&* *Dominæ*
" Margaritæ *Vxoris ejus filiæ* Johannis *Domini* Dinham *Militis: Qui quidem*
" Nicolaus *obiit Sexto die Menfis* Decembris, *Anno Dom.* 1470. *Et prædicta*
" *Domina* Margareta *obiit* 13 *die Menfis* Decembris, *Anno* 1471.

There was another Sir *John Carew* of *Devonfhire*, as the hiftorian calls him, who was an eminent foldier, and ferved K. *Hen.* 8. at fea, againft the French; what relation he had to either of the gentlemen aforementioned I cannot fay; but probably he was a younger brother to Sir *Philip* or Sir *Edmund Carew*. When the Lord Admiral *Howard* had prepared a great fleet, the King, *Hen.* 8. went himfelf to *Portfmouth* to fee it, where he appointed captains, for one of his chiefeft fhips called the *Regent*, Sir *Thomas Knevet*, mafter of his horfe, and Sir *John Carew*: who engaging with a French Carrick of great force, they enter'd her, which when her gunner faw, he defperately fate fire to the powder, and blew them both up; when Sir *Thomas Knevet*, and Sir *John Carew*, with feven hundred men, were all drown'd or burnt." *Prince*, pp. 148, 150.

* In the 26th Edward 3. 1354, Sir Hugh Courtenay, and Sir Thomas his brother, were commiffioned by the King, to arm and array all perfons, Knights, Efquires and others, within the counties of Devon and Cornwall, and to conduct them to the fea-coaft, to oppofe an invafion apprehended from the French.—*Cleaveland.* And, the following year, the King fent to Exeter " his Letter Patent under his great feal bearing date 25. *Martii*, whereby he required the fpeedy fupply of three fhips, and every one of them threefcore mariners and twenty archers, which the city foon procured, and delivered them over to one *Gervis Aldlamy* then *Vice Admiral* of *Devon*, who conducted them to *Sandwich*, and there prefented them to *John Montegomer* Lord High Admiral of *England*."—*Izacke's* Mem. of the city of Exeter.

† See *Carew*, f. 114.

‡ So *Tonkin* fays (in his MSS.) whether from family-tradition, or papers I cannot determine.

§ " During the warlike raignes of our two valiant *Edwards*, the firft and third, the *Foyens* addicted themfelues to backe their Princes quarrell, by coping with the enemy at fea, and made returne of many prizes: which purchafes hauing aduanced them to a good eftate of wealth, the fame was (when the quieter conditioned times gaue meanes) heedfully and diligently employed, and bettered, by the more ciuill trade of marchandife; and in both thefe vocations they fo fortunately profpered, that it is reported, 60. tall fhips did, at one time, belong to the harbour, and that they affifted the fiege of Callais, with 47. faile. Heereon, a full purfe begetting a ftout ftomack, our Foyens tooke heart at graffe, and chauncing about that time (I fpeake vpon the credit of tradition) to fayle neere Rye, and Winchelfea, they ftifly refufed to vaile their bonets at the fummons of thofe townes; which contempt (by the better enabled fea-farers, reckoned intolerable) caufed the Ripiers to make out with might and mayne againft them; howbeit, with a more hardy onfet, then happy iffue: for the Foy men gaue them fo

But our hiftories tell us, that "King John, after being wounded in the face, was taken prifoner by one of his own fubjects, whom he formerly banifhed, and who now fought for his enemies." It is poffible, that Sir John Trefry might have affifted in taking the French King prifoner, or have been appointed as a guard over the captive Monarch. Some fignal act he moft, doubtlefs, have performed, to merit fo proud an armorial bearing, and a title fo honourable to a foldier. That Sir WILLIAM BASSET was created a Knight-Banneret, on this memorable occafion, we are not fure: but the records of the family inform us, that he was a brave officer in the French wars under Edward III. and that the King in reward for his fervices, gave him liberty to* *crenallate* his houfe at Tehidy, and granted him two weekly markets, and two fairs yearly to be held in his town of Redruth. That on his return to England, the Duke landed at Plymouth, with his royal captive, and many of the French nobility, is a fact which I muft not omit; tho' unenlivened by one traditionary anecdote.|| In thefe enterprizes, more glorious than ufeful,‡ the national treafury muft have fuffered diminution; and might have been exhaufted but for a timely fupply from the "Silver Mines" of Devon and Cornwall.†

The

fo rough entertaynment at their welcome, that they were glad to forfake patch, without bidding farewell: the merit of which exploit, afterwards entitled them Gallants of Foy: and (it may bee) they fought to eternize this memorable fact, after the Greeke and Romane maner, by inuefting the towne of *Golant* with that name: notwithftanding, *quære*, whether a caufeleffe ambition in the pofteritie turned not rather Golant into Gallant, for their greater glory!!! Moreouer, the proweffe of one *Nicholas*, fonne to a widdow, neere Foy, is defkanted vpon, in an old three mans fongs, namely, how he fought brauely at fea, with *Iohn Dory* (a Genowey, as I coniecture) fet forth by *Iohn* the French king, and (after much bloudfhed on both fides) tooke, and flew him, in reuenge of the great rauine, and crueltie, which hee had forecommitted, vpon the Englifh mens goods and bodies. Yet their fo often good fucceffe, fometimes tafted the fawce of croffer fpeeding; for *Tho. Walfingham* telleth vs, that Sir *Hugh Calueley*, and Sir *Th. Percy*, deputed to gard the fea, by *R.* the 2. *Anno.* 1379. chanced there to meete a *Cornifh* barge, belonging to Foy harbour, which hauing worne out his victuals, and time, limited for the like feruice, was then fayling homewards, neither would be entreated by thofe knights, to ioyne companie with them: howbeit they bought this refufall verie deare. For no fooner was the Englifh fleete paft out of fight, but that a Flemmifh man of warre lighted vpon them, and (after a long, and ftrong refiftance) ouermaftered them as well, at laft in force, as they did at firft in number, tooke the Barge, funk it, and flaughtered all the Saylers, one onely boy excepted, who in the heate of the bickering, feeing which way the game would goe, fecretly ftole aboord the Flemming, and clofely hid himfelfe amongft the ballaft. Ouer a while, this Pirate caft Anker in an Englifh harbor, where the boy, hearing his countrimens voice, that were come aboord, rifeth from his new buriall, bewrayeth the fact, and fo wrought meanes, for their punifhment, and his owne deliuery." *Carew*, f. 134, b. 135, b.

* *Crenallare* is the word ufed in the patent —— to fortify with battlements. We are not told, whether the men of *Redruth*, (vaffals, of Sir William Baffet) were partakers of their leader's glory. But as they probably followed him to the field of Creffy or of Poictiers, (or perhaps both) it is likely, that they fought valiantly by his fide, to the credit of their Chieftain, and the honour of their county. *Lefkeard* enjoyed feveral confiderable privileges by favor of the Black Prince, who, as Duke of Cornwall, is faid to have occafionally refided there, at Prince's Court. And, in return (tradition fays) that town and the country round it raifed a large body of young and active men, who entered into the fervice of their Duke, and followed his fortunes in the wars.

|| "At *St. Michael's Mount*, (as *Froiffart* faith) landed *Sir Robert Knolls*, a valiant commander of the Black Princes, in the French wars temp. Edward 3, (who drew the traitor Sir Perducas d'Albert from the French to the Englifh army, to which afterwards he returned again moft perfidioufly) when he had been highly inftrumental in taking the forts of Froyns, Roach-Vandower, Ville Franche, and other places for the Englifh. From hence he went to London by land, was gracioufly received, and plentifully rewarded for his good fervices by King Edward 3d." W. H. (MS.) vol. 1. p. 40.

‡ In thofe days of Chivalry, the national advantage or utility of a warlike expedition was too mean a confideration; an enterprize was undertaken, purely for applaufe; and to win the fmiles of the fair, a caftle or a kingdom was attacked with indifcriminate ardour. An exploit of the Duke of Lancafter, hitherto unnoticed, I believe, in our Englifh hiftories, may well illuftrate thefe pofitions: it was fimply a piece of knight-errantry. It is recorded in the Chronicle of Don Alonzo XI. and Mr. Carter was the firft to publifh it in this country. The battle of Tarifa, fought on the 30th of October, 1342, between the Moors, and Don Alonzo XI. King of Spain, where the latter proved victorious, had raifed the reputation of Alonzo to fuch a pitch, throughout Chriftendom, that Henry Plantagenet Duke of Lancafter, Earl of Derby, Lincoln, and Leicefter, great grandfon to Henry III. and grandfather of Henry IV. commanding at this time the Englifh forces in Guienne, obtained leave from *Edward* III. to ferve a campaign under Don Alonzo in the fiege of Algeziras: of his arts of chivalry the chronicle of Don Alonzo XI. makes particular mention; an anecdote, which reflects honour on the Englifh in general; a nation famed through all ages for honor, virtue, and noble deeds of arms, and on the auguft defcendants of this

have

The times of RICHARD II. are little noted in the Chronicles of the weft of England, except for the wars with France.‡ But (what I think worthy of obfervation) they produced an

brave prince, whofe valour and martial fpirit brought him fo many hundred leagues to ferve in the dangerous fiege of a town, defended by 30,000 men, and covered by the whole power of Granada, in a camp fickly and wanting neceffaries. On his arrival in Spain, being informed that a battle was daily expected to be fought between the Chriftians, and the united troops of the Benemarines and the King of Granada, he haftened his march, and made fuch diligence, that, when he arrived in Seville, only the Earl of Salifbury and four of his knights had been able to follow him; they were honourably received in that city by the Englifh factory, and lodged at their houfe. Henry brought with him feveral companies of horfe, and was received by Don Alonzo XI. with all the marks of efteem due to his high birth. He foon fignalized his valour in an action, wherein the impetuofity of his courage carried him beyond his followers, and into the midft of the Barbarians, but on being furrounded he drove them back to the town; two Englifh knights, out of an excefs of valour, followed them within the gates, fhewing the aftonifhed Barbarians that undaunted fpirit of our forefathers, which, tranfmitted without blot or blemifh to their fons, has raifed the Britifh empire to its prefent pitch of greatnefs: the Moors fought, as the chronicle tells us, to take them prifoners, and would not flay them: thereby evidencing a great fenfe of honour and courage in themfelves, who could thus refpect it in an enemy. The Duke of Lancafter, in one of thefe combats, had two of his Knights flain, and was wounded himfelf by an arrow in the face; which honourable fcar he carried with him to the grave. He was the champion of the Englifh caufe in France, and learned the art of war under the invincible banners of his coufin Edward the Black Prince; for his fuperior virtues he was ftiled the good Duke. His glorious career was fhortened by the plague in London, in 1361, five years before the birth of Henry the fourth, fon of his daughter Blanch and John of Gaunt." *Carter's* Journey from Gibraltar to Malaga, 2 vols. octavo, 1777, vol. 1, p. 168.

† *See Fuller*, p. 245. I muft not pafs this reign, without the obfervation, that Edward III. was a politic though an arbitrary Prince. Among other ftrong meafures, he feized the goods of the Ciftercians, and of fome other orders. He levied by his own authority an additional tax of 40s. on a fack of wool, which, for many years, amounted to 60,000l. per ann. And he became the fole merchant of all the *Tin in Cornwall* and *Devon.*

‡ When the French, in the year 1377, the firft of Richard II. attacked Carifbrook caftle without fuccefs, and threatened other parts of the Southern coaft with invafion, fome troops haftily drawn together by the prior of Lewes, to repel them from the coaft of Suffex, were defeated, while thofe under the abbot of Battle had better fuccefs at Winchelfea. After various orders addreffed to the Earl of Salifbury to take the neceffary meafures for the defence of the Ifle of Wight, [*Rymer*, VII. 139;] to the *Bifhop of Exeter*, for defence of *Dartmouth*; to the *Abbot of Bucfaft* and others who held lands adjoining; to the Abbots of *Taviftock* and *Buckland*, the prior of *Plymton* and *Modbury*, and to *John*, *Vicar of Plymton*, for that of *Plymouth* [ib. 145, 146,] all this not being deemed fufficient, an order was at length iffued to array the *Clergy*, which I fhall here give in the words of the original:

"De Clero arraiand.

"Rex ven. in Chrifto patri S. eadem gratia archiepifcopo Cantuarienfis, totius Angliæ primati, falutem.

"Satis informati eftis qualiter inimici noftri Franciæ, & alii fibi adherentes, facinora fua erga nos & ligeos noftros licet indirecte de die in diem circumquaque oftendentes cum magna claffe navium, cum maxima multitudine armatorum & bellatorum fupra mare congregati, diverfas villas fuper cofteris regni noftre Anglie invaferunt, & eas per arfuras & homicidia ligeorum noftrorum deftruxerunt, & ultra hoc nos & regnum noftrum prædictum ac populum noftrum per terram & per mare deftruere, et ecclefiam Anglicanam fubvertere cum omnibus viribus fe conantur. Per quod volentes falvatione dicti regni & populorum noftrorum, ac ecclefiæ fanctæ contra malitiam ipforum inimicorum, operante Altiffimo, providere per diverfas commiffiones affignavimus certos & fideles noftros in fingulis comitatibus regni noftri prædicti ad arratandum & arraiari faciendum omnes homines defenfabiles, inter ætates fexaginta & fexdecem annorum exiftentes, viz. quemlibet eorum juxta ftatum & facultates fuas: & eos arraiatos, armatos, & munitos, in arraiatione hujufmodi teneri faciendum, fic quod femper prompti fint & parati ad proficifcendum in defenfionem regni noftri prædicti ubi ac quotiens & quando ex hoftium incurfibus periculum immineat, aut neceffe fuerit aliquale. Advertentes vero quod vos, & cæteri prælati, ac totus clerus dicti regni, una cum aliis fidelibus noftris, ad refiftendam dictis inimicis pro falvatione fanctæ ecclefiæ & ejufmodi regni manus tenemini apponere adjutrices, vobis in fide & dilectione quibus nobis tenemini firmiter injungimus & mandamus quatenus, confideratis gravibus dampnis & periculis imminentibus per aggreffus inimicorum noftrorum prædictorum, omnes abbates, priores, religiofos, & alias perfonas quafcuqnue veftræ diocefis, quacunque dilatione poftpofita, armari & arraiari, & annis competentibus, viz. quemlibet inter ætates prædictas juxta ftatum, poffeffiones & facultates, fuas muniri & eos in millenis, centenis, & vintenis poni faciatis, ita quod prompti fint & parati ad proficifcendum ad mandatum veftrum una cum aliis fidelibus noftris contra dictos inimicos noftros infra dictum regnum noftrum ad ipfos cum Dei adjutorio debellandum, expugnandum, & deftruendum, & ad eorum malitiam & proterviam propulfandam & conterendam. Et hoc ficut nos & honorem noftrum ac veftrum, & falvationem fanctæ ecclefiæ, & regni noftri diligatis nullatenus omittatis.

"Tefte rege apud Weftmonafterium 25 die Julii, per ipfum regem & confilium.

"Confimilia brevia diriguntur Alexandro, archiepifcopo Eboaum, Angliæ primati, & fingulis epifcopis in Anglia & Wallia, fub eadem data." *Rymer*, ib. 162, 163.

In 1378, the Englifh fleet was attacked by a Spanifh fquadron. Part of the Englifh fleet feems not to have engaged: and Philip and Peter Courtenay who commanded the fhips that fought, were charged with temerity. Philip efcaped, tho' much wounded; and Peter was taken with a few of his men. In this fight, perifhed a great number of gentlemen of the weft.* In the mean time the French fleet defpoiled the coafts of Cornwall. They deftroyed Plymouth. See *Nic. Trivet et Adam Murimuth, Annal.* vol. II. p. 143, 144. *Holinfhed*, vol. II. p. 419. *T. Walfingham*, pp. 212, 213, *Vit. R. Ricardi*, II. pp. 6, 7. *Froiffart*, c. 327. *T. Otterbourne*, p. 148.

* Sir

* Sir *Peter*, Knight of the Garter, called by *Dugdal*, Sir *Piers de Courtenay*, was the fixth fon of *Hugh*, the fecond of that name, Earl of *Devon*. He was younger brother to to the Arch-bifhop *Courtenay*, by the fame parents.

This gentleman was a true fon of *Mars*, and actuated with fuch heroic fire, that he wholly addicted himfelf unto feats of arms. The firft proof he gave of his valor, was in a fea fight, againft the Spaniards, in the expedition of the great Duke of *Lancafter*, when he went to challenge the crown of that country, in right of *Conftance* his fecond wife, daughter and heir of *Don Peter the Cruel*, about the year of our Lord 1378. At what time he was affifted by Sir *Philip Courtenay*, Kt. his valorous brother, who was the firft founder of that truly honorable family of the name, which this day florifheth, (and God grant it always fo to do) at *Powderham* Caftle in this county. In which fight, Sir *Philip* was fore wounded, but efcaped the hands of his enemies. After which, in 7 K. R. 2. he was conftituted Lord Lieutenant of *Ireland*, for ten years.

Sir *Peter Courtenay* aforefaid, was alfo fore wounded in that fight, and taken prifoner: but for his enlargement, he had a grant from the king, of the benefit of the marriage of *Richard*, the brother and heir of *Thomas de Poinings*.

His next fcene of action, was the court of *France*; in which he followed that manly exercife of jufts and tournaments; now juftled out of fafhion by your carpet Knights, who regard no arms, but thofe which are for embraces; wherein he behaved himfelf fo bravely, that he was much honoured by the King of *France* himfelf. Hence, in the 7th of K. *Rich.* 2. he had licenfe to fend into *France*, by *Northampton Herald*, and by *Anlet Purfevant*, eight cloths of fcarlet, black, and ruffet, to give to certain noble men of that realm. As alfo, two horfes, fix faddles, fix little bows, one fheaf of large arrows, and another fheaf of crofs-bow arrows, for the King of *France's* keeper: likewife a grey-hound, and other dogs All which were for prefents to the French, in refpect to the great honor that king had done him, at fuch time as he combated there, with a Knight of that realm.

Here I fhall crave leave to fpeak fomething, as to the manner and magnificence wherewith thefe jufts and tournaments were wont to be folemnized.

And this, from that particular one held here in *England*, *A.* 1390, of which we have this account in Sir *Richard Baker's* Chronicle. ' in the 13th year of *K. Rich.* 2. a royal juft was proclaimed, to be holden within *Smithfield* in *London*, to begin ' on *Sunday* next after the feaft of S. *Michael*; which being publifhed, not only in *England*, but in *Scotland*, in *Almaigne*, ' in *Flanders*, in *Brabant*, and in *France*, many ftrangers came hither. Amongft others, *Valerian* Earl of St. *Paul*, that ' had married *K. Richard's* fifter; and *William*, the young Earl of *Oftervan*, fon to the Earl of *Holland* and *Heinault*. At the ' day appointed there iffued forth of the *Tower*, about three a clock in the afternoon, fixty courfers apparalled for the jufts; ' and upon every one an efquire of honor riding a foft pace. After them came forth four and thirty ladies of honor, *Froifard* ' faith, three fcore, mounted on palferies, and every lady led a knight with a chain of gold. Thefe Knights being on the ' King's part, had their armor and apparel garnifhed with white hearts and crowns of gold about their necks. Undoubtedly ' on the other part, whofoever undertook to perform it againft the King, they were but very little lefs glorious and magni- ' ficent.' They came riding through the ftreets of *London* and *Smithfield*, at what time we need not queftion, but this our valiant knight, Sir *Peter*, or Sir *Piers Courtenay* made one. The jufts lafted divers days, fome fay four and twenty; which were grac'd all the time with the king and queen's royal prefence; who lay at the bifhop's palace by St. *Paul's* church, and kept open houfe for all comers.

In the 11th of *K. Richard* 2. was Sir *Peter* made chief chamberlain to the King, a place of great honour and truft; whofe fee is an hundred pound yearly, and fixteen difhes each meal, with all the appurtenances. But his martial mind was more intent upon glory in the feat of arms, than upon the foft dalliances of a court life. He obtained therefore the fame year, licenfe to go again to *Calais*, with *John Holoildod*, Efquire, to challenge the French for the performance of a certain feats of arms and behaved himfelf bravely there. Whereof the enfuing hiftory, which I have met with in a certain manufcript, contains a full demonftration; which I fhall here relate, with very little variation, in the words of my author.

' In the reign of *Charles* the 6th, *King* of *France*, *A. D* 1390, were divers noble knights in this court, men at arms, and ' of great prowefs; three whereof were of great name, *Monfieur de Bauciquant*, *Monfieur Raynant de Roy*, and *Monfieur de* ' *St. Pie*, all gentlemen of the king's chamber; who had proclaimed a great tournament, to be held the 20th of *Novemb.* ' 1389, and valiantly performed it accordingly: at which were prefent an hundred gentlemen at arms of the Englifh nation: ' if our Sir *Peter* were not there at firft, he came foon after to *Paris*; and after he had refted a few days, he challenged ' *Monfieur Tremouly*, a noble gentleman, who having obtained leave of the *King*, accepted the fame, and appointed the day ' and place.

' The time being come, the *King*, affociated with the Duke of *Burgundy*, and other high eftates, were prefent to behold ' it; the firft courfe was exceedingly well performed by both parties, with high commendation; but the *King* inhibited any ' farther proceedings, feemingly offended with our knight, who had made fute to do his utmoft. Sir *Peter* herewith grieved ' thought good to leave the court and country; at which the *K.* was very well pleafed, and fent him an honourable gift at ' his departure (the Duke of *Burgundy* did the like) and commanded *Monfieur de Clary*, a great Lord of his train, to accom- ' pany him to *Calais* then in Englifh hands.

' By the way thither, they vifited *Valerian*, the third of that name, Earl of St. *Paul*, who had married *King Richard's* ' half-fifter *Maud*, daugher of Sir *Thomas Holland*, and widow to *Hugh Courtenay*, the younger fon of *Hugh* Earl of *Devon*, ' Sir *Peter's* eldeft brother, where they had fair reception; and fitting one night at fupper, communing of various arguments, ' among other things, the Earl afked Sir *Peter*, *how he liked the realm of* France, *and his opinion of the worth of the nobility* ' *thereof?* To whom Sir *Peter*, with a fomewhat fower countenance, replied;

That he found in *France* nothing to be compared to the magnificence there was in *England*; tho' for friendly entertainment, he had no caufe to complain; but for the caufe that moved him to come into *France*, he returned unfatisfied. For I proteft, *fays he* before this honourable company, that if *Monfieur de Clary* had come into *England*, and challenged any of our nation, he fhould have been fully anfwered. Whereas other meafure hath been tendered to me in *France*; for when *Monfieur Tremouly* and I engaged our honor, after one launce broken, the *King* commanded me to ftay. I have therefore faid it, and whe ever I come will fay, that in *France* I was denied reafon, and leave to do my utmoft.

' *Monfieur de Clary* efpecially, was much moved at thefe fpeeches; yet having it in charge from the *King*, to conduct Sir ' *Peter* fafe to *Calais*, for the prefent he forbore. But the Earl replied, *Let me tell you Sir* Peter, *it appears to me, that you*

depart

an armed aſſembly perhaps the only one in hiſtory that can find a full juſtification in imperious neceſſity. I refer to that memorable inſurrection of the confederate lords, in 1387. They were a formidable body. The king was apprized of their coming. And at Weſtminſter, on the

E throne,

'*depart from* France *with much honor, in regard, the King did vouchſafe to entreat you to ſtay the fight; whom to obey, is* '*both wiſe and commendable.*'

'Sir *Peter* having now taken his leave of the Earl, paſſeth on his journey with *Monſieur de Clary*; and as ſoon as they were 'entered the Engliſh territories, he heartily thanked him for his noble company: but *Monſieur de Clary*, having admitted a 'deep impreſſion to be made in his mind, by Sir *Peter*'s eager ſpeeches at the Earl of St. *Paul*'s began thus to accoſt him:

Now Sir, I have done my duty, in performing the king my maſter's commands, in conducting you to your friends. However, before we part, I muſt remember you of thoſe inconſiderate ſpeeches you lately uttered, in contempt of the nobility of *France*; and that you may have no cauſe to boaſt when you arrive in *England*, that you were not fully anſwered, Lo! here I am, this day, or to-morrow, (tho' inferior to many other of our country) to do you reaſon: not out of any malice to your perſon, or vaingloriouſly to boaſt of mine own valor, but to preſerve the fame and luſtre due to the French nation; which never wanted, ſure, gentlemen at arms, to anſwer any Engliſh challenge whatſoever.

You ſpeak well and nobly, *quoth our Knight*, and with very good will I accept your challenge: and to-morrow I will attend you, armed with three launces, according to the French cuſtom.

'Upon this agreement and reſolution, Sir *Peter Courtenay* went for *Calais*, there to furniſh himſelf with arms and ac-'coutrements proper for the combat. And the Lord *Warren* then governor there, was made privy to the buſineſs.

'The next day he returned according to his promiſe, to meet *Monſeur de Clary* between *Calais* and *Bulloigne*; with 'whom went the lord governor and other gentlemen, to behold the combat.

At the firſt courſe, either party broke well; but at the ſecond, by default of the Engliſh knight's armor, he was hurt in 'the ſhoulder; which moved the Lord *Warren* to tell *Monſieur de Clary*, *you have done diſcourteouſly to hurt* Courtenay, *his* '*armor being broken.* To which he anſwered, *I am ſorry*; *but to govern fortune is not in my power: it might have hapned* '*to me, what befel him*; and ſo they parted.

Of which action, perhaps Sir *William Dugdal* may be underſtood, when he ſaid, *that Sir* Piers de Courtenay *did not ably manifeſt his military ſkill and valor, at a tournament held in* France, *to his high renown.*

However *de Clary* came off with *Courtenay*, his welcome to his King, upon his return, was very ſharp and ſevere; an argument he had not acquitted himſelf to expectation. Nor did Sir *Peter*'s action better pleaſe the King of *England*; for there was a meſſage brought him from K. *Rich.* 2. *that he the ſaid Sir* Peter Courtenay *now at* Calais, *ſhould forbear to exerciſe any feats of arms with the French, without the ſpecial leave of* Henry de Percy, *Earl of* Northumberland.

Theſe things being well over, in the 14th of the ſame king, Sir *Peter* was made conſtable of *Windſor* Caſtle: and in his 16th year, when divers knights came out of *Scotland*, to challenge the Engliſh to certain feats of arms, one —— *Darrel* challenging Sir *Peter*, they ran at one another with ſharp ſpears. For all which his brave exploits, he was, by K. *Rich.* 2. made one of the knights of the moſt noble order of the garter.

It was not long after this, when this noble Chevalier had another combat with a far more mighty champion than any of thoſe afore-mentioned, by whom he was ſoon foil'd, and that was death; which took him off by an unhappy ſtroke in the flower of his age, in the 10th year of the reign of *K. Hen.* 4. *A. D.* 1409.

Where he died is not certain; but he lieth interr'd in the cathedral church of St. *Peter, Exon*, about the middle of the body of it, near his father the Earl of *Devonſhire*'s tomb, where a fair grave-ſtone, richly inlaid with gilded braſs, containing the portraicture of the ſaid Sir *Peter*, arm'd cap-a-pe, might heretofore be ſeen: whoſe Epitaph, ſo much of it as remaineth, here followeth.

Devoniæ *Natus Comitis, Petruſque vocatus*
Regis Cognatus, Camerarius intitulatus.
Caliſiæ Gratus, Capitaneus enſe probatus.
Vitæ privatus, fuit hinc ſuper Aſtra relatus.
Et quia ſublatus, de Mundo tranſit amatus.
Cœlo firmatus, maneat ſine fine Beatus.

Which verſes are thus tranſlated in *Izacke's* Exeter:

The Earl of *Devonſhire*'s ſon, *Peter* by name,
Kin to the *King*, Lord Chamberlain of fame.
Captain of *Calais*, for arms well approved;
Who dying, was above the ſtars removed.
And well beloved, went from the world away,
To lead a bleſſed life in heaven for aye."——*Prince*, pp. 159, 161.

"In 1379, *Sir John Arundel*, who had bravely repulſed the French, when they landed in Devonſhire, failed for Bretagne, with a conſiderable reinforcement; but being overtaken with a violent tempeſt, his ſquadron was diſperſed; and the greateſt part was ſhipwrecked on the coaſts of Ireland, Wales, and Cornwall. Himſelf, and a thouſand men at arms, periſhed. To note the ſumptuouſneſs of thoſe times, this Sir John Arundel was ſaid, in his furniture to have two and fifty new ſuits of apparel of cloths of gold and tiſſue, all loſt in the ſea." *Baker's* Chron. p. 137.

"It was uſual to raiſe money upon their eſtates for redeeming them from captivity, when gentlemen ſerved in the wars. Thus *John de Aclane*, anceſtor of the preſent Aclands of Devon, ſerving in their wars of France, 9 *Richard* II. 1385, conveyed his

throne, he awaited their approach. There they appeared in arms before their ſovereign; and throwing themſelves on their knees, profeſſed their determination to root out the traitors of their country. And in this reſolution they perſevered; not deſiſting from their purpoſe till they had cleared the throne and its avenues from favourites that too juſtly incurred their indignation. Such was the LADY MOHUN, Sir THOMAS †TRIVET, and Sir ROBERT TRESILIAN. The Lady whoſe manners were uncommonly licentious, was immediately baniſhed; and Sir Thomas taken into cuſtody. Treſilian had made his eſcape. But, lying in diſguiſe in an apothecary's ſhop at Weſtminſter, where he obſerved the tranſactions of Parliament, he was betrayed by one of his own ſervants; and after much ignominious uſage, was drawn through the city, and (according to *Walſingham*) *hanged* at Tyburn.* To the death of King Richard, I ſhould not as a provincial

his eſtates in Aclane, Gratton, Barnſtaple, Little-Bray, and Southmolton, to Thomas Affeton, John Stafford, and John Colyn, to raiſe money for his redemption, in caſe he ſhould be taken priſoner, without ſale of his lands." (The *Acland family* papers.)

" *Hawley* of Dartmouth, was at the head of an expedition againſt France. In his time it was, *Rich.* 2. being then *King* of *England*, that the French raiſed a powerful army, and equipped a formidable navy of twelve hundred ſail of ſhips, with deſign to tranſport them hither, to the entire conqueſt of this kingdom; though by God's providence, and much by this gentleman's endeavours in particular, they were wholly diſappointed herein. To repel this threatening danger, the Engliſh fitted out what ſhips they had, under two Admirals, who yet did nothing worthy of their fame or place.

At this time, the hiſtorian tells us, *the townſmen of* Portſmouth *and* Dart, *i. e.* Dartmouth, *manned forth a few ſhips at their own peril and charge; wherewith entering of the river* Sein, *upon which the renowned cities of* Roan *and* Paris *are ſituate, they ſunk ſome of their enemies ſhips, and took others: among theſe, one of the goodlieſt that* France *had. The ſucceſs* (ſays Speed) *anſwered their hopes; and they were enriched with the ſpoils of their adverſaries; whom thus they compelled to bear the charge of their proper miſchief.* This happen'd in the 11th of *K. Rich.* 2. reign, *A. D.* 1387, at what time Mr. *Hawley* might be near fifty years of age. So that in theſe brave exploits, we need not queſtion but he was a chief and principal actor, not only in the ſetting forth of thoſe ſhips and forces, or a good part. of them, at his own proper charges, but alſo in his perſonal command and conduct of them. Which action, at that time, might be ſo pleaſing to the *King*, and of that conſequence to the nation, that it is likely enough his Majeſty might ſend for him to confer ſome honour or royal reward upon him. And becauſe we find no particular title he was diſtinguiſhed withal, 'tis not improbable but he might decline all perſonal favours, with the humble deſire only, *that his town might wear the badge of the royal bounty.*" *Prince*, p. 360.

One of John Hawley's wives, was the daughter and heireſs of Sir *Robert Treſilian*, Lord Chief Juſtice of England. *Weſtcote's* MSS. in Chagford.

† Thomas Trivet is not (ſays *Carew*) to be forgotten as a writer; though he have graven his memory in a fairer letter, by building the coſtly bridge at Bridgewater, of which ſometimes he was Lord. *Carew*, f. 59, 59 b.

Camden calls *Trivet* a nobleman of Cornwall: (ſee *Britan.* in Somerſet) and *Philemon Holland* adds, that he founded the hoſpital of St. John and Dunkeſwell-Abbey. But *Tanner* in his Not. Mon. ſays, that this abbey (which is in Devon) was founded A. D. 1201, by William Briwere, and therefore Trivet was only a benefactor to it. He was probably the father of *Nicholas* Trivet, of whoſe annals an excellent edition was publiſhed at Oxford in 1719. Ann. 1388, " Sir Thomas Trivet died with a fall from his horſe." *Baker*, p. 146.

* Sir Robert Treſilian, was probably born at Treſilian, in the pariſh of Newlyn. *Fuller*, indeed (ſee Worth. in Cornwall, p. 200) ſuſpects to the contrary. " Some conceive, Sir Robert Treſilian, chief juſtice of the king's bench, 5 R. 2. to be a Corniſhman; tho' producing no other evidence ſave *Tre*, the initial ſyllable of his ſurname, as a badge of Corniſh extraction." But *Fuller* did not know, that we had ſeveral places of the name in this county, and a family of Treſilian. Some ſay, that Treſilian was born in the pariſh of Berian.§ According to *Speed*, the manner of his death was extraordinary " Being apprehended (A. D. 1388) and brought to the Parliament, which began at Candlemas in the forenoon, he had ſentence (ſays *Speed*) to be drawn to Tybourne in the afternoon, and there to have his throat cut; which was done accordingly." Robert Treſilian was knight of the ſhire for Cornwall, 42 Edw. 3. See *Speed's* Chron. pp. 616, 724, 733. *Hearne*, vol. 2, p. 443. With reſpect to the character of *Treſilian*, he was juſtly executed (ſays *Wood*) by act of parliament, for pronouncing their acts revocable at the king's pleaſure. Yet ſays *Speed* (Chron. p. 624) the articles in thoſe times ſentenced for treaſonable by the moſt eminent lawyers, did extend themſelves ſo farre, that the prince ſeemed to have too greate meanes left to worke miſchiefe to the peeres and people: and that we may ſee the conſtant humour in lawyers, to judge with the will of the greateſt, the Lord William Thyrning, chiefe juſtice of the common bench, the Lord Walter Clopton chiefe juſtice, and others, being demanded their opinions upon the ſame articles for which Sir Robert Treſilian had loſt his life, and for which others had been ſo

§ Feb. 10, 1793, died at a very advanced age, at the ancient family reſidence at Trevidar, in the deanry of St. Berian, Mrs. Mary Pendar, relict of the late Mr. P. of that place, and eldeſt ſurviving daughter of the late Mr. Treſilian, of Treſider, in the ſame deanry, who was the laſt heir-male of the ancient family of that name. This family, in the reign of Charles I. poſſeſſed conſiderable property in many parts of the county of Cornwall, the reſidue of which is now confined to the precincts of that deanry. The late aged lady left only two daughters, though many grand-children, and is ſuppoſed to be deſcended from the ſame family as the chief juſtice of England.

vincial writer even allude; if a curious memoir of Sir John Fortefcue (who may be ftiled by way of diftinction *the lawyer of the weft*) did not tend to illuftrate the obfcure fubject. There are fome indeed who have reconciled, as they conceive, the ftarving of the King with his fall by the weapons of the murderer: almoft ftarved to death, he was then, it feems, affaffinated. But his affaffination was, I think, a fiction.‡

In the time of Henry IV.† *Sir John Cheyney* of Bodanan, in this county, was fpeaker of the Houfe of Commons;¶ and *Sir Robert Hill* was one of the juftices of the court of Common Pleas. He was probably of the family of Hill once feated at Truro; if we may judge from his coat-armour.‖ It was in this reign, that *Sir William Hankford*, of Annery, the lord chief

juftice,

fo terriblie cenfured by the Glocestrian faction, affirmed (as Trefilian and others did) that the faid commiffion was againft the royal prerogative, and the procurers thereof were all traitors.". *Hume* is one of thofe, who pretend to juftify the conduct of Trefilian. There can be little doubt that ftrong temptation was thrown in his way; and that Richard defcended to the meaneft acts, not only in the election of his §parliament, but in influencing the opinions of his judges. Trefilian, however, betrayed pufillanimity as well as depravity in his opinions and practices. And whatever Hume may offer in his vindication (See *Hift.* vol. III. pp. 19, 43. edit. 1773.) the parliament of that age faw him in his true colours, a proftituted judge, a venal hireling. (See *Parliament. Hift.* vol. I. pp. 433, 434.) He fcrupled not, in fhort, to commit any crime, to purchafe the fmiles of royalty. Againft the Duke of Lancafter, for inftance, who had been accufed of treafon, Trefilian undertook to *give fentence* before the Duke could be brought to trial; before he could be even arrefted. And tho' he might have legally claimed the privilege of his Peers. See *Walfingham*.

‡ The dubioufnefs of hiftory too fully appears in the difcordance of our old writers in relating the circumftances of Richard's death. The report of our countryman Sir John Fortescue fhall clofe the evidence. That Richard was affaulted and murdered by armed men, is exprefsly told by *Fabian*, *Hall*, *Holinfhed:* and in "the firft part of the life and reign of King Henry IV." 4to. 1599, Sir *John Hayward* ftates, that "after being fallen to the ground, the king groaned forth" a dying fpeech. The account of Richard's affaffination is, alfo, adopted by Shakfpeare. On the other hand, *Harding* who is fuppofed to have been at the battle of Shrewfbury, in 1403, intimates that Richard was *ftarved to death*. "Men fay'd *for-hungred* he was." Chron. 1543, fol. 199. So alfo *Walfingham*, who wrote in the time of Henry V. and *Polydore Vergil*.* The *Percies* in the manifefto which they publifhed againft Henry IV. in the 3d year of his reign the day before the battle of Shrewfbury, exprefsly charge him with having "carried his fovereign lord traiteroufly within the caftell of Pomfret, without the confent or the judgement of the Lordes of the realm, by the fpace of *fiftene daies* and fo *many nightes*, with *hunger*, *therft*, and *cold*, to *perifhe*." But nothing can be more decifive than *Stowe's* account, from a MS. of Sir John Fortefcue. Richard (fays *Stowe*) "was imprifoned in Pomfrait caftle, where xv dayes and nightes they vexed him with *continuall hunger*, *thirft and cold*, and finally bereft *him of his life*, with fuch a kind *of death* as never *before that time* was known in England, faith Sir John Fortiscute." This information of Sir John Fortefcue is probably contained in his "*declaration touching the title of the houfe of Yorke*." A work which was never publifhed, and which is yet fomewhere I believe exifting in MS. Sir John Fortefcue was called to the bar a few years after the death of Richard. As he lived, therefore, fo near the time, his teftimony is of great weight. With refpect to Richard's death, however, I cannot but remark, that Sir John Fortefcue's mode of expreffion feems to imply more than fimple ftarving; confirming almoft the popular idea, as reported by *Polydore Vergil* and *Baker*, p. 155, that "Richard was ferved with coftly meat like a king, but not fuffered once to touch it."

† *King Harry* paffage, which goes directly acrofs the *Fal*, as that of Tolverne goes obliquely, and is therefore (we may be fure) prior in time to Tolverne paffage, is faid by tradition to be denominated from one of our royal Harries, who in fome troubles of his reign retired into Cornwall, and *fwam the river on horfeback*, though about 400 or 500 yards broad: and fome fay he was Harry the 4th.

¶ *Sir John Cheyney* of Bodanan, in St. Teath, was chofen fpeaker of the Houfe of Commons, 1ft and 6th of Henry IV. "The Parliament 6th Henry IV. was called *indoctum parliamentum*; for that, in the writ of fummons, there was a claufe, no lawyer fhould be chofen therein." *Hakewell's* Cat. of the fpeakers, p. 202. *Hals's* MS. in St. Teath.

‖ *Arg. a Chev. betw. 3 water bougets Sab. a mullet, or.* See *Prince's* Worthies, p. 366.

§ Tyrrell fays, "The king, by certain indirect practices, and tampering with the fheriffs of feveral counties, whom he had now made for this purpofe, caufed them to return fuch knights of fhires, without any due elections, as he had before named, and fent down to them; and this is worth our obfervation, becaufe it is the firft example of any king's making ufe of an arbitrary and illegal power in this kind." p. 964. And we are informed, in the Parliamentary Hiftory, that Richard's council of ftate commanded the fheriffs "to fuffer none to be returned as knights or burgeffes in parliament, but fuch as the king and his council fhould nominate." Vol. I. p. 432.

* Fame necatus fuiffe dicitur, uti etiam nunc conftans fama eft, quæ teftatur cibaria in fingulos dies more regio adpofita fuiffe, quo fic facinus occultaretur, fed efurienti non licuiffe, non modo deguftare verum etiam ne attingere quidem. Quod certe crudelitatis genus dixerim haudquaquam in Henricum hominem temperatum cecidiffe, cum morte ipfa pejus fit, in aqua perire fiti. Hæc oportuit non omittere, ut vulgo etiam fatisfieret, qui facile aniles fabellas ad pofteros fermone propagat." *Polyd. Vergil* pp. 1087, 1088.

juftice, awakened his countrymen, on a memorable occafion, to a juft fenfe of the laws as paramount to the will of princes.† With refpect to war, I have only to ftate, that Plymouth was now burnt by the Bretons.*

Whether

† "*Sir William Hankford*, Knight of the Bath, and Lord Chief Juftice of England, was born, moft probably, at the antient feat of the family, whence the name is derived, called *Hankford*, in the hamlet of *Bulkworthy*, a chappel of eafe to *Buckland Brewer*, in the north-weft parts of Devon. The firft I have met with of this name, is *William* of *Eaft-Hankford*, in Bulkworthy aforefaid, mentioned in a deed fo antient that 'tis *fans-date*; the next is *Warinus de Hankford*, who was witnefs to a deed of *Roger de Putford*, and *Robert* his brother, of land in *Little Bovey*, in the days of *K. Hen.* 3. An argument he was a perfon of fome note at that time. In which tything of Bulkworthy, Mr. *Rifdon* tells us, Sir *William Hankford* had a dwelling-houfe bearing his name, which, together with his building a chappel in that place, may induce us to conclude he was born there.

However, from hence he afterward removed, and (whether upon the account of match or purchafe, I know not, tho' *Rifdon* fuggefts the former) find his habitation at *Annery*, in the parifh of *Monklegh*, near Great Torrington. A pleafant and noble feat it is, on the weft fide of the *Turridge*, over which it ftands, and takes a delightfome profpect of that river. The houfe, now gone to decay, was heretofore ftately and magnificent, and famous for a large upper gallery, wherein might be placed thirty ftanding-beds, fifteen of a fide, and yet not one to be feen there; nor could you from one bed fee another: for the gallery being very long, and wainfcotted on each hand, there were feveral doors in it, which led into little alcoves or appartments, well plaiftered and whited, large and convenient enough for private lodgings.

This place had fometime lords of its own name, and was antiently held by *Ofbert*, firnamed *de Annery*. After that, it was the *Stapledons*, where they had their dwelling. Since, it yielded habitation, for feveral generations following, to the honourable family of *Hankford*; here lived the famous judge of that name, of whom now I fhall proceed to fpeak.

Sir *William Hankford* was in his time a very eminent lawyer; for which reafon, *A.* 14 *K. Rich.* 2. 1391, he was made one of the King's ferjeants at law; and on the 6th of *May*, in the 12th of that reign, one of the Lords Juftices of the court of *Common Pleas*, in which honourable ftation he continued the fhort remainder of that unfortunate Prince's reign. When *Henry* of *Bullingbrook* afcended the Englifh throne, by the title of *K. Henry* the 4th, this gentleman was made Knight of the *Bath* at his coronation, and confirmed by him in the fame feat of judicature, during all his rule, which was fourteen years. When *K. Henry* the 5th fucceeded to the crown of *England*, Judge *Hankford* was called higher up, and *A.* 1 *Regnifui*, made Lord Chief-Juftice of the *King's Bench*, and fo remained all that fhort but glorious reign of about ten years. When this heroick prince yielded to fate alfo, *Dugd.* tells us, Sir *William Hankford* was conftituted in the fame high office by *K. Hen.* 6. in the beginning of his reign: near about which time, death gave him his *Quietus eft*, as we may hereafter obferve: of whom this is farther remarkable (and whether it may be parallel'd by any other example, I cannot tell), *That he was a judge in the reigns of no lefs than four Princes that fucceffively fway'd the Englifh Scepter.*

This is that noble and famous jufticiary (tho' fome would afcribe the honour hereof to another of our countrymen, Sir *John Hody*, which cannot be, for that he was not a judge until thirty years after) that dared to do juftice upon the King's fon, who afterwards was the glory of the Englifh nation, by the name of *Hen.* 5th. The ftory is thus: he, when he was yet Prince, commanded Judge *Hankford*, upon the bench, to free a fervant of his, arraigned for felony, at the bar; which when he would not do, he offered to take the prifoner away by force: being withftood alfo herein by the judge, the Prince ftep'd to him and ftruck him a blow on the face. Whereat, nothing abafhed, Judge *Hankford* told him boldly, *that he had not done this affront to him, but to the King his father, in whofe place he fate; and if he would not obey his fovereign's laws now, he afked him, who fhould obey his when he was king? wherefore*, fays he, *in the King your father's name, I commit you prifoner to the King's ward, the Fleet.* Whereat the Prince abafhed, quietly obey'd the judge's fentence, and fuffered himfelf to be led to prifon. *You would have wondered*, fays the hiftorian, *to have feen how calm the Prince was in his own caufe, who in the caufe of his companion had been fo violent.* When the King his father was advertifed thereof, after he had duly examined the circumftances of the matter, he rejoyced, that he had a fon fo obedient to his laws, and a judge of fuch integrity, as to adminifter juftice without fear or favour.

The praifes of this reverend jufticiary have been highly celebrated, and very defervedly, for his gravity, fobriety, wifdom, and juftice. Fair ornaments for men in authority, but moft efpecially neceffary in thofe who fit in the feat of judgment; yea! they are required by Almighty God, and expected among all nations, Pagan as well as others. So a poet directs them:

A manibus refeces Munus, ab aure Preces.

Thus tranflated to my hands:

To finger bribes in any cafe deteft;
And let thine ears be fhut againft requeft.

The

* In 1403, the king married Joan, lately widow to Montford Duke of Britany. The Bretons, conceiving an ill opinion of this marriage, fent a fleet to fea, landed in the weft and burnt Plymouth. To revenge this affront, the Plymouthians, thro' William de Wilford, Admiral of the Narrow Seas, feized forty fhips laden with iron, oil, foap, and wine, and then burnt the like number in the harbours of Britany, reducing the towns of Penmarch and St. Matthew, and wafting with fire and fword a great part of the coaft. In the mean time Admiral de Caftel, who commanded the enemy's fleet, fteered for Devonfhire, where landing, he attacked Dartmouth, but was defeated by the county militia, with the lofs of 400 men, and 200 taken, among whom were himfelf and two other perfons of diftinction. *T. Walfingham*, p. 561. *Stowe*, p. 329. *Holinfhed*, vol. II. p. 524.

The prefent judge, doubtlefs, was eminent for all thofe laudable qualities which are mentioned of him; yet furely fomewhat was defective in him (as who among the fons of men is perfect on this fide heaven?) if that be true which fome authors have related of him: then in him we may plainly fee, as in a mirror, how frail a thing a man is, and that his life is often either the prologue or cataftrophe to a woful tragedy; for in the laft act of his laft fcene, wherein it might be expected he fhould have fhewn his greateft wifdom and fortitude, he fell, not only fhort of himfelf, but of a much weaker and meaner perfon. Being weary of his life, 'tis faid, upon direful apprehenfions of dangerous approaching evils, he fell into a defperate refolution; as if,

Triftior eft Letho, Lethi mora.

He that muft die, hates lingering ftay,
And death were doubled by delay.

He became witty in finding out a fafe way for the prefervation of his goods and chattels, and getting rid of that; for thus is it ftoried of him.

On a fit time for the purpofe, he called to him the keeper of his park, which adjoyn'd his houfe at Annery, and charged him with negligence in his office, fuffering his deer to be killed and ftolen; whereupon he left it in a ftrict charge with him, that he fhould be more careful in his rounds by night; and that if he met any one in his walk that would not ftand and fpeak, he fhould fhoot him, whoever he was, and that he would difcharge him. This the keeper directly promifed, and too faithfully performed. The judge having thus laid the defign, meaning to end his doleful days, in a dark tempeftuous night, fit for fo black an action, fecretly convey'd himfelf out of the houfe, and walked alone in his park, juft in the keeper's way; who being then in his round, hearing fomebody coming towards him, demanded, *Who was there?* No anfwer being made, he required him to ftand; the which when he refufed to do, the keeper fhot and killed him upon the place; and coming to fee who he was, found him to be his mafter.

This is the ftory, which is authenticated by feveral writers, and the conftant tradition of the voifenage in thofe parts: and I myfelf have been fhewn the rotten ftump of an old oak, under which he is faid to have fallen, called by the name of *Hankford's* oak unto thefe days.

The occafion of which fad tragedy, is varioufly reported; fome afcribe it to thofe tumultuous and dangerous times in which he lived, when *Henry* the 4th contended with, and at length difmounted, *K. Richard* the 2d; at what time the fword was unfheath'd, and the voice of the law could not be heard for the hideous noife of warlike inftruments: and tho' he knew, perchance, to whom he ought juftly to adhere, yet he did not know to whom he might fafely. And, moreover, terrify'd he was with the fight of infinite executions and bloody affaffinations, which caufed in him continual agonies; and upon apprehenfion what his own fate might be, he fell into that melancholy, which haftened his end.

Others reprefent the matter otherwife, that this judge having, as was faid before, committed the Prince to prifon in his younger years, was afraid he would take a too fevere revenge thereof when he came to the crown: the thought and confideration whereof, filled him with fuch infuperable melancholy, that it provoked him to take this courfe, for the putting a period to his own days. And this we know, that dreadful have been the effects of this black aduft humour, when predominant, as might be confirmed from divers fad examples out of authentick hiftory.

Now fome, it may be, (as one defcants hereupon) may chance to term this a refolution equal to that of the antient Romans, *Cato*, *Pomponius Atticus*, and many others; and fay alfo with them, *that 'tis extream folly to live long in pain, want, or difhonour, and only to wifh death when nature affordeth a man remedies to eafe himfelf at his pleafure*; according to that of *Epicurus*, approved herein by that great moralift *Seneca*, *Malum eft in neceffitate vivere*; *Neceffitas nulla eft*; *quippe pateant undiq*; *ad Libertatem viæ multæ, breves, faciles: agamus Deo gratias, quod Nemo invite teneri poffit*, I grant, *faith he*, 'tis a mifery to live in neceffity, but there is no neceffity to live fo; there are many quick and eafy means to free ourfelves: let us therefore, *faith the Heathen*, thank God, that no man can be conftrained to live againft his will, or longer than it fhall pleafe himfelf. To which, agrees that of *Quintilian*, *Nemo nifi fua Culpa diu dolet*, no man endures pain and forrow long, but thro' his own default. Thefe fentences, indeed, may be alledged rightly, and accord fitly, with meer human reafon and philofophick arguments; which may undertake to juftify the practife, not only as lawful and convenient, but as laudable and noble. This, as it muft be acknowledged, hath been fo held, not only among Indians, Medes, Perfians, Greeks and Romans, but the Jews alfo; witnefs the old man *Rhafis*, termed the father of the Jews. Nay! among Chriftians, fome have been canoniz'd faints, as *Pelagia*, *Appolonia*, and others, tho' they have contributed to their departure out of this vale of mifery before their time.

Thus have I reprefented the opinion herein of fome others; but far be it from my thought to juftify or excufe fo black a crime: the facred rites of our religion allow of no fuch leud practife; chriftianity yields not its votaries, upon any occafion, any difpenfation in this matter, but utterly abhors and condemns the practife with fuch indignation, that fo far as punifhment can be inflicted on the dead, he that is *Felo de fe*, fhall be treated in an ignominious manner, be buried in a ditch bottom or a highway, *with the burial of an afs*, and all his goods and chattles confifcated to the king. Nor is felf-murder, whatever may be thought, an act of that true courage and bravery fome may fuppofe; rather is it an inftance of pufillanimity and cowardife: fo true is that of *Jofephus*, *he that would live longer, or die fooner, than he ought, is equally a coward.* Even the poet could fay;

Fortius ille facit, Qui mifer effe poteft.

Far more ftout and brave is he,
That dares miferable be.

To conclude this matter; however wife, learned, or judicious, this reverend judge was reputed, fhould this be true, it muft be granted, terror brought him to that pafs, that he could not determine rightly how to bear or get out of the danger he was in; for, trufting to his own wifdom, he found that of the poet true;

Sick, to myfelf I ran for my relief;
But ficker of my phyfick than my grief.

Thus

Whether the *peaceful virtues or the military, be the fubject of obfervation, the *Courtenays* and *Arundels* make the firft figure in almoft every reign.† But in that of HENRY V. *Sir John Colfhul*, of Tremedart, Knight, tho' hitherto fcarcely recognized in the background of hiftory, fhould be brought into full light, the foremoft of all. Valiantly fighting, he fell on the plains of Agincourt. This is certainly a fact. Yet our hiftorians have paffed it in filence. His body was brought over from France, and buried in the church of Duloe.‡ The name of *Trelawny* fhould

Thus have fome authors made their comments upon this reverend judge's fuppofed violent end. But what if, after all, this finely contrived ftory fhould be found a romance, aud without any bottom of truth? Upon a due confideration of circumftances, I fuppofe, it will fo appear; which I fhall be glad to illuftrate, for the clearing of the memory of the dead from fo foul an afperfion, and the honour of thofe royal and noble perfonages which defcended from him, however long fince laid in their graves.

That he was not induced hereunto upon the account of the former furmife, to wit, *the bloody and cruel executions which happened in the latter end of K.* Rich. *2d's reign*, is clear, in that he lived in great honour, and ferved no lefs than three Princes, in one of the higheft feats of judicature, for many years after, even more than two reigns.

As to the fuggeftion, that this fhould be occafioned by his fears of what might befall him, upon *K. Hen.* 5th's coming to the crown, for imprifoning of him when Prince: we find that heroick King was fo far from refenting of it to his prejudice, that he feem'd to honour and applaud him for it the more, for he advanced him to a higher ftation than he was in before, making him chief juftice of his own bench, and continued him in that honourable office all his reign. Nor was he in the leaft difgrace with *K. Hen.* 6. but conftituted by him in the fame place, in the beginning of his reign; foon after which he died.

To all which, there is yet a farther circumftance to add, which will not a little expofe the improbability of the ftory, and that is the piety and devotion, according to the temper of that age, this reverend perfon was addicted to: a material teftimony whereof remains vifible to this day, and that is his building at his own charges, the chappel of *Bulkworthy* (now their parifh church) for the glory of God, and the eafe of the inhabitants of that place: as did appear from his arms in one of the windows, there lately, if not ftill, to be feen, with this *Motto* under-written.

Orate pro bono Statu Willielmi Hankford, qui iftam Capellam fieri fecit.

i. e. Pray for the good eftate of *William Hankford*, who caufed this chappel to be erected.

To conclude. This learned and reverend judge, which way foever it happened (though moft likely in a good courfe of nature, in a good old age) yielded to fate at his houfe at *Annery*, on the 20th of December, in the year of our Lord 1422, being the laft of *K. Hen.* 5th, and the firft of *K. Hen.* 6th. After which, his remains were honourably interred in the parifh church of *Monklegh* aforefaid; where, in an Ifle belonging to the family, is a noble monument erected to his memory, having this Epitaph engraven thereon, in a plate of brafs;

Hic jacet Willielmus Hankford Miles, quondam Capitalis Jufticiarius Domini Regis de Banco. qui obiit xx. *die Menfis Decembris, Anno Domini* M.C.C.C.C.X.X.II. *Cujus Animæ propitietur Deus,* Amen.

He is portraicted kneeling in his robes, together with his match: and the matches of fome of his anceftors are infculpt on brafs; out of his mouth proceeds this prayer,

Miferere mei Deus, fecundum magnam Mifericordiam tuam.

Over his head is this infcription,

Beati qui cuftodiunt judicium & faciunt jufticiam omni tempore.

A book in his hand hath this,

Miferere mei Deus fecundum magnam jufticiam Divinam.

Near hereunto is the ftatue of Sir *Richard Hankford*'s fon, wrought in armour, kneeling on his knees; on whofe furcoat are his arms. Then the portraicture of his lady, on whofe upper veftments *Hankford*'s and *Stapleton*'s armories are curioufly cut in brafs." *Prince*, pp. 361, 362, 363, 364.

* *John Hals* of Trembethow in Lelant, was ferjeant at law; and one of the twelve judges, 9 Henry V. *Tonkin's* MSS.

† "7. Henry 5. there was an indenture made, between Hugh Courtney, Earle of Deuon, Lieutenant to the King, for a fea voyage, in defence of the realme: and Sir John Arundel of Trerice, for accompanying him therein. He was fheriffe of Cornwall, 8 Henry 5." *Carew*, f. 145. b. 146.

‡ In the King's atchievements in France, the Earl of Cornwall ftood foremoft in conduct and valour. *Walfingham.* Thomas Beaufort, third fon of John of Gaunt by his third Duchefs Lady Catherine Swineford, uncle to Henry V. commanded the rear guard of the army at the battle of Agincourt; and afterwards defended Harfleur, and in a pitched battle, defeated the Earl of Armignac. Ann. 1416, he was creared *Duke of Exeter.* Was it in confequence of his atchievements in conjunction with military men from *Exeter* or its neighbourhood, that this title, in particular, was conferred on him? See King's remarks on the abbey church of Bury St. Edmunds, in the Archæol. vol. III. p. 314. "Thomas Weftcote, of Weftcote, in Marwood, addicted himfelf to feats of arms, which endeared him to thofe puiffant Princes, Henry IV. and Henry V. He married Elizabeth the daughter and heir of Sir Thomas Littleton, of Frankley, in Worcefterfhire. Their fon who changed his name from Weftcote to Littleton, was afterwards the famous Sir Thomas Littleton, one of the judges of the Common Pleas." *Prince*, pp. 584, 585.

ſhould here, alſo, be mentioned with honour. So eminent was Sir John Trelawny in the wars of France, that Henry V. 27 September, in his 7th year at Giſors, in Normandy, granted him 20l. yearly for life, as a juſt recompence for his ſignal ſervices. And Henry VI. was pleaſed to confirm it to him again in the firſt year of that King's reign, and granted him, as 'tis ſaid, in augmentation to his arms, three oaken or laurel leaves, the ſymbols of conqueſt. He was certainly the firſt of the family, who bore that addition. Under the picture of Henry V. which ſtood formerly over the great gate, at Launceſton, was this obſolete rhyme:

"He that will doe ought for mee,
"Let him love well *Sir John Tirlawnee*."*

The conflict between Henry VI. and the fourth Edward, produced repeated ſhocks through the iſland, which were felt at its extremeſt ſhores: Cornwall was but too ſenſible of the commotion. And that the French, with their accuſtomed promptitude and treachery, took an early advantage of the inteſtine troubles of England, our county can fully atteſt.‡ "In 1457, the Lord of Pomier, a Norman, encouraged by the civill warres, wherewith our realme was diſtreſſed, furniſhed a navy within the river Sayne, and with the ſame in the night, burned a part of Foy,§ and other houſes confyning. But, upon approach of the countrys forces, raiſed the next day by the ſherife, he made ſpeed away to his ſhips, and with his ſhips to his home."† For

* The Trelawny family papers.

‡ John Nanſon, of Nanſon, ſheriff of Cornwall, 7 Henry VI. at firſt, as tradition faith, was a ſervant to one of the Eriſeys, temp. Henry, and in that Prince's wars with the French, was by him promoted to a Captain's poſt in that expedition; wherein he behaved himſelf with ſuch valour and conduct, always attended with ſucceſs, that he was highly rewarded by that Prince, with much lands in England and France. Upon which foundation and by his thrift and good conduct, he laid up a very great eſtate in land; and particularly was the purchaſer of the manor and barton of Trethuell and Tregerryn, in Padſtow, where he ſeated himſelf. He was again, becauſe of his great advancement by his Prince's bounty made ſheriff of Cornwall, 18. Henry VI. *Hals*, p. 107. The *Arundels* recur to notice in this reign. 8 Henry VI, John Earl of Huntingdon ſtiling himſelf Lieutenant-General to John Duke of Bedford, Conſtable and Admiral of England, wrote to *Sir John Arundel*, then Vice-Admiral of Cornwall, for the releaſe of a ſhip which he had arreſted by virtue of his office. *Carew*, f. 146. Sir John Arundel, of Trerice, (as *Holinſhed* tells) having with the Lord Camois and Sir George Seimor, the government of Gaſcoigny, 29 Henry VI. they manned towns, gathered people, and comforted the fainting hearts of the Gaſcoigners."

§ *Carew*, f. 136. "1458, The French under Lord Fulnoy burnt many villages and ſmall towns, on the weſtern coaſts." *MS Not.* of Plymouth. Ann. 1459. "The Earls of March, Saliſbury, and Warwick, got into Devonſhire, where, by means of John Dynham, Eſq. (who was afterwards Lord Treaſurer of England, to Henry VII.) they were ſhipped from Exmouth to Guernſey, and ſo to Callice." *Baker*, p. 195.

† From their various ſucceſſes at ſea, "the people of *Fawey* grew unſpeakably rich, proud, and miſchievous. Which occaſioned the Lord Pomier and other Normans to petition John King of France to grant them a private commiſſion of mart and arms, to be revenged on the Pyrates of Foye town: which accordingly they obtained, and carry'd the deſign ſo ſecret, that a ſmall ſquadron of ſhips, and many bands of marine ſoldiers were prepared and ſhipped without the Foye men's knowledge. They accordingly put to ſea out of the river Seyne, in the month of *July*, 1457, in 35. Henry VI. and with a fair wind failed thence croſs the Britiſh Channel, and got ſight of Foye harbour; where they lay off at ſea 'till night; when they drew towards the ſhore and dropt anchor, and landed their marine ſoldiers, and ſeamen, who at midnight approach'd the ſouth weſt end of Foye town, where they kill'd all perſons they met with, ſet fire to the houſes, and burnt one half thereof to the ground, to the conſumption of a great part of the inhabitants riches, and treaſures, a vaſt deal of which were gotten by their pyratical practices. In which maſſacre and conflagration the women, children, and weakeſt ſort of people, forſook the place and fled for ſafety into the hill country. But the ſtouteſt men, under conduct of *John Treffrye*, Eſq. fortified themſelves as well as they could in his then new-built houſe of Place, yet extant, where they ſtoutly oppoſed the aſſaults of their enemies, whilſt the French ſoldiers plundered that part of the town which was unburnt, without oppoſition, in the dark. The news of this French invaſion in the morning flew far into the country; and the people of the contiguous parts as quickly put themſelves in arms; and in great multitudes gathered together, in order to raiſe the ſiege of Fowye; which the Frenchmen obſerving, and fearing the conſequence of their longer ſtay, having gotten ſufficient treaſure to defray the charge of their expedition, as haſtily ran to their ſhips as they had deliberately entered the town, and as privately returned into France as they had clandeſtinely come into England: with ſmall profit and leſs honour. See *Baker's* Chronicle, and *Tonkin's* MS. Fowey, pp. 375, 376, 377.

"The

For their courageous defence of Fawey, againſt the French invaders, the *Trefrys* were juſtly celebrated; eſpecially a lady of the family.*

Among our men at arms under Henry and Edward IV.|| I ſhould number ‡John Duke of

" The town of Foye being thus conſumed by fire, and plundered by the French ſoldiers and ſeamen, the inhabitants former wealth and glory reduced to poverty and contempt, they politickly caſt themſelves at the feet of Richard Nevill, Earl of Warwick, who pitying their diſtreſs'd condition, and being Lord High Admiral of England, granted ſome of them new commiſſions for privateering and taking French ſhips, on promiſe of their juſt and righteous proceedings, and renouncing the trade of Piracy. Whereupon, in few years they ply'd their ſea buſineſs ſo effectually, that they increaſed their riches to ſuch degree, that they began to repair and rebuild their damnified houſes, and in the ſtones of many of them, in memory of the Earl of Warwick's favour and bounty towards them, there are cut his arms, badge, and cognizance." *Hals*, p, 135.

* " One of the Treffrys about 145 yeares ſithence valiantly defended his dwelling againſt the French, which time they had ſurpriz'd the reſt of the town of Foy." *Carew*, f. 134 b. The Lady Trefry, in the abſence of her huſband Sir John Trefry (who was then at court as cupbearer to Edw. IV.) defended her houſe in Fowey, for ſix weeks againſt the French, after they had ſeized on the reſt of the town; in memory of which, and for its better ſecurity in future, ſhe built the tower adjoining, as I have heard (ſays Tonkin) from the late John Trefry, Eſq. *Tonkin's* MSS.

|| In the 7th vol. of the Archæologia, Art. 5, is an illuſtration of an unpubliſhed ſeal of Richard Duke of Glouceſter, by the Rev. Dr. Milles. It is in braſs, and in the moſt perfect preſervation. It was found at St. Columb, in this county, in a lot of old braſs and iron. Richard, Duke of Glouceſter, was conſtituted *Admiral of England, in the reign of* Edward IV. *which office is here expreſſed.* We have a very neat engraving of the ſeal, and ſome hiſtorical obſervations.

‡ *John* Duke of *Exeter*, was a moſt eminent perſon, as well in merit as in title. Notwithſtanding which, and that by his mother he was half-brother to *K. Rich.* 2d, and, by his wife, brother-in-law to *K. Hen.* 4th, then on the throne; yet being found in conſpiracy with his brother the Earl of *Kent*, and other Lords, for the depoſing and death of the ſaid K. *Henry*, and reſtoration of K. *Richard*, he was beheaded, and in Parliament adjudged to loſe his honour; and his lands, caſtles, and other poſſeſſions, were confiſcated to the King. He left iſſue *Richard* his eldeſt ſon, who after his father's death, was ſeized of a great eſtate, which fell not under confiſcation, as *Bovey-Tracy*, *Northlien* (ſo *Dugd.* for *Northlieu*) *Barnſtaple*, *Holdeſworthy*, *Langacre* (it may be *Lang-tree*) *Comb-Martin*, *Fremington*, with the hundred, *South-Molton* with the hundred, *Dartinton*, *Blackborn-Both* (ſo *Dugd.* for *Blackburgh-Bolhay*, both not far from *Cullumpton*) and *Winklee*. But this *Richard* dying unmarried *December* 3, *A.* 4, *K. Hen.* 5th, eighteen years after his father, *John* his ſecond brother became his heir; and the ſame year was reſtored in blood, as heir to *John* his father and *Richard* his brother.

Being reſtored in blood, and to the Earldom of *Huntingdon*, he was conſtituted general of all thoſe men at arms and archers, at that time employed in the King's fleet at ſea, againſt his enemies, being then retained to ſerve with three bannerets, nine knights, thirty-ſeven men at arms, and ſeven hundred archers, for the fourth part of a year. After that, he was retained again to ſerve the King (*Hen.* 5th) in his voyage-royal into *France*, for one whole year, with forty men at arms and an hundred archers. The year after, he was made general at ſea, and aſſiſted that King in his ſiege of *Caen* in *Normandy*, but had not made proof of his age till the 6th of *Hen.* 5th, at what time he was near thirty years of age. Soon after which, he was ſent to view certain defenſible places in thoſe parts of *France*; which in a ſhort time he manfully reduced to the King's obedience: and being at the ſiege of *Roan*, he lay before the gate of the caſtle called *Beauvice*. After that, upon taking of *Pontaiſe* by *Capitan de la Bouch*, he intercepted thoſe of that garriſon, who endeavoured to get to *Paris*. He was alſo in the great fight againſt the French, who came to raiſe the ſiege of *Freney*; in which were ſlain by the Engliſh near five thouſand of the enemy, and ſix hundred taken priſoners.

After this, *A.* 7. *K. Hen.* 5. being governour of *Pontoiſe*, he had ſpecial commiſſion to ſubdue all the caſtles and ſtrongholds in *Normandy*, which held out againſt the King. And being with the King *A.* 8. *K. Hen.* 5. at the ſiege of *Melon*, which laſted above fourteen weeks, upon his ſurrender, was conſtituted governour thereof. And by reaſon of other his ſpecial ſervices, he was made conſtable of the tower of *London*. But paſſing, the year after with *Thomas* Duke of *Clarence*, over a marſh, not far from the caſtle of *Beaufort* (where, by diſorder, he fell into the enemies hands) he had the fate to be taken priſoner, and the Duke himſelf with many others ſlain. After which he continued ſome years in thoſe parts; but upon the death of *Elizabeth* his mother *A.* 4 *K Hen.* 6. which was 1425, doing his homage, he had livery of thoſe lands, whereof ſhe died ſeized.

K. Hen. 5th, (the glory of *England*) being dead, he grew into favour alſo with that good King, *Hen.* 6. in the 6th year of whoſe reign, in conſideration of the ranſom which he paid for his redemption from impriſonment, and his good ſervices, he obtained a grant of 123l. 6s. 8d. *per Ann.* to be paid out of the *Exchequer*. Near two years after this, he married; his firſt wife was *Anne*, widow of *Edmund Mortimer*, Earl of *March*, daughter to *Edmund* Earl of *Stafford*; and being the ſame year retained to ſerve the King with three knights, ſeventy ſix men at arms, and two hundred and forty archers, he went thereupon into *France*. Taking ſhiping with the *King* at *Dover*, and landing at *Calais*, he was ſent by the Duke of *Bedford*, then regent of *France*, to the ſiege of *Campeigne*. And the next enſuing years he attended at the royal coronation of *King Henry* 6th, then ſolemnized at *Paris*.

After this, he obtained the *King's* ſpecial licence, that himſelf, and *Anne* his wife might receive full profit of all their lands and lordſhips in *Ireland*, notwithſtanding their abſence from the realm for three years. And the year following, the ſaid *Anne* his wife being dead, he obtained licenſe to marry *Beatrice*, the widow of *Thomas* Earl of *Arundel*, illegitimate daughter to *John* King of *Portugal*: at which time alſo, he had the grant of the office of Lord High-Marſhal of *England*, to hold during the minority of *John*, ſon and heir to the late Duke of *Norfolk*, and went again into *France*. And being ſent ambaſſador

of Exeter, and Sir William *Kerfewell, ‡Bonville, and †Fulford, Borlafe, ||Arundel, and
F ¶Floier;

ambaffador to the city of *Arras*, *A.* 13 *Hen.* 6. to treat of peace with the French, he had licenfe to carry with him gold, filver, plate, jewels, robes, twenty four pieces of woollen cloth, and other things, to the value of fix thoufand pounds fterling: a great treafure in thofe times.

The year after this, *A.* 14 *Hen.* 6. he was joined in commiffion with the Earl of *Northumberland*, for guarding the eaft and weft marches towards *Scotland*; as alfo conftituted Admiral of *England* and *Aquitain*. Next was he retained to ferve the *King*, *A.* 16 *Hen.* 6. as Lieutenant of *Guien*, for fix years, with two bannerets, fixteen knights, two hundred and eighty men at arms, and two thoufand archers, for the defence of thofe parts. Before the expiration of which time, in confideration of his continual fervices in the wars of *France*, both in the time of *K. Henry* the fifth, and the then prefent *King Henry* the fixth; as alfo by reafon he had been taken prifoner, and put to a large ranfom for his liberty, he obtained a grant to himfelf, *A.* 19 *Hen.* 6. and to the heirs male of his body, of five hundred marks, to be yearly received out of the ports of *London*, &c. being the fame year joined in commiffion with divers other lords, and fome of the judges of the land, to enquire of all manner of treafons and forceries, which might be hurtful to the King's perfon.

Not long after which, viz. 21 *K. Hen.* 6. he was, by letters patents, bearing date at *Windfor* 6th *Jan.* advanced to the title of, Duke of *Exeter* (which dignity his father loft by attainder, 1 *Hen.* 4th) with this fpecial priviledge, *that he and his heirs Male fhould have place and feat in all Parliaments and Councils, next to the Duke of* York *and his heirs male.* Three years after, *A.* 24 *Hen.* 6th, was he conftituted Lord High Admiral of *England*, *Ireland*, and *Aquitain* for life: his fon *Henry* being joined with him for life in the grant. And the year after that, made conftable of the tower of *London*, in like fort, with his fon *Henry*.

This moft noble Duke married a third wife, though in what year I do not find, *viz Anne*, daughter of *John Mountague*, Earl of *Salifbury*, who furvived him many years.

At laft this great perfon, after he had feen all the grandeur of this world, and was himfelf a good part thereof, yielded to fate near about the 26th year of the reign of *K. Hen.* 6th, 1447, not being fully arrived at the 50th year of his age.

By his teftament bearing date 16th *July*, 25 *Hen.* 6th, he bequeathed his body to be buried in a chappel, within the church of St. *Katharine*, befide the tower of *London*, at the north end of the higher altar, in a tomb there ordained for him and *Anne* his firft wife, as alfo for his fifter *Conftance*, and *Anne* his other wife, then living.

He bequeathed alfo to the high altar of the faid church a cup of byrel, garnifhed with gold pearls, and precious ftones, to put in the facrament: alfo a chalice of gold, with the whole furniture of his chappel: appointing that another chalice, two bafons, two candlefticks of filver, with two pair of veftments, a mafs-book, a paxbred and a pair of cruets of filver fhould be delivered to that little chappel, for priefts to celebrate divine fervice therein, and pray for their fouls. To the priefts and clerks, and other of the houfe of St. *Katharine*, for their great labour and obfervance on the day of his *obit* and day of his burying, he bequeathed forty marks; ordaining, that four honeft and cunning priefts fhould be provided, yearly and perpetually, to pray for his foul in the faid chappel, and for the foul of *Anne* his firft wife, the foul of his fifter *Conftance*, and the foul of *Anne* his prefent wife, when fhe fhould pafs out of this world, and for the fouls of all his progenitors. To his daughter *Anne* he bequeathed his white bed with *Popinjayes*; and to his fon *Henry* all the ftuff of his wardrobe. And departing this life 5. *Aug.* next enfuing, which was the year of our Lord 1446, he was buried in the chappel aforefaid.

Anne his laft wife furvived him many years, as appears from her laft teftament, bearing date the 20th of *April* 1457; by which fhe bequeathed her body to be buried in the chancel of the faid church of St. *Katharine's*, expreffly forbidding her executors from making any great feaft, or having a folemn herfe, or any coftly lights, or largefs of liveries, according to the glory and vain pomp of the world at her funeral; but only to the worfhip of God, according to the difcretion of *John Pinchback*, D. D. one of her executors. She gave to the mafter and every brother of the faid college of St. *Katharine*, particular legacies; further appointing, that her executors fhould find an honeft prieft to fay mafs and pray for her foul, her Lord's foul, and all Chriftan fouls in the chappel where her body fhould be buried, for the fpace of feven years next after her deceafe; for which he was to receive every year twelve marks. But to return to the Duke.

He had iffue, by *Anne* his firft wife, only *Henry*, his fon and heir; and by *Anne* his laft wife a daughter called *Anne*, married firft to *John* Lord *Nevil*, fon and heir to *Ralph Nevil*, fecond Earl of *Weftmoreland*, of that family; by whom having no iffue, fhe took to hufband Sir *John Nevil*, Kt. Uncle to her former hufband.

Henry, the only fon and heir to his father *John* Duke of *Exeter*, inherited his father's titles with his lands. He was a very brave foldier, but unfortunately engaging on the weakeft fide, (viz. the fupport of the tottering houfe of *Lancafter*) he perifhed under the ruins thereof. Fighting manfully at *Barnet-field* with the Lancaftrians, he was fore wounded and left for dead, from feven o'clock in the morning, till four in the afternoon. Recovering of his wounds, he fled beyond fea; but was reduced to very great extremity, for tho he defcended from the royal family, and had married the fifter of K. *Ed.* 4- yet it is reported by *Comines*, *that he faw him in fuch great diftrefs, that he ran on foot bare-legg'd after the Duke of* Burgundy's *train*(who had married his wife's fifter) *begging his bread for God's fake.* He was at length found dead (13 *Edw.* 4. 1473) in the fea, betwixt *Dover* and *Calais*, tho not known how he came thither.

This *Henry* married *Anne*, daughter of *Richard* Duke of *York*, and fifter to K. *Edw.* 4. which *Anne*, at her own fuit, was divorced from him, 12. *Nov.* 1472, 12th *Edw.* 4. and having no iffue furviving, fhe afterwards became the wife of *Sir Thomas Saintleger*, knight for the body to K. *Edw.* 4th, who had fometime their habitation at *Dartinton-houfe*, in this county." *Prince's* Worthies, pp. 371, 372, 373.

* "The houfe of Carfwell, (near Modbury) antiently yielded feveral eminent perfons, fuch was *Robert Kerfwel* of *Exeter*, reckoned the firft among thofe antient gentlemen there, that deferved well of the common-wealth. He was the laft chief fteward of that city, before they had a mayor, now above five hundred years fince. The chief magiftrates of which city in the Saxon and Danes times were called *Port-Reeves*; after the conqueft, bailiffs, or ftewards

wards until K. *John*'s days, who in the 2d year of his reign incorporated that antient burrough by charter, under the diſtinction of a mayor and citizens.

But the moſt memorable perſon I have met with of this houſe, is Sir *William Kerſwel*, or *Carſwell*, a great warrior in the days of K. *Hen.* 5. and K. *Hen.* 6. whom he bravely aſſiſted in their wars, with many noble exploits. Among ſeveral others of them, now buried in oblivion, theſe few are come to hand: that he, with half a dozen others (when the Engliſh army there, after a long ſiege, were not able to force a certain caſtle in *France*) fell upon this ſtratagem. They attired themſelves in countrymens habits, and carrying bags of proviſions on their backs, in which they had privily hid their arms, ſo found admiſſion into the caſtle; where ſeizing on the captain, they fought open the gates, and let in the Engliſh, who lay in ambuſcado by for that purpoſe. Another time, as the Engliſh lay before the ſtrong town of *Ponthoiſe*, in the ſame kingdom, in a great ſnow, this gentleman, with ſeveral others, came by night in their white ſhirts undiſcovered home to the walls; which they ſoon ſcaled, ſlew the guards, and ſubdued the place. He is ſaid to have been a perſon of that prodigious ſtrength, that he would go near, with one ſtroak of his ſword, to cleave a man down the back.

Nor was he a perſon of leſs loyalty and faithfulneſs to that pious prince his ſovereign, K. *Hen.* 6. who at the battle of St. *Albans* being in danger to be taken by his enemies, this gentleman deſperately undertook his reſcue, by ſlaying, with his own hand, ſeveral of thoſe which oppoſed in his way. For all which his good ſervices at home and abroad, he had the honour of knighthood conferred upon him, and ample poſſeſſions at a place called *Caverefwell* in *Staffordſhire*, near the river *Blith*, where this Sir *William* built him a caſtle, which from him hath ever ſince been called by that name. At his death, he left it to his daughter and heir married into the noble family of *Montgomery*; from whom it came to Sir *John Port*, Kt. as *Glover Norrey* king of arms tells us.

In the church belonging to this place Sir *William Carſwell* lieth interred, under a fair monument, on which this inſcription was ſometime legible.

Willielmus Careſwell de Caverefwell Miles:
Caſtri ſtructor eram Domibus Foſſiſq; *cemento*
Vivus dans operam jam Claudor in hoc Monumento.
A. D. M.C.D.L.X.V." *Prince*, p. 433.

‡ "Upon a marriage with Sir *Thomas Pine's* daughter, and co-heir, the family of *Bonvil* tranſplanted itſelf from *Wiſcombe* to *Shute*, where it long flouriſhed. A very ſweet and noble ſeat; adorned in thoſe days, (as ſtill it is) with a fair park, and large demeſns. There was a great eſtate belonging to it, not only in *Devonſhire* (too tedious to be particulariz'd) but in *Somerſet*, *Dorſet*, and *Cornwal*. In which laſt county, their ſeat, was at *Trelawn*, near *Weſt-Loo*; the pleaſant habitation of the Right Reverend Father in God Sir *Jonathan Trelawny*, Bart. the preſent Lord Biſhop of this Dioceſs; whoſe undaunted zeal for the church of *England*, and the liberties of his country, will be read in the records of the tower of *London* (unto which, with ſix others of his venerable order, he was committed by K. *Jam.* 2. for humble-petitioning) to all generations. So that Lord *Bonvil*, in the 14. K. *Hen.* 6. *A.* 1435. was no leſs than 920l. in the ſubſidy-book.

Lord *Bonvil* was in his time a great ſoldier: who making proof of his age, in 2 K. *Hen.* 5. had livery of his lands. In the 5. *Hen.* 5. being then a knight, he went in that expedition then made into *France*, and was of the retinue with *Thomas*, Duke of *Clarence*, the King's brother. In the 11 K. *Hen.* 6. he was made ſheriff of *Devonſhire*: and in the 4th, he had livery of the mannor of *Meryet*, in Com. *Somerſ.* In the 21 K. *Hen.* 6. he was retained to ſerve the King, for one whole year, in his wars of *France*, with twenty men at arms, and ſix hundred archers; being at that time alſo made ſeneſchal of the dutchy of *Aquitane*. And meriting ſo well for his ſervices in thoſe wars, and otherwiſe, *A.* 28 *H.* 6. he had ſummons to Parliament, amongſt the barons of the realm; and ever after to his death. And in 31. of that reign, in conſideration of his further ſervices, he was conſtituted governour of the caſtle of *Exeter*, for life: his title was Lord *Bonvil*, of *Chuton*; which place deſcended to him from his mother, who brought it into this family. And moreover, he was admitted companion of the noble order of the garter.

In 32 K. *Hen.* 6. he was made Lieutenant of *Aquitane*. And in the 33. of that King, there fell out a ſhrewed diſpute between *Thomas Courtenay*, Earl of *Devonſhire*, and this Lord *Bonvil*, about a couple of hounds; which could by no mediation of friends be qualified, or appeaſed; until it was valiantly try'd by a ſingle combat, on *Cliſt-Heath*, near *Exeter*, wherein (as *Dugd.* tells us), this Lord prevail'd. But another writer ſaith, that after they had well try'd one the other's ſtrength and valour with their naked ſwords, they at laſt, as was ſaid of the two Kings *Edmond* and *Canutus*, in the iſle of *Olney*, near *Glouceſter*, *A.* 1016 lovingly agreed, and embraced each other, and ever after continued in great love and amity.

Not long after this, the civil wars breaking out in *England*, between the two famous houſes of *York* and *Lancaſter*; notwithſtanding the honour, and perſonal obligations, this noble Lord had received from K. *Hen.* 6. he was always found on the ſide of his enemy, the Duke of *York*. But whether induced hereunto from a principle of meer conſcience, towards what he apprehended the right line, or by the ſubtile inſinuations of *Nevil*, Earl of *Saliſbury*, whoſe daughter he had married up to his grand-ſon *William Bonvil*, Lord *Harrington*, I ſhall not take upon me to determine.

But in that battle, fought at *Northampton*, between the *Yorkiſts* and *Lancaſtrians*, that unfortunate Prince K. *Hen.* 6. was taken priſoner; and, among others, was committed to the care and cuſtody of this Lord *Bonvil*. After which, 'tis obſerv'd, he was never proſperous: as if he had been pick'd out as an example of the inſtability of fortune: for all theſe miſchiefs ſoon ſucceeded to the neck of one the other, as if (ſaith Mr. *Camd.*) a fury had haunted for revenge. He was an eye-witneſs of the untimely death of his only ſon, (nobly married to the Lord *Harrington's* daughter and heir) and of *Bonvil*, Lord *Harrington's* grand-child, both ſlain before his face, in the battle of *Wakefield*: and preſently after, to make his old age as miſerable as could be, whilſt he was in expectation of better fortune, himſelf was taken priſoner, in the ſecond battle of St. *Albans*: and though his own party had then the better, and King *Henry* had promiſed him he ſhould receive no bodily hurt; yet, ſuch was the indignation of the Queen towards him, as alſo of the Duke of *Exeter*, and the Earl of *Devon*, that being now in their power, however they had loſt the day, never reſted till they had taken off his head; which happen'd in the 39th and laſt year of the reign of *K. Hen.* 6. *A. D.* 1460. Notwithſtanding, this Lord's memory was *q. e poſtliminio*—as it

¶Floier; and, among our courtiers, *Vyvyan and Billing. That after the battle of Barnet-field, *Sir Walter Borlaſe* was there made a Knight-Banneret by EDWARD the 4th, is the conſtant tradition in that family. And formerly were painted in the glaſs window over Treluddero ſeats, in Newlyn church, the arms of Borlaſe with ſeveral quarterings, ſupported by two angels;

F 2 which

it were reſtored to him by act of Parliament, after his death, 1 *Ed.* 4. declaring him innocent. And in regard he had ſtood up ſo ſtoutly againſt the *Lancaſtrians*, *Elizabeth*, his widow, that ſame year, had likewiſe an aſſignation of a very large dowry out of his eſtate in *Somerſet*, *Dorſet*, *Cornwal*, and *Devon*; by name, *Combe-Pyne-Seton*, *Combe-Pyne*, *Down-Umphra-vile*, *Charletone*, *Head and Pole*, *Northcote*, with divers lands in *Birches*, *Sydeford*, *Axminſter*, and *Toregge*, all in this county.

The Lord *Bonvil*, thus falling by the hand of violence, his corps, it ſeems, was perſerved to a decent ſepulture; for *Camden* tells us, upon what authority he beſt knows, that *William Bonvil*, and his lady, lye inter'd in the chancel of the church of *Chuton*, in the county of *Somerſet*.

This noble family, in the male line, thus extinct, this vaſt eſtate fell to *Cicely*, this Lord *Bonvil* his grand-ſon's only daughter and heir, married unto *Thomas Grey*, Lord Marqueſs of *Dorſet*, half brother, by the mother, to *K. Edw.* 4. which by the attainder of the Duke of *Suffolk* fell to the crown; part of which, in this country, came afterward to be purchaſed of Q. *Mary* by Sir *William Petre*, her principal ſecretary of ſtate; who exchanged the houſe at *Shute*, with the park and lands about it, for other of like value, with one of the anceſtors of the honourable Sir *John Pole*, Bart." *Prince*, pp. 73, 74.

† Sir Thomas Fulford, ſon of Sir Baldwin, commanded a part of *Queen Margaret's army*, and was taken priſoner at the battle of Towton Field, and beheaded in 1461.

|| Sir John Arundel of Trerice, Knight, 11 Edw. IV. on Queen Margaret's landing in England, after the battle of Barnet-field, brought the forces of Cornwall and Devon to her aſſiſtance.

¶ "*William Floier* of *Exeter*, was an eminent ſoldier, as may appear from that agreement made between the Duke of *Clarence* and him, to attend him into *Normandy* with three archers and thirty ſpears. Which Duke of *Clarence*, younger brother to K. *Edw.* 4th, was very unfortunate; being at laſt, after many turmoils in the world, drowned in a butt of Malmſey. The occaſion of which expedition into *Normandy* was this, K. *Edw.* being now quietly ſettled in his throne at home, was prevailed upon by his brother-in-law the Duke of *Burgundy*, to look abroad, and make a deſcent upon *France*, for the recovery of that kingdom, lately loſt by the misfortunes of his predeceſſor. Great preparations were made accordingly, and a vaſt army raiſed; the greateſt that ever ſet ſail out of *England* before. All things in readineſs, K. *Edw.* in the 14th year of his reign, 1474, repaired to *Dover*, and embarqued himſelf and forces for *Calais*, having with him 1500 noblemen and men at arms, all of them mounted, and moſt of them barbed; who with the archers on horſeback, made up the number of 15000, beſides a great many foot; having before ſent his herald *garter* king at arms to the French king, with a letter of defiance, in caſe he would not preſently yield up the whole realm of *France* into his hands, as his juſt right and due.

Now to ſerve his King and country in this action, was Mr. *Floier* retained in the quality of a captain; as may appear from that charter of agreement made between the Duke of *Clarence* and him; a copy of which hereafter follows: but firſt I ſhall exhibit a tranſcript of that loving letter the Duke ſent him, in order to his ſigning of the ſaid agreement.

The Duke of *Clarence*, Earl of *Warwick* and *Sarum*, and Great Chamberlain of *England*.

Truſty and wel-beloved we greet you well! whereas at our laſt being in the weſt parts, ye agreed to go in our retinue in my Lord's voyage over ſea, with ſuch number of archers as is contained in an indenture that we ſend unto you, by our ſervant *John Halwel*, bearer hereof, wherein ye ſhew your ſelf of right loving diſpoſition towards us, whereof we thank you heartily. It is alſo that we having conſideration of the labor and coſt that ſhould be unto you, to come to *London* or hither to ſeal the indenture, have, for your more eaſe, ſent you the ſame, praying you to ſeal the one part thereof, and to deliver it to our ſervant. Geaven at our caſtle of *Warwick* the 14th day of *Febr.*

Thus endorſed;

To our truſty and well-beloved *William Floier*.

The indenture followeth in theſe words:

This indenture made betwixt the right high and mighty Prince, *George* Duke of *Clarence*, on the one part, and *William Floier* of *Exeter*, in the county of *Devon*, on the other part, *Witneſſeth*, that the ſaid *William* is retain'd and beliſt towards the ſaid Duke, to do ſervice of wars unto the King our Sovereign Lord, in the ſaid Duke's retinue, in the Dutchy of *Normandy* and realm of *France*, for one whole year, with three archers well and ſufficiently habited, armed, and arrayed; taking wages for himſelf, xij d. by the day, with rewards accuſtomed, after the rate of a C. *Marcs* in a quarter for xxx ſpears, and for every the ſaid archers vj d. by the day; with divers other conditions and agreements. Dated the xiv. of *Decemb.* in the xiv. year of the reign of our Sovereign Lord King *Edward* the iiijth.

Which indenture we need not queſtion was ſign'd and ſeal'd by Mr. *Floier*, and he went accordingly; but what exploits he or the army did in this expedition we do not find, for that the Engliſh and the French came to terms of accommodation without comeing to a battle; and as for any other eminent actions of his, what ever they were, the memory of them died with him." *Prince*, pp. 309, 310.

* Leland calls *Richard Vyvyan* of Trelowarren, a gallant courtier, ſet forth by Somerſet, Lord Herbert. It appears, from a record in the tower, (Franc. 8 Edw. IV. No. 3.) that Richard Vyvyan of Trelowarren, attended on the Earl of Worceſter, deputy of Ireland, in ſervice of the King, into that realm. Sir Thomas Billing was one of the twelve judges in the reign of Edw. IV. and contemporary with judge Littleton. It is ſuppoſed that he was the grandſon of John Billoun (or Billing) who was knight for Cornwall, 24 Edw. III.

which are ſaid to be the arms of this Sir Walter.* But I mean not to exclude from their juſt ſhare

* Immediately after the battle of Barnet, intelligence was brought to Edward, that Queen Margaret was landed at Weymouth, and that the Corniſh and Devonians, urged on by Courtenay Earl of Devonſhire, were hourly flocking to her ſtandard. Courtenay fell in the battle of Tewkeſbury, that followed this ſame year. *Speed.* "It was not long after the diſcomfiture of the adherents of Henry VI. at Barnet field, that John Earl of Oxford, one of the principal on the weaker ſide, arrived at St. Michael's Mount, by ſhipping; and diſguiſing himſelf and his followers in pilgrim's habits, thus got entrance and maſtered the garriſon, and ſeized the place. This port he a long time maintained, till reaſonable conditions forced him to a ſurrender." *Carew,* f. 155.

"Richard de Vere, (ſays *Hals*) *i. e.* of the great or greater, (as if derived from the Corniſh *Veor,* great) the 11th Earl of Oxford, married Alice, one of the daughters and co-heirs of Sir Richard Sergreaulx, Knight, Lord of Colquite and Killygarth, widow of Guy Seyntabyn, ſheriff of Cornwall, 22 Richard 2d. 1399; from whoſe heir on her begotten, ſhe paſſed her lands to her ſecond huſband, the Earl of Oxford; who had iſſue by her John de Vere the 12th Earl of Oxford, who married Elizabeth daughter of Sir John Howard, Knight, the which John had iſſue by her John the 13th Earl of Oxford. The which John, the 12th Earl, was the chief of thoſe Barons, that oppoſed the precedence in parliament of the Lords ſpiritual, tempore Hen. 6th, the which parliament-roll in the tower of London, is thus endorſed, "memorandum, the Lords ſpiritual alleged, that foraſmuch as they were ſpiritual Barons, they ought to have the right of precedence of the Lords temporal, for it was well known how far things ſpiritual exceeded carnal or temporal." To which this Earl of Oxford replied on behalf of the Lords temporal, that "whatſoever right or privelege they had, or could challenge (ſee Brooke on Oxford Earl), it came from them and their anceſtors, and their almſdeeds, who had been the worthy founders and benefactors of the Lords ſpiritual;" and further ſaid, it was an unſeemly thing for maſters to be inferiour to their ſervants, who were depended of regal, honourable, and noble families, which moſt of the ſpiritual Barons were not." [This proud Earl, in the undiſtinguiſhing ſpirit of his mind, unconſciouſly put a piece of ſophiſtry upon the Parliament; in ſtating the Peers to be the endowers of the Biſhopricks, when the Kings alone were; then from premiſes ſo falſe arguing as falſely, that what was thus given for the endowment of Biſhopricks, was not given to God, and to Biſhops as his ſupreme miniſters, but was given to the Biſhops for their own ſakes, and was merely an alms done to them; and finally conſidering the Biſhops from both falſities united, to be only the ſervants of the Peers. Such reaſoning might well ſuit the head of an Earl, equally illiterate and ir-religious! The crown erected and endowed the Biſhopricks, while the Peers merely augmented the parochial benefices, with an addition of Glebe to the Tithes. And the crown placed the Biſhops with the Peers in Parliament, and gave them the precedence of the Peers there, in reverence to religion and to God.] Which matter being fully underſtood, and indifferently heard, the Lords temporal, by means of the logick (rare logic!) and rhetorick of this Earl, had then the precedence of place in Parliament given them. But alas! this bold demand, queſtion, and argument of his (in direct contradiction to the uſages of Parliament, and the laws of the land, which had prevailed ever ſince the introduction of Chriſtianity; even thoſe very laws and uſages, upon which the temporal Peers themſelves had a right to a ſeat in Parliament,) was a project for that reaſon rather pitied than admired by his beſt friends. For, though it ſucceeded well in one Parliament, it got him many enemies in another, (all indeed, that adhered to law or uſage, and that retained a reverence for religion); ſo that in the Parliament held the 2d November, 1462, tempore Edw. 4th, this Earl and his ſon Aubry, were attainted of treaſon againſt that King, in the behalf of Henry 6th, and both beheaded without trial or anſwer, (*Baker's* Chron. p. 204.) (So fell he in direct violation of uſage, law, and religion; who violated all to deprive the Biſhops of their precedence, as the firſt eſtate of Peers in Parliament. See Hiſt. of Man. II. 4to. 389, 391.

——— Nec lex eſt juſtior ulla,
Quam necis artifices arte perire ſuâ.)

Whereupon John his ſecond ſon ſucceeded, and was the 13th Earl of Oxford; who, as his father had done before, adhered to the intereſt of King Henry 6th, againſt Edward 4th, and was at the battle of Barnet-Heath, 1471; and had with the Marquis Montacute, the command of the right wing of King Henry's horſe, under Richard Earl of Warwick, general of his army. And when in the battle it appeared, the vanward of King Henry's horſe had ſomewhat worſted King Edward's party, by the valour of the Earl Oxford; the news preſently fled to London, that Warwick had obtained the victory. But alas; "Fama eſt mendax;" for, immediately after, a ſtrange misfortune befel the Earl of Oxford and his men, in the latter part of the encounter, they having a ſtar with ſtreams on their liveries, as King Edward's ſoldiers had the ſun. The General Warwick's men by reaſon of a great miſt, raiſed (as was thought) by the magick art of Frier Bungey, miſtaking the badges, ſhot at the Earl of Oxford's men, which were of their own party, to their great hurt and deſtruction. Whereupon the Earl, ſeeing how matters went, cried out treaſon, and forthwith fled with 800 men. Whoſe departure gave King Edward opportunity, to obtain a total victory over his enemies.

[The hiſtory ſhould have begun with this Earl of Oxford, and not have run back to his father and his brother, eſpecially not to his father's motion in Parliament againſt the biſhops. But the author apparently ran up the current of time ſo high, with the mere view of introducing this motion. Such were his principles of polity, and ſuch was his injudiciouſneſs of mind.]

Whereupon the Duke of Somerſet, and the Earl of Oxford, fled to Jaſper Earl of Pembrook, in Wales, for ſafety and protection; from whence Oxford, and a convenient number of men of arms, ſhipped themſelves from Milford Haven, and with a fair wind ſailed down St. George's Channel, turned the Land's End, and came ſafely to anchor in this Mount's Bay. Where, as ſoon as the Earl and his men had diſguiſed themſelves, in pilgrims' and friers' apparel, under which all had lodged a ſmall ſword and a dagger; they went on ſhore, pretending that they were pilgrims, that had come a long pilgrimage from the remoteſt part of this kingdom, to perform the penance impoſed upon them by the father-confeſſors, and to perform their vows, make oriſons, and oblations to the altar of St. Michael, who preſided there. Upon which pious pretext, the monks and inhabitants opened their gates, and let them into the caſtle; where they were no ſooner entered, but, as De la Pomeray,

ſhare in military honours, many other warlike characters of the weſt.* Theſe were times peculiarly

Pomeray, had done before, they ſhowed their weapons, diſcovered their impious fraud, and made known who they were, and their deſigns to kill all perſons that made reſiſtance, or oppoſed King Henry 6th, for whom the Earl of Oxford was come to take poſſeſſion of this Mount, and would keep it to his uſe. Whereupon the monks and the ſmall garriſon, were neceſſitated to comply with their demands, and yield them a quiet poſſeſſion thereof. Which forthwith the Earl put in better repair; and, by the intereſt of King Henry, and the Earl's friends and relations in thoſe parts, his grandmother, being Sir Guy Seyntaubyn's widow, and Selgreaulxe's coheir; he ſoon got ammunition, proviſion, and ſoldiers ſufficient for their defence. As ſoon as King Edward 4th heard of the ſurprize of St. Michael's Mount, by the Earl of Oxford, he iſſued forth his proclamation, proclaiming him, and all his adherents traytors; and then conſulted how to regain both to his obedience. And, in order thereto, he forthwith ſent to Sir John Arundel of Trerice, Knight, then ſheriff of Cornwall, to reduce and beſiege (beſiege and reduce) the ſame, by his poſſe comitatus. Which gentleman, purſuant to his orders, and by virtue of his office, ſoon raiſed a conſiderable army of men and ſoldiers, within his bailiwick, and marched with them towards St. Michael's Mount. Where being arrived, he ſent a trumpeter to the Earl with a ſummons, of ſurrender of that garriſon to him, for King Edward upon mercy; eſpecially, for that in ſo doing, in all probability, he would prevent the effuſion of much Chriſtian blood.

To this ſummons of the trumpeter, the Earl ſent a flat denial; ſaying further, that rather than he would yield the fort on thoſe terms, himſelf and thoſe with him were all reſolved to loſe their lives in defence thereof. Whereupon the ſheriff commanded his ſoldiers being very numerous on all parts, to ſtorm the Mount and reduce it by force. But alas! maugre all their attempts of this kind, the beſieged ſo well defended every part of this rocky mountain, that in all places the ſheriff's men were repulſed with ſome loſs; and the beſieged iſſued forth at the outer gate, and purſued them with ſuch violence, that the ſaid Sir John Arundel, and ſome others were ſlain upon the ſands at the foot of the Mount, to the great diſcouragement of the new-raiſed ſoldiers, who quickly departed thence, having loſt their leader; leaving the beſieged in better heart than they found them, as much elevated at their good ſucceſs, as themſelves were diſmayed at their bad fortune. This Sir John Arundel, (as Mr *Carew*, in his ſurvey of Cornwall, 119, tells us,) had long before been told by ſome fortune-teller, he ſhould be ſlain in the ſands; wherefore, to avoid that deſtiny, he removed from Efford, near Stratton on the ſands, where he dwelt, to Trerice, far off from the ſea; yet by this misfortune, fulfilled the prediction in another place. [He was buried in the Mount Church. *Price's* MSS.]

In like manner Cardinal Wolſey was foretold by ſome prophet, to beware of Kingſton; and therefore, he always ſhunned and avoided that town in Surry, in his way to court; but maugre all his endeavours to ſhun fate, he was at laſt ſeized, by order of King Henry the 8th, by Sir William Kingſton, his lieutenant of the tower of London, to be brought up there, in order to be tried for his life; the very ſight of which gentleman ſo ſtruck to his heart, in remembrance of the prediction aforeſaid, that he died on his journey two days after, (ſee *Fox* and *Fuller*,) or poiſoned himſelf to death.

King Edward, upon news of this tragical accident, forthwith ordered letters patent to be drawn, for making John Forteſcue, Eſq. ſheriff of Cornwall, in the place of Sir John Arundel, ſlain as aforeſaid. Who, being accordingly ſworn in that office, received the ſame commands, and took the ſame meaſures for reducing the Mount, as the former ſheriff had done, by ſummons and aſſault; but was always and in all places, repulſed with diſhonour and loſs; the ſame being as ſtoutly defended within, as it was aſſaulted without. The fort (thus) appeared invincible. All which circumſtances being tranſmitted to the King by Mr. Forteſcue, the ſheriff, the King, for prevention of further bloodſhed, ordered him to have a parley with the ſaid Earl of Oxford, and know what his deſigns and expectations were. Who, thereupon ſent a meſſenger to him, for that purpoſe, from whom he received this reſolute and deſperate anſwer: "That, if the King would pardon the offences of him, and his adherents, and grant them their lives, liberties, and eſtates, *that* then he would yield up the fort to his uſe; otherwiſe, they would fight it out to the laſt man." Which anſwer, being ſent up to the King, he granted their requeſt; and forthwith ordered a proclamation of free pardon to be made unto them, under the broad ſeal of England. Which with all convenient ſpeed was ſent down, and by Mr. Sheriff Forteſcue, delivered to the Earl, to the great quiet and content of all parties. Whereupon the fort was yielded to him for the King's uſe, and the Earl of Oxford was ſoon after ſent priſoner to the caſtle of Hamms, in Normandy, (though he was promiſed "liberty" under the broad ſeal of England.) Where he was continued a priſoner till the firſt year of King Henry 7th, 1485; with whom he (having eſcaped from priſon, I ſuppoſe) came into England, and led the vanward of his army, at Boſworth Field, againſt King Richard the 3d, where he was ſlain. After the death of this Earl's firſt wife, he married Elizabeth daughter of Sir Richard Scroop, Knight, widow of William Lord Beaumont, by whom he had no iſſue; ſo that, he dying the 4th Henry 8, left John, the ſon of George Vere, his brother, his heir and ſucceſſor, and the 14th Earl of Oxford. King Edward attributed this ineffectual long ſiege of St. Michael's Mount, either to the cowardice or diſloyalty of the ſheriffs and country-people of Cornwall. But there was no juſt cauſe for this conjecture, ſince Sir John Arundel and ſeveral of his men, loſt their lives about it. At other times, he would ſay, the inhabitants were more affected to the houſe of Lancaſter, than that of York. Whereupon, when the ſaid Mr. Forteſcue went out of office, after a four years ſervice, he made his brother, Richard Duke of Glouceſter, ſheriff of Cornwall during life, for that he was often heard to ſay, he looked upon Cornwall, only as the backdoor of rebellion. So that thoſe ſeveral perſons, ſet down in the catalogue of ſheriffs of Cornwall, after Forteſcue, were not abſolutely ſheriffs, but deputies under the ſaid Duke; viz. Daubeny, Carneſew, Willoughby, Nanſon, Grenvill, Fulford, Trefry, Terrill, and Houghton." *W. Hals*, (MS.) Vols. I. II. pp. 44, 49. In the MS. Hiſt. of the Mount, which I call *Price's*, we have little more than an abridgment of the above, at pp. 30, 31, 32.

* During the conteſt between Edward IV. and Henry VI. Exeter was the ſcene of hoſtility. And, in the diſplay of *character*, (which I am always fond of contemplating) the ſiege of Exeter was peculiarly fertile. "Exeter was in troubles (ſays *Hooker*) in the tenth year of King Edward the fourth, Anno 1470, (*Izacke* ſays 1469.) when the iſſue of affairs between this King and King Henry VI, was doubtful; the whole realm being then in the utmoſt confuſion, and rent in

culiarly inauſpicious to the purſuits of literature. Yet it was at this conjuncture, that William of Worceſtre made his tour; apparently indifferent to the horror of war. In the year 1473, we find him in Devon and in Cornwall; ſurveying ſome places with accurate attention, and calmly ſetting down thoſe obſervations, to which the antiquary has recourſe as curious; though they indicate very little learning, and leſs acuteneſs. In the vicinity of Truro, Worceſtre notices the two rival caſtles of Polwhele and Moreſk. The caſtle of Polwhele, in an inland ſituation, was the property of a gentleman, then in the ſervice of *the King*, as we are expreſſly informed: the caſtle of Moreſk, on the ſea-ſhore, was occupied by a tenant of the Duke of Cornwall.

The latter ſtood on the great Dutchy Manor. The former, unconnected with the Dutchy and independent on the Dukes, had towered on a commanding ſcite for ages. But we are told by Worceſtre, who paſſed the night there with OTHO Phelip (de Polwhele)† that the caſtle of

in pieces by different parties, ſome following King Edward, and ſome following King Henry. In the time of theſe troubles the Dutcheſs of Clarence, the Lords Dinham and Fitzwalter, and the Baron of Carew, who took part with King Henry, came to this city, accompanied with a thouſand fighting men. The Dutcheſs was then great with child, and lodged in the Biſhop's palace; and the Lords lodged in the houſes of ſome of the Canons, within the cloſe. But Sir Hugh Courtneie, Knight, (*Izacke* calls him Earl of Devon) who was of King Edward's party, hearing of theſe Lords, &c. being here, forthwith raiſed an army, marched hither, and laid ſiege to the city; breaking down the bridges, and ſtopping up all the avenues by which proviſions could be brought to the ſame. Being encamped about the city, he ſends a meſſage to the mayor, requiring the gates to be opened, and entrance given to him and his troops; or that he would deliver unto him the lords and gentlemen that were therein. On the other hand: theſe noblemen, either miſtruſting the mayor and citizens; or not willing to truſt to their courteſy, and be under their protection, deſired the keys of the city gates might be delivered to them, and that all things be done by their order and appointment.

The mayor and his brethren, therefore, conſulting together what was beſt to be done in this perplexed ſtate, reſolved neither to conſent to the requeſts of thoſe who were without, nor to the demands of them who were within. But giving good words to both parties, they pacified them; and kept cuſtody of the city, being the chamber of the King, and parcel of the revenues of the crown; which they were in duty and allegiance bound to maintain for his uſe.

With all ſpeed they therefore rampired up the gates, fortified the walls, appointed guards, and did every thing requiſite to put the city in the beſt ſtate of defence poſſible. Yet in proceſs of time, for want of due forecaſt, proviſions began to wax ſhort; and a famine, 'twas feared, would be the conſequence (which neither the commons could or would endure), if ſome method to prevent the ſame was not hit upon. Yet they had that regard to their own faith and ſafety, that they patiently ſubmitted to endure every want, till ſuch time as it ſhould pleaſe a good God to bring about their deliverance; which he effected in about twelve days after the ſiege was begun, by the mediation of certain canons of the Cathedral. Soon after this followed the battle of Edgecourt; wherein the Duke of Clarence and the Earl of Warwick being worſted, they fled unto this city; and entering the ſame the 3d day of *April*, 1470, lay in the Biſhop's Palace a few days. Meanwhile they cauſed ſhips to be prepared at Dartmouth, and took paſſage to Calais. The King being informed which way his enemies were gone, purſued them with an army of 40,000 men, and came to this city the 14th of *April* 1470, having in his company divers great Lords, namely, the Biſhop of Ely, Lord Treaſurer of England, the Duke of Norfolk, Earl Marſhal of England, the Duke of Suffolk, the Earl of Arundel, the Earl of Wiltſhire, ſon to the Duke of Buckingham, the Earl of Shrewſbury, the Earl Rivers, the Lord Haſtings, the Lord Grey, of Codnor, the Lords Audley, Saye, Stourton, Mountjoy, Stanley, Dacres, and Ferrers, and the Baron of Dudley; with a great number of knights and gentlemen. But they came too late; for the Duke and Earl were gone to ſea, as above related.

The mayor being advertiſed of their coming, gave order to every citizen and inhabitant, being of ability, to provide himſelf a gown of the city's livery, which was then of red colour, and to be in readineſs for receiving the King; which was accordingly done. And when he was come near to the city, the Mayor being attended by 400 perſons, in good and ſeemly apparel, went to the ſouth gate, and without the ſame attended the King's coming. On his arrival the Mayor did his humble obeiſance; and Thomas Dowriſh, Eſq. then recorder of the city, made an oration, congratulating his coming to the city: which ended, the Mayor delivered unto him the keys of the gates, and the maces of his office, and therewith a purſe of 100 nobles in gold; which he took very thankfully. The money he kept, but the keys and the maces he delivered back to the Mayor, who bore the mace through the city bare-headed before him, until he came to his lodgings. (*Izacke* ſays, that the Queen and Prince being likewiſe then there, the city preſented to them 20l. a piece in gold.) After the King had reſted here three days he ſet out on his return to London."

† "Jones Polwhyle de = Alicia, fil. et unica
"Polwhyle, 37. Henr. VI. | hæres Oth. Lukie.

"OTHO Polwheile de = Maria fil. et unica hæres
"Polwheile, fil. et hær. | Walter Killigrew."

* * * * * * * * * * * *

See Pedigree, in Hiſt. of Cornwall, Vol. II.

of Polwhele was reduced to ruins: and it was ſo reduced, probably, by the adherents of Queen Margaret.

In the conteſt between RICHARD III. and the Earl of Richmond, the gentlemen of Cornwall and Devon were for the moſt part, hoſtile to Richard. The King, however, with the activity natural to his character, came down to Exeter, and tried all the means in his power to conciliate the affections of the people. But, ſuſpecting diſloyalty from his own obſervation of the movements of the nobility, and ſtruck by a circumſtance which he conſidered as ominous, he left the city with a melancholy preſentiment of his fate. Of the incident to which I allude, *Shakſpeare* has made a poetical uſe:

> " *Richmond!*—When laſt I was at Exeter,
> The mayor in courteſy ſhew'd me the caſtle,
> And call'd it, *Rougemont:* at which name I ſtarted;
> Becauſe a bard of Ireland told me once,
> I ſhould not live long after I ſaw *Richmond*."†

Among thoſe who were ill-diſpoſed to favour the pretenſions of Richard, were *Courtenay* and *Edgecumbe*. And men of ſuch influence, were truly formidable.

> " My gracious ſovereign, now in Devonſhire,
> As I by friends am well advertized,
> *Sir Edward Courtenay*, and the haughty prelate,
> Biſhop of Exeter, his elder brother,
> With many more confederates, are in arms."*

In theſe times, the great majority of the people of Cornwall (as well as the iſland at large) were much attached to their lords or leaders: " and ſo much were they addicted (ſays *Carew*) to the name of COURTENAY, that they readily followed Sir Edward Courtenay and his brother, Peter Biſhop of Exeter, what time they aſſiſted the Duke of Buckingham in his revolt againſt Richard the third." But, on the diſperſion of the Duke of Buckingham's army, ſuch a panic ſeized the Devonians and the Corniſh, that throwing down their arms, they fled, ſome into ſanctuaries, and others beyond ſea, particularly into Britany.‡ From the circumſtance of his favouring

† Malone's *Shakſpeare*, vol. vi. p. 565. " In 1484, Richard III. came to Exeter, but in a very ſecret manner, whom the mayor and his brethren received in the beſt manner they could, and preſented him a purſe of 200 nobles, which he thankfully accepted. During his abode there, he went about the city, and viewed the ſame. At length he came to the caſtle; and when he underſtood that it was called Rugemont, ſuddenly fell into a dump, and (as one aſtoniſhed) ſaid, " Well, I ſee my days be not long." He ſpake this of a propheſy told him, that when he came once to Richmond, he ſhould not live long after: which fell out in the end to be true; not in reſpect to this caſtle, but in reſpect of Henry Earl of Richmond, who the next year following met him at Boſworth Field, where he was ſlain. Finding, during his ſtay here, that the gentlemen of this country were not well affected towards him; and hearing alſo, after his departure, that the Marquiſs of Dorſet, the Biſhop of Exceſter, and ſundry other gentlemen of rank and fortune, were in a confederacy againſt him, in favour of the Earl of Richmond, he ſent down John Lord Scroope with a commiſſion to keep a ſeſſion; who ſat at Torrington: and then and there were indicted of high treaſon Thomas Marquiſs of Dorſet, Peter Biſhop of Exceſter, Thomas Sentleger, and Thomas Fulford, Knights, as principals; and Robert Willoughby, and Thomas Arundell, Knights, John Arundell, Dean of Exceſter, David Hopton, Archdeacon of Exceſter, Oliver Abbat of Buckland, Bartholemew Sentleger, William Chilſon, Thomas Greenfielde, Richard Edgecombe, Robert Burnbie, Walter Courtneie, Thomas Brown, Edward Courtneie, Hugh Lutterell, John Crocker, John Hallewill, and 500 others, were indicted as acceſſaries. All which fled, and ſhifted for themſelves, ſome into Britaine (in France) and ſome elſewhere, ſaving, Sir Thomas Sentleger, and one Sir John Rame, who were brought to Exceſter, and there, at the Carfox, beheaded." *Hooker*.

* *Shakſpeare*, vol. vi. p. 589.

‡ *Moore*.

favouring the Earl of *Richmond, Sir Richard Edgecumbe was narrowly purfued by the fervants of the crown. And in the days of our hiftorian Carew, there was a tradition in the neighbourhood, that Sir Richard concealed himfelf in thofe thick woods at Cuttayle, which overlook the river. In this fituation, whilft his enemy was clofe at his heels, he put a ftone in his cap and tumbled it into the water. His purfuers, looking down to the fpot whence the noife iffued, and feeing a cap fwimming on the water, fuppofed that he had defperately drowned himfelf, and gave over the purfuit. Sir Richard efcaped into Britany, with† many of his neighbours.

After the battle of Bofworth, Sir Richard Edgecumbe, Sir Edmund Carew, and Sir Hugh Trevanion,‡ among others, received the honour of knighthood in the field: and on the acceffion of the Earl of Richmond (now HENRY VII.) to the crown, Sir Richard Edgecumbe was made one of the privy council, and ftill more fubftantially rewarded by the whole hereditary eftate of Sir Henry Trenowth, of Bodrigan,§ Knight, and with the caftle and lordfhip of Totnes, and other lands of John Lord Zouch, all forfeited by attainder on the part of King Richard the third.‖ In the mean time, the name of ARUNDEL, and indeed others

¶of

* "I have heard the inhabitants about Caufam Bay report, (fays Carew,) that the Earl of Richmond (afterwards Henry the feventh) while he hovered upon the coaft, here by ftealth refrefhed himfelf; but being advertized of ftraight watch kept for his furprizing at Plymouth, he richly rewarded his hoft, hied fpeedily a fhipboard, and efcaped happily to a better fortune." *Carew*, f. 99.

† On his return, he built a chapel on the very fpot where he had concealed himfelf, in grateful remembrance of his fingular delivery. "Sir Richard Edgecombe (fays *Cleaveland*) was concerned in the infurrection that was made by the Bifhop of Exeter, Sir Edward Courtenay and other gentlemen of the weft againft Richard the 3d; and when the Duke of Buckingham's army whom they had a defign to join, were difperfed, and he taken and put to death; the weftern gentlemen were forced to difperfe to fave their lives; and Sir Richard Edgecombe went to his own houfe and hid himfelf, and King Richard fent a party of men to feize him. Sir Richard hearing of their coming, fled to a wood near his houfe," and eluded his purfuers, as above mentioned. "Sir Richard got over into Britany, to the Earl of Richmond; and afterwards came over to England with him, and was at the battle of Bofworth, and was in great favour with him, when he became King of England; and the King as foon as he came to the throne, gave him the caftle and honour of Totnes, which came to the crown by the attainder of John Lord Zouch: the King alfo made Sir Richard Edgecombe, comptroller of his houfehold, and of the privy council, and employed him in divers ambaffies. He was fent ambaffadour to the King of Scots, and into Britany, where he died." *Cleaveland*, p. 289.

‡ It is fuppofed, Sir Hugh Trevanion was made a Knight Banneret at this conjuncture. The fword with which he was dubbed, is ftill to be feen at Carhayes; and his arms are cut in ftone there, over the door in the firft court, with a lion and a ftag for fupporters; and this motto under it: *Loyante mon Orgueil.*

§ He was knighted by King Edward 4, or King Richard 3, by the name of Sir Henry Bodrigan. Siding with King Richard 3, at the battle of Bofworth Field, he was, with many others, attainted of treafon againft King Henry VII. And in order to fhun juftice, he made his efcape after the battle aforefaid, and fecretly repaired to Bodrigan; where he was kept clofe for a feafon; but not fo private but King Henry's officers got notice thereof, and at an appointed time befet the fame in queft of him. Which underftanding, he by a back-door, fled from thence, and ran down the hill to the fea-cliff near the fame, the officers purfuing fo quick after him, that he could not poffibly make his efcape. As foon therefore, as he came to the cliff, above an hundred foot high, he leap'd down into the fea, upon the little graffy ifland there, without much hurt or damage. Where inftantly a boat which he had prepared in the Cove, attended him there, which tranfported him to a fhip that carried him into France. Which aftonifhing fact and place, is to this day well known and remember'd by the name of Herry Bodrigan's leap, or jump. But notwithftanding his own efcape beyond the feas; this lordfhip and his whole eftate, were forfeited and feiz'd by King Henry 7, for attainder of treafon; and the greateft part thereof, he fettled upon Sir Richard Edgcumb, and his heirs forever; whofe property are ftill in poffeffion thereof. This Sir Richard Edgcumb but four years before, on fufpicion of being confederated with the Earl of Richmond againft King Richard 3, (as tradition faith) was fhrewdly fought after, and perfued by means of this very Sir Henry Bodrigan, in order to be taken into cuftody; who from his houfe at Cutteel, made alfo a wonderful efcape, and got into France, to the Earl of Richmond." *Hals*, p. 151. Sir Henry Bodrigan fled into Ireland. What became of him afterwards is uncertain. Some fay, that he came over to affift John Earl of Lincoln, and was flain with the Earl, at the battle of Stoke. With him, however, terminated the greatnefs of the family. It is faid that Sir Henry forfeited an eftate of ten thoufand pounds a year. See *Tonkin's* MSS.

‖ "On 5 December, 1485, 1ft Henry VII. the King, fully confiding in the loyalty, care, and induftry of Sir *Richard Edgecombe*, Knight, comptroller of his houfehold and of his privy council, appointed Sir Richard, with *John Arundel*, Dean of of St. Peter's Church, in Exeter, one of his privy council, and *John Baldifwell*, L. L. D. clerk of the council, to meet and treat with all captains, lieutenants, officers, perfons paying tribute or inhabitants in the town of Callis, tower of

Rifebank,

Rifebank, tower and caftle of Guynes, caftle of Hammes, and marches thereof, relating to all matters that concerned the crown of England in the faid places, and to admit all perfons therein to their allegiance.* In 2 Henry VII. Sir Richard Edgecombe was fheriff† of Devon; and that year brought aid to the King at the battle of Stoke, near Newark; where John Earl of Lincoln, the Lord Lovell and their adherents were vanquifhed. After which, the King removing to Lincoln, and thence into Yorkfhire, came about the middle of Auguft to Newcaftle-upon-Tyne; where, as *Stowe* writes, he fent ambaffadors into Scotland, Richard Fox, Bifhop of Winchefter, D. Privy-Seal, and Sir Richard Edgecomb, Knight, comproller of his houfe, to conclude a peace or truce with James King of Scotland. It appears that the Englifh ambaffadors were honorably received, and would have concluded a peace with the Scotch Monarch, had his people been averfe to it; that they made a truce for feven years; and that Henry VII. ftayed at Newcaftle till their return. *Fuller's* Worthies, p. 270.

3d Henry VII. Sir Richard Edgcombe was fent into Ireland, being a perfon of fingular prudence, (as Sir James Ware obferves, in his annals of Ireland, p. 10.) to take the oaths of allegiance and obedience, as well of the nobility, gentry and prime officers, as of the commonalty of the realm; and brought over with him 500 armed men. Among the manufcripts in the Cotton Library, is a journal of his expedition, containing many particulars, unobferved by our hiftorians, both of England and Ireland. I fhall recite, therefore, the moft material part of this journal, which Mr. Anftis, a native of Cornwall, and Garter King at arms, believed to have been written by himfelf. On 23d June, 3 Hen. 7. Sir Richard Eggecomb, Knt. took fhipping at Mount's Bay, in Cornwall, in the Anne, of Fowey, and arrived at Kingfale, the 27th. He landed there 28th of June, at the requeft of the Lord Courcy, and of the Portreve, who delivered him the keys of the town in the King's name; and he then gave them the King's pardon, and alfo took the oaths of allegiance and fealty, of the Lord Thomas Parry. The fame night he embarked and failed towards Develyn, (Dublin) and the 29th croffed the feas, the wind being contrary. 30th June, at fix in the morning, he arrived at Waterford, and landed in the afternoon, when the mayor and worfhipful men, honourably received him; and he lodged at the mayor's houfe. 1ft July the mayor had him about the city, fhewed him the walks and reparations, and then went to Guildhall, where the council was affembled; and the mayor fhewed him the ftate of the city, and difpofition of divers great men, and of the common people, telling him, he underftood that he had brought with him the King's pardon for the Earl of Kildare, always an enemy to their city. At night he went on board, and put to fea July 2, failing towards Develyn, the wind contrary. 3d July, with great difficulty, and tempeftuous fea, he made Lambay Ifland, on the coaft of Develyn, and fent a man on fhore, to enquire for the Bifhop of Cloconnen, or Thomas Dartas, or Richard the King's porter, with an intent to notify his arrival, and to have knowledge of the difpofition of the country, and of his fure coming to land. 4th July, Thomas Dartas, came on board Sir Richard, and told him, the Earl of Kildare was gone on pilgrimage, but that he would be there in four or five days, and defired him to ftay at Develyn in the mean feafon, to take his eafe. 5th July, Sir Richard landed at Malehide, where he was received by Mr. Talbot, who made him good chear; and in the afternoon, the Bifhop of Meath, and others came to him, and accompanied him to Develyn, where the Mayor, and principal perfons of the city, received him at the Black Frier's Gate, and they lodged him in the faid Friers. 6th July, Sir Richard waited for the Earl of Kildare, and other Lords of Ireland coming to him. 7th and 8th July, he continued there, preparing matters he had to deliver to the Lords, and the Archbifhop of Develyn came to him. 9th, the Bifhop of Cloconnen, and the Treafurer of Ireland, came to him to his lodgings. 10th July, he ftill waited for the Earl of Kildare's arrival there, as he did the 11th, to his great cofts. 12th July, the Earl of Kildare came to St. Thomas's Convent, within the walls of Develyn, with 200 horfes, and fent the Bifhop of Meath, and the Baron of Slaa, with divers others, to Sir Richard, who conveyed him to the Earl, where in a great chamber he received and welcomed him. Howbeit Sir Richard made not reverence to him, and the Lords there affembled; but openly delivered the Earl the King's letters, which being read, they all went to a privy-chamber, when he declared his meffage from the King, and the caufe of his coming, but divers of the Lords being abfent, they took five days to anfwer; and that night the Earl went to his place called Mayoneth, twelve miles from Develyn; and Sir Richard continued in his lodgings. 13th July, Sir Richard went to Chrift-Church, and there caufed the Bifhop of Meath, to declare as well the Pope's Bull of accurfing, and the abfolution for the fame, as the King's pardon to fuch as would do their duty; and that day the Archbifhop of Develyn, Bifhop of Meath, and divers great men, dined with Sir Richard at his lodgings. Monday 14th July, Sir Richard, at the requeft of the Earl of Kildare, went to Mayoneth, where the Earl entertained him with good chear, promifing to conform in all things to the King's pleafure, fo as to content the mind of Sir Richard. 15th July, he continued with the Earl, where came the chief of the Lords, and others of the council, and had great communications, but nothing was done that day, and Sir Richard was put off till the next day. Wednefday 16th July, Sir Richard expected that the Earl would have done as was agreed over night; but he, the faid Earl and his council, made unreafonable delays, which difpleafed Sir Richard, who plainly and fharply told them of their unfitting demeanour. And that day the Earl, with the Lords and council, and Sir Richard came again to Develyn. Thurfday 17th July, the Earl and other Lords, held a great council at St. Thomas's Convent, where they agreed to become the King's true fubjects, as they faid; and would give fureties, as could be devifed by the King's laws, but would not affent to the bond of Nifi; and certain of the faid council came three or four times that day to Sir Richard, and required him to leave off calling for the bond, with which he not complying, and giving fhort anfwers, angry words arofe that day, fo no conclufion was taken. The fame day, the Lord Gormanfton dined with Sir Richard at his lodgings. Friday 18th July, the Earl of Kildare, and council affembled, and in the afternoon gave Sir Richard for anfwer, that they would in no wife be bound in the faid bond of Nifi, and rather than do it, they would become Yryfhe every of them. The faid Sir Richard, hearing that the common voice in Develyn, and all the country, was that the King of Scots was dead; and confidering the danger of leaving them in their erroneous opinion, he at laft condefcended, that the Earl of Kildare, and all the Lords of the land, fhould be fworn on the facrament, for their affurance unto the King, in fuch a form as fhould be devifed by the faid Sir Richard; and that night, Sir Richard devifed as fure an oath as he could. Saturday

G

* *Rymer's Fœdera*, vol. 12, p. 279. In the ftatute of Refumptions made 1ft of Henry VII. there is an exception, that the fame fhall not extend to Sir Richard Eggecomb, Knight, for the offices of Feodary of the Dutchy of Cornwall, the conftablefhip of the caftle of Launcefton, and of the caftle of Hertford, and manor of Bufhy, in the county of Hertford.

† *Stowe's* Annals, p. 273.

day 19th July, Sir Richard fent to the faid Earl, and council the oath; who made great queftions and doubts thereon. So in the afternoon Sir Richard went in perfon to them, but they making great delays, came to no conclufion. Sunday 20th July, the Earl and council, agreed to be fworn upon the holy facrament, to be the King's true liegemen, from thenceforth, according to the oath agreed on, between them and Sir Richard, which was to be certified to the King, under their feals; and offered to be fworn in the afternoon, to which Sir Richard would not confent; but would have them be fworn in the forenoon, and that a chaplain of his own fhould confecrate the hoft, as they fhould be fworn upon; and fo deferred it to the next day. At night the treafurer of Ireland, and Lord Gormanfton, fupped with Sir Richard. Monday 21ft July, Sir Richard went, at the defire of the Earl of Kildare, to the Monaftery of St. Thomas the Martyr, where the Lords and Council were affembled, and in the great chamber, called the King's Chamber. Sir Richard firft took homage of the faid Earl, and of other Lords. After which the faid Earl went into another chamber, where Sir Richard's chaplain was at mafs; and in mafs time the faid Earl was fhriven, and affoiled, from the curfe he ftood in by virtue of the Pope's Bull, and before the agnes of the faid mafs, the hoft was divided into three parts; and the prieft turning about, holding the three parts upon the patten, in the prefence of many, the Earl holding his right hand over the hoft, made his folemn oath of allegiance to King Henry the Seventh, and likewife the Bifhops and Lords. All which being done, the Earl with the faid Sir Richard, Bifhops and Lords, went into the church of the faid Monaftery, and, in the chair, the Archbifhop of Develyn began Te Deum, and the choir with the organs fung it up folemnly; and all the bells in the church did ring, which done, the Earl and greateft part of the Lords, went with Sir Richard, and dined with him, and had much good chear; Sir Richard at the faid Earl's homage, put a collar of the King's Livery about his neck, which he wore throughout the faid city of Develyn. Tuefday 22d July, Sir Richard went about nine of the bell in the morning, to the Guildhall within the city, where the Mayor, Bailiff, and Commonalty, were affembled; and they were fworn to the King, according to fuch form as they had certified under their common feal. Wednefday 23d July, Sir Richard, about eight of the bell, went to the Earl of Kildare, to a place of Canons, called All Hallows, within Develyn; and there had a long communication with him and his council, and after dinner Sir Richard rode twenty-four miles, thence to Drogheda. Thurfday 24th July, Sir Richard took fealty of the Mayor, and town of Drogheda, in the Guildhall, and took fureties for their good abideng towards the King and delivered to them the King's pardon, and lay all that day in the town, and had good chear. Friday 25th July, Sir Richard rode to Trymme, and took fealty of the portreve, burgeffes, and commonalty of the fame. Saturday 26th July, Sir Richard returned to his lodgings, in the Black Friers, in Develyn. Sunday 27th July, he dined with the Recorder of Develyn, and had a great dinner; at which was prefent the Archbifhop of Develyn. Monday 28th July, he continued at Develyn waiting the coming of the Earl of Kildare, and of the Lords, to have their letters, and certificates, to the King. For Sir Richard would in no wife deliver to the Earl the pardon, till he had delivered the aforefaid certificate and obligation. Tuefday 29th, the Earl of Kildare and Lords fpiritual and temporal, came to All-Hallow's Priory, within Develyn; to whom Sir Richard came, and had with them long communication; and underftanding that certain perfons, noted to be the chief caufers of the great rebellion, lately in Ireland; and Juftice Plunket, and the Prior of Kylmaynam, to be among the chiefs; thereupon great inftances were made by the faid Earl, and Lords, to receive them to the King's Grace, which Sir Richard refufed, and that day the Earl and Sir Richard, and many other Lords, dined with Walter Ywers, and in the afternoon they met at St. Mary's Abbey, without Develyn; where Sir Richard took the fealty and homage of many gentlemen; and the Archbifhop of Armac, came to Sir Richard's lodging, and made both his fealty and homage. Wednefday 29th July, the faid Earl, Sir Richard, and the Lords fpiritual and temporal, met at our Lady Church of the Daines in Develyn; and great inftance was made to Sir Richard, to accept of Juftice Plunket, and the Prior of Kilmaynam's fubmiffion to the King's Grace; the faid Sir Richard anfwered fharply, that he knew better the King's commands and inftructions, than they, and gave the Juftice and Prior, fearful and terrible words, infomuch that the faid Earl and Lords, would give no reply, but kept their peace; and after the great ire paft, the faid Earl and Lords laboured, with fuch fair means and proffers, as Sir Richard agreed to admit Juftice Plunket to the King's Grace, and took his homage and fealty; but refufed the Prior of Kylmaynam unto the King's Grace; and then departing unto his lodging, he took with him divers judges, and other noblemen, and went to the Caftle of Develyn, and there put in poffeffion, Richard Archibell, the King's fervant, into the office of Conftable of the faid Caftle; which the King's Grace had given unto him by his letters patent; from the which office, the faid Prior of Kylmaynam had wrongfully kept the faid Richard, by the fpace of two years, and more. And before he departed out of the faid church of Daines, the faid Earl of Kildare, delivered to the faid Sir Richard, both his certificate, upon his oath, under the feal of his arms, as alfo the obligation of his fureties. And there the faid Sir Richard, in the prefence of all the Lords, delivered unto him the King's pardon, under his great feal, in the prefence of all the Lords, and there took his leave of the faid Earl, and Lords fpiritual and temporal. And that day, after dinner, the faid Sir Richard departed out of Develyn, to a place called Dalcay, fix miles from Develyn, where his fhip lay. And the Archbifhop of Develyn, Juftice Bermyngham, and the Recorder of Develyn, with many other nobles, brought him thither; and that night he took his fhip, and lay at Rode all that night, the wind being contrarious unto him; and the fhips fo lay, that he could not get into them without peril. Thurfday the laft day of July, the fhips were gotten out of the faid road, and becaufe the wind was contrarious, he could make no fail; and that night lay befide a place, called Houthe. Friday the firft day of Auguft, the wind being ftill contrarious, the faid Sir Richard caufed the mafter and mariners to take fail, and traverfed in the fea, till it was about four of the clock at afternoon; and the wind began to rife, being ftill contrarious; fo that he was fain to return again to a road, called Lambry, an Ifland about ten miles from Develyn, and there ftay all night. Saturday the fecond day of Auguft, fuch an huge and great tempeft arofe, that no fail might be made, the wind being ftill contrarious. Sunday the third day of Auguft, the aforefaid tempeft endured ftill, and the aforefaid Sir Richard lay that day about the aforefaid ifle; and there he and his company avowed great pilgrimages, that God would ceafe the tempeft, and fend a fair and a large wind. Monday the fourth day of Auguft, the forefaid tempeft endured ftill, and at afternoon, that day, the wind began to come large; but it blew fo much and the coafts were fo jeopardous of fands and rocks, that the fame night the mariners durft not jeopard to take the fea, but lay ftill at anchor about the faid Ifle. Tuefday in the morning, the fifth day of Auguft, the faid Sir Richard made fail, and failed a kenning, and more into the fea; and the wind began to come fo contrarious, and fo many great damages were on every fide, that he was fain to go again to the faid Ifle of Lambrye; and that day at afternoon the wind began to come large and incontinent, the faid Sir Richard caufed fail to be made, and all that afternoon

¶of patriot worth, had an equal claim to refpect, with that of Edgecombe or of Courtenay. We find the Queen, by her letter advertizing John Arundel, of Trerice, Efq. "that fhe was brought in childbed of a Prince."† The reign of Henry the feventh, by no means paffed in tranquillity. But it feems to have owed much of its difturbance to the fiery fpirits of the Cornifh: and in feveral affairs of high importance, in matters that feemed to fhake the throne to its foundations, Cornwall had the honour or the difgrace, of giving the prime impulfe to the national movements. Our annalifts on this fide of the Tamar, have taken no notice of the impoftor Lambert, who landed in Cornwall, raifed a large body of men in this county, marched to Exeter, and laid fiege to the city.‡ No fooner was this impoftor unmafked, than Perkin

G 2 Warbeck,

noon failed on his way, and at night the wind calmed and came again contrarious, and therefore came to an anchor in the open fea, and there lay all night. Wednefday the 6th day of Auguft, the wind being contrarious, the faid Sir Richard caufed the mafter and mariners, to traverfe in the fea homeward; and with great pain that day came againft a rock, called Tufkard, and there lay at anchor all that night, in the open fea; and the wind blew right fore, and was right troublefome weather. Thurfday the 7th of Auguft, the wind came reafonably large, and that day the faid Sir Richard failed, till he came open upon Saynt Yves, in Cornwal; and becaufe the wind fell, the mafter and mariners durft not venture to pafs by the great fea, and perilous jeopardies, at the Land's End; and therefore, all that night, they traverfed in the fea; and that night many fuddain fhowers and winds fell. Friday the 8th day of Auguft, the wind and the fea being troublous, the faid Sir Richard and his fhips came into the haven of Fowey, and there he landed, and went a pilgrimage, to a chapel of Saynt Sauyour; and that night all his company landed. The title of the manufcript, (Titus, b. II, in the Cotton Library,) from whence this was taken, is, original letters and papers concerning Ireland, until the end of Edward VI. and Queen Mary. Sir Richard Edgecomb is ftiled, Privy Councellor, and Comptroller of the Houfehold, to the King. And a further account is given of the names of thofe in Ireland, who took the oath. The recognizances of the Lords fpiritual and temporal. The certificates. The oath of fidelity and allegiance. The oath, devifed by the Lord Chancellor, for the Earl of Kildare. The homage they performed. The Lords of Ireland, certificates to the King of their taking the oaths, and doing allegiance and homage. The recognizance, in a large penalty, to obferve their oath of fealty and allegiance. The bond and condition. The condition for the towns corporate. The bond Nifi, the oath that at laft the Earl of Kildare, and the other Lords fpiritual and temporal took. And fo provident was the King, that Sir Richard Eggecombe had only 300l. fterling allowed him, for his cofts and expences, into, and from the faid kingdom." *Anftis's Regift.* of the Order of the Garter, vol. I. p. 364.

"In 4 Hen. VII. the King reciting, that by advice of his council, he intends to fend into Britany, an army for its relief, he therefore, in full confidence of the loyalty, care, and induftry of Sir Robert Willoughby de Brooke, Knt. Sir *Richard Edgecombe*, Knt. and *Thomas Greynvile*, Knt. commiffions them to fummon and examine what number of archers, armed and arrayed at the King's expence, the county of Cornwall could provide, and to article with them, to review them, and to certify the number of archers that all earls, barons, knights and others are to find, before the Quindenes of Hillary next. Dated at Maydefton, 23d Dec. 1488, 4 Hen. VII." *Rymer's* Fædera, tom. 12, pp. 355, 356.

"Sir Richard Edgcombe was by commiffion bearing date 11th December, 4 Hen. VII. in confideration of his loyalty, induftry, forefight, and care, appointed with Henry Aynfworth, L. L. D. fecondary in the office of privy-feals, to treat with Anne Duchefs of Brittany, refpecting a truce, ceffation of arms, alliance and trade. Alfo, on the 23d December, the King reciting, that by advice of his council, he was fending an army into Britany for its relief. He, therefore, in full confidence of his loyalty and care, was commanded, with Edward Earl of Devon, Robert Lord Willoughby of Broke, and Thomas Greenvile, Efq. to fummon and examine, what number of archers, armed, and arrayed at the King's expence, the county of Cornwall could provide; and to article with them for the fervice, and to review them, and to commit to writing the names of the faid noblemen, knights, and others, and the number of archers they are to find, and to certify the King thereof, before the Quindenes of Hilary next. *Rymer's* Fœdera, vol. 12, pp. 348, 355, 356, 357. *Stowe* relates, that Sir Richard Edgecomb was alfo, fent with John Abbot, of Alington, and Chriftopher Urfwick, to the French King, to offer King Henry's mediation to compofe the differences, between the Duke of Britany, and that monarch. They went firft to the French King, and after to the Duke of Britany; in which fervices, Sir Richard Edgecomb departed this life at Mortlaix, in that Province. *Stowe's* Annals, p. 474.

¶ John Trevelyan of Trevelyan, who had been attainted together with Amyas Pawlet, 1ft Rich. III. was reftored by act of Parliament, 1 Hen. VII. *Rot. Parl.* Carew mentions Sir *John Naphant*, as by birth a Cornifhman; though by inhabitance a Califian, where Henry VII. ufed his fervice in great truft; and Cardinal Wolfey owned him for his mafter. *Carew*, f. 61.

† 3 Henry VII. *Carew*, f. 146.

‡ "*Richard Symons* a crafty prieft took into his tuition one *Lambert*, a witty Dutch boy, perfwading him that he was the only fon of the Duke of Clarence, and the firft heir male of the houfe of York, and therefore inheritable to the crown, who by the advice of his fuppofed Aunt, the Lady Margaret, fifter to King Edward the fourth, and Dutchefs Dowager unto Charles the deceafed Duke of Burgoyn, he (feigning himfelf to be Richard Duke of York, Edward the fourth's fecond fon) arrived in Kent, where being difappointed, failed into Scotland, and from thence into Cornwall, where being fafely landed, and aided with three thoufand men of the meaneft of the people, marched towards Exeter, and befieged it, where, when his fair fpeeches and rhetorical arguments could not perfwade the inhabitants thereof to furrender the city into his hands, he fcaled

Warbeck, a much more formidable rival of the reigning monarch, made pretenſions to the throne. And it is remarkable, that both Lambert and Perkin endeavoured to uſe Cornwall, as an engine for putting their deſigns into execution. We are informed, that not without ſilent and ſecret relation to Perkin's pretences, the Corniſh reſiſted the levy of ſuch payments, as were aſſeſſed for the Scottiſh wars; and that when the collectors came among the Corniſh, they found them "*a ſtout, big, and hardy race of men,*" tumultuouſly aſſembled, and inflamed by one Thomas Flammock, a lawyer, and Michael Joſeph, a blackſmith or horſe-farrier, of Bodmin, like firebrands of rebellion.* In 1497, (ſays *Carew*) "the Corniſhment† repining at a ſubſidy lately graunted Henry the ſeventh, by act of parliament, were induced to rebellion by *Thomas Flammock*, a gentleman, and *Michael Joſeph*, a blackſmith, with whom they marched to Taunton, there murdering the Provoſt of Perin, a commiſſioner for the ſayd ſubſidy, and from thence to Welles, where James Touchet, Lord Audely, degenerated to their party, with which encreaſe they paſſed by Sariſbury to Wincheſter, and ſo into Kent. But by this time, Lords and Commons were gathered in ſtrength, ſufficient to make head againſt them, and ſoone after, Blackheath ſaw the overthrow of their forces, in battell, and London, the puniſh-

ment

ed the walls, and fired the gates thereof, which proving unſucceſsful to him, diſcontentedly departed, and marched eaſtward. The King hearing of this uproar, comes to Exeter, (guarded with an army) in perſon, and having by the way defeated the rebels, and taken many of them priſoners, cauſed them to be brought before him in St. Peter's church-yard (lodging in the Treaſurer's Houſe, where a window between the gate of the ſaid houſe, and the north tower of the Cathedral was erected on purpoſe for the King to behold the ſaid rebels) where they appeared bare-headed, in their ſhirts, and halters about their necks. The King in hope of their reformation and future obedience, graciouſly pardoned them, chuſing rather to waſh his hands in milk by forgiving, than in blood by deſtroying them." *Izacke*, p. 102. According to *Baker*, (p. 244) this happened after Perkin's rebellion. "King Henry, being come to Exeter ſtayed there a few days, about examination of the rebels, and execution of the chief offenders; when the King viewing out of a window made for the purpoſe, after he had pauſed awhile, made a ſpeech unto them, exhorting them to obedience: and in hope they would afterward be dutiful ſubjects, he pardoneth them all. Whereat they made a great ſhout, crying all "God ſave King Henry!" though ſome of them afterwards, like ungrateful wretches, fell into new rebellions." "Lambert was taken into the King's kitchen, to turn the ſpit in the turn of his fortune, and at laſt made one of the King's falconers." *Baker*, p. 238.

* See *Speed*, p. 963, from *Polydore Vergil, Stowe* and *Holinſhed.* According to *Bacon*, the Blackſmith was moved by ambition, believing ſuch an action would add a luſtre to his memory, and that his clowniſh loquacity would procure him the firſt place among the people. The attorney having gained credit by his profeſſion, had ſo far won upon their opinions, than they valued their refuſal of the ſubſidy, and their meeting to be legal and meritorious. The Corniſh, not being all provided with bows and arrows, armed themſelves with ſuch tools as belonged to their ſeveral trades. At Horwood (near Bideford) "that valiant Blackſmith, *Michael Joſeph*, in his way to Taunton, left a badge of his trade on the church door." *Riſdon.* And the inhabitants to this day ſhew a piece of iron faſtened to the church-door; which they call "*Michael Joſeph's badge.*

† The Corniſh conceived that they had no concern in a tax which was raiſed on account of the Scotch war. They had a notion that the northern people were bound by their tenures to defend themſelves. They declared againſt the King's Miniſters; who, they ſaid put him upon fleecing his ſubjects.§ And when they had recourſe to arms, they purſued their route with firmneſs and regularity, committing no devaſtations on their way. This, they maintained as a common cauſe; and they flattered themſelves, that the men of Kent, in particular, would join them in an enterprize ſo intereſting to all. Tho' the King had encamped an numerous army in St. George's Fields, yet the approach of the Corniſh to Deptford, occaſioned a great ſenſation in the city of London. By theſe obſervations, I do not mean to offer an apology for Flammock, or his followers. They were rebels; but not "a rebel route." Their plan was boldly projected, and perſeveringly purſued: its failure was owing to the unuſual quiet of the men of Kent, the inflammability of whoſe ſpirits on ſuch an emergence was no unreaſonable expectation.

§ This inſurrection was not a mere "*rebel route.*" There were ſome gentlemen of conſequence implicated in Flammock's affair. Pencarow gave name and original to an old family of gentlemen, ſurnamed de Pencarow, who, ſiding with Richard 3, againſt Henry 7, as ſome ſay (but others will have it with Flammock, in his inſurrection againſt that King) loſt this place, and other lands, by attainder of treaſon, having before conveyed a great part of his eſtate to Henry, the firſt Lord Marney, of Colquite, to procure a reprieve, or pardon of his life from that King. *Hals*, p. 109.

ment of their feducers by juftice."|| In the fame year, Perkin Warbeck landed in ‡Cornwall, and proceeding to Bodmin, there collected "a rebel rout:" and he was daring enough to march to Exeter, and lay fiege to the city. That Perkin Warbeck was actually the Duke of York,

|| *Carew* f. 97, b. 98. See *Speed*, pp. 964, 965. *Rapin*, vol. 1. pp. 679, 680, 681, 683, 683, 984. In *Kennet's* Complete Hift. of England, (vol. 1. f. 618) the Provoft of Penryn, whom the Cornifh flew at Taunton, is called "an officious and eager commiffioner for the fubfidy." *Hals's* account of Flammock's rebellion is as follows: "Thomas Flammock, a lawyer, in the reign of Henry VII. 1496, together with Michael Jofeph, a fmith of thofe parts, ftirred up the Cornifh to rebellion, under pretence of the feverity of the land tax, though it was but a fubfidy of 120,000l. charged by act of parliament for one year on the 37 fhires in England towards the Scotch war; which could not amount to above 2500l. on this county. But the real defign of this infurrection, was to depofe King Henry, and in his ftead to fet up Henry de la Pole, Earl of Suffolk, the true heir male of the Houfe of York, fifter's fon to King Edward IV. Which being well underftood by the inhabitants of Cornwall, gave Flammock and Jofeph opportunity to raife an army fo formidable, that John Baffet, of Tihiddy, then fheriff, with his poffe comitatus, durft not encounter them. Wherefore, they marched with their army confifting of about 6000 men, from Bodmin, to Launcefton, and from thence into Devon; where alfo, they appeared fo tremendous, that Sir William Carew, Knight, then fheriff thereof, with his poffe comitatus, would not venture a battle with them; but fuffered them (either thro' fear or affection) to pafs through his Bailiwick into Somerfetfhire, and fo to Taunton there; in which place they flew the Provoft Perrin, a commiffioner for the fubfidy, and then advanced to Wells; where James Twitchet, Lord Audley, knowing the myftery of their defign, confederated with them, and became their general. Soon after they publifhed their declaration of pretended grievances, chiefly concerning the faid land tax, and wholly laying the blame of that exaction upon John Morton, Archbifhop of Canterbury, and Reginald Braye, Knight, two of the King's council, whom they would have removed from their ftation. Upon which pretence (and the fecret referve aforefaid) the people, being better affected to the Houfe of York than Lancafter, fuffered thofe rebels quietly to march from Wells to Salifbury, from Salifbury to Winchefter, and fo into Kent; where they expected great affiftance. But contrary to promife, no perfon came to their help. But on the contrary: for the King there appeared in arms againft them, the Earl of Kent, the Lord Aburgain, Sir John Brook, Lord Cobham, and divers other gentlemen, with great force to ftop their farther proceedings that way. On which difappointment, the rebels turned their march towards London, and encamped upon Blackheath. There they were foon encountered by Giles Lord Daubeny, King Henry's general, who after a fhort conflict with them, and the lofs of 300 foldiers on the King's part, and 2000 on the rebel's fide, the remainder fell into defpair, threw down their arms, craved mercy and yielded themfelves prifoners. The King pardoned many, but of the chief authors of the infurrection none. The Lord Audley was committed to Newgate, and from thence drawn to Towerhill in his coat-armour, (painted on paper) reverfed and all torn, where he was beheaded. Flammock and Jofeph were hanged, drawn, and quartered, and had their heads and quarters pitched upon ftakes, fet up in London and other places, June 26, 1496." *Hals*, p. 24. "Sir John Seymour was one of the commanders of thefe forces, that vanquifhed the Lord Audley, and the Cornifh rebels at Blackheath, 12 Henry VII. Where for his valiant deportment, he was knighted by the King in the field of battle." See *Collins*. vol. 1. p. 27. [Edit, 1735] "Three hundred on the King's fide were flain; moftly by arrows, for the Cornifh ufed very ftrong bows and arrows of a yard in length." See *Hollinfhed*, *Bacon*.

‡ "September 1497, Perkin landed at Whitfand-Bay, in Cornwall, with four little barks, and only 140 men. Three thoufand Cornifh in arms, received him at Bodmin. He had three chief counfellers, a broken mercer, a taylor, and a fcrivener. They proceeded to Exeter." See *Bacon*, *Hollinfhed*, *Speed*. "About the year of our Lord 1496, when James the 4th, King of Scotland, upon a truce with King Henry the 7th, of England, had expulfed from Scotland that counterfeit fham Prince Perkin Warbeck, the pretended Richard of Shrewfbury, youngeft fon of King Edward the 4th, who had before been murdered in the Tower of London; to whom he had given in marriage his near kinfwoman, the Lady Catherine Gordon; he, together with his wife and family, failed from thence over into Ireland, to feek friendfhip of the rebels and all others well-affected to the Houfe of York. Where being arrived, and fortune favouring him according to his expectation, news was brought him there, that the Cornifh rebels were ready to renew their former hoftility, and venture their lives in battle upon the title of the Houfe of York, againft that of Lancafter, had they a valiant and able general to lead them; notwithftanding Flammock and his confederates, under the fame engagement, were defeated and executed 1495. Thefe tidings were acceptable to Perkin, who thereupon confulted his privy counfellers Hearne, Aftley, and Skelton, a mercer, a taylor, and a fcrivener, all bankrupts. Thefe all agree *nemine contradicente*, that his four fhips of war fhould forthwith be rigged and manned for an expedition into Cornwall, which accordingly being prepared, himfelf with his lady, and 120 foldiers embarked thereon, and being favoured with a fair wind, took his leave of his Irifh friends, and in the month of September 1499, 15 Henry the 7th (*Carew's* Sur. Corn. p. 98), came fafely to anchor in St. Michael's Mount's Bay. Where, foon after, he landed and went up to the Mount, and made himfelf known to the monks and other inhabitants, publifhing himfelf to be the true and real Richard of Shrewfbury, the true head of the Houfe of York. Which the monks greatly affected to that title, were fo very ready to believe, that they yielded up the mount and garrifon without refiftance into his hands; who prefently renewed the old fortifications, and put the fame into a better pofture of defence.—Which having done, himfelf with a band of foldiers marched from thence to Bodmin, where the rendezvous of Flammock's rebels in thofe parts formerly was; in which place, by falfe words and promifes, he fo prevailed with the difcontented rebels of that town and contiguous country, that he foon got together without money or reward, at leaft three thoufand men that could bear arms: thefe he divided into companies and bands and regiments, under captains, majors, and colonels, expert in war to inftruct them in military difcipline; till at length his army grew to 6000 well-armed foldiers. Thereupon King Henry the 7th, having notice of Perkin's landing and formidablenefs in thofe parts, ordered Sir Peter Edgecomb, Knight, then fheriff of Cornwall, whofe father,

ther, Sir Richard Edgecomb, Knight, was one of that King's privy counfellers, and (that King) had comparatively been raifer to his great eftate by his boons and favour: that he fhould forthwith, by virtue of his office, raife the country, and give battle to this counterfeit Richard of Shrewfbury, and his confederate rebels. Whereupon the fheriff did as he was commanded, and raifed an army of 20,000 men, as tradition faith; and led them towards Bodmin. But when they approached near, and faw Perkin entrenched at Caftle Kynock, on the eaft-hill of Bodmin Downs, with the body of his army, and divers troops of horfe, and bands of foot placed towards Lanhydrock, and the roads from Cardinham, in order to refift and oppofe the fheriff; his men refolved to march no further, but to return from whence they came, without giving battle. Which accordingly they did, notwithftanding the fheriff's threats and commands to the contrary, in great terror, confufion and aftonifhment. But, whether this fear proceeded from the cowardice of the fheriff and his men, or their difaffection to the Lancaftrian dominion of King Henry, is uncertain; for the like fact was committed two years before, by the poffe comitatus of John Baffet, then fheriff, which he had raifed to fupprefs Flammock's rebellion.—Upon news of this flight and difbanding of the fheriff's army, Perkin was faluted by his foldiers and confederates as King of England; and foon after, not only in this camp, but in divers places of Bodmin town, was proclaimed by a trumpeter and others, King of England and France, and Lord of Ireland, with great fhouts and acclamations of the people and bonfires; by the name of Richard the 4th. And 'tis reported he affumed majefty with fuch a boon grace and affable deportment, that immediately he won the affections and admiration of all that made addreffes unto him; in which art of kingfhip he had long before been educated and inftructed by his pretended Aunt, Margaret Dutchefs of Burgundy, fifter to King Edward the 4th; which he had alfo acted to the good liking of all that faw him in the Burgundian, Irifh, Scots, and French courts. And moreover, befides his magifterial port and mien, being an incomparable counterfeit, a natural crafty lier and diffembler, ("qui nefcit diffimulare nefcit regnare," as the old proverb faith); fo that, in fhort time, he grew fo popular and formidable about Bodmin, that no power durft oppofe him there. But alas! this Cornifh regniculum gave him no content; for his pride and ambition put him upon further expedients, viz. to get poffeffion of the whole kingdom of England, and reduce it alfo to his obedience. In order to which, with a well-prepared army of 4000 men, and 2000 of other forts, he marched out of Cornwall into Devon; where met him alfo great numbers of volunteers of that county and Somerfet, that joined with his forces. The dread whereof, fo terrified James Chudleigh, Efq. then fheriff of Devon, and the power of his Bailywick, raifed to ftop his march to Exon; that they durft not give him battle or obftruct his paffage, till he came before that city, pitched his camp and laid fiege thereto.—Upon whofe approaches, the citizens fhut their gates, and prepared to defend themfelves; when, foon after, he fent a meffage or fummons to them, in the name of Richard the 4th, King of England, commanding to furrender the fame to him upon their allegiance. But the citizens fo ridiculed his pretended title, and flighted his fummons; that by his own meffenger they gave him defiance; at which time Dr. Richard Redman, was Lord Bifhop of Exon, William Burgoigne, Efq. recorder; William Froft, mayor; Francis Gilbert, fwordbearer; John Bucknam, William Wilkinfon, John Doncafter, and Richard Howel, were ftewards or bayliffs; John Cladworthy, John Bonefant, Philip Bullock, John Wilkin, Nicholas Auburne, John Atwell, William York, Thomas Lanwordaby, Philip Binks, John Slugg, Thomas Andrews, Thomas Oliver, and others aldermen. (See *Ifacke's* Memorials of Exon, 1499.)*—Soon after this defiance given, Perkin and his foldiers furrounded the city-walls, and attempted to fcale the fame in feveral places, daily for fome time; but always repulfed with confiderable lofs, by the valour of the citizens. During which fiege, they fent to King Henry, for his aid and affiftance, in this great diftrefs. Whereupon the Lord Daubeny was ordered to raife forces, and march towards Exeter therewith; in order to remove the fiege thereof. But, before he came, Edward Courtenay 16th Earl of Devon, and the Lord William his fon, accompanied with Sir Edmund Carew, Sir Thomas Fulford, Sir William Courtney,

* (To ufe the words of *Holinfhed*,) "determined firft of all to affaie the winning of Excefter."—"Then hafting thither," continues our author, "he laid fiege to it; and wanting ordnance to make batterie, ftudied all waies poffible to breake the gates; and what with cafting of ftones, heaving with iron barres, and kindling of fire under the gates, he omitted nothing that could be devifed for the furtherance of his purpofe. The citizens perceiving in what danger they ftood, firft let certeine meffengers downe by cords over the wall, that might certifie the King of their neceffitie and trouble. And herewith taking unto them boldneffe of courage, determined to repell fire with fire, and caufed fagots to be brought and laid to the inward parts of the gates, and fet them all on fire; to the intent that the fire being inflamed on both fide the gates, might as well keepe out their enemies from entering, as fhut in the citizens from fleeing out; and that they, in the meane feafon, might make trenches and rampires to defeat their enemies inftead of gates and bulworks. Thus by fire was the citie preferved from fire. Then Perkin of verie neceffitie compelled to forfake the gates, affaulted the towne in diverfe weake and unfortified places, and fet up ladders to take the citie. But the citizens, with help of fuch as were come forth of the countrie adjoining to their aid, fo valiantlie defended the walles, that they flue above two hundred of Perkin's fouldiers at that affault. The King having advertifement of this fiege of Excefter, hafted forth with his hoft, in as much fpeed as was poffible, and fent the Lord Daubeneie with certaine bands of light horfemen before, to advertife all men of his comming at hand. But in the meane feafon, the Lord Edward Courtneie, Earl of Devonfhire, and the valiant Lord William his fonne, accompanied with Sir Edmund Carew, Sir Thomas Trenchard, Sir William Courtneie, Sir Thomas Fulford, Sir John Halewell, Sir John Croker, Walter Courtneie, Peter Edgecombe, William Saint Maure, with all fpeed, came into the citie of Excefter, and holpe the citizens; and at the laft affault was the Earle hurt in the arme with an arrow, and fo were many of his companie, but verie few flaine. When Perkin faw that he could not win the citie, when he faw it was fo well fortified with men and munitions, he departed from thence, and went unto Taunton." "Henry (marching hither to fupprefs Perkin Warbeck) whom having vanquifhed, he entred the city, and lodged here certain days in the treafurer's houfe of the cathedral church, and adjoyning to the north tower thereof, he heartily thanked the citizens for their faithful and valiant fervice done againft the rebels, promifed them the fulnefs of his favour, and (for an addition of honour to the faid city) gave them a fword taken from his fide, and *alfo a cap of maintenance*, commanding that for the future in all publick places within the faid city, the fame fword fhould be born before the mayor as formerly, as for the like purpofe his noble predeceffor King Edward the fourth had done, and the faid cap to be worn accordingly, whereupon a fword-bearer was elected and fworn to attend that office. *Izaac's Exeter.*

York, is maintained by Horace Walpole: and there is great plaufibility in his arguments. Yet, on this fubject Walpole and Hume have both advanced pofitions which are by no means tenable.* In the prefent reign the Cornifh hiftorian is acquainted with no other memorable occurrences; excepting, indeed, the nuptials of Prince Arthur and the Lady Catherine of Spain.†

The

ney, Sir John Halwell, Sir John Crocker, Walter Courtney, Peter Edgecomb, William St. Maure, Richard Whiteleigh of Efford, (fheriff of Devon the year after), Richard Hals, of Kenedon, John Fortefcue, of Vallapit, James Chudleigh aforefaid, and other gentlemen of thofe parts, had raifed a confiderable army of foldiers; with which they marched towards the rebels. At the fight of whofe approach, Perkin and his hoft were as much difpirited then, as they were elevated before. Whereupon he called a council of war, in which it was unanimoufly agreed upon, that it was not advifable to give them battle, being at leaft 10,000 fighting men; but to diflodge from their trenches, and leave the fiege of that place, and forthwith to march into Somerfetfhire, a county better affected to King Perkin, where he might raife more foldiers. Accordingly, this order of council was obferved and put in practice: fo that, the night after, Perkin and all his army marched towards Taunton; where he muftered his men, as if he meant to give battle. But when by the mufter-roll he faw, what numbers of men had deferted him in his nightly march from Exon, falling then much fhort of 6000; and further notice being brought him, that King Henry was in purfuit of him, with a much greater army, he forefaw the worft, and doubted that fortune would favour him no longer in his military and regal practices; and therefore contrived for the prefervation of himfelf, with 60 horfe-troopers, to forfake his army by night, and fly to the Abbey of Beaulieu, in Southampton, as refting upon the name and privilege of the place, where he took fanctuary. As foon as King Henry underftood Perkin had deferted his foldiers, and had taken fanctuary at Beaulieu; he forthwith ordered a band of foldiers to guard and furround that abbey, to prevent his efcape beyond the feas; from whence it appears, that at that time the privilege of fanctuary was allowed to traitors. So that Perkin, defpairing of getting thence, fubmitted to the King's mercy, and was committed prifoner to the tower of London; from whence he made an efcape, and fled to the Priory of Sheen at Richmond. Where, on condition of making a true confeffion who he was, in a pair of ftocks fet before Weftminfter-Hall door, and true anfwer make to fuch queftions as fhould be demanded, the Prior got the King's pardon for him; and accordingly he fat in the ftocks a whole day before Weftminfter-Hall Door, afterwards on a fcaffold in Cheapfide, openly reading; declaring, and giving manufcripts under his own hand; wherein he told his parentage, the place of his birth, the paffage of his life, that he was a cheat, an impoftor, and by what ways and means he was drawn into thofe treafonable and bloody attempts and practices, &c. After which he was again committed to the tower of London; where endeavouring to make an efcape, he was afterwards with others, executed at Tyburn. After Perkin took fanctuary at Beaulieu, his foldiers from about Taunton and elfewhere, were all brought to Exon; where King Henry, in St. Peter's Church-yard, pardoned them all, on their promife of being good fubjects afterwards. But fome of them were not fo good as their word. King Henry alfo then fent the Lord Daubeny to St. Michael's Mount, for Perkin's wife, the Lady Catherine Gordon, whom he brought to King Henry; who commiferating her youth, birth and beauty, beftowed a competent maintenance upon her; which fhe enjoyed during that King's life, and long after, to her dying day." *Hals's* MS. Hift. of the Mount, pp. 49, 53. To her hufband's falfe title had been given the name of the *White rofe*: it was now transferred to her beauty, with no difputed meaning. Vid. Franfc. Bacon. Oper. Moral. et Civil. tom. [Londin. 1638.] pp. 67, 108. Bacon dedicates his works: Illuft. et excell. Princ. Carolo Princip. Wall. Duci Cornubiæ, &c. &c.

* See *Hiftoric Doubts*, pp. 82, 93. Edit. 2d.

† Principio Anni fequentis, qui erat Regis Decimus Septimus, Domina Catharina, Ferdinandi & Ifabellæ, Regis & Reginæ Hifpaniæ, Filia quarta, Angliam appulit, apud Portum Plimmouthi, Secundo die Octobris; et decimo quarto Novembris infequentis, Principi Arthuro nupfit; Matrimonio in Templo D. Pauli folenniter celebrato. Princeps, tunc Annorum erat circitèr quindecim, Sponfa autemejus circitèr octodecim. Modus eam in Angliam recipiendi; Modus Ingreffûs ejus in Londinum; Atque Nuptiarum ipfarum Celebritas, magnâ et verâ cum Magnificentiâ peracta funt; five Sumptus fpectetur, five Splendor, five Ordo. Præcipuus vir, qui univerfum Apparatum curavit, erat Foxus Epifcopus; qui non folùm prudens erat Confiliarius, in Negotiis tam Belli quam Pacis, verùm etiàm bonus Præfectus operum, bonus itidem Magifter Cæremoniarum: Denique omnia erat, quæ competerent parti Activæ, & pertinerent ad Servitium Aulæ, aut ftatûs, Magni Regis. Nuptiarum harum Tractatus feptem Annorum Opus erat; cujus partìm cauffa erat Ætas tenera Principum, præfertim ipfius Arthuri. Sed vera cauffa fuberat, quod hi duo Reges, prudentiffimi fcilicet, et profundi Judicii, ftabant diù alter in fortunam alterius intuentes; fatis gnari, Tractatum ipfum intereà, Opinionem ubique creare arctæ inter illos Conjunctionis, & Amicitiæ; quod ipfum utrinque utile erat rebus amborum Regum, licet liberi adhuc manerent. Verùm in fine, cùm utriufque Regis Fortuna, indies magis profpera & fecura evaderet; atque cùm circumfpectantes nullam invenirent Conditionem meliorem, Tractatum Matrimonii concluferunt.—Summa Dotis (quæ in Regem tranflata erat per viam Renunciationis,) fuit Ducenta Millia Ducatorum. Quorum centum Millia folvi debebant, poft decem dies à Solennizatione Matrimonii: Altera veró centum Millia, æquis portionibus, proximis duobus Annis. Pars tamen poterat per Jocalia, aut per Vafa aurea & argentea, repræfentari; et Ratio inita eft, quo pacto jufte & indifferentèr æftimarentur. Reditus autem Principiffæ affignatus fuit tertia pars Principatûs Walliæ & Ducatûs Cornubiæ, & Comitatû Ceftriæ, pofteà per Metas feparanda. Verùm, fi contigerit eam Reginam Angliæ fore, indefinitus relinquebatur; ita tamen, ne minor foret, quam ulla Regina Angliæ antehàc frueretur.—In Spectaculis & triumphis Nuptialibus, multa ex Ariftonomiâ defumpta funt. Sponfa enim per Hefperum adumbrata eft, Princeps autem per Arcturum: fed & vetus Rex Alphonfus, (qui inter Reges maximus fuerat Aftrologus, atque fimul ex Progenitoribus Principiffæ,) introductus eft, ut Fortunam Nuptiarum prædiceret. Certè, quifquis is fuerit,

qui

The firſt occurrence we have to notice in the reign of Henry VIII. is an act, which was paſſed in 1512, to prevent perſons from being queſtioned for their conduct in Parliament. This was occaſioned by the behaviour of the Stannary Court of Cornwall, which ſeverely fined, and cruelly impriſoned, Mr. Strode, a member who had introduced to the houſe a bill concerning tin.† From the Senate, we are again hurried to ſcenes of war. About this time the fleet under Sir Edward Howard received from the weſt conſiderable reinforcements; among which were ſent from Plymouth two capital ſhips, the Regent, commanded by Sir Thomas Knevet,

iſtas nugas concinnaret, ultra Pedantium ſapuit. Sed pro certo ducas, Arthurum illum Regem Britannum, ad Fabulas uſque celebrem, atque Proſapiam Principiſſæ Catharinæ, à Familia Lancaſtrenſi, extractam, nullo modo oblivione præterita fuiſſe. Verum, (ut videtur) non fauſta res eſt, Fortunam ex Aſtris petere. Nam Princeps iſte Iuvenis, (Qui, eo tempore, in ſe trahebat, non ſolùm Spes & Affectus Patriæ ſuæ, verùm etiam Oculos & Expectationem Exterorum) poſt paucos Menſes, ineunte Aprile, apud Caſtrum de Ludlow obiit, quo miſſus erat, ut cum Aulâ ſuâ reſideret, tanquàm Princeps Walliæ. Hujus Principis, eò quod citò mortuus eſt; et quia in more Patri erat, Liberos ſuos modicè illuſtrare, exigua manet Memoria. Illud tantùm traditur, eum bonarum Literarum ſtudioſiſſimum fuiſſe & magnos in iis profectus feciſſe, ſupra Annos ſuos, & ſupra Conſuetudinem Principum magnorum.—Dubitatio quædam temporibus ſequentibus oborta eſt, cùm Divortium Henrici Octavi, & Dominæ Catharinæ, tantas turbas in orbe concitaverat, utrùm Arthurus carnalitèr cognoviſſet Catharinam uxorem ſuam; quo iſta pars, de Cognitione carnali, caſui infereretur. Verum autem eſt, Catharinam ipſam rem negaſſe; vel ſaltem Advocatos illius & rei inſtitiſſe, & ut firmamentum cauſæ non contemnendum omitti noluiſſe; etſi plenitudo Poteſtatis Papalis in diſpenſando, Quæſtio fuiſſet primaria. Iſta autem Dubitatio per longum tempus duravit, reſpectu duarum Reginarum quæ ſucceſſerunt, Mariæ & Elizabethæ; quarum Legitimationes erant inter ſe incompatibiles, etſi Succeſſio ipſarum, vigore Actûs Parlamenti, ſtabilita fuiſſet. Tempora autem quæ Mariæ Reginæ Legitimationi favebant, credi volebant, nullam fuiſſe carnalem cognitionem. Non quod videri vellent abſolutæ Papæ Poteſtati quicquam derogare, vel eo caſu diſpenſandi; ſed Honoris tantùm cauſſâ, atque ut Caſus magis eſſet favorabilis, & molliùs laberetur. E contrà, Tempora, quæ Legitimationi Reginæ Elizabethæ favebant, (quæ & longiora, & recentiora fuerunt,) contrarium defendebant. Illud certæ Memoriæ eſt, interceſſiſſe Tempus ſemeſtre, inter Mortem Principis Arthuri, & Creationem Henrici, in Principēm Walliæ; Quod eò pertinere Homines interpretabantur, quò ſpatium illud temporis, in certo poneret, utrùm Catharina ex Arthuro gravida facta fuiſſet. Quin & Catharina ipſa, novam à Papâ Bullam procurari fecit, ad Matrimonium meliùs corroborandum, cum clauſulâ illâ, (Vel forſan Cognitam) quæ in priore Bullâ comprehenſa non erat. Datum etiàm in Evidentiis fuit, dum Cauſſa Divortii tractaretur, Scomma quoddam facetum; Nimirum quòd Arthurus manè cùm è lecto Principiſſæ ſurrexiſſet, potum poſtulaſſet, præter Conſuetudinem ſuam; Cumque Generoſus quidam è Cubiculo ſuo, qui potum ei porrigeret, ſubrideret, remqne notaſſet; Princeps jocans, ad eum dixiſſet, Se in medio Hiſpaniæ, qnæ calida eſſet Regio fuiſſe; iter autem ſuum ſitibundum eum reddidiſſe; quodque ſi Adoleſcens ille, è tam calido Climate veniſſet, potum avidiùs hauſiſſet. Quinetiàm Princeps fuerat Annorum circiter ſexdecim, cùm mortuus eſt, & Corpore ſanus & robuſtus.—Februario ſequente, Henricus Dux Eboraci factus eſt Princeps Walliæ, & Comes Ceſtriæ & Flintæ; Etenim Ducatus Cornubiæ, ſtatuto ad eum devolutus eſt. At Rex Ingenio tenax, & non libentèr Reditus novos, ſi alibi nupſiſſet Henricus, aſſignaturus; ſed præcipuè propter affectum ſuum, quo & Naturâ, & propter Rationes politicas, Ferdinandum proſecutus eſt, Affinitatis prioris continuandæ cupidus, à Principe obtinuit, (etſi non abſque aliquâ Reluctatione, qualis eâ Ætate, quæ Duodecimum Annum nondùm complevit, eſſe poterat,) ut cum Principiſſa Catharina contraheretur: Secretâ Dei Providentiâ ordinante, ut Nuptiæ illæ, magnorum Eventuum & Mutationum Cauſſa exiſterent." *Bacon's* Hiſt. pp. 118, 119, 120. "The Lady Catherine of Spain, was ſent by her father K. Ferdinand, with a puiſſant armada of ſhips into England; where ſhe arrived at Plymouth, 2d October, and 14th November, was eſpouſed openly to *Prince Arthur*, both being clad in white; he, of the age of fifteen, ſhe of eighteen. At night, they were laid together in one bed; where they lay as man and wife all that night, When morning appeared, the Prince (as his ſervants about him reported) called for drink, which before time he had not uſed to do; whereof one of his Chamberlains aſking him the cauſe, he anſwered merrily, ſaying "I have been this night in the midſt of Spain which is a hot country, and that makes me ſo dry;" tho' ſome write that a grave matron was laid in bed between them, to hinder actual conſummation. The Lady's portion was 200,000 Ducats, her jointure the third part of the principality of Wales, Cornwall, and Cheſter. At this marriage was great ſolemnity and royal juſtings." *Baker*, pp. 245, 246. On the 17th November, 17th Henry 7. 1501, *Thomas Greynvile* was made one of the Knights of the Bath, at the marriage of *Arthur*, Prince of Wales. See *Anſtis's* Obſervations on Knighthood of the Bath, p. 46. On the ſame occaſion *Sir John Trevelyan*, of Trevelyan, was created a Knight of the Bath, together with Sir William Walgrave, Sir John Scrope, of Caſtlecomb, Sir John Paulet, Sir Richard Ware, of Heſtercomb, and others. See *Anſtis's* Hiſt. of Knights of the Bath, N. 60, Append. Ann. 1505. Henry 7. Into the creek of *Armouth*, ſo dangerous on account of the rocks at its entrance, was driven Philip King of Caſtile. See *Polydore Vergil, Anglican. Hiſt.* l. xxvi. *Bacon's* Works, vol. II. p. 349. According to ſome accounts the King and Queen of Caſtile were driven by a ſtorm into Falmouth. See *Rapin*, pp. 688, 689. In the ſame year, Sir Thomas Trenchard and Sir John Carew, deſired the Archduke Philip, who had been driven hither by a ſtorm, to remain at Sir Thomas's houſe, till they could inform the King of his landing. *Stowe.* I have ſaid nothing of the French in this reign. But *Norden* (p. 61.) ſpeaks of John Polrudden, of Polrudden, in St. Auſtel, as having been "taken out of his bed by the French, in the time of Henry 7, and carried away with violence."

† *Hume*, from Pub. Acts.

Knevet, and *Sir John Carew*, and the Sovereign, by Sir Charles Brandon. The commanders in the Regent, although it was a much ſmaller ſhip, attacked and boarded the French Admiral. The action laſted for ſome time with equal vigour on both ſides. The French and Engliſh fleets ſtood ſome time in ſuſpence, as ſpectators of this dreadful ſingle combat. At length the French Admiral finding himſelf overpowered, ſet fire to his ſhip. Both ſhips blew up almoſt at the ſame time: and Sir John Carew* and Sir Thomas Knevet, with more than 1600 men, periſhed.

* *Baker's Chron.* This was *Sir John Carew*, of *Bereferrers*. See Sir *W. Pole's* MS. Catal. of Knights in the reign of K. Henry 8.—"There were in the chief ſhip, *the Regent*, of a thouſand tons, Sir Thomas Knevet, maſter of the horſe, and Sir John Carew, with 700 men." See *Polydore, Speed, Stowe*. Of Thomas Carew, Prince has given a full and ſatisfactory memoir. "*Thomas Carew*, Eſq. the firſt that ſettled this name at *Bickleigh*, in this county, was born at *Mohuns-Ottery*, near Honiton. He was the ſecond ſon of Sir *Edmund Baron Carew*, by *Katharine* his wife, daughter and one of the heirs of Sir *William Huddesfeild*, Kt. attorney general to K. *Hen.* 7. Which Sir *Edmund* being a brave ſoldier, and at the ſiege of *Terwin*, in *France*, when K. *Hen.* 8. ſate down before it with a great army, was, in the fifth year of that King's reign, as he ſate in council there, unfortunately ſlain by a cannon ball that came from the town. This *Thomas* proved a ſon worthy of ſuch a father, being alſo of a martial ſpirit; whereby he got great honour and renown in the wars, as in the ſequel of this diſcourſe will appear.

But before we come to that, it may not be improper here, to give a brief account of a ſofter enterprize; which, however in the iſſue it proved ſucceſsful enough, yet for the preſent it adminiſtred an occaſion of trouble, that haſtned him on into the wars, ſooner than he intended.

You may pleaſe to know then, that *Bickleigh* in this ſhire, was ſometime the inheritance of the honorable family of the *Courtenays* of *Powderham* Caſtle; which was wont to be a portion for a younger ſon of that houſe. At length it came to be ſettled upon *Humphry*, the youngeſt ſon of Sir *Philip Courtenay*; who dying before his father, left his only daughter and heir unto his care. Sir *Philip* entruſted her over unto Sir *William Carew* (*Thomas's* eldeſt brother) who had married his eldeſt ſon's daughter, Couſin-German to this lady. Mr. *Thomas Carew* living with his brother, became very familiar with this young fortune, courted her, and won her good will; which having obtained, he ſecretly by night, carried her away and married her. This he did, not only contrary to Sir *Philip* her grand-father, and Sir *William* his brother, their likeing and approbation, but to the high diſpleaſure of them both: for the better pacifying whereof, after due time of conſideration, he concluded, nothing would conduce more thereunto, than abſence. Being young and luſty, of an active body, and a courageous mind, having in him, the inherent ſeeds of hereditary virtue, he reſolved for the wars; and ſoon found an occaſion ſuitable to his inclination and reſolution; which thus hapned.—The Scots taking the advantage of K. *Hen.* 8th's abſence in *France*, invaded *England*. Againſt whom, *Thomas* Earl of *Surry* (whom the King had made his Lieutenant in the North at his departure) raiſed a potent army, of five and twenty thouſand men; unto whom, his ſon, the Lord *Howard*, Lord Admiral of *England*, having the King's navy at ſea, brought a great ſupply of good ſoldiers, well appointed for the war; among whom was this Mr. *Thomas Carew*. The Earl marched his army from *New Caſtle*, and pitched his hoſt beſide a little town under *Flodden* Hill, a mountain lying in the north of *Northumberland*, on the borders of *Scotland*, betwixt the rivers of *Till* and *Tweed*; on the top whereof K. *Jam.* 4. with his Scottiſh forces, well near an hundred thouſand men, lay ſo ſtrongly encamped, that 'twas impoſſible to come near them without great diſadvantage.

Before the battle began, a valorous Scottiſh Knight made a challenge to any Engliſh-Gent. to fight with him for the honor of his country; I ſuppoſe 'twas the ſame, who by Mr. *Speed* is called *Andrew Barton*; unto whom, he tells us, the Lord Admiral ſent word, he would in perſon juſtify his action againſt him, and abide to the laſt drop of his blood in the van gard of the field. Mr. *Carew* begged the favor of the Admiral, that he might be admitted to the honor of anſwering the challenge. It was granted him; they both met in the place appointed; where, to his high commendation, and great endearment with the Lord Admiral ever after, Mr. *Carew* got the victory; which was, it ſeems, only an earneſt of that which enſued: for ſoon after this, followed the famous battel, called the Battel of *Flodden-Field*; wherein the Scots were totally routed, their King with a multitude of noblemen and gentlemen, and thirteen thouſand of the common ſoldiers ſlain, (ſome ſay but eight) and near as many taken priſoners, with the loſs only of about a thouſand Engliſh.

It is a memorable, but ſcarce credible thing, ſays the hiſtorian, which *Buchanan* relates, concerning this K. *Jam.* 4th, K. of *Scotland*: that intending to make this war with England, a certain old man, of venerable aſpect, and clad in a long blue garment, came unto him; and leaning familiarly on the chair wherein the King ſate, ſaid this to him: *I am come to thee, O King! to give thee warning, that thou proceed not in the war thou art about*; *for if thou doſt, it will be thy ruine.* Having ſo ſaid, he preſſed through the company, and vaniſhed out of ſight; ſo that by no enquiry, it could be known what became of him. But the King was too reſolute to be affrighted with phantoms, and no warning could divert his deſtiny; which had not been deſtiny, if it could have been diverted. Thus he.

To proceed with Mr. *Carew*. His courage and conduct had gotten him great favor, as was ſaid, with the Lord Admiral; but after the battel was over, there hapned another occaſion, which greatly encreaſed it, and fixed him deeper in his affection. For my lord taking Mr. *Carew* in company with him, as he rode forth upon ſervice, deſcryed a band of Scots coming towards them: the Admiral, at a very ſtrait narrow paſſage of a bridge, was in danger to be entrapped and taken: to prevent which, Mr. *Carew* inſtantly entreated him to exchange his armor and martial attire with him, that by ſuch mean, if need were, he might make the eaſier eſcape; the which, the Admiral well conſidering of, ſoon conſented to.

The enemy coming on to this narrow paſſage, Mr. *Carew*, in his rich habit, well mounted, croſſed the bridge with his horſe; and for a time, ſo valiantly defended the ſame, that no man could paſs; that way gaining time, the numbers be-

In the great church of St. Malos, is a reprefentation of this battle cut in ftone. The French admiral was made a faint. And his memory, it feems, is preferved in the Romifh Calendar, under the title of St. Donne. " Markajew (fays *Carew*) now felt the Frenchmen's fiery indignation." But, " the fmoke of thofe poor houfes" alarming the country, " made the place over hote for the enemies any longer abode."* In that romantic interview in the Vale of Audrens, between the monarchs of England and France, which to defcribe, would require rather the talents of the poet than of the hiftorian, I fhall furnifh an inftance, I fear, of genuine bathos, by naming as one of the fupporters on the fide of the King, a gentleman of Cornifh extraction, *Nicholas Carew*,†—unlefs, indeed, I carry my readers to the pavilion of the cloth of gold, and refign them, amidft " the turneys and the trophies," to " love-darting eyes!"‡ This was a period fruitful in Knights and Knight-errantry. The Knights of Malta, fome of whom were Cornifh or Devonian, are, at once, prefented to memory, and may with propriety be noticed here, as they were firft the object of Henry's fondeft attention, and afterward of his religious hatred. It appears, that our capricious monarch gave the Grand Mafter L'Ifle Adam, twenty thoufand crowns, and thus enabled him to take poffeffion of the ifland of Malta.¶ In the fequel, Henry robbed and perfecuted the order. Ingley, Adrian Forreft, ADRIAN FORTESCUE, and Marmaduke Bohu*s* [Bohu*n*] Englifh Knights, refufing to renounce the faith of their anceftors, perifhed

tween them being very unequal, for the Lord Admiral's efcape. However, Mr. *Carew* himfelf was at laft taken prifoner, to the no little joy of the enemy, who thought they had taken the General himfelf; as indeed by the richnefs of his armor they had reafon to imagine. But in fine, finding themfelves deceived, they carried him to the caftle of *Dunbar*, lying twenty Scotch miles to the *Eaft* of *Edenburgh* in *Scotland*; where he was courteoufly entertained by the lady thereof: who having a brother then a prifoner in *England*, hoped by the advantage of an exchange, to have him delivered to her again.—This lady then was always affable and courteous to her prifoner; but the keeper of the caftle was of a malicious and churlifh nature, and dealt moft cruelly with him. As an inftance of which, on a time, as Mr. *Carew* was fitting by the fire-fide in his chamber, he came fuddainly upon him, with his fword drawn, and an intention to murther him; which he timely perceiving, took up the chair whereon he fate to defend himfelf; which, ufing his beft fkill to defend his life, he managed fo well, that he gave his keeper a deadly wound; whereupon, more help called in, he was prefently caft into a deep dungeon, and kept there in fuch hard and cruel manner, that he fell dangeroufly fick; and what did moft afflict him, was a dyfentery, or a long tedious flux, which never quite left him to the time of his death. However, at length he was redeemed, and fo returned to his mannor at *Bicklegh*. After which, the Lord Admiral never forgot the noble fervices Mr. *Carew* did him, but ever entertain'd him with all courtefy and friendfhip; made him his Vice-Admiral, and affifted him in all his affairs." *Prince*, pp. 176, 177.

* *Carew*, f. 156. " In 1514, when war had been proclaimed againft the the French King, a fleet of French men of war, confifting of thirty fail with fome marine regiments of foldiers therein, coafting in the Britifh Channel, at length came into the Mount's Bay, and there dropt anchor; when, foon after, they landed a confiderable number of feamen and foldiers, and marched in hoftile manner towards this town. Which the inhabitants obferving, they forfook their houfes, and fled to the hill country; whereby the Frenchmen became peaceably poffeft thereof, and plundered the fame for fome days; till they underftood that John Carmenow, of Fentongollan, Efq. was marching towards them with his poffe comitatus, to give them battle. When inftantly they fet the town on fire, and the houfes of the contiguous part of the country; and burnt the fame totally to the ground, to the great lofs and damage of the inhabitants; and forthwith fled to their fhips for fafety and protection. And thereupon the fhips hoifted anchor, and put forthwith to fea again; where they had not long been, till Sir Anthony Oughtred, Knight, and Admiral at fea, with a fquadron of thirty men of war, met and gave them battle, to their great lofs of men and fome fhips of war, whilft the reft of their fleet ran away, and fled into the haven of Breft for fafety." Whitaker's *Hals*, MS. vol. 1. pp. 35, 36.

† Sir William Coffin of Portledge, was one of the eighteen affiftants to King Henry VIII. at the tournament held between him and the French King, before Guifnes in France, in 1519. The Portlege MSS.

‡ Montfaucon in his work, entitled, " *Les Monumens de la Monarchie*," Pl. 30, vol. 4, has given a reprefentation of the meeting of Henry VIII. and Francis I. on the "*field of the Cloth of gold*," between Guifnes and Ardres.§ The kings are on horfeback, followed by their refpective attendants; and thofe of Henry are principally archers mounted on horfes, carrying their long-bows with them.

¶ This curious fact feems to give this country fome legitimate claim, after the deftruction of the order by the French, to the ifland of Malta.

§ If the reader wifh to fee an account of this fuperb affair, he will find it defcribed in Robertfon's Charles V. vol. 2.

perifhed by the axe of the executioner. Thomas Mytton and Edward Waldegrave, imprifoned in a horrible dungeon, chofe rather to die with honour in their confinement, than to purchafe their liberty by perjury and apoftafy. Richard and James Bell, John Noel, and others preferred the confolations of religion to the pleafures of a court, and paffed the remainder of their days in exile.* In thefe hafty fketches, where events are taken up, chiefly for the fake of illuftrating the characters of our weftern worthies, I have named a few gentlemen of diftinction: but of fome of thefe, more remains to be faid: and there are others, whom it would not be eafy to introduce in hiftorical connexion.†

Among

* See Ancient and Modern Malta, by Louis de Boifgelin, Knight of Malta. 3 vols. 4to. *Robinfons*, 1804.

† Edgcumbe and Arundel were ftill names of high refpectability. In 2d Henry VIII. *Sir Peirs Edgecombe* with Robert Willoughby de Broke, Knt. *John Arundel, Knt.* and Richard Carew, Knt. they or any three of them, were impowered to array and review all men at arms, archers, and others, who were to accompany Sir Thomas Darcy, Knt. captain of the caftle of Berwick, in his expedition againft the Moors and other infidels; and to certify to the King, and his council, the number of men at arms, archers and others.§ In 5 Hen. VIII. Sir Peirs Edgecombe, was in the expedition againft France, and was there made a Knight Banneret for his gallant behavior in the fieges of Therovene, and Tournay, and the battle that enfued called by our hiftorians, the battle of *Spurs*, from the fwiftnefs of the French in running away.‡ 11th Hen. VIII. the King wrote to Sir John Arundel of Trerice, that he fhould give his attendance at Canterbury, about the entertaynment of the Emperour, whofe landing was then and there expected. 14th Hen. VIII. John Arundel of Trerice, Efquire, tooke prifoner, Duncane Campbell, a Scot, in a fight at fea, as our chronicle mentioneth, concerning which, I thought it not amiffe, to infert a letter fent him from Tho. Duke of Norfolke (to whom he then belonged) that you may fee the ftile of thofe dayes.

"Right welbeloued, in our hearty wife we commend vs vnto you letting you wit, that by your feruant, this bearer, wee haue receyued your letters, dated at Truru the 5 day of this month of April, by which we perceyue the goodly valiant, and ieopardus enterprife, it hath pleafed God of late to fend you, by the taking of Duncane Camel and other Scots on the fea; of which enterprife we haue made relation vnto the King's highneffe, who is not a little joyous and glad, to heare of the fame, to giue you thanks for your faid valiant courage, and bolde enterprife in the premifes: and by thefe our letters, for the fame your fo doing, we doe not onely thanke you in our moft effectuall wife, but alfo promife you, that during our life, wee will bee glad to aduaunce you to any preferment we can. And ouer this, you fhall vnderftand our faid Soveraigne Lords pleafure is, that you fhall come and repaire to his Highnefs, with diligence in your owne perfon, bringing with you the faid captiue, and the mafter of the Scottifh fhip; at which time, you fhall not onely be fure of his efpeciall thanks by mouth, and to know his further pleafure therein, but alfo of vs to further any your reafonable purfuits vnto his Highnefs, or any other during our life, to the beft of our power, accordingly. Written at Lambeth, the 11th day of Aprill aforefaid.

To our right welbeloued feruant, JOHN ARUNDEL of Trerice." *Carew*, f. 146, 146, b.

"35th Henry VIII. the King wrote to Sir John Arundel of Trerice, touching his difcharge from the Admiralty of the fleete, lately committed vnto him, and that he fhould deliuer the fhip which he fayled into Sir Nicholas Poynts. The fame yere the King wrote to him againe, that he fhould attend him in his warres againft the French King, with his feruants, tenants, and others within his roomes and offices efpecially horfemen. Our letters from the King thefe are, whofe date is not expreffed, neither can I by any means hunt it out. One to his feruant John Arundel of Trerice, Efquire, willing him, not to repaire with his men, and to wayte in the rereward of his army, as hee had commaunded him, but to keepe them in readineffe for fome other feruice. Another to Sir J. Arundel of Trerice, praying and defiring him to the court, the quindene of Saint Hillarie, next wherefoever the King fhall then bee within the realme." *Carew*. "K. Henry VIII. came into Cornwall to view, build, and fortify the cafles of St. Mawes and Pendennis, againft the French; when he made *Talverne*, the chief place of his refidence. Hence, perhaps, King *Harry*-paffage." Carew calls Sir John Arundel of Talverne, "the kind and valiant Sir J. Arundel." f. 142. "At the coronation of Anne Bullen Sir Thomas Arundel was made Knight of the Bath." *Baker*, p. 282. Of other remarkable names occurring in this reign, I fubjoin a few particulars. In 1530, Mr. *William Hawkins* (father to the great navigator Sir John Hawkins) fitted out a ftout fhip, the Paul, of Plymouth, and failing to the coaft of Guinea and Brafil, began a practice which, although it has been fince very profitable to his country, has covered it with difgrace; that of feizing the unfortunate natives of Africa and tranfporting them to foreign fhores, there to end their days in flavery. See *Hiftory of Devon*. "Ann. 1531. about this time was a call of eleven ferjeants at law; among whom was *John Denfel*. They kept their feaft at Eley Houfe five days together; where on the laft day the King and Queen dined. This John Denfel, of Denfel, in the county of Cornwall, was of Lincoln's Inn, and died the 3d of Jan. 1535, and lieth buried within the church of St. Giles in the Fields, in Middlefex; leaving by Mary his widow, the daughter of Sir —— Lucas, in Warwickfhire, Knight, two daughters and coheirs. *Ann*, the eldeft married to Sir William Hollis of Haughton, in the county of Nottingham, Knight, grandfather unto John Hollis, Knight, Earl of Clare, &c. deceafed; and *Alice* the other daughter married unto Mafter Refkimer." *Baker*, p. 280. Ann. 1542. "During the Parliament, George Ferrers gentleman, fervant to the King, and Burgefs for the town of Plymouth, in going to the Parliament Houfe, was arrefted in London, by a procefs out of the King's Bench, for a debt, wherein he late afore condemned as furety for one Welden, at the fuit of one White. Which arreft being fignified to *Sir Thomas* ‖*Moyl*, Knight, fpeaker then of the Parliament, and to the

Knights

§ See *Fuller* in Devon, and *Rymer*, vol. 13, p. 296.

‡ MS. in Bibl. Cot. Claud. C. 3. p. 81.

‖ He was an anceftor of the *Moyles* of Bake.

Among the rebels that disturbed the short reign of EDWARD the SIXTH, we are forced to include the lower orders of the people in Cornwall; and, according to the Lord Protector,* one or two of our principal families. But I fear, a greater number of gentry were implicated

Knights and Burgesses there; order was taken, that the serjeant of the Parliament, called Saint-john, should be sent to the Counter, in Bread-street, (whither the said Ferrers was carried) and there demand to have him delivered. But the officers of the Counter not only refused to deliver him, but gave the serjeant such language that they fell at last to an affray; at which time the sheriffs coming they also took their officer's part; so as the serjeant was fain to return without the prisoner: which being signified to the Speaker and the Burgesses, they took the matter in so ill part, that they would set no more without their Burgess: and therefore, rising up, they repaired to the upper house, where the whole case was declared by the Speaker before Sir *Thomas Audeley*, Lord Chancellor, and the Lords and Judges there assembled; who judging the contempt to be very great, referred the punishment thereof to the House of Commons itself. Whereupon returning to their places upon new debate of the case, they took order that their serjeant should once more repair to the sheriffs of London, and demand the prisoner, without carrying any writ or warrant for the matter: on this second demand the sheriffs became more mild, and delivered the prisoner without any denial. But the serjeant had further in charge, to command the sheriffs and clerks of the Counter to appear personally the next morning before the House of Commons. Where appearing, they were charged by the Speaker with their contempt, and compelled to make immediate answer, without being admitted to any council. In conclusion, the sheriffs and White who had caused the arrest, were committed to the Tower; the officer that did the arrest, with four other officers, to Newgate; but after two or three days, upon the suit of the mayor, were set at liberty. The King commended the wisdom of Parliament in maintaining the priveleges of their house." See *Baker*, pp. 289, 290. *John Cosowarth*, of *Cosowarth*, Esq. is said to have been a brave soldier, both by sea and land. "He was knighted by Henry 8, for that with equal courage and hazard, he took down the Pope's Bull, set up at Antwerp against his sovereign." *Tonkin's* MSS. *Sir Richard Greynfyld* was marshall of Calais, and served in the wars under the Earl of Hertford, before Humbletue with 200 soldiers; and was also at the *siege of Bologne*, 36th Henry 8th. (The Anstis MS. Collection.) Sir *John Tregonwell* was bred at Broadgate's Hall, afterwards principal of Vine Hall or Peckwater's Inn, Oxford, and admitted there, Dr. of civil laws, June 23, 1552. Being an eminent and learned man in his profession, he was employed to be proctor for Hen. 8, in that memorable cause of his divorce from Queen Catharine, in which he behaved so well, that the King not only knighted him, but gave him a pension of 40l. per ann. and on the resignation thereof, with the paying down of a thousand pounds, conferred on him and his heirs the rich demesne and scite of Middleton or Milton, a mitred Abbey, in Dorsetshire, possessed at this day by his posterity. He died in the year 1564, (7 Eliz.) and was buried in the church of Middleton. His male line ended in a daughter married first to Col. Lutterel, of Dunster Castle, in Somerset, and secondly to Sir Jacob Banks, Knight, a Swede by birth, and naturalized here, and captain of a man of war in King William and Queen Anne's reign, whose eldest son by her, Tregonwell Banks, Esq. now enjoys the estate." *Fuller's* Worthies in Cornwall. *Athen-Oxon.* p. 666. *Tonkin's* MSS. *Sir William Godolphin* was a person of great note in the reign of Henry VIII. who for his services conferred on him the honor of knighthood, and constituted him warden and chief steward of the Stannaries. *He lived to a great age*, was several times chosen one of the Knights of the Shire for Cornwall, in the Parliaments of Henry VIII. and Edward VI. and was also sheriff of this county in 21st, 25th, and 30th Henry VIII. 3d Edward VI. and 10th Elizabeth. He likewise acquired much fame, by his conduct and intrepidity in several military commands, particularly at the siege of Bologne. *Carew* ranks this Sir William among the Worthies of Cornwall. "He demeaned himself (says Carew) very valiantly beyond the seas; as appeared by the scars he brought home; no less to the beautifying of his fame, than the disfiguring of his face." His brother *Thomas Godolphin* was, also, at the siege of Bologne: and on Thursday 14th August, 1544, he, Mr. Harper, and Mr. Culpeper were hurt with one shot from the town. His "Nephew, of the same name and dignity hath so inriched himself with sufficiency for matters of policy, by his long travell, and for martial affaires, by his present valiant carriage in Ireland; that it is better knowne, how far he outgoeth most others in both, than easily to be discerned for which he deserveth principal commendation himself." *Carew*, f. 61, 62. It seems to have been in the French war of Henry VIII. that Murth was carried away from his own house a prisoner to France. One of the ancestors of Mr. Murth (whose demesnes were situated near Polpera) "within the memorie of a next neighbour to the house called Prake, (burdened with 110 years age) entertained a British miller, (a miller of Britany) as that people, for such idle occupations, prove more handie, than our owne. But this fellowes service befell commodious in the worst sense. For when, not long after his acceptance, warres grewe betweene us and France, he stealeth over into his country, returneth privily backe againe with a French crew, surprizeth suddenly his master and his ghests, at a Christmas supper, carrieth them speedily unto Lantreghey, and forceth the gentleman to redeeme his enlargement, with the sale of great part of his revenues." *Carew*, f. 131, b. We have, from tradition, a similar story of Mr. *Woollcombe*.

* The following curious MS. is well worthy the inspection of the public. It is a letter from the Duke of Somerset, Protector, to the ambassador, and Sir Philip Hobby, resident with the Emperor. This copy was compared with the MS. in the Cotton Collection, "Galba. b. 12." "Knowing that all such as be ambassodors abroad are not only desirous of news for the love they bear to their own country naturally, desiring often to hear of the estate of it, but also to confirm or confute such rumors as be spread in the parts where they lie, we have thought good to impart what sithe our last letters hath chanced. The Devonshire men are well chastised and appeased; three other of their Captains have voluntarily come in, and simply submitted themselves to Sir Thomas Pomeroy, Knight. Wise and Harrys who before were fled and could not be found; and the country cometh in daily to my Lord Privy Seal, by hundreds and by thousands, to crave his pardon, and be put in some sure hope of grace. Burry and some one or two more of their blind guides that escaped from the sword, have attempted in the mean season to stir up Somersetshire, and have gotten them a band or camp, but they are sent after, and we trust by this, they

cated in this disgraceful affair, than the Lord Protector was willing to allow. According to *Carew*, the insurrection of the Cornish was first occasioned by " one *Kilter*,† and other his associats of a westerne parish, called St. Keveren, who imbrued their wicked hands in the guiltles blood of one *M. Body*, as he sate in commission at Helston, for matters of reformation in religion: and the yere following it grew to a general revolt, under the conduct of *Arundel*, *Wydeslade* [or *Wynslade*,] *Resogan*‡ and others, followed by 6000 men. With this power they

they have as they deserve. The Earl of Warwick lieth near to the rebells in Norfolk, which faint now, and would have grace gladly, so that all might be pardoned, Keate and the other arch traitours in the number; upon that is a stay and they daily shrink so fast away, that there is great hope that they will leave their captains destitute and alone, to receive their worthy reward, the which is the thing we most desire to spare as much as may be the effusion of blood, and that namely of our own nation. In Yorkshire a commotion was attempted the week last past, but the gentlemen were so soon upon them, and so forwardly that it was straight suppressed; and with weeping eyes, the rest upon their knees, they wholly together desired the gentlemen to obtain their pardons; the which the King's Majesty hath so granted unto them, as may stand with his highness honour: so that for the inner parts, (thanks be to the Almighty God) the case standeth in good points. The causes and pretences of these uproars and risings, are divers and uncertain, and so full of variety almost in every camp, as they call them, that it is hard to write what it is; as ye know is like to be of people without head and rule; and that woud have that they wot not what. Some crieth pluck down *inclosures and parks, some for their commons, others pretend the religion, a number woud have rule another while and direct things as gentlemen have done, and indeed all have convayed a wonderful hate against gentlemen, and taketh them all as their enemies. The ruffians among them and souldiers which be the chief doers look for spoil. So that it seemeth no other thing but a plague and a fury amongst the vilest and worst sort of men; for *except only* DEVON *and* CORNWAL, (*and* they not past *two or three*) in all other places, not one gentleman or man of reputation was ever amongst them, but against their wills and as prisoners. In Norfolk gentlemen and all serving men for their sakes, are as evil handled as may be, but this broil is well asswaged, and in manner at a point shortly to be fully ended, with the Grace of God.—On the other part of the seas, we have not so good news, for the French King taking now his time and occasions of this rebellion, within the realm, is come unto Bullingnois, with a great number of horsemen and footmen, himself in person: and as we are advertised of the letters of the 24th of this present, from Ambletuse or Newhaven, the Almain Camp, or Almain Hill, a peece appertaining to the said Ambletuse, was that day delivered to the French, by traiterous consent of the captain of the camp, their variance falling or feigned, between the captain and the souldiers, so that they are now besieged very near and in manner round. Howbeit, they write that they trust the peece itself of Newhaven will be well enough defended, God assisting them, who be in as good and stout courage as any men may be, and as desirous to win honour, and give a good account of their charge. Thus we bid you heartily farewell." 24 August, 1549.

† There is a place called *Kilter*, in St. Kevern, the property of John Oliver Willyams, Esq. of Carnanton.

‡ *Wynslade*, *Bochym*, *Quarme* and several others, were gentlemen of considerable property. "The manor of Mythi-an, *i. e.* of Whey, a notable grange for cows and milk, (otherwise, if the name be compounded of My-Thyan (Saxon) my servant, or villain) by inheritance was formerly the lands of *Winslade* of Tregorick, in Plynt; an Hereditary Esquire of the White Spur, who forfeited the same, with much other land, by attainder of treason, tempore Edvardi 6. So that he himself or Queen Mary, gave those lands to Sir Reginald Mohun, of Hall, Knight, or his father, who settled them upon his younger son." *Hals*, p. 3. " Bochym gave name and original to an old family of gentlemen, surnamed De Bochym, temp. Hen. 8. who were Lords of the Manor and Barton, till such time as John Bochym, temp. Edw. 6. entered into actual rebellion against that Prince, under the conduct of Humphry Arundell, Esq. governor of St. Michael's Mount, and others; whose force and power being suppressed by John Lord Russel, Lieutenant-General of that Prince, at Exon, and those rebels attainted of treason, their lands were forfeited to the crown. Whereupon King Edward 6, gave this barton and manor to Reginald Mohun, Esq. sheriff of Cornwal 6th Edward 6, who gave this barton of Bochym, to one of his daughters, married to Bellot, now in possession thereof. The Manor of Bochym he settled upon his great-grandson William Mohun, Esq. now in possession thereof. Lastly, by this rebellion Bochym lost not only his lands, but his life also." *Hals*, p. 79.—" Nancar, (Duchy) *i. e.* the Vally Rock, or the Rock in the Vally, is the dwelling of Mr. Walter Quarme, Clerk; whose father Robert Quarme, Gent. married Judith, eldest daughter of Thomas Ceely, Esq. and had issue by her six sons and seven daughters; Walter Quarme aforesaid, his eldest son, married Grace, daughter of Samuel Gayer, Gent. and had issue by her six sons and as many daughters. The family of Quarme, was in all likehood an ancient British Tribe, and was never totally ruin'd by the Romans, Danes, Saxons, or Normans. However, a great many of that tribe about the year 454 or 455, (when Hengist and Horsa had betray'd King Vortigern in the first place, and afterwards conquer'd him and his son Guortimer,) departed the Island of Great Britain, and went into Armorica, now called Little Britany, in France: in which Province a great many of their posterity and name are at this day, to confirm it. The ancestors of that House from which Walter Quarme is lineally descended lived, in good wealth and honour, either at or soon after the coming in of William the Norman, at a seat of theirs in the Southams, in the county of Devon. About the year 1045, the heir of the family married a daughter and heiress of Sir William Crispine, and had with her the barton and manor of Woodhouse and Alwynton, which has a famous royalty and was a

* The enclosing of waste lands, was the chief cause of those troubles in Norfolk. See Hist. of Norwich, in 8vo. printed at Norwich, by John Crouse, 1768.

marched into Devon, besieged and assaulted Excester, and gave the Lord Russel (employed with an army against them) more than one hot encounter, which yet (as ever) quayled in their overthrow."* During the time of this insurrection in the west, the island of St. Nicholas, is said

a brave lordship; the said Quarme being then possessed of other brave manors and estates, viz. the manor of Dartmouth, and the manor of Westcomb, &c. This manor of Westcomb, was sold to the Earle of Oxford, in the first year of K. Edward 6, Anno Dom. 1546; and was for purchasing a pardon for Roger Quarme, who was engaged with the discontented Papists that then rose in arms in Cornwal and Devon, and besieged Exeter. This first broke the estate of the family. The manor of Dartmouth went to a younger son of the family, and some estate in the city of Exon; the former soon sold, and the latter wrongfully destroy'd in the time of King James I. The manors of Woodhouse and Alwynton were first leased for years to John Bickford, of Devon, Gent. and then Anno 1625, sold to his son William Bickford, Merchant, and continued to his heirs, until this and other estates, purchased by the sale thereof, descended to the foresaid Robert Quarme. The forementioned Sir William Crispine, had the like bearing in his arms with Quarme, they differing only thus: Sir William bore Argent and Sable; Quarme, Argent and *Gules*. *Hals*, pp. 76, 77.

* *Fol.* 98. "To Bodmin (says *Carew*) flocked the rebels from all quarters of the shire, pitching their campe at the town's end. And here they imprisoned such gentlemen as they had plucked out of their holes and houses; untill the fortune of warre gave verdit with right of justice, for their well deserved evill speed." f. 124. "They pitched their camp on *Castle-Kynock*." *Hals's* MSS. "The Priory or Abbey of St. Michael, being dissolved by act of Parliament, and given to the King, 33 Hen. 8, 1533, he gave the revenues and government of the place to Humphry Arundell, Esq. of Lanherne family; who *enjoyed the same till the first year of King Edward 6th*, 1549, when King Edward set forth several injunctions about religion. Amongst others this was one, viz. that all images, found in churches for divine worship or otherwise, should be pulled down, and cast forth out of those churches; and that all preachers should persuade the people from praying to Saints or for the dead, (and) from the use of beads, ashes, processions, masses, dirges, and praying to God publickly in an unknown tongue. And, least there should be a defect of preachers, homilies were made and ordered to be read in all churches. Pursuant to this injunction, one Mr. Body, a commissioner for pulling down images in the churches of Cornwall, going to do this duty in Helston church; a priest, in company with *Killtor of St. Kevorne*, and others, at unawares stabbed him in the body with a knife, of which wound he instantly fell dead in that place. And though the murderer was taken and sent up to London, tried, found guilty of wilful murder, in Westminster-Hall, and executed in Smithfield; yet the Cornish people flocked together in a tumultuous and rebellious manner, by the instigation of their Priests in divers parts of the shire or county, and committed barbarities and outrages in the same. And though the Justices of the Peace, apprehended several of them, and sent them to jail; yet they could not, with all their power, suppress the growth of their insurrection. For, soon after, Humphry Arundell aforesaid, governour of the mount, sided with those mutineers, and broke out into actual rebellion against his and their Prince. Who (the mutineers) chose him for the general of their army, and for inferiour officers, as captains, majors, and colonels; John Rosogan, James Rosogan, William Winslade, of Tregarrick, or St. Agnes at Mithian, John Payne of St. Ives, Robert Bochym of Bochym, and his brother, Thomas Underhill, John Salmon, William Segar; together with several priests, rectors, vicars, and curates of churches; as John Thompson, Roger Barret, John Woolcock, William Asa, James Mourton, John Barrow, Richard Bennet, and others; who mustered their soldiers according to the rules of military discipline, at Bodm*a*n, where the general rendezvous was appointed. But no sooner was the general, Arundell, departed from St. Michael's Mount, to exert his power in the camp (camp!) and field aforesaid, but divers gentlemen, with their wives and families, in his absence possessed themselves thereof. Whereupon he dispatched a party of horse and foot, to reduce his old garrison; which quickly they effected, by reason the besieged wanted provision and ammunition, and were distracted with the women and children's fears and cries; so that they yielded the possession to their enemies, on condition of free liberty of departing forthwith from thence with life, though not without being plundered.—The retaking of St. Michael's Mount by General Arundell, proved much to the content and satisfaction of his army at Bodm*a*n, consisting of above 6000 men; which they looked upon as a good omen of their future success, and the first-fruits of the valour and conduct of their general. Whereupon, the confederates daily increased his army with great numbers of men from all parts, who listed themselves under his banner, which was not only pourtrayed, but by a cart brought into the field for their encouragement, viz. the Pyx under its canopy, that is to say, the vessel containing the Roman Host or Sacramental Sacrifice or Body of Christ, together with crosses, banners, candlesticks, holy bread and water, to defend them from Devils and the adverse power, (see Fox's Martyrologie, page 669); which was carried wheresoever the camp removed. Which camp grew so tremendously formidable at Bodman, that Job Militon, Esq. then sheriff of Cornwall, with all the power of his bailywick, durst not encounter with it, during the time of the general's stay in that place. Which gave him and his rebels opportunity, to consult together for the good of their publick interest, and to make out a declaration or manifesto of the justice of their cause, and grounds of taking up arms. But the army in general, consisting of a mixed multitude, of men of divers professions, trades, and employment, could not easily agree upon the subject-matter and form thereof. Some would have no Justices of the Peace, for that generally they were ignorant of the laws, and could not construe or English a Latin bill of indictment, without the Clerk of the Peace's assistance; who imposed upon them with other attornies for gain, wrong sense and judgment. Besides, in themselves they were corrupt and partial in determining cases. Others would have no Lawyers nor Attornies; for that the one cheated the people in wrong advice or counsel, and the other of their money by extravagant bills of costs. Others (would have) no Court Leets or Court Barons; for that the cost and expence in prosecuting an action at law therein, was many times greater than the debt or profit. But generally it was agreed upon among them, that no inclosures should be left standing, but that all lands should be held in common. Yet what expedients should be found out, and placed in the rooms of those several orders and degrees of men and officers; none could prescribe.—However,

ever, the priefts, rectors, vicars, and curates, the priors, monks, friers, and other diffolved collegiates, hammered out feven articles of addrefs for the Kings Majefty; upon grant of which, they declared their bodies, arms, and goods fhould be at his difpofal, viz.

I.—That Curates fhould adminifter Baptifm at all times of need, as well week days as holy days.

II.—That their children might be confirmed by the Bifhop.

III.—That Mafs might be celebrated, no man communicating with the Prieft.

IV.—That they might have refervation of the Lord's Body in churches.

V.—That they might have holy bread and water, in remembrance of Chrift's body and blood.

VI.—That Priefts might be un-married.

VII.—That the fix articles, fet forth by King Henry 8, might be continued, at leaft till the King came of age. Now thofe fix articles were invented by Stephen Gardiner, Bifhop of Winchefter, who was the baftard fon of Lyonell Woodvill, Bifhop of Salifbury, by his concubine Eliz. Gardiner, the which Lyonell was the fifth fon of Richard Woodvill Earl Rivers, 1470; and therefore called his Creed.

That the body of Chrift is really prefent in the Sacrament, after confecration.

That the Sacrament cannot truly be adminiftered under both kinds.

That Priefts entered into Holy Orders might not marry.

That the vows of chaftity, entered into upon mature deliberation, were to be kept.

That private Maffes were not to be omitted.

That Auricular Confeffion was neceffary in the church of God.

To thefe demands of the Cornifh rebels the King fo far condefcended, as to fend an anfwer in writing to every article, and alfo a general pardon to every one of them, if they would lay down their arms (fee Foxe's Acts and Monuments, Book 9, p. 668.) But alas! thefe overtures of the King's were not only rejected by the rebels, but made them the more bold and defperate; efpecially, finding themfelves unable longer to fubfift upon their own eftates and monies, or the bounty of the country, which hitherto they had done. The General therefore refolved, as the fox, who feldom chucks at home, to prey upon other men's goods and eftates farther off; for his army's better fubfiftence. Whereupon he diflodged from Bodman, and marched with his foldiers into Devon; where Sir Peter Carew, Knt. was ready to obftruct his paffage, with his poffe comitatus. But when they faw the order and difcipline of the rebels, and that their army confifted of above 6000 fighting-men defperate, well armed, and prepared for battle; the Sheriff and his troops permitted them quietly to pafs through the heart of that country to Exon. Where the citizens, upon notice of their approaches, as formerly done, fhut the gates and put themfelves in a pofture of defence. At which time Dr. John Voyfey was Bifhop of Exon, viz. 10th July, 1549, John Blacaler was mayor, William Tothill was fheriff, Lewis Pollard, recorder; William Beaumont, fword-bearer; John Drake, Geffery Arundell, Henry Maunder, John Tooker, were bayliffs or ftewards; Thomas Preftwood, John Maynard, John Webb, William Hals, Hugh Pope, William Hurft, Nicholas Limmet, Robert Midwinter, Henry Booth, John Berry, John Britnall, John Tuckfield, John Stawell, Edward Bridgeman, Thomas Grigg, John Drake, Thomas Skidmore, John Bodley, and others, (all which had before that time been mayors), ftewards or bayliffs of the city (fee *Ifack's* Memorials of Exon, page 122).—Things being in this pofture, the General Arundell fummoned the mayor and citizens, to deliver their town and caftle to his dominion.* But they fent him a flat denial. Whereupon forthwith he ordered his men, to fire the gates of the city, which accordingly they did. But the citizens on the infide fupplied thofe fires, with fuch quantities of combuftible matter fo long; till they had caft up a half-moon on the infide thereof. Upon which, when the rebels attempted to enter, they were inftantly fhot to death or cut to pieces. Their entrance being thus obftructed at the gates, they put in practice other expedients, viz. either to undermine the walls or blow them up, with barrels of gunpowder, which they had placed in the fame. But the citizens alfo prevented this their defign, by countermining their mines, and cafting fo much water on the places where their powder-barrels were lodged, that the powder would not take fire. Thus ftratagems of war were daily practifed, between the befieged and the befiegers; to the great hurt and damage of each other—King Edward being informed by his council of this fiege, and that there was little or no dependence upon the valour or conduct of the Sheriff of Devon and his bailywick, to fupprefs this rebellion or raifing the fiege of Exon; granted his commiffion to John Lord Ruffel, created Baron Ruffel, of Taviftock, by King Henry 8, Lord High Admiral and Lord Privy Seal, an old experienced foldier, who had loft an eye at the fiege of Montrule, in France, to be his General for raifing foldiers to fight thofe rebels. Who forthwith, purfuant thereto, rofe a confiderable army, and marched with them to Honyton. But, when he came there, he was informed, that the enemy confifted of ten thoufand able fighting men, well armed; which occafioned his halting there longer than he had intended, expecting greater fupplies of men, that were coming to his aid under conduct of the Lord Grey, which at length arrived and joined his forces. Whereupon he diflodged from thence, and marched towards Exon; where, on the way, he had feveral fharp conflicts with the rebels, with various fuccefs, fome times the better and fome times the worfe; though at length, after much fatigues of war, maugre all oppofition and refiftance of the rebels, he forced them to raife their fiege, and entered the city of Exon with relief, the 6th of Auguft, 1549, after thirty-two days fiege, wherein the inhabitants had valiantly defended themfelves, though in that extremity they were neceffitated by famine, to eat horfes, moulded cloth, and bread made of bran. In reward of whofe loyalty, King Edward gave to the city the manour of Exeyland, fince fold by the city for making the river Exe navigable.—After raifing the fiege as aforefaid, the General Arundell rallied his routed forces of rebels; and gave battle to the Lord Ruffel and the King's army, with that inveterate courage, animofity, and refolution, that the greateft part of his men were flain upon the fpot; others threw down their arms on mercy. The remainder fled, and were afterwards many of them taken, and executed by martial law. The General Arundell, and fome of the chief officers aforefaid, were fent up to London, and there executed. Sir Anthony Kingfton, Knt. a Gloucefterfhire man, after this rebellion was made Provoft Marfhal, for executing fuch weftern

* The rebels, commanded by Arundel, laid fiege to the city; boafting, that they would fhortly meafure all the filks and fattins in it by the length of their bows. After the lofs of about 1000, they were forced to raife the fiege and return to Launcefton. Arundel was taken and executed. *Holingfhed. Stowe.*

ſaid to have afforded a ſafe protection to many of his Majeſty's loyal ſubjects. But among thoſe, who were not ſo fortunate as to gain an aſylum, were Sir Richard Grenville and his lady. In this "commotion (ſays *Carew*) S. Richard Greynuile the elder did, with his ladie and followers, put themſelues into the caſtle of Trematon, and there for a while indured the rebels ſiege, incamped in three places againſt it, who wanting great ordinance, could haue wrought the beſieged ſmall ſcathe, had his friends, or enemies, kept faith and promiſe: but ſome of thoſe within, ſlipping by night ouer the wals, with their bodies after their hearts, and thoſe without, mingling humble intreatings with rude menaces, he was hereby wonne, to iſſue forth at a poſterne gate for parley. The while, a part of thoſe rakehels, not knowing what honeſtie, and farre leſſe, how much the word of a ſouldier imported, ſtepped betweene him and home, laid hold on his aged vnweyldie body, and threatned to leaue it liueleſſe, if the incloſed did not leaue their reſiſtance. So proſecuting their firſt treacherie againſt the prince, with ſuteable actions towards his ſubiects, they ſeized on the caſtle, and exerciſed the vttermoſt of their barbarous crueltie (death excepted) on the ſurpriſed priſoners. The ſeely gentlewomen, without regard of ſexe or ſhame, were ſtripped from their apparrell to their very ſmockes, and ſome of their fingers broken, to plucke away their rings, and Sir Richard himſelfe made an exchange from Trematon Caſtle, to that of Launceſton, with the gayle to boote."* Of the proceedings of Sir Anthony Kingſton, the Provoſt Marſhall of the King's army, on the occaſion of this rebellion, tradition hath preſerved memorials,† not much to his credit.—There are letters directed

weſtern rebels as could be taken or were made priſoners in Cornwall and Devon; together with all ſuch who had been aiders or affiſters of them in that rebellion. Upon whom, according to his power and office, he executed martial law with ſport and juſtice, as Mr. Carew and other hiſtorians tell us. And the principal perſons that have come to my knowledge, over whoſe miſery he triumphed, was Boyer the mayor of Bodman, Mayow, of Glevyan, in St. Columb, whom he hanged at the Tavern ſign poſt in that town, of whom tradition ſaith his crime was not capital; and therefore his wife was adviſed by her friends to haſten to the town, after the Marſhall and his men had him in cuſtody, and beg his life; which accordingly ſhe prepared to do. And, to render herſelf the more amiable petitioner before the Marſhall's eyes, this dame ſpent ſo much time in attiring herſelf, and putting on her French hood, then in faſhion; that her huſband was put to death, before her arrival. In like manner the Marſhall hanged one John Payne, the mayor or portreeve of St. Ives, on a gallows erected in the middle of the town; whoſe armes are ſtill to be ſeen in one of the fore-ſeats in that church, viz. in a plain field three pine-apples. Beſides thoſe, he executed many more in other places in Cornwall; that had been actors, affiſters, or promoters of this rebellion. Laſtly, 'tis further memorable of this Sir Anthony Kingſton, that in Sir John Heywood's Chronicle, he is taxed of extreme cruelty in doing his Marſhall's office aforeſaid. Of whom Fuller in Glouceſterſhire, gives us this further account of him; that afterwards, in the reign of Queen Mary, being detected with ſeveral others of a deſign to rob her exchequer, tho' he made his eſcape and fled into his own country, yet there he was apprehended and taken into cuſtody by a meſſenger; who was bringing him up to London, in order to have juſtice done upon him for his crime; but he, being conſcious of his guilt, and deſpairing of pardon, ſo effectually poiſoned himſelf, without having *Capiſtrum Kingeretur* the reward of his deſert, viz. the girt of an halter." *Hals's* MS. *W.* vol. II. pp. 53, 57.

* *Carew*, ff. 111, 112. "Sir *Rich. Greinvile* the elder [ſays *Carew* in another place, ſee f. 62.) did enterlace his home-majiſtracy with martiall employments abroad: whereof the King teſtifyed his good liking by his liberality. Which domeſtical example encouraged his ſonne *Roger* the more heartily to hazard, and the more willingly to reſign his life in the unfortunate Mary Roſe."—His ſon again, the ſecond *Sir Richard!*"—[Here Carew ſpeaks of the ſignal action in the *Revenge*, all the circumſtances of which will be related in a ſubſequent page.] "Laſtly, his ſon *John* took hold of every martiall occaſion that was miniſtred him, untill in ſervice againſt her Highneſſe enemies, under the command of Sir Walter Ralegh, bedde ocean become his bed of honour." f. 62.—Of this family, how many died violent deaths!—A peculiar fatality ſeems to have attended it!

† Sir Anthony Kingſton married Mary, the widow of Sir William Courtenay, and lived at Cadhay; which was his wife's jointure, as well as Honiton. "This Sir *Anthony Kingſton* was Provoſt-Marſhal of the King's army that defeated the rebels in Devonſhire, in the reign of King Edward VI. and he was eſteemed by many cruel and barbarous in his executions. One *Boyer* mayor of Bodmyn in Cornwall, was obſerved to be among the ſeditious, but was forced to it, as were many others: the Marſhal wrote him a letter that he would dine with him at his houſe upon a day which he appointed; the mayor ſeemed glad, and made for him the beſt proviſion that he could: upon the day he came, and a great company with him, and was received with great ceremony. A little before dinner, he took the mayor aſide, and whiſpered him in the ear, that an execution

directed to Sir John Arundell, of Trerice, "from the King's counſell; by ſome of which it appeareth, that hee was viceadmirall of the King's ſhippes, in the weſt ſeas, and by others, that hee had the goods and lands of certaine rebels giuen him, for his good ſeruices."* Sir *Thomas Arundel*, a younger brother of Lanherne-Houſe, married the ſiſter of Queen Catherine Howard, and was a Privy Counſellor of Edward the ſixth: but from his attachment to the Lord Protector, with the Lord Protector he loſt his head.†

Of the events of QUEEN MARY's reign, Cornwall from its remoteneſs, was little elſe than a ſpectator. It is a happy circumſtance, when "good people are out of harm's way."‡ The

I treaty

execution muſt that day be done in the town, and therefore required him that a pair of gallows ſhould be made, and erected againſt the time that dinner ſhould end. The mayor was diligent to fullfil his command, and no ſooner was dinner ended, but he demanded of the mayor, whether the work was finiſhed? The mayor anſwered, that all was ready: I pray you, ſays the Provoſt, bring me to the place; and therewith took him friendly by the hand, and beholding the gallows, he aſked the mayor, whether he thought them to be ſtrong enough? Yes, ſaid the mayor, doubtleſs they are: well, ſaid the Provoſt, get you up ſpeedily, for they are prepared for you. I hope, anſwered the mayor, you mean not as you ſpeak. In faith, ſaith the Provoſt, there is no remedy, for you have been a buſy rebel; and ſo he preſently hung him up. Near the ſaid place dwelt a miller, who had been a buſy actor in that rebellion, and fearing the coming of the Provoſt-Marſhal, told his ſervant, that he had occaſion to go from home; and therefore told him, if any ſhould enquire after the miller, that he ſhould ſay that he was the miller, and ſo he had been for three years before: ſo when the Provoſt came and called for the miller, his ſervant came forth, and ſaid that he was the man: the Provoſt demanded how long he had kept the mill? theſe three years, anſwered the ſervant: then the Provoſt commanded his men to ſeize him, and to hang him on the next tree: then the fellow cried out, that he was not the miller, but the miller's man. Nay, Sir, ſays the Provoſt, I will take thee to thy word; if thou art the miller, thou art a buſy knave; if thou art not, thou art a falſe lying knave; whatſoever thou art, thou ſhalt be hanged. When others alſo told him, that the fellow was but the miller's man; what then, ſaid he, could he ever have done his maſter any better ſervice than to hang for him? and ſo without more ado he was diſpatched.—In 1555, the 3d of Queen Mary, there was a Parliament called, and this Sir Anthony Kingſton was, ſaith Dr. Burnet, a great ſtickler in it; and it muſt be for the Proteſtant Religion againſt the court, ſeeing that he hanged up ſo many in King Edward's time for their riſing in rebellion for their old religion; and being a bold daring man, he one day, during the time of the ſitting of the Parliament, took away the keys of the houſe from the ſerjeant, which, it ſeems, was not diſpleaſing to the major part of the houſe, ſince they did nothing upon it, ſaith Dr. Burnet; but the day before the Parliament was diſſolved he was ſent to the tower, on the 9th of December, and lay there 'till the 23d of that month, and then he ſubmitted and aſked pardon, and was diſcharged. But he was the next year accuſed to have engaged in a deſign with ſome others to have robbed the Exchequer of 50,000l. whereupon ſix of the confederates were executed for felony, and Sir Anthony Kingſton died in his way to London from Devonſhire, as they were bringing him up; and if he had not, he would, in all probability, have been ſerved in the ſame manner that he ſerved the mayor of Bodmyn, the miller, and many others." See *Baker's* Chronicle, p. 305; *Burnet's Hiſt.* of the Reformation, vol. 2, p. 324; and *Cleaveland's* Courtenay, pp. 293, 294.—*Carew* ſeems to apologize for the conduct of the Provoſt-Marſhall. "Sir Anthony Kingſton hath left his name more memorable then commendable, amongſt the townſmen of Bodmin, for cauſing their maior to erect a gallows before his owne doore, upon which (after having feaſted Sir Anthony) himſelfe was hanged. In like ſort (ſay they) he truſſed up a miller's man thereby, for that he preſented himſelfe in the others ſtead, and ſaying he could never do his maſter better ſervice. But mens tongues, readily inclined to the worſt reports, haue left out a part of the truth, in this tale, that the reſt might carrie the better grace. For Sir Anthony did nothing herein, as a Iudge by diſcretion, but as an officer by direction; and beſides, hee gaue the maior ſufficient watchwordes of timely warning, and large ſpace of reſpite (more then which, in regard of his owne perill, he could not afford) to ſhift for ſafety, if an vneſchewable deſtiny, had not haltered him to that aduancement. As for the millers man, he equalled his maſter, in their common offence of rebellion, and therefore it deſerued the praiſe of mercy, to ſpare one of the two, and not the blame of crueltie, to hang one for another." *Carew*, f. 124.—Carew is here a bad advocate. If Sir Anthony intended to execute the mayor, was it not perfidiouſly cruel to lull his victim into a falſe confidence, by dining with him familiarly? Was not this, deceit combined with barbarity? Was it not the monkey and the tiger, blended in one animal, playful and treacherous, wanton and ſanguinary—the French aſſaſſin, laughing in the midſt of murder, not the Engliſh judge, ſhedding tears of pity over thoſe whom the law condemns to die? If Sir Anthony did not intend to execute the mayor, would he have ventured to partake of the mayor's entertainment? Muſt he not have felt and thought, that ſuch familiarity was likely to excite a ſuſpicion of partiality, and even diſloyalty in himſelf? And would he not therefore, have avoided all open communication with the culprit, and have warned him in private to make his eſcape from the place? He could eaſily have conveyed a ſecret hint to the mayor, and a hint as effectual as ſecret.

* *Carew*, f. 147.

† In 1551, the Protector was ſent to the tower, with Sir Thomas Arundel and others. They were accuſed of a conſpiracy, in which Arundel was to have ſeized on the tower. Sir Thomas Arundel was much lamented. His jury was ſhut up a whole day and a night. And thoſe who were for acquitting him, were compelled by the fury of the reſt, only that they might ſave their own lives, and not be ſtarved. At length he was condemned and beheaded." *Carew*, f. 61.—*Hayward, Speed, Heylin.*

‡ Say the authors of *Magna Britannia*, on Cornwall's eſcape from the minions of perſecution.

treaty of marriage between Philip and our Queen, occafioned a confiderable ferment in the country: and a confederacy of fome moment was formed between the Duke of Suffolk, Sir Thomas Wiat and *Sir Peter Carew*; the firft of whom was to raife the midland counties, the fecond, the county of Kent, and the third, Cornwall. But ere the defign was ripe for execution, the project in the weft was difcovered: and *Carew* fled into France.* After a pretty general alarm, the Duke of Suffolk was feized and imprifoned; and Wiat condemned and executed; but not before he had accufed the Princefs Elizabeth and the Earl of Devon of being acceffaries in the Cornifh infurrection; in confequence of which, tho' Wiat, on the fcaffold, recanted the accufation, the Earl and Princefs were fent prifoners to the tower.‡

From

* Sir Peter was taken and brought a prifoner to England. But he lived many years after, and died in Ireland. *Baker*, p. 318.—Sir *Thomas Moyle*, with Sir Thomas Finch and others, was fent, the firft of Philip and Mary, to fupprefs Wyat's rebellion.—The Prideaux Carew [a MS. of the Rev. Prideaux Brune] at f. 110, b.

‡ COURTENAY, ARUNDEL, and EDGCUMBE ftand foremoft in this reign, as in moft others. The COURTENAYS. Boconnoc belonged to the Courtenays Earls of Devon. At the death of Earl Edward, it became the fhare of William de Mohun thro' Ifabel Courtenay. This Edward, who flourifhed in the reign before us, was propofed for a hufband to Queen Mary. And the propofal feems to have coincided with the inclination of the Queen, tho' by no means with that of the Earl of Devonfhire, who had a tender regard for the Princefs Elizabeth. In the Britifh Mufeum is a MS. paper, entitled "A relation how one Cleber, 1556, proclaimed the *Ladie Elizabeth*, QUENE; and her beloved bedfellow, *Lorde Edward Courtneye*, KYNGE!!" MS. *Harl.* 537, 27.—Prince has given us a very interefting memoir of Edward the laft of the Courtenays poffeffor of Boconnoc. "This Lord *Edward*, (fays he) was the no fortunate fon of a very unfortunate father; for however, at firft, he was greatly in favor of K. Hen. 8, and had, by his royal bounty, feveral eftates confer'd upon him, and was advanced, from being the Earl of Devon, to be Marquefs of Exeter; yet, afterwards, he fell into his great difpleafure, being accufed, for holding correfpondency with Cardinal *Poole*, and other the King's enemies beyond the feas, and confpiring the King's deftruction. Hereupon, he was committed to the tower, the 5th of November, the 30th of K. Hen. 8, 1538; and, on the 3d of January following, being brought to his tryal, before *Thomas Lord Audley*, fitting high-fteward for that time, he was found guilty, and received fentence of death. Though the King had long favored him as his kinfman, yet, 'tis faid, in regard of his near alliance to the crown, he became fo jealous of his greatnefs, whereof the Marquefs had given fome teftimony, in his fo fuddain raifing divers thoufands againft the Yorkfhire rebels, that he gladly entertained any occafion to cut him off. Whereupon he was foon beheaded, and attainted in the Parliament, held the next enfuing year.—This noble Lord Edward, as if he muft partake of his father's guilt, becaufe he did of his blood, was hereupon committed to the tower, where he remained a prifoner divers years, viz. from the latter end of the reign of K. Hen. 8, unto the beginning of the reign of Q. Mary; who, in the firft year thereof, coming to the tower, had at her entrance there, prefented to her *Thomas* Duke of *Norfolk*, the Dutchefs of *Somerfet*, *Stephen Gardiner* Bifhop of *Winchefter*, and this *Edward* Lord *Courtenay*: who all kneeling down, the Queen kiffed them, and faid, thefe be my prifoners; and caufed them prefently to be fet at liberty. And on the 3d of September, the fame year, fhe reftored the Lord *Courtenay* to the honor of his family, and created him Earl of Devonfhire, at her Palace of Richmund.—This moft noble young Earl, was a perfon of lovely afpect, of a beautiful body, fweet nature, and loyal defcent, all which concurring in him, the Queen caft an obliging countenance upon him; and, as 'twas generally conceived, intended him an hufband for herfelf. Of which, report hath handed down unto us this confirmation, that when the faid Earl petitioned the Queen, for leave to travel; fhe advifed him, rather to marry, enfuring him, that no lady in the land, how high foever, would refufe him for an hufband; and urging him to make his choice where he pleafed, fhe pointed herfelf out unto him, as plainly as might confift with the modefty of a maiden, and the Majefty of a Queen.—Hereupon, the young Earl, whether becaufe his long durance had fome influence on his brain, or that naturally his face was better than his head, or out of fome private fancy and affection (which is moft probable) to the Lady Elizabeth, or out of a loyal bafhfulnefs,§ not prefuming to climbe fo high, but expecting to be called up; is faid, to have requefted the Queen for leave to marry her fifter, the Lady Elizabeth, afterwards the moft glorious ftar in the Britifh orb, or indeed the whole weftern horizon, Queen of England. Unhappy it was for both, that his choice went fo high, or no higher; for who could have fpoken worfe treafon againft Mary, though not againft the Queen, than to prefer, in affection, her fifter before her? Upon this, he was ever after fufpected; and the Princefs Elizabeth (innocent Lady!) did afterwards dearly pay the fcore of this his indifcretion. But what did greatly contribute to their troubles, was a falfe accufation laid to their charge, by Sir *Thomas Wiat* of Kent; who having raifed confiderable forces, to oppofe (as he pretended) Q. Mary's match with Philip of Spain, being fuppreffed, and taken prifoner, in hopes of his life, he accufed this noble Earl, and the lady Elizabeth, the Queen's fifter, as privy to his confpiracy: whereupon the matter was fo urged againft them both, by Gardiner, Bifhop of Winchefter and Lord Chancellor, that they were both committed to the tower. At which place, I fuppofe it was, fhe was baited with this queftion, *What fhe thought of thefe words of Chrift*, this is my body? *Whether they did not imply the true Body of Chrift in the Sacrament?* to which catching queftion, after fome paufing, the royal Princefs returned this difcreet anfwer:

Chrift was the word that fpake it:
He took the bread and brake it:
And what the word did make it,
That I believe, and take it.

§ Baker fays, that her Lutheranifm was the exception againft *Courtenay*, as the hufband of Queen Mary. *Baker*, p. 318.

From a tranfient view of Queen Mary's days, we obferve, that one feature of the times, was a fpirit of chivalry, diftinguifhable both in the gallantries of love, and the enterprizes of

I 2 war.

However, they were, by Wiat's accufation, committed to the tower, they were foon after releafed; for at his death, he cleared them both, and protefted openly, that they were altogether innocent, and never had been acquainted with his proceedings.—Nor was this favor of Q. Mary to this noble Earl, an effect only of a private affection; but in regard of his royal defcent, florifhing youth, and courteous difpofition, he was one of the three, then propofed to her for an hufband, by her council; the firft, was Cardinal Poole, four and fifty years old, as old for a batchelor, as fhe for a maid (being then feven and thirty years of age); but he was laid afide, as not fo likely for procreation: the fecond, was this Lord Courtenay, Earl of Devon, a goodly gentleman, but there was this exception againft him, as if enclining, as was thought, to Lutherifm: the third took effect, Philip Prince of Spain, the Emperor Charles the 5th's eldeft fon.—When thefe matters were well over, the Earl's humor returned upon him to travel; and he obtained leave of the Queen to go and fee foreign countries. An undertaking, well manag'd, no lefs profitable than delightfom; as what not only furnifhes the tongue with variety of good difcourfe, but the mind alfo with experience and underftanding. Hereupon this noble Earl fitted himfelf for his journey; and leaving England, he travelled into Italy; where having feen feveral other places, he came at length to Padua, where he died, not without fufpicion of poifon, on the 4th of October, 1556.—His honorable remains, after his deplorable deceafe, were repofed in St. Anthony's Church in that city, where a noble monument was erected to his memory, having this infcription.

Anglia quem genuit, fueratq, habitura Patronum
  Corteneum celfa hæc continet arca Ducem:
Credita caufa necis, Regni affectata Cupido;
  Reginæ optatum tunc quoque Connubium,
Cui regni Proceres non confenfere Philippo
  Reginam Regi jungere poffe rati.
Europam unde fuit juveni peragrare neceffe
  Ex quo Mors mifero contigit ante diem.
Anglia fi plorat, defuncto Principe tanto
  Nil mirum, Domino deficit illa pio.
Sed jam Corteneus Cœlo fruiturq; Beatis
  Cum doleant Angli, cum fine fine gemant.
Cortenei Probittas igitur, Præftantia, Nomen,
  Dum Stabit hoc Templum, vivida Semper erunt.
Angliaq; hinc etiam Stabit, Stabuntq; Britanni
  Conjugii optati Fama perennis erit.
Improba naturæ Leges Libitina refcindens,
  Ex æquo Juvenes, præcipitatq; Senes.

This Lord Edward was the laft Earl of Devon, of this moft noble and antient family, which had enjoy'd the title for no lefs than ten defcents together; with the interpofition only of Humphry Stafford, Lord Stafford of South-wick; who by K. Edw. 4, was created Earl of Devonfhire; and had granted him the honors of Okehamton and Plimton, with the lands thereunto appertaining. But he did not enjoy the honor above three months: for having dealt traiteroufly with the faid King, he was apprehended at Bridgewater, in Somerfetfhire, and beheaded: he died without iffue.—Whereupon, Sir Edward Courtenay, fon of Sir Hugh Courtenay of Boconock, fon of Sir Hugh Courtenay of Haccombe, younger fon of Sir Edward Courtenay, brother of the Earl of Devonfhire, was, by K. Henry 7. in the firft year of his reign, reftored, and made Earl of Devonfhire. —There were three of this name that fucceeded him in the Earldom; but Edward, the laft, dying without iffue, the lands were divided among the heirs of Edward's four fifters, that was advanced to the Earldom, as was faid, by K. Hen. 7. Thus difpofed of in marriage; Elizabeth, to John Tretherf; Mawd, to John Arundel of Talvern; Ifabel, to William Mohun; and Florence, to John Trelawny, the anceftor, in a direct line, of the prefent honorable, and right reverend Father in God, Sir Jonathan Trelawny, Baronet, Lord Bifhop of this diocefs." *Prince*, pp. 185, 187.

In another place (Prince informs us) "Edmund, fecond fon of *Thomas Tremayne*, Efq. became a fervant to Edward Earl of Devon, and Marquefs of Exeter, and a great fufferer for his inviolable fidelity to his noble mafter. For when the Marquefs of Exeter and the Lady Elizabeth, (afterwards Queen of England), were committed to the tower in Queen Mary's days, upon an accufation of being privy to Wyat's confpiracy, Mr. Edmund Tremayne was fet on the rack, thereby to exhort from him a confeffion of their guilt. Wherein approving their innocency and his own fidelity with invincible refolution, he was, upon the Lady Elizabeth's advancement to the throne, in recompence thereof, made one of the clerks of her Majefty's Privy Council. He had, alfo, an honorary falary fettled upon him by the city of Exeter, for the good offices it had received and expected from him. This gentleman married Eulalia, daughter of Sir John Saintleger, by whom he had iffue two fons named Francis, who both died without iffue." *Prince's* Worthies, p. 570.—Coryat, defcribing St. Antony's Church, at Padua, thus notices the monument of Edward Courtenay, Earl of Devon. "In the Cloyfter, I obferved a monument that made me even lament." "Truely it ftrooke great compaffion and remorfe in me to fee an Englifhman fo ignobly buried. For his body lieth in a poore wooden coffin, placed upon another faire monument, having neither epitaph nor any other thing to preferve it from oblivion: fo that I could not have known it for an Englifhman's coffin, except an Englifh gentleman my kinde friend Mr. George Rooke, had told me of it, and fhewed me the ftone." *Coryat's* Crudities, vol. 1, pp. 176, 177. [Octavo Edit. 1776.]—The ARUNDELS. "The Queene wrote to Sir *John Arundell* of Trerice, praying and requiring that hee with his friends and neighbours, fhould fee the Prince of Spaine moft honourably entertained, if he fortuned to land in Cornwall. Shee wrote to

war. This will be more apparent in the reign of ELIZABETH. And, perhaps, the heroic paffion was cherifhed, in no fmall degree, by the mode of education then prevalent among the higher claffes.

to him (being then Sheriffe of Cornwall) touching the election of the knights of the fhire, and the burgeffes for the Parliament. Shee likewife wrote to him, that (notwithftanding the inftructions to the Juftices) he fhould mufter, and furnifh his feruants, tenants and others, vnder his rule and offices, with his friends, for the defence, and quieting of the countrie, with ftanding of enemies, and any other employment, as alfo to certifie, what force of horfe and foote hee could arme." *Carew*, f. 147, b.—The EDGECUMBES. Sir Richard Edgecumbe who flourifhed in the time of Queen Mary, was the moft diftinguifhed of this noble family. "This gentleman (fays *Prince*) was of a truly great and generous difpofition, as may farther appear from that particular hiftory of his life, I have been fo happy to light upon, in manufcript, written by his grandfon *Richard Carew*, Efquire, (intituled, *A friendly remembrance of* Sir Richard Edgecombe; now in my poffeffion; where are alfo feveral poems, written by the fame Richard Carew, Efquire, with a learned letter againft the fupremacy of the Pope, and other things) the celebrated author of the Surveigh of Cornwal: whofe own language, though fomwhat antiquated, I fhall here prefent to the reader's view, and the example he defcribes, to his imitation.—Many (faith he) have been more heedful to rehearfe the times of their anceftors births and deaths, the number of their wives and children, and the pomp of their wealth and offices; than to exprefs the vertues of their minds, fhining in the uprightnefs of their lives, and haughtinefs of their enterprizes. This refpect hath the fooner emboldned me to fupply that want, which I fee utterly unfurnifhed by any other, in behalf of one, who becaufe he was by nature my grandfather, and in good-will my father, I could not but bear him a dutiful and affectionate mind, whilft he lived; and reverence his remembrance being dead.—I will therefore, among many of his virtues, rehearfe only thofe, which were chiefly noted of others, and are fitted for us to follow; namely, his *Knowledge*, *Courtefy*, and *Liberality*.—His knowledge confifted in learning and wifdom.—His learning may be divided into divine and profane; that is to fay, religion and the liberal fciences.—Touching his religion, I will not ftand long therein, becaufe I count it a hard matter, for any to judge of another man's heart; and the days wherein he moftly lived, favored of Romifh ruft; yet, if guefs may be given by outward fhew, his upright dealing bears witnefs, that he had the fruits of a good confcience. Befides, in his lifetime, he kept an ordinary chaplain in his houfe, who daily and duly faid fervice: and at his death, he had the grace to call upon God.—His learning in the arts, he attained by his ftudy in the Univerfity of Oxford, where he fpent fome part of his youth; not idly, nor only whilft he baited his horfe (as the fcholarly-minifter anfwered the bifhop's ordinary); but both orderly and profitably: for he could tell, as I guefs, by certain rules of aftrology, what any man's errand was, that came unto him. And in endicting of letters he was fo fkilful, that being on a time at the quarter-feffions, where was fome difference about the form of one, to be fent up to the Lords of the Council, he ftep'd down from the bench, and at a fuddain penned it fo well, to all their likings, as, without farther amendment, they allowed and fent it forth: yea, the Lord Cromwel, in this point, gave him fpecial commendations. He had alfo a very good grace in making Englifh Verfes, fuch as, in thofe days, paffed for current; which flowing eafily from his pen, did much delight the readers. The fharpnefs of his wit was alfo feen in his apophthegms; of which, though I have heard many, I only remember two, the one, that Ingratus was Latin for a Prieft (underftand him, reader, of them of thofe times); and the other, that where the good-man did beat his wife, there Cupid would fhake his wings, and fly out of doors.—For his wifdom, I will only give a tafte, or effay thereof, that by fome parts, the whole may be guefs'd. For he that would take upon him, to difcourfe of every point, muft needs be a wife man himfelf. He ufed, what occafion foever he had of expences, to keep always a hundred pounds in his cheft untouch'd: and yet he would never be long indebted unto any man, neither break promife of payment. Wherein he furely dealt far more difcreetly than thofe, who having fair revenues, are notwithftanding fo beggarly, that when any coft is to beftowed, for their own profit, the benefit of the Prince, or behoof of their country, they are forced to take it up at fuch hands, as turneth to their great lofs; or elfe to leave themfelves utterly difcredited, their country unhelped, and their Prince unferved. What grief of mind it procureth them, when they are forced to bewray their want, and to fend pofting up and down with all hafte and lefs fpeed; what fpeech of the people it caufeth (who commonly caft their eyes on their betters to pry on their doings); and how little truft it gaineth among their creditors, to be ever borrowing and never paying, I need not tell them; fince by proof they know it fufficiently already. Neither boots it to warn them by words, when by fuch wounds and ftripes to their good name and confciences, they will not learn to falve the fame in time. Auguftus the Emperor hearing a Roman Knight to be dead, who being in his life-time accounted rich, was at his end found fo poor, as the fale of his goods was not able to countervail the charge of the debts, willed his bed to be bought for himfelf; *For I am well affured* (quoth he) *I fhall eafily take my reft in that bed, where one owing fo much could quietly fleep.* What eafe they have to lye fnorting fo in the carelefnefs of their affairs, I know not; but this I know, that they can give no greater caufe of forrow to their friends, rejoycing to their enemies, or utter difliking to the whole world. And this much I have ventured to fay the rather, that by difplaying the harms of the contrary, his careful forefight in preventing the fame, might the better appear.—He was alfo very careful to have provifion made before-hand, of all things belonging to his houfhold, for two years at leaft; and would very willingly beftow his money that way, whenfoever any good pennyworth was to be had, though he did not prefently need it. Befides, he was fo careful for his pofterity, as at his death he left 400l. of old gold in his cheft, for the fuing of his fons livery. It was moreover noted in him, that whatfoever he did, he would be always girt with a fword, or at leaft with a hanger; which that he did not do of curiofity, as if he would be like Julius Cæfar (he held a fword in one hand and a book in the other, with this motto, *Ex utroq, Cæfar*), who carried his commentaries in his bofom, his pen in his right-hand, and his launce in his left; or to imitate Alexander the Great, who flept always with his fword by his bed-fide, and Homer's Iliades under his pillow, the plainnefs of the reft of his life doth fufficiently witnefs: his reafon thereof was, (as I have heard) that fome part of his oath of knighthood did bind him thereunto.—Another point of his wifdom was, that he continually maintained one at London, to be a folicitor of his caufes; and to fend him advertifement, with the fooneft, of all occurrences from the court, and elfewhere; wherein if order were given him, for any bufinefs, concerning the fervice of his Prince or country, or that his help were

claffes. It was a cuftom at this time, to educate young gentlemen and ladies in the houfes of the great. And fome of the principal gentry of Devon and Cornwall were brought up with the

were craved in behalf of his friend, he would not flack any time, nor overflip any fit occafion, for difpatch thereof. For his friends, he would deal as advifedly, and follow it as effectually, as if the matter were his own. In his Princefs's fervice, he was ready with the foremoft, to execute her commandments; and prepared with the fooneft, to return anfwer.—And whenfoever he was to meet at any place, for his country's affairs, he would always come with the firft, and depart with the laft, faying, *it were better that one man fhould tarry for many, than many for one.*—Laftly, he was in fpeech very fpare, and in counfel very fecret; and yet was not his fecretnefs towards his friends fo clofe, but that he would lovingly impart unto them whatfoever was convenient; nor his filence in fpeech fo great, but that he could entertain every one with courteous words, according to their calling; ufing to his betters, reverence; to his equals, kindnefs; and to the meaner fort, affability. And as he was naturally given to believe the beft of every one, fo could he fcarcely be drawn to miflike any, of whom he had been once well perfwaded.—Yea, even to fuch as were his enemies, being in diftrefs, he rather lent a hand to take them up, than a foot to tread them down, as by this ftory following may plainly appear. There was a Knight, [Trevanion] dwelling in the fame fhire, with whom, for divers caufes, in King Edward's days, he had fundry quarrels; which as at firft they bred inward mifliking between them, fo at laft they brake forth into open hatred. This Knight, in the troublefome change of Queen Mary's reign, partly for religion, and partly for other caufes, was clap'd into prifon: and though the matters difcovered againft him were hainous, and his enemies (at that time bearing great fway) very grievous, yet he obtained fo much favor, as to be tryed by certificate, from the gentlemen of the chiefeft authority in his country, for his behaviour therein. According to whofe report to the council, he was to be either delivered, or more ftraightly to be dealt with. This granted, he conceived very good hope of every other's friendly advertifement; and feared only the hard favor of our Sir Richard; who he doubted would ufe the fword of revenge (then put into his hands) to his enemies deftruction. It hapned, that upon return of their anfwer he was delivered; and being at liberty, to the end he might know, how his countrymens minds were affected towards him, he by means, procured a copy of all thefe advertifive letters; in perufing of which, he found that fuch as bore him faireft countenance, wrote moft againft him; and that Sir Richard Edgecombe's certificate made moft for him: fo as, in all likelihood, his greateft enemy in fhow, was the chiefeft caufe of his deliverance in deed.—I would ftay here in praife of this noble mind, who fhewed his valor in conquering his own affections; his vertue in abftaining from revenge, being offered; and his chriftianity in doing good for evil; but that I am carried forth with no lefs wonder at this Knight's thankfulnefs: who pretending as though he wift not of this courtefy, to the outward fhew, continued his wonted enmity until the next Chriftmas after.—At which time, on a night, word was brought to *Mount Edgcomb*, that a company of armed men were lately landed from Plymouth, marching up to the houfe. Sir Richard, having heard before, that this Knight was in that town, and miftrufting, he had picked out this time to come and fet upon him unawares, refolved to fhew himfelf neither difcourteous to them he knew not, through fear; nor yet to lie open to his enemies, if they pretended any fuch practice, through heedlefnefs; he therefore caufed his gates to be fet wide open, and placed his fervants on both fides the gate and hall, where they muft pafs, with fwords and bucklers: but they coming in, turned this doubt into paftime, for their armor and weapons were only painted paper, as by nearer approaching was perceived; and inftead of trying their force with blows, in fighting with men, they fell to make proof of the ladies fkill in dancing.—Thefe paftimes at laft being ended, they were led into another room to be banquetted: where this Knight taking off his vizard, and difclofing himfelf to Sir Richard Edgcomb, uttered, *That having known the great courtefy fhewn him in his trouble, befides his looking, and countrary to his deferving, he was come thither to yield him his moft due thanks for the fame; affuring him, that he would from thence forth, reft as faithful a friend, as ever before he had fhewd himfelf a profeffed enemy.* In witnefs of which his true meaning, and to ftrengthen the friendfhip newly begun, in good-will, with a faft knot of alliance, he there prefented him a young gentleman his nephew, a ward, and the heir of his houfe (who being of fair poffeffions, came amongft the other company, mafked in a Nymph's attire) to match with one of his daughters; which marriage afterwards came to pafs. And here I fhould alfo run out into commendation of this rare thankfulnefs, fave that this Knight's many other fhews of his right noble mind, are fo well known, that they need not, and fo great, that they cannot, be praifed enough.—I will therefore let them pafs, and fhut up this part of Sir Richard's courtefy, when I have fpoken a word or two of his foft nature; the rather, becaufe I have heard fome difcommend this his mildnefs, who were themfelves fooner to be pitied for their ignorance, than to be anfwered for any weight of their frivolous reafons. For if this gentlenefs of difpofition, and familiarity of behaviour, were a fault, neither would *Cyrus, Artaxerxes, Auguftus*, and many fuch like famous Princes, have ufed it. Neither would *Trajan* have anfwered to one, who reproved him of the like, that he being an Emperor, behaved himfelf towards his fubjects, as he would (if he were a fubject) that his Emperor fhould behave himfelf towards him. Befides, that it getteth good-will, appeareth by *Q. Minutius*, the Roman Conful, who was no lefs beloved of his country for his gentlenefs, than proud *Appius* hated for his roughnefs. And that it doth our country better fervice, was well known in the troublefom times at Rome, when the common people, being grieved with the nobilities oppreffions, and the cut-throat dealings of ufurers, and thereupon refufing to obey the Magiftrates in taking weapons for defence of the country; this notwithftanding, *Servilius*, with his gentle fpeech and fair ufage, brought them to appear at the Mufters; and after a fharp battle, to return with a glorious victory over their enemies. But of this enough.—His liberality refted chiefly in houfekeeping and gifts. What provifion he made for houfe keeping, is before fhewed; which being carefully procured, was both orderly and bountifully fpent: and as he wanted not ftore of meat, fo had he a fufficient company of fervants, to attend him at his table; the moft part gentlemen by birth, and all of them both trained in fervice, and courteous to fuch ftrangers as haunted the houfe; who when they came, found themfelves fo well entertained, that this good Knight was feldom or never unvifited. Yea, if he underftood of any ftrangers come into the country, of any calling, either by fea or land, he would freely invite them home. And thefe, by reafon of Plymouth, his neighbor town, were not a few; fo that at one time,

the Courtenays of Powderham, and the Granvilles of Stowe. Hence were diffused a lively sense of honour, of personal dignity and of family-distinction: hence that fondness for adventure, which threw a romantic colour over the transactions both of public and of private life.* In the various

time, besides many other great personages, he received into his house, the Admirals of England, Spain, and Flanders. And this he did for some good space. (*Id.* Survey of *Cornwal*, pag. 100.) A passage the more remarkable, for that the Admirals of those Nations, never met before so amicably at one table; nor ever since, unless perhaps *Anno* 1605, near to Cadiz in Spain, at what time the English and Dutch fleets lay there.—Neither could these great guests cause him to forget the poor, who were daily as duly served as himself. Moreover, whosoever (either his servant or otherwise) had brought him word of any thing to be bought, at a reasonable price, or had done any errand or service for him, was sure of a liberal reward.—Strangers arriving in the Haven, were presented with such things as he had: and the poor, whom he met, received whatsoever came first to hand. It hapned once, that a beggar craved an alms of him, to whom, instead of a shilling, he gave a piece of gold of ten; the beggar perceiving that he was mistaken, and doubting his displeasure, came crouching, and began to tell how he was deceived, offering him the gold again. But Sir Richard, loath to have his alms known, would not hear him; but bid him, *away, knave, and if I catch thee any more here* (quoth he), *&c.* So that the poor fellow, shrewdly hurt by this repulse, quietly departed.—This beggar, for his truth, in my judgment, deserved to possess the hoarded treasures of many a covetous gruff; and the knight, for his liberality, was worthy to find the heavenly treasure.—But to draw this tedious discourse to an end, he resembled the Emperor *Titus*, called, for his good disposition, *the delight of the world*; who sitting, on a night, at supper, with his acquaintance, and remembring that he had bestowed nothing on any man that day, cryed out upon a suddain, *Friends! I have lost a day.* These his vertues procured his favour of his Prince and the council, who in times of danger, chiefly committed to him, and a very few others, the government of the shire where he dwelt: they got him love among his neighbors, who counted nothing too dear for him; and coming home in their shipping, from far countries, would hale his house with two or three pieces of ordnance; and present him with the best things they had. And lastly, they purchased him credit among strangers, who would commonly call him, *the good old Knight of the Castle.* These few things I have touched amongst many, which in him were worthy the noting."—Thus far that worthy author; whom we could farther have wished, that as he hath given a fair account of the life of this worshipful Knight, so he had also given us the history of his death and funeral! together with the time when, and place where he was buried.—Whether he hath any sepulchral tomb, or monument, although I much endeavored it, I could not inform my self. However, the latter part of that epitaph which the fore-quoted author, Mr. *Carew*, made for the wife, or daughter, of this gentleman, (in his poems on various occasions, in number above one hundred and thirty manuscripts) with the change only of the article, would very well have fitted his marble.

The blessings large which fortune gave, I dare not call his own,
Nor from himself the fear of God, so sought and kept, was grown:
Yet this I boldly may avouch, and truth shall it maintain,
His heart dame vertue so possess'd, that vice was banish'd clean.

Then give me leave, ye sacred nymphs, of him alone to boast;
Who whil'st he liv'd, in words and deeds, did honor vertue most.
And grant unspighted eke of you, each top of stately hill,
Each *Edg* of *Comb*, each pit of vale, may sound his praises still."—*Prince*, pp. 283, 286.

* Tradition tells us, that Sir William Courtenay in the time of Elizabeth, had the superintendance of several young people of the west, at Powderham Castle. And it is said, that those gentlemen having robbed in a wanton frolic some people upon the road as they were going to market, were tried at the assizes for the robbery; when Sir William Courtenay was upon the bench to intercede for them with the judge. In the course of the trial, Sir William incensed at some expression of the judge, stood up, and threatened, as he grasped his sword, that he wou'd make the judge's shirt as red as his scarlet gown. Sir William, however, considering what he had done, took horse and rode post to London, and fell on his knees before Elizabeth. "Courtenay (said the Queen) what have you been guilty of now?" On his reciting the transaction, the Queen refused to pardon him; resenting so flagrant an affront on the representative of her person: but the image of a once favoured Courtenay, soon recurred to memory: and her severity was softened into forgiveness. *Cleaveland*, pp. 297, 298.—In a letter from Lord Lansdowne to William Henry Earl of Bath, at the camp in Flanders, Sept. 4, 1711; we have a good sketch of the manners of the Cornish gentry, of former times. "Whilst you are pursuing honour (says *Lord Lansdowne*) in the field, in the earliest time of your life, after the example of your ancestors, I am commanded by the Queen to let you know, she has declared you her Lord Lieutenant of the county of Cornwall; the Earl of Rochester to act for you, till you are of age. You are placed at the head of a body of gentry, entirely disposed in affection to you, and your family: you are born possess'd of all those amiable qualities which cannot fail of fixing their hearts: you have no other example to follow, but to tread in the steps of your ancestors. You are upon an uncommon foundation in that part of the world: your ancestors, for at least five hundred years, never made any alliance, male or female, out of the western counties: thus there is hardly a gentleman, either in Cornwall or Devon, but has some of your blood, or you some of theirs. I remember, the first time I accompany'd your grandfather into the west, upon holding his Parliament of Tinners, as warden of the Stannaries, when there was the most numerous appearance of gentry of both counties that had ever been remember'd together; I observ'd there was hardly any one but whom he called Cousin, and I could not but observe at the same time how well they were pleased with it. Let this be a lesson for you when it comes to your turn to appear amongst them. Nothing is more obliging than to seem to retain the memory of kindred and alliances, tho' never so remote: and in consequence, nothing

various expeditions of Granvile, of Champernowne, and of other cavaliers of the weſt, to aſſiſt foreign powers, to relieve diſtreſs, or to diſcover new regions, there was a ſpecies of knight-errantry, ſuch as the calculating prudence of the preſent day would treat with ſcorn or ridicule. Sir Richard Granvile (vice-admiral of England in the reign of Elizabeth) was one of thoſe famous Engliſhmen who in the year 1566, went into Pannonia, to ſerve the Emperor Ferdinand againſt the Turks; and was afterwards preſent at the memorable battle of Lepanto,* with Don John of Auſtria. The incurſion into France, in 1569, had all the features of a cruſade. To relieve the French Proteſtants in France, Elizabeth (we are told) permitted Henry Champernowne to lead thither one hundred Engliſh gentlemen who had volunteered their ſervices. In this number, was the famous Walter Raleigh, then a very young man, tho' affording a fair promiſe of future eminence.† In lending aid to Portugal, England had a romantic intercourſe with her King.‡ In 1585, Sir Richard Granvile reduced Virginia, to her Majeſty's obedience, and added it to her dominions.§ In 1587, the nation was ſtruck by an incident, which all our annaliſts and

thing more diſobliging, than a forgetfulneſs of them: which is always imputed to an affected, diſdainful ſuperiority and pride.—There is another particular, in my opinion of no ſmall conſequence to the ſupport of your intereſt, which I would recommend to your imitation: and that is to make Stowe your principal reſidence. I have heard your grand-father ſay, if ever he liv'd to be poſſeſs'd of New-hall, he would pull it down, that your father might have no temptation to withdraw from the ancient ſeat of his family. From the conqueſt to the reſtauration, your anceſtors conſtantly reſided amongſt their country-men, except when the publick ſervice call'd upon them to ſacrifice their lives for it.—Stowe, in my grand-father's time, till the civil wars broke out, was a kind of academy for all the young men of family in the country: he provided himſelf with the beſt maſters of all kinds for education; and the children of his neighbours and friends ſhared the advantage with his own. Thus he, in a manner, became the father of his country, and not only engaged the affection of the preſent generation, but laid a foundation of friendſhip for poſterity, which is not worn out at this day.—Upon this foundation, my Lord, you inherit friends without the trouble of making them, and have only to preſerve them: an eaſy taſk for you, to whom nature has been ſo liberal of every quality, neceſſary to attract affection, and gain the heart.—I muſt tell you, the generality of our countrymen have been always royaliſts: you inherit too much loyal blood to like them the worſe. There is an old ſaying amongſt them; that a Godolphin was never known to want wit; a Trelawney, courage; or, a Granville, loyalty: wit, and courage, are not to be miſtaken; and to give thoſe families their due, they ſtill keep up to their character: but it is the misfortune of loyalty, not to be ſo clearly underſtood, or defined. In a country ſubject to revolutions, what paſſes for loyalty to-day, may be treaſon to-morrow." Vol. 3, pp. 178, 179, 180.

* But I find him returned in 1568; for he then granted to John Hals, of Efford, Eſq. all thoſe lands in Eaſt-Buckland, ſome time the inheritance of his grandfather. See Camden's Elizabeth, in Hiſt. of England, vol. 2, p. 99. Thomas, *Lord Arundel* of Wardour, when a young man, behaved ſo valiantly againſt the Turks in Hungary, that he merited from Rodolph II. Emperor of Germany, *the honour of a Count of the Empire*, Ann. 1595, 38 Eliz.—"for that he had behaved himſelf manfully in the field; as alſo in the aſſaulting of divers cities and caſtles, ſhewed great proof of his valour; and that in forcing the water-tower near Strigonium, he took from the Turks their banner with his own hand," (as are the words of that Emperor's charter.) So that every of his children and their deſcendents of both ſexes, ſhould for ever enjoy that title; have vote in all Imperial Diets; purchaſe lands within the dominions of the Empire; liſt any voluntary ſoldiers, and not be put to any trial but in the Imperial Chamber. But the year after on his return home, a queſtion ariſing among the Peers, whether that dignity ſo conferred by a foreign Potentate ſhould be allowed here, as to place and precedence or any other privelege; occaſioned a warm diſpute, which *Camden* mentions in his hiſtory of Elizabeth. This hiſtorian tells us, that the Queen, being aſked her opinion in the caſe, anſwered, "that there was a cloſe tie of affection between the Prince and the ſubject; and that as chaſte wives ſhould have no glances but for their own ſpouſes, ſo ſhould faithful ſubjects keep their eyes at home, and not gaze upon foreign crowns. That ſhe for her part, did not care her ſheep ſhould wear a ſtranger's mark, nor dance after the whiſtle of every foreigner." It was voted therefore, in the negative; which induced King James, 3d of his reign, in conſideration of Arundel's ſingular merits, to create him a Baron of this realm, by letters patent, bearing date the 44, Maii, 1605, with limitation thereof to the heirs male of his body.

† See *Camden's* Elizabeth.

‡ In 1580, the King of Spain ſeizeth the kingdom of Portugal; when the King of Portugal came to England, and lay awhile at Mount Edgecombe. Plymouth MS.—In 1584, the King of Portugal comes to Plymouth. Plymouth MS.—In 1589, Sir James Norris and Sir Francis Drake failed from Plymouth with the King of Portugal, to endeavour to reſtore him, but could not: they came to the gate of Liſbon. Plymouth MS.

§ Of which a Narrative by Theodore de Bry, was printed at Frankfort, in 1590, intitled "Admiranda Narratio, fida tamen, de commodis et incolarum ritibus Virginiae, nuper admodum ab Anglis, qui a Domino *Richardo Granvile*, Equeſtris ordinis viro eo in Coloniam A. D. 1585, deducti ſunt, inventæ," &c.—Ann. 1591. After other ſervices performed with great honor

and hiftoriographers have either mifreprefented or but imperfectly recorded, till one arofe, to whom all his predeceffors in hiftory, were but as fparrows to the eagle. My allufion to Mary Queen of Scots, and her vindicator, muft be inftantly perceived. That partial, that difingenuous writer, *Echard*, labours to extenuate the offences of Elizabeth, in her maffacre of a Princefs, as fpotlefs in heart, as fhe was bright in perfonal beauty. But with all his cafuiftry, he is unable to fupprefs facts. That the Queen actually figned a warrant for the execution of Mary, after long deliberation, is not to be diffembled. The fubfequent fluctuations of her mind, and her diftrefs and melancholy, were partly feigned, and partly real: they were feigned for political purpofes, and real, from the reproaches of confcience. Over the blood of murdered innocence, fhe flung the deep fhade of hypocrify. She fent, it feems, *our* WILLIAM KILLIGREW to Davifon, with an order that the warrant fhould not be drawn. But the warrant was drawn already: it was fealed too. Yet tho' drawn, and tho' fealed, was it beyond revocation?—The conduct of England with refpect to her foreign connexions, had long excited the jealoufy of Spain: and *the menaced invafion of this country, the preparations for which were, every year, more formidable, awakened fear and roufed to vigilance all Cornwall even in 1575.† That the Little Dinas, in the Parifh of St. Anthony-

honor and fuccefs, he was at laft, flajn near the Azores Iflands; having with one of the Queen's fhips alone, fuftained a fight for fifteen hours againft the whole naval power of Spain. This happened in 1591. See *Hiftory of Queen Elizabeth*, in Hiftory of England, vol. 2, p. 565.

* " There was a prophefy (fays Sir Francis Bacon) before the year 88, which I do not well underftand:

There fhall be feen upon a day,
Between the Baugh and the May,
The black fleet of Norway.
When that is come and gone,
England build houfes of lime and ftone,
For, after, wars you fhall have none.

It was generally conceived to be meant of the Spanifh fleet that came in 88. For that the King of Spain's furname, as they fay, is Norway." *Bacon's Effay's*, p. 209. [Edit. 1663.]—A little before the Spanifh armament put to fea, the Ambaffador of his Catholic Majefty had the confidence to propound to Queen Elizabeth, in Latin verfe, the terms upon which fhe might hope for peace. Which are as follows, with an Englifh tranflation by Dr. Fuller.

' Te veto ne pergas bello defendere Belgas:
' Quæ Dracus eripuit nunc reftituantur oportet:
' Quas pater evertit jubo te condere cellas:
' Religio Papæ fac reftituatur ad unguem.'

' Thefe to you are our commands:
' Send no help to the Netherlands:
' Of the treafure took by Drake,
' Reftitution you muft make;
' And thofe abbies build anew,
' Which your father overthrew:
' If for any peace you hope,
' In all points reftore the Pope.'

" The Queen's extempore return:
' Ad Græcas, bone rex, fient mandata calendas.'

' Worthy King, know, this your will
' At latter-lammas we'll fulfil.'

Betham's Baronetage of England, vol. 1, Art. Sir Francis Drake.

† On the alarm of the threatened Spanifh invafion, in 1575, Lord Burleigh feems to have greatly exerted himfelf, in gaining information with refpect to the coafts, and a variety of other particulars. See *Muf. Brit.* 18, D. 111. P. 284, Plut. xxvii. D. Cod. Sec. xvi. Lord Burghley Bibl. Reg. containing maps of counties of England, draughts of fea ports, and juftices of various counties. The number of all the counties, cities, parfonages, and vicarages within the faid counties and cities of the Realme of England, extracted out of her Majefty's (Queen Eliz.) the Queen's recordes of firft fruits and tenths remaining in the Exchequer: with notes and remarks by Lord Burghley, and maps of each county, 1575, 1576, 1577.

CORNWALL.—*Juftices of the Peace.*

Richard Grenefield, Miles,	Henry Killigrew,	Richard Carewe,	Richard Edgcumb,
Francis Godolphin, ditto	Richard Chamand,	Thomas Bellott,	Thomas Nofworthy,
Peter Edgcumb,	Peter Courtney,	William Power,	George Grenefielde,
William Mohun,	John Carminew,	Thomas Chiverton,	Richard Trevanion.

A map of Cornwall, and a drawing of the harbour of Falmouth.

DEVONSHIRE.

DEVONSHIRE.—*Justices of the Peace.*

Lord Edward Seymour,	John St. Leger,	William Poole,	Edward Drewe,
William Periam, Judge of the Queen's Bench,	Peter Edgcumb,	Bernard Drake,	John Drake,
	Robert Ourry,	George Cary,	Thomas Hatch,
William Courtney, Miles,	Christopher Coppleston,	John Eveleigh,	Edmund Waldron,
Robert Denys, ditto,	Hugh Fortescue,	John Parker,	Thomas Devenishe,
Johan. Gilbert, ditto,	Gawen Champernoone,	Thomas Carewe,	Richard Edgcumb,
Arthur Bassett, ditto,	Thomas Monche,	John Stukeley,	Humphrey Speccott,
Amias Poulett, ditto,	John Fortescue,	Richard Bampfilde,	John Cole,
Richard Grenefield, ditto,	Richard Sparrey,	Edward Yarde,	Robert Hill,
John Chichester, ditto,	Thomas Southcott,	Edward Meredithe,	William Mohun,
Thomas Drake, ditto,	Thomas Risdon,	Humphrey Smith,	Walter Devenishe.

With a colour'd map of Devon, 1575, and a note of the places of descent and exposed to danger, viz. Plymouth, Salcomb, the Sandes in the parishes of Stokenham, Slapton, and Stoke, four miles; next to these towards Dartmouth, Blackpool, the harbour of Dartmouth, Torbay, Brixham, Paington, Cockington, and Tor-Mohun, four miles; Budleigh-Salterton, one mile and half; Woollecomb, and Georgeham, two miles; and the following towns made magazines, Exeter, Totnes, Dartmouth, Plymouth, Barnstaple, Plymton, Tavistock, Southmolton, Bideford, Tiverton, Columbton.

The three divisions of the county of Devon, East, North, and South. In each, Colonels and Captains were appointed, viz.

EAST.—*Colonels,*
Sir *William Courtenay*, and Sir *Robert Denys.*
Assistants.—Kirkham, Giffard, Waldron, Acland, Argenton, &c.

NORTH.—*Colonels,*
Hugh Fortescue, and *Hugh Pollard.*
Assistants.—Stuckley, Monche, Cary of Clovelly, Sprowl, Gutchens.

SOUTH.—*Colonels,*
Sir *John Gilbert*, and *Cary* of Cockington.
Assistants.—Champernon of Axmynster, Halse of Plympton, Slanning of Roborough, Eyles Edward Seymour, Gawen Denbury, Fulford, Randall of Exon.

The number of men to be raised is 5000. Posts to be set up at several stages, viz. Staines, Hertford-Bridge, Basingstoke, Andover, Salisbury, Shaftesbury, Sherborne, Crewkherne, Honyton, Exeter, Ashburton, Plymouth. In Devon 258 Parsonages.—116 Vicarages.

The waie from St. Burine in Cornwall, to London.

From St. Burine to the Mount	20 Miles
From the Mount to Fowey	12
From Fowey to Bodnam	20
From Bodnam to Lannefton	20
From Lannefton to Ocomton	15
From Ocomton to Crokekernwell	10
From Crokekernwell to Exester	10
From Exester to Honiton	12
Erom Honyton to Chard	10 &c. &c.

By this it will be perceived, that we reckon miles very differently at present.

A note what powder and match was appointed to be kept in store in every corporate towne, within the county of Devon.

	last	*matches*		*last*	*matches*
Excester	2	1000	Tavistock	1000	200
Totnes	1	500	Torrington	600	150
Dartmouth	1200	250	Southmolton	400	100
Plymouth	1	500	Biddeford	300	60
Barnesteple	1200	250	Tyverton	600	150
Plymton	500	1000	Culhamton	400	100

A note of his Majesties store of ordonnance, powder, match, &c. &c. remayning in the Lord Lieutenants, and deputy Lieutenants hands.

Imprimis of cast iron pieces { 2 Sakes, 2 Mynions, 2 Falcons } Mounted upon cariages with their wheeles shodde with iron, and furnished with ladells and sponges and ramers. Six spare exeltrees, three pair of wheeles shodde with iron, twenty bullets of iron shott of each sort, being in all sixty.

The posts were paid in 1595.

London per diem	os. 20d.	Total per diem 45 shillings
Staines	2s. od.	
Hartford-Bridge	os. 20d.	
All the rest	2s. od.	
Plimouth	os. 20d.	

K A

Anthony-Meneg, was early fortified, in expectation of the enemy, we have traditional authority for aſſerting.* Yet, in 1588,† there were not above one hundred and twenty ſail of men of war, in all England, to encounter the invincible Armada: and not above five of them all, except the Queen's great ſhips, were 200 tons burthen: ‡nor did they exceed thoſe rates, in all that Queen's time.§ The grand fleet of England was ſtationed at Plymouth: and the chief command of it was given to Charles Lord Howard of Effingham, Lord High Admiral; whoſe Vice-Admiral was Sir Francis Drake, and Rear-Admiral, Sir John Hawkins. Effingham, having

" A note of ſuch armour bought by the whole pariſh of Conſtantine, this preſent 23d of Auguſt, Anno Eliz. Reg. 26, 1584.

Item 2 pair of Cattletts
Item 8 Wynnians
Item 2 Burganetts
Item 4 Skulls
Item more 2 old Munnians
Item 1 Calyver
Item 2 Swords and 2 Daggers
Item 4 Girdles
Item 1 pair of Almain Rivetts.

A note where the pariſh armour is in keeping, 23d day of April, Anno Eliz. Reg. 1588.

Item with Mr. Dynham, one Munnian,
Item with Mr. Ryſe, one Munnian,
Item with William Richards, one Munnian,
Item with Cuthbert Lenderiow, one Skull,
Item with George Harvy, a Skull and a Girdle,
Item with William Chindower the elder, a Girdle,
Item with William Robyn, a Calyver,
Item with Thomas Tregove, a Dagger,
Item with Edmund Medlen, a Sword and a Dagger,
Item with Richard Boſſawſack, one Munnian,
Item with John Trefaker, a Skull,
Item with Michael Tremain, a Munnian,
Item with Mr. John Pendarves, a Munnian,
Item with John Treliggan, a Munnian.

A note of certain arms bought by the pariſh, 15th of April, 1590.

Item 4 Pikes,
Item 1 Muſket, Flaſk and Furniture, Tuchbox, Wynnion, Mould and Reſt.
Item 1 other Muſquet, bought by Will. Richard, for the pariſh, with Flaſk, Touch-box, Mould and Reſt.
Item 2 Halbets
Item 1 Burgenett, with Mr. Trevanian,
Item a Sword, Dagger, and Girdle,
Item 1 Cap for a Skull,
Item with Mr. Pendarves, 1 Halbet,
Item with William Richard, 1 Muſquet, Flaſk, and Touch-box, Mould and Reſt.
Item with William Jordan, 1 Muſquet, furniſhed."

July 1803.—A true copy from Conſtantine Regiſter,

JOHN VINCENT, Curate.

* The beacon on Roſcruge in St. Anthony, is ſuppoſed to have been thrown up in Elizabeth's time, when the Spaniſh Armada was expected. The Dinas, which contains about twenty acres, is joined to the main land by a narrow iſthmus, and commands the entrance into both the harbours of the Helford and Gillan or Dura, the ancient name of Gillan. Steep and very difficult of acceſs from the ſea, it is eaſily defended from an attack from the land. The poſſeſſion of it has at all times been conſidered of much conſequence: and it was in Mr. Hals's opinion a place of refuge for the ancient Britons in times of danger. That it was poſſeſſed by the Romans, is evidently proved by the great number of Roman coins already mentioned, as found in its vicinity. It was probably a place of refuge in the unhappy diſputes between the houſes of York and Lancaſter, in the troubles occaſioned by Perkin Warbeck, and in Kilter's inſurrection; and, I have obſerved above, fortifications were erected here by Elizabeth againſt the Spaniards. We ſhall ſee the Dinas again fortified in the grand rebellion.

† See *Churchill's Voyages*, vol. 3. Edit. 1704.

‡ I cannot forbear noticing here an account in Rymer's *Fœdera*, of Penryn being ſaved by a company of ſtrolling Players. Rymer ſays that " ſome time before the year 1588, the Spaniards were landing to burn the town, juſt at the nick when a company of ſtrollers with their drums and their ſhouting, were ſetting Sampſons upon the Philiſtines; which ſo ſcared them, that they ſcampered back to their galleons, as apprehending our whole Tilbury camp had lain in ambuſh, and were coming ſouſe upon them."

§ A liſt of the Engliſh fleet, with the names of the ſhips and captains, &c. From the Royal Library, 1588.

	Tons.	*Captains.*	*Mariners.*
Revenge,	500	Sir Francis Drake, V. Admiral,	250
Victory,	800	Sir J. Hawkins, R. Admiral,	400
Galleon Dudley,	250	James Erizey,	100

From Barnſtaple, Merchant ſhips converted into Frigates 3
From Exeter 2
From Plymouth ſtout ſhips, every way equal to the Queen's men of war 7

Abſtract of the numbers of every ſort of the armed men in the counties throughout the kingdom, 1588. (From Brit. Muſ. *Harleian* Collect.)

	Ablemen.	*Armed.*	*Trained.*	*Untrained.*	*Pioneers.*	*Launces.*	*Lighthorſe.*	*Petronels.*
Devonſhire,	10,000	6,200	3,660	2,540	600	120	0	22
Cornwall,	7,760	3,600	1,500	2,100	0	4	96	0

having received intelligence that the Armada* was in fight, immediately weighed anchor, and failed out of the harbour, but not without great difficulty, as the wind blew hard into Plymouth Sound.† On the next day, he faw the Spanifh Navy drawn up in the form of a crefcent, failing flowly through the Channel, and extending feven miles from one extremity to the other. He engaged a part of them off the Start-Point; and day after day, from the lightnefs of his fhips and dexterity of his failors, did great execution among the heavy veffels of Spain; failing round them, approaching and retiring with a velocity that filled them with amazement.—In the fummer of 1589, the Earl of Cumberland with a ftout fquadron, failed to the Tercera Iflands, where he did the Spaniards incredible mifchief. He reduced the ifland of Fayal, forced the ifland of Graciofa to a compofition, and feized feveral rich fhips: among the reft was one, the cargo of which was valued at upwards of an hundred thoufand pounds, but which, on its return, was loft in the Mount's Bay.‡—The year 1591, is chiefly memorable in the eyes of Cornifhmen for a fignal exploit of Sir Richard Grenville.§ But, whilft *Grenville* aftonifhed us by one

defperate

* "The Duke of Medina Sidonia, Admiral of the Spanifh Armada, was fo affected with the fight of Mount Edgcombe, (fays *Fuller*) though beholding it at a diftance off at fea, as to referve it for his own poffeffion, in the partage of this kingdom, which in hopes and expectation they had already conquered." *Fuller's* Worth. in Cornwall, p. 196.

† The firft land the Armada fell in with, was the Lizard, which they miftook for the Ram's head; as it was towards night they ftood off to fea till the next morning. In this fpace of time, they were defcried by a Scots pirate, a Captain Fleming, who bore away immediately for Plymouth, and gave the Lord Admiral notice, to the prefervation of the Englifh fleet. So little had the Englifh heard of the Spaniards, that their fleet had not only been returned into port, but feveral of the fhips laid up, and the feamen difcharged. The Admiral, however, failed on the firft notice, and though the wind blew hard into Plymouth Sound, got out to fea. The next day, July 20, the Spanifh navy appeared, drawn up in a half moon. See *Stowe*, p. 741. *Monfon's* Naval Tracts, p. 172. *Speed*, p. 860. *Phenix Brit.* [4to. 1731.] p. 346. *Strype*, vol. 3. *Grot.* Hift. Belg. l. 1. p. 118.—During the whole of Sunday, and the fucceeding day, this unwieldy armament continued in fight of Penlee Point, Mount Edgcumbe, the Hoe, and all the adjacent fhores; but afterwards proceeding to the eaftward, it was furioufly affailed by the Britifh fleet; and the deftruction thus commenced, being completed by a violent ftorm, the entire expedition was fruftrated. Many natives of Devon and Cornwall were among the brave feamen who manned the Englifh fhips on this occafion.

‡ *Hackluyt's* Voyages, vol. 2. p. 143. *Purchas's* Pilgrims, vol. 4. p. 1142. *Monfon's* Naval Tracts, p. 176.

§ Amidft numberlefs heroic atchievements of our brave countrymen, the memorable tranfaction, to which I allude, has efcaped the obfervation of Campbell, in his Lives of the Englifh Admirals. In contemplating fuch a character as Sir Richard Grenville, it is worth while to be circumftantial, to be minute in detail, to hold in contempt the charge of prolixity.—This hero was the fon of Sir Roger Grenville, Knt. by Thomafine, daughter of Thomas Cole, of Shute, Efq and was born, about the year 1540 His father was unfortunately drowned in Portfmouth harbour, whilft he was a child, and his mother marrying a fecond hufband, it is probable he was educated under the infpection of his grandfather, Sir Richard Grenville, Knt.; who alfo, ended his life, together with his lady, unfortunately through the hardfhips inflicted on them by the rebels, temp. Edw. 6th, after he had been forced to deliver up to them his Caftle of Trematon, leaving the greateft part of his large eftate to his grandfon. Our Richard, being of an active, enterprizing, and martial genius, when he became mafter of himfelf, procured a licence from Q. Eliz. in the eighth year of her reign, to go into the fervice of the Emperor, againft the Turks, in Hungary, where he gave many proofs of his courage. It is faid, that he was engaged in the glorious victory over the Turks at Lepanto. He ferved to the conclufion of the war, returning to England with a reputation, the natural confequence of his noble behaviour. Soon after he engaged himfelf and his fortune in affifting towards the reduction of Ireland, in which he behaved fo much to the fatisfaction of the Queen, and the Lord Deputy Sir Henry Sidney, that he was, in the eleventh year of her reign, made fheriff of Cork, during her royal pleafure. Upon his return to England, he was elected a knight of the fhire for Cornwall, to the Parliament fummoned to meet April 2d, 1571. In the 18th Eliz he was high fheriff of that county, and an active member, in that Parliament which met Nov. 23d, 1584, for the fame county. About this time he was deeply engaged with his kinfman, Sir Walter Raleigh, in his project of planting America, and foon after commanded a fleet of feven fmall fhips for the purpofe of making difcoveries, with the title of general, according to the cuftom of thofe times. This fleet failed from Plymouth, April 9, 1595, and, May 12, came to an anchor in the Bay of Mofquito, in the Ifland of St. John de Porto Reio, where they landed, built a fort, and foon after took two valuable prizes. June 1, they anchored before the town of Ifabella, on the north fide of Hifpaniola, where they were well entertained by the Spanifh governor. On June 20, they fell in with the coaft of Florida, (Virginia) where Sir Richard left a colony of 100 men, under Mr. Ralph Lane. In his return to England, he gave chafe to a Spanifh fhip of 300 tons burthen, which he found it impoffible to take any otherwife than by boarding her; and this method, in the opinion of his own people, was impracticable; as, by fome accident, they, at that time, had no boat: however, nothing was impoffible to a temper refolved as Sir Richard's; he

caufed

caufed fomewhat of the fafhion of a boat to be conftructed, of fuch boards as were ftowed about the fhip, and boarded the Spaniard, his awkward machine finking by her fide as foon as he and his companions had forced themfelves up the fide. In this prize the general arrived at Plymouth October 18, amidft the acclamations and congratulations of a great concourfe of his friends and others. Some time after, Sir Richard, with three fail of fhips, made a fecond voyage to Virginia, according to a promife he had made the infant colony; but they had, according to their own requeft, been taken from the country by Sir Francis Drake, who touched there, in his return from the Weft Indies to England, fome little time before Sir Richard's arrival. However, to preferve the right of the crown, and the proprietor, he left, with their own confent, furnifhed with all neceffaries for two years, fifteen of his men, on the ifland of Roanoak. In his outward bound paffage he took feveral of the enemy's fhips; and in his voyage home, he landed on the Azores iflands, and plundered feveral villages. He was preparing for a third voyage to his favourite Virginia; but the intelligence the Queen had received, of a defign of the Spaniards to invade her dominions, provided other and more neceffary employment. On this occafion he acted as one of the ftanding council of war, which confifted of nine members; the other eight being Lord Grey, Sir Francis Knolles, Sir Thomas Leighton, Sir Walter Raleigh, Sir John Norris, Sir Richard Bingham, Sir Roger Williams, and Ralph Lane, Efq. Sir Richard Grenville was entrufted with the care of the county of Cornwall, in the memorable year 1588; and the Queen's commands, for that purpofe, prevented, no doubt, his making a great figure on his proper element in the famous fea fight, that rendered all the Spanifh defigns abortive.—In the year 1591, the Queen fent a fquadron to the Weftern Iflands, to intercept a rich Spanifh fleet, which had remained in the Weft Indies all the year before, through the dread of falling into the hands of Sir John Hawkins, and Sir Martin Frobifher. The fquadron confifted of feven fail of the Queen's fhips, viz.

Ships.	*Tons.*	*Men.*	*Commanders.*
Defiance,	500	250	Lord T. Howard, Admiral.
Revenge,			Sir R. Grenville, Vice-Admiral.
Nonpariel,	500	250	Sir Edward Denny.
Bonaventure,	600	250	Captain Crofs.
Lion,	500	250	Captain George Fenner.
Forefight,	300	160	Captain Thomas Vavafor.
Crane,	200	100	Captain Duffield.
Raleigh Bark,			Captain Thynne.

Befides fmall veffels and tenders.

The King of Spain, mafter of a refined policy, and who fpared no expence for intelligence, had early notice of the force of this fquadron, and thereupon fent orders for the galleons to return very late in the year; and, at the fame time, fitted out a great fleet in his European ports. He judged that, as the galleons would ftay fo long, the Englifh fquadron would be obliged to return home for want of provifions; by which he would avoid fighting; or on failure of this project, which indeed was the cafe through the care ufed in fending ftore-fhips from London, then his next refource was, to provide a fleet of ten times the force of that of the Englifh, which was to meet and convoy the galleons home, and which, by the delay of the galleons, he had time to effect.—On the 31ft of Auguft Capt. Middleton, who had kept the Spanifh fleet company for three days, the better to difcover their force, gave intelligence of it to the Englifh Admiral, who was at anchor under the ifland of Flores, and before he had concluded his account, their Armada appeared in fight. It may be judged the Englifh fleet were in fome confufion, as part of their feveral crews were on fhore, getting ballaft, filling water, and collecting frefh provifions; feveral of the fhips were alfo not properly ballafted, and near half their men difabled, by the fcurvy and other diftempers. The Admiral confidering the great difproportion of the fquadrons, weighed, however, immediately, and put to fea, and the reft of his fleet followed his example. Sir Richard Grenville, in the Revenge, weighed laft, for he ftaid to take on board thofe that were on fhore, and whofe affiftance he ftood in need of, as he had near ninety of his people fick. The Admiral and the reft, though with great difficulty, recovered their wind; but this Sir Richard was not able to effect: whereupon fome of his officers advifed him to cut his mainfail and caft about, and truft to the failing of his fhip, as the Spanifh fquadron had already got upon his weather bow. This Sir Richard peremptorily refufed, faying, *He would much rather die than leave fuch a mark of difhonor on himfelf, his country, and the Queen's fhip*; and adding, he had hopes to pierce through the two fquadrons, and force that of Seville to give him way. The Spanifh Admiral being in the wind, then bore down upon him, which becalmed the Revenge fo, that fhe could neither make way, nor feel her helm; and in this fituation the fhips under his lee luffed up in order to lay him on board. He was boarded firft by the Spanifh Admiral the St. Philip, and foon after by four others, two on the larboard, and two on the ftarboard; but the Spanifh Admiral met with fo warm a fire, from the Revenge's lower tier of guns, loaded with crofs-bar fhot, that fhe foon fell off, and the reft as roughly treated, followed his example. A little while after, a fmall victualler fell under the lee of the Revenge, and her captain afked Sir Richard, what he would command him, to which with his accuftomed greatnefs of mind, he anfwered, *fave yourfelf and leave me to my fate*.—The unequal conflict began about three in the afternoon, and by the break of day the next morning, Sir Richard had repulfed the enemy no lefs than fifteen times, notwithftanding they continually fhifted their veffels, and attacked him with frefh men. This heroick chief was wounded in the beginning of the action, notwithftanding which, he kept the deck till eleven at night, and then receiving a fhot in the body, he was carried down to be dreffed; and whilft that was performing, he received another dangerous wound in his head, and the furgeon was killed by his fide. The Englifh now began to want powder, their fmall arms were all broken, forty men, the beft of 103, which were all that were capable of affifting, were killed, and almoft all the reft wounded; their mafts fhot over-board, rigging cut to pieces; and, in fhort, nothing but a hulk remained, unable to move, but as the fea directed, and the enemy furrounding them on every fide. In this forlorn fituation, Sir Richard exhorted his men to yield themfelves to the mercy of heaven, rather than the Spaniards, and not to fully the reputation they had acquired, by feeking to preferve their lives for a few hours, or a few days. To this the mafter-gunner, and many of his feamen affented: and this gunner, a refolute and bold fellow, ftood ready to execute his commander's orders, which were to fplit and fink the fhip. But other officers, of a contrary opinion, interpofed: and, whilft they argued the cafe with Sir Richard, who was not at all moved by their reafons, the mafter went on board

desperate action; *Carleil* was admired for his prudence and good conduct, during a series of years.* In 1595, the Spaniards made a descent on the Cornish coast,† where they burnt some small

board the Spanish Admiral, Don Alphonso Bacan, who, finding none of his fleet inclined to board the Revenge again, for fear of being blown up, immediately offered to spare all their lives, to send them home to England, and that no ransom should be taken, but from such as were able to afford it.—When the master returned to the Revenge, he soon persuaded all, but the master-gunner, to accept these conditions, who would have thrown himself on his sword, if he had not been seized and locked in his cabin. As soon as the Revenge was in the power of the Spaniards, the Admiral sent to remove Sir Richard, out of a place that resembled a slaughter-house, more than a ship; and when his design was mentioned to the brave Vice-Admiral, he said, "they might do with his body what they pleased, for he esteemed it not." As they carried him over the side, he swooned; but recovering, desired the company to pray for him. On board the Spanish ship, to which he was carried, he was very respectfully treated, but did not live above the third day. The last words he spoke, were in Spanish to this effect: *Here die I,* Richard Grenville, *with a joyfull and quiet mind, for that I have ended my life as a true soldier ought to do, fighting for his country, Queen, religion, and honour, my soul willingly departing from this his body, leaving behind the lasting fame of having behaved, as a valiant soldier is in duty bound to do.* His death was sincerely lamented even by his enemies, struck with such an example of true fortitude and heroism.—This victory cost the Spaniards very dear; for the Admiral of the fly-boats, and the Ascension of Seville, sunk by the side of the Revenge; a third vessel, returning to the road of St. Michael to refit, sunk there; and a fourth was run ashore by the crew, to save themselves: and so warmly had this handful of English plyed their arms, that the Spaniards lost above 1000 men. To the honour of Old England, be it remarked, that this conquest of the Revenge was atchieved by fifty-three sail of ships, most of them larger than herself, and at least 10,000 soldiers and mariners. The Revenge was afterwards lost, in a great storm, with seventy Spaniards, and some of the captive English on board; in which storm many Spanish ships also perished, so that of this great Armada, consisting of 140 sail, but 32 or 33 arrived in Spain or Portugal. Thus fell the brave Sir Richard Grenville, who, as a valuable writer says, "did not throw away the Queen's ship, any more than his life, but forming a true notion of the duty of a man in his station, upon such an occasion, he chose to risk all, rather than sacrifice the glory of the English flag, as well knowing, that if the worst should happen, and himself and ship should be lost, yet the Queen and nation would be no losers, the superior loss of the enemy considered." "Our learned countrymn John Evelyn, having related this action in a few words, cries out, *than this, what have we more! what can be greater?* Indeed I think nothing that is recorded in any history, in any language. Yet this man is without any monument, and very little pains have been taken to do justice to his memory. May every virtuous reader pay it the just tribute of a tear, and may the British flag never want, what it lately had,‖ an officer of the same name and spirit to support its glory."—"RICHARDUS GRENVILLUS, Mil. Aur. in the Heroologia; 8vo." [*Granger*, vol. 1, pp. 245, 246.] In the engagement already related, he displayed that enthusiam, or rather madness of courage, which has often decided the fate of an empire. Sir Sydney Smith and Sir Edward Pellew, are the Grenvilles of the present day. The famous Sir Bevil Grenville (who will hereafter be noticed) was the grandson of Sir Richard.

* Captain Christopher Carleil, Esq. *Robert Boissard, Sculpt, small half sheet.* This belongs to a curious set of English Admirals, by the same engraver. CHRISTOPHERUS CARLEIL OR CARLISLE. In the Heroologia, 8vo. Christopher Carlisle, a Cornish gentleman, son-in-law to Sir Francis Walsingham, [*Biog. Britan.* p. 2465.] served with reputation in the Prince of Orange's fleet in the Low countries; and in that of the Protestants in France, commanded by the Prince of Conde in person. He was afterwards, by the great Duke of Muscovy, appointed Admiral of his fleet destined to act in 1584, against the King of Denmark. He was employed by Sir John Perrot in Ireland, to defend the western part of that kingdom against the incursions of the Scots. The next year, he had the command of the land forces, sent on board the fleet commanded by DRAKE, to the West-Indies; where he gave the highest proofs of his military capacity, and had a principal hand in taking the towns of St. Jago, St. Domingo, Carthagena, and St. Augustine. Ob. 1593. See *Granger's* Biogr. Hist. vol. 1. pp. 239, 240.—It is impossible to pass the name of Drake in this place without an observation or two on that hero of the west. In the various memoirs of Sir Francis Drake, I believe his picture in the townhall at Plymouth, has been never described. —It is probably an original and is in good preservation. He is here represented as low as to the waist, in a black gown with a turned down collar, and straight sleeves and cuffs, with quill'd ruffles at the wrist turned back on them. He has a short quill'd ruff round his neck with a long and massive gold chain. A medal of Queen Elizabeth, in profile suspended by a ribbon hangs upon his breast; his right hand rests on a terrestrial globe, his hair is auburn, his whiskers and piked beard are sandy, his complexion fair and ruddy. His *arms* are painted above, in the right hand corner of the picture, viz. *Sable*, a fesse wavy between two blazing stars of ten points *arg*. Crest, a ship in full sail, upon a globe upheld by the arm of Providence, issuing from a cloud, on the dexter side. Motto upon the right of the arms, on a scroll *Auxilio divino.* Ditto upon the left, *Sic parvis magna.* Behind the head, and in the left angle of the picture.—Ætat. suæ. 53, Anno. 1594. Under the picture, upon the right, are these lines in the black letter:—

Sir Drake, whome well the world's ends knowe
  Which thou didst compass rounde
And whome both poles of heaven ons saw,
  Which North and South do bound
The Starrs above will make thee known
  If men here silent were,
The Sunn himself cannot forgett
  His fellow traveller.

And

‖ Captain Thomas Grenville, of the Defiance, brother of Earl Temple, killed in his country's service, May 3, 1747.

ſmall *towns. Their force, embarked in four gallies, was not conſiderable. This ſquadron was commanded be Don Diego Brochero. The ſpirit of the nation, rouſed by this inſult, was

And upon the left, in the ſame character, the following,

Great Drake whoſe ſhippe about the world's wide waſt
In three years did a golden girdle caſt,
Who with freſh ſtreames refreſht this Towne, that firſt
Though kiſt with waters yet did pine for thirſt.
Who both a pilot and a Magiſtrate
Steer'd in his turne the Shippe of Plymouth ſtate
This little Table ſhewes his face whoſe worth
The world's wide Table hardly can ſett forth.

Ætatis ſuæ 53
Ano. 1594.

The following lines are painted upon a ſeparate Tablet, which hangs beneath the Picture upon its right.

Thou y^t in eighty eight that dreadfull yeere
Amōgſt the greatſt thy ſervice madſt appeare
Thou that refreſhdſt this thirſty town with ſprȳgs
Thou whoſe meaſt āctiōs weare admir'd by kings;
Thou that wert fitt for couſell and for warr,
Thou y^t borē heere yet madſt thy name fear'd farr;
After thou earth and ſea hadſt meaſur'd eaven
Didſt in thy laſt diſcovery ſaile for heaven.

The following are upon another Tablet under the picture upon the left hand.

What fitter name than Drake could he obtain
Whoſe worth ennobled hath both land and maine?
The maine with goldē wings he flew throughout
Whoſe watery armes ye world intwines about:
The firſt y^t taught (what none had done before)
A Carrack to ſalute the Engliſh ſhore.
On land his ſword the choiceſt gold did gleane
From St. Domingo, Jago, Carthagene:
And that our Drake might David paralel
A maſſe of man a gyant he did quell.
May wee not thē Drake ye tenth worthy call
Or rather ſtile him abſtract of thē all.

FITZ GE.

Upon the ſame ſide, and upon another ſmall Tablet, are theſe Latin lines.

Drake peragrati novit quem
terminus orbis,
Quemque ſimul mundi vidit
uterque polus.
Si taceant homines facient te
Sydera notum.
Sol neſcit comitis immemor
eſſe ſui
Plus ultro Herculeis inſcribas
Drake Columnis
Et magno dicas Hercule
Major ero.

† This was the firſt time, and I believe the laſt, that a Spaniard ever ſet his foot on the ſhores of England as an enemy, if we except the incident of 1597. Twenty-two cheſts of the Pope's bulls and pardons, which had been ſeized in Cornwall, were afterwards brought to Plymouth and publicly burnt in the market-place.

* "Penſans, by interpretation, the Saints head, is a market towne, (ſays *Carew*) not ſo regardable for his ſubſtance, as memorable for his late accident of the Spaniards firing, which fell out in this manner:—The three and twentieth of July, 1595, ſoone after the ſun was riſen, and had chaſed a fogge, which before kept the ſea out of ſight, four gallies of the enemy preſented themſelues vpon the coaſt, ouer-againſt Mouſehole, and there in a faire bay, landed about two hundred men, pikes and ſhot, who foorthwith ſent their forlorne hope, conſiſting of their baſeſt people, vnto the ſtragled houſes of the countrie,

countrie, about halfe a mile compaſſe or more, by whome were burned, not onely the houſes they went by, but alſo the pariſh church of Paul, the force of the fire being ſuch, as it vtterly ruined all the great ſtonie pillers thereof: others of them in that time, burned that fiſher towne Mowſehole, the reſt marched as a gard for defence of theſe firers. The inhabitants being feared with the Spaniards landing and burning, fled from their dwellings, and verie meanely weaponed, met with Sir Francis Godolphin on a greene, on the weſt ſide of Penſance, who that forenoone comming from his houſe, for pacifying ſome controuerſies in thoſe weſtern parts, and from the hils eſpying the fires in that towne, church, and houſes, haſtened thither: who foorthwith ſent to all the captaines of thoſe parts, for their ſpeedie repaire with their companies, and alſo ſent by poaſt to Sir Francis Drake, and Sir Iohn Hawkins (then at Plymmouth with a fleete bound for the Indies) aduertiſement of the arriuall of theſe foure gallies, and of their burnings, aduiſing to looke to themſelues, if there were any greater fleete of the enemies at ſea, and to ſend weſt with all haſte, what ſuccours by ſea and land they could ſpare. Then Sir Francis Godolphin aduiſed that weake aſſembly, to retire into Penſance, and to prepare it for defence, vntill the comming of the countrie forces that hee ſent for. But they finding themſelues in number ſomething aboue a hundred, wherein were about thirtie or fortie ſhot, though ſcarce one third of them were ſeruiceable, inſiſted to march againſt the enemies, to repell them from farther ſpoyles of their houſes.—But while they were marching towards them, the Spaniards returned aboord their gallyes, and preſently remooued them farther into the Bay, where they anchored againe, before and neere a leſſer fiſher towne, called Newlyn.—There againe with all ſpeede they landed, and imbattelled in the ſlope of a hill, about foure hundred pikes and ſhot, ſending about two rankes of ſoldiers, three in a ranke, vp to the top of the hill, to diſcouer what forces or ambuſhes of the countrey might lye in view: who eſpying none but thoſe that were returned with Sir Frauncis Godolphin, from their forementioned fruitleſſe march, gaue notice thereof to their imbattelled company. Wherevpon they forthwith marched towards Penzance.—Vpon their moouing, Sir Fraunċis Godolphin moued alſo to enter Penzance before them: and aſſoone as that weake number were entred into the open greene being of three quarters of a mile length, the Gallyes ceaſed not to ply them all that way with their ordinance from their prowes, as buſily as they could. Of which ſhot, though none were hurt, but onely a conſtable vnhorſed without any harme, ſauing the ſhew on his doublet of the bullets ſliding by his back, yet many in fearefull manner, ſome fell flat to the ground, and others ranne away.—Sir Fraunċis ſent after thoſe that were entred Penzance before him, that they ſhould make their ſtand at the market place, himſelfe ſtaying hindmoſt, to obſerue the enemies order, and which way they would make their approach. Which done, he found at the ſaid market place but onely two reſolute ſhot, who ſtood at his commaund, and ſome ten or twelue others that followed him, moſt of them his owne ſeruants; the reſt, ſurpriſed with feare, fled, whom, neither with his perſwaſions, nor threatning with his rapier drawne, hee could recall.—Finding himſelfe thus abandoned, and the enemies entred the towne in three parts, he was then forced to depart, the enemies beginning their fire ſome houſes behinde him. The towne thus fired, as alſo the forementioned little fiſher towne Newlyn, they returned againe to their gallies.—By this time, towards the evening, the Corniſh forces encreaſed in nomber, and amended in heart, encamped themſelues on the greene, neere to the towne of Markeſew and S. Michael's Mount, for defence thereof, and there ſpent out the night. The next day the enemy made ſhowe to land againe on the weſt ſide of the bay; but ſeeing the people, though few in number, yet reſolute to reſiſt, they deſiſted from their enterprize: and beſides, finding themſelues annoyed by the ſhooting of bullets and arrowes into their gallies where they roade at anchor, they were forced to remoue them farther off.—Soone after, viz. on the 25th of Iuly in the morning, came thither Sir Nic. Clifford, Sir H. Power, and certaine other captaines, who were ſent by the generals from Plymmouth to the campe: as ſome of her Maieſties ſhips were alſo ſent, who being come as farre as the Lizard head, and thoſe captaines to the camp, matters there goe on in prouident and orderly ſort, a plot is layd for intercepting the enemy by ambuſh, if he thruſt on ſhore againe, whereto neceſſity muſt ſoone haue preſſed him, for reneuing his conſumed ſtore of freſh water: but within one houre after the arriuall of theſe captaines, the winde, which was vntill then ſtrong at ſouth-eaſt, with miſt and rayne, to haue impeached the gallies returne, ſuddenly changed into the northweſt, with very fayre and cleare weather, as if God had a purpoſe to preſerue theſe his rods for a longer time. The winde no ſooner came good, but away pack the gallies with all the haſt they could.—Thus haue you a ſummary report of the Spaniards glorious enterpriſe, and the Corniſh mens infamous cowardiſe, which (were there any cauſe) I could qualify by many reaſons, as, the ſuddenneſſe of the attempt, the narrowneſſe of the country, the openneſſe of the towne, the aduantage of the gallies ordinance on a people vnprepared againſt ſuch accidents, through our long continued peace, and at that very time, for the moſt part, eyther in their Tynne-workes, or at ſea, who e're the next day made reſiſtance, euen with a handfull, and entred a vowed reſolution, to reuenge their loſſe at the next encounter, if the enemy had landed againe.—So might I likewiſe ſay, that all theſe circumſtances meeting in any other quarter of the Realme, would hardly haue produced much better effects. But I will not ſeeke to thruſt my countrymen into any other folkes company, for ſhifting them out of ſight.—Verily ſuch ſudden ſurprizes worke more indignity then dammage, and more dammage then diſgrace, and haue ſo beene euer conſtrued. Moſcho, a head citie in a populous dominion, was burned by the roguing Tartars, anno domini 1572. The Capitoll, a head fortreſſe, in a populous citie, was taken by ſlaues and outlawes, anno vrbis, 292. and yet who therefore exalteth the Tartars valiancy, aboue the Moſchouite, or the Romanes ſlaues and outlawes, aboue their maſters? Beſides, ſuch nap taking aſſaults, ſpoylings, and firings, haue in our forefathers daies, betweene vs and Fraunce, beene very common; and yet, who is ſo witleſſe, as to twite eyther of both, for the ſame?—But leaſt hold can the author, and actor of this Tragedy take, to build any vaunt thereon: for oftentimes ſmall troups of ours, againſt farre greater forces of theirs, yea (ſometimes) after forewarning, and preparance, haue wonne, poſſeſſed, ranſacked, ſynged, captiued, and carried away the townes, wealth, and inhabitants, not onely of their Indies, but of Portugall and Spaine it ſelfe. Which Nombre de dios, S. Domingo, Cartagena, the lower towne of the Groigne, Penecha, the ſuburbs of Liſbone, and Cales will teſtify, beyond all exception. But our countrymen leauing reaſon and example, excuſe themſelues by deſtiny. In fatis they ſay (and not in fatuis) it was, that the Corniſh people ſhould vndergo this misfortune; for an ancient prophecy, in their owne language, hath long run amongſt them, how there ſhould land vpon the rock of Merlin, thoſe that would burn Pauls Church, Penſants, and Newlyn. And indeed, ſo is the rocke called, where the enemy firſt ſtept on ſhore." *Carew*, f. f. 157, 157, 158. See *Stowe's Annals*, p. 771.

was

was resolved to retaliate the blow. And, on board a fleet of one hundred and twenty-six ships of war, was soon embarked more than 7000 land forces. This armament which set sail from Plymouth, was commanded by the Earl of Essex, and the Lord High Admiral Effingham. And it was strengthened by a Dutch squadron of 24 ships. The design of the expedition, was to destroy the Spanish fleet in the Port of Cadiz, and to make themselves masters of that rich city: and this they fully accomplished.—In 1597, the Spaniards were meditating great designs against England. With their squadrons from Corunna and Ferrol, they purposed to make a descent in Cornwall, and possess themselves of the port of Falmouth. The Spanish Admiral joined his ships, and proceeded with them to the isles of Sylleh, within sight of the Cornish shore. But suddenly a storm arose which dispersed his whole fleet.*—In the year 1599, "the Spaniards vaunts (as *Carew*† expresses himself) caused the Cornish forces to advance at West Stonehouse a kind of fortification, and to plot the making of a bridge or barges over that strait, for inhibiting the enemies accesse by boats and gallies, into the more inward parts of the Haven. But it may be doubted, whether the bridge would have proved as impossible, as the sconce fell out unnecessarie." In this Spanish war, Falmouth, it seems, was plunged into disgrace, thro' the rapacity of a female of the family of Arwinick, who robbed two Dutch ships in the harbour, of Spanish money, and murdered the Spanish factors.‡—From the rebellious state of Ireland,

* *Sir William Monson's* Nav. Tracts, pp. 173, 174. *Burchet's* Nav. Hist. p. 365. In 1597, happened a curious incident which Carew hath recorded. "At Causam Bay, of late years, part of the Cornish forces twice encamped themselves, planted some ordinance, and raised a weak kind of fortification, to contest if not repulse, the landing of the expected enemy: and a strong watch is continually kept there, ever since one thousand five hundred and ninety seven: at which time a Spaniard riding on the Bay, while most of the able people gave their attendance at the county assizes, sent some closely into the village, in the dark of the night, who hanged up barrels of matter fit to take fire, upon certain doors, which by a train should have burned the houses. But one of the inhabitants, espying these unwelcome guests, with the bounce of a caliver chaced them a board, and removed the barrels before the trains came to work their effect. The inginer of this practice, (as hath since appeared by some examinations) was a Portuguese, who sometime sailed with Sir John Borowghs, and boasted to have burned his ship: for which two honourable exploits, the King of Spain bestowed on him two hundred ducats." f. 99.—"The Syllene Isles are often robbed by the Frenchmen and Spaniards," says Harrison. Of these Isles, the governor was *Francis Godolphin*, who succeeded his uncle Sir William Godolphin, in the ancient inheritance of the family, and was knighted by Elizabeth at Richmond, on Sunday 20th November, 1580. His knowlege in the laws, his love of justice and equity, and his attachment to her Majesty's government, raised him to all the posts of honor, which he could hold consistently with a country life: for he perferred retirement to the court, where his great abilities might have have further advanced him. He was returned member of Parliament for Cornwall, 31st Eliz. and for Lestwithiel, 35 Eliz. In that reign, he was the first in the commission of the peace and of the Quorum; as also the first in the Lieutenancy of the county of Cornwall, and colonel of a regiment of twelve companies armed with 470 pikes, 490 muskets, and 240 calivers. With respect to Sylleh, (*Carew* says) it was her Majesty's order, "reduced to a more defensible plight, and governed by Sir Francis Godolphin, who with his invention and purse, bettered his plot and allowance, and therein so tempered strength with delight, and both with use, as it served for a sure hold and a commodious dwelling." *Carew*, f. 85.

† *Carew*, f. 100, b. "In 1599, our west country was apprehensive of the Spaniards; and therefore made gates and barricadoes, and had 4000 men and some horse under the command of the Earl of Bath." *MS. Notices* of Plymouth.

‡ "In the Spanish wars (says *Hals*) in the latter end of the reign of Queen Elizabeth, Jane Killigrew, widow of Sir John Killigrew, went from the house of the Killigrews of Arwinick, aboard two Dutch ships of the Hanse Towns, always free traders in times of war, driven into Falmouth harbour by cross winds, laden with merchandizes on account (as was said) of Spaniards, and with a numerous party of *Ruffians*, slew the two Spanish merchants on board the same, and from them took two hogsheads of Spanish pieces of eight, and converted them to her own use. In consequence of which, these offenders were tried and found guilty, at Launceston, of wilful murder, and had sentence of death passed accordingly upon them, and were all executed except the said Lady Killigrew, the principal agent and contriver of this barbarous fact. This woman by the interest of Sir John Arundel of Tolverne, Knight, and his son-in-law, Sir Nicholas Hals, of Pengersick, Knight, obtained of Queen Elizabeth a pardon or reprieve, which was seasonably put into the Sheriff of Cornwall's hands. At the news whereof, the other condemned wretches aforesaid, at the gallows, lamented nothing more than that they had not the company of "that old Jezebel *Killigrew* at that place," and begged Almighty God that some remarkable judgement might befal her and her posterity, and all those who were instrumental in procuring her pardon. And observed hereupon it was that her grandson Sir William Killigrew spent the whole paternal estate of his ancestors; as did Sir Thomas Arundel, Knight, son

Ireland, the Spaniards judged, that a defcent upon that country, might be effected with more aufpicious omens than they had hitherto experienced in their projects of invafion. They, accordingly, landed in Ireland in 1602, and took Kinfale. And they were joined by Tiroen, and a great number of Irifh under him. But they were routed, and the Spanifh leader Alphonfo made a prifoner. And D'Aquila, in a conference with SIR WILLIAM GODOLPHIN* complained of the cowardice and treachery of the Irifh.† With the fervices of Sir William Godolphin in Ireland, I fhould mention thofe of SIR ARTHUR CHAMPERNOWNE;‡ *Sir George*

L

Cary;

fon of Sir John Arundel aforefaid, and John Hals, Efq. fon of Sir Nicholas Hals, Knight, in their own times." *Hals's* MSS. —Yet the Killigrews maintained the dignity of their family in the perfon of *Sir Henry Killigrew*. This gentleman (fays *Carew*) "after ambaffades and meffages, and many other employments of peace and warre, in his Princes feruice, to the good of his countrey, hath made choyce of a retyred eftate, and reuerently regarded by all forts, placeth his principall contentment in himfelfe, which, to a life fo well acted, can no way bee wanting." *Carew*, f. 61.—It feems that a lady of erudition in thefe times, had no repulfive qualities, as at the prefent day. From the very circumftance of her learning, fhe had the power of attracting admirers. Sir Anthony Cook, Schoolmafter to King Edward the fixth had given fuch a learned education to his five daughters, that he married them all to men of confequence—the firft, to the great Lord Burleigh, the fecond to the Lord Keeper Bacon, the third to Sir Thomas Hobby, who died Ambaffador in France, the fourth to Sir Ralph Roulet, and the fifth to *Sir Henry Killigrew*.

* *William Godolphin*, eldeft fon and heir of Sir Francis, was one of thofe gentlemen of quality who accompanied Robert Earl of Effex, in his expedition to Ireland againft the rebels, in 1599; and for his valor at Arclo, was with William Courtenay, Efq. knighted by that Earl, on his return to Dublin. He fet out with great reputation; having, befides a very liberal education, travelled into moft parts of Europe, and attained feveral languages. On the Spanifh invafion, in the latter end of the year 1600, he was in fuch efteem with Lord Mountjoy, Lord Deputy of Ireland, that he entrufted him with the command of his own brigade of horfe, in the decifive battle between the Queen's forces, and the Spaniards and rebels fought 24th December, within a mile of Kinfale. This victory was principally owing to Godolphin; who broke through the whole body of the Spaniards, entirely routing them, and taking their leader prifoner: on which the Irifh threw away their arms and fled. In this action, our hero was flightly wounded in the thigh with a halbert. But, in fix days after, he was fo well recovered from the wound, that when Don John D'Aquila, commander of the Spaniards in the town of Kinfale, offered a parley, defiring the Lord-Deputy to fend fome gentleman of fpecial truft and fufficiency in to the town to confer with him, and receive his propofals, Godolphin was employed in the negociation, which was brought to a conclufion the 2d of January, 1601, on the Spaniards confenting to quit all places in that kingdom. Sir William afterwards performed various fervices againft the rebels; and 20th March, 1601-2, was fpecially appointed to confer with the Earl of Tyrone, and received according to the Earl's requeft, his humble fubmiffion to her Majefty. In 1603, he commanded in the province of Leinfter; and on the defeat of the rebels, returned to England, foon after the death of Elizabeth.§

† See *Baker's Chronicle*, p. 395. It is remarkable, that the French general Hubert, lately "*complained of the cowardice and treachery of the Irifh!*"

‡ "Sir Arthur Champernowne, Knight, was the fecond fon of John Champernowne of Modbury, Efq. by Catherine his wife, daughter of Sir Richard Edgcombe of Mount Edgcombe, Knight, and younger brother of Sir Richard Champernon of Modbiry, Knight, that married Elizabeth, daughter of the Lord Chief Juftice Popham; who, by an high fplendid way of living, greatly exhaufted the eftate: he, dying without iffue, left the remainder thereof to Sir Arthur; who, by an happy marriage with Amy, daughter and heir of John Cruckern of Childhay, did, in fome good meafure, repair it again.—This gentleman was a good foldier, and an eminent commander, in the Irifh wars; he ferved there, under that every way brave, but unfortunate general, the Earl of Effex, then Lord Lieutenant of Ireland; whofe father, Walter Devereux, (the firft Earl of Effex, of this name) was fometime Earl-Marfhal of that kingdom; who, blafted with envy, and oppreffed with grief, fell into a bloody flux, which foon ended his life; when he had firft defired the ftanders by, to admonifh this fon, fcarce ten years old, *to have always before his eyes, the fix and thirtieth year of his age, as the utmoft term of his life*; *which neither himfelf, nor his father before him, could outgo*; nor did the fon attain unto it. A little before his death, this noble Earl fell into this pious prophetical ftrain of devotion, not unfit to be here recorded.—*Oh! Lord, fave that noble realm of* England: *but the miferies, that fhall fhortly fall on it, are many*; *I know, I know them, this night hath God fhewed them unto me. And great is the caufe that it fhould be plagued*; *for the Gofpel of Jefus Chrift is bountifully and truly preached unto them, but they are neither Papifts nor Proteftants*; *they are of no religion, but full of pride and iniquity: there is nothing but infidelity, atheifm, atheifm*; *no religion, no religion! they learn*, faid he, *all to policy, and let go religion*; *but I would to God they would learn to religion, and let go policy. O Lord! Blefs* England.—After which he foon exchanged this life for a better. His fon Robert, Earl of Effex after him, efcaped not alfo, the dreadful effects of envy, which purfued him likewife into Ireland, where he was Lord Lieutenant; after he had exhaufted a great treafure, and wafted a brave army, inftead of returning with a noble conqueft, he ftole home into England, after a fufpicious treaty with the enemy, before he was expected, or before he was welcome. But, before he went, this moft noble Earl, confirmed the honor of knighthood upon

fome

§ On the deceafe of Sir Jonathan Trelawney, Knight, he was elected unanimoufly member of Parliament for Cornwall, to the firft Parliament called by James I. See *Carew*, *Stowe*.

Cary;* and §*Carew*, Earl of Totnes. The Low country-wars, were to many of the Cornish† a school

fome Devonfhire gentlemen, that had fignalized themfelves by their valor and conduct there; among which, Sir Arthur Champernon was one, advanced to this honor by the Lord Lieutenant there, *A. D.* 1599.—Sometime after (moft likely on the death of his elder brother,) Sir Arthur returned into England, and retired to his feat at Modbiry, where he married, and left a fair eftate to his pofterity; which now florifhes at Memland, &c.—The prefent heir married, firft, the eldeft daughter of Richard Hillerfdon, late of Memland, Efq. fans-iffue; fecond, Mary, the daughter of Mr. John Wife of Totnes, Gent. and fole heir to her mother, the daughter and one of the heirs of Lewis Full, of Stoke-Gabriel, Gent.—Sir Arthur was not only fkilled in affairs of war, but in many other ingenious arts; particularly in architecture, as may be inferred from that model of a pleafure-houfe, Mr. *Carew* tells us, he had from him, of great curiofity: where that author was pleafed to beftow this character upon him, that he was a perfectly accomplifhed gentleman.—He died at Modbiry aforefaid, about the beginning of the reign of King James the firft, and lieth there interred, among his anceftors, without any funeral monument.—Chambernon of Clift-Chambernon, gave, Gules a Saltire Verrey between twelve Crofs-Croflets." *Prince*, p. 193.

* "*Sir George Cary*, Knight, and Lord Deputy of Ireland, was born at Cockinton Court-Houfe; an antient, but pleafant feat, near adjoyning to Torbay, which lieth from it a mile, to the fouth, as doth Totnes, five miles from, to the weft.—He was the eldeft of fix fons, of Thomas Cary of that place, Efq. who was fecond fon of Robert Cary, of the fame, by Jane his firft wife, daughter of Sir Nicholas Baron Carew, on whom his father fettled Cockinton, in whofe iffue it defcended home to the prefent age. John Cary, the eldeft fon of Robert aforefaid, married Anne, daughter and heir of Edmund Devick or Devyock, of Keckbear, in the parifh of Okehamton, Efq. and fettled there. His pofterity continued in that place feveral defcents; of which race, Anthony (if it be not miftaken for Lancelot) Cary, Efq. gave a bountiful gift to the town of Okehampton, viz. the fum of fixty pounds, to continue in ftock, to be employed for the better education of poor children, in trades and occupations. This family is extinct.—By Agnes, his fecond wife, Robert Cary, of Cockinton aforefaid, (fhe was the daughter of Sir William Hodie of Pilfden, in Dorfetfhire, Lord Chief Baron of the Exchequer) had iffue William Cary of Ladford, in the parifh of Shebear, near the Turridge. This family, likewife, is gone.—By his third wife, Margery, daughter and heir of Foukroy of Dartmouth, the faid Robert had iffue Robert, unto whom he gave Clovelly, in the north-weft part of this county: whofe pofterity continues there this day in great repute.—Sir George Cary aforefaid, upon what motive or encouragement I do not find, went into Ireland, where he grew in great efteem with the government, and was preferred treafurer of wars, an high and honorable poft in that kingdom; whofe fallary was 638l. 15s. per annum; befides which, he had the command of a band of foot, or horfe, or both, which amounted to many fcores more: here we find him in this ftation, *An.* 1599, at what time, he was alfo one of the Lords of her Majefty Q. Elizabeth's Privy Council, for that kingdom. In this office and truft, doth Sir George Cary continue feveral years, even to the death of that glorious Princefs of happy memory. And then the Lord Mountjoy, Sir Charles Blount, (a very learned, wife, and noble gentleman, afterwards created Earl of Devon) at that time Lord Deputy there, being willing to go for England, to congratulate King James the firft, upon his coming to this crown, and to be nearer the beams of that new rifen fun, in our hemifphere, in his inftructions to Sir Henry Davers, whom he fent exprefs to the faid King, recommended to his Majefty Sir George Cary, treafurer at wars, as the fitteft perfon to fucceed him in that high and honorable place; urging this alfo as a reafon, that Sir George Cary had already been Lord Juftice of that kingdom: of whom this is farther added, 'that howfoever he be no foldier, yet is well acquainted with the bufinefs of the war, wherein he had been ever very induftrious to advance the fervice: which indeed is a very honorable character.'—The Lord Deputy Mountjoy, therefore, having, for the prefent, pretty well fettled the Province of Munfter, and, for the greater quiet of that kingdom, publifhed an act of oblivion, for all grievances, his lordfhip received letters from the King, fignifying, that he was chofen one of his Majefty's Privy Council in England; and was licenfed to come over; and had authority to leave Sir George Cary, the King's Deputy there, during his abfence; which was accordingly done.—Sir George Cary took up this honorable fword, in a ftormy tempeftuous time, when that kingdom was ftrangely actuated with the fpirit of rebellion; which occafioned him much trouble, during that little fpace he had held it. And the public treafure of the kingdom being then reduced to a very low ebb, he was forced to make payments of brafs and leather money, which brought great clamors and reproaches, upon him, even from his own friends and countrymen; fo hard a matter is it for one to pleafe a multitude: and fuch unjuft tafk-mafters are they, to exact brick without ftraw. Sir George did not continue in this government much more than a year; and then Sir Arthur Chicefter, another of our noble countrymen, with better fortune, fucceeded him therein.—Not long after this, Sir George Cary returned into England, and retired to his feat at Cockinton; where, being grown fomwhat aged, he refolved to live the refidue of his days to God and himfelf. And knowing how pleafing a facrifice to God, charity and good deeds are, he purpofed to do fomething for the poor; and accordingly he fet about the building of feven alms-houfes for their ufe and comfort; *i. e.* fo many feveral apartments, all under one roof, for feven poor people of that parifh; every one having a ground-room, and a chamber over; with a little diftinct herb garden enclofed with a ftone-wall: to each of which alfo, he allowed 1s. per week, with a new frize gown, and a new fhirt or fhift yearly, at Chriftmas; as may more fully appear from the deed, whereof here follows an abftract.—

'Sir George Cary of Cockinton, Knight, by his deed under hand and feal, bearing date 11th day of September, in the 6th year of the reign of K. James I. did grant to feveral feoffees in truft, an annuity of 30l. per ann. iffuing out of his manors of Cockinton and Chilfon, by quarterly payments for ever; for and towards the reparation of feven alms-houfes at Cockinton, there newly erected by the faid Sir George Cary: and for and towards the relief and maintenance of feven poor people, then, and at all times afterwards inhabiting therein, every poor man and woman to be paid one fhilling every week; and at Chriftmas, yearly, a new frize gown, and a new fhirt or fmock: and the overplus of the 30l. per an. if any, fhall be employed to the ufe of fuch of them as fhall be fick; and for fuch other neceffary occafions, as in the difcretion of the feoffees fhall be thought fit.' And the deed farther declares; 'That the owners of Cockinton houfe fhall for ever thereafter, nominate

nate fuch poor people as fhall be placed into the faid alms-houfes; fo as fuch nomination be made within twenty eight days after any of the houfes be void, by death, or otherwife; and fo as the choice be of the pooreft fort of the inhabitants of the parifh of Cockinton: and if there fhould be any neglect or default therein, by the fpace of the twenty eight days fully expired, that then the Bifhop of Exeter for the time being, is to elect and nominate any fuch poor perfon as he fhall think fit.' Thus the deed.

Thefe houfes are commodioufly fituated, near the church, and near Cockinton houfe aforefaid; which is a generous piece of charity, if the will of the founder be fo faithfully executed, as it was pioufly intended; as I queftion not for the future but it will, it being the beft way that I know, to obtain God's bleffing upon the whole eftate, out of which this annuity iffues, and the poffeffors of it.—Sir George Cary, fome eight years after this, yielded to fate; and lieth interred in a vault in Cockinton church, being buried there, *A.* 1615, *Feb.* 19. Altho' he was twice married, he had no iffue that furvived him: firft, he married Wilmot, daughter and heir of John Gifford of Yeo, the divorced wife of John Bury of Colaton, near Chimly in this county; by whom he had iffue one fon, Sir George Cary, Knight, a brave foldier, married, but flain in the wars of Ireland, without iffue, before his father's death; and one daughter, married to Sir Richard Edgecombe, of Mount-Edgecombe fans-iffue. Secondly, he married Lucy, daughter to Robert Lord Rich, Earl of Warwick; but having no iffue by her, he adopted George, (third fon of his fecond brother, Robert, fo one; fifth fon of his fourth brother, John Cary, fo another tells us) whom he made his heir. An elder brother to which George, was Sir Edward Cary, fometime of Stantor, near adjoyning, knighted in the Irifh wars; whofe grandfon, Edward Cary, Efq. now florifhes at Tor-Abby in great efteem, who was the eldeft fon of Sir George Cary of that place, Knight." *Prince*, pp. 196, 197.

I am obliged to Mr. Cornifh of Totnes, for copies of two letters which were written by Queen Elizabeth, to Sir George Cary, at this conjuncture. "The originals were fent to me (fays Mr. Cornifh) from Tor-Abbey. I have as many as will make a handfome volume: you will be the beft judge by the materials in your poffeffion, whether they will enrich your work, or if fairly relevant. I affure you they coft me no little trouble in decyphering." Hiftorians have told us, that Effex returned in great terror and precipitation: but I believe the letter that caufed that fudden return, has never yet met the public eye.

Copy of a letter written by Queen Elizabeth, to Sir George Cary, Treafurer of War in Ireland, dated the 7th of March, 1598.

"Truftie and well beloved, wee greete you well.

"Whereas we have made choice of our coufin the Earle of Effex, our Marfhall of England, to be Lieutenant of our Kingdom of Ireland, and have appointed unto him (befides in allowance of ten pounds by the daie contain'd in our eftablifhment, fign'd with our hand, and delivered to you) all the ordinary entertainment heretofore allow'd by us to our deputies of that realme, which are contain'd in an other eftablifhment fign'd by our Privy Counfel, and is alfo deliver'd to you. We do therefore, will and require you to make payment to the faid Earle, or his affigns of his faid entertainment due to himfelf, and to his company of fifty horfe, and fifty foot, with the officers, after the rate in the faid eftablifhment contain'd, from the day of the date hereof, until our pleafure fhall be otherwife made known to you; and thereof to deliver unto him by way of imprefs, (if he fhall demand it) as much as his faid entertainment for himfelf, and his faid fifty horfe and fifty foot, with their officers, doth amount unto for the fpace of two months; the fame to beafterwards defalked upon his entertainments; and further, whereas heretofore our deputies of that our realme have had an allowance from us, of one thoufand pounds yearly, out of a compofition made with our fubjects inhabiting our pale there in line of Chefte, being two thoufand and one hundred pounds by the year; we do likewife will and require you from the time of the faid Earle's receiving of the fword, there to make payment unto him, of the like fum of one thoufand pounds yearly, out of that compofition, or proportionally according to the time he fhall remain there; and our pleafure is that our juftice of that our realme now being, and our Lieutenant of our armie there fhall have the full entertainment ordinarily allowed to our deputy of that our realme, by equal parts in fuch manner as now they have, untill the day of their delivery up of the fword, all imprefts firft deducted which in that realme they have before our arrival receiv'd.—And further, whereas we have appointed an allowance of twenty fhillings by the day, to our late treafurer Henry Wallop, Knight, during the time of his ftay there, we do require you that uppon warrant from our Lieutenant, you make payment thereof unto him; and this our letter fhall be your fufficient warrant and difcharge in this behalf. Given under our fignett att our Mannor of Richmonde, the 7th day of March, in the one and fortieth year of our reign."

"To our truftee and well beloved Sir George Cary, Knight, our treafurer at warres in our realme of Ireland."

Copy of a letter from Queen Elizabeth, to the Earle of Effex, 14th September, 1599.

"Right truftie and right welbeloved coufin and counfellor, and trufty and welbeloved we greet you well; having fufficiently declared unto before this time, how little the manner of your proceedings hath anfwered either our direction, or the world's expectation, and finding now by your letters, by Cuff, a courfe more ftrange, and if ftranger may be, we are doubtfull what to prefcribe you at any time, or what to build upon your writting to us in any thing, for we have clearly difcern'd of late that you have ever (to this hour) poffefs'd us with expectations, that you would proceed as we directed you, but your actions alway fhew the contrary, though varied in fuch fort as you were fure we have no time to countermand them.—Before your departure no manner of counfel was held found, which perfwaded not prefently the main profecutions in Ulfter, all was nothing without that, and nothing was too much for that; this drew on the fudden tranfportation of fo many thoufands to be carried out with you as when you arrived, we were charged with more than the lift on which we refolved, the number of three hundred horfe alfo, (above the thoufand which was affented to) which were only to be in pay during the fervice in Ulfter, hath been alfo put in charge ever fince the firft journey, the pretence of which voyage, as appear'd by your letters, was to do fome prefent fervice in the interim, whilft the feafon grew more commodious for the main profecution, for which purpofe you did importune with earneftnefs, that all manner of provifions might be haften'd to Dublin, againft your return. Of this refolution to defer your going into Ulfter, you may well think that we woud have made ftay, if you had given us more timely warning, or if we coud have imagined by the contents of your own writings, that you woud have fpent nine weeks abroad. At your return when a third part of July was pafs'd, and that you had underftood our miflike of your former courfes, and made your excufe of undertaking it only in refpect of your conformity to the counfel's opinions, with great proteftations of haft into the north; then we receiv'd another letter of new reafons to fufpend that journey yet a while, and to draw the army into The fruit whereof was no other at your home comming, but more relations of further miferies of our army and greater difficultys to perform the Ulſter war. Then follow'd from you and the counſel a new demand of two thouſand men, to which if we woud aſſent you woud ſpeedily undertake what we had ſo often commanded; when that was granted, and your going outward promiſed by diverſe letters, we receive by this bearer now freſh advice, that all you can do is to go to the frontier, and that you have provided only for twenty days victual, in which kind of proceeding we muſt deal plainly with you, and that counſel that it were more proper for them to leave troubling themſelves with influencing us, by what rules our power and their obedience are limited, and to bethink them (if the courſes have been only derived from their counſel) how to anſwer this part of theirs, to traine us into a new expence, for one end; and to employ it uppon another, to which we never woud have aſſented; if we coud have ſuſpected it, ſhoud have been undertaken before wee heard it was in action; and therefore, we do wonder how it can be anſwered, ſeeing your attempt is not in the capital traytors country, that you have increaſed. But it is true as we have often ſaid, that we are drawn on to expence by little and little, and by proteſtations of great reſolutions in generalitys, till they come to particular operations; of all which courſes, whoſoever ſhall examine any of the arguments uſed for excuſe, ſhall find that your own proceedings beget the difficulties, and that no juſt cauſe do breed the alteration. If lack of numbers, if ſickneſs of the army be the reaſons, why was not the action undertaken when the army was in better ſtate; if winter approach, why were the ſummer months of July and Auguſt loſt; if the ſpring was too ſoon and the ſummer that followed otherwiſe ſpent: if the harveſt that ſucceeded were ſo neglected, as nothing hath been done; and if it be true that in the winter nothing muſt be done: then ſurely muſt we conclude, that none of the four quarters of the year will be in ſeaſon for you and that counſel to agree of Tyron's proſecution, for which all our charge was intended.—Further we require you to conſider, whether we have not great cauſe to think, that the purpoſe is not to end the war, when yourſelf have ſo often told us, that all the petty undertaking in Leinſter, Monſter, and Connaught, are but loſs of time, conſumption of treaſure, and waſte of our people, untill Tyrone himſelf be firſt beaten, on whom all the reſt depend. Do not you ſee that he maketh the war with us, in all parts by his miniſters ſeconding all places where any attempt be offerd? Who doth not ſee that if this courſe be continued, the wars are likely to ſpend us and our kingdom beyond all moderation; as well as the report of the ſucceſs in all places hath blemiſh'd our honour, and encouraged others in no ſmall proportion. We know that we cannot ſo much fail in judgment, as not to underſtand, that all the world ſaith, how time is dally'd, though you think that the allowance of that counſel, (whoſe ſubſcriptions are your echoes) ſhall ſerve and ſatisfie us. How woud you have derided any man elſe, that ſhoud have followed your ſteps. How often have you told us, that others which preceeded you, had no intent to end the war; how often reſolved us, that untill Longfoile and Balliſhannon were planted, there woud be no hope of doing ſervice uppon the capital rebells. We muſt therefore let you know, that as it cannot be ignorance, ſo can it not be want of means, for you had your aſking; you had choice of times, you had power and authority, more ample than ever any had or ever ſhall have; it may well be judged with how little contentment we ſearch out theſe and other errors, for who doth willingly ſeeke for that which they are ſo loth to find; but how ſhould that be hidden that is ſo palpable. And therefore, to leave that which is paſt, and that you may prepare to remedy matters of weight hereafter, rather than to fill your papers with many impertinent arguments, being in your general letters, ſavouring ſtill of many points of humour that concerne only the private of you (our lieutenant) We do tell you plainly, that are of that counſel, that we wonder at your indiſcretion, to ſubſcribe to letters which concerne our public ſervice, when they are mixed with many private, and directed to our counſel table; which is not wont to handle things of ſo ſmall impottance. To conclude, that you will ſay though the army be in liſt nineteen thouſand, that you have them not; we anſwer then to you our treaſurer, that we are ill ſerv'd, and that there need not ſo frequent demands of full pay; if you will ſay that the muſter maſter is to blame, we much muſe then, why he is not puniſhed; tho' ſay we might to you our general, (if we woud ex ore proprio indicare) that all defect by muſters, (yea in never ſo remote garriſons) have been affirm'd to us, to deſerve to be imputed to the want of care in the general. For the ſmall proportion you ſay you carry with you, of three thouſand five hundred foot, when lately we augmented you two thouſand more; it is to us paſt comprehenſion, except it be that you have left too great numbers in unneceſſary garriſons, which do increaſe our charge, and diminiſh our army, which we commande you to reforme, eſpecialy ſince by your continual report of the ſtate of every province, you deſcribe them all to be in worſt condition, than ever they were before you ſet foot in that kingdom; ſo that whoever ſhall write the ſtory of this year's action, muſt ſay, that we were at great charge to hazard our kingdom; and you have taken great pains to prepare for many purpoſes, which periſh without undertaking.—And therefore, becauſe we ſee now by your own words, that the hope is ſpent of this year's ſervice, uppon Tyrone and Odonnel, we do command you and our counſel jointly, to fall into preſent deliberation, and thereupon to ſend us over in writing, a true declaration of the eſtate to which you have brought our kingdom, and what be the effects which this journey hath produced, and why theſe garriſons which you will plant (as far within the land in the Brenny and Monoghan, as others whereof we have written) ſhall not have the ſame difficulties. Secondly, we look to hear from you and them jointly, how you think fit that the remaine of this year ſhall de employ'd, in what kind of war, and when and with what numbers; which being done and ſent us hither in writing, with all expedition, you ſhall then underſtand our pleaſure, in all things fit for our ſervice; until which time we command you to be very carefull to meete with all inconveniencys that may ariſe in that kingdom, where the evil effected will grow ſo inſolent upon our ill ſucceſs, and the good ſubjects grow deſperate, when they ſee the beſt of our preſerving them.—We have ſeen a writing in form of a cartell, full of challenges that are impertinent and of compariſons that are needleſs, ſuch as hath not been before this time preſented to a ſtate, except it be done now with a hope to terrifie all men from cenſuring your proceedings. Had it not been enough to have ſent us the teſtimony of the counſell, but that you muſt call ſo many of thoſe that are of ſlender experience, and none of our counſel to ſuch a form of ſubſcription. Surely, however you may have warranted them, we doubt not but to let them know what belongs to us, to you, and to themſelves; and thus, expecting your anſwer, we end. At our Manor of Noneſuch, the 14th of September, in the 41ſt year of our reign, 1599."

"To our right truſty, and right well-beloved couſin and counſellor, the Earle of Eſſex, our lieutenant and governour general of our kingdom of Ireland, and to the reſt of our counſel there."

§ "*George Carew*, Baron of *Clopton*, and Earl of *Totnes*, was born in this county; but whether at Upton-Hilion, near Crediton, or at Exeter, in the houſe there, belonging to the Arch-deaconry of Totnes, or where elſe, I am not able to determin.

termin. He was second son of George Carew, D. D. who was third son of Sir Edmund Carew, of Mohuns Ottery, Knight, by Katharine his wife, daughter of Sir William Huddesfeild. Which Sir Edmund was a brave soldier, and knighted for the gallant service he did unto King Henry 7. at Bosworth-feild. He had four sons, all famous men; as first, Sir William, who by Joan his wife, daughter of Sir William Courtenay of Powderham, had issue George Carew, drown'd at sea in the Mary Rose, *A.* 37 K. Henry 8. Sir Philip, a Knight of Malta, and Sir Peter, an eminent soldier in the Irish wars; who all died without issue whereby Mohuns-Ottery fell to their sister and heir; whose daughter and heir brought it to Southcot.—Second, Sir Edmund had issue Thomas Carew of Bicklegh. Third, George Carew, D. D. and fourth, Sir Gawen Carew of Wood in this county, Kt. a great courtier, belonging to Queen Elizabeth.—George (however the genius of the family enclin'd the others generally to arms) addicted himself to the arts; and became a member of the University of Oxford, spending some time in the house then called King Henry the eighth's hall, since swallowed up of Christ-Church. How long he continued is uncertain; but certain it is, that having been resident here a while, he betroth'd in marriage a noble young gentlewoman, of excellent vertues, who being a little after snatch'd away from him by immature death, he took the stroke so tenderly, that he resolv'd to leave his country, and travel beyond sea. After some time, returning into England, he took holy orders; with this especial aim, that he might be no more obnoxious to love, and the contingencies of matrimony. However, at length he chang'd his resolution, and married Anne, daughter of Sir Anthony Harvy, Kt. by whom he had two famous sons, Sir Peter, an excellent soldier, and Sir George, Earl of Totnes; and one daughter, married to Walter Dourish of Dourish in the parish of Sanford, Esq. from whom, in a direct line, is descended the present heir of that antient name and family.—Before I proceed to the Earl, I shall crave leave to speak something farther of his father, Dr. George Carew. He was, first, Arch-deacon of Totnes; then Dean of Bristol; next, Chantor of the church of Salisbury; after that, Chaplain and Dean of the chappel to Q. Eliz. then Dean of Christ-Church in Oxford, *Anno.* 1559; afterward Dean of Exeter; and lastly, Dean of Windsor. From all which preferments, growing rich, he purchased a good estate, rebuilded the house of Upton-Hilion aforesaid; which he left unto his son, Sir Peter (having bought the site and demesns himself); who dying without issue, left it to his brother, the Earl of Totnes; who sold it to the ancestor of Sir Walter Young, Baronet, whose now it is. But to go on.—George Carew, the younger son of the Dean, for his better education, went to Oxford, where he became gentleman-commoner of Broad-Gates-Hall, now Pembrook-College, *An.* 1572, and of his age fifteen. At the same time, two of his name are said to have studied in University College; which hath given occasion to some, to challenge this person for theirs. However, this gentleman being more delighted in martial affairs, than in the solitary shades of a study, left the University, without taking any degree, and betook himself to travel.—The first place, we find, he went into was Ireland, at that time the scene of noble actions; where he had soon a command given him in the wars, which he diligently pursued against that noted rebel, the Earl of Desmond, a subdolous man; who occasioned great disturbance to the English government in that kingdom.—This gentleman having behaved himself very well in Ireland, his merits, at length, were made known to Q. Elizabeth of gracious memory; upon which she made him one of her council there, and master of the ordnance in that kingdom. In which last employment, he behaved himself with great renown in various expeditions; as he did likewise, some years after, in his voyage to Cadiz in Spain.—Sometime after this, he returned to England; and coming to Oxford, he was, in company with other persons of quality, as Ferdinando Earl of Derby, Sir John Spencer, &c. in the year of our Lord 1589, in the month of September, created master of arts.—Sometime after this, he went back into Ireland again; and when that unhappy kingdom was, in a manner, over-run with a domestic rebellion, and a Spanish army, Sir George Carew was made Lord President of Munster for three years; at what time, joyning his forces with those of the Earl of Thomond, he took divers castles and strong holds, in those parts; as Logher, Crome, Glane, Carigroile, Ruthmore, &c.; and at length brought the titular Earl of Desmond, one of the most active rebels there, to his tryal. How greatly this carriage and conduct of his, pleased his gracious mistress Q. Elizabeth, may appear from that letter sent him by her Majesty, *An.* 1601, written with her own hand. A copy whereof here follows:

My faithful George,

If ever more services of worth, were performed in shorter space, than you have done, we are deceived among many eye-witnesses: we have received the fruit thereof; and bid you faithfully credit, that whatso wit, courage, or care may do, we truly find, they have all been thorowly acted in all your charge. And for the same, believe, that it shall neither be unremembred, nor unrewarded: and, in the mean while, believe, my help, nor prayers, shall never fail you.

Your soveraign, that best regards you, E. R.

After K. James I. of blessed memory, came to the crown of England, Sir George Carew was called home; and in the first year of his reign, was constituted governor of the isle of Guernsy and Castle-Cornet. In the third year of that King, he was advanced to the dignity of a baron of this realm, by the title of, the Lord Carew of Clopton: he having married Joice, daughter and co-heir to William Clopton of Clopton, in the county of Warwick, Esq. Afterwards, he became vice-chamberlain and treasurer to Q. Anne, consort-royal to K. Jam. I. then master of the ordnance throughout England, and of the privy-council to that prince.—Upon the death of K. James, when Charles the first succeeded in the English Throne, he was, by that gracious King, on the 5th of Febr. in the first year of his reign, created Earl of Totnes, in his own country; the same place whereof, before, his father had been the arch-deacon. At what time he was under this most honorable character, that he was a faithful subject, a valiant and prudent commander, an honest counsellor, a gentile scholar, a lover of antiquities, and a great patron of learning. For amidst his busy employments there (what is not a little observable) as an argument of his affection to that kind of study, he wrote an historical account of all the memorable passages which hapned in Ireland, during the term of those three years he continued there, under this title:—*Pacata Hibernia*: or, *The History of the late Wars in* Ireland. London Print. Folio, 1633, with his effigies before, and these verses under it:

'Talis erat vultu: sed linguâ, mente, manuq;
'Qualis erat, qui vult dicere, scripta legat.
'Consulat aut famam, qui linguâ mente, manuvé
'Vincere hunc, famâ judice, rarus erat.

which

Which may thus be rendred into English:
Such was his face; but's tongue, his mind, his hand,
Who best would know, from's works must understand.
Him who excels, in tongue, in hand, in mind,
Though fame herself be judg, 'tis rare to find.

Of which history, containing those three years transactions in Munster, that he was there, the said Earl's own exploits are not the least part.—This work, while he lived, was first, reserved for his own private satisfaction. Secondly, preserved for the furtherance of a general history of the kingdom of Ireland, when some industrious writer should undertake a compleat description of those affairs. And lastly, out of his own retired modesty, it was by him held back from the stage of publication, lest himself, being a principal actor in many of the particulars, he might be thought to give utterance to his private merit and services; however justly memorable.—After the Earl's death, this book came into the hands of his faithful and trusty servant, if not his natural son, called Thomas Stafford, for his good services in Ireland also knighted, by whom, being first offered to the view and censure of divers learned and judicious persons, it was at length published.—Besides his Pacata Hibernia, this noble Earl hath, in four large volumes, collected several chronologies, charters, letters, muniments, and other materials belonging to Ireland; which, as choice rarities, are at this day reserved in the Bodleian Library.—He also made several collections, notes, and extracts for writing the history of the reign of K. Hen. 5. which were remitted into the history of Great Britain, published by John Speed; of which author, and his work, one hath given this remarkable character: for stile and industry (saith he) it is such, that for one who (as Martial speaks) had neither a Græcum χαιρε, nor an Ave Latinum, it is without many fellows in Europe.—This noble Earl ended his days at the Savoy, in the Strand, near London, on the 27th of March, 1629, being then of the age of seventy three years, and near ten months. Soon after his death, his body was conveyed to Stratford, upon Avon, in Warwickshire, in which stood Clopton-House, the seat of his lady's family; and was interred at the upper end of an isle, on the north-side of that parish church, among the ancestors, and near the place where she herself was afterwards laid.—Over whose grave, and to whose memory, a very stately monument was soon after erected, by the care and kindness of Joice his lady; adorned by Ursula, the wife of Henry Nevil, of Holt in Leicestershire, Esq. this lady's sister's daughter; as may be seen from this inscription:

'*Georgio Totonesiæ Comiti &*
'*Comitissæ Jocosæ Guil. Clopton*
'*Arm. Cohæredi, Materteræsuæ*
'*Optime Merenti.*
P.
'*Vrsula uxor Henr. Nevil de*
'*Holt Leicef. Arm.*

A very lively draught of this noble monument, may be seen in Sir William Dugdal's Antiquities of Warwickshire; where the Earl and his Countess are represented, lying side by side, in their robes and coronets, under a noble arch, adorned with their coats of arms, in the midst whereof is a fair marble table, containing this large epitaph.

D. O. M.
Et
Memoriæ Sacrum.

Qui in spem immortalitatis, mortales hic deposuit exuvias Georgivs Carew, antiquissima nobilissimaq; Ortus Prosapia: eadem scilicet Mascula stirpe qua illustrissimæ Giraldinorum in Hibernia & Windesoriensium in Anglia familiæ à Carew-Castro in agro Penbrochiensi Cognomen fortitus est. Ab in eunte Ætate Bellicis Studiis innutritus, Ordines in Hibernia adhuc Juvenis contra Rebellem Desmoniæ Comitem primum duxit. Postea Elizabethæ fœliciffimæ Memoriæ Reginæ in eodem Regno Consiliarius, & Tormentorum Bellicorum Præfectus fuit. Quo etiam munere in variis Expeditionibus, in illa præsertim longe celeberrima qua Cades Hispaniæ expugnatæ sunt Anno MDXCVI. fæliciter perfunctus est. Demum cum Hibernia universa domesticæ Rebellionis & Hispanicæ Invasionis incendio flagraret, Momoniæ Præfectus per integrum Triennium, contra Hostes, tam internos quam externos multa fortiter, fideliterq; gessit. Tamdem in Angliam revocatus a Jacobo Magnæ Britanniæ Rege, ad Baronis de Clopton dignitatem evectus, Annæ Reginæ Procamerarius & Thesaurarius, Tormentorum Bellicorum per totam Angliam Præfectus, Garnseiæ Insulæ Gubernator constitutus, & in Secretioris Consilii Senatum Cooptatus est. Jacobo deinde ad Cœlestem Patriam evocato, Carolo filio usque adeo Charus fuit, ut inter alia non vulgaria Benevoli affectus indicia, ab eo Comitis de Totnes honore Solenni investitura exornatus fuerit.—Tantus vir, Natalium Splendore illustris, Belli & Pacis artibus Ornatissimus, magnos Honores propria virtute consecutus, cum ad plenam & adultam Senectutem pervenisset, Pie, Placideq; Animam Deo Creatori reddidit Londini in ædibus Sabaudiæ.

Anno Dominicæ Incarnationis juxta Anglicam Computationem MDCXXIX die Martii xxvii.
Vixit Annos lxxiii Menses fere x.

Joisia Clopton, cujus Effigies hic cernitur, antiqua Cloptonorum Familia, filia primogenita & Hæres ex Semisse, Gulielmi Clopton de Clopton Armigeri, Conjux Mæstissima viri charissimi & optime Meriti cum quo vixit Annos xlix, Memoriæ pariter ac suæ, in Spem fæliciffimæ Resurrectionis, Monumentum hoc, quo Supremo Munere, non sine Lachrymis Consecravit. Illa vixit Annos lxxviii & xiiii die Januarii obiit Anno Dom. M.DC.XXX.VI.

Of which noble Earl, I shall only add that honorable character, given of him by Dr. *Fuller*, in his England's Worthies, 'that for state-affairs, George Carew, privy counsellor of England, Scotland, and Ireland, was as able a man, as the age, he lived in, produced.'—This Earl had an elder brother, whose name was Sir Peter Carew, a very noble knight, as *Camden* calls him, and of approved virtue. He was also, an excellent soldier, and did great service to the crown of England, in the kingdom of Ireland; where he died, and was buried at Waterford, Dec. 15, 1575.—Notwithstanding which, there is a noble memorial erected to him, and Sir Gawen Carew his uncle; and another to Sir Peter Carew of Mohuns-Ottery, Kt.

(a

ſchool of honour. "Maſter *William Lower* (ſays *Carew*) late captain of Sir Frauncis Vere's companie in Netherland, hath opened the war-ſchoole with a great many Corniſh young gentlemen, that under his conduct ſought to conforme themſelves to his patterne, everie way accompliſhed with all the due parts of honour."* Thomas Bonython of Bonython, Eſq. was, alſo, a captain in the Low-country-wars. *John Carew* of Penwarne, in Mevagiſſy, Eſq. (ſon to Peter Carew) ſignalized himſelf in the Low-country-wars, and at the famous ſiege of Oſtend, in 1601; where his right hand was ſhot off by a cannon ball, in lieu of which he had a wooden hand with ſprings: this is ſtill preſerved at Heligan.‡ Though, in the reign of Elizabeth, Cornwall will admit of few additional

(a great ſoldier likewiſe) at the upper end of the north ambulatory, in St. Peter's church, at Exeter, in, or near, the Lady Mary's Chappel; on one of which are found theſe words:

Viro
Nobiliſſimo D. Petro Carew
Equiti Aurato,
Eſt hoc Structum Monumentum:
Qui Obiit Roſæ in Laginia Hiberniæ 27
Novem. Sepultus autem Waterfordiæ
15 *Decem.* 1575.
Terra Cadaver habet ———" *Prince*, pp. 196, 199.

† In enumerating a few of thoſe gentlemen who ſerved her majeſty abroad, I am reminded of *Sir Thomas Baſkerville*, who from the connexion of the Polwheles with his family, may here, perhaps, not improperly be introduced; eſpecially as the following lines to his memory, occur in a MS. volume of poems by John Polwhele; of which poems further notice will be taken in the philological department of the work.—" In memorye of the right worthye and valiant gentleman Sir Thomas Baſkerville, Knighte, cheif commander of her Majeſties forces in Picardye, in the ſerviſe of the French Kinge; who deceaſed there 4th June, 1597.

Theſe ar the glories of a worthye praiſe,
Which, noble Baſkerville! heere nowe ar reade;
In honour of thy life and latter daies,
To number thee amongſt the bleſſed dead.
A pure regarde to the immortall parte,
A ſpotleſs minde, a bodye prone to paine;
A givinge hande, and an undaunted hearte,
And all theſe vertues voyde of all diſdaine.
And all theſe vertues, yet not ſoe unknowne,
But Netherlands, but Indies, Spaine, and France
Can witneſſe that theſe honours were thine owne,
Which they reſerve thy merrit to advance;
That valour ſhould not periſh voyde of fame,
Nor noble deeds but leave a noble name.

This monument is behinde the high altar in the cathedrall church of St. Paul, in London. He was my wives neere kinſeman, deſcended from Earſly Caſtle, in Herefordſhire. John Polwhele."—This much for my poetical anceſtor. I ſhall only remark, that in a book entitled, " the State of the Proteſtants of Ireland, under the late King James's Government," by Dr. William King, Biſhop of Derry," I found at p. 330, *Baſkerville Polwheel*, Purſuivant in Chancery. [See Oct. Edit. being the third with additions.] At p. 386, occurs *Barth. Polwheele*, member for the borough of Caryesfort, in Ireland. This name is introduced among thoſe of the knights, citizens, and burgeſſes returned to the Parliament, beginning the 7th of May, 1689.

* *Carew*, f. 62, b.

‡ " In S. Ewe the ſeat of his great grandſon John Tremayne, Eſq. of which accident and of Carew's unbroken courage, Camden, in his Annals of Elizabeth, has made this honourable mention. " Nec tacendus Joannes Carew ab Antonio Cornubienſis Adoleſcentulus, qui inter erumpendum, brachium majoris tormenti impetu avulſum et longius projectum, ſociis condolentibus, infracto animo, ſine omni doloris ſenſu in oppidum altera manu retulit, et chirurgo monſtrans, Ecce, inquit, brachium quod hodie univerſo corpori inſervivit." To which let me add, what his grandſon, the late Lewis Tremayne has often told me, that he gave it to his landlady to bury it with theſe words: " Here, landlady, this is the hand that cut the pudding to-day." For tho' Camden calls it an arm, it was the hand only taken off about the wriſt." *Tonkin's* MS.—" *William Mohun*, Eſq. of Trencreek, was a captain under Sir Walter Raleigh, in ſeveral expeditions; particularly his laſt unfortunate one to Guinea." *Tonkin's* MS.—" Captaine *George Wray* by a rare temperature of vertues, breathed courage into his ſoldiers, purchaſed love amongſt his acquaintance, and bred diſmay in his enemies." And " Captaine *Hender* was the abſoluteſt man of war for preciſe obſerving marchall rules which his dayes afforded, beſides his commendable ſufficiencie of head and hand for invention and execution." *Carew*, f. 62. b.—" John Drake of Aſh, by Amey his wife, daughter of *Roger*

additional obſervations; yet the attention of the Queen was by no means engroſſed by war or commerce. To the religious eſtabliſhment—to Proteſtantiſm as oppoſed to Popery, Elizabeth was oſtenſibly a zealous friend: but ſhe was a mere ſtate-religioniſt.§

Before

Roger Grenville of *Stowe*, (anceſtor of the Right Hon. John Earl of Bath, ſays *Prince*) had iſſue Sir Bernard Drake," who diſtinguiſhed himſelf as a ſoldier in Elizabeth's reign. See *Prince* pp. 244, 245, 246.

§ Among the Prieſts and Jeſuits who are exhibited in the black catalogue of criminals by Proteſtants, and in the bright liſts of Saints and Martyrs by papiſts, *Granger* mentions *Cuthbert Mayne*. He was executed at Launceſton, in 1579. Of this perſon, is preſerved an engraved portrait, 4to. Mezz. *Granger*, vol. 1. p. 226.—But Mayne was not the only Corniſhman who felt the ſeverity of Elizabeth's law againſt Papiſts; though he was the firſt of all her ſubjects, againſt whom it was put in execution. Francis Tregian, a gentleman who had harboured Cuthbert, was condemned to the loſs of his eſtates, and to perpetual impriſonment. Of this circumſtance *Tonkin* has given us a very full account. "Mr. Carew (ſays *Tonkin*) tho' it happened in his time, doth not mention the great misfortune which befell *Francis Tregian*, Eſq. tho' it ended in the total ruine of this wealthy and flouriſhing family. In giving an account of which, I will be as brief as the thing will bear. Mr. Camden has touched on it, in his Annals of Queen Elizabeth (*A. D.* 1577, Reg. 19): "Hactenus ſerena tranquillitas Pontificiis in Angliâ affulſit, qui, quàdam miſericordi connoventia ſua ſacra inter privatos parietes, licetilla legibus interdicta pecuniariâ mulctâ inflictâ, quodam modo impuné celebrârant; nec regina vim conſcientiæ afferendam cenſuit. Verum poſtquam illud fulmen excommunicationis Romæ in reginam fuiſſet ejaculatum, in nubes et tempeſtates ſerenitas illa paulatim abiit, legemque elicuit anno 1571, contra eos, qui ejuſmodi Bullas, Agnos Dei, et Grana Benedicta, Papalis obſequii teſſeram, in regnum intulerint, aut aliquem Romanæ eccleſiæ reconciliarint, ut diximus. Primus hâc lege tenebatur Cuthbertus Mainus ſacerdos qui, Pontificiæ contra Principem potentiæ aſſertor pervicax, without any overt-act, as far as appears here, againſt the new law, by bringing in his Bulls, &c. or by reconciling any to the church of Rome, ("ad Fanum Stephani (Launſton vulgò vocant) in Cornwalliâ ſupplicio affectus, et Trugionus nobilis qui eum hoſpitio acceperat," only had entertained him in his houſe), "fortunis everſus, perpetuoque carceri adjudicatus." And that you may ſee what a noble fortune he loſt, it being his hard hap to be the firſt, as Cuthbert Maine to ſuffer death, ſo he to loſe his eſtate and liberty, by this ſevere law; and being, beſides, myſelf deſcended from this gentleman's ſiſter, Jane Tregian married to Thomas Tonkin of Trevaunance; I ſhall here ſet down an abſtract of an exemplification of the inquiſition taken at Lanceſton 5 Car. 1, on the lands, &c. of the ſaid Mr. Tregian; of which I ſhall give only the ſubſtance here, [referring myſelf for a fuller account to my fol. book, vol. 2, p. exemplif. penes me] "Inſpeximus etiam," &c. Inquiſitio indentat. capt. apud Lanceſton in Com. prædict. on Monday the 1ſt of March, An. 5. Car. before William Wray, Knight; Walter Langdon, Knight, James Bagg, Knight, Nicholas Burlace, Eſq. Peter Huſſey, Eſq. and William Stowell, Gent. commiſſioners, &c.; on the oaths of Sampſon Manington, Eſq. Robert Dodſon, Eſq. Nicholas Leach, Eſq. Chriſtopher Pollard, Gent. Humfr. Lower, Gent. Richard Lanyon, Gent. Francis Rawle, Gent. Timothy Browning, Gent. John French, Gent. Oliver White, Gent. James Hoſkins, Gent. Richard Bettiſon, Gent. Degory Prowſe, Gent. John Rawlyn, Gent. and Roger Edgcombe, Gent. That the ſaid Francis Trugeon, in the ſaid commiſſion named was indited, convicted, and attainted of Præmunire as in the ſaid commiſſion is contained, on the ſaid 20th of April, 19 Elizabeth; and alſo on Monday aforeſaid, in the ſaid 4th week in Lent, An. 21 Elizabeth, was ſeized of

	£.	s.	d.
The Manor of Digembris alias Degembris in Poch. de Newlyn, et alibi, quæ valent per ann. in omnibus exitibus ultra repriſas, ...	21	4	8
The Manor of Trewithgy cum Ptiis in Poch. de Probus, &c.	15	2	0
The Manor of Tregyn alias Tregion, cum Ptiis in Poch. de St. Ewe, ...	4	0	0
The Manor of Tremolla alias Tremolleth, cum Ptiis in Poch. de Northill, Linkinhorne et Liſkeard, &c.	5	12	8
The Manor of Bodmin alias Bodman, et Heyland, cum Ptiis in Poch. de Bodman et Loſtwithiel, &c. ..	13	0	0
The Manor of Landegey and Lanner, cum Ptiis in Poch. de St. Key, et alibi, quæ valent, &c.	36	10	8
The Manor of Carvolghe alias Carvaghe, cum Ptiis in Poch. de Morva et St. Jes, et alibi, ...	4	14	6
The Manor of Tollays alias Tollgus, cum Ptiis in Poch. Redruth et St. Juſt, et alibi, ...	23	10	0
The Manor of Truro et Tregewe, cum Ptiis in Poch. de Kenwyn et Truro, et alibi quæ valent, ...	22	15	4
The Manor of Bedocke alias Beſacke, cum Ptiis in Poch. de Lazacke, et alibi, &c.	11	8	1
The Manor of Wolvedon alais Gowlden, cum Ptiis in Poch. de Probus et Tregony, et alibi, &c.	242	13	10
	400	11	9
The Manor of Treleigh cum Ptiis in Poch. de Redruth, &c.	4	4	0
The Manor of Eaſt Drays cum Ptiis in Poch. de St. Nyoth and St. Cleere, four parts in five, quæ valent,	10	0	0
The Manor of Kalenſo cum Ptiis in Poch. de Hilary et Sythney, four parts in five, quæ valent, &c. ..	10	11	6
The Manor of Elerkey and Lanyhorne alias Rewyn Lanyhorne in Poch. de Ruan et St. Veryan, one half, quæ valent, ...	17	17	3
The Manor of Penpoll alias Penpole, cum Ptiis in Poch. de St. Germyns et Quethiocke, one half, quæ valent, &c.	32	14	8
The Manor of Bunerdake, cum Ptiis in Poch. de St. Ive, one half, quæ valent, &c.	4	10	6
A Burgage in Leſkeard, &c. cum Ptiis, ...	1	0	0
Severall Tenements in Rogervei et Leſtreiake in Germow et Brake, ...	0	10	4
A Tenement in Trewerrys alias Tregwerys in Poch. de Probus, ...	0	2	0

A Tenement in Villâ de Grampont, et valet, &c.	0	8	0
The Manor of Rofemodens alias Rofemodros, cum Ptiis, in Poch. de Buryan St. Hillaric Pawle et Gwynnier, four parts in five, quæ valent, &c.	15	0	0
	96	18	3
The other fide	400	11	9
In all	497	9	0

The faid jorors farther fay, that the faid Francis Tregian was not poffeffed of any other lands and tenements, "prædicto die Aprils, 19. Elizab. aut die quæ in quartâ feptimanâ Quadragefimæ, 21 Eliz. feu unquam poftea tenuit," as far as could any way appear to them at the taking of this inquifition. "Et Jurator. predict. ulterius dicunt quod Georgius Cary Miles, Marefchallus &c. &c. nuper Reginæ Elizab." by letters patent of the great feal of the faid Queen, to the faid Sir George Cary, Knight, and his heirs male, of all the aforefaid Manors, &c. bearing date at Weftminfter, 27th June, An. 21, Eliz. did enter into all the faid premifes, and did poffefs the fame till the 5th November An. 36, Eliz.; and that the faid premifes "valent per Ann. in omnibus Exitibus ultra reprifas £.340. (I don't know how to reconcile this with the former fum) and that the faid Sir George Cary on the faid 5th November, 36 Eliz. did fell the faid Manor of Rofemodres to one Ezekiel Groffe of Trelodevus, in the parifh of Burienne, Gent to have and to hold to him and his heirs for ever, for the fumme of £.700 leg. mon. Angl." and that from thence to the 7th Sept. or thereabouts, in the 1. Jacob. the faid Sir George Cary was poffeffed of all the other aforefaid Manors, &c. which were worth yearly, viz. £.325, (when the faid Sir George, being then Lord Hunfdon, died); and that then the moft noble Lady Hunfdon, widow, [who had thefe eftates in jointure, it feems,] after the death of the faid George Cary her hufband, did poffefs the fame to the 29th June in the 5. Jacob. when fhe did fell and convey all the faid Manors, &c. (except the Manor of Rofemodros aforefaid) to Francis Trugeon, Jun. Efq. the fon of the aforefaid Francis Trugeon, Efq. (who was, I fuppofe lately dead) [but who, from the epithet of Junior to his fon, appears to be actually alive,] for the fumme of £.6500 leg. mon. Angl.; and the faid Francis Trugeon was not only to poffefs and enjoy the aforefaid Manors, &c. in the county of Cornwall aforefaid, but alfo all thofe in the counties of Devon, Somerfet, and elfewhere in the kingdom of England, which had been the lands, &c. of the faid Francis Trugeon, the father. [By which it appears, that *thefe in this inquifition were not the whole eftate* of the faid Francis, but only *thofe which he had in this county*, beyond which thefe jurors could not go]; [and that Francis the father had never been deprived of thofe out of this county] and the faid Francis Trugeon the fon, did accordingly enter on, and enjoy the fame, to or about (from the faid 29th June, 5 Jacob) the month of January in the faid 5 Jacob. when the faid Francis Trugeon was convicted of recufancy, fecundum formam Statuti in de editi, &c. and then, by reafon of fuch conviction, two parts of the premifes aforefaid, were feized into the hands of the late King James; and the faid King, by his letters patent bearing date in or about the month of February, in the 6th of his reign, and under his great feal of England, did grant the faid two parts to George Bland, Efq. for the term of 41 years at a yearly rent, as by the faid letters patent doth more fully appear; and the faid Francis Trugeon being thus feifed afterwards, to wit, in St. Hilary Terme in the 7th of the faid King James, a fine was levied in the Court of King's Bench, Weftminfter, between Humphrey Victor Querent, and the faid Francis Trugeon, the fon, Efq. —— of the Manors of Wolvedon, Treworgye, Degembris, Befacke, Trurow, Tolgoofe, Kalenfa, Carvath, Bodmyn, Tregeyn, Landygey, Eaft-Dreanes, and Tremolleth, and of the half of the Manors of Penpoll, Bunardake, Elerkey et Rewean Lanyhorne, "com Ptiis in cum. Cornubiæ exiften." parcell of thofe which had been fo forfeited by the faid Francis Tregian, the father, in the faid Queen Elizabeth's reign. And the jurat aforefaid farther fay, that the faid Francis Tregian the fon did poffefs the fame, and receive the rents, &c. (the faid two parts, by the faid King James demifed as aforefaid, excepted) from the faid 29th June, 5. Jacob. to Trinity Term, in the 8th of the faid King James. And the jurat aforefaid farther fay, that the faid Francis Tregian the fon, did receive after the faid 29th June, 5 Jacob. for the fines lands and tenements by him demifed; and granted within his manor of Penpoll aforefaid, the fumme of £.1700, leg. mon. Angl.; and that the faid Dame Elizabeth Cary, during her widowhood, "feu dum fuit fola," did receive of William Williams for the fine of a Meffuage and Tenement in the Manor of Treworgye, the fumme of £.30, leg. mon. Angl.; and that the aforefaid Ezekiel Groffe of Camborne, Gent. at the time of the taking of this inquifition, was poffeffed of the Manors of Kalenfo, Carvath, et Tolgoofe, befide the aforefaid Manor of Rofemodros; and that John Cooke of St. Allyn, Gent. was poffeffed of the Manor of Trurow; and that William Coryton, Efq. was poffeffed of parcel of the half of the Manor of Penpoll; and that John Moyle, Efq. was poffeffed of a Tenement, called Out Crew, parcell of the faid Manor of Penpoll; and that, as for the reft of the faid Manors, &c. abovementioned, who were then poffeffed of the fame, the jurator. aforefaid, knew not, &c. Infpeximus a certificate of the faid commiffion and inquifition, &c.; delivered into "Cancellariam noftram 30th Mart. 5. Car." We therefore, at the requeft of our well-beloved fubject John Arundell, Efq. have caufed the fame to be exemplified by thefe prefents: Tefte meipfo apud Weftmon. decimo nono die Julii An. Regni noftri nono.

CESAR.

"Examinatur Pnos { Ro. Roche, et Johem Page } Clericos.

Note, here, that you are not to judge of the real value of Tregian's eftate by this return, which is only of the conventionary rents; except it be in the Manor of Gowlden, where the demefne is valued as well as the rents; and probably all the demefne that he had, including Tregian, Trewithgy, &c.; fome of which were then in demefne, by reafon that they are not named in the value of the feverall Manors. And this muft be farther obferved, that thefe jurors returned only the antient rents, &c. as was ever ufuall in fuch cafes. I have heard feverall intelligent people fay, that the eftate of this family in this county only, was worth at the leaft £.3000 per ann. befides a great fumme they were poffeffed of in ready money: which enabled them

Before JAMES was univerfally acknowleged as our rightful Sovereign, one of the reprefentatives of a houfe defervedly refpected beyond moft others in Cornwall or Devon, I mean *Sir Robert Baffet*, was no mean competitor for the crown, tho' in his ambitious aims he was unfortunate. At Heanton-Court, lived Sir Robert Baffet. Defcended by his grandmother from the Plantagenet, and confcious of his royal blood, he made fome pretenfions to the crown of England, in the beginning of the reign of James I. but not able to make them good, he was forced to fly into France to fave his head. To compound for which, together with his high and generous way of living, he greatly exhaufted his eftate; felling off with White-Chapel, (the ancient houfe) no lefs than thirty manors of land.* It is conjectured, tho' I do not know with what degree of probability, that the connexion of Sir W. Raleigh with Baffet, was one caufe of Sir Walter's† difgrace and death. Mr. Oldys, fpeaking of James's diflike

to make fuch a noble houfe here, of which the ruins are ftill magnificent; among which, under an old tower, they ftill fhow the place, where Cuthbert Mayne the Prieft was found concealed.|| As for Francis Tregian the father, Efq. he was (faith Norden's Defcription of Cornwall, p. 58) "nere twenty years imprifoned; but he is now at libertie," [releafed at laft by Elizabeth herfelf about 1597], and liveth with fufficient glorie nere London; having no ufe of his lande, which was in the handes of the late Lord Hunfdon, Lord Chamberlaine to her late Majefty. [This fhows Norden to have written after Sept. 1603, when Lord Hunfdon appears above to have died; and Tregian the elder, to be then alive.] "The gentleman's reliefe is thought to grow by the bounty of fuch as affecte his parte." [It grew, as appears above, from the eftates which he was ftill allowed to retain in Devon, Somerfet, and elfewhere in the kingdom of England; which enabled him, by his fon, to redeem his Cornifh eftates from Lady Hunfdon, at the expence of £.6500, on the 29th June, in the 5th of King James or 1608; and which equally enabled him when Norden wrote, juft before in all probability, to "live with fufficient glory nere London.]—Francis Tregian the fon, finding that he could not ftem the tide; but that either thro' malice, or eagernefs of thofe that were gaping after his eftates, (or rather through the growing fpirit of perfecution againft the Papifts, from the gunpowder plot of November 5, 1605,) he was once more (in January 1608) outed of the beft part of it; he made the beft of a bad market, raifed what he could by compounding, (as I believe) with the crown, (for this affair is left in the dark,) and fhipped himfelf off for Spain, (after Trinity term in the 8th of King James, or 1611, when he appears above to have difcontinued to poffefs his third fhare; having from the 29th of June, 1608, when he redeemed the eftates, to Trinity term 1611, when he fold them, received £.1700 for fines in his Manor of Penpoll only) where, as 'tis faid, he was very well received on account of his, and his father's fufferings for his religion, and made a grandee of that kingdom. Where his pofterity ftill flourifh, by the title of Marqueffes of St. Angelo: but whether this be true or not, I cannot affirm; having it only by tradition; [a tradition that ftill remains in general to this day.] However, we hear no more of him in this county. *Tonkin's* MSS. [*Whitaker's*]

* *Wood's Athenæ Oxon.* vol. 1. col. 366. *Prince*, pp. 113, 114.

† "In order to extenuate the conduct of King James I. in the cafe of Sir Walter Raleigh, Mr. Hume feems to have been much inclined to blacken the character of that celebrated perfon.‡ And his principal authority for much of what he fays upon this fubject, is King James's "Declaration of the demeanour and carriage of Sir Walter Raleigh, Knight, as well in his voyage, as in and fithence his return; and of the true motives and inducements which occafioned his majefty to proceed in doing juftice upon him, as hath been done." But notwithftanding what our hiftorian hath urged to make this royal publication§ appear of "undoubted credit," it is certain, that an artful defence, of an odious and unpopular meafure,

|| Tradition ftill reports, but only with a voice reflected faintly back from fome old perfons now fhrouded in their graves, that the Sheriff, fent to examine the houfe for Mr. Mayne, defignedly made a very flight examination, and then fat down to drink with Mr. Tregian; that, in this exercife of hofpitality and mirth, Mr. Tregian was fo far thrown off his guard, as to joke the Sheriff upon his examination, even to alledge he had not examined one room, and at laft, to fhow him the privy as a room unexamined; that the Sheriff fired upon this very unfeafonable jeft, declared he knew where the Prieft was, and went immediately to Mr. Mayne's lurking-place, the confeffional at the further end of the chaplain's room.

‡ Hift. vol. vi. p. 31, 34, 35, 36, 37. edit. 1763.

§ In the preamble to this declaration it is faid, "although Kings be not bound to give account of their actions to any but God alone; yet fuch are his majefty's proceedings, as he hath always been willing to bring them before fun and moon, and carefully to fatisfy all his good people with his intentions and courfes, giving as well to future times, as to the prefent, true and undifguifed declarations of them." Harleian Mifcellany, vol. iii. p. 18. It appears, that Sir Walter Raleigh was apprehenfive that fomewhat would be publifhed after his death to traduce his memory: for when he was upon the fcaffold, he particularly requefted lord Arundel, "to defire the King, that no fcandalous writing to defame him, might be publifhed at his death."—Mr. Hume fpeaks of the King's declaration rather ambiguoufly, and in a manner that might lead his readers to fuppofe, that this was fubfcribed by fix privy-counfellors: but the fact is, it was not fubfcribed by any privy counfellor. Reference is made in the declaration to examinations taken in the prefence of fix privy-counfellors, which examinations were fubfcribed by them, and made ufe of in drawing up the declaration. But the declaration itfelf was not fubfcribed by any of them. See the edition of this, in 4to. printed by Norton and Bill, in 1618.

dislike to Raleigh, says:* "There were not wanting still other particulars, which might render Raleigh obnoctious to a man of the King's jealous disposition: for (according to Sanderson§) 'he had, at the time of his Majesty's accession to the throne, the daughter and heir of Basset to his ward, who was to be married to his son Walter, her estate worth three thousand pounds per annum; but she was (after his condemnation, we suppose,) taken from him, and married to Mr. Henry Howard, who died suddenly at table; and she was afterwards married to the Earl of Newcastle, who professed he would never have wedded her, if young Walter Raleigh had been alive; conceiving her before God to be his wife, for they were married as much as children could be.' Now these Bassets [continues Oldys] were those of Umberlegh and Heanton-court, in Devonshire; who, being descended from the Plantagenents, laid some claim at this very time of the King's entrance to the crown of England." The ward of Sir W. Raleigh was Elizabeth Basset, daughter and heiress of William Basset of Blore, of Staffordshire. And Oldys should have said, that the Bassets of Umberleigh and Heanton were from the same stem as those of Blore. Among other personages of Cornwall and Devon, whose characters flung a lustre on the times, were *Sir Jonathan Trelawney*,† *Carew of Clopton*, (already noticed)‡ *Sir Arthur Chichester*,¶ *Sir Thomas Ridgeway*,** *Lord Robarts*,

sure, is not very implicitly to be relied on. Indeed, King James himself has, in some degree, borne testimony to the merit of Sir Walter Raleigh, though to his own dishonour: for soon after Sir Walter's execution, the King beginning to see that he should probably be deluded by the Spanish ministry, made one of his ministers write to his agent in Spain, to let that court know they would be looked upon as the most unworthy people in the world, if they did not now act with sincerity, since his majesty had given so many testimonies of his; and now of late, "by causing Sir Walter Raleigh to be put to death, chiefly for the giving them satisfaction. Farther, to let them see how, in many actions of late, his majesty had strained upon the affections of his people, and especially in this last concerning Sir Walter Raleigh, who died with a great deal of courage and constancy. Lastly, that he should let them know how able a man Sir Walter Raleigh was, to have done his majesty service. Yet, to give them content, he hath not spared him, when, by preserving him, he might have given great satisfaction to his subjects, and had at command, upon all occasions, as useful a man as served any Prince in Christendom.‖"

* P. cxlix. of the Life prefixed to his History of the World, edit. 1736.

§ Reigns of Mary Queen of Scots and her son James I. 4to, 1656, p. 12.

† "Sir Jonathan Trelawney was a person of great honor and interest, a knight well spoken, staid in his carriage, and of thrifty providence. (*Carew*, p. 63.) The House of Commons, to shew their respect for him attended his funeral at St. Clement's Danes, where he was interred, as appears by what follows from their journal.

"Die Ven. 22 June 1604.

"It was informed, that Sir Jonathan Trelawney, one of the Knights of the shire for Cornwall, died yesterday, being suddenly suffocated with a flux of blood, which came by breaking a vein with vehement coughing, and was said to be found sick and dead in a quarter of an hour; and thereupon moved by Sir John Hollis, that the Members of the House do attend his burial to-morrow in the afternoon, which was so ordered."

‡ "*George Carew* was knighted not by Queen Elizabeth, (as *Wood* says vol. 1. p. 452) but by King James, who in January 1605, sent him ordinary Embassador into France, where he behaved himself to the credit of the English nation." This is *Tonkin's* Statement. See his MSS. "Ann. 1605. In the hall at Greenwich, richly hung with arras, James created (among others) Thomas Cecil, Earl of Exeter, *Sir George Carew* (vice-chamberlain to the Queen) Lord Carew of Clopton, Mr. Thomas Arundel, Lord Arundel of Wardour." *Echard.*

¶ "*Sir Arthur Chichester*, Knt. baron of Belfast, and Lord Deputy of Ireland, was born at Ralegh, near Barnstaple. He was the second son of Sir John Chichester, of that place, Kt. by Gertrude his wife, daughter of Sir William Courtenay, of Powderham, Kt. They were wonderfully blessed in a noble issue, male and female: having five sons; four whereof, were knights; of which, two also were lords, viz. a baron, and a viscount; and eight daughters, all married to the chiefest families in these parts: as first, Elizabeth to Hugh Fortescue of Phillegh, Esq. secondly, Dorothy to Sir Hugh Pollard of Kings-Nimpton, Kt. thirdly, Elenor to Sir Arthur Basset of Vmberlegh, Kt. fourthly, Mary to Richard Bluet of Holcomb-Rogus, Esq. fifthly, Cicilia to Thomas Hatch of Aller, Esq. sixthly, Susanna to John Fortescue of Buckland-Phillegh Esq. seventhly, Bridget to Sir Edmund Prideaux of Farway, Bart. all in Devon; and eighthly, Vrith to —— Trevillian of Nettlecombe in Somerset, Esq.—The grandfather of this Sir John Chichester, had two wives successively; first Margaret, daughter and heir of Hugh Beaumont of Youlston, Esq. from whom proceeds the present honorable family, that now inhabits there.

‖ Life of Sir Walter Raleigh by Mr. Oldys, prefixed to his History of the World, edit. 1736. p. 232, and British Biography, vol. iv. p. 71.

there. Secondly, Joan, daughter of Robert Brett of Whitstaunton in Somerset, and of Pillond near Barnstaple, in Devon, Esq by whom he had issue, first, John of Widworthy in the east, and secondly, Amias, of Arlinston in the north parts of this county; whose posterities, in both places, florish in worshipfull degree this day.—As to the knightly family of this name, which resides at Hall in Bishop's-Tawton, whereof Francis Chichester, Esq. batchelor of laws is the now Lord, that issued out of Ralegh house, four generations before these last mentioned. The first that settled there was Richard, third son of Richard Chichester, of Ralegh, by Alice his wife, daughter and heir of John Wotton, or Watton, of Widworthy; with whom that inheritance came into this family. Which Richard, was the grandson of John Chichester, and Thomasin Ralegh his wife, the first of this name, that possess'd Ralegh. Richard Chichester aforesaid, married Thomasin daughter and heir of Simon Hall of Hall, by whom he had this fair inheritance. Whose posterity, match'd into many eminent houses, as Gough of Aldercomb in Cornwal, Ackland of Ackland, Marwood of Westcot, Basset of Umberlegh, Strode of Newnham, Pollard, Carew, &c. and yet prospers well in this place.—Having premised these things, for our better understanding of the fair spreading of this noble family, I shall now proceed unto him, whom we ought chiefly to commemorate, Arthur Lord Chichester of Belfast, in the kingdom of Ireland; whom, to pass over in silence, were to drop one of the chiefest ornaments of our country.—This gentleman spent some part of his youth in the University, which being a too sedentary sort of life for his active genius, he went into the wars; and at every place where his sovereign's service required, there he was, by sea and land, in England and in France; in the last of which, for some notable exploit done by him, in the presence of the French King, Hen. 4. he was by that puissant Prince, honored with knighthood.—While he followed feats of war in France, his next brother, being also of a martial spirit, fought glory and renown in Ireland; whose valor and puissance there, were rewarded with knighthood. So that he came to be distinguished from his elder brother, who was of the same name and degree, (but rarely found at once in the same family) by the title of Sir John Chichester the younger. He being at length traiterously murdered there, Sir Arthur, not so much to revenge his brother's death, as to recover that kingdom, then in a desperate condition, put himself into that service. In which employment, he manifested to the world, valor and wisdom, so fairly and evenly tempered, that his generous actions expressed an extraordinary sufficiency. For he was effectually assistant, first to plough and break up that barbarous nation by conquest, and then to sow it with seeds of civility; when by K. James 1. he was made Lord Deputy of that kingdom, A. D. 1504. He managed his affairs with such prudence and resolution, that all the swarms of brooding rebels were in a little time, either vanquish'd and executed, or, upon submission, pardoned, and received to mercy. For which his great services, he was, by K. James aforesaid, honored with the title of Baron of Belfast in the kingdom of Ireland: unto whom one applys these verses, written, he says, by a learned poet, on Joseph in Ægypt, only with the transmutation of the names:

> With all these honors, and with wealth conferr'd,
> With great applause, Chichester is preferr'd,
> To rule all Ireland; which with great dexterity,
> Wisdom and worth, care, courage and sincerity,
> He executes ——

'Tis true, good laws and provisions had been made by his predecessors, to the same purpose before; but alas, they were like good lessons set for a lute out of tune, useless, until the lute was fitted for them. And therefore, in order to the civilizing of the Irish, in the first year of his government, he established two circuits, after the manner of the English nation, for justices of assize, the one in Connaugh, and the other in Munster. And whereas the circuits in former times, only encompassed the English pale, as the Cynosura doth the pole, henceforward, like good planets in their several spheres, they carried the influence of justice round about the kingdom. Insomuch, in a short time Ireland was so cleared of thieves and capital offenders, that so many malefactors have not been found in the two and thirty shires of Ireland, as in six English shires in the western circuit.—This noble Lord, during his Lieutenancy in Ireland, reduced also the mountains and glins on the south of Dublin (formerly Thorns in the English Pale) into the county of Wicklow: and in conformity to the English fashion, many Irish began now to cut their mantles into cloaks. And so observant was the eye of this excellent governor, over the actions of suspected persons, that the Earl of Tyrone was heard to complain, that he could not drink a full carouse of sack, but the state in a few hours after was advertised thereof.—After that this noble person had continued there many years together, no less than eleven, as a certain author tells us, in this principality, the stile thereof being Prorex Hiberniæ, K. James his master, called him home; out of no displeasure or disaffection, but rather, as knowing his great abilities, to employ him elsewhere: for soon after his return, he sent him his ambassador to the Emperor and the German Princes. In his journey thither, or from thence (which is not very material) he touch'd at Mainchine, as my author calls it; or, as I suppose, Manheim, a city of the Lower-Palatinate; a place much indebted to the prudence of my Lord Chichester, for the seasonable victualling of it. While he was there, his Lordship, with the rest of the city, was besieged by Count Tilly, the Emperor's general; upon this, my Lord sent the Count word, that it was against the law of nations to besiege an ambassador. Tilly return'd, he took no notice that he was an ambassador. Upon which, my Lord Chichester replied to the messenger, had my master sent me with as many hundred men, as he hath sent me on fruitless messages, your general should have known, that I had been a soldier as well as an ambassador.—At his return into England, K. James entertain'd him with great commendation, for having so well discharged his trust; so that he died in favor with God and Man, in as great honor as any Englishman of our age. about the year of our Lord God 1620.—From which account, given by the historians, a late writer hath made these observations on him: That my Lord Chichester was stout in his nature, above any disorder upon emergencies; resolv'd in his temper, above any impressions from other Princes; and high in his proposals, beyond the expectation of his own. There is a memorable observation of Philip K. of Spain, called El Prudente, the Prudent; that when he had design'd one for ambassador, the man came faintly and coldly to him, to propose somthing for his accommodation. of whom he said, how can I expect that this man can promote and effectuate my business, when he is so faint and fearful in the solicitation of his own?—Yet was not my Lord Chichester more resolute in Germany than wary in Ireland; where his opinion was, that time must open and facilitate things for reformation of religion, by the protestant plantations, by the care of good bishops and divines, by the amplification of the college, the education of wards,

wards, an infenfible feifure of Popifh Liberties, &c. In a word, this brave gentleman had an equal mind, that kept up it felf between the difcourfes of reafon, and the examples of hiftory, in the enjoyment of a good fortune, and in conflict with bad.—Where this nobleft Lord lieth interr'd, we are expresfly told, that dying about the time that K. James the firft did, he was buried at Belfaft in Ireland, to the great grief of his country; becaufe it was in fuch a time, as moft required his affiftance, courage, and wifdom; which are often at odds, and feldom meet; yet in him fhook hands as friends, and challenged an equal fhare in his perfections. Alex. Spicer, his chaplain, and, I think, a native of Exeter, wrote elegies on his death. Whether his brother and heir, the Lord Edward Chichefter, might afterwards bring over, and lay his remains in the fepulchre belonging to his houfe at Eggesford, I know not; only this is certain, that in a little oratory adjoyning to the very little church of Eggesford, on the north fide of the chancel, I faw this memorial of him; to wit,—A head cut out in coarfe marble, where his face is reprefented to the life, yielding a look ftern and terrible, like a foldier.—They who are fkill'd in fculpture, aver it to be an excellent piece of art.—This right noble Lord, although once married, unto Letice, daughter of Sir John Perrot, Lord Deputy of Ireland, left no iffue behind him; he made therefore, his youngeft brother his heir, viz. Sir Edward Chichefter, Kt. who fucceeded him in his eftate and in his honor; being created Baron of Belfaft aforefaid, A. 1624; but exceeded him in his title, being made Vifcount of Carrickfergus in the fame kingdom; as his fon Arthur did them both, who was advanced to the Earldom of Donnegal, which continues in his pofterity unto this day, and may it ftill continue.—This right honorable Lord, Edward Vifcount Chichefter, was alfo a very worthy and eminent perfon; well accomplifh'd, as well for war as peace. He was very ferviceable in the wars of Ireland, and gave good proofs of his valor there; for which he was knighted, and made governor of Carrickfergus aforefaid. And he gave no lefs demonftration of his wifdom and fagacity; on which account, he became one of his Majefty's moft honorable privy council for that kingdom." *Prince*, pp 199, 200.

** "*Sir Thomas Ridgeway*, Kt. and Bar. and Earl of London-Derry, in the kingdom of Ireland, was born, either at Torwood in the parifh of Tor-Mohun, on the eaft fide of the famous Bay of Tor, where it hath a delightfome profpect thereof; or elfe at Tor-Abby, ftanding in the mouth of the faid Bay; a very pleafant and gentile feat alfo, where feveral windows of the houfe yield a fweet and lovely view of the whole Bay, from which it ftands about a quarter of a mile. This Abby, after the diffolution, became the poffeffion of this noble Earl's anceftor; who re-edified thofe almoft decayed cells to a new and better form. He was the fon of Thomas Ridgeway of Torwood and Tor-Abby, Efq. by Mary his wife, eldeft daughter of Thomas Southcot, Efq. who was co-heir to her mother, Grace, the daughter of Barnhoufe of Marfh near Crediton. The other co-heir of Barnhoufe became the wife of Sir Anthony Rows of Halton in Cornwal, and of Edmerfton in Modbiry in Devon, Kt. a gentile family of antient refidence in this fhire; which Thomas was the fon and heir of John Ridgeway of Torwood, Efq, by Elizabeth Wentford his wife; a gentlewoman deferving fingular commendation. Higher than this I cannot carry the pedigree of this noble family in a direct line, altho' the flourifhing thereof in thefe parts is of a much antienter date.—The firft of the name I have met with, was Matthæus Ridgeway alias Peacock; he was a feoffee in truft to John Shillingford, for his lands in Farrendon-Shillingford (in the parifh of Farrendon near Exeter) and elfewhere, A. 38 Hen. 6. which was the year of our Lord 1460.—The next I find was Stephen Rudgeway, one of the ftewards of the city of Exeter, A. 6 K. Edw. 4. 1466. fome years after which, he was advanced to the higheft truft and command in that city, being chofen mayor thereof in the fourth year of the reign of King Hen. 7. 1489, now above two hundred years ago. Which gentleman was a benefactor to Grendon's Alms-Houfe, commonly called the Ten Cells, being fo many partitions for ten poor women, lying in Prefton-ftreet within the faid city.—I prefume this name, as moft antient ones were, was originally local, and at firft taken up from that place of their habitation; tho' from what particular place it might be I can't fay, for I find two places in this county fo called; the one is Ridgeway, near Plymouth, and the other is Ridgway in the parifh of Owlfcombe near Honiton. Whether of them had inhabitants fo named I do not find; tho' 'tis not improbable but that they had. But omitting a farther profecution hereof for the prefent, I proceed.—This noble gentleman, of whom we are fpeaking, Thomas Lord Ridgeway Earl of London-Derry, was a perfon of extraordinary eminence both in peace and war. The firft truft I find he had, was that of the poffe comitatûs of Devon, committed to him by Q. Elizabeth of pious memory, in the 32d and 42d years of her reign, if there be no miftake in the catalogue found in Sir William Pole's and Mr. Rifdon's manufcript of Devon. And all, as well print as manufcript, agree, that he was high fheriff of this county A. 42d of her reign 1600, in which year he was honoured by that gracious Princefs with the degree of knighthood.—Nor was he in lefs grace or favour with K. James the firft of bleffed memory, her royal fucceffor, who well underftanding his excellent parts, his great and comprehenfive judgment, his apt and dexterous addrefs, his refolution and conduct in bufinefs, imploy'd him in his moft weighty emergent affairs in Ireland, and advanced him to fome of the higheft places of truft and command in that kingdom; which as they were arguments of that great confidence the King repofed in him, fo were they alfo of his own great fufficiencies; he was one of the Lords of his Majefty's moft honourable privy council there, deputy-treafurer of that kingdom, commander-general and treafurer of wars therein, for feveral years together. So we have him reckon'd among the officers-general that were there in the year 1613; at what time my Lord Chichefter Baron of Belfaft (another great ornament to this country) was Lord Deputy of Ireland, and had been fo for many years beyond all example of former times; as, fays my author, the very next perfon unto whom, in that lift of officers-general, is reckon'd Sir Thomas Ridgeway, treafurer at wars. All which high and weighty places he fill'd with honour and fidelity.—About this time it was that the province of Vlfter, in the north-parts of that kingdom, by the frequent mutinies and rebellions of the old native Irifh, became uneafy to the Englifh government; for a total fuppreffion whereof, and the better planting therein a colony of the Englifh nation, K James the firft was pleafed to propofe great encouragements to fuch as would tranfport themfelves and families thither; as accordingly many did out of divers places of England. For the better carrying on of which plantation (De Plantatione .egni noftri Hiberniæ ac potiffimum Vltoniæ quam noftris jam Aufpiciis atq; Armis feliciter fub obfequii jugum redactam, &c. Ex Patent. Baron. apud Sylv. Morg. Lib. 5. C. 2. p. 12.) Peace being now happily fettled in that province, that wife King thought it fit to inftitute a new title of honour, in the 9th year of his reign over England 1611, call'd Baronet, q. Little Baron, (it being made the next in degree to a Baron of the realm) which honour is hereditary, and defcends from the

*Robarts,** *Sir John Eliot,*† *Sir William Noye.* It was at the close of this reign, that Sir William stood forward as the champion of civil liberty. But his extensive knowlege of the laws of his country, that enabled him to supply Parliament with precedents, on which to ground their

the father to the heirs-male of his body lawfully begotten, as that of a Baron doth; for which, each one was obliged to pay in the Exchequer, so much money as would, for three years at 8d. per Diem, pay thirty foot solders, to serve in the province of Vlster, in that kingdom; which sum amounts to 1095l. and with the fees it commonly ariseth to 1200l. for which reason they have given them the arms of Vlster, viz. A finister hand gules in a canton of their shield; or in an escotcheon of pretence; by which hand is signify'd administration of justice, as a certain author tells us.—Into which number our Sir Thomas Ridgeway was very early admitted, viz. Novemb. 25, 1612, he being then the second of that degree in the county of Devon.—After this, he having deserved very well of the crown, not only by his eminent services in the support thereof, but his signal industry and charges in promoting the plantations thereabout; his Majesty K James the first was pleased as a peculiar mark of his royal favour, to advance him to the high degree of a Peer of that realm, and bestowed upon him the title of, Earl of London-Derry; the best built city in the north of Ireland, lying in the province of Vlster, near Lough-Foyl; so call'd from a colony of Londoners, near about this time planted therein. It is seated in a Peninsula of about forty acres of ground, on one side environ'd with a river, and on the other impassible with a deep and moorish soyl, strongly situated by nature, and stronger by art: of late become wonderfully famous for the admirable defence it made in the siege laid against it, A. 1689, the reverend Mr. Geo. Walker rector of Donaghmoor being governour thereof, against 20,000 Irish, for an hundred and five days together; whom neither the number nor rage of the enemies without, nor those more cruel ones within, famine, sicknefs, and the fatigues of war, could ever make to think of surrendering, when they only reckon'd upon two days life; but being within that space relieved by sea, the Irish withdrew the siege. Into which province this noble Lord carried several persons out of Devon, as his servants and attendants, whose posterity, or some of them, arrived to great wealth and honour there, in which they still flourish." *Prince*, pp. 548, 549.

* 22d James, *Sir Richard Robarts* was created Lord Robarts of Truro.

† "*Sir John Eliot*, Knight, was born at Port Eliot in St. Germans, and baptised April 20, 1592. Being the only son of Richard Eliot of that place, Esq. by Bridget Carswell his wife, he became a gentleman commoner of Exeter College in Michaelmas Term 1607 at fifteen years of age; left the University without a degree after he had continued there about three years, went to one of the Inns of Court and was made a barrister. In 1618, May the 10th, he received the honour of knighthood from King James at Whitehall; and ever after to the time of his death, was returned a member of Parliament. But shewing himself there, an active man for the public, a zealous assertor of the ancient liberty, (as he thought) of the subject, and an enemy to favourites and their encroachments; he was several times committed to custody, particularly to the Tower with Sir D. Diggs in 1626, for his speech by way of epilogue on the Duke of Buckingham's impeachment, as Sir Dudley was, for the prologue. And being soon after released, Sir John made a speech to clear himself as to the particulars laid to his charge. In the same year, he was imprisoned in the Gatehouse at Westminster, for refusing to part with money on the loan: and therefore in a petition to the King (his counsel refusing to assist him otherwise) he set forth the illegality of the said loan, or of any tax without a Parliament; alledging farther, that his conscience could not submit to it, and praying for his liberty; which tho' he could not then obtain, he was however, released soon after (perhaps upon his submission) and chosen a member of the next Parliament which met March 17, 1627. In which, June 11th, making a speech, intended against the Duke of Bucks, he was enjoined silence by the speaker. On which, warm debates following, the house adjourned by the King's command, till the next morning. Soon after the dissolution of this Parliament, Sir John was sent to the Tower, where he died Nov. 27, 1632, as appears by the inquisition taken after his death, and was buried in the chapel belonging thereto. His family had from the Parliament which met in 1640, 15 Charles I. 5000l. given to them for his sufferings, 3 Charles I 1627, for opposing the illegalities of that time; which vote passed in 1646. See *Wood Ath. Ox.* col. 464. Echard, in his History of England, has left a severe reflection on this knight's character, for stabbing Mr. *Moyle* of *Bake*: and the matter of fact is too true. I have myself seen his submission to Mr. Moyle under his own hand, attested by some of the principal gentlemen of the county: and the original is now to be seen at Bake, in the present Mr. Moyle's custody. All that can be said in his excuse (if an assassination can bear any) is that Mr. Moyle had highly injured him. And the late Walter Moyle, Esq. would often say, that his ancestor in some measure deserved it, for his ill representations of Sir John to his father: and there has been ever since a good understanding between the two families. Sir J. Eliot, besides his printed speeches and debates (which may be seen in Rushworth's Collections, vol. 1.) has left many things in MS. as the report of the committee on the Stannaries, of which he was chairman, verses, &c. being chiefly invectives against the Duke of Buckingham, to whom he bore a most inveterate enmity; all which I have seen at Port Eliot." *Tonkin's* MS. p. 156.—It may scarcely be worth noticing, that Sir Thomas Edmunds, Knight, and treasurer of the household to King James the first, was the fifth son of Thomas Edmunds, head-customer of the Port of Plymouth, and of the Port of Fowey, in 1562. *Sir William Pole's* famous Statesmen of Devon MS. *Westcot's pedigrees*, MS.—Pennant mentions at St. Mary's Overie's (St. Saviour's) Southwark, an epitaph on *John Trehearne*, porter to James I. who is there told of the reversion he is to have in Heaven:

In thy King's Court good place to thee is given,
Whence thou shalt go to the King's Court of Heaven.

Some account, pp. 50, 51, of London. Edit. 1793. *Trehearne* is Cornish to the very bone.—About the latter end of the reign of James, *Owen Phippen* to whose memory a monument is erected in Truro church, displayed that spirit of adventure which was so fashionable in the voyages of this and the preceding reign.

their claims, was afterwards directed to the ſupport of the prerogative.‡ The paths of legal ſcience

‡ William Noye (according to *Hals*,) was born at Pendre, in the pariſh of Berian; and was prevented only by death from building a "noble houſe here, having brought vaſt quantities of ſuitable materials to this place, in order thereto." *Hals's* MSS. in Burian. But it appears, that, at one time, he made Carnanton in (Pider) Mawgan, his reſidence. *Carnanton* (ſays *Hals*) "was lately the dwelling of William Noye of Pendre, Eſq. farmour thereof; who was firſt bred a ſtudent at law, in Lincolns Inn; afterwards haueinge taken his degrees therein, he was choſen Member of Parliament for the towne of St. Iues or Mitchel, in Cornwall, in which capacitie he ſtood for ſom Parliaments, in the begininge of the reigne of Kinge Charles I. and was ſpecially famous for beinge one of the boldeſt, and ſtouteſt champions of the ſubjects liberty in Parliament, that the weſterne parts of England afforded; which beinge obſerued by court party, Kinge Charles was advized by his cabinet councill, that it wold be a prudent courſe to divert the force and power of Noye's ſkill, logick, and rhetorique, an other waye; by giuinge him ſom court preferment. Wherevpon Kinge Charles made him his Atturney Generall 1631, by which expedient he was ſoone metamorphized, from an afferter of the ſubject's liberty and property, to a moſt zealous and violent promoter beyond the laws of the deſpotick and arbitrary prerogatiue or monarchy of his Prince; ſoe that like the image of Janus at Rome, he looked forward and backward; and by means thereof greatly enriched himſelfe.—Amongſt other things he is reflected vpon by our chronologers, for beinge the principal contriuer of the ſhip money tax, layd by Kinge Charles, vpon his ſubjects for ſettinge forth a nauye, or fleet of ſhipps at ſea, without the conſent of Lords or Commons in Parliament; which moneys were rayſed by writt to the ſheriffs of all countys and commiſſioners, and for a longe tyme brought into the exchequer twenty thouſand pound per menſem, to the greate diſtaſt of the Parliament, the layety and clergye, who declard againſt it as an vnlawfull tax. Neuerthelefs all the twelve judges after Noyes death, except Hutton and Crooke, gaue their opinions and hands to the contrary; in Hamdens caſe, viz. Branſton, Finch, Dauenport, Denham, Jones, Trevor, Vernon, Barkley, Crawley, and Weſton. See *Baker's* Chron. printed 1656. Howeuer, out of kindneſs to the cleargye, the Kinge writ to all the ſherriffs of England, requiringe that the cleargye poſſeſſed of parſonages or rectorys, ſhold not be aſſeſſed aboue a tenth part of the land rate of their ſeuerall pariſhes; and that regard ſhold be had to vicars accordingly, by which rule the quanto or ſume of this ſhip money tax by the month may be calculated. But I ſhall conclude this paragraph of Noye, in the words of Hammon Le Strange, Eſq. in the life of Kinge Charles I, viz. Noye became ſoe ſervilly addicted to the King's prerogatiue, by ferretinge vp old penal ſtatutes, and diviſinge new exactions; for the ſmall tyme he enjoyed his power, that he was the moſt peſtilent vexation to the ſubject, that this latter age afforded, &c. He dyed about the yeare 1635; and lyes burid in the church of St. Maugan, with an inſcription on a ſtone to this purpoſe: here lyes the body of Wm. Noye, Eſq. ſome tyme Attorney Generall, to King Charles I. This gentleman writ that excellent booke of the lawe, called Noy's Reports. He had iſſue, Edward Noye, his eldeſt ſon, kill'd in a duell ſoon after his father's death; and Humphry Noye his ſecond ſon, of whome in his father's will, whereby his eſtate was ſettled on thoſe his children, I am told are thoſe expreſs words written, Imp. I giue all my lands and tenements, &c. next, and immediately after my deceaſe to my ſon and heire apparent Edward Noye, &c.; and for want of his legal iſſue, to my ſecond ſon Humphry Noye, and his heirs to be ſquander'd, or ſcatter'd, for that I can hope noe better; which foreſight or prediction afterwards accordingly came to paſs. He married Heſter daughter of the Lord Sands of Hantſhire, and by her had iſſue two ſons. William Noye ſtill aliue at Saliſbury, who married ——— and hath iſſue; and Humphry Noye that dyed without iſſue male; and Katherine married to William Davies, gent. of St. Earth; Jane to Richard Davies, his younger brother; and Bridgman to John Williams of Roſworthy, Eſq. ſome tyme commiſſioner for the peace, tempore Queen Anne, in whoſe right he is now in poſſeſſion of this barton of Carnanton, but by her he had noe iſſue. After her deceaſe he married Dorothy daughter of Peter Daye, Gent. and by her hath iſſue, and giueth for his armes, the paternal coate armour of the Williams, of Dorſet or Wiltſhire, his grandfather cominge from thence a ſteward to the Arundells of Lanherne. Humphry Noye, Eſq. aforeſaid, after he had by ill conduct, riot, and exceſs, diveſted himſelfe of the greate eſtate left him by his father the Attorney Generall, liued for many years on the charitie of his friends; and by virtue of his beinge a commiſſioner for the peace, and moſtly chairman at the ſeſſions, got ſeverall ſums of money by vnrighteous practices, in countenancinge and defendinge, excuſinge, or acquitting felons and other criminals at that tribunal, of which at laſt beinge detected, he was deſeruedly ſtruck out of the commiſſion of the peace, by John Earle of Radnor, Cuſtos Rotulorum; after which growing ſcandalous for theſe and other miſdemeanors, he was ſlighted by his former friends, and put to great hardſhips, to get a ſubſiſtance neceſſary for the life of man. (His creditors vpon mortgadges a beinge in poſſeſſion of his whole eſtate.) Howeuer it happen'd ſome tyme before his death, that vpon puttinge his hand and ſeale with his creditors, for convayinge the manor of Amelt and Trylly, in Penwith, to his ſon in lawe Mr. Dauies, on marryage with his daughter Katherine aloreſaid, he had by them pay'd him in caſh 100l. in conſideration thereof. Soon after the receipt of which money, he ſickned and dyed at Thomas Will's houſe, in St. Colomb Towne, and left 80l. in caſh, about the yeare 1683; which was more money then he was poſſeſt of at one tyme for above twenty year's before; and the laſt words that he was heard to ſpeake, as his ſoule paſſed out of this life, was—"*Lord where am I goinge now!*" The name Noy, Noi, Noye, ni, nay, Welſh, as ſome think, doth not ſignifie after the Engliſh, one that is a malevolent perſon that hurts or anoy's others, as was generally ſaid of the Attorney Generall Noye; that he acted ſutable to his name: for I aſſure the reader the monoſilable Noye in the Corniſh, Britiſh, Welſh, and Armorican tongues, from whence it is deriued, is quite of another import and ſignification, and is the ſame as nepos, nepotis, nepotulus in Latin, viz. a nephew, brother, or ſiſter's ſon. See *Floyd* upon the Latin words aforeſaid, and neptis, a neice, in Corniſh noith, armorice niſes, a ſhee or female woman ſoe related. The Attorney Generall on a day hauenge Kinge Charles I. and the principle officers and nobillitie of his court, at a diner at his houſe in London, at which tyme the arch poet Ben Johnſon, and others, beinge at an inne, on the other ſide the ſtreet, and wantinge both meate and money for their ſubſiſtance, at that exigent reſolued to trye an expedient, to gett his dinner from the Atturney Generall's table, in order to

ſcience generally lead to opulence if not to honour. But an occurrence in this reign, more intereſting, perhaps, to Cornwall, as it involves the fate of one of its firſt families, meets us in a very different road. My readers may recollect *Sir Thomas Arundel* of Talverne, as engaged in a viſionary purſuit which ruined his ancient houſe. An iſland was announced by the Quixotes of the age to be floating ſomewhere in the American ocean, and was denominated Old Brazil. Of this iſland, Sir Thomas was conſtituted by the King, the ſole proprietor: and the grant of James ſerved only to ſanction abſurdity. Thus did Arundel annihilate that fortune, which deſcended to him from a long ſeries of anceſtry. From Henry VI. to James I. had the Arundels graced Talverne, the ſeat of their anceſtors, with knightly dignity and ſplendour.*

to which, by his landlord at the Inn aforeſaid, he ſent a white timber plate or trencher to him, when the Kinge was ſate downe to table, wheron was inſcribed thoſe words:

When the world was drown'd
Noe deer was found,
Becauſe there was noe park;
And heere I ſitt,
Without e're a bitt,
Cauſe Noyah hath all in his Arke.

Which plate beinge preſented by the Atturney Generall to the Kinge, produced this effect; that Johnſon had a good diſh of venſon ſent him back by the bearer to his great content and ſatisfaction; on which aforeſaid plate by the King's direction, Johnſon's rhymes were thus inverted or contradicted:

When the world was drown'd,
There deer was found,
Although there was noe park;
I ſend thee a bitt,
To quicken thy witt,
Which com's from Noya's Arke.

William Noye, anagram, I Moyle in law. He was the blowcoale incendiary or ſtirrer vp of the occaſion of the ciuill wars between Kinge Charles, and his Parliament, by affertinge and ſetting vp the King's prerogatiue to the higheſt pitch, as Kinge James I. had done before, beyond the laws of the land as aforeſaid; and as counſill for the Kinge, he proſecuted for Kinge Charles I. the impriſoned members of the Houſe of Commons 1628, viz. Sir John Ellyot, Mr. Coryton and others, who after much coſt and trouble he gott to be fyned 2000l. each, the others 500l. and further to be ſentenced, notwithſtandinge they payed thoſe fynes, not to be deliuerd from priſon, without ſubmiſſion and acknowledgement of their offences, and ſecurity to be put in for their good behaviour for the future. *Hals's* MSS. in Mawgan."—"William Noye was bred in Lincoln's-Inn, where he was a moſt ſedulous ſtudent. In his early time he was a ſtout champion for the liberties of the ſubject againſt the prerogatives of the King; but being made Attorney General in 1631, an employment which however he did not ſue for, he countenanced the King's demand of ſhip-money, by which he incurred the hatred of the public. He died in 1634, much regretted by the court party. He is ſaid to have been a man of cynical humour, an indefatigable plodder, and ſearcher into ancient records, by which he became an eminent inſtrument both for and againſt the King's prerogative." *Noorthouck's* Hiſtorical and Claſſical Dict. 2 vol. 8vo. London, 1776.—"Sir †William Noy, Attorney General; C. Johnſon, p. 8vo. William Noy, Attorney General to Charles I. large ruff. Before his Complete Lawyer, 8vo. William Noy was for his quick apprehenſion, ſolid judgment and retentive memory, equal at leaſt to any of the lawyers of his time. But with all theſe great, he had no amiable qualities; he was illnatured, haughty and unpolite. He had the principal hand in the moſt oppreſſive expedients for raiſing money for the King, and ſeems not to have had the leaſt notion of public ſpirit. He was, in a word, a man of an enlarged head, and a contracted heart.‡ See an acconnt of his learned and judicious works in the Athenae Oxon. Ob. 9 Aug. 1634." *Granger*, vol. 2, pp. 225, 226.

* See *Price's* MSS.

† In Archbiſhop Laud's "Diary," where his death is noticed, he is ſtyled *Mr.* William Noy.

‡ *Howel* informs us, that his heart was literally contracted, that "it was ſhrivelled like a leather penny purſe, when he was diſſected." See *Howel's* Letter to Lord Savage, vol. 1. p. 241.

END OF THE FIRST PART.

TREWMANS, PRINTERS, EXETER.

PART THE SECOND.

It was with every appearance of prosperity, that Charles ascended the throne. But scarcely had he seated himself there, before he began to project schemes which his people disapproved, or in the execution of which his Parliament refused to assist him. The expedition into Spain was one of his favourite plans, which he was determined to execute, in spite of every opposition. And in the first year of his reign, he made a visit to Plymouth in order to prepare for this expedition. Of the royal progress we have yet a few traces in family-papers, or the tradition of the country; particularly at Totness, and at Ford then the seat of the Reynells, where Charles was entertained in festal state.* But we has en to the times when his progress into Devon and Cornwall had in its character, no feature of festivity. On the first open rupture between Charles and the Parliament, whilst hostilities were commencing on either side, the disposition of the Devonians was by no means flattering to royalty. Not so the temper or the feelings of the Cornish. The forces which the King sent into the west under the command of Sir Ralph Hopton, had been joined in this county by Sir Bevil Granville and were seated at Truro. The east of Cornwall was possessed by Sir Alexander Carew, of E. Anthony, and Sir Richard Buller, of Morval, both members of the House of Commons. And except Pendennis-Castle (the governor of which was Sir Nicholas Slanning) the committee of Parliament believed themselves masters of Cornwall. Secure in the possession of Devon, they now drew off their forces to Launceston, to prevent the escape of Sir Ralph Hopton and his adherents, whose power they thought contemptible. But recruited with a body of 3000 foot (the Posse Comitatus) Sir Ralph marched to Launceston; Buller retreated before him; Saltash received the King's troops, and Lord Mohun (whose landed property in this county was considerable) declaring for the King, was admitted to a joint command of the royal forces, with Sir Ralph Hopton, Sir John Berkley, and Colonel Ashburnham. This was early in the winter of 1642; not long after which, General Ruthen, the rebel governor of Plymouth, made an irruption into Cornwall at a bridge six miles above Saltash, and pushed on to Leskeard. The King's army, at first inferior in numbers, fell back upon Bodmin, but now joined by the trained bands, advanced towards Leskeard: and Sir Ralph Hopton drew up his men upon Bradock-down, where meeting the enemy, he put him completely to the rout: Ruthen fled to Saltash; and Leskeard was the same day taken.[A] Sir Ralph and Lord Mohun did not remain inactive but proceeding to Saltash took it by assault; and Ruthen escaped by water to Plymouth; whilst Sir J. Berkeley and Colonel Ashburnham went at the head of the volunteer regiments to attack the Earl of Stamford at Tavistock. That about this time some of the Cornish proposed to the Parliament, the formation of a treaty for securing the peace of Cornwall and Devon—that such a treaty was framed but proved ineffectual—that on the 11th of March, Mr. Prideaux and Mr. Nicholls, two Cornish members of the House, were sent down to break the pacification—that Major General Chudleigh, in the beginning of May, came by surprize upon Launceston, the headquarters of the loyalists, but was soon forced to retreat into Devon—that not

* See the Palkian MSS. at Haldon-House.

[A] Jan 19, 1642. See HEATH, p 4[illegible], and DUGDALE's view of the Troubles, p. 116. About the latter end of this month we observe the faithful Lords and Commons rallying round the sacred person of majesty: and the magnificent hall of Christ-Church, was the Senate-house of the nation.—There assembled. on Jan. 27, 1643, the Lords and Commons addressed a letter to the Earl of Essex, deploring the miseries of war, and inviting the Earl to second their exertions for the restoration of Peace. The Cornish members present were, THE EARL OF BATH, LORD MOHUN JOHN HARRIS, Esq. JOHN JANE, Esq. RICHARD EDGCOMBE Esq. JONATHAN RASHLEIGH, Esq R. EDGCOMBE, Esq. WILLIAM GLANVILL, Esq. F. GODOLPHIN, Esq. A. MANATON, Esq. R. VIVIAN, Esq. JOHN POLWHEELE, Esq. JOHN ARUNDELL, Esq. THOMAS LOWER, Esq. RICHARD ARUNDELL, Esq. WILLIAM CONSTANTINE, Esq HENRY KILLEGREW, Esq. WILLIAM BASSET, Esq. SAMUEL SANDYS, Esq. JOHN DIGBY, Esq. See King Charles' Works, Vol. 2, pp. 375, 376, 384, 385.

long after, the Earl of Stamford marched into the north of Cornwall, and (thence dispatching Sir George Chudleigh with a party of horse to Bodmin to prevent the High Sheriff from coming to the assistance of the army at Launceston) encamped on the brow of a steep hill near Stratton—these are the chief occurrences and military movements which preceded one of the most memorable battles on record in the west of England. It was on the 15th of May, that the King's generals, determined to engage the enemy, though with inferior force, and on very disadvantageous ground, took their station within a mile of Stratton hill. The next morning saw this little force divided into four detachments—those four detachments the same moment mounting the hill—saw them all gaining the summit with equally invincible bravery, the summit on which the enemy was posted, and saw the rebels at once intimidated and discomfited—some put to the sword, many made prisoners, and the rest rushing headlong down the declivity. Among the prisoners, was Chudleigh, among the fugitives, Stamford.[cc] The camp, with all the baggage, ordnance and ammunition, was of course abandoned to the royalists. Till the battle of Lansdowne and the siege of Bristol, nothing remarkable occurred, to attract the notice of the Cornish historian. Leaving garrisons at Saltash and Millbrook to check incursions from Plymouth, the King's Generals had marched into Somersetshire, to join Prince Maurice and the Marquis of Hertford; not long after which, they distinguished themselves at Lansdowne where fell Sir Bevil Granville, and at Bristol where Colonel John Trevanion and Sir N. Slanning, governor of Pendennis were slain.[D] In 1644, the Queen's retreat to Pendennis-Castle, whence she embarked for France [AA]—the

[cc] He fled to Exeter.—Sir Ralph was created Lord Hopton, of Stratton. After his death Sir J. Berkeley was created a Baron by Charles II. with the same distinction—which, as he had shared the glory of the action, he equally merited.—In Mr. Brune's library at Place near Padstow, is a valuable collection of original letters; among which we have the following letter from Sir William Waller. It appears to have been written in consequence of a confidential letter from Sir Ralph, (not then Lord) Hopton. Struck by its fine sentiments and uncommon elegance, I seized it with avidity for my history. It unites the urbanity of the gentleman, the steadiness of the hero, and the religiousness of the christian, and it well illustrates a remark of JACKSON, "that when men spoke from their real feelings, the language of the last and the present century hath been nearly the same." See Jackson's "Thirty Letters."

To my noble friend, Sir Ralph Hopton, at Wales.

Bath, June 16, 1643.

Sir,

The experience I have had of your worth, and the happiness I have enjoyed in your friendship are wounding considerations, when I look upon the present distance between us. Certainly my affections to you are so unchangeable, that hostility itself cannot violate my friendship to your person; but I must be true to the cause wherein I serve. The old limitation, USQUE AD ARAS, holds still; and where my conscience is interested all other obligations are swallowed up.

I should most gladly wait upon you, according to your desire; but that I look on you, engaged as you are in that party beyond a possibility of retreat; and consequently incapable of being wrought upon by any persuasions, and I know the conference would never be so close between us, but that it would take fire, and receive a construction to my dishonour.

That great God, who is the searcher of my heart, knows with what reluctance I go upon this service; and with what a perfect hatred I detest a war without an enemy. But I look upon it as Opus Domini, and that is enough to silence all passion in me. The God of peace, in his good time send us peace; and in the mean time fit us to receive it. We are both on the stage: and we must act the parts that are assigned us in this tragedy. Let us do it in a way of honour, and without personal animosities:—but, whatever be the issue, I shall not willingly relinquish the dear title of

Your affectionate friend and faithful servant,

W. WALLER.

[D] In consequence of these atchievements, Cornwall received from the King a complimentary letter, dtaed 10 Sept. 1643, from his camp at Sudeley-Castle—which as it is preserved in many of our churches, I shall not insert here.

[AA] "April 17, 1644, the Queen began her journey to the west, where, the 16th of June in Exon, she was delivered of the illustrious Princesse Henrietta Maria, since married to the Duke of Orleans, brother to the King of France. But the poor Queen was forced thence the next sunday after which she was delivered (being the former sunday about ten of the clock, when the minister was in first prayer at St. Peters, who then gave thankes for a son as I remember well, but after sermon for a daughter.) Frighted by Essex, she went in her litter for Cornwall, and arrived at Brest, the 15th of July, 1644." Extract from a MS in possession of Mr. Cholwich, Faringdon-House. It was written by Samuel Sainthill, and bears date 1659.—See Walker's Hist. Discourses p. 41. and Hist. of Devon, vol. I.

Earl of Essex marching into Cornwall, at the instance of Lord Robarts, of Lanhydroc, disputing the pass at Newbridge with Sir Richard Granville, taking possession of Launceston and Saltash—and pressing on to Bodmin, and Lestwithiel and Fawey, where he fixed his headquarters—Sir Richard Granville retiring before Essex, and after a skirmish with Lord Robarts at Lestwithiel, retreating to Truro—and the King himself, in pursuit of Essex, are incidents which, glancing over, we come to the first of August, when his majesty[OP] entered Cornwall at Polston-bridge, passed through Launceston and slept at Mr. Manaton's, Trecarrel in Lezant—whilst his army were quartered around him in the fields. On the next day he drew up his men on Carraton-down, in Linkinhorne; where, joined by Prince Maurice, he marched to Leskeard. On the fourth of August, a party of the King's horse took Boconnoc (Lord Mohun's seat) by surprise, and there made Essex's Lieutenant Colonel and other officers of the Parliament, prisoners. On the 7th, advancing from Leskeard, the King encamped at the entrance of Bradock-down—and on the 8th, we find him in occupation of Boconnoc-house.[LLD] From the menacing aspect of the two armies, a renconter of serious moment, might have been expected. But, as the military actions of the present year were a few sharp skirmishes at most, we shall just cursorily notice the relative situation of the King's foot in the fields between Boconnoc and the heath and his horse about St. Veep; and Essex occupying Lestwithiel and Fawey, and the intermediate ground for his horse: whilst Sir R. Granville pressing on from Truro to Grampound and thence to Bodmin, on the 11th of August, seized Lanhydroc and Resprin-bridge, and on the 13th the pass at St. Veep, the Ford below it, View-Hall over against Fawey-haven, and Pernon-fort at its mouth—the king riding on the 17th of August to inspect the passes on the river towards Fawey, and the garrisons at Hall and Pernon-forts, on the 21st, drawing near Lestwithiel, when Sir R. Granville took Restormel-Castle—on the 26th General Goring and Sir Thomas Basset possessing themselves of St. Austle, the western part of St. Blazey, and a place on the river called the Par, where chiefly the Parliament army was supplied with provisions &c.; so that Essex (seeing the extent of the King's line to Grampound, Fawey and St Blazy-bridge) began to project an escape—on the 31st, Sir William Balfour passing the King's quarters, and with the whole body of the horse getting safe out of Cornwall by Carraton-down, Pillaton, and Saltash—on the same day Essex quitting Lestwithiel, (while his soldiers, in the true spirit of republicanism blew up the church) and on the next, proposing a parley with the King (now encamped very near the rebel army) but before he could receive an answer taking ship at Fawey and with Lord Robarts reaching Plymouth in security—General Skippon (with whom the Parliament forces had been left in charge, above 6000 men) delivering up to the loyalists the whole of their arms, artillery, and ammunition—Sir R. Granville, in pursuit of the Parliament horse, and in possession of Saltash.—And, on the 2nd of September, the King returned to Boconnoc, on the 4th, marched to Leskeard, and on the 5th advanced to Tavistock. For 1645, we have little more to remark, than that Charles II. then Duke of Cornwall, spent a great part of the autumn and the winter in this county; residing chiefly at Laun-

[OP] See ITER CAROLINUM, in Colectanea Curiosa, Vol. 2 pp. 425 456. His Majesty's march with his armies towards the west &c began on Sunday the 2nd of June, 1644. On Wednesday, July 24th, 1644, His Majesty reached Chard, and on Monday, September 23rd, returned to the same place.

[LLD] This he made his Head-quarters.—He had invited Essex to submission, but to no purpose. And a general battle was now looked for.—Here among others We are told Dr Thomas Wykes, Dean of Berian paid his respects to the King. The Dean, it seems, was famous for his puns; one of which Dr. Pope, in his "Life of Bishop Ward," hath recorded.—"Dr Wykes, being well mounted, was near His Majesty. The King spoke thus to him: "Doctor, you have a pretty nag under you: I pray, how old is he?"—To which he, out of the abundance of the quibbles of his heart returned this answer: "If it please your Majesty, he is in the 2nd year of his REIGN (REIN.)" The good King did not like this unmannerly jest, and gave him such an answer as he deserved; "Go, you are a fool." p. 59.

ceston and at Truro.[BB] It was so late, indeed, as March 2nd, 1645-6, that he embarked at Pendennis for Sylleh.[CC] In the mean time Sir R. Granville was employed in fortifying Launceston—but all to no purpose. Dissention between himself and Goring, had operated to the prejudice of the royal cause. And such was his aversion from his antagonist, that it was proclaimed in all our churches, if any of the Lord Goring's forces entered Cornwall, the bells should ring out, and the whole county rise, to expel them from beyond its borders. Actuated by the same evil spirit, Sir Richard refused submission to Lord Hopton when made commander in chief of the western army, and for this act of disobedience was committed to Launceston-prison by the Prince.[AW] We have now only to record a series of disasters—Lord Hopton defeated by Sir Thomas Fairfax at Torrington, retiring to Stratton and pursued by the enemy,—at Launceston, Colonel Edgecumbe (whose loyalty as Clarendon insinuates was mere pretence) uniting his trained bands with Fairfax's forces—Bodmin abandoned to the Parliament General—Cromwell with a large party of horse occupying the pass at Wadebridge—and Fairfax finally in possession of Truro. Every hope of success was now expiring with the royalists. Mount Edgcumbe had surrendered to the Parliament; Prideaux, the high sheriff, Trelawney, Trevanion, Coryton, and Sawle had submitted to necessity: and Lord Hopton, since all his officers and army were in a state of mutiny, had given the horse (nearly 3000) leave to capitulate,[B] after he had sent his ammunition and foot to Pendennis and the Mount, and had himself repaired to the Mount in company with Lord

[BB] It was, (at the latter end of the year) from Tiverton, that CROMWELL wrote the following letter to Col. Ciely, then at Pendennis-Castle. The original is among the family-papers of the Rev. George Moore of Grampound, who very obligingly copied it, for my purpose.

Sr.

its the desier of Sr. Gilbert Pickeringe that his deceased Brother Col. Pickeringe should bee enterred in your guarrison, And to the end his funeral may bee sollemnized with as much Honor as his memorie calls for, you are desired to give all possible assistance therein, the particulars will be offered to you by his Maior, Maior Gubbs with whome I desier you to concurr herein, And believe itt sir you will not only lay a huge obligation upon myselfe, and all the officers of this Armie, But I dare assure you the General himselfe will take it for an especial favor and will not lett itt goe without a full acknowledgment: But what neede I prompt him to soe honorable an action whose owne ingenuitye wil be argument sufficient heerin, wherof rests assured

Your humble servant

December 10th 1645. Oliver Cromwell.

Teverton.

[CC] Thence sailed to Jersey, and from Jersey to France.—Whilst at Truro he sent to Rashleigh, Polwheele and Saule a letter, bearing date Feb. 24, 1645-6.—In this letter, he called upon those gentlemen to raise the Posse Comitatus &c. &c.

[AW] Whence he was sent to St. Michael's Mount. There he remained till all Cornwall had submitted to the Parliament; when he retired by the Prince's leave to the continent lest he should fall into the enemy's hands.—See Clarendon, Sprigge's England's Recovery, Whitelocke and, particularly Mercurius Belgicus, for the occurences of January 19, 22. in 1642;—of May 16, July 5, August 20, September 3, in 1643;—of May 12, June 5, 22, August 1, 25, 30, 31, September 2, 5, 12, 17, October 7, 16, December 23, in 1644;—and of January 18, 1645.

[B] "Tresillian-Bridge (situated between the parishes of St. Erme, Probus and Merther) is memorable (says Hals) for a Treaty of Peace Hostility between the Lord Hopton and Sir T. Fairfax—see Hals's MSS. No. 6.—among the Polwhele family papers, I possess a letter in the hand writing of Fairfax, which I have copied as follows—It originated it seems in the gratitude of the general recovered from illness by a younger brother of John Polwhele, Dr. Degory Polwhele M. D.

To all officers and soldiers under my command.

These are to require you on sight hereof, to forbeare to prejudice John Polwheele, of Treworgan, in the County of Cornwall, Esq. either by plundering his house, or takeing away his horses, sheepe, or other cattall, or goods, or by offering any violence to his person, or the persons of any of his familie as you will answer to the contrarie. Provided hee bee obedient to all ordinances of Parliament. Given under my hand and seale att Truro this 18th Day of March, 1645-6.

FAIRFAX.

According to the family tradition, the troops did not abstain from violence. I still possess the large brass boiler in which many whole sheep were boiled by the rebels, after the date of the protection.

Capel, and thence embarked with the first fair wind to join the Prince in Sylleh. Cornwall was exerting her utmost nerve in favour of her King; but was at length exhausted: and PENDINAS was the last strong hold in England (except perhaps one)[v] that surrendered to the Parliament. To its good old governor John Arundel [w] of Trerice, it was chiefly indebted for its fame of fidelity.[x] Over the melancholy scenes that followed, the insolence of the victorious army, the mock-trial and murder of the King, we would willingly drop the curtain. But it must not be dissembled, that Cornwall, amidst all her loyalty, produced for the trial of Charles both a judge and a witness; for his prison, a gaoler; and for his death, an executioner. In Carew, we sat in judgement on our sove-

[v] According to Tonkin, the "Dinas" sustained a siege of several months after the taking of Pendinas. But if the Weekly Intelligencer may be depended on, the "Dinas" was in the hands of the usurpers before March 19, 1646; and Pendinas not till some months after.—The "Dinas" had surrendered even before St. Michael's Mount. It appears from some papers at Trelowarren, that the fortifications of the Dinas had been repaired, and additional works erected by the voluntary exertions of the inhabitants of Meneage.—Each of the 12 parishes which compose that division of Kirrier turning out alternately for the purpose. A number of men under the command of Mr. Bogans of Treleage in St. Keverne who had accepted a commission from Charles, posted themselves in a most advantageous situation at Gear in Mawgan, with an apparent determination of defending that important pass: But the Parliament troops advancing and shewing themselves in much greater force than was expected, Major Bogans' men deserted him without coming to action.—Some betook themselves to the Dinas, the greater part dispersed, and Major Bogans himself fled to Hilters Clift, in St. Keverne, and concealed himself in a cave in the rocks. This event is still remembered in Meneage, by the name of the Gear rout. The parliament forces then marched on towards the Dinas; and concluding that their appearance might intimidate the garrison there, as it had done the encampment at Gear, a party of horse were detached with orders to advance to the entrance of the fortification.—When they reached Tendero, a shot from the Dinas killed one of their horses, and the dismounted trooper got on horse-back behind his comrade, but a second shot killed that horse likewise; on which they retreated. The Dinas was soon after invested by land and sea, six ships being sent from Plymouth for that purpose.—The garrison soon found their case desperate, and those gentlemen who were most obnoxious to the Parliament, and had least reason to expect favourable terms, escaped in boats in a dark windy night, and the possessor of Tendero, who acted at first as gunner, became commanding officer and capitulated. His estate of Tendero near the Dinas was restored to him as well as his other property, and his belt hangs in a room there to this day.

[w] Sylleh still holding out under the auspices of Godolphin and Sir John Granville, was not reduced till 1651; when Granville was taken among the prisoners.

[x] Lewis Tremayne, of Heligan in St. Ewe, Lieutenant Colonel, was in the castle of Pendinas during the siege; whence he made almost a miraculous escape by swimming over from one of the blockhouses to Trefusis-point, through all the enemy's fire. He suffered much, and was forced to keep close, during most of the usurpation. Tonkins MSS.—Sir John Killigrew, with his own hands, set fire to his noble mansion at Arwinick, that the rebels laying siege to Pendinas, might find no shelter there. This heroic action was well rewarded by Charles II. but the house was never rebuilt.—John Polwhele severely suffered by fine and imprisonment: He paid more than £2000 besides being depriv'd of his estates for several years.—I shall close these transactions with a list of the commissioners' names for the county of Cornwall, as extracted from a manuscript of Simon Cottell, esq, treasurer for the said county in the civil war. Many of the commissioners were officers in the King's western army. "John Grylls, esq. sheriffe January 17, 1642. Frauncis Basset, esq sheriffe: Nathaniell Luggar, esq. pro. vic. January 17, 1643. Richard Prideaux, esq. sheriffe: Richard Filles, esq. sub. vic. January 17, 1644. Frauncis Basset, esq. sheriffe: John Grills, esq. pro vic. January 17, 1644.—— The Right Honourable Warwick Lord Mohun, Ralph Hopton, esq. afterwards Lord Hopton, Sir John Trelawney kt. and bart., Sir William Wrey kt. and bart. Sir Richard Greenvile kt. and bart, Sir Bevil Greenvile kt., Sir Nicholas Slanning kt Sir Richard Vivian kt., Sir William Courtney kt., Sir John Berkley kt., Sir Peter Courtney kt., Sir Samuell Cosowarth kt., John Arundell of Trerise esq. Ezechiell Arundell esq., William Arundell esq., William Godolphin, Humphry Noye esq., Francis Godolphin, John Roscarrocke esq, Charles Roscarrocke esq., Richard Courtney esq., Reskimmer Courtney esq, Henry Killegrew esq., William Killegrew esq., Charles Trevannion esq.. Peirce Edgecombe esq. William Corryton esq., Walter Langdon esq., Renatus Bellott esq., Nicholas Crisp esq,. Ezechiell Grosse esq., John Digby esq., William Ashburnham esq., Jonathan Rashley esq., Francis Hawley esq., John Taverner esq., Francis Polwhele esq, William Pendarves esq, John Greenvile esq., George Waldrond esq., Nicholas Hawke esq., Thomas Hitchings esq., Paul Speccott esq., Giles Hambley esq., John Rowe esq., Symon Cottell esq., Obadiah Reynolds secretary to Simon Cottell esq, John Lower esq., Roger Sleeman esq., George Heale esq., Richard Hawke esq., John Hicks esq., Ambrosse Mannaton esq., Tymothy Browning esq., William Painter esq., John Tresaher esq., Symon Payne esq., Stephen Barbar esq., John Hutchings Hanniball Bugany esq. Christopher Wrey esq. William Cotton esq., John Benoke esq, Nathaniell Jewell esq., John Plumbleigh esq., Oliver Saule esq., Charles Grills esq., Nevill Blighe esq., Joseph Jane esq."

reign; in Williams,* we bore witness against him; in Peters, we murdered him. And in Francis Rous,[AA] we invested a usurper with the regal power.—That Charles II. was ready to reward those who were immediately instrumental in bringing him back to the throne of his fathers, is well known. The Earl of Bath and the Duke of Albemarle are proofs of his alacrity in conferring honours: but they furnish no evidence of his gratitude. On this happy emergence, few were recompensed for their services or sufferings. The project† of the Knights was an invidious scheme.—To the historian of Cornwall and Devon the sceptre of Anne must shine with more than common splendour: If Devonshire boast her MARLBOROUGH, Cornwall had equal reason to rejoice in her GODOLPHIN.[B] We pass to the rebellion of 1715, when many Cornish gentlemen were sent to the Tower, on suspicion of being friends to the Pretender; and among others, Sir FRANCIS VYVYAN of Trelowarren.‡—The debates on Triennial Parliaments mark the reign of George II. But they are detailed at so great a length in the histories of England, that just to touch upon them here, may be sufficient; though the spirit and address of our great patriot Sir JOHN ST. AUBYN, must instantly occur to every cultivated mind, as forming the most distinguished part of those parliamentary discussions.--The years 1758 and 1759, are blazoned in the annals of the country by the glorious atchievements of BOSCAWEN.—With respect to later transactions, I shall only remark, that the activity of Cornwall on every public occasion, has been not less apparent, than the acknowleged wisdom of her councils. If, at one conjuncture, a ST. AUBYN, a GLYNN or a PITT, have stood foremost in the ranks of our political worthies; a BASSET [ONO] or a GREGOR have been no less conspicuous, at another: and a PELLEW and a VIVIAN have still raised us to a prouder preeminence.

* Among the witnesses examined against the king, January 25, 1648--9, was Robert Williams of the parish of St Martin in the county of Cornwall, husbandman, aged about 23 years. Clarendon, Vol. 7, p. 762.

[AA] A younger son of Sir Anthony Rouse, of Halton kt., and member for Truro.

† List of the projected knights of the Royal Oak, with the value of their estates pr. annum, A. D. 1660. [From a MS of Peter le Neve Esq., Norroy.] Cornwall. Francis Buller esq. 3000l., Ellyott of Port-Ellyott esq. 2500l., Samuel Pendarvis esq. 1500l., Col. Godolphin esq. 1000l., Col. Penrose esq. 1000l., Col. Boscawen esq. 4000l., Col. Hallett esq, 800l, Edmund Prideaux esq, 900l, Charles Grylls esq, 700l, Oliver Sawle esq, 1000l, Joseph Tredenham esq, 900l, John Vivyan esq, 1000l, Charles Roscarrocke esq, 800l, William Scawen esq, 800l, Peirce Edgecombe esq, 2000l, James Praed esq. 600l.

[B] Of the great contested election in this county, in the reign of Anne, many curious particulars are remembered;—not the least remarkable of which, is, that thirty-seven of the family of DAVIES voted on the Tory side; though not one remains at present possessing a freehold of forty shillings.—The late Mrs. GIDDY, of Tredrea, was in some measure the last of the race; and I may add, one of the good old times that are gone. She brought a considerable fortune into the Giddy family; in whom we have an uncommon instance of wealth united with every mental accomplishment—with every excellence both of the head and heart.

‡ It would appear invidious, as we approach so near our own times, to mention the names of those Cornish gentlemen who were most active in detecting and apprehending their neighbours the Jacobites.—It was about the time of evening service when the emissaries of——arrived at Trelowarren: Sir F. Vyvyan begged permission to read prayers to his family; and after having gone through the service with his usual composure of mind, resigned himself prisoner into their hands. He was conveyed to the tower; where he was detained a considerable time, and was forced to pay many thousand pounds for his enlargement. The late Miss Ann Vyvyan was born there.

[ONO] I allude to the projected French invasion of 1779: and the zeal, judiciousness, and adroitness of Sir Francis Basset, now Lord de Dunstanville and Basset, at this crisis of alarm in calling up an army, from the mines of Cornwall, conducting them to Plymouth, and regulating their labour at the foss, must be always considered with respect and gratitude.—Of Pellew (now Lord Exmouth) I had almost said that his naval honours are eclipsed by the military fame of Sir Hussey Vivian!—Truro is justly proud of both.

CIVIL AND MILITARY CONSTITUTION.

BOOK III. CHAPTER II.

I. WE have seen the county divided into hundreds; and these hundreds subdivided into parishes.—Under this arrangement, it were easy to speak with precision of private property, of the possessors of estates, of titles, of the government of Cornwall, and of the county and its towns as represented in parliament.

II. 1. In the distribution of private property, it appears that thirty acres usually made a farthing, nine farthings a Cornish acre, and four Cornish acres a knight's fee.[A] 2. On a retrospective glance to the Cornish families from the conquest to Edward I. we must observe, that few which are recorded in Domesday, occur at the conclusion of that period. There was so great an alienation in property, from forfeitures during the contests between the Norman kings and the kings of France, that many of our nobility and gentry, who had lands both in Normandy and England, lost their estates by espousing the party of one of these princes. The crusades occasioned many estates to be sold, and more mortgaged to their full value at least, and never redeemed, to enable their owners to equip themselves for their romantic expeditions, of which the monastic clergy much availed themselves. By these and other casualties, and the arbitrary power of our princes, and from families terminating in females, we may account for the obliteration of the Domesday namse.—In the period immediately before us, we regret also, the extinction " or the low estate" of numerous families that had served their country in arts and arms; whilst the landed interest hath gradually given way to the commercial; and foreign luxuries succeeded to homebred hospitality.[ooo]

III. Of our titled gentry, we enumerate the names of the Rev. Sir Harry Trelawny of Trelawny, Sir Viell Vyvyan of Trelowarren, Sir John St. Aubyn of Clowance, Sir Arscott Ourry Molesworth of Pencarrow, Sir William Lemon of Carclew, Sir Christopher Hawkins of Trewithan, Sir William Pratt Call of Whiteford-House, Sir Joseph Copley of Bake, Sir Edward Buller of Trenant-Park, and Sir Rose Price, Barts.—

[A] See Carew (Edit. as before) for extent Cornub. f. 45-2-49 —and Tonkin's (Tehidy) MSS.

[ooo] Of our gentry, I should enter into a full account, but for Mr. Arundell's promised work; which from his ingenuity and accurate acquaintance with the subject, we anticipate as a complete history of Cornish houses.—Of the old British families still existing, are the Carlyons, the Boscawens, the Glynns, the Penwarnes, the Polwheles, the Prideauxs, the Trelawnys, the Trefusis, the Vyvyans: Among those from Normandy or Britanny are the St. Aubyns, the Bassets, the Borlases, the Lanyons: Among those of respectable but no high Cornish origin, Code or Coode, Tucker, and Taunton. Among the extinct families, the Bellots, the Bevilles, the Bodrigans, the Carminows, the Chamonds, the Connocks, the Eriseys, the Granvilles, the Gaverigans, the Godolphins, the Lowers, the Lukies, the Carnsews, the Lunys, the Mohuns, the Keskymers, the Roscarrocks, the Trencreeks, the Tonkins, the Trefrys, the Tregians, the Tresawells, the Killigrews form a various and melancholy groupe.—See pedigrees, at the end of this chapter.

Grenville of Boconnoc, Eliot of Port-Eliot, Trefusis of Trefusis, Basset and De Dunstanville of Tehidy-Park, and Pellew (Lord Exmouth) Barons—Boscawen of Tregothnan, Viscount—and Edgcumbe of Mount Edgcumbe, Earl.

IV. From our nobility, we ascend to the Duke of Cornwall; which prompts the consideration of our government.—We have seen that the territory comprising the *Dutchy*, was anciently a *Monarchy*, a *Principality*, a *Dukedom*, and a little before and also after the Norman conquest, an *Earldom*. And it continued to be an Earldom, till the 11th of Edward III. when it was constituted a *Dutchy*. It was first conferred on Edward, son of Edward III. surnamed the Black Prince. The creation was to the said Edward and the first begotten sons and heirs apparent of him and his heirs, Kings of England, forever. And to this day the eldest sons of the Kings of Great Britain are Dukes of Cornwall from their birth, and are entitled to have livery of their Dutchy lands and hereditaments whilst infants as if they were of full age.* 2. As Cornwall derived its chief importance from its tin—it had been divided into four stannary-districts—Fawey-moor, Blackmoor, Tywarnheyl and Penwith, so called from the principal tinworks at the time of the division.* To encourage the searching for tin, it was expedient to divide the tin-grounds themselves into separate portions. This was called bounding, as the limits of those separate portions of ground, were the Bounds—little pits dug in the ground about a foot wide and deep, at the extreme angles of the land.* The rights of bounds in Cornwall seem to have been ascertained by a charter of Edmund earl of Cornwall; and by this charter, also, were granted two coinages yearly, at Midsummer and Michaelmas. But the charter of Edward I. commands, that all tin, whether white or black, or wheresoever found or wrought within the county, be weighed at Lestwithiel, Bodmin, Leskeard, Truro, or Helston, and that the tin be coined in the said towns yearly before the day of St. Michael.‡ Thus settled as it was by charters, this tin-establishment could not have long endured without appropriate laws, and courts of justice for putting these laws into execution. The laws by which the tin-mines were governed, were long vague, and property in the mines precarious: and the tinners of Cornwall and Devon were accustomed to meet on Hingeston-hill near Callington every seventh or eighth year to concert measures for their mutual interests. But Edward I. made the tinners of Cornwall a distinct body from those of Devonshire.§ And he confirm'd the authority of the *Custos*¶ of the Stannaries; (an officer probably of high antiquity) recognizing him as one general Warden¶ over both counties, to do justice in law and equity. From his decision there lay an appeal to the Duke of Cornwall in council only, or for want of a Duke of Cornwall, to the crown. And the Lord Warden was empowered to appoint a regular Vice-Warden for each county; whose office it was to hold his court for the determination of stannary disputes, every month; and also a steward for each of the stannary districts in each county,

* With respect to the first creation of the king's eldest son, Duke of Cornwall, the erecting of that county into a Dutchy, and assigning him lands, manors, castle, &c· in divers counties; ample information may be derived from Selden's titles of Honour, vol. 3, p. 30, 776 (Dr. Wilkin's edition of Selden's works, London 1726.) and the Prince's case in 8. Coke's reports. * See Gibson's Caaden, Carew f. 13, and Borlase's Nat. Hist. p. 192.

† See Pryce's Mineralogia, pp. 137—141

‡ In the time of Charles II. to the coinage towns of Liskeard, Lestwithiel, Truro, and Helston, was added Penzance, for the convenience of the western tinners.

§ See Pearce's Stannary Laws·

¶ See charter of Edward I.

¶ Camden is much in error when he speaks of a Warden now first appointed. p, 5. Carew seems to refer the office to earlier times.—

who was to hold his court for the district every three weeks, and decide by juries of six persons with an appeal reserved to the Vicewarden; thence to the Lord Warden; and thence finally to the Duke of Cornwall.[A] The Vicewarden's, was a court of equity; answering to the court of chancery. The Steward's court, is a court of law; answering in a great measure to the court of King's bench. It resembles, in its process, the hundred-court. The Vicewardens of Cornwall and Devon, appointed by the Lord Warden, have been generally of consideration in the country.[B]

[A] With respect to the revenues of the Duchy of Cornwall, I cannot omit a curious document with which I am favoured by Benjamin Tucker Esq. of Trematon-Castle, Surveyor-general of the Duchy of Cornwall.—The following is a list of sixteen Duchy Manors which were sold by Queen Elizabeth and recovered by Prince Henry, the property of the Duchy being inalienable: so that the purchasers lost all their money; which, extraordinary as it may appear, has never yet been shewn in any history of the County—

Names of Manors.	When voted or granted.	To whom.	For what sum. £	s.	d.
Port Looe	16 Elizabeth 1574.	Henry Welby Esq., and George Bligh gent.	granted		
Leigh Durant, Bonyalva	44 Elizabeth 1602.	Thomas Harriet, and John Shelbury, gents.	1165	1	9
Tinton, Bucklawren, Carnedon Prior, Climsland Prior, Stratton Sanctuary	44 Elizabeth 1602.	Francis Lord Norris, Rowland Lytton, and Thomas Bellot, gents.	5901	17	5
Eastway, Northill, Tregamere, Landreyne, Treverbyn Courtenay	44 Elizabeth 1602.	Michael Stanhope, esq., and Edw. Stanhope, L. L. D.	1370	12	7
West Anthony, Trelowia, Landulph	37 Elizabeth 1595.	Gallio Merriett, esq. and Henry Lindley, esq., (afterwards knights)			

[B] List of the Lord-Wardens and Vice-Wardens from Edward VI.

Lord-Wardens.	Vice-Wardens.
Temp. Edw. VI. Edward Duke of Somerset	Sir Thomas Smith
1553. John Earl of Bedford	Sir William Godolphin
1554. Edward Lord Hastings of Loughborough	
About 1560. Francis Earl of Bedford	
1584-1603. Sir Walter Raleigh	William Carnsew, esq.; Sir Francis Godolphin; Sir Richard Grenville
1603-1629. William Earl of Pembroke	William Coryton, esq.
1630. Philip Earl of Pembroke and Montgomery	William Coryton, esq.; John Trefusis, esq.
1660. Sir John Granville (afterwards Earl of Bath	Sir Richard Prideaux; William Scawen, esq.; Sir John Trelawny, bart.; Sir Joseph Tredenham; J. Waddon, esq.
1701. Charles Earl of Radnor	Hugh Tonkin, esq.
1702. John Granville esq. (afterwards Lord Granville)	Sir Richard Vyvyan, bart.
1705. Francis Lord Rialton (afterwards Earl of Godolphin)	
1708. Hugh Boscawen esq. (afterwards Visc. Falmouth)	Walter Moyle, esq.; John Gregor, esq.; Thomas Hearle, esq.
1734. Col. John Schutz	Thomas Hearle, esq.; John Hearle, esq.
1742. Thomas Pitt esq., of Boconnoc	John Hearle, esq.; Christopher Hawkins, esq.; Francis Gregor, esq.
1751 James Earl of Waldgrave	John Hearle, esq.
1761.————	Rev. Walter Borlase, L. L. D.
1763. Humphrey Morice esq.	Rev. Walter Borlase, L. L. D.
1776.————	Henry Rosewarne, esq.
1783.————	John Thomas, esq.
1783. George Visc. Lewisham	John Thomas, esq.
1798. Sir John Morshead bart	John Thomas, esq.
1800. Rear-Admiral John Willet Payne.	John Thomas, esq.
1803. Thomas Tyrwhitt esq, (now Sir Thos. Tyrwhitt kt.	John Thomas, esq.
1812. Francis Charles Seymour, Earl of Yarmouth.	John Thomas, esq.

3. For that part of our government, whether military or civil, which we share in common with the realm, I should mention Lord Lieutenants,[c] Sheriffs,[D] Justices of the Peace.[E] Camden speaks of

[c] Lords Lieutenants and Custodes Rotulorum. 1660. In the 12th year of Charles the 2d, John Earl of Bath, was constituted Lord Lieutenant of this county, and John Lord Robarts of Truro (afterwards Earl of Radnor) Custos Rotulorum. 1692. In the 4th of King William and Queen Mary, Charles Lord Viscount Lansdowne, eldest son to John Earl of Bath, was joined in the lieutenancy of the Counties of Cornwall and Devon, with his father, and of Custos Rotulorum, also. 1696. In the 8th of William 3d, Charles Bodville, Earl of Radnor, was constituted Lord Lieutenant and Custos Rotulorum of Cornwall. 1702. The 1st of Queen Anne, John Granville esq. second son of John Earl of Bath (soon after created Lord Granville of Potheridge in Devon) was constituted Lord Lieutenant and Custos Rotulorum of Cornwall, during the minority of William Henry Earl of Bath, his nephew. 1705 In the 4th of Queen Anne, Sidney Lord Godolphin (soon afterwards Earl of Godolphin) Lord High Treasurer of England, was constituted Lord Lieutenant and Custos Rotulorum of Cornwall, in his own right. 1710. In the 9th of Queen Anne, Lawrence, Earl of Rochester (her Majesty's uncle) was constituted Lord Lieutenant and Custos Rotulorum, of Cornwall, during the minority of William Henry Earl of Bath. And after the Earl of Bath's death, May 17, 1711, whom the Earl of Rochester preceded, and 2d of the same month, his son Henry Earl of Rochester was constituted Lord Lieutenant and Custos Rotulorum of Cornwall. 1713. In the 1st of George I. Charles Bodville Earl of Radnor, was constituted Lord Lieutenant and Custos Rotulorum of Cornwall. 17— In the of George, on the death of Charles Bodville Earl of Radnor, his nephew, Henry Earl of Radnor (only son to Russel Robarts, Esq,) was constituted Lord Lieutenant but no Custos Rotulorum and Nicholas Vincent of Trelevan gent. was made Custos Rotulorum. 1726. Mr. Vincent dying the 1st of July, 12 George, the Honourable Richard Edgcumbe of Mount Edgcumbe Esq. was made Custos Rotulorum; and continued so by George 2d, the 1st year of his reign—Henry Earl of Radnor dying unmarried at Paris, Jan. 1740, he was constituted Lord Lieutenant. Richard Edgcumbe was succeeded in both offices by his eldest son Richard Lord Edgcumbe; and on his death George the second son took them; and on his death Richard the present Earl and grandson of the first Lord was appointed, and still holds both offices.

Sheriffs from Edward I. to the present day.

EDWARD I. 1275, John Wigger. 1276, Idem. 1277, Robert de Chini [Chenduit of Bodannen in Endelion.] 1279, William de Muncketon, 5 years. 1284, Alexander de Sabridsworth, 3 years. 1287, 1288 Simon de Berkely. 1289, Edmund Comes Cornubiæ to 1300. 1301, Thomas de la Hide. 1302, Robert de Elford. EDWARD II. 1310, Peter de Gaveston Comes Cornubiæ 3 years. 1313, Thomas de la Hide. 1314, Thomas de Excedekney de Antony, arm. 1315, Richard de Polhampton, [qu. Buchampton.] 1316, Richard de Hewish. 1317, Henry de Wellington [of Giddesham in Devon.] 1320, Isabella regina, consors regis, quæ habet officium vice Com. 1321,——. 1322, Nullus titulus in rotulo. 1323,——. 1324, Isabella regina, [Carew fo. 50.] 1325, John de Treiagu de Fenton-gollan, [probably appointed by the king, or the bishop of Exon. In Rymer's Fœdera, is an order from the king, for taking the county of Cornwall (and other counties) from the queen, and giving it in charge to Walter bp. of Exeter or his deputy—dated Sept. 18, 1324, Porchester.] EDWARD III. 1327, Isabella regina, regis mater, for 5 years. 1332, William de Botreaux. 1333, Idem. 1334, John Petit de Ardevora. 1335, Idem. 1336, Joh. de Chudeleigh 1337, John. Hamley. 1338, John. Petit de Ardevora. 1339,——, 1340, Edward, dux Cornub. et Comes Cestiæ fil. regis primogen. 1341, Hen. Terril, Rog. de Prideaux. 1342, Edward dux Cornubiæ. 1343, Idem. 1344, Guliel. Pipehard. 1345, Edward dux Cornubiæ, nine years. 1354, Johannes Northcot. 1355 William de Austell, 4 years. 1358, Edward dux Cornubiæ, to the end of this king's reign. RICHARD II. 1378, Nicholas Wampford. 1379, Rad. Carminow de Carminow. 1380, Otho de Bodrigan. 1381, William Tallbot. 1382, Johannes Bevill de Gwarnick in Powder. 1383, Wal. Archdeacon, Miles de Antony et Castro de Lanyhorne. 1384, William Fitzwater, miles. 1385, Richard Kendall de Treworgy. 1386, John. Bevill. 1387, Nicholas Wampford. 1388, John Colyn. 1389, Richard Sergeaux, knight, [of Killigarth or Colquite, or of Lanreath in Helland.] 1390, Thomas Peverell de Park in Egloshayle. 1391, Will. Talbot. 1392, John Colyn. 1393, John Colshull de Tremadart, [Binnamy Castle, in Stratton, his original residence.] 1394, Joh. Herle [de Prideaux.] 1395, James Chuddelegh. 1396, Will. Talbot. 1397, Joh. Bevill, 1398, Joh. Colshull. 1399, Guy Seyntalbyn de Clowance. HENRY IV. 1400, Hen. fil. regis promogen. et J. Rheynes. 1401, Henry fil. regis, 4 years. 1405, John Cole. 1406, Henry Princeps, 6 years. HENRY V. 1413, John Rederow. 1414, Idem. 1415, William Talbot. 1416, Oto Trevarthyn, miles. 1417, Henry Fullford. 1418, John Arundell, miles, de Lanherne. 1419, Stephen Dernford de Rame. 1420, John Arundel de Trerice, miles. 1421, John Arundel, miles, de Trerice. 1422, John Arundel, miles. HENRY

VI. 1423, Thomas Carminow. 1424, William Talbot. 1425, John Herle, miles. 1426, John Arundel, miles. 1427, ——. 1428, John Nanfan. 1429, Thomas Carminow. 1430, Robert Chambleyn. 1431, James Chuddeleigh. 1432, ——. 1433, John Herle, miles. 1435, Thomas Bonevill de Trelawn. 1435, John Yerd. 1436, Thomas Whalesbrow de Whalesbrow. 1437, Ren. Arundel. 1438, John Coleshul. 1439, Johannes Nanfan. 1440, Johannes Mundy. 1441, Thomas Whalesborough. 1442, Johannes Blewet, de St. Colan. 1443, John Arundell. 1444, Nich. (vel Mich.) Power. 1445, John Champernowne de Inswork, 1446 Johannes Austell or de Austell. 1447, Henry Fortescue. 1448, Johannes Trevilyan. 1449, Johannes Basset, de Tehiddy. 1450, Johannes Nanfan. 1451, Thomas Butside, (Budockshed de Budeaux.) 1452, William Daubeney. 1453, Thomas Whalesborough. 1454, Johannes Petit. 1455, John Cornworth. 1456, Johannes Nanfan. 1457, John Arundell. 1458, Johannes Whalesborough. 1459, Johannes Trevilyan. 1460, ——. EDWARD IV. 1461, Richard Champernoun de Halwin vel Inkworth (Ro) 1462, Ren. Arundell de Lanherne. 1463, Idem. 1464, Thomas Bere, (forsan de Killigarth in Talland.) 1465, Alver Cornburg. 4466, Will. Bere. 1467, Johannes Colshall, miles. 1468, Johannes Sergeaux, arm. 1469, Alver. Cornburg. 1470. Johannes Arundell, miles, de Trerice. 1471, Johannes Fortescu, arm. 4 years. 1475, Richard dux Gloc. Vic. ad terminum vitæ. 1476, Johannes Fortescue arm. 1477, Egid. Dawbeney. 1478, William Carnsew, forsan de Bokelly in St. Kew. 1479, Robert Willoughby, miles. 1480, Richard Nanfan. 1481, Thomas Greenvill de Stowe. 1482, Thomas Fulford. RICHARD III. 1483, Johannes Treffry, de Fowey. 1484, James Tyrrel, miles de Trerice, (Stripe in his notes on Buck's history says, that Richard III. gave Tyrrel the wardship of Robert Arundel and management of his estates, Trerice &c. &c.) 1485, William Haughton, miles. HENRY VII. 1486, Thomas Greenvill. 1487, Johannes Tremayne de Tremayne. 1488, Alexander Carew de Anthony. 1489, Richard Nanfan. 1490, Johannes Trefry, miles. 1491, Johannes Roscarrock de Roscarrock in Endelion. 1492, Thomas Tregarthyn, de Tregarthyn. 1493, Richard Vivian, de Trevidren in Beryan. 1494, Walter Enderby, arm. 1495, Petrus Bevill. 1496, Ed. Arundell, arm. 1497, Johannes Basset. 1498, Peter Edgecombe miles, de Cuttayle. 1499. Idem. 1500, Johannes Trefry, miles. 1501, William Trefry arm. 1502, Peter Bevill. 1503, William Trevanyon, de Carhays. 1504, Johannes Godolphin, de Godolphin. 1505, Richard Vivian arm. 1506, Peter Edgcombe miles. 1507, Michael Vivian arm. de Trevidren. 1508, William Trevannion arm. 1509, Thomas Trevanion miles. HENRY VIII. 1510, Johannes Arundel miles, de Tolvern. 1511, Ro. Graynfield arm. 1512, William Carnsew arm. de Bokelly in St. Kew. 1513, Jac. Erisey arm. de Erisey, (he drove the French invaders from Marazion.) 1514, Johannes Carminow arm. de Fenton.gollan. 1515, Johannes Carew arm. 1516, William Trevanion miles. 1517, Peter Edgecombe miles. 1518, Johannes Basset miles. 1519, Ro. Greenfield arm. 1520, Johannes Arundel arm. de Trerice. 1521, Johannes Skewys arm. de Skewys in Cury. 1522, Johannes Basset miles. 1523, Ro. Greenfield arm. 1524, Johannes Arundel arm. de Trerice. 1525, William Lower arm. 1526, Richard Penrose arm. de Penrose. 1527, Richard Greenfield arm. 1528, Johannes Trevanion arm. [Hu.] 1529, Johannes Chamond arm. de Lancels. 1530, William Godolphin arm. 1531, Chr. Tredinoke arm. de Tredinoke, (Tredinnick in Breage.) 1532, Johannes Arundel arm. de Trerice. 1533, Hugh Trevanion miles. 1534, William Godolphin miles. 1535, Peter Edgecombe miles. 1536, Johannes Reskymer miles, de Reskymer. 1537, Johannes Chamond miles. 1538, Hu. Trevanion miles. 1539, William Godolphin miles. 1540, Johannes Reskymer arm. 1541, Johannes Arundel arm. 1542, Johannes Arundel miles. 1543, Hu. Trevanion arm. 1544, Richard Chamond arm. 1545, Richard Greenfield arm. 1546, Thomas St Albin arm. 1547, John Trelawney arm. de Pool. EDWARD VI. 1548, Job Milaton arm. de Pengersick. 1549, Rich. Chamond arm. 1550, Will. Godolphin miles. 1551, Ric. Roscarrock arm. 1552, Hu. Trevanion miles. 1553, Reg. Mohun arm. de Hall. MAR. REG. 1554, Joh. Arundell miles de Trerice. 1555, Joh. Arundell miles de Lanherne. 1556, Ric. Edgecombe arm. 1557, Joh. Reskymer arm. 1558, Joh. Bevill arm. ELIZ. 1559, Joh. Carminow arm. 1560, Reg. Mohun arm. 1561, Joh. Trelawney arm. 1562, Ric. Roscarrock arm. 1563, Ric. Chamond arm. 1564, Henry Chyverton arm. de Kerrys in St. Paul. 1565, Hu. Trevanion arm. 1566, Will. Milliot arm. (Milaton last heir male of Pengersick.) 1567, Joh. Trelawny arm. 1568, Joh. St. Aubyn arm. 1569, William Godolphin miles. 1570, Pet. Edgcombe arm. 1571, Henry Curwen miles. 1572, Will. Mohun arm. 1573, Pet. Courtney ar. de Trethurfe. 1574, Joh. Arundel ar. de Trerice. 1575, Joh. Bevill ar. 1576, Geo. Keckwich ar. de Catchfrench.

1577, Ric. Grenvill ar. 1578, Will. Mohun ar. 1579, Will. Lower ar. 1580, Fr. Godolphin ar. 1581, Joh. Arundell ar. 1582, Johan. Fitz. 1583, Ric. Carew ar. 1584, Geo. Grenville ar. de Penheale. 1585, Tho. Coswarth ar. de Coswarth. 1586, Joh. Roscarrock ar. 1587, Joh. Wrey ar. de Trebigh. 1588, Ant. Rouse ar. de Halton. 1589, Tho. St. Aubyn ar. 1590, Will. Bevill ar. de Killygarth. 1591, Walt. Kendall ar. de Treworgy. 1592, Geo. Keckwich ar. de Catchfrench. 1593, Ric. Champernoun ar. 1594, Tho. Lower arm. 1595, Jonathan Trelawny ar. 1596. Car. Trevanion ar. 1597. Barnardus Grenville armiger. 1598, Willus Bevill, miles, Peter Courtney [Fuller] 1599, Willus Wrey, arm. 1600, Franciseus Buller arm. de Tregarrick. 1601, Hannibal Vivian, arm. 1602, Antonius Rowse, miles, Halton. JAMES I. 1603, Arthur Harris, arm. 1604, Franciscus Godolphin miles. 1605, Nichas Prideaux arm, de Solden. 1606, Degorius Chamond arm. 1607, Johnes Arundell arm. 1608, Johnes Rashleigh arm. and Joh. Acland. m. Fuller. 1609, Christ. Harris miles. 1610, Ric. Edgcumbe miles. 1611, Ric. Buller miles. 1612, Wills. Wrey miles. 1613, Wills. Coryton arm. 1614, Rich. Robarts arm. of Truro. 1615, Johs. Chamond arm. 1616, Wills. Code arm. 1617, Franciscus Vivian arm. 1618, Rich. Carnsew arm. 1619, Reskymer Bonython arm. 1620, Nichas Glynn arm. 1621. Samuel Pendarves arm. of Roscrow. 1622, Johes Speccot, miles. 1623, Rich. Geddy arm. of Trebursy in S. Petherwin. 1624. Johnes Moyle, arm. CHARLES I. 1625. Thomas Wyvell arm. St. Stephens, near Saltash. 1626. Johes Trefusis arm. de Trefusis. 1627, Jonathan Rashleigh arm. 1628, Georgius Hele, arm. Bennets in Whitstone. 1629, Johes Rowe, arm. 1630, Johnes Trelawney miles et baronetus. 1631, Johnes Prideaux arm. 1632, Nichas Lower, miles. 1633, Carolus Trevanion arm. 1634, Hugo Boscawen arm. 1635, Johnes Seyntaubyn arm. 1636, Rich. Buller miles. 1637, Franciscus Godolphin, miles. 1638, Franciscus Godolphin de Treveneage. 1639, Rich. Trevill arm. 1640, Francus Wills arm. 1641, Johnes Grylls arm. of Court in Lanreath. 1642, Franciscus Basset arm. 1643, Franciscus Basset arm. 1644, Rich. Prideaux arm. 1645, Johnes Seyntaubyn arm. 1646, Ed. Herll arm. 1647. Ed. Herll arm. 1648, Ed. Herll, arm. CHARLES II. 1649, Petrus Kekewich arm. 1650, Johnes Lampen arm. 1651, Andreus Trevill arm. 1652, Rich. Lob arm. 1653, Rich. Trevill arm. 1654, Jacobus Praed arm. 1655, Ed. Nosworthy arm. 1656, Ed. Nosworthy arm. 1657, Anton. Nicholls arm. 1658, Petrus Jenkyn arm. . 1659, Nichas Cossen arm. Roseveth in Kenwyn. 1660, Nichas Cossen arm. 1661, Pearce Edgcumbe arm. 1662, Carolus Grylls arm. (of Court in Lanreath.) 1663, Oliver Sawle arm. 1664, Edmond Prideaux, arm. 1665, Josephus Tredenham, arm. 1666, Thomas Darrell, arm. 1667, Joh. Seyntaubyn, arm. 1668, Joh. Vivyan, arm. of Truan. 1669, Fran. Gregor, arm. 1670, Joh. Connock, arm. 1671, Walterus Moyle, miles. 1672 ,Johannes Nicholls, arm. 1673, Richus Trevill, arm. 1674, Petrus Kekewick, arm. 1675, Nichus Glynn, arm. 1676, Sam. Cavell, arm. of Treharrock in St. Kew. 1677, Franciscus Trefusis, arm. 1678, Willus Jennings, arm. 1679, Thomas Coke, arm. Tregassow, in St. Erme. 1680, Johannes Cotton, arm. Botreaux Castle. 1681, Willus Pendarves, arm. Pendarves. 1682, Christ. Bellot, arm. 1683, Sir Vyell Vyvyan, Bart. Trelowarren. 1684, Sir John Coryton, Bart. JAMES II. 1685, Sir Richard Edgcumbe, Bart. 1686, Jonathan Rashleigh, arm. 1687, Humphrius Borlase, arm. de Treluddro 1688, Humphrius Borlase, arm. WILLIAM & MARY. 1689, Willus. Bond, arm. 1690, Johannes Morth, arm. 1691, Johannes Molesworth, M. et B. 1692, Johannes Buller, Jun. arm 1693, Humphrius Nicholls, arm 1694, Willus. Williams, arm 1695, Johannes Tregeagle, arm de Trevorder 1696, Franciscus Wills, arm [Johannes forsan] 1697, Johannes Barrett, arm 1698, Richardus Erisey, arm 1699, Edmond Prideaux, arm 1700, Stephen Robins, arm 1701, Carolus Grylls, jun. arm. QUEEN ANNE 1702, Gregorius Peter, arm. de Harlyn. 1703, Johnes Williams de Bodenick, arm 1704, Rich. Tregeare arm 1705 Iohnes Williams, de Truthan, arm. 1706, Hugo Piper, de Tresmarrow, arm 1707, Emanuel Pyper, arm de Leskard 1708, Francus Basset, arm de Tehidy 1709, Sam Enys, arm de Enys 1710, Paul Orchard, arm de Aldercumb. 1711, Iohnes Worth, arm de Penryn. 1712, Iohnes Cole, arm de Cartuther 1713, Ed. Herll, arm de Landew. GEORGE I. 1714, Ed. Amy arm de Botreaux-Castle. 1715, Ios Silly de Helligan, arm. 1716, Francis Gregor, esq Trewarthenick. 1717, William Adis, esq. 1718, Dennis Arscott, esq de Ethy. 1719, Iohn Arundel, esq de Trevelver in St Minver. 1720, Erasmus Pascoe, esq. Trevassick, Phillack. 1721, Geo. Robinson, esq. Bochim. 1722, Edward Hoblyn, esq.

Croan. 1723, Richard Polwhele, Esq. Polwhele. 1724, Reginald Haweis, Esq. Killiow. 1725, Thomas Long, Esq. Penheale. 1726, John Collins, Esq. Treworgan. GEORGE II. 1727, Samuel Phillips, Esq. Mear, *mort.* and J. Phillips, residue of his year.] 1728, George Dennis, Esq. de Trenant. 1729, John Saltren, Esq. Treludrick, in Egloskerry. 1730, John Hill, Esq. de Lidcot. 1731, Nicholas Donnithorne, Esq. St. Agnes. 1732, Samuel Gilbert, Esq. Tackbear, in Bridgerule. 1733, Edward Crewys, Esq. 1734, James Tillie, Esq. Pentillie. 1735, William Symonds, Esq. of Hatt, Botesfleming. 1736, Ferdinando Wallis, Esq. Fentonwoon, Lanteglos. 1737, John Moyle, Esq. Bake. 1738, John Hony, Esq. Menheniot. 1739, Sir Francis Vyvyan, Bart. 1740, Francis Llewellin Leach, Esq. Trethewell. 1741, John Fortescue, Esq. Penwarne. 1742, William Lemon, Esq. Truro; [he bought Carclew of Kempe.] 1743, Nicholas Glynn, Esq. Glynn. 1744, John Hicks, Esq. Trenethick. 1745, John Pearse,* Esq. Stithians. 1746, John Tremayne, Esq. Heligan. 1747, Henry Peter, Esq. Harlyn. 1748, Edmund Cheyne, Esq. Launceston. 1749, Henry John, Esq. Camborne. 1750, Humphrey Prideaux, Esq. 1751, John Enys, Esq. Enys. 1752, John Trewren, Esq. Trewardreva, Constantine. 1753, William Morshead, Esq. Cartuther. 1754, John Glanville, Esq. Catchfrench. 1755, Francis Beauchamp, Esq. Pengreep. 1756, John Sawle, Esq. Penrice. 1757, John Luke, Esq. Treviles. 1458, Swete Nicholas Archer, Esq. Truro. 1759, Robert Lovell, Esq. Trefusis. 1760, Sir Christopher Treise, Knight, Lavethan. GEORGE III. 1761, Nicholas Kempe, Esq. Rosteage. 1762, Philip Enough, Esq. Falmouth. 1763, John Harrison, Esq. Wearde. 1764, Hender Mounsteven, Esq. Lancarfe. 1765, William Churchill, Esq. Redruth. 1766, Thomas Treffry, Esq. Fowey. 1767, John Carew, Esq. Anthony. 1768, Francis Kirkham, Esq. Croan. 1769, John Blewett, Esq. Marazion. 1770, Hugh Rogers, Esq. Helston. 1771, John Call, Esq. Whiteford. 1772, James Vivian, Esq. Pencalenick. 1773, William Harris, Esq. Camborne. 1774, John Price, Esq. Penzance. 1775, Peter Bown, Esq, Mawnan. 1776, John Elliot, Esq. Trebursey. 1777, Richard Gully, Esq. Tresillian. 1778, John Stackhouse, Esq. Pendarves. 1779, Thomas Vivian, Esq. jun. Trewan. 1780, Darell Crabbe Trelawney, Esq. Coldrinick. 1781, Sir John St. Aubyn, Bart. Clowance. 1782, John Coryton, Esq. Crocadon. 1783, Christopher Hawkins, Esq. Trewithen. 1784, Joseph Beauchamp, Esq. Pengreep. 1785, Weston Helyar, Esq. Newton. 1786, Michael Nowell, [Knight,] Falmouth. 1787, Samuel Thomas, Esq. Tregols. 1788, Francis Gregor, Esq. Trewarthenick. 1789, Robert Lovell Gwatkin, Esq. Killiow. 1790, Richard Hichens, Esq. Poltair. 1791, Sir William Molesworth, Bart. Pencarrow. 1792, Davies Giddy, Esq. Tredrea. 1793, Francis Glanville, Esq. Catchfrench. 1794, Edward Archer, Esq. Trelask. 1795, Ralph Allen Daniell, Esq. Truro. 1796, John Enys, Esq. Enys. 1797, William Slade Gully, Esq. Trevenen. 1798, James Buller, Esq. Shillingham. 1799, Edmund John Glynn, Esq. Glynn. 1800, Matthew Mitchell, Esq. Hangar. 1801, Edward Collins, Esq. Truthan. 1802, Thomas Carlyon, Esq. Tregrehan. 1803, Thomas Rawlings, Esq. Padstow. 1804, Sir Lionel Copley, Bake, refusing to act, T. Rawlings held the office till April 3, when was appointed John Trevanion Purnell Bettesworth Trevanion, of Caerhayes. 1805, Samuel Stephens, Esq. of Tregenna-Castle. 1806, Thomas Graham, Esq. Penquite. 1807, Sir William Pratt Call, Bart. Whiteford. 1808, John Tillie Coryton, Esq. Crocadon. 1809, Hon. Charles Bagnall Agar, Lanhydrock. 1810, Richard Oxnam, Esq. Rosehill, Penzance. 1811, William Lewis Salisbury Trelawney, Esq. Penquite. 1812, John Vivian, Esq. Pencalenick. 1813, John Coleman Rashleigh, Esq. Prideaux. 1814, Rose Price, Esq. [created a Baronet of Trengwaynton, in this year, 1814.] 1315, Sir Vyel Vyvyan, Bart. Trelowarren. 1816, Sir Arscot Ourry Molesworth, Bart. Pencarrow.

[E] *The names of such as were in the commission of the Peace for the County of Cornwall at the death of George I.*

"Sir Fran. Hen. Drake, of Buckland'Monachor. in Dev. bart.; Sir Wm. Carew, of East Anthony, bart.; Sir John St. Aubyn, of Clowance, bart.; Sir Wm. Coryton, of Newton Ferrers, bart. sworn: Sir Jo. Moles-

* Nicholas Pearse, his grandfather, died full 100 years old. At his funeral, it was ascertained that his age was 103, when on the coffin (immediately before the interment) the figure 3 was added to 100—standing thus, 1003. Future antiquaries, on the re-appearance of the coffin, might speculate on an age even exceeding that of Methuselah.

Lord Lieutenants in the days of Elizabeth, as extraordinary magistrates, constituted only in times of difficulty and danger. Yet they were certainly appointed 2, 3 Edw. VI. and 4, 5 Phil. and Mary, by patent under the great seal. On the abolition of military tenures after the restoration, the power of Lord Lieutenants was as-

worth, of Pencarrow, bart. sworn; Sir Jo. Trelawny, of Trelawn, bart.; Sir Francis Vivyan, of Trelowarren bart.; Sir Nich. Trevannion, of Molinnick, kt.; Rich. Edgecombe, of Mount Edgecombe in Devon; John Trevannion, of Carhays, sworn; John Francis Buller, Morvall; Charles Trelawny, of Hangar; Fran. Scobell, of St. Austle; Charles Grylls, of Trebarth; Alexander Carew, of Harrowburg; Edward Elliott of Treberzy; Francis Manaton, of Killaver, sworn; Edm. Prideaux, of Padstow, sworn; Sam. Ennys, of Ennys, sworn; Arthur Arscott. of Tetcott inDevon, sworn; Warwick Mohun, of Luny, sworn; Darrell Trelawny, of Coledrinnick; Geo. Spry, of St. Anthony; Phillip Rashley, of Menabilly; Andrew Wheeler, of Hengar; Lewis Tremain, of Heligan; Martin Kelligrew, of Arwinnack; William Glynn, of Glynn, sworn; Edward Penrose, of Penrose; Jo. William, of Treworgye, sworn; Edward Bennet, of Hexworthy, sworn; Jo. Borlace, of Pendean, sworn; Jo. Peters, of Halwin, sworn; Joseph Silly, of Helligan; Jonathan Webber, of Ambell; Peter Kekewich, of Hall, sworn; Jo. Worth, of Penryn, sworn; Tho. Hearl, of Penryn, sworn; Jo. Ennys, of Ennys, sworn; Sam. Foot, of Truro, sworn; Jo. Sandys, of St. Keverne; Jo. Robins; Joseph Fortescue; Arthur Fortescue, of Pencoss, sworn; Joseph Sawle, of Penrice; Francis Gregor, of Trewarthynock, sworn; William Addys, of Whitford; Francis Foot, of Verian; John Roberts; Tho. Savill, Dep. Gov. of Pendennis Castle; James Tilly, of Pentilly, sworn; Rob. Corker, of Falmouth; Tho. Coppleston, of Bowden, Devon; Mark Batt, of Muttenham; Jo. Harris, of Kennegie; Rich. Elliot, of Port Elliot, now Molenick, in St. Germans; Geo. Dennis, of Dulo, sworn; James Keigwin, of Mousehole, sworn; Will. Bickford, of Dunsland, Devon, sworn; John Oliver, of Trevarnoe; John Moyle, of Bake; John Treise of Levethen, sworn; Edward Hoblyn, of Croan; John Glanvill, of Catchfrench; Sam. Phillips, of Macre; Jeffery Murth, of Tallant; Walter Kendall, of Pellyn, sworn; Tho. Fisher, of Lansallas; Christoph. Hawkins, of Trewinnard, sworn: John Hicks, of Trevethick; Richard Polwheel, of Polwheel; Charles Valence Jones, of the West, sworn; Roger Wollacombe, of Langford Hill; Kelland Courtenay, of Tremere, in Lanivet; John Saltern, of Treludick, sworn; Edmund Bickford, of the Inner Temple; William Arundell, of Trangventon, sworn." From the Prideaux *Carew*, at ff. 96, 97.

Those who were in the commission of the Peace in 1803.

Hon. John Eliot, Hon. William Eliot, Sir Harry Trelawny, Sir John St. Aubyn, Sir William Lemon, Sir Lionel Copley, Sir John Morshead, Sir Christopher Hawkins, Sir W. Pratt Call, Sir Edward Pellew, Sir Francis Buller, William Carpenter D. D., William Flamank, John Jago, Charles Mayson, Edward Pole, Philip Lyne L. L. D., John Cudlipp M. D., Stephen Luke, Edward Archer, esq. Samuel Archer, A. Bickford, James Buller, John Buller, John Buller, Frederick Wm. Buller, Edward Buller, Thomas Carlyon, Arthur Champernowne, Edward Collins, John Coryton, John Tillie Coryton, John Phillips Carpenter, Reginald Pole Carew, William Clode, Jonathan P. Coffin, William Carlyon, Ralph Allen Daniell, Zachary Hammett Drake, John Eliot, William Ellis, John Enys, Francis Enys, Thomas Edwards, Wm. Fortescue, John Inglett Fortescue, Davies Giddy, Walter Raleigh Gilbert, Francis Glanville, Edmund John Glynn, Thomas Graham, Francis Gregor, Robert Lovell Gwatkin, William Slade Gully, John Gould, jun. John Hawkins, David Hearle, Weston Helyar, John Hosken, Richard Hichens, William Hickes Horndon, Francis John Hext, Thomas Hext, John Hext, Joseph Hocken, Wrey I'Ans, Richard Johns, Arthur Kelly, Arthur Kelly, jun. John Kempe, Arthur Kempe, Samuel Kekewich, John Lemon, Charles Lemon, Matthew Michell, Jonas Morgan, William Morshead, Nicholas Harris, Paul Orchard, John Penhallow Peters, Thomas Pascoe, Thomas Phillips, William Praed, Rose Price, Humphry Prideaux, Arthur Puckey, Hoblyn Peter, Henry Peter, Edmund Prideaux, Benjamin Pender, Francis Pender, Edward Parson, Philip Rashleigh, John Coleman Rashleigh, Francis Rodd, Francis Hearle Rodd, John Rogers, John Rowe, Thomas Reed, Thomas Rawlings, John Rogers jun. Hugh Rogers, Thomas Spry, William Stackhouse, John Stackhouse, Edward William Stackhouse, Samuel Stephens, William Lewis Salisbury, John

certained by Parliament: And the present military laws are formed on those statutes which were then enacted; by which a certain number of inhabitants of every county are chosen by lot for three years, and officered by the Lord Lieutenant, Deputy-Lieutenants, and other principal landholders under a commission from the crown. The sheriffs of Cornwall are appointed by its dukes, in council. [o]

V. Respecting the Parliamentary representation of Cornwall, or its towns, I shall enter into no detail. [F] That in our representatives, we occupy a large space in the House of Commons, (no less than forty-four members from the county, and its borough towns) should not pass unnoticed. [MM] Of the families, which

Thomas, John Trevenen, Thomas Trevenen, Arthur Tremayne, Lovell Todd, John Hearle Tremayne, John Trevanion Purnell Bettesworth Trevanion, George Treweeke, Edward Trelawney, Vyell Vyvyan, Thomas Vyvyan, John Vivian, (Truro) John Vivian, Stephen Usticke, John Oliver Willyams, James Willyams, James Brydges Willyams, Richard Wymond, John Allen, William Borlase, John Bennett, Edward Baynes, Charles Prideaux Brune, Richard Buller, John Buller, Charles Dayman, Benjamin Forster, George Fortescue, Edward Giddy, Edmund Gilbert, William Gregor, Richard Gerveys Grylls, Richard Hennah, Robert Hoblyn, John Francis Hearle, Richard Hichens, Cadwallader Jones, John Kingdon, Nicholas Kendall, Charles Kendall, Charles Trevanion Kempe, John Kempe, Charles Lemon, Charles Lethbridge, John Molesworth, Edward Morshead, Charles Marshall, Thomas Penwarne, Henry Pooley, John Pomeroy, Richard Polwhele, Joseph Pomeroy, John Phillips, Jonathan Rashleigh, Coplestone Radcliffe, Edward Rodd, William Sandys, John Stephens, George Pender Scobell, William Stackhouse, James Tonkyns, Henry Hawkins Tremayne, Jeremiah Trist, Thomas Trevenen, John Trefusis, Henry Vivian, Thomas Wills, Simon Webber, Robert Walker, John Wood, Philip Webber.

[o] *The Duke of Cornwall's council in* 1816.

The Rt. Hon. William Adam, H. R. H's. chancellor; Duke of Northumberland; Earl of St. Vincent; Earl of Moira; Lord Keith; Lord Hutchinson; Lord Erskine; Earl of Yarmouth, Lord-Warden of the stannaries, and Steward of the duchy in the counties of Cornwall and Devon; Sir Thomas Tyrwhitt, kt.; General Hulse, H. R. H's. treasurer; The Rt. Hon. John M. Mahon, secretary and auditor; The Rt. Hon. R. B. Sheridan, receiver-general of the duchy; Benjamin Tucker, esq., surveyor-geveral; Major Gen. Sir Benjamin Bloomfield; Michael Angelo Taylor, esq.; Frederick Beilby Watson, esq.; John Nesbitt, esq.; Joseph Jekyll, esq., H. R. H's. attorney-general; William Draper Best, esq., H. R. H's solicitor-general.

[F] See Browne Willis, Brady and Burgh.—The following is an extract from Burgh's Political Disquisitions. Vol. I. p. 392.

"The collectors of the debates of the commons have given us a curious list of pensions, and pensioners, and their characters in the pension parliament, from a scarce tract published at the time, entitled, a seasonable argument to persuade all the grand juries in England to petition for a new parliament. Or, a list of the principal labourers in the great design of power and arbitrary power, &c. A reward of £200 was offered by proclamation for discovering the author. He gives an exact account of all the emoluments and advantages enjoyed by above 200 members. His manner is whimsical enough. I will copy a few of his articles for the reader's amusement.

CORNWALL. Sir Jonathan Trelawney, bart. one who is known to have sworn himself into £4000 at least in his account of the prize office. Controuler to the duke, and has got, in gratuities, to the value of £10,000 besides what he is promised for being informer.

LANCESTON. Sir Charles Harbord, surveyor-general. He got £100,000 of the king and kingdom, was formerly a solicitor of Staple's Inn, till his lewdness and poverty brought him to court.

DEVONSHIRE. Sir Copleston Bampfield, bart. much addicted to tippling, presented to the king by his pretended wife, Betty Roberts, in Pall Mall.

HONITON. Sir Peter Prideaux. Constant court dinners, and 300l. per annum pension.

This was in one of the parliaments of Charles II. of whom the author observes, that he is thought to be the first king who bought the votes of members of parliament."

[MM] In the reign of Edward I. the county and the six boroughs only of Launceston, Leskeard, Lestwithiel, Bodmin, Truro, and Helston returned members to parliament. In the reign of Edward VI. Saltash, Camelford, West-Looe, Gram-

had the honour of producing persons, to represent their native county from Edward I. to Elizabeth, it is remarkable, that not one exists at the present day,—except Basset, Tremayne, and Polwhele. †

Of St. Aubyn, who lives in the gratitude of his countrymen, it were difficult to speak in more appropriate terms than his epitaph on the Crowan-monument.

If we look for his parallel, we cannot but fix our eyes on one of the present members for Cornwall. Sir William Lemon indeed, has passed through perilous times, such as the antagonist of Sir Robert Walpole never saw: And, with a power possest by few, he has been able not only to reconcile contending parties, but to conciliate to himself their esteem and affection. In him we justly admire the old country gentleman, faithful to his king without servility—attached to the people without democracy. Whilst many fearful of incurring the suspicion of republicanism, abandoned the cause of liberty, Sir William stood firm in the ranks of independence, and had even the resolution to express his dissent from the minister at that unheard of moment, when opposition to administration was considered as synonymous with disaffection from government. Such was the conduct, resulting from a strong mind, a sagacity in judging of the probable issue of things, and in penetrating the views of men, and from a conscious feeling of integrity. Open and unaffected, however, as he always was, there were none who could mistake his principles: Candid, courteous, and benevolent—there were none who could do otherwise than applaud them. It is to this undissembling spirit, this urbanity of manners, and suavity of disposition, united with that intrepidity, we are to ascribe his success in pleasing all, though he flattered no man's prejudices, and did homage to no man's opinions. That Cornwall cannot boast of others, resembling Sir William Lemon, I would by no means insinuate. Without such characters, we could never after so long a struggle with difficulties in history unexampled, have attained our present height of prosperity and glory.

pound, Bossiney, St. Michael, and Newport were admitted to the like honour. In Mary's reign, Penryn and St. Ives. In Elizabeth's, Tregoney, St. Germans, St. Mawes, East Looe, Fawey, and Kellington. It must be remarked, that Tregoney East-Looe, and Fowey occur once under Edward III.—See Br. Willis, III. 1——176.

† William Basset occurs once under Edward II. a colleague with John Lercedekne, and twice under Edward III. a colleague. first with John Lercedekne, and next with John Crochard; John de Tremaen (ancestor of our present member) appears under Edward III. no less than twelve times, associated with John Whalisbron, James de Trewenhard, John Riskarrek, Will. de Trewinnard, Ric. Cergeaux, John Hameli, Will. Polglas, John Hamely, Ric. Cerseaux, John Hamly, Nic. Wainford, and Otto Bodrugan; and under Philip and Mary we see John Polwhele, de Polwhele, in company with John Arundel de Lanheron. We first observe the name of Edgcumbe in the reign of Elizabeth, Richard Edgecombe, his colleague John Trelawny; then Peter Edgecombe, with Ric. Chamond, with Will. Mohun, with Francis Godolphin, and with Will. Bevill, knight. Under Car. II. we hail in unison with Francis Robarts, Richard Edgecombe, knight of the Bath; and under Will. III. Ric. Edgecombe, with John Speccot. Of the ancestors of the present worthy Sir Harry Trelawny, of Trelawny, bart., the first I have noticed is John Trelawney, the companion of Richard Edgecombe. Then comes Jonathan Trelawney; under James I. Jonathan Trelawney, knight: and under Car. II. Jonathan Trelawney. Of the Corytons, we have the name once under James II., twice under Car. I., and once under Car. II. Of the Bullers, once under Car. I., and once under Anne. Of the Carews, once under Car. I., once under Car. II., once under Will. and Mary, once under Geo. I, and once under Geo. II. The Boscawens first come forward under Car. I., and are of frequent occurrence till they attain the peerage. I observe Trefusis only in the reign of Car. I. Vyvyan (Sir Richard) first occurs in the reign of Anne, and in that of Geo. I. St. Aubyn.

CODE, DE MORVALL. ‡

ARMS.—1*st, Argent, A Chev. Gules, between 3 Heathcocks, Sab. crested, jelloped, and legged, of the 2d.*—
2d. Gules, 3 *Crescents, Argent.* No Crest.

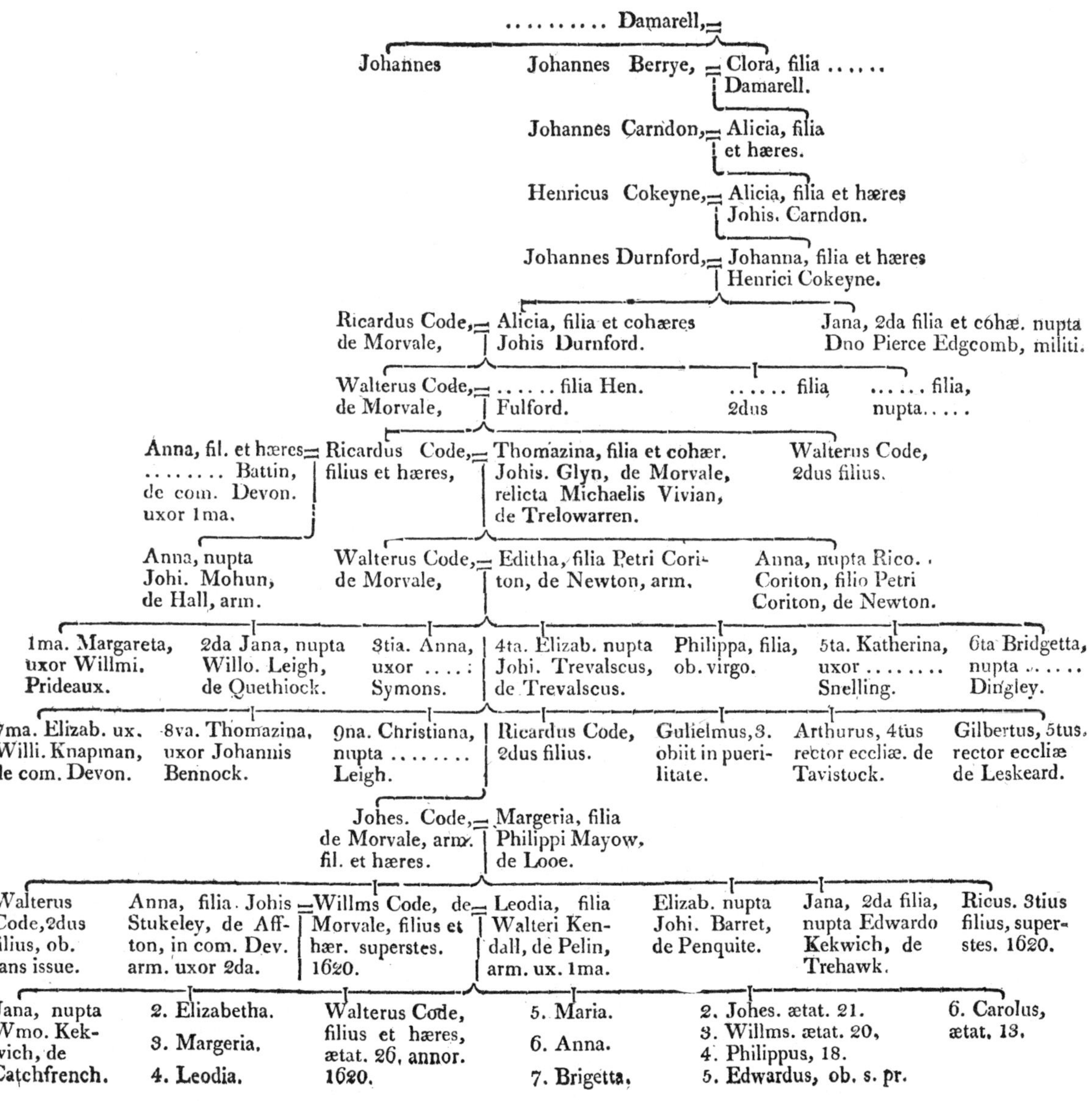

TUCKER DE IN PAROCHIA DE ✝

ARMS.—*Barry wavy, Argent and Azure, A Chev. Crenelle, Or, Embattled. Or, Charged with 5 Guttes or Drops, Sable, between 3 Sea-horses, naiant, Argent.*
His CREST.—*An Arm, couped, Gules, (on which are 3 Bars-humet, Or,) the Hand clenched, and holding a Buttle-Axe, the Handle, Or, the Point, Proper.*

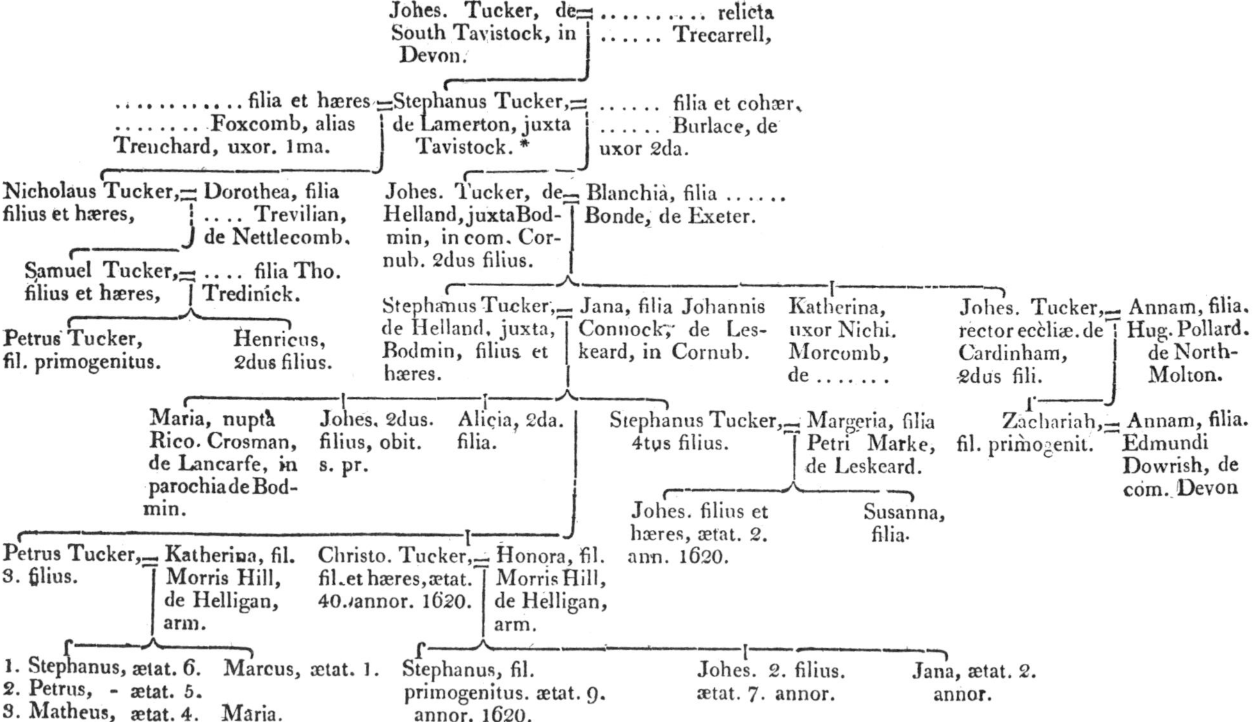

* *HENRY, REX.*

Henry, by the Grace of God, King of England and of France and Lord of Ireland, To all manner of Our Subjects, as well of the Spirituall Preheminence and Dignitie, as of the Temporall Authority. These Our Letters heiring or seeing, Greeting.—Forasmuch as we be credibly informed that our trusty Subject, Stephen Tucker, of Lamerton, in our County of Devon, Gent. for certain Diseases and Infirmities, which he hath and daily sustayneth in his head, he cannot convéniently without his great danger be discovered of the same, We let you witt, that of Our Grace especiall in tender Consideration, thereof, We have by these Presents licensed the said Stephen Tucker to use and weare his Bonnet upon his head, As well in our Presence as elsewhere att his Libertye. Wherefore We will and Command you and every of you to permit and suffer him so to doe, without any your Challenges, Lettes, or Interruptions to the coutrary, as yee and every of you tender our Pleasure.——— Given under our Signet, at our Manner of Woodstock, the 2d day of July, in the 10th year of Our Reigne.

LOWER, de St. WINNOW, &c. ‡

ARMS.—1st. *Sable, A Chev. between 3 Roses, Argent:* Lower.
2d, ...

Philippus Lower, de ......
=

Johannes Lower, filius et hæres. =

Johannes Lower, filius et hæres. =

Philippus Lower, filius et hæres. =

Richardus Lower, filius et hæres. =

Willms. Lower, filius et hæres. =

Johes. Lower, de Polscotes, in parochia de = Jana, filia 2da Willmi. Moyle, militis.

Ricardus Tresithney, = Johanna, filia et hær. Johis. Tregonnon,

NicholausLower, de Polscotes, = Amy, fil. et cohær. Rici. Tresithney, de ......

Willms. Lower, de St. Wynow. = Elianora, fil. 2da Johis. Pentire, de Pentire.

- Nicholaus Lower, de Trelaske, 2dus filius. = Jana, filia, et cohær. Tho. Upton.
  - 1. Gratia, uxor Johis. Polwheele, arm.
  - 2. Jana, uxor Johis. Lampen.
  - 3. Catherina. uxor Rogeri Tubb.
  - Thomas Lower, de Trelask, filius et hæres. = Margareta, filia Edmundi Percivall, de com. Somerset.
    - Petrus Lower, de Trelask, arm. superstes. ann. 1620. = Honora, fil. et hær. Willmi. Abbot, de Hartland, in com. Devon.
      - 1. Margareta.
      - 2. Elianora.
      - Thomas Lower, de Trelask, arm. duxit Eulaliam, fil. Arth. Tremaine, de Collacomb, arm. =
        - Thomas Lower, fil. et hær. ætat. unius, ann. 1620.
        - Maria, ætat. 3. annorum.
      - 2. Willms.
      - 3. Petrus.
      - 4. Georgius.
      - 5. Nicholaus
    - Jana, filia.
- Willms. Lower, 3. filius.
- Johes. Lower, de St. Wynow, filius et hæres. = Margareta. fil. Tho. Upton, de Trelask, et cohæres.
  - Willms. Lower, de St. Wynow, fil. et hæres. = Agneta, filia Thos. Trefry, de Fowey, arm.
    - Thomas Lower, filius et hær. superstes. 1591. = Jana, filia, et hær. Willmi Roskymer.
      - Willms. fil. et hæres.
      - 2. Johes.
      - 3. Nicholaus.
    - Walterus 5. filius.
    - Henricus Lower, 2dus fil. duxit = Elizab. relict Anton. Fox, deHighampton, Devon.
    - Edwardus Lower, 3. fil. de Tremere, in St. Tudy, superstes, 1620. = Maria, fil. Hump. Nicoll, de Penvose.
      - Katherina, uxor Francisci Courtney, de Lanivet.
      - 2. Agneta.
      - 3. Elizabet.
      - 2. Willms.
      - 3. Edwardus.
      - 4. Gracia.
      - 5. Jana.
      - 4. Nicholaus.
      - 5. Philippus.
      - Humphredus Lower, fil. et hæres. ætat. 21. annor. 1620.
    - Ferdinando Lower, de Lezant, 4tus fil. supers. 1620. = Lora, filia Willmi. Kelly, de Northlew, in Devon.
      - Jana, fil. et cohær. uxor Tho. Grosse de Leskerd.
      - Barbara. 2da fil. et cohær. nupta Nico. Ley, de Quethiock.
      - Elizab. 3. fil. et cohær. nupta Nico. Cock, de South-Petherwin.
  - Johannes 2dus fil.
- Thomas Lower, 4tus fil. duxit = Janam, fili. Johis. Trevenen, de ..
  - Johes. Lower de Polmakin, in parochia de = Margareta. filia. Jacobi Luke, et cohær. ... Beauchamp.
    - Johes. fil. et hær. ob. ante patrem.
    - Georgius Lower, 2dus. fil.
    - Jana, uxor Georgii Carminow de Fentongollan.
  - Marcus 2ds fil.

CARNSEW, de BOKELLY, in St. KEW.

ARMS.—1*st, Sab. a Goat passant, Argent, (attired & tripped, Or.)*.. CARNSEW.
2*d, Or, a Bull passant, Sable*.. TRECARNE.
3*d, Paly of Six Argent & Azure, on a Bend, Gules,* 3 *Cinque-foils, Or*.. STRADLING.
4*th, Argent, on a Fess, Sable,* 3 *Cheveronds, sideways of the First*.. TRENOWTH.
5*th, Sable, a Chev. Ermine, between* 3 *Pair of Wings, conjoined, Argent*.. NANFANT.
6*th, Argent, on a Chev. Sab.* 5 *Bezants, between* 3 *Torteauxes*.. TREJAGO.
7*th, Gules, a Lion rampant regardant, Argt. between* 9 *Acorns, Or*.. CHENDUIT.
8*th, as the* 1*st.*
CREST.—*On a Cap of Maintenance, doubled, Ermine, a Greyhound, passant regardant.*

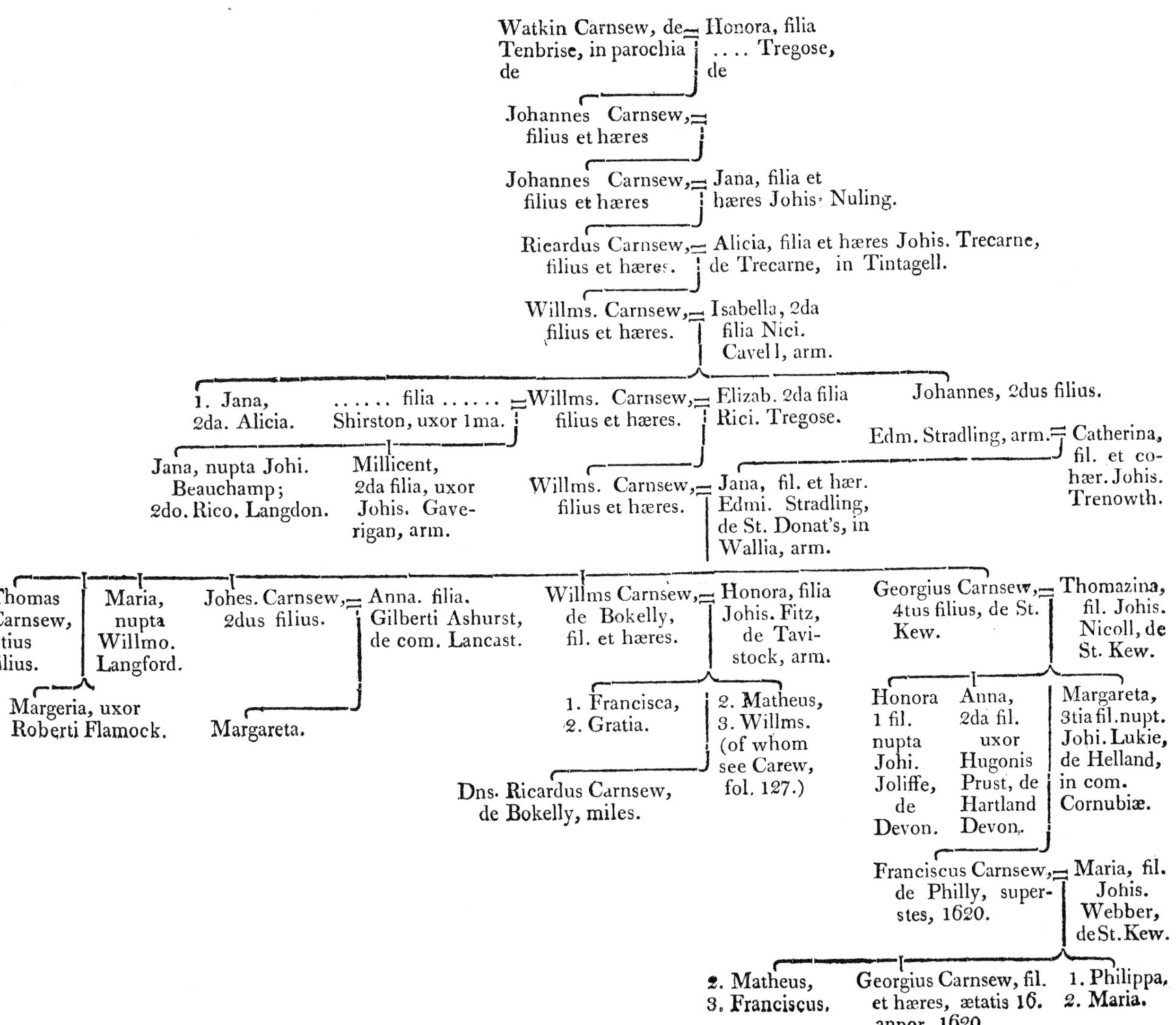

RELIGION.

BOOK III. CHAPTER III.

I have already spoken of the Bishopric of Exeter,[A] of the Archdeaconry of Cornwall, of the eight Deanries into which the Archdeaconry is divided, of our Parish Churches, and of our religious foundations. I have now to state, that the parishes in our archdeaconry are 203—of which 85 are rectories, 100 vicarages, and 18 donatives or curacies[B]—that the Archdeacon's* visitations are held every year about a month after Easter at

[A] See History of Devon, Vol. I. pp. 214—222, 283—291, 312—314, and Hist. of Cornwall, Vol. II. pp. 97—132. That our See was originally at Bodmin, (as commonly reported) I was by no means assured, and therefore stated it as a very doubtful point. But Whitaker has since proved, in "the Cathedral of Cornwall," that it was first established at St. Germans and that it continued there till Canute; when the Sees of St. Germans and Crediton were united.

[B] In Cornwall the following 25 benefices are in the Patronage of the Bishop of Exeter.

DEANRY OF EAST.	£	s.	d.
Quethiocke V. yearly tenths	£ 1	11	1
Lawhitton R.	1	18	8
Lezant R.	3	4	0
WEST. TRIGG MAJOR.			
Morwinstow V.	1	7	1
TRIGG MINOR.			
Egloshayle V.	1	12	0
St. Tethe V.	1	4	0
PYDRE.			
St: Enedor V.	1	13	4
St. Evall V.	0	13	4
St. Merin V	1	10	8
St. Newlin V.	1	13	4
St. Colan V. its certified value	40	0	0

POWDRE.	£	s.	d.
St. Allen V. its yearly tenths	0	17	4
Guerrans R.	1	11	3
St. Goran V.	2	0	0
Kenwyn and Kea V.	1	12	0
St Probus &c. &c. V.	1	7	8
Tywardraith V.	0	18	8
St Feocke V. its certified value	45	0	0
KERIER.			
St. Gluvias &c. V.	2	2	8
Milor and Mabe V. its yearly tenths	1	13	6
Manaccan V. its certified value	48	0	0
Mullion V.	34	18	11
Sithney V.	48	0	0
PENWITHE.			
Gwinear V. its yearly tenths	1	4	0
Zenor V. its certified value	35	0	0

* **Archdeacons of Cornwall See Le Neve's Fasti, &c. &c.**

A. D.

1096 Alnothus. He died Id. Jun. 1098. Martyrlog. Eccles. Exon. MSS. 12 W. 2.

A. D.
1110 Ernaldus. Reg. Exon. 10 Hen. 1.
1135 Hugh de Ang. Reg. Abbat de Tavistoc. MS. penes Duc. de Bedf. f. 81. 1. Stephen.
1143 William Reg. Exon. 8 Steph.
1150 A——— Reg. Plymton 15 Steph.
1157 Walter. He died 2 Cal. Maii. 1157 Martyr. Eccles. Exon. 4 Hen. 2.
1171 Peter. He died 7 Id. Sept. Mart. Eccles. Ex. 17 Hen. 2.
1180 G. Reg. Abb. Tavist. MS. f. 21. 26 Hen. 2
1192 Walter. He died 9. Cal. Jul. 1216. Mart. Eccl. Ex. 3 Ric. 1
1243 John. He subscribed as a witness to the deed, whereby the Vicars of Exon were erected in 1243 28 Hen. 3.
1264 Galfrydus de Bysimano. He resigned in 1264. Reg. Bronescombe.
1264 Robert de Tefford succeeded in the same year. Reg. Bronescomb.
1274 John de Esse was collated Aug. 23, 1274, and died in 1284. R. Br. 2 Edw. 1
1284 Henry de Bollegh was collated 8 Id. Jul. 1284. Reg. Quiv. 11. Edw. 1
1296 Will. de Bodringham 1296 Chron. Dunstable MS. 24 Edw. 1
1300 Adam de Carleton 1300. Reg. Abb. de Tavist. MS. f. 249. 28 Edw. 1
1327 Nicholas de Scotton. Pat. 2. p. 1. 2 Edw. 3
1346 John S. Paul 1346. Reg. Beke Epi. Lincoln. 20 Edw. 3
1349 Will. de Cusantia Feb. 15, 1349. Pat. 24, p. 1. 24 Edw. 3
1371 Thomas de Orgrave. He resigned 1376. Reg. Brentingham
1376 Robert de Bradbroyk was collated Mar. 3, 1376. resigned 1381
1381 Nicholas de Braybrook collated July 26, 1381. 50 Edw. 3
1397 Edward Dauntesey collat. July 14. Reg. Stafford. 20 Rich. 2
1411 John Oram, Reg. Staff. 11 Henr. 4
1413 John Bremer collated Apr. 3. Reg. Staff. 1 Henr. 5
1419 Will. Fylham May 29. Chancell. of the Church 1436 R. Lacy. 7 H. 5.
1436 Walter Trengoff collat. Oct. 2, R. Lacy. 13 H. 6
1444 Richard Helier Feb. 20. R. Lacy. 22 H. 6
1446 Henry Trevihen Nov. 19. 24 H. 6
1448 John Selot, Mar. 20. Reg. Lacy. 26 H. 6
1462 Thomas Mark, July 12. Reg. Nevill, p. 47. 2 Edw. 4
1499 Will. Sylke L. L. D. resigned for the Precentorship. Reg. Redmayne
1499 Thomas Harris L. L. D. Apr. 15, Precentor 1509.
1509 Barnard Oldham Dec. 16. Treasurer 1515. Reg. Oldham
1515 John Fulford Apr. 18. Reg. Oldham. 7 Hen. 8. A. D. Exon.
1515 Hugh Ashton Sept. 28. R. O. 7 Hen. 8.
1516 Richard Sampson L. L. D. Feb. 3. resigned 1528. 8 Hen. 8. Reg. Exon
1528 Rowland Lee L. L. D. Sept. 8. Bp. of Lichfield and Cov. 1534. Reg. Old. 20 H. 8.
1534 Thomas Bedall June 11 installed 26 H. 8. Reg. Oldham
1537 Thomas Winter Oct. 8.
1543 Rowland Taylor L. L. D. martyr. Burnt at Hadleigh in Suffolk. Tanner's Not.
1543 John Pollard
1554 John Rixman A. M.
1555 George Harvey March 2 resigned 1563 2 and 3 Phil. and Mary.
1563 Roger Alley Oct. 13. R. Voysey 5 Eliz.
1574 Nicholas Marston, June 10. Reg. V. 16 Eliz.
1603 Thomas Somaster died 1603. He was A. D. of Cornwall 1602. See Carew.
1603 William Hutchinson S. T. P. Sept. 5. R. Exon 1 Jac. 1.
1616 Jasper Swife S. T. P. July 20. exchanged for Totten in Nov. 14 J. 1.
1616 William Parker Nov. 27. R. Exon 14 Jac. 1.

Launceston, Leskeard, Bodmin, Truro, Helston and Penzance—and that the Deans rural† are expected to visit annually all the Churches within their deanries.

For our Religious houses, we had colleges or collegiate churches at St. Neots; at Endelion; at Crantoc; at St. Columb; at Probus; at St. Teath; at St. Piran; at Penryn; at Constantine; at St. Berian. And not long before the Reformation, a college was founded by Thomasine Bonaventure at Week St. Mary. Our principal monasteries, were the *Austin*-priories of St. Germans, Launceston, and Bodmin. The Austin monks had a cell at Lancels subject to Hertland, and a cell also at St. Anthony in Roseland subject to Plymton.—The *Benedictines* had an alien Priory at Tywardraith, to which there was a cell at St. Anthony in Menege; a Priory at Talcarne, and at St. Michael's Mount, and a cell at Lamana in Talland. The *Cluniacs* had a cell at St. Carrock in St. Veep. The *Cistercians* had a cell at St. Keverne. The *Knights-Hospitalers* had a Receptory at Trebigh, in St. Ives. The *Black Friars* had a convent in Truro. The *Grey Friars* had a convent at Bodmin.[B] There was a nunnery at Leskeard, and at Truro, (the *Poor Clare's;)* at Tresilian-bridge; at Trugan (as Hals says) perhaps Tregonian, in St. Michael-Penkevil; and at St. Michael's mount. There were hospitals at Launceston; at Newport; in Menheniot; in Bodmin those of St. Anthony and St. George; near Bodmin, that of St. Lawrence; and in Sithney a hospital under the government of a Prior, dedicated to St. John the Baptist. The suppression of alien Priories was gradual, for the most part in the reigns of Henry IV. V. VI.—It paved the way for the dissolution of religious houses in the reign of Henry VIII.[N]

1628 Martin Nansogg coll. Jan. 27, but not installed. 3 Car. 1.
1631 Rob. Peterson Jul. 23. per. mortem Parker. Reg. Ex. 6 Car. 1. Collation never took effect.
1633 Rob. Hall, treasurer Aug. 21. 8 Car. 1. Reg. Exon.
1641 George Hall, Oct. 8. per. resignationem Rob. Hall 17 Car. 1.
1660 Edward Cotton, Sept. 15 per. resign. Georgii Hall 12 Car. 2.
1672 Edward Drewe, M. A. Sept. 5. per resign. Cotton died 1714. 24 Car. 2.
1714 Lancelot Blackburne Jan. 26. 1 Geo. He held it with the Deanry and with the Bishopric of Exon.
1724 Stephen Weston Jan. 23. He held it with the Bishopric till 1732
1732 C. Fleetwood. Feb. 15.
1737 Geo. Allanson. Sept. 14.
1741 John Sleech. Aug. 26.
1788 Geo. Moore. Feb. 16.
1807 William Short.

† The office of the Dean Rural is to visit the Churches, Chapels, Parsonages and Vicarage Houses, within his Deanry; to see that the edifices be kept in decent repair, and the Churches and Chapels provided with proper furniture, utensils and ornaments, and to report to the Vicar General, or, within the Archdeaconry of Cornwall, to the Archdeacon by composition;—but the Archdeacon is finally to report to the Vicar-General. For this purpose the Clergy of each Deanry, at their annual visitations, elect one of their body (generally by rotation), who takes an oath before the Vicar-General, or one of his Surrogates, for the due execution of his office. The advantages resulting from this office are obvious—The houses of the Clergy are, in general, kept in good order, and briefs for the rebuilding or repair of Churches, so frequent in other parts of the kingdom, are here almost without an example.

[B] Carew mentions a House of Friars at Launceston.

[N] See Speed p. 1053.

CIVIL, MILITARY, AND RELIGIOUS ARCHITECTURE.

BOOK III. CHAPTER IV.

THE materials for building with which we are furnished in different parts of the county, seem to have determined not only the general appearance of our houses, but the mode of their construction.—Where stone-quarries are scarce, we have good houses of [A] mud: And where [B] slate is plentiful, we seldom see roofs of thatch.

1. In the neighbourhood of the Denyball quarry, even the meanest huts are covered with fine blue slate. And we have excellent specimens of the thatched cottage in Cornwall. But the seats of the Cornish gentry, have little to boast, in point of architecture. At the commencement of this period, we observe many grand and noble piles, which were, manifestly, derived from the opportunity of seeing, during the Crusades, the various refinements and improvements in foreign countries; when at length the idea of the castle was nearly swallowed up in that of the palace. In the time of Edw. I. *Bodrigan-Castle* is said to have been the most magnificent in the county. Till the year 1786, (when they were pulled down) stood the hall, and the kitchen, with a timber roof, and the chapel which had been converted into a barn.—In the reign of Edw. III. arose the spacious hospitable mansion, embattled only for ornament, and containing vast combinations of ill-matched rooms put together as if they had been added at various times and by chance. Of the structure at *Tehidy* in those days, there are no remaining vestiges. It appears from the family-papers that William Basset was permitted by Edward III. to *kernellate* his house at Tehidy: The present

[A] Cob-walls (if supported by a good foundation of stone-work) are very lasting, and the houses thus built are drier and warmer than others. The cob is a composition of earth and straw, wetted up somewhat like mortar, and well-beaten and trodden together: and probably, the word cob is derived from κοπτος, contusus. After a cob-wall is raised to a certain height, it is allowed time to settle; when the mason lays on another range of cob.—An old cob-wall is excellent manure.—These cob-built houses are usually covered with thatch or reed. And with this combed wheaten straw, the thatcher is enabled to finish his work much more neatly than can be done in those counties, where no reed is made, but where the straw in which the long hath scarcely been separated from the short, is fastened to the roof, rough as it comes to hand. The eves of the cottage roofs, are seldom so regularly shorn in other counties, as in Cornwall.

[B] Slating, or healing of houses with slate, seems in Cornwall and Devon a trade in itself. Before the discovery of our slate-quarries, the roofs of houses were generally covered with shingles: in the Eastern counties they are covered with tiles.

E. Harding Ex.

TRELOWARREN.

The Seat of Sir Carew Vyvyan, Bart. Engraved at the expence of Viel Vyvyan Esq.r to whom it is inscribed, by his obedient Servant R. Polwhele.

London, Pub.d by the Rev.d R. Polwhele, August 1.st 1804.

buildings (chiefly of Cornish free-stone) were begun in the year 1736 by John Pendarves Basset, and finished in 1739, in which year he died. Erected from designs by Edwards, they consist of a square and spacious dwelling house in the centre, and four detached pavilions at the angles. On the East side of Trelawny house we have some remains of the castellated mansion built by Lord Bonville in the reign of Henry VI. Travelling through Cornwall in 1478, William of Worcester speaks of *Turris Blekennock* (or Boconnoc)—and of a castle at Godolphin ["*Godollen*"] in ruins. The mansion that succeeded the castle, was called Godolgan and then Godolphin-Hall. The portico was built of white moor-stone from Tregoning, by Francis Earl of Godolphin. William of Worcester notices, also, the dilapidated castle of *Polwhele*, and the castle of of Morysk near Truro in ruins. Of the age of Henry VII. is *Cotehele*, situated on the West banks of the Tamar; an irregular stone building inclosing a small quadrangle, the entrance to which is through a square gateway tower on the south. Beyond the buildings which form the North side of the quadrangle is a large square tower. The windows to the East and South are narrow, arched at the top, and darkened with iron gratings. Those towards the quadrangle and in the North tower are wide and square. In the windows of the hall (42 feet by 22) is preserved in painted glass, the coat armour of the Edgcumbes and their alliances. About the time of Henry VIII. we may observe the regular quadrangular edifice. Of *Pengersick-Castle* all that remains, is a square embattled tower. The paintings with which an upper apartment in this tower was ornamented, I have specified elsewhere, as curious relics of the age of Henry VIII. *Rialton-House,* in St. Columb Minor, was built by Prior Vivian, who died in 1533. Its remains bear testimony to its grandeur of other days. There is a chamber still called the Prior's Chamber. A large arch which seems to have been the principal entrance, is embellished with shields and inscriptions. The old hall and chapel of *Trecarrell* in Lezant, and the old hall of *Benallack* in Constantine are still in existence. Most of the great buildings in the reign of Elizabeth, have a style peculiar to themselves both in form and finishing: the Grecian manner is adopted, though much of the old Gothic is retained. Neither of these tastes, however, predominates; while both thus indistinctly blended compose a fantastic species, hardly reducible to any class or name. One of the characteristics of this species of architecture, is the affectation of large and lofty windows; where (says Bacon) "you shall have sometimes faire houses so full of glass, that one cannot tell where to go to be out of the sun." I do not know that Cornwall was in any great degree "illuminated" by the architects of Elizabeth. To them, perhaps, is attributable *Place-House* in Fawey, the ancient seat of the Treffrys. It has still a large bow-window, richly adorned with Gothic tracery. And in its hall cieled with oak, there is the date, under a coat of arms, of 1575. The castellated feature of the building is very striking. At *Golden,* in Probus, the Tregians had planned a fabric equal to that of the Treffrys. [B] In 1592, *Padstow-Place* was built by Nicholas Prideaux, and was lately re-edified by its present worthy possessor, the Rev. Charles Prideaux Brune. In *Trelowarren* there is a venerable and (if I may so express myself) an inviting aspect, which reminds us of ancient hospitality. It has a fine Gothic air without loftiness: It has more of comfort than magnificence. Francis Vyvyan esq. father of Sir Richard Vyvyan, who was created a baronet in 1644, is said by Hals to have built this mansion. But, according to Borlase, it was not a new edifice: The greater part of the old building was preserved.

[B] "Mr. Tregyan hath a Manor Place richly begon and amply but not ended, caullid Wulvedon, alias Goldoun." Leland's Itin. III. f. 12. And see Carew f. 143.

At the Restoration, most of the seats of gentlemen in Cornwall, were either newly built or materially repaired. During the Usurpation and the persecution of their owners (almost all loyalists) they were greatly dilapidated, and almost went to ruin. This accounts for the general renovation of so many houses, on the joyful return of the owners to their estates. It was about this time (or some years before) that the Lord Robartes new-built *Lanhydroc*—a quadrangular[D] building remarkable at this day for its gallery, through the whole length of which (116 feet) the cieling and cornices are ornamented with a variety of scriptural subjects. *Stowe* in Kilkhamton was a noble edifice of this era—the seat of the Granvilles. But Stowe and the Granvilles are now no more. The residence of this illustrious house, once the pride of Cornwall, and the resort of the western gentry, hath been long laid even with the ground—" so that corn may grow and nettles spring, where Stowe once stood."* It was in the reign of Charles II. that Hugh Boscawen, Esq. built his seat at *Tregothnan*.† The present Lord Falmouth is now rebuilding Tregothnan-House, with the free stone of Newham-quarry. In its resemblance to the old castellated mansion we recognize the period of the third Edward; whose " embattled roofs" were rendered interesting by the hospitality of their possessors. The turrets of Edward are again arising: and there will be ample space for the display of the same old English spirit. *East Anthony-House* was built of Pentuan-stone, by Gibbs the architect. It was finished in 1721.‡ " Mr. Trevanion has bestowed a great deal of money in buildings at *Caerhayes*. But as no regularity is observed, it may more properly be called a pleasant romantic seat, than a complete habitation. And though it faces the south, yet it lies too much under the hill, and consequently is damp and cold in winter." So said Tonkin. And that the present John Trevanion Purnell Bettesworth Trevanion entertained the same opinion, is evident from his entensive castle-wise erections not yet completed.. *Pencarrow* is coeval with the old house at Caerhayes. [A] I might here mention *Newton*, the seat of the Corytons, and several other houses as good family mansions, equal to almost any of those already specified. *Nanswhydden*-house, of the Grecian order, was built chiefly of the schist of the neighbouring quarries. It cov-

[D] " In the year 1644, John Lord Roberts, being disgusted on some occasion or other with the Town of Truro, left the barony-house there, and new-built a large one at Lanhydroc, quadrangle ways, to which he added afterwards a noble gatehouse, and enclosed a very handsome park, well wooded and watered by the river Fawey." Tonkin's MSS.

* It is remarkable that the cedar wainscot with which the Earl of Bath fitted up the chapel in Kilkhamton was purchased by Lord Cobham, and applied to the same purpose at Stowe in Buckinghamshire.—The stone carved work which ornaments the town-hall at Southmolton, as well as Castle-hill, and many other places in the neighbourhood, are among the relics of this magnificent mansion.—The House in short was sold piecemeal: so that scarcely a vestige remains of it. A man of Stratton, indeed, lived long enough to see its site a cornfield before the building existed, and after the building was destroyed, a cornfield again.

† " It is said, that on the purchase of Fentongollan, he pulled down the noble old mansion, the lofty tower and fine chapel there, and carried the stones to Tregothnan, to build his new house. But he had built his house at Tregothnan before he laid Fentongollan in ruins." Tonkin's MSS.

‡ "At East Anthony, Sir William Carew hath lately built a stately house of Pentuan-stone, and hath adorned it with gardens corresponding with it. From the bowling-green above the house, is a beautiful prospect of the river and all the adjacent country." Tonkin's MSS.

[A] " In Pencarrow is dug a quarry of bright clear freestone that works with tool, plane, or hammer to what shape or form the mason pleaseth. It is equal to any stone in Cornwall, as may be seen by the beautiful house Sir John Molesworth is now building with it." Tonkin's MSS.

Js. Bourne del. J. Walker sc.

St. AUSTEL.

Published by R. Polwhele March 25th 1803.

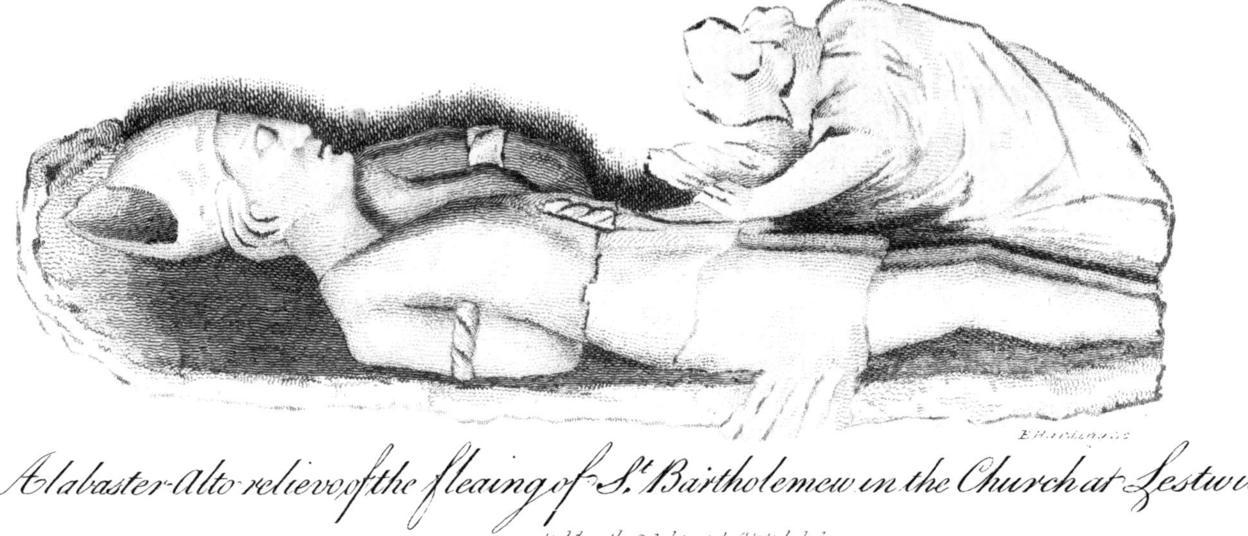

Alabaster Alto relievo, of the fleaing of St. Bartholemew in the Church at Lestwithiel

Pub.d as the Act directs by C. R. Polwhele

S. I. Neele sc. 352 Strand.

A View of the Chancel of the Parish Church of Crowan in the County of Cornwall.

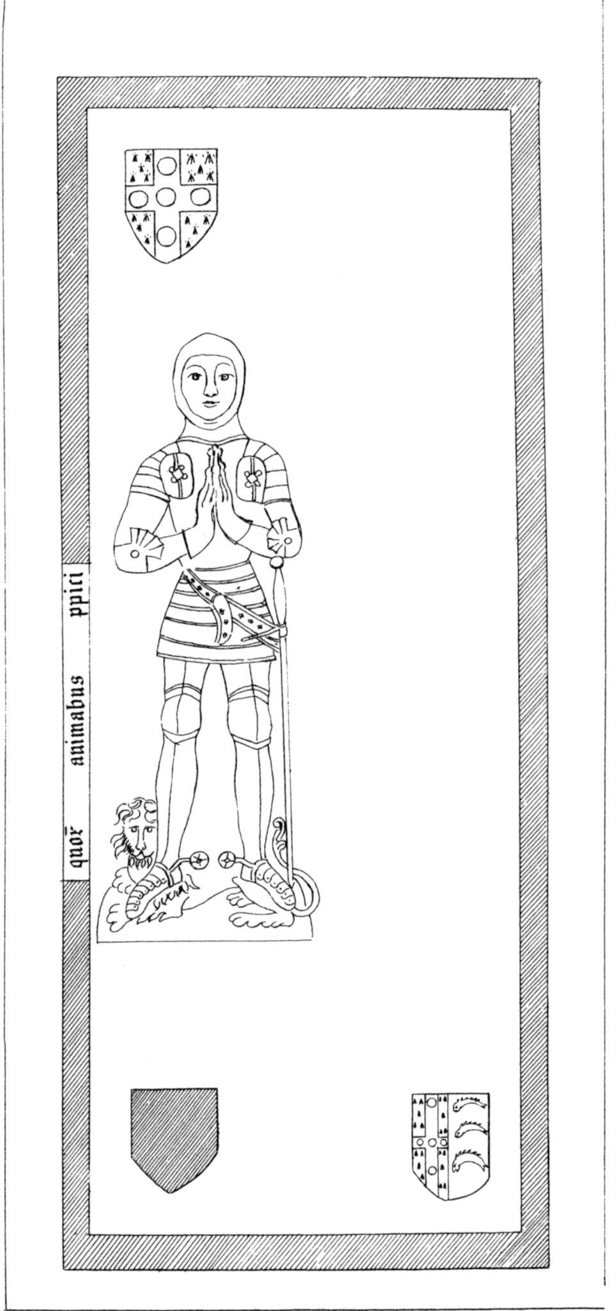

S.I.Neele sc. 352 Strand.

Geffry S^t. Aubyn, and Elizabeth his Wife, Daughter and Heiress of Pier Kymyel of Clowance; from a Monument in the Parish Church of Crowan in the County of Cornwall. Obit 1400.

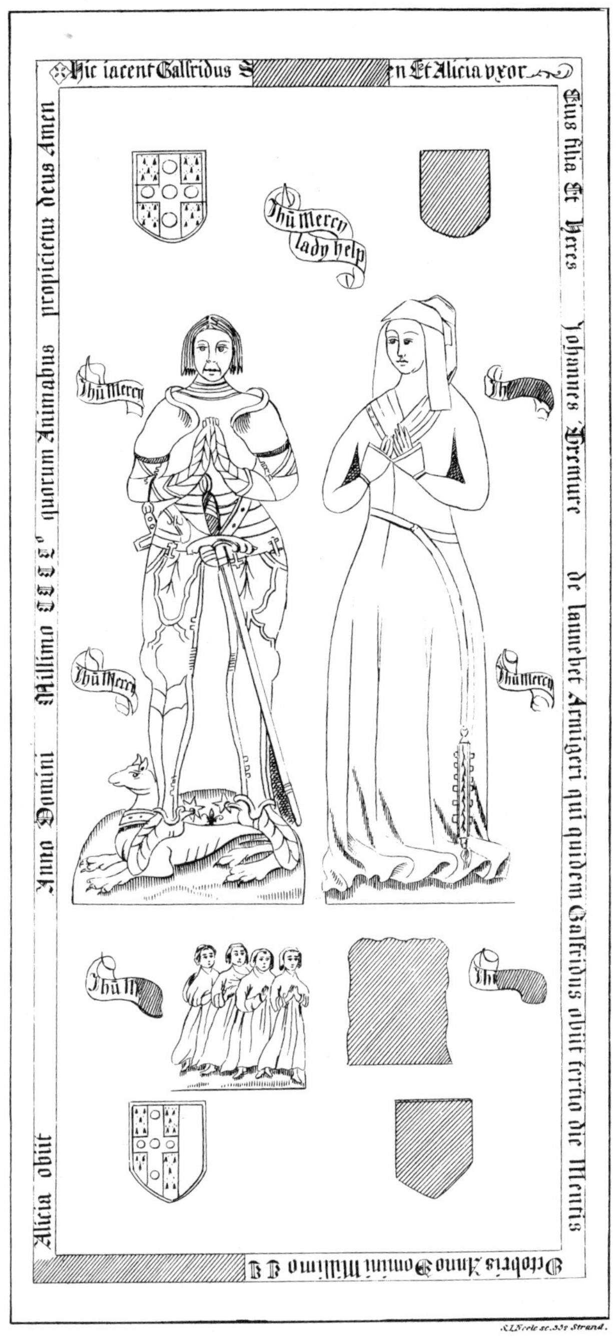

Sr. Geffry St. Aubyn of Clowance and his Wife Alice Daughter and Coheiress of John Tremere from a Monument in the Parish Church of Crowan in the County of Cornwall.

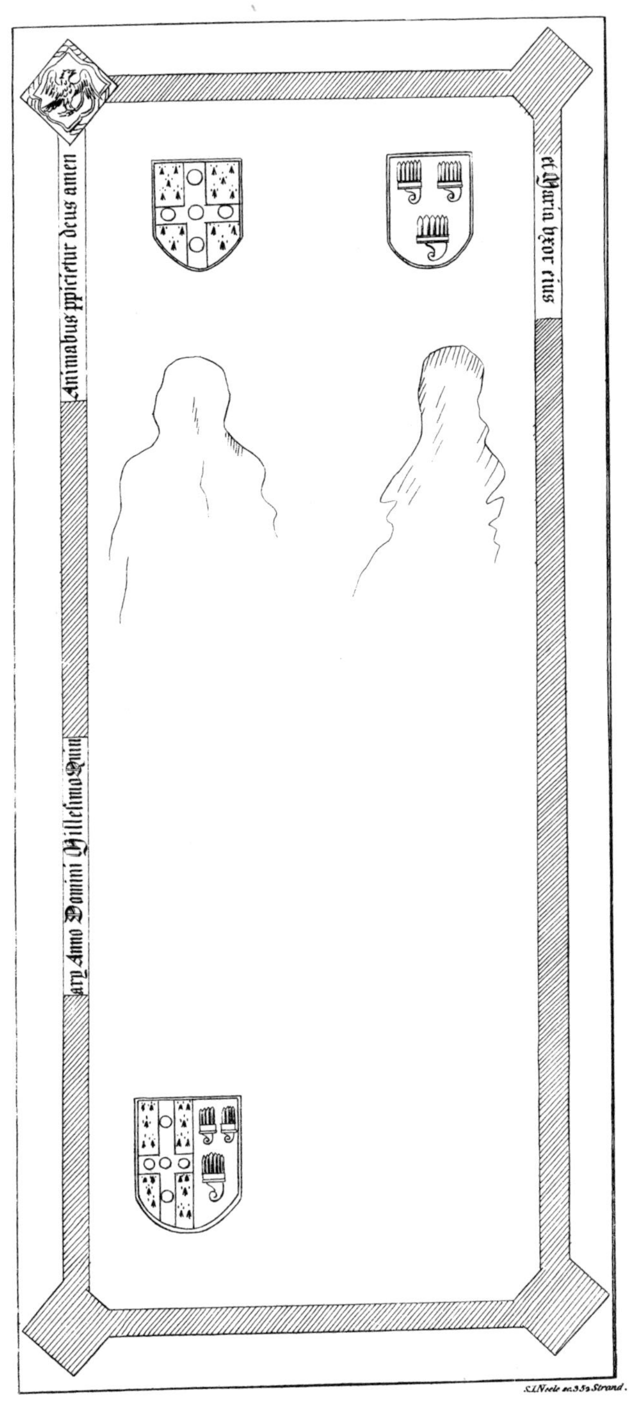

Thomas St. Aubyn of Clowance Esqr. and his Wife Mary Daughter of Sir Thomas Grenville of Stow, Knt. from a Monument in the Parish Church of Crowan in the County of Cornwall.

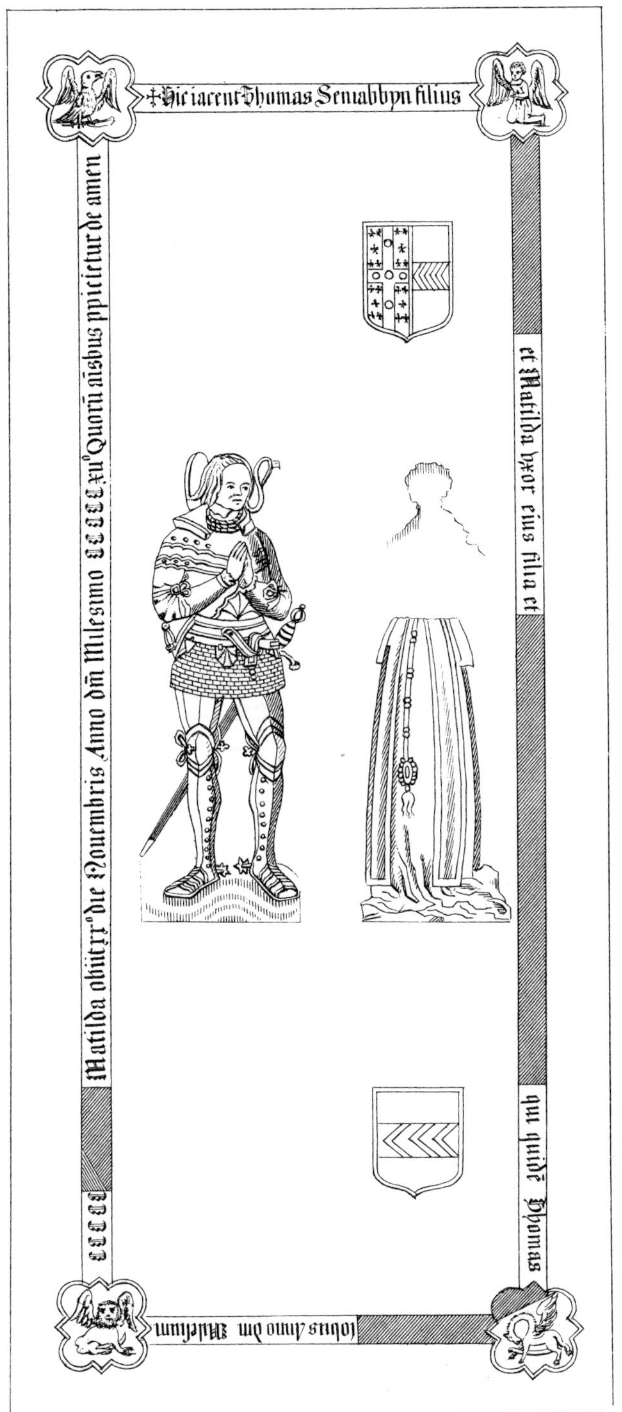

S. I. Neele sc. 352 Strand.

Thomas St. Aubyn of Clowance Esqr. and his Wife Matilda second Daughter & Coheiress of John Trenowith of Fentongolleth in Cornwall Esqr. from a Monument in the Parish Church of Crowan in the County of Cornwall:

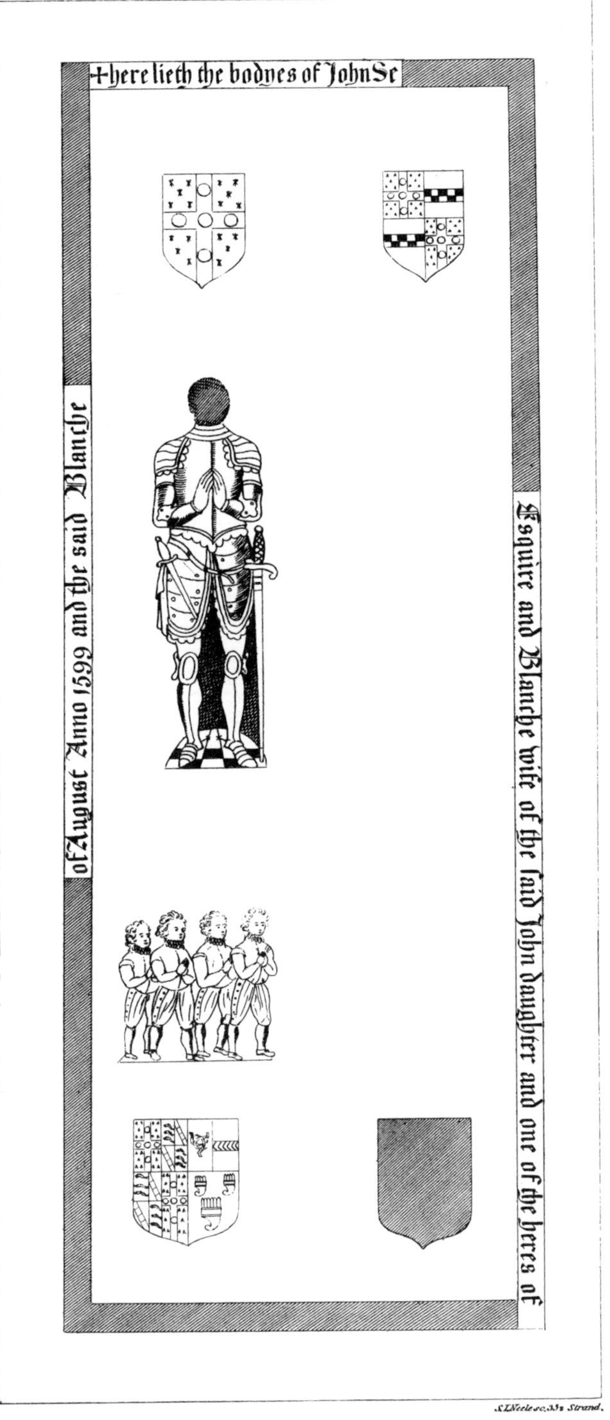

+here lieth the bodyes of John Se
Esquire and Blanche wife of the said John daughter and one of the heres of
of August Anno 1599 and the said Blanche

S.I. Neele sc. 352 Strand.

John S.Aubyn of Clowance Esq. and Blanch his Wife Daughter and Heiress of Thomas Whittington. from a Monument in the Parish Church of Crowan in the County of Cornwall.

S.I.Neele sc 352 Strand.

Thomas S^t. Aubyn of Clowance Esqr. and His Wife Zenobia Daughter of John Mallet of Wooley in Devonshire Esqr. from a Monument in the Parish Church of Crowan in the County of Cornwall.

In memory of
mas Seynta
Esq who dyed th
13 day of S
Anō
S. I. Neele sc. 352 Strand.

Thomas S^t. Aubyn, 2^d Son of John S^t. Aubyn of Clowance Esqre.
a Colonel for the King in the Civil Wars. from a Monument
in the Parish Church of Crowan in the County of Cornwall.

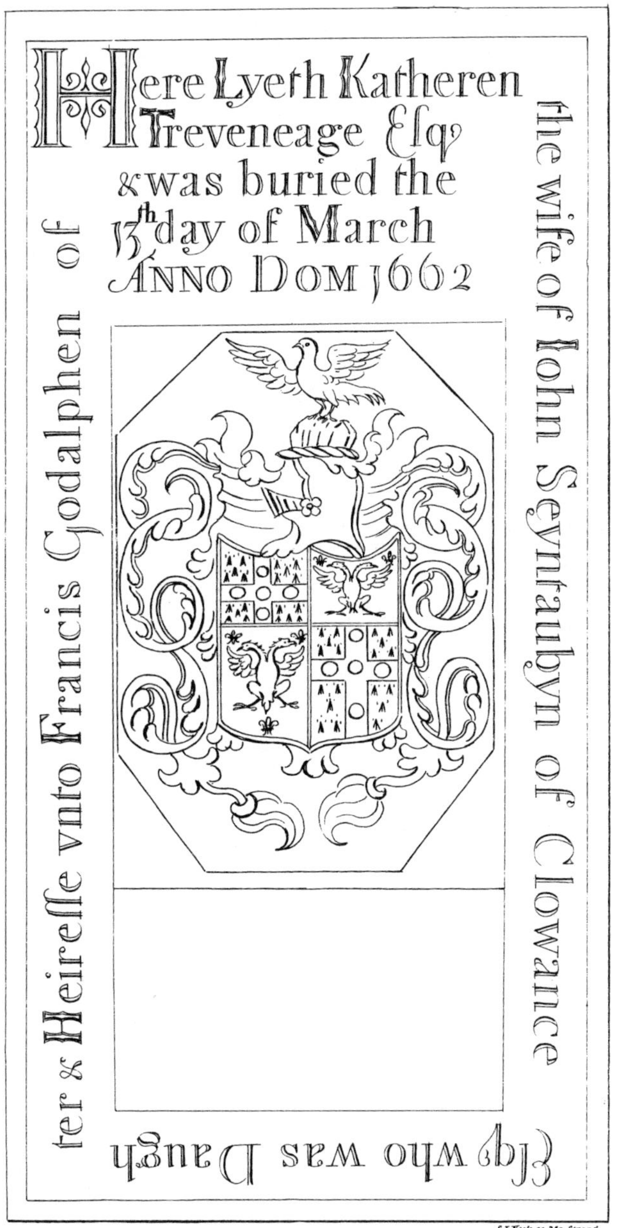

Here Lyeth Katheren
Treveneage Esq
& was buried the
13th day of March
Anno Dom 1662
the wife of John Seyntaubyn of Clowance
Esq who was Daugh
ter & Heiresse vnto Francis Godalphen of
S.I. Neele sc. 352 Strand.

*John St. Aubyn of Clowance and of St. Michael's Mount Esqr.
and Catharine his Wife. Daughter & Heiress of Francis Godolphin
of Trevenege in the County of Cornwall. from a Monument in
the Parish Church of Crowan in the County of Cornwall.*

John St. Aubyn of Clowance Esqr. & Catharine his Wife, Daughter of Sir John Arundel of Trerice, in the County of Cornwall Kt. from a Monument in the Parish Church of Crowan, in the County of Cornwall.

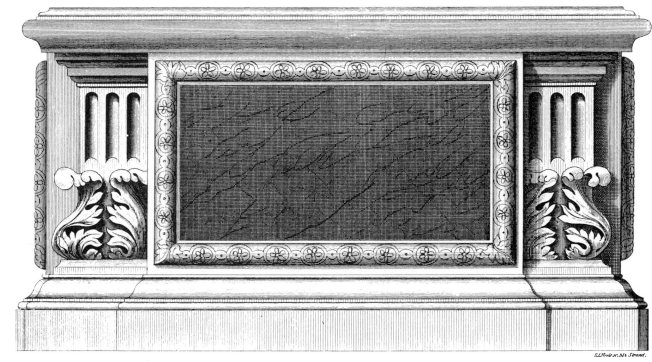

S. I. Neele sc. 352 Strand.

Sir John St. Aubyn of Clowance and of St. Michaels Mount Bart.
from a Monument in the Parish Church of Crowan in the County
of Cornwall. The First Baronet.

Here lyeth the Body of
S^R JOHN S^T AUBYN
of Clowance in the
County of Cornwall Bar^t
who departed this Life
the 20th day of June
Anno Dni 1714 in y^e 45th
year of his Age
S.I. Neele sc. 352 Strand.

Sir John St: Aubyn of Clowance and of St. Michaels Mount Bar^t from a Monument in the Parish Church of Crowan in the County of Cornwall.

— *The First Baronet.* —

PRO PATRIA
SEMPER
To the memory of SIR JOHN S^T AUBYN Baronet, who
by his descent from a long line of worthy Ancestors, and
a Father eminently distinguished by honest Zeal and pru
dent moderation was recommended to the important
trust of representing in Parliament the County of Cornwall,
and justified the Confidence of his Electors by unshaken
constancy of principle, uniting with the dignity of his
public Character the domestic virtues of tenderness
and friendship, this Monument was erected by his
disconsolate Widow.
He was born the 12th of Nov.r 1726. He died the 12th of Oct.r 1772.
S.I.Neele sc 352 Strand.

Sir John St. Aubyn of Clowance and of St. Michaels Mount Bar.t from a Monument in the Parish Church of Crowan in the County of Cornwall.

The 4th Baronet.

ered a large extent of ground, and rose to a great elevation. Approached by flights of steps, it stood proudly supported by Ionic pillars. There was the same order of architecture within, in the staircase, the marble chimney piece of the library &c. This stately mansion was built by Mr. Hoblyn, at the expence of more than £25,000. Nineteen years in building, it was consumed by fire in a few hours. || *Carclew* is a neat building of the Ionic order, faced with granite: It has a regular portico. I must not conclude this cursory survey of our Cornsh gentry, "seated amidst rural repose" without noticing *Glynn*, and *Trelissick*; the latter, so finely harmonizing in architectural elegance, with the picturesque beauties of the place. The word itself *Tre-lis-ick* is descriptive of the natural situation.

2. Of our ancient church-architecture I can give few examples, to raise in the minds of my readers ideas of the sublime or the graceful. I shall class a few of our sacred edifices (the ages of which have not been ascertained) under different centuries, as their architecture may seem to correspond with the modes of building that prevailed at different periods. But nothing can be more fallacious than such conjectural dates, where time has silenced the voice of tradition. The south aisle of *St. Germans* church, (rebuilt in 1261) and the nave of *St. Anthony* church (in Meneg) which has pointed arches with foliated capitals, may be mentioned among the instances of early Gothic architecture. The church of *Kilkhamton* is said to have been built by an ancient baron of the Granvilles. It consists of three aisles, divided by slender pillars supporting obtuse Gothic arches, and was probably reedified in after days.—Dr. Borlase in a letter to Dean Lyttelton calls it "a light, airy, modern church." [aaa] The church at *Fawey* was built and endowed about the year 1350. [A] The windows of *Sheviock* church, and the east window of the church of *St. Ive*, point to the fourteenth century. The church of *St. Austell* [o] (with its singular tower) and the beautiful Gothic spire of Lestwithiel (which might have done honour to Truro) may be referred to nearly the same period.† Of the St. Aubyn monuments in *Crowan* church, here presented to observation, the most ancient bears the date of 1400. *Launceston* church (nearly in the centre of the town) originally a chauntry-chapel, was in the reign of Henry IV. re-edified. It is built with square blocks of granite, and every stone is enriched with carved ornaments. *Kellington* church, spacious and lofty, was almost wholly re-built about the middle of the fifteenth century by Nicholas de Asheton. The spacious church of *St. Cleer* consists of a nave, and two aisles. Each aisle is separated from the nave by four very large pointed arches supported by pillars with highly ornamented capitals, and from the chancel by a pointed arch, lower than the others. The tower is 97 feet high, with large and lofty pinnacles. The church of *Bodmin* (or the greater part of it) was erected in 1475. *St. Agnes* church, as built in 1484, consisted of three roofs, a small tower and spire.§

|| See Vol. V. of this work, p. 94.

[aaa] MS. in my possession.

[A] By Treffry.

[o] In the vicinity of St. Austell, most of the churches and towers were built of the Pentuan freestone.

† See the flaying of St. Bartholomew to whom Lestwithiel church is dedicated.

§ It was then large enough for the inhabitants; but at present far from it. In 1712 it was intended to enlarge this church (as also that of Redruth.) But nothing was done, except a small aisle, built by Mr. Tonkin for the use of himself and family. Tonkin s MSS.

Cornwall was much indebted to the munificence of Henry VII. for its churches, a large part of which seem to have been rebuilt in the fifteenth and sixteenth centuries. *St. Kew*, *St. Berian*,* and *Padstow*, are said to belong to the fifteenth century; and the churches of *Camborne*, *St. Just* in Penwith, and *St. Neot's*‡ to the sixteenth. There is an elegant lightness in the architecture of *Truro* church, and a profusion of decoration, the character of the later Gothic. The time when this church was erected, is ascertained by the date of 1518, in one of the windows of painted glass on the south-side. Its modern spire,[o] of plain moorstone, is ill suited to its fine old vestibule, or any other part of this venerable edifice. It should be viewed at a distance only, as a picturesque object. The tower of Probus church was "builded (says Carew) within compasse of our remembrance, by the well-disposed inhabitants."‖ Its height to the battlements is 108 feet. At each angle is a double buttress, which lessens in ascending, and terminates in a foliated pinnacle. The top of the tower is ornamented with 40 pinnacles, disposed in eight clusters. The plinth cornices and upper story are richly embellished with foliage, fleur de lis, &c. &c. St. Budeaux church was built in 1566. The earliest date on the monument of Grylls, in the church of *Lanreath*, is 1607. The new church at *St. Piran*, built under the inspection of John Thomas, Esq. of Chiverton, does credit both to his taste and his liberality. The cold and comfortless aspect, however, of the new church at *Kea*, (better according with its interior nakedness, than the font of old St. Kaius, there preserved) reflects, perhaps, no great honour on the architect; though the painting over the altar is certainly correct in design and beautiful in execution. Not that it will atone for plain round windows, and a room without pillars. But the days of "superstition" are passed away, and the temples of God, whether churches or conventicles, are reduced upon the same footing—large rooms, equally accommodated to the purpose of public worship, or of public business—now re-echoing to the preacher, and now to the debating society. At *Trevenson* near Pool in Illogan, was lately built an elegant chapel, at the expence of Lord De Dunstanville.

Of our monastic buildings, we have few traces, except at *St. German's*, *Lanivet*,[A] and *St. Michael's*

* St. Berian church, of granite, consists of three aisles, which are divided from the east end by a roodloft: this roodloft of oak has a profusion of gilding and carvings of huntsmen, hounds &c. &c. The S. porch is ornamented with embrazures and pinnacles.

‡ See Forster's St. Neot pp. 6—26, and Whitaker's Arianism p. 330.

[o] In 1776 July 9, was laid the last stone in Truro spire by John Bland, the architect. The height under ground 9 feet, thence to the battlements, 70—thence to the top, 50—in all 129 feet.

‖ There is a tradition, that a Mr. Andrew, an ancestor of the late Rev. Dr. Andrew, was the architect.

[A] Near the church of Lanivet are the remains of an ancient house and a tower which were formerly inhabited by nuns; and still the name of St. Bennet remains, to whom this religious house was said to have been dedicated. It is romantically situated; is well wooded and watered, and exceedingly retired. Some painted glass, being the armorial bearings of the founders, is still remaining, among which I think I can trace those of the family of Chiverton, who formerly resided at a place of that name in Piran-zabulo which is now the seat of John Thomas esq. Vice-Warden of the stannaries of Cornwall. There is a good well in the area between the house and the tower: and a pure stream of water issues out from the base of the tower, where the steps for ascending it are placed. The entrance into the tower, from the west, is through a large Gothic arch way, and a similar one is on the east side, and immediately over the latter are evident traces of the roof that connected the tower with the chapel, which composed the northern side of the quadrangle. The apartments of the Lady Abbess are still very evident, being of a more ornamented architecture than the rest. The proprietor of the house and tower is said to be a Mr. Grose, who as he has been told that the stone of which the tower is built is worth £200, intends to pull it down under the pretence that it is about to fall. A great part of the buildings have been destroyed in the memory of persons now living, for the purpose of building Mr. Grose's dwelling-house at some distance.

Mount. The garden of W. R. Gilbert, Esq. occupies the site of the Priory-Church at Bodmin.[B]

3. Of the towns in Cornwall an architect would say little; though an antiquary might, with Mr. Whitaker, describe "the glory" of Tregoney from the days of the Romans to the reign of King John; and thence pass to *Truro* rising upon Tregoney; and thence to *Falmouth*—we cannot add—eclipsing Truro.[CD] In Truro, Sir William Lemon's house, built by his grandfather, and Mr. Daniell's, built of Bath stone (a present from Allen of Prior-park) are the only private houses which a traveller would stop to notice with a moment's observation; though this town may be mentioned for the variety of its structures, from the old manerial residence of the Robartes family (now defaced in its front,) and the Red Lion Inn (built by the first of the Truro Footes, though not the birth-place of our comedian) to the new buildings in Lemon-street, or Richards'-row, or Bennallack-place.—The town of *Padstow*, consisting of schist and slate, was anciently (as we have seen) a place of distinction. It sunk, after a few centuries, to decay. And many have been its elevations and depressions from Edward I. to this moment. Within the last forty years, it has greatly increased in buildings and inhabitants, and is now flourishing as a mercantile town chiefly through the influence of Thomas Rawlings esq. His newly-erected house, substantial in its materials, and compact in its construction, seems to promise durability to the town which it adorns.

But, whilst we thus flatter ourselves with ideas of permanence, we must not forget *Nanswhyden*—we must remember *Stowe*. The superb edifices which have perished—the splendid families which have been extinguished, call forth the most affecting sentiments of melancholy. And we contemplate with a sigh, and "not without a fear" the fleetingness of mortal prosperity—the awful uncertainty of human grandeur. Under such dispensations of mysterious wisdom, we learn important lessons: They humble our pride, and instruct our reason.

[B] There is a tradition that on the dissolution, when the monks still lingering at the monastery, persevered in the exhibition of their mummeries, the people of Bodmin exasperated against them set fire to the building: And some relics, now in Mr. Gilbert's possession, have evident marks of fire.

[CD] See Whitaker's Tonkin's MSS. Vol. IV. pp. 217, 218, 219.

AIR, WATERS, AGRICULTURE.

BOOK III. CHAPTER V.

In the fifth chapter of the former periods I considered Cornwall, first as presented in its *natural* state, and secondly as subjected to human cultivation.

And here, the air and climate, and the soil, our waters, birds, fish and quadrupeds, *first* occur to observation; and *secondly* our pasturage and agriculture, as the county is divided into unenclosed and enclosed ground, and the enclosed ground is seen in the farm, the plantation, the garden, and the picturesque union of the whole.

I. 1. As Cornwall approaches so near to an island, it must be subject to all the disadvantages as well as benefits of an insular situation; for the area of water being superior to that of the land, the air is not only moister than over great tracts of land, but the weather in general more subject to rain. Accordingly a dry summer is a rare thing; and when other parts of England suffer by drought, Cornwall has seldom reason to complain. Our rains, however, are rather frequent than excessive; and it has been generallyobserved, that there is seldom a day so thoroughly wet, but there is some intermission; which may be owing to the hilly, narrow, ridge-like form of the county, over which the winds make a quick and short passage, and leave not the clouds to hang in one place, as they do where the ground is more level and champaign. The most prevalent winds are those which blow from the intermediate points of west and south: These winds advancing to the land, over so large a plain of water as the Atlantic ocean, not only bring rain, but frequently very hard gales. Hence the air of Cornwall must necessarily partake of the salts of the sea in a great degree, so as that it corrodes iron very shortly, in situations on the coast. This saltness of the air is also very unfavourable to shrubs and trees; and near the shores, especially in a western aspect, a tree or plantation is permitted to rise very little above its shelter; for after a storm from these quarters we usually find the young shoots of plants shrivelled, and to the taste of a pungent saltness. Under shelter, and at a few miles distant from the sea, trees suffer less; and those of a more robust nature such as the sycamore, ash, spanish chesnut, and beech attain to a respectable growth.

To the prevalence of the sea air, and in some degree to our more southern latitude may be attributed the general mildness of our winters. The snow seldom lies more than three or four days, and we are scarcely ever visited by those excessive hail storms, which sometimes desolate more inland districts. As our winters are usually mild, our spring for the same reason shews itself early in buds and blossoms. [A] We have a languid kind of spring indeed throughout the winter. In the midland counties, however, the repose of four or five winter months imparts to vegetation a vigorous spring unknown to our equable seasons. Again our summers are not so hot, (though we lie so far to the south) as in the more inland counties, the sea air equally assuaging the heats of summer, and moderating the winter colds. From the intense heat of the sun, the harvests [B] are earlier to the eastward. Our climate is undoubtedly healthy. We suffer not from sluggish exhalations, such as infest low, flat, and marsh countries. The prevalence of the winds seldom permits any mist to rest long, but promotes a constant current and circulation of air. Nor does the saltness of the atmosphere impair health; for as many instances of long life are to be found in this county especially on the high promontory lands, as in any part of England, perhaps owing to our more constant and equable state of the weather with respect to heat and cold.[C]

2. The vegetable soils of Cornwall may be distinguished into three sorts, the black and gravelly, called by the Cornish *growan*, the shelfy slatty earth, and the stiff reddish loam. The black soil prevails in the more inland and mountainous parts of the county. It runs in a line nearly east and west through the more northern parts of the parishes of St. Cleer, St. Neot's, Lanlivery, Roche, and St. Stephens, principally on the tops and sides of the hills. It is a lax, cold soil, and on the higher grounds so destitute of vegetative powers, that its produce is little more than dwarf heath and starved moss. In crofts, further down from the hills, it serves as wintering for black cattle, where they pick up a scanty livelihood among the sedge-grass, and other marsh plants. The second soil is the shelf, the superficies of which is a fine vegetable mould, and the substratum a soft slatty rock. This is better calculated than the former both for wheat and grass, but it is so porous that in the opinion of some farmers, it looks for rain every third or fourth day, and is seldom disappointed, and as seldom overdrenched, its shelfy bottom easily disposing of any moisture. It prevails on the uplands throughout the hundreds of West and Powder. The stiff red loam is the next general soil. It is most common on level grounds; and being of a closer texture, is more retentive of the vegetative qualities, and consequently more productive than either of the former. These three sorts of soil are not always equally and specifically distinct from each other, but in different places are so mixed, that the black partakes more or less of the loam, and the loam of the black, and the shelf of either or both: Neither are they found always in separate peculiar tracts, but oftentimes so intermixed that the same tenement exhibits different strata of these soils. This is observable in several instances in the parish of Probus, where in general the southern lands are upon a yellowish shelf, and the north upon a dunstone. The parish of Cuby

[A] Memorandum on an old account book of Thomas Glynn, esq. late of Helston. "27 March 1750. I had a gooseberry pye; the gooseberries were gathered yesterday by Jane Blewett, who now lives with me as a servant, and was eat by Dr. Peters and my own family: the goosberries were as big as white kidney beans."

[B] Harvest is much later than formerly, in Cornwall and Devon. A gentleman of the South Hams writes thus: "my father has been told by an old man of the neighbourhood, of strict probity, that when he was a boy, he reported, upon his return from Kingsbridge fair, as a surprizing circumstance, that he had seen a standing field of wheat: now this fair always was, and now is held on the 20th of July."

[C] With respect to the irregularities of the air, "though it be commonly said Winter's thunder is summer's wonder, Yet I can with truth affirm (says Tonkin) that there has not been one winter for the last thirty-five years, without frequent thunder in this county, both before and after christmas. And this November, Sunday 29, 1735, Mr William Trevithick, of Trevisa in St. Enoder, had two oxen and a cow killed with lightning." Tonkin's MSS.

consists, one half of shelf, and the other half of a stiff loamy clay intermixed with spar, with a substratum of slatty stone. The parish of St. Ewe exhibits a variety of these soils.[AB]

Cornwall abounds in clays, the low and level lands of almost every estate producing some kind or other of them: But they do not effervesce with acids. At Liscus in Kenwyn, there is a yellow micaceous clay with which the lighter lands are successfully manured for wheat. A few other instances of the use of this fertilizing substance occur in the district. But the only real marle is in the parish of Veryan. This is a rich slatty marle, the immediate superstratum of a limerock discovered not many years ago. It effervesces strongly with acids, and 100 parts contain 42 of lime and 58 a mixture of silex, clay, and iron. It dissolves readily on exposure, but when thrown into the fire makes no crackling noise. In the parish of St. Stephens Brannel there is a saponaceous white clay on the tenement of Carloggass; that ingredient in the porcelain manufactory, several hundred tons of which are sent coastways every year into Staffordshire.

Cornwall produces likewise a variety of ochrous earths, which are found to mix well with oils. A vein of pale yellow ochre was not long since discovered in the cliffs near the Deadman point in Gorran, which appears to be a valuable earth for painting in oil, as well as water colours.

The sands of this county are perhaps more various and plentiful than in any other district of Great Britain. Every little cove or bay produces specimens correspondent in a great measure to the adjacent cliffs. In some situations these sands are more favourable than others to the interests of agriculture in proportion to their mixture with salts, lime, shells, and coral. The lands on the river of Looe experience this variety; and the shelly sand procured from the neighbourhood of Looe island is more valuable than the slatty sand collected at Looe bar. In Carreg road in the harbour of Falmouth a coral sand is procured by dredging, to which the lands on each side of this fine navigable river are greatly indebted. All those sands effervesce in the marine acid, and crackle much in the fire.

3. Few countries are in general so well supplied with water as Cornwall, and few where its value is more appreciated. The mining interest can assert this. But agriculture reaps little or no advantage from its application, except we take into the account the services derived from our maritime situation and the several navigable rivers of this county. The naturalist may be amused with the variety of our mineral and chalybeate waters. But of irrigation few instances occur: and these for want of accurate attention are imperfectly conducted. Some meadow lands belonging to Mr. Puckey of Liskeard have, however, been greatly improved by this commendable practice: and the Rev. Mr. Jope of St. Cleer has experienced the very good effects of it. A well managed meadow on a farm of the Rev. Robert Walker, in St. Winnow, exhibited a pleasing specimen of the great advantages derivable from the judicious application of a rich water proceeding from his farm yard. So frequent are our rills, that these advantages may be obtained in a greater or less degree upon al-

[AB] Where an attentive husbandman may easily distinguish them, and appropriate to each its proper culture. To the black and slatty soils, stiff, earthy, and calcarious manure, such as may warm, strengthen, and consolidate them. In the parish of St. Stephens, in a lane leading from Brannel to the church town, there is a greasy dun-coloured loam, well calculated for the high growan lands on the northern part of this parish. The discreet and industrious farmer will equally appropriate to the red and loamy soil, that species of earth, or quality of manure that may loosen, quicken, and open it. The management of these soils must be different, and the product and fertility will be in proportion to the remedy applied to their natural defects: Where the loose soils are strengthened and consolidated, the necessary moisture will be retained; and the fertility of the stronger and more compact loams will be furthered by a mixture of opening and loosening manures.

most every large farm. Some lands appear to be pecularly favourable to this practice. The grounds both above and below Lestwithiel court the experiment, and some rich low land in the neighbourhood of Leskeard. But the most extensive practice of this kind is observable at Glynn.

4. Of the indigenous plants peculiar to Cornwall, are the *ligusticum cornubiense*, the *erica vagans*, and the *illecebrum verticillatum*. Though no where else occuring in England, the ligusticum cornubiense is found at Mount Athos. The *sibthorpea europea*, which this island produces no where but in Cornwall and Devon, is a native of Thessaly and of Crete. And it is remarkable, that the *panicum dactylon* (of the sands between Penzance and Marazion), is to be seen in Greece; and the *corrigiola littoralis* (on the banks of Lopool) on the Bosphorus. The *herniaria glabra* growing plentifully on hedges at the Lizard, is almost peculiar to Cornwall; as it is found only here and in the vicinity of Newmarket.[D] The tamarisk (through adopted by Withering as such) can scarcely be

[D] The habitats of these and others are as follows. Class 1. (Order monogynia) Hippuris vulgaris; Marazion-marsh. 2, (monogynia) Veronica spicata; near Penzance. Veronica Chamœdrys; near Penzance. Pinguicola villosa; marshes, frequent. Utricularia minor; Tretheage-marsh between Helston and Truro, Marazion bog. 3, (monogynia) Valeriana rubra; old walls, &c. Cornwall and Devon. Iris pseudacorus; near Penzance. Schoenus mariscus; near Penzance. Schoenus albus; frequent. 3, (digynia) Panicum dactylon; sands between Marazion and Penzance. Avena nuda, "prope Belerium copiose seritur." Hudson. Arundo arenaria. 4, (monogynia) Exacum filiforme; below St. Blazey-bridge and near St. Ives. 5, (monogynia) Myosotis scorpioides; near Penzance. Anchusa sempervirens; near Leskeard. Lycopsis arvensis; near Penzance. Primula vulgaris, liver-coloured variety; near Poltair. Primula veris; near Cotehele, and near Hayl, plentifully. Campanula hederacia; in Cornwall and Devon, frequent, Illecebrum verticillatum; between Senan and the Land's end. 5, (digynia) Gentiana campestris; Piran round. Chenopodium bonus Henricus; Polwhele. Salsola fruticosa, Devon and Cornwall, frequent. Herniaria glabra; at the Lizard-point. Ulmus campestris. Eryngium campense; near the ferry from Plymouth into Cornwall, and near Penzance. Ligusticum cornnbiense: from the time of Ray, this plant seems to have eluded the researches of botanists; and for a long time only one specimen was known to exist. But Mr. Pennington at length discovered it near Bodmin, very plentiful in a field which had then been ploughed after having lain fallow from time immemorial. See Withering's Arrangement, 3rd edit. vol. ii. p. 297. 5, (trigynia) Corrigiola littoralis; west bank of Loe pool near the bar of sand. 6, (pentagynia) Linum angustifolium; in Cornwall and Devon, frequent. 6, (monogynia) Allium ampeloprasum; Goonhilly downs. Hyacinthus nonscriptus; near Penzance. Scilla verna; near St. Ives, plentifully. Scilla autumnalis; at the Lizard-point, plentifully. Asparagus officinalis; on a peninsula at Kynan's cove. 8, (monogynia) Erica vagans, Goonhilly downs, fir plantation opposite Penrose, &c. 8, (tetragynia) Adoxa moschatellina; banks of a rivulet near Castle-horneck. 10, (trigynia) Silene anglica, Stellaria Holostea; near Penzance. Arenaria verna; on the side of the path leading down to the soap-rock, and near Penrose. 10, (pentagynia) Cotyledon umbilicus: near Penzance. Sedum acre; near Penzance. Sedum anglicum; frequent in Devon and Cornwall. Sperguta laricina; in Cornwall and Devon, frequent. 11, (trigynia) Euphorbia peplis: some years since between Penzance and Market-jew. Euphorbia Portlandica; common on the shores of Cornwall. Euphorbia paralias; between Penzance and Market-jew. 12, (trigynia) Sorbus aucuparia. Sorbus domestica; mountainous parts of Cornwall. 13, (mongynia) Papaver cambricum; in St. Anthony (Meneg) under the cliff near the church. It grows all round the kelpkiln, as if the kelp were favourable to its growth. Papaver maritimum; hedge between Hayl and Camborne. Nymphæa alba; Marazion-marsh. It extends itself by long runners, which form a root at the end, and send up leaf-stalks in deep water. The root is bulbous: It is one of the most beautiful of the English plants, and may be propagated by transplanting the bulbous roots in winter. 13, (trigynia) Aquilegia vulgaris; near Bodmin, Goldsithney, Falmouth, banks near the Loe, and hedge near St. Erth. 14, (Angiospermia) Bartsia viscosa; marshes of Cornwall and Devon. Antirrhinum cymbalaria; near Penzance. Antirrhinum monspessulanum; hedges near Penryn. Schrophularia scorodonia; sea-shore near St. Ives. Digitalis purpurea. Sibthorpia europea; banks of rivulets and borders of wells, frequent. 15, (Siliculosa) Lepidium ruderale; near Truro. Lepidium anglicum; near Truro and Penryn. Cochlearia officinalis; frequent in Cornwall. (Siliquosa) Brassica oleracea; near Penzance, &c. 16, (Decandria) Geraniun columbinum; fields near Penzance. Geranium sanguineum; at Kynans cove. (Polyandria) Lavatera arborea; in Cornwall and Devon, frequent. 17, (Decandria) Genista pilosa; sides of the path leading down to the soap-rock. Ulex nanus. Anthyllis vulneraria; Penzance. Trifolium ornithopodioides; near Penzance and Marazion. 18, (Polyandria) Hypericum androsæmum; in our woods and hedges. 19, (Polygamia æqualis) Tragopodon porrifolium; many places in Cornwall. Santolina maritima; between Penzance and Marazion. (Polygamia superflua) Gnaphalium dioicum; on Newmarket heath and in Wales and Cornwall. Tussilago petasites; Veryan Churchyard, &c. &c. Inula Heleneum; near St. Ives. (Monogamia) Viola lactea; heaths between Leskeard and Lestwithiel. 20, (Diandria) Orchis pyramidalis. Orchis mascula. 21, (Tetrandria) Littorella lacustris; banks of the Loe in abundance, forming during the summer a grass-like margin to the lake. In the winter, it is always under water, being considerably below the high-water-mark. 22, (Tetrandria) myrica gale; frequent in Devon and Cornwall.

numbered among our indigenous plants. Abp. Grindall who died in 1583 first brought it into England. It was planted at St. Michael's Mount; whence a branch of it was carried to the Lizard, and stuck into a hedge. [L]

5. With respect to our birds, the *Corvus Graculus* (the Cornish chough) seems the only bird plentiful here, and scarce in most other parts of the island.† It much frequents the Lizard point; where it breeds in the cliffs.

6. For our fish, the pilchard and the mackarel in particular, "bless our lucky shores," in great abundance. But rare or uncommon fish sometimes excite the wonder of the fishermen and attract the attention of the naturalist. [ooo]

23, (Diœcia) Ilex aquifolium; frequent in our woods and hedges. 24, (Filices) Osmunda regalis; near Poltair. Asplenium marinum; Cornwall and Devon, frequent. Asplenium lanceolatum: in Cornwall abundant, particularly near St. Ives. (Algæ) Lichen niger; near St. Ives abundant. Lichen lunatus——Ulva coccinea; near Plymouth and Falmouth. Ulva dichotoma; Devon, Cornwall. Ulva articulata; Cornwall, Devon, Dorset, &c. Fucus natans, Fucus sanguineus, Fucus concatenatus, Fucus tamariscifolius, Fucus crispatus, Fucus tomentosus, Cornwall, Devon.—For the Fuci, see "Nereis Britannica."

[L] See Hunter's Evelyn's Silva, II. 35 (edit. 1736) Granger's Biog. Hist. of England, I. 204, (3rd edit.) and Withering's Arrangement II. 318 (3rd edit.)—An old man of the Lizard informed my friend Mr. James (late of St. Keverne) that in his father's time, a person came from the Mount with a branch of the Tamarisk, which he used for a whip, and that he carelessly stuck it into a hedge there: where it has been propagated, and grown ever since. The hedge, if it be remembered rightly, is part of an enclosure belonging to the last house at the Lizatd-point.

† A very large eagle was killed in Piranzabulo in 1698—Since that time, eagles have been more than once shot at, in that neighbourhood; and one I think killed. The goshawk, the kite, and the buzzard are scarce. The people here call the moor-buzzard a kite. The kestrel is frequent, commonly called a creshawk; in old Cornish, krysat. Of owls, the long-eared (strix otus) was once shot near Fawey. The carrion-crow; not very plentiful. The hooded or Royston-crow; a bird of passage, generally comes and goes with the wood-cock, and from its frequenting Market-jew in particular is called in the west of Cornwall, the Market-jew crow. The nutcracker; very rare. The roller; one shot near Helon-Bridge many years ago. A white bird larger than a thrush, but supposed to be a degenerate variety of the cuckoo, was taken up in an exausted state in the parish of Stratton, in June, 1813. The great spotted woodpecker; two have been seen in Cornwall. The king-fisher; very scarce. The hoopoe; several have been killed. The partridge; I have been informed that Charles Rashleigh, esq. of St. Austell, procured from abroad, some of the red-legged, and turned them loose, and that they have multiplied. The quail; some scattering ones: Mr. James once found a nest with seven eggs, he has also seen two bevys, the one of eleven, the other of five. The land-rail; never abundant. The bustard; one killed near Padstow in the lands of Edmund Prideaux, esq. in 1710. Turtle-dove; scarce. Starling; it breeds in the cliffs: in winter vast flocks. Missle-thrush: scarce. Fieldfare; vast flocks about November. Redwing; comes and goes with the fieldfare. Ring-ousel; a few about Michaelmas. Water-ousel: Mr. James saw one in the parish of Manaccan. Oriole; he saw one, and heard of another. Reed-bunting—Tawny-bunting—Brambling—Woodlark—Redstart—Yellow-wren: scarce. Golden-crested wren; frequent in hard winters. Sedge-bird—Sandmartin; scarce. The Bee-eater, meropsapiaster: rarely seen in England; four were seen, and two shot, in the parish of Madron, in 1807. Of water-fowls, the Bittern; scarce. Woodcock: nest sometimes found. Snipe; nest often. Sandpiper; not common. Golden-plover; amazing flocks in winter. Long-legged plover; very scarce. Ringed dotterel; scarce. Oyster-catcher; not common. Spotted Galinule; very scarce. Coote—Grebe—Puffin—Arctic Gull—Great Tern—Lesser Tern—Shear water; scarce. Stormy petrel; Mr. James saw two near Porthoustock. Goosander; very scarce. Wild Swan; in hard winters. The common wild Goose; in hard winters; "In the winter of 1710, I had five (says Tonkin) brought me one morning; killed at one shot in Mellingey moors under Lambrigan; they were fat and very good meat. Willoughby speaks of a tame goose, more than 80 years old. But Tonkin memorizes a gander of Charles Huddy of Trenthoweth, in Probus, which, according to tradition, was 300 years old; He died in 1688. Mr. Huddy had at Trenoweth a picture of this gander; under which were some rhymes intimating his great age, and his constancy in getting ten goslings at a time every year, even in the very year in which he died.

[ooo] "Of whales I have seen many" says Mr. James, "but cannot say of what sort. Of the lamprey and of the angel or monk fish I never saw but one. For the porbeagle, see Borlase, p. 265; and for the Beaumaris shark, see Pennant's Brit. Zool. Vol. III, p. 118, 8vo. edit. Lond. 1776. I never saw but one, which was caught near the Manacles. The

The Porbeagle

Length 3 Ft. 5 In Depth 8 In

Pub.d as the Act directs by G R Polwhele

Span Mackerel

Pub.d as the Act directs by G.R.Polwhele

7. Of quadrupeds, our small breed of horses, our small black cattle, and our black-nosed sheep may be mentioned, perhaps, as indigenous.[BA]

II. Removed as we are at a distance from a state of nature, it would be more difficult than useful to discriminate with precision between the wildness that speaks no cultivating hand and the artificial improvements of man. I have in some instances, therefore, intruded on the division now before us.

1. In the reign of Edward I. Cornwall measured 1,500,000 acres. It contains now no more than 758,484.

2. It has been calculated, that nearly a fourth part of the county from 150,000 to 200,000 acres consists of *unenclosed* lands, which are appropriated to no other use, than a scanty pasturage for a miserable breed of sheep and goats throughout the year; and about 10,000 acres, to the summer pasture of cattle and sheep.*

3. Of our *enclosed* lands, the general appearance and nature of the fences, are the first object of attention to the traveller. In some places, we have specimens of a good hedge, consisting of about three feet of stone surmounted with turf or earth about three feet more, and exhibiting on its sides various sorts of herbaceous plants and flowers, primroses, daises, violets, kingcups—and on its top shrubs and trees, the black and white thorn, the hazel, holly, privet and rose—the sycamore, ash, elm, and oak, and (what in winter is very pleasing to the eye) a profusion of moss and ivy. Our most profitable enclosures are on the sea-coasts, and

Great Weever: I never saw but two, which were sent to me by the fishermen of Coverick, to know what they were. Cepola: Five were thrown on shore in the parish of St. Keverne during a heavy gale of easterly wind in the winter of 1797; two of which I took home. This fish has a slender tapering shape, about twelve inches long, and hardly one thick; semi-transparent, of a fine rose colour. It had no scales. Common in the Mediterranean, but I believe never before known on the British coast. Bellows or Trumpet fish: One thrown on shore on Parr-sand, St. Austel bay, in the spring of 1804. It was about five inches and a half long, and an inch and half broad. Covered with rough scales, it has a long snout, almost equal to one third of the whole length. It has a small aperture at the end, which has a covering connected to the lower part, and must be raised upwards in order to shut it, and when it is opened this is let down. The eyes are large, and their iris is white; and on the back there rises a very strong spine of great length, to which there corresponds a furrow on the back part. On the edges there are a row of teeth which turn upwards, and the spine can be erected, or laid down at pleasure, but not directly upright, for it always inclines towards the tail. It is common at Rome; but the only one ever found on the British shores. For the Spanish Mackerel, see Pennant III. 266.—Crabs: Their claws actually perform the office of hands. I once saw a crab in Gillan harbour (St. Anthony-Meneg) seize the head of a gray mullet (which had been thrown over the side of a French vessel) and holding it with one of the claws, pick the eatable parts off with the other, and convey the morsels to its mouth.

[BA] Goonhilly was once famous for a breed of excellent horses, occasioned, it is said, by a Barbary horse, turned loose there by one of the Erisey-family. The estate of Erisey joins the down —Sheep: The Leicester and Southdown introduced. Deer, Stag: Some few straggle out of Devon into the eastern part of Cornwall. Cat, wild: sometimes seen in the Eastern part of the county. Domestic Cat: A Cat belonging to a family west of Penzance had been remarked for her gentle disposition: And, a lucky concurrence suggesting the experiment, a young duck hatched by a magpie, was substituted for her kittens. The cat received it kindly, and took every care of an offspring so dissimilar from her own. The cat would frequently call. and the young duck come to her; when if it happened to be wet in dirty weather, she would express great disgust, but never failed in the end, to lick it clean: And the duck would nestle under her like a kitten. The same cat afterwards nursed a young rabbit, and once rescued it from a large and fierce dog. On another occasion perceiving her adopted charge in danger, she flew at a second dog, but unfortunately falling into a pan of hot milk, was scalded so much, as to occasion her death—in 1802.—Marten: very scarce. One was killed some years ago near Bodmin. Stoat, or Ermine: very scarce. Dormouse: scarce. Mole: I have seen several of a fine buff colour.—Seal: scarce on the South, but numerous on the North coast.

* "The midland country from Brownwilley to Launceston yields great quantities of grass all the summer season: so that from all the other parts of the county, vast numbers of black cattle are brought, both to graze and feed. As also Bodmin-moors and all that middle land between Launceston and Bodmin. To both which, great numbers of the like sort of cattle are brought down by the Devonshire graziers likewise." Tonkin's MS.—See Worgan's Agricult. Survey.

along the banks of the navigable rivers. Tonkin's 'Agricultural glance' (as it may be termed) discovers much sagacity. I prefer the following to volumes which have since been written on the subject. "In the W. part of the county from the Landsend to Penryn, on the S. and St. Agnes on the N. the sod is mostly inclinable to a growan, and is fitter for pasture, milch-kine, barley, pillis, and oats, than for wheat; except that part of it, called Meneage, which is excellent for all kind of grain, but more especially barley, and lies on a blue iron stone; and some few parishes besides in which is a mixture of what they call penny-shelf the best bottom of any, and growan. The northern coast, where the N. W. winds have not overwhelmed with sand the most neighbouring parts to the sea (which sandy shores are covered with millions of small snails of all sorts of shapes in their shells, affording excellent food to the sheep that greedily lick them up) lies mostly on a penny shelf; more to the inland, of a mixture of clay, and in some places, of a deep fat mould; and is excellent for all kind of grain, especially wheat; as it likewise produces an exceedingly sweet pasture for breeding sheep. And this sort of soil variously intermixed but more shallow and on the shelf towards the sea, continues from Piran-sands to Tintagel, which part of the county, in the summer-season, as being much more on a level than the south part, and having the advantage of the Gannel and the beautiful river Alan, is by far the pleasantest of any: and were it better wooded I should not stick to compare it with the finest countries in the kingdom. From Tintagel to Hartland, and most of the hundreds of Lesnewth and Stratton, the soil inclines to a deep clay, and a colder bottom, though not without several veins of good land The southern coast, from Penryn to Plymouth harbour, is full of little hills, with a mixture of penny-shelf clay, and fat mould, and yields a very good produce of corn and grass to the painful husbandman; to which the plenty of most sorts of dressing does not a little contribute. The middle part of the shire answers to Mr. Carew's description of it: Only this I must add, that since his time, the several sorts of grass seeds have been introduced every where with good success: So that meadow land is not so much wanted here as formerly."‡ The rent of lands is very variable; depending on local circumstances and the different springs of human industry. In the neighbourhoods of Truro, St. Austell and Lostwithiel, rents run so high as from 3* to 5 or 6l. per acre of 160 poles or yards of 18 feet square. But the rack tenant at a lease of from 7 to 21 years, pays upon an average about 18s. per acre, and in general when his rent was much below that average the lands were in a state of wretched management, and where he paid considerably higher, the rent operated as a stimulus to proportionate industry.†

4. The Cornish farms are small, as compared with those in the midland counties. The largest are Norton near Stratton of about 900 acres, Roscarrock in Endellion, Trerice in Newlyn, and Bodrigan near Mevagissey—the last three, about 600 acres. The Cornish farm is not, like that of the eastern, partitioned out into lands for pasturage[OR] and for agriculture; whilst each partition is kept distinct for a long series of years; but small as it is, we find its fields (even its coarser outgrounds for sheep) broken up and tilled, in

‡ Tonkin's MSS. * Some land near Penzance is let for £18 per acre; near Truro, for £12. But this is rare.

† A great stimulus to the improvement of our lands, is the leasing of estates to farmers,—the lease determinable in 99 years, or with the lives of three persons named in the lease, which is a grant of the Duchy Church-lands, or manors of private gentlemen. For this lease of three lives, the taker usually pays on the average about 16 years value of the real annual profit of the estate, besides a reserved conventionary rent to the lord of about a twentieth part or 1s. in the pound.

[OR] I am acqvainted with one or two instances of dairy cows near Truro producing nearly three pounds of butter a day for several months after calving, and long afterwards, not less than two pounds. But the most remarkable is the Manaccan cow, late the property of Nathaniel Roskruge. This cow was bred on Tregonwell in Manaccan and bought by

regular rotation.[CDE] At Bodrigan there remains a spacious barn which would contain 1000 bushels of wheat in the straw. And the barn at Trewothack in St. Anthony-Meneg, is a fine stone building, 90 feet long by 19, and about 16 feet high.

5. Of plantations, Borlase says, "we have several laid out in a more rural manner than was formerly the custom" and he particularizes "Anthony, Port-Eliot, Trewithan, Tregothnan, Carclew, Nanswhydden, Tehidy, Clowance, Trelowarren, Trevetho, Enys, and Castlehorneck."* I can only add, that Lord De Dunstanville has enriched Tehidy, Lord Falmouth, Tregothnan, Sir V. Vyvyan, Trelowarren, Sir William Lemon, Carclew, Mr. Enys his seat of Enys, and Mr. Daniell, Trelissick, with a variety of firs and forest trees, planted to a great extent, and disposed with taste.

6. Of orchards many parts of the county, present but a cheerless prospect. Here, around Truro, in St. Clements and in Kea particularly, our apple-trees are gone to decay. Our "*raciest*" cyder is, at the present day, produced in the hundred of Stratton, and in that of East where it borders on the Tamar, from an apple called the *duffling*, and in the neighbourhoods of Fawey and Lestwithiel.[L]

Roskruge, when young; after which he kept her as a dairy cow. While in milking, being surprized at the great produce of this cow he was induced to try the weight of butter produced from one common meal of milk, which weighed 33 ounces; at which rate a day's produce was 66 ounces, making 4lbs. 2oz. avoirdupoise weight. When fat, she was killed, and weighed 7cwt. She had two calves at a birth, male and female, which were reared for labour, after which they were fed and killed, weighing 10cwt. each. For sheep, I must observe, that (notwithstanding our strangers from Leicestershire) the Towan mutton is still prized on account of its high flavour. The large sandy common in Gunwallo called the Towan, has been already noticed: But Tonkin mentioned Kelsey with distinction. "Kelsey in Cuthbert means the dry neck; and such is the character of the estate, a dry promontory of land covered mostly with sand, and famous for feeding the sweetest mutton in Cornwall. The old Earl of Radnor, when in the country, would admit no other to his table." Tonkin's MS. Our farmers have, of late years, considered their hoggery as of prime importance. In 1805, a pig was killed at Killiow, weighing 48 score. In 1806, Mr. Anthony Hocky of St. Issey killed a pig weighing 44 score and 8 pounds. And a pig bred at Enys was sold to a Mr. Reed of Constantine, who fed the same. And when killed in 1814, it weighed 40 score and 18lbs.

[CDE] Our principal manures are sea-sand, the earthridges, dung and sea-weed and bruised or damaged pilchards and the refuse salt used in curing them. "Of oats (says Tonkin) we have a sort plentifully sown in the west parts of the county called Pilez, the avena nuda of Ray. Its name in Cornish signifies bald or bare: whence I take it to be originally Cornish. Plot mentions it, as sown in one place in Staffordshire." Tonkin's MS. Of late years, potatoes have been cultivated on a large scale. In the neighbourhood of Penzance, two crops are produced within the year; and an acre has been known to yield, of the kidney or golden dons 300 (winchester) bushels, the first crop and of the apple-potatoe 600 bushels, the second crop; whence Truro and its vicinities are generally supplied before the end of May.

* Natural History, p. 218.—"The trees most proper for propagation are agreed to be Oak, Ash, and Elm. The Elm more especially, in such places as are fit for it; as being of such general use for pumps and in the mines. And when they like the soil, they are very quick growers. The sycamore too is well worth cultivation (though not of such general use) as they grow in the most exposed places. The late Mr. Paynter of Boskenna has shewn what industry will do; since at his seat there by means of furze-ricks for shelter at first, he has raised a very fine tuft of trees in a place where scarcely a bush grew before. The Scotch Fir will likewise thrive well with us; as may be seen in those fine plantations of the Hon. R. Edgcombe esq. at Mount Edgcombe, who hath been a great raiser of all sorts of trees; and the late Samuel Kempe esq., at Carclew in Mylor; and as myself have done with success at Lambrigan, and several others, in many places of this county. George Dennis esq hath at his seat of Trenant in Duloe, several prosperous trees of that sort of fir, which the gardeners from its fragrant scent call the Balm of Gilead, and makes a very beautiful tree; which were originally planted by Mr. Dandy of Trewan in the said parish of Duloe. And there is a fine one brought from thence now growing in the garden of Court in Lanreath, late the seat of Charles Grills esq.; as also some at Mount Edgcombe, given by Mr. Dennis. The silver fir thrives too very well with us, of which sort there are several fine trees now growing at Carclew aforesaid. But I cannot say the same of the spruce fir, which will not bear the weather with us, at least from what I have seen of it in many places, and have had the experience of, myself. Mr. Moyle, in the 1st vol. of his works p. 421, speaks of a fir-tree in his garden at Bake, which the late Mr. Stephens of Menhinnet (a curious botanist) took to be a non-descript—the cones which it bears every year hanging downwards." Tonkin's MS.

[L] "Orchards and gardens are much improved of late all over the county; and in our table and cyder fruit, we may vie with most other countries. The Redstreak, indeed, seldom makes a good tree with us: but the Whitesour, Hopskin, &c. do mighty well. And our cyder itself, is so well managed as to come up in many places, especially in the east

In the mean time, the cherry-orchards of Calstock and Stoke-climsland or the strawberry-fields of that neighbourhood have not lost their celebrity: And with black cherries or mazards, Truro is supplied from the East, as with "golden dons" from the West. And Kea, where apples were once abundant, is now in plums (as heretofore) prolific.[v]

7. The union of the farm and the garden in a picturesque manner, may be instanced in the seats of Cornish gentlemen. Few or none, indeed, of these seats, exhibit perfect models of the picturesque: But there are many claim our notice from their fine situation, or the taste displayed in shewing their unpromising features to the best advantage. In the disposition of the ground, the wood or the water, Cornwall never witnessed, till the generation before us, the design of the artist; in some degree owing to the circumstance, that gentlemen had too great a regard for the old familiar features of their places, to admit of any material alteration. At present, (if not equal in fame to Mount Edgcumbe,) Boconnoc, Tregothnan, Tehidy, Trelisick, hath each its appropriate beauties.[P]

and south, to the cyder of the Southams in Devon. And the planting of good cyder fruits is what we ought chiefly to encourage, having so many pleasantly seated and well sheltered bottoms fit for such plantations: So that, indeed, there are few parishes in the whole county but have some such bottom or other." Tonkin's MS. Of Cornish apples I can enumerate a few, such as the Borlase's Pippin (first introduced by Borlase at Treluddero), the Slade's Pippin, the Blanchet, the Hasling, the Jany-gimblet, the Stubbart, the Whitesour, the Bel-bone, the Jacky-Johns, the Cobble-dick-longcr-skins, the gilliflower, first produced I believe in the Polwhele-orchards and the cloth-of-gold, once existing there but now extinct. The Cornish apples sent to Mr. Forsyth, from Penzance, from Mr, John Duncan, are as follows: The Cornish nonpareil, rather under the middle size. It is a little flatted, and of a russet colour. This is a very good apple and keeps till the middle of March. The Cornish Pearmain of a middling size and long shape of a dull green colour on one side, and russet on the other. This is a very good apple and keeps till the latter end of April. Harvey's Russet, so called in Cornwall; a large russet-coloured apple, with a little red towards the sun. This is a famous kitchen fruit, and tolerably good, raw. It has a musky flavour. The Hollow-eyed Rennet, the Red Sweet, the Spaniard, the Treworder Rennet. See Forsyth on Fruit-trees, edit 2 pp. 79—118. The Blue-pippen is often sold in the Penzance markets. The Godolphin apple is a very handsome large fine fruit, streaked with red on the side next the sun and of a yellowish colour on the other side. It is in eating from the latter end of September to December. I found this apple growing in the garden of the late Lord Godolphin St. James's Park, and have given it the name of the Godolphin-apple, as I have not been able to find it in any catalogue. Forsyth's Treatise p. 91. This apple is frequently seen in the Helston markets.

[v] "For vines, the slate or penny-shelf is found to be as good a bottom as the limestone; witness the white muscadine growing on such a bottom, in the garden of Edmund Prideaux, Esq. at Padstow; which ripens at least a fortnight sooner than any other in the neighbourhood. But the truth of it is, we have wines at so cheap a rate from France, that gentlemen think it scarcely worth their while to propagate the vine for that end. The Hon. Richard Edgcumbe has lately planted a vineyard at Mount Edgcumbe, which hath all the advantages of nature and art." Tonkin's MS.

[P] Of our ancient parks Carew says: "Cornwall was stored not long since with many parks of fallow deer, four of which took a fall together, viz. Cary-bullock, Liskerd, Restormel, and Lanteglos. (temp. Henr. VIII.) "Parks yet remaining, are in E. Hundred, Pool, Sir Jon. Trelawnyes newly revived; Halton, M. Rouse's, lately impaled; and Newton, M. Corington's, almost decayed. In W. Hundred, Boconnock, Sir Reginald Mohun's. In Powder, Caryhayes, M. Trevanion's. In Stratton, Lancels, M. Chamond's. In Kerier, Trelowarren, M. Vivian's; and Merthir, M. Reskymir's." f. b. 23. "Pool, Lancels, Halton, Trelowarren, and Merthyn (not Merthir) have been long since disparked. But we have at present, (besides Newton, Boconnoc, and Carhayes, which are still kept up) in Penwith, Trevetho, Mr. Praed's; in Kerier, Godolphin, the Earl of Godolphin's, and Tremogh, Mr. Worth's; in Powder, Tregothnan, Lord Viscount Falmouth's; in Pider, Lanhydroc, the Earl of Radnor's; Treluddro, the late Mr. Borlase's (now left to ruin though a park by patent) Trevaunance, the Writer's hereof; in W. Hundred, Pincheley, the Earl of Radnor's; in E. Hundred, Bradridge, Mr. Coster's: Werington, Sir Wm. Morice's; and Mount Edgcomb, Mr. Edgcomb's." Tonkin's MS. The parks now in existence are, in E. Hundred, Werington and Mount Edgcumbe; in the West, Boconnoc, Lord Grenville's; in Pyder, a small park at Place, Mr. Brune's; in Powder, Tregothnan, Lord Falmouth's; Caerhayes, Mr. Trevanion's; Penrice, Mr. Sawle's; and in Kirrier, Carclew, Sir W. Lemon's.

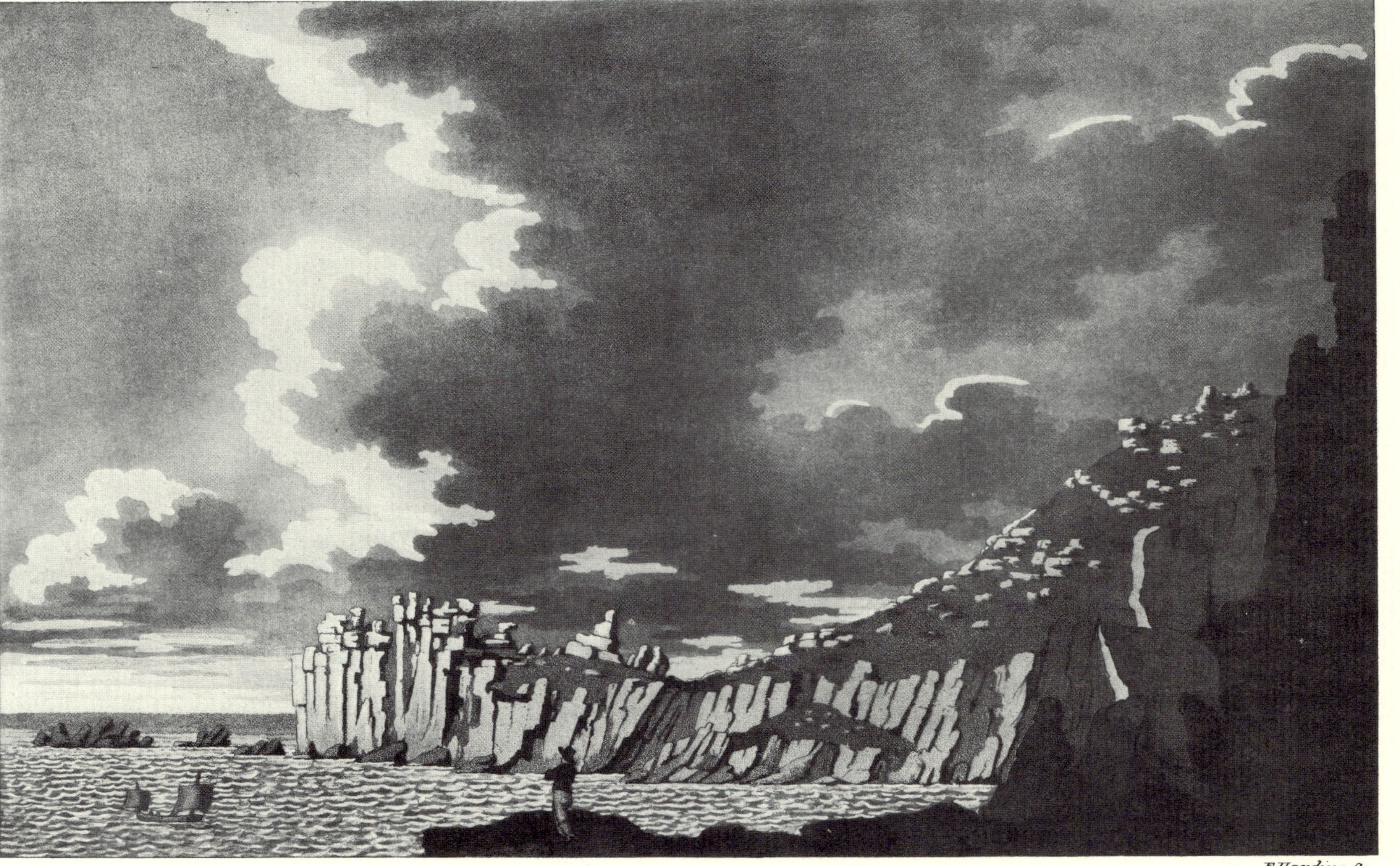

E Harding Sc

The Lands End

Pub.[d] as the Act directs by G.R. Polwhele

The Logan or Rocking Stone, near the Lands End.

Pub.d as the act directs by G.R.Polwhele

MINING.

BOOK III. CHAPTER VI.

I. I have already described our hills of granite (that mountainous chain which has been called the jugum Ocrinum) as running from Dartmoor through the centre of Cornwall to the sea at the Landsend.* The *granite* displays itself here and there in various shapes and elevations; as amidst the wild scenery of Rowtor and Brownwilley; in the Cheesewring of Linkinhorne, where rock piled upon rock rises to the height of 32 feet; in the country between Roche and Lestwithiel, (where the hills consist entirely of granite or rocks of a granitic nature peeping above the soil in various places, and forming rude grotesque crags)†—in the kairns and mighty masses of Karnbre; in the enormous oval stone on the tenement of Mên in Constantine, which (33 feet long and more than 14 feet high) on the points of two other rocks, seems ready to crush them with its weight; in the hills of Tregoning, Breage and Godolphin; in the conic form of the Mount of St. Michael rising as out of the sea and gradually diminishing from its broad base to its summit;[ABC] and in the rocks of Cape-Cornwall, Castle-Treryn,[OB] and the Landsend.[CD]

* Elevation of hills &c. above the sea-level (according to Colonel Mudge, Davies Giddy esq. &c. &c.) from Portreath up to Brownwilley—Clift near Portreath, 180 feet; St. Michael's Mount, 267; Trevose-head, 274; the Dudman, 379; Maker-heights, 402; St. Berian, 415; Lansallos, 514; St. Stephen's-down, 605; St. Agnes-beacon, 621; Bodmin-down, (quarter of a mile E. of the turnpike-gate) 649; Bindown, 658; Karnminnis, 805; Karnbonellis, 822; Cadenbarrow, 1011; Hensbarrow, 1026; Kitt-hill, 1067; Carraton-hill, 1208; Brownwilley, 1368.

† Roche-rock itself is not a granitic but a shorl-rock.—And north of St. Blazey, there are considerable ridges, some of which are composed of detached blocks wholly dissimilar with respect to their constituent parts. The quartz, feltspar, and mica are not only in very different proportions, but different in texture, and are partially mixed with shorl and hornblende.

[ABC] Its height from low water-mark to the top of the chapel tower is about 260 feet—its circumference at the base nearly a mile. It consists of clay-slate and granite. The whole north-base is clay-slate—the upper part entirely of granite, or pseudo-granite, according to De Luc.—That the Mount was inland, in the time of Diodorus, I have not a doubt. It could not have been the Ictis; however its present peninsularity may answer to the description of the historian.

[OB] At Castle-Treryn, the groupe of granite rocks rising in pyramidal clusters to a great height, overhang the sea. The Logan-stone in the parish of St. Just "in the large heap of rocks called Bosworlas Lehan," is a mass of granite, as is another "on the top of the granitic rocks called Castle-Treryn." See Borlase p. 180. Near St. Just Churchtown, Dr. Berger observed many blocks of shorlrock scattered on this part of the granitic plain.

[CD] The clift at the Landsend is rather bold and broken, than elevated; here like basaltic columns, there formed into arches.

In St. Stephens Brannel, we meet with what is called the Cornish *china stone.**

On each side of the great ridge of granite, there are lower *killas* hills, declining northward and southward to the sea. Towards the coast, the killas passes into an argillaceous slate.

In the mean time, the *slate* (or the helling-stone of Cornwall) is to be found—among other places—between the Tamar and Leskeard, at Tintadgel, in the Dennybal quarries, at Padstow, and in St. Anthony in Roseland. But the Dennybal slate is " perhaps the finest in the world."

The scarcity of *lime* is a marked feature of this county. It is discovered between the Tamar and Leskeard in thin stratifications, at Padstow in larger masses, and in Crantoc and Lower St. Columb to the north, and in Veryan and Caerhayes to the south. The limestones both to the north and the south resemble each other.

Among our *freestone* quarries, those of Pentuan and Newham near Truro are the most remarkable.

Sandstone occurs in St. Ives bay, at Pendean cove in St. Just and at other places, where the observations of the ingenious Dr. Paris have evinced its recent formation.†

Of the *iron-stone,* St. Keverne presents unmanageable masses, and Tolcarne near Penzance is a striking specimen.

The southern part of Meneg, is what we call the *serpentine* country. And the serpentine well deserves particular attention, as it occurs no where else in England. It occupies the whole extent of Goonhilly downs, and terminates about half a mile before we reach the Lizard point. Its grotesque appearances in the rocks of Mullion and of Kinance Cove, its variegated colours and spots (resembling the serpent's skin) its dark green or brown suffused with shades of red, and its fine polish from the beating of the waves, cannot escape the eye of the most negligent observer.

The *steatite,* a mile and half N. W. of the Lizard, is considered by Dr. Thomson, as serpentine itself in a state of decomposition.‡

Of precious stones, the only product of Cornwall, is the white topaz. In the rock at St. Michael's Mount, it is sprinkled over the granite. In the slate-quarries of Dennybal have been found the largest transparent and colourless rock-crystals; in the mines of St. Agnes, the finest groupes of the same substance; at Hewas in St. Mewan, crystallizations of amethystine quartz; at Trevascus in Gwinear, the stalactital chalcedony;

* Among the burrows of a mine near Helstone, the late ingenious Mr. Cookworthy discovered a sort of earth, which partly gave occasion to his porcelain manufactory at Plymouth. This substance had the distinguishing characters of the kaolin of China, which is described to be a white, unctuous, unvitrifiable earth, and is considered by the Chinese as the bones of China ware, or what gives it its firmness and consistency in the fire. The petunse, or vitrifiable ingredient (says Mr. Cookworthy) which the Chinese consider as the flesh, since it gives the body, transparency, softness of texture and lustre in the breaking was yet to be discovered. In his search after this, Mr. C. found a stone which would vitrify, but, after some pretty expensive experiments, was satisfied it would not answer. This was a compound stone, having a small mixture of limestone particles in it. Some time after this he perceived that our western granite or moorstone was of the genus of the stone he was enquiring after; as it was sufficiently vitrifiable. On giving a piece of this stone a white heat in a crucible, it melted: and the white parts of the stone were of a beautiful glossy semidiaphanous white, but the black particles burning red as containing iron, and being by any practicable art inseparable from the white part, it was plain the common moorstone would not answer in so elegant a ware as the porcelain, where the perfection of the white is its merit and excellence. At length he discovered what he wanted near St. Austell.

† See his excellent little book, entitled " A Guide to the Landsend;" particularly at pp. 106, 107, 108, 109, 110.

‡ For the manufacture of porcelain, we must add the steatite of the Lizard to the granite and decomposed feltspar of St. Stephen.

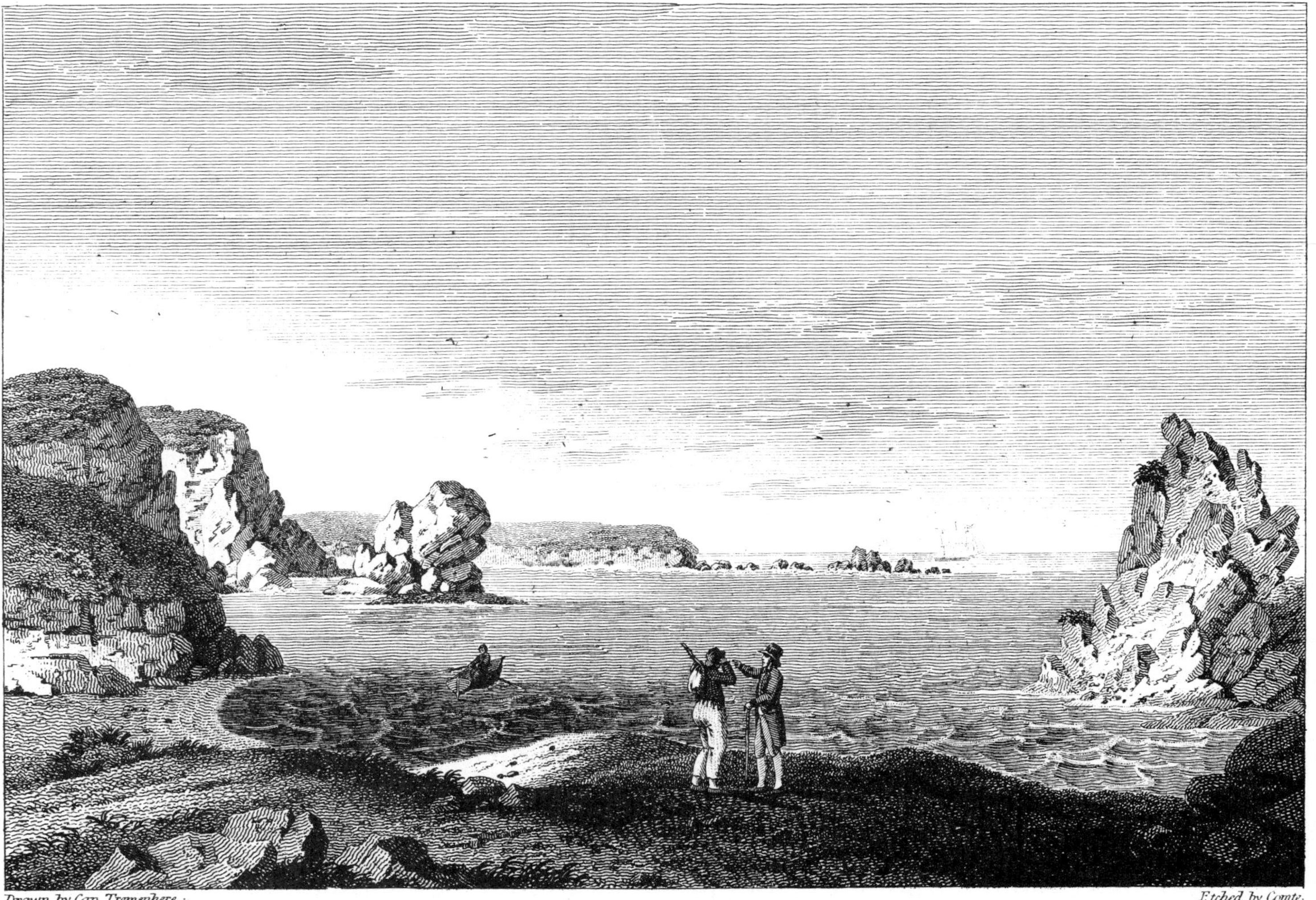

Drawn by Cap. Tremenhere. *Etched by Comte.*

The Lizard, from Kinans Cove.

Published Oct. 1. 1804, by Rev. Mr. Polwhele.

T.S.

KINANS.

Published by R. Polwhele March 25th 1803.

MULLION ISLAND.

Published by R. Polwhele March 25th 1803.

Drawn by Cap. Tremenhere. Etched by Comte.

Tolcarn, near Penzance.

Published Oct. 1. 1804. by Rev. Mr. Polwhele.

crystals of axinite in Lanlivery and at Trewellard a little north of Botallack in St. Just where they were first discovered in Cornwall; at Stennagwyn in St. Stephens, that rare mineral hydrargillite or wavellite—at Stennagwyn, also, at Godolphin-ball in Breage, and at St. Michael's Mount, phosphat of lime, and in the mines of St. Agnes, the cubic, with bevilled edges, and octaedral crystals of fluor or fluat of lime.

2. I spoke of the granitic ridge that runs through the whole length of our peninsula, and of the lower killas-hills. It is in that granite and this killas, that we boast our mines of tin and copper, the richest in the world. Our most ancient tin-mine is *Drakewill's* on Hengeston-down: It has been in working 150 years. Our most productive tin-mines in Borlase's time were Polgooth in St. Mewan, Polberou in St. Agnes, and Poldice (now worked as a copper-mine) in Gwennap. About the year 1800, were worked in Cornwall 28 tin-mines, of which 7 were in St. Agnes, 4 in Wendron, 3 in Gulval, 2 in Lelant, 2 in Redruth, and 2 in Piran-zabuloe: And among the mines producing both tin and copper, there were 4 in Redruth, 4 in Gwennap, 3 in St. Agnes, and 2 in St. Neot. And one was worked for tin and cobalt in Madron.[A] At this moment our richest tin-mines are *Huel Unity* in Gwennap, *Cook's Kitchen* in Illogan, *Trevenen* near Helston, and *Botallack* in St. Just. For the depth of the mines, it is observed that tin rarely continues worth working beyond 50 fathoms deep, while copper is seldom wrought in great quantities till past that depth to 100 fathoms. In the mean time, there are found in the strata of some of our vallies large quantities of tin-ore; which, at very distant periods, had been washed from the higher grounds and there deposited: These are our *streamworks*, the most ancient of which I have already noticed. The principal streamworks of the present day, are in St. Mewan, Creed, Probus, Ladock, Carnon, and Piranzabulo.[B] The Carnon-stream is nearly a mile in length, and 300 yards broad. An adit, a little above Carnon-stream, which has been driven to the W. part of North Downs, a distance of nearly 10 miles, drains, by its various branches, the mines of Chacewater, North Downs, Huel-Unity, Huel-Garland, Huel-Pink, Huel-Jewell, Huel-Hope, Huel-Daniell, Poldice, Huel-Virgin, the United Mines. And the water that issues from the adit, drives the wheel in Carnon-works. We have no native tin. But woodtin, a variety of the oxid of tin, is almost peculiar to this county, and has as yet been found only in the alluvial strata of Roche, St. Columb, St. Dennis, St. Austel, St. Mewan, Ladock and Madron.* In the mines of Huel-Rock in St. Agnes and Huel-Speed near St. Ives, I have been told that tin was discovered about 30 years ago, in the state of sulphuret,† com-

[A] See Borlase's Nat. Hist. p. 188, and Berger's Phys. Structure of Cornwall and Devon, published in the Trans. of the Geol. Society.

[B] Native gold is found in all our streamworks. Borlase notices "a piece of gold in possession of William Lemon, Esq. of Carclew, which weighed in gold coin three pounds three shillings, or fifteen pennyweights ond sixteen grains." It was found in the parish of Creed, and brought to him in September, 1756. p. 215. Mr. Rashleigh's piece of gold (which Mr. Wills shewed me about four years ago at Truro) was less in weight. It was from Carnon.

* "This variety has hitherto been found only in Cornwall. It occurs always in fragments, which are generally rounded. Colour brown; sometimes inclining to yellow, streak yellowish grey. Opaque. Texture fibrous. Hardness 9. Specific gravity 7. 0. Before the blow-pipe becomes brownish red; decrepitates when red hot, but is not reduced. Klaproth obtained from it 63 of tin; and in all probability it is an oxide of tin nearly pure." Thomson's System of Chemistry, IV, 79, 8vo. Edin. 1802.

† Dr. Paris tells, that sulphuret of tin has never been found any where throughout the world but at St. Agnes.—See Thomson's Chemistry, IV, 77.

bined with the sulphuret of copper: And Mr. Gregor informs me, that he pointed out a few years since " a large vein of sulphurated tin at Stennagwyn in St. Stephens."

Our first successful copper mines, are said to have been those of Albalanda or Blanchland in Kea. In Borlase's time, our " first and greatest" copper-mines were *Chacewater* in Kenwyn; *North-downs* in Redruth; *Huelros* in St. Agnes; *Dalcooth, Bullen-garden, Roskaer, Huel-Kitty, Entral and Longclose* in Camborne; *Huel-Fortune* in Ludgvan; the *Pool* in Illogan; *Metal-works* and *Trejeuvyan* in Gwennap; *Binner-downs* and *Clowance-downs* in Crowan; *Huel-Cock* and *Rosmoran* in St. Just; and *Herland* mine in Gwinear. About 1800, the number of our copper-mines was 45—of which, 11 were in Gwennap, 6 in St. Agnes, 5 in Camborne, 4 in Gwinear, 4 in St. Hilary, 3 in Germoe, 3 in Crowan, 3 in Illogan, and 2 in St. Neot. In Gwinear one mine was worked for copper and silver, and one in Camborne for copper and cobalt. The chief copper mines now working are Gunnis Lake in Calstock; Crennis near St. Austel; Huel-Towan in St. Agnes; Huel Unity, United Mines, Huel Damsel, Treskerby and Poldice in Gwennap; Dalcooth in Camborne; Huel Alfred near Hayle; and Huel Abraham in Crowan.—The deepest now at work, are Crenver and Oatfield 200 fathoms; Cook's Kitchen, 210 and Dalcooth 228 fathoms. But our most remarkable copper mine, is the Crown Engine of Botallack in St. Just, Penwith. Here, the miner was at the outset, forced to lower a gigantic steam engine down a precipice of more than 200 feet to carry on his operations under the bed of the vast Atlantic! The workings of this mine extend at least 70 fathoms in length under the sea. Over the heads of the miners, the Atlantic ocean rolls its roaring waves!—In some places, the sea actually penetrates through, and by its filtration is deprived of a great proportion of its salts. In the mines of Gwennap, we have the red oxid of copper, and varieties of arseniat of copper;* and the sulphuret of copper, more particularly in the mines of Camborne which are remarkable for their fine crystallizations of this ore. In the serpentine rocks of Mullion and Landewednac occur veins of native copper. The ore of Crown-engine is the grey and yellow sulphuret of copper, which sometimes occurs in prismatic crystals. At St. Michael's mount, has been found the triple sulphuret of copper, antimony and lead.

Towards the sea-coast, are veins of *lead* intersecting the lower Killas-hills.† Of all our lead-mines, Tonkin gives the preference to the Garras. About 20 years before his time, the ore from the Garras was very rich in silver. The mine, it seems, was discontinued, but was resumed in 1726; when " though it did not turn to any great account, it was richer in silver than any other in the county." In our lead-mines, we have the crystallized carbonet and phosphat of lead, and from Huel Unity in Gwennap, the arseniat of lead.

Of those emphatically called *silver*-mines, (Wheal Duchy, Huel Mexico, and the Herland mine) Wheal

* " When arsenic acid is digested on copper, the metal is oxidated and dissolved; and a bluish-white powder is formed which consists of the arseniate of copper. This salt may be formed also by pouring arsenic acid into acetite of copper, or by precipitating nitrat of copper by means of an alkaline arseniat. Arseniat of copper has been lately found native in considerable quantities in the mine of Huel Gorland in the parish of Gwennap in Cornwall; and a very interesting description and analysis of it have been published by the Count de Bournon and Mr. Chenevix in the Philosophical Transactions for 1801," Thomson's Chemistry, II. 506, 507.

† Lead " anciently and lately worked (says Borlase) in St. Mewan, Boconek, Piran-sands, St. Agnes, Crowan, Sithney, Gwinear, St. Issey, St. Columb, Illogan, and Camborn. The works most noted formerly are those of Penrose, Penwortey Trevascus, Relistian, and Guarnek." See Woodward's Cat. I. 217, 218. and II. 30. and Tonkin's MSS. Garras-mine was again discontinued. It is now worked afresh. But does it produce, as formerly, one hundred and forty ounces of silver in a ton of lead?

Duchy in Calstock (discovered in searching for copper) has been worked with most success. The whole lode is from 6 to 12 inches wide—the part containing silver from 1 to 4. It runs E. and W. the direction of other similar veins in the neighbourhood. Some of the ores contain from 60 to 70 parts in 100, of pure silver. About £5000 worth of silver, a year or two ago, had covered the expence of the undertaking in its early stages. In Cubert, Huel Mexico produced, some time since, large quantities of rich horn silver and crystallized in tubes.

Woodward mentions iron as found in Temple, Lanivet, Piran-zabulo, St. Dye, at the Lizard-point, in Gwinear, and in Morvah. We have the brown iron stone and brown hæmatites from Lanhydroc and St. Just; the cupreous arseniat of iron in the mines of Gwennap, and all the known crystallizations of the common sulphuret and arseniat of iron, and the usual oxides, the specular from the Lizard and St. Just, the spathose from the Lizard, and the magnetic from St. Just. The oxid of uranium, in the form of uran-glimmer at Stennagwyn in St. Stephens, is a discovery of the Rev. W. Gregor; as was the ferriferous oxid of titanium in the form of a sand at Manaccan. In the cliffs near Crown Engine, there is a black crystallized shorl in which titanium has been detected also by Mr. Gregor. And at the Crown Engine is found iron crystallized in four sided prisms, which is supposed by Count de Bournon to contain titanium. Wolfram, or the ferriferous oxid of tungsten, is found in the mines of Kithill near Kellington, and in various tin-mines in the west of Cornwall. It was first detected by Dr. Paris, at the Mount on the south base below high water mark. Tungsten, or the oxid of tungstic acid combined with lime, has been found only at Pengelly, in Breage.

In Pillaton and Endelion, we have the sulphuret of antimony from the mines of that metal. And in the mine of Huel-boys in Endelion was found a triple sulphuret of antimony, lead, and copper.* Of bismuth, cobalt, arsenic and manganese, we have the common ores, abundant. In Crown-Engine, is sulphuret of bismuth imbedded in jasper.

II. 1. For the working of our Cornish stone, whether blocks on our moors, or stones in the quarry, I shall only state, that the *granite*† is exported from Cornwall for bridges and other public buildings—that the *granite of St. Stephen's* and a *fine white clay*, (already described) from some pits in the same parish are exported in large quantities from Charles-town for the porcelain manufacture in Staffordshire—that for the same purpose the *steatite* of the Lizard is exported by the Worcester china manufacturers; and that the Denyball slate is exported from Port-Isaac (about five miles distant from the quarry) in large quantities.

* See Phil. Tran. for 1804.—For the greater part of the above information, I am indebted to my most valued friends the Rev. W. Gregor, and Davies Giddy, Esq. That my acquaintance with Dr. Paris of Penzance is but of late date, my readers perhaps have cause to regret; as I am sure his liberality and openness of communication can only be equalled by his talents and his science. Penzance may well felicitate herself on the presence of such a man, by whose exertions chiefly the "Geological Society" is going on more and more towards perfection. That Truro, however, will soon become a formidable rival to Penzance, or rather that she will be enabled to cooperate powerfully with her sister, in the promotion of science, we have good ground of expectation; as the present County-Library-room is intended for the repository of the most select specimens of mineralogy, under the auspices of a gentleman of true scientific genius. The books will probably be removed thence to an apartment in the Coinage-hall. The room where they now are, is a part of the house of John Vivian, Esq. And the gentleman to whom I allude, is, of his three sons, the second—John Henry Vivian. We know, how the eldest, Sir Hussey, fought the battles of his country! And of the youngest son, Thomas, I have the pleasure to say, that his classical attainments are most respectable.

† In Mr. Rashleigh's elegant grotto, is a table inlaid with 32 polished specimens of Cornish granite. In Borlase's time the Denyball quarry was 300 yards long and 100 wide, and the deepest part "from the grass" 40 fathoms. See Nat. Hist p.94

2. In the former chapters, I have had occasion to point out the ancient mode of working our mines. The present method of working them by shafts and adits commenced about 300 years ago; and the art of blasting with gun-powder about 150 years since. But before Newcomen's steam-engine about 1710, a shaft could be worked to a very inconsiderable depth: The water interrupted the progress of the miners; fifteen fathoms was a deep tin mine; and till within some few years, fifty was so accounted. With respect to the process, our present method of stamping and dressing the tin-ore, is said to have been introduced by Sir Fr. Godolphin. Tin had been smelted from time immemorial in the county. But Sir Bevil Granville is memorized as the first who made the experiment of melting our tin with "fire of sea-coal, to save wood, and keep the tin from wasting in the blast."* In 1705, Mr. Lyddell obtained a patent for smelting tin in iron furnaces, and set up works at Angarrack in Phillack. The use of reverberatory furnaces soon followed, and the blowing-houses grew into disuse. At St. Austell only, they stood their ground. In 1811, a new blowing-house was erected near Penzance.[B] In one view, then, we observe, that the tin-ore, when collected, is broken, washed, stamped by mills, and dressed, then smelted and cast into blocks, and carried on mules to one of the coinage towns. There each block, weighing 320 pounds, is examined by a piece broken from the corner of the block, and is impressed with the arms of the Duchy. This stamp implies permission to vend the tin as pure. In 1602, the profits of the coinage of tin in Cornwall amounted to £2,623 9*s.* 8*d.* Dr. Borlase published his Natural History in 1759. "For the last four years (says he) the tin has amounted on an average to £190,953 19*s.* 3½*d.* Of this the Duke of Cornwall receives about £10,000 yearly." The tin raised in 1799, 1800, and 1801, amounted, each year, on an average, to 16,820 blocks—whence the Duke's revenue was £9,620. The quantity raised in 1811, was 14,043 blocks, in 1812, 16,698.

It is in the copper mines, that we are to contemplate the grand effect of our mining operations. And Cornwall affords a piece of machinery, well worthy admiration, in the Chacewater steam-engine. It may be seen about 3 miles S. of Redruth; a double engine on the improved principle of Boulton and Watt.† Its

* See Tonkin's Carew [MS] p. 34. and Lloyd's Mem. of Loyalists, p. 469.

[B] Calennick smelting-house consists of ten reverberatory furnaces, each six feet high, and 12 feet long. Culm is used as a flux, in proportion of one eigtht to the ore, of which nearly 600 cwt. is smelted within six hours, yielding about 350 cwt. of tin.

† The improved engine of Watt was introduced into Cornwall about 1778. Whilst the powers of the steam-engines have been computed equal to 40,000 men, the application of whims have saved, it is said, the labour of 10,000 more. "Steam-engines are of so recent a date that Mr. Lemon erected the second ever built in Cornwall about seventy years since on Wheal Fortune in Ludgvan: the first was set up in Breage. Whims are not more than half a century prior to steam-engines. I remember a carpenter who used to boast of being the first builder of one to the westward of Hayle. Previous to these inventions and the occasional use of wheels which may be somewhat older, all the water was discharged from mines by manual labour, applied through windlasses or chain pumps perfectly similar to those still retained on board large ships. An improvement in mining scarcely less important than that owing to hydraulic machines was effected by the introduction of gunpowder. For accustomed as we now are to the use of this powerful agent, it has became difficult to conceive how the workmen of former times made their way through rocks almost impervious to gunpowder itself. They are said to have fallen on many expedients equally inconvenient and tedious, such as making large fires in contact with the hard stone; driving wooden plugs into holes bored after the present manner and waiting for their gradual expansion: But in ordinary cases they seem chiefly to have relied on instruments called feathers and tearers; each consisting of two half cylinders, and a long slender wedge: these were placed in a perforation adapted to their size, and the wedge driven between them. I have never been able to ascertain when gunpowder was first used in the Cornish mines; but the date cannot be anterior to the middle or perhaps the latter part of the seventeenth century." Extract of a letter from Davies Giddy, M. P.

dimensions the cylinder 66 inches, the box 19 inches in diameter, the depth of the engine shaft 128 fathoms—from the adit to the bottom 90 fathoms. It makes 8 strokes in a minute, and at every stroke raises 108 gallons of water to the adit—It raises at the same time 60 gallons of water 10 fathoms high, for the purpose of condensing the steam. The coals consumed in 24 hours are about 8 chaldrons. It is equal to the power of 1008 horses—In one instant it may be stopped by applying the finger and thumb to a screw. But the steam-engine, invented by Mr. Trevithick, now in full course of working on the Herland Mines, in Gwinear, confirms, in every respect, the high opinion expressed by several scientific men on the day on which it was set to work, " that it has not, in our day, had an equal"—if " using only a third part of its steam, it go 13 strokes ($10\frac{1}{2}$ feet stroke) per minute, and lift, at each stroke, 92 gallons of water, which will amount to 1,722,240 gallons per hour; and if in this operation it burn no more than two bushels of coals." In the mean time, one of the same size, (a 33 inch cylinder) on Bolton and Watt's construction, will burn about the same quantity, and not do, even at the very extent of its power, a fifth part of the duty.[A]

In 1758, Borlase informs us, that for 14 years then past, the copper mines had produced £160,000 per annum.† In 1806, the total produce of the Gwennap mines was 2962 tons. Crennis yields about £2060 a month: And of Huel-Alfred the monthly expenditure amounts to about £3500 which it has defrayed, and returned besides a clear profit of £120,000 to the adventurers. The greater part of the copper-ore is smelted in Wales. The only copper smelting-house in Cornwall, is at Hayle; where about 6000 tons are smelted annually.* We should notice the rolling-mills at St. Erth, where bars of copper are reduced into sheets of any thickness. It is computed, that the mines nf Cornwall support a population of nearly sixty thousand, exclusive of artizans, tradesmen and merchants in St. Austel, Truro, Penryn, Falmouth, Redruth and Penzance.

[A] Extract of a letter from my friend Davies Giddy in 1802. "Mr. Richard Trevithick has obtained a patent for moving carriages by the force of Steam. His machine consists of a fire-place, boiler and cylinder suspended near the centre of a waggon, from whence the power is transferred to the wheels by means of toothwork and cranks. If this contrivance answer the expectations of many persons well informed on mechanical subjects, it will become of great national importance; and assisted by iron-railed roads may prove eminently useful in the mining district of Cornwall; where a sum little short of a thousand pounds a week is now paid for transporting copper ore and coals to the sea-coast and the mines.

† Note of Copper Ores produced and sold from the Cornish mines in the years 1799, 1800, and 1801.

	Tons of Ore.			Tons produced in fine Copper.
1799....	52043	sold for at the mines	£467,166............	
1800....	56223	————	560,140............	
1801....	57198	————	471,872............	5310.

* Hayle copper-house built with square masses of the scoria, which for the purpose of building &c. is cast into moulds as soon as it comes out of the furnaces.

MANUFACTURES.

BOOK III. CHAPTER VII.

"AS the mines and the pilchard fishery are the chief support of the labouring poor not employed in husbandry, we have no manufactures of any consequence in Cornwall, except those of coarse woollens and carpets." So said the first merchant in this county, in a letter to me, containing much valuable information on the conduct of the mines.

There is a considerable serge manufacture at Padstow and at Lestwithiel: And the carpet manufactory commenced at Truro about the year 1791, by Tippet, Martyn, Turner and Co. and continued under that firm until the year 1800, since that period carried on by Martyn and Turner, and then Plummer, who have machinery &c. sufficient to manufacture one thousand yards of carpetting per week from 1*s.* 8*d.* to 7*s.* 6*d.* per yard value. As they prepare the wool from the sheep's back through every process until it is manufactured, they employ from five to seven hundred men, women, and children weekly.—The commencement of the late war occasioned great stagnation to the trade—The Brussell's carpetting which they manufacture is considered by the trade to be equal if not superior in quality and colours to any manufactured in the kingdom.*

* The coarse mats of Cornwall, commonly called Piran broadcloth, from the great quantities made from the rushes growing on the sand banks in Piranzabulo, are scarcely worth mentioning. See Carew fol. 18. There are manufactures of leather at Leskeard &c. (noticed by Campbell I. 344)—paper and gunpowder mills in the neighbourhood of Penryn—and kelp from 100 to 200 tons a year, and spinning of wool in the Sylleh isles.—Speaking of the Sylleans, Campbell observes, "Their alga marina, fucus, or oreweed serves to feed both their small and great cattle, manures their lands, is burned into kelp, is of use in physic, is sometimes preserved, sometimes pickled, and is, in many other respects very beneficial to the inhabitants."

COMMERCE.

BOOK III. CHAPTER VIII.

I. AS introductory to the state of our commerce, I had brought together a volume of facts relative to our roads and posts, our rivers, canals and harbours. But I can advert to our roads and posts only; selecting a few particulars.

1. Such was the bad condition of the western roads little more than a century ago, that they scarcely admitted of wheel-carriages in travelling. The stannary-court of the Earl of Bath, the Lord Warden, which was held about 150 years since, at "Crockerentorre" on the wilds of Dartmoor, was attended by a cavalcade of three hundred gentlemen. They were all, it is said, well-mounted; little regarding the inclemency of the weather, whilst they held their open court amidst the rocks of the desart. It was not, indeed, more than fifty years ago, that our first gentry resigned the saddle for the more luxurious chaise or coach. In 1756, was set up "a *three days* stage machine from Bath to Exeter."* We have now coaches scarcely to be enumerated from London to the Landsend. There is one (if not more) which travels from London to Falmouth in 41 hours.

2. It appears, that *posts*, when first projected, were for the service of the prince: And the use made of post-houses, was only to furnish horses; the rate of which was, in the reign of Edward VI. fixed at one penny a mile. In the reign of Elizabeth, Mr. Randolph was chief postmaster. In 1635, Charles published a proclamation, regulating the rates of postage, forbidding private posts, and pointing out what we stile the north and west roads.† In 1644, the parliament bestowed the foreign office on the Earl of Warwick, and the inland on Edmund Prideaux, Esq., who in this year was supposed to collect about £5000. It is to

* "The three days stage machine from Bath to Exeter will set out from the Lamb Inn in Stall-street, on Thursday the first day of April next, at nine o'clock, and continue so to do every Thursday during the summer; will arrive at the Oxford Inn in Exeter every Saturday, and set out from thence to Bath every Monday. Passengers to pay 23 shillings each &c. &c." Bath Journal March 22, 1756.

† See Rymer's Fœd. XIX. 649. and Campbell, II. 255.

him, our countryman, that we owe the regular establishment of the post-office.‡ From this time to the act passed by queen Anne for its improvement, the annual receipt of the post-office gradually increased to £111,461. The scheme of the cross-posts seems to be the next thing of consequence in the history of the post-office; an improvement, for which the nation is indebted to the great and good MR ALLEN. And it is with pleasure I have to record, that the hospitable possessor of *Prior-Park*, (that friend of genius and of virtue) was a native of St. Blazey in this county. He was the "low-born Allen" of Pope. But his commercial genius soon broke through the obscurity of his birth. Pursuing the subject before me, I am led to state, that placed under the care of his grandmother, who kept the post-office at St. Columb, he here discovered a turn for business, a cleverness in arithmetic, and a steadiness of application which seemed to indicate his future eminence—that the inspector of the post-office coming into Cornwall, and among other towns visiting St. Columb, was highly pleased with the uncommon neatness and regularity of young Allen's figures and accounts, and expressed a wish to see the boy in a situation where ingenuity and industry might have a wider scope and more ample encouragement—that not long afterwards, Allen's friends consented to his leaving Cornwall—that at Bath he was chiefly patronized by General Wade; and that there, by his project of the cross-post, for forming which he obtained a grant from government, he laid the foundation of his fortunes.* It was in 1764, that Mr. Allen died—in which we observe—still marking the progressive improvement of our post-offices, their product, inland and foreign, was no less than £432,048. From Mr. Allen's time to the present, there is nothing which, in this slight outline, I am required to notice; except Mr. Palmer's reform in the administration of the post-office—which is, indeed, of vast national importance. In his plan, presented in 1783 to Mr. Pitt, Mr. Palmer observed, that the post, instead of being the swiftest, was almost the slowest conveyance in the country; and that though, from the great improvement in our roads, other carriers had proportionably mended their speed, the post jogged on as heretofore. And, that

‡ The "Gazet" was published by authority in 1665 at Oxford, where the court had taken up their residence. It was there printed by Leonard Lichfield to the fourteenth number; and then reprinted and continued in London by Thomas Newcomb who became the sole printer and publisher of this paper. A complete set of the Gazet no where, perhaps, exists: But there are a few numbers of it in the library of All Souls, Oxford. At its commencement, Sir Francis Godolphin used to send a messenger every week to Exeter for this paper; which was the only Gazet that came into the west of Cornwall, and was laid on the table of the great hall at Godolphin for the inspection of the clergy and gentlemen of the neighbourhood. Sir Rose Price's MSS.

* How far the following anecdote may be deserving of credit, I do not know; but it was communicated to me by a most respectable correspondent "In a severely contested election for the county, in which the candidates were Edgcumbe, Boscawen, Glanville, (of Stowe) and Trevanion; Mr. Boscawen called upon Mr. Allen, and asked for a pint of his beer, requesting Mr. Allen to drink with him. Mr. Allen being naturally obliging felt no hesitation in complying with the request of the stranger. Mr. Boscawen (who was incog.) took an occasion to enquire the news of the neighbourhood and day; and the election being then most predominent, the subject was immediately introduced. After conversing in a more cursory manner, Mr. B. began to enquire into the general opinion of the private characters of the candidates, which Mr. Allen as freely gave him. Mr. B. then enquired who this Boscawen was, and what Allen thought of him? Allen observed, "he is much respected I believe in his neighbourhood, but in his public capacity we all suspect him to be unsound." The conversation having proceeded thus far, several of Mr Boscawen's attendants came up and addressed him in his proper form. Mr. Allen felt abashed and apologized for the freedom which he had ignorantly taken. "Give me your hand my honest friend" (cried the gentleman) "you have given me no offence, here is your money for the beer. I hope soon to undeceive the country, and prove that Boscawen is not unsound." It was not long after this that Mr. Allen removed to Bath, where I need not pursue him; and some relation of his succeeding him in the public-house, (some say his son-in-law, named Tucker) his name and family have long been forgotten in St. Blazey." See Hurd's Warburton for a further account of Allen.

Engraved by H^y Meyer.

To

Ralph Allen Daniel Esqr.

this print of his relation

Ralph Allen of Bath, Esqr.

is inscribed by R. POLWHELE.

the post (he added) was very unsafe, the frequent robberies of it, sufficiently proved. In the mean time, (he stated) the conveyance of parcels through stage-coaches and diligences was at once expeditious and secure. "It is advised, therefore (said he) to contract with the masters of these diligences, to carry the mail, and have a guard to protect the same. By such means, it is presumed, letters might be delivered in nearly half the time they now are from many parts of the kingdom." Mr. Palmer's plan was adopted in all its material points: And the acceleration and extension of the posts, are far greater than he would venture to promise. The mails are now conveyed not only in half their usual time to most parts of the kingdom, but in one third, and even one fourth of the time in many of the cross-posts. In 1783, when this regulation was proposed, the gross receipt of the post-office, annually was about £500,000. But the revenue was soon increased to a considerable amount. Thus the mail-coach was really the very perfection of carriages. And at this day, it runs its course with unvaried regularity, from one end of the island to the other—in Cornwall, over its whole mountainous range, from the Tamar to its utmost town.

2. In the mean time, our peninsularity points out our dependance, not on travelling so much as navigation, and shews, in a commercial light, our best roads and vehicles of little importance, when compared with our ships and our harbours.[D]

II. At the time when Campbell made his report of the products of Cornwall, they were said to amount, in the whole, to about half a million per ann. Three fifths of this were supposed to arise from the tin and copper mines; another from the rest of the mines and native commodities; and the remaining fifth was held to be about the value of our manufactures and fisheries.*

[D] "The many harbours and creeks of Cornwall furnishing the inhabitants with every means for foreign imports, and their many mines of tin, copper, lead bringing these in money to supply materials therewith to which we may add our fish and wool—few counties in England can pretend to vie with this, either for the necessaries or superfluities of life. Fuller, in his works, saith that God may be said in this county to rain meat (such the plenty thereof) and give dishes, too, made of pewter, which hath tin for the father, and lead for the mother thereof." Tonkin's MSS.

* Campbell vol I. p. 344.—"Great as this sum may appear (says our author) I conceive it to be rather below the real income, and that, in a very few years, the annual produce of this rich, and yet improveable county, might be at least doubled, by very easy and none of them very expensive establishments—such as erecting an office of assay in each of the coinage-towns, where the worth of the ores might be settled with certainty and their values certified by authority—founding a school and endowing a single college for the education of youth in mechanics and metallurgy, and for the comfortable maintenance of a few persons capable of teaching in those branches of knowledge, or who may distinguish themselves by new inventions in regard to machines, or by discoveries in respect to minerals and metals—putting the exportation of tin under a proper regulation, or encouraging the manufacturing of it here which might be done with vast advantage both to Cornwall and the country in general—allowing coals to be imported from Wales duty free, or under small duty; which would enable the people in this county to melt their own copper as well as tin, and to make other improvements from which they are now precluded. And possibly some hundred acres, in proper parts of the county, might be assigned out of the dutchy lands, for maintaining wood for this service only, the profits of which woods would defray the expence of the two former establishments. If the soil or air of Cornwall be thought unfriendly to timber, I reply, that it was disforested by king John: And trees will doubtless grow if those whose salaries depend on their produce, be appointed overseers of the woods. This would put it in the power of the Cornish to erect saltworks also, which would be beneficial to their fisheries, and turn to vast profit many of their minerals, that are now useless or advantageous only to foreigners. And though there be no great hope of producing any rich wines in Cornwall, yet the juice of the Cornish grape might be profitably

Our pilchard fishery affords employment for at least 12000 persons: And the capital engaged, has been estimated at £400,000.[A]

Herrings seldom pass the Landsend; abundant as they are in the Bristol channel. The herring-fishery is carried on, at St. Ives, on a large scale.

employed in turning their own copper into verdigris." I need not add, that some of these schemes have been happily carried into execution. But the speculations of strangers are often visionary.

[A] For the following description of the seine-nets and process of taking the pilchard at Mullion in the Mounts-bay I am indebted to my ingenious friend, Mr. Head surgeon at Helston. "The pilchards seldom make their appearance in the Mounts-Bay before the latter end of July; but more generally in the first and second weeks of August: at which season the seans are prepared to take them, which is sometimes done in immense quantities. The stop sean is a net about 220 fathoms in length, and from 10 to 14 or 16 in breadth. It is fixed both at its upper and lower part to a strong double rope through its whole length; this they call setting the sean. The head rope is buoyed up with a great quantity of cork fixed on it at about 10 inches distance, and the foot rope is sunk by means of hollow leads, placed at the distance of about three feet asunder, through which it runs. A boat of about eight tons burthen is appropriated to carry this net, which is placed with great care in a chamber in the stern of the boat; and so folded as to be thrown overboard with great expedition by two men, the most skilfull and strongest of the whole crew. The man who throws the head rope overboard is denominated the master seiner, and the other the foot rope man. The rest of the crew consists of the bow man (who seated at the bow oar, and having his eyes upon the huer directs the motion of the boat) and five other rowers of proved abilities. The ends of both the head and foot ropes are fixed at about five fathoms from each end of the net, to a strong rope of from 40 to 50 fathoms long. These ropes are denominated the warps, as by them the ends of the net are brought into contact as will be shewn by and bye. The other boats necessary to this fishery, are one of rather smaller dimensions than the sean boat; which carries the tuck sean, and whose crew consists of 5 or 6 men at most—and a smaller boat with a crew of three men denominated the cock boat. Each of the boats is furnished with several coils of strong rope, and a proportionate number of anchors and grapnells, for the purposes to be mentioned presently. The nets and every other apparatus, with the crews being got onboard, they now proceed to the place of their destination. This is generally some sandy bay into which the pilchards are expected to come, in their progress round the coast. The sean boat and follower or tuck-sean boat, anchor at about three or four hundred yards from the shore; whilst the cock boat proceeds to sea to the distance of a quarter of a mile, more or less, where the master of the cock boat keeps a good look out for the game. The huer in the mean time, takes his station upon the highest clift, near the boats so as perfectly to command a view of the sea to a considerable distance. The huer is the person upon whom the success of the fishery chiefly depends; as in addition to his discovering the fish when they approach the coast, he has the entire direction of the sean boat whilst inclosing them. He should therefore be a person who in addition to a quick and piercing eye for seeing the shoals at a distance, should possess an even temper not easily ruffled by trifling disappointments; a vigilant and active mind; with strength of body capable of enduring great fatigue; and firmness and good-humour to keep his crews in proper subordination, and to make them love and respect him; above all other things he should be a perfectly sober man in his own person, thereby not only to show a good example to the men under his command, but that if any of them should at any time get intoxicated, which they scarce ever fail to do when an opportunity offers, he may with the greater propriety correct them for it by imposing such fines at may be thought adequate to the offence. Thus qualified, and thus situated, he patiently waits the approach of the pilchards. On espying the shoal in its approach to the shore he is immediately on the alert; he holds in each hand a bush or branch of a tree with which to make the necessary signals to the different boats. When the shoal has proceeded so far as to give him a reasonable hope that he shall be able to catch it he makes the signal for the sean boat to weigh her anchor and to get the tarpaulings with which the sean is at other times covered, removed. Each man is now at his post and the most eager expectation is depicted in every countenance, but in none so forcibly as in that of the huer, who as the fish move in different directions, expresses by various turns of his own, the greatest anxiety, the liveliest hope, and when finally successful, the happiest exultation that can possibly be conceived. An unconcerned spectator indeed must be possessed of a great degree of apathy to view this scene and not take a lively interest in it; as it sometimes happens that a shoal of fish shall keep both huer and his crews busily employed for several honrs, and perhaps at last give them the slip. When however the shoal is so situated as to induce the huer to hope for success, he makes the signal to the sean boat for throwing the net overboard. The rowers immediately begin to pull with all their might, whilst the master seiner throws the warp overboard with a buoy fix-

Of the dried ling of Sylleh and of Mousehole, the former is generally preferred.*

ed at its extremity; as soon as it is all out he and the foot rope man, begin to throw out the net with the greatest expedition; the boat in the mean time proceeding with the greatest possible velocity, in order to surround the shoal; directed in its course by the orders of the bowman, whose eye is intently fixed upon the signals from the huer. As soon as the warp is thrown overboard from the sean boat, the cock boat takes her station upon it, and there waits till the whole of the stop sean is out. As soon as this is accomplished, the people in the cock boat begin to beat the water with their oars, in order to prevent the fish from approaching this part of the sean, as it still remains open: sometimes indeed to a considerable distance; when it becomes necessary to warp the two ends of the sean together in order to secure the pilchards. When the net is brought close at the ends, the head rope of each end is tied together with a piece of rope-yarn; this is repeated at the distance of every ten or twelve feet, till they have tied up about as many fathoms; by which means the foot ropes are brought close also, and the fish are now completely secured. A large anchor is now carried out from this doubled end of the sean, by which means it is secured from moving, or shifting its situation materially. The tides however require some attention; as, if nothing further were to be done, they would draw the net together, and by pressing the pilchards into a firm and compact body would force up the leads from the ground, when every fish would escape; and the greater the quantity of pilchards the more certain would this event be. To prevent this accident, three or four, or more grapnels are fixed to long warps of 30 or 40 fathoms more or less; which warps being tied firmly to the cork rope of the sean, in as many different places, the grapnels are then carried to the full extent of the warps and thrown into the sea; by which means the sean rides without being affected by the different currents of the tide. They then tie up a small quantity of the head rope from the fixture of each warp, in the same manner as was done by the ends of the net. Thus are the pilchards secured in the sean. Here it is the custom if the shoal is a good one (i. e. large) for all the seaners to collect in a body, and salute the huer with three hearty cheers. The next business is to take up the pilchards in order to their being removed to the cellars for curing. This is performed by another net called the tuck sean. This net is not above half so long as the stop sean, but of a different shape, being considerably deeper in the middle, or cod, than at either of the ends: it is also corked but not leaded. The boat with this net on board, proceeds to the inside of the sean; and being drawn forward by the head rope of the stop sean, the men throw the net overboard close to the stop net; tying the head rope of the tuck sean to the head rope of the stop sean, every three or more fathoms till the whole is thrown overboard. Thus a double wall of netting is formed as far as the tuck sean reaches. The tuck sean boat is now carried about ten or fifteen fathoms from the middle part of the tuck sean, and fastened with a hawser fixed to her midships, to the opposite side of the stop sean; by which means her broadside is brought towards the cod of the tuck sean. From twelve to fourteen of the seaners now go into her and begin to haul up the foot rope of the tuck sean from each end; cutting the cords by which it is fastened to the stop sean as they proceed. When they have got the whole of the foot rope into the boat, the pilchards are completely inclosed in the cod of the net as in a large bag; and nothing more remains but to take them into the boats which are always in waiting, to have them conveyed to the cellars. In this manner shoals of 2000 hogsheads have been taken at a time; but it is not often that the adventurers are so very fortunate; a shoal of from 200 to 500 hogsheads being thought a good catch." Another correspondent says: "it often happens that they enclose from 500 to 2000 hogsheads at a time when it requires several weeks to take them up: It has been known many times (particularly in the year 1790) that after the fish were enclosed they have sent to France for salt, which has arrived home in time to cure the said fish; but this is a great risk, as, after they are enclosed they are often lost by means of bad weather or strong tides. In some seasons the pilchard fishery has produced upwards of 60,000 hogsheads, each of which has contained from 2500 to 3900 fish of five score to the hundred, the number depending on the size of the fish; which in the first instance are salted in the fishermen's cellars and spread in regular rows and a layer of salt between each row of fish, so that it requires about eight bushels of of foreign salt, of 56 pounds to a bushel to cure a hogshead of pilchards in a proper manner to bear the hot climate of Italy, where they are often kept twelve months: After remaining in salt for about 32 days, the fish are packed in regular rows in the casks and pressed very hard by means of a lever and stones at the end thereof; the cask is then filled a second and a third time, and after the third repacking and well pressed, the cask is headed up and fit for export. Pilchards are a very fat fish, so that in consequence of being so pressed, the fish will not only keep longer and better (and the cask contain double the quantity of fish) but a hogshead of oil is extracted from every ten to twenty hogsheads of fish, perhaps on the average out of fifteen when the fish are fine and caught in the months of July and August, but the fish taken in September and October seldom produce so much, perhaps one out of twenty. When the fish are taken out of salt, near half the eight bushels remain, with which the fishermen cure fish either the same or the following season: The salt that then remains after being used twice, is found to be of great use for mixing with earth to manure the land. A hogshead of pilchards I apprehend is nearly equal to three barrels of herrings, as it contains about four hundred and a quarter of dry fish. In some seasons it has been sold (cask included) so low as 18s., at others, so high as 34s. exclusive of the bounty which is always the property of the fish curer."

* In Fuller's Worthies, we have a curious notice, respecting the salmon: "The nature of the salmon is, that if in the night he see any light, as of a candle or lightning, he will come to the top of the water and play in and out. The Cornish men used to take salmon and trout by tickling them under the bellies and so throwing them on the land."

Of our oysters, those at Helford have been famous for ages. The scallop, once very fine at Helford, has disappeared. But oysters are still plentiful, for the supply of Truro and other parts of Cornwall, and even of Southampton, whither we send them fresh and good in our fishing-smacks; though we shall never, perhaps, retrieve the art of the epicure Apicius, ho sent to the emperor Trajan from Italy into Persia, oysters that, when eaten there, were as fresh as on the day when they were taken.

Of our tin and copper, I have already spoken.[AB]

[AB] The following extract from "Minutes of evidence before the Committee"&c. &c. on the copper-business, 1799" may not be unacceptable to those who would compare the present with the state of the trade about sixteen years ago. "On the part of the Cornish miners it has been proved that in the last seven years the ores sold from the mines have amounted to £2237291; Cost, £2195123; Profits, £42168; against which profits must be placed the unsatisfied claims of Messrs. Boulton and Watt for the use of their engines, which are not much short of the whole sum That the capital employed in the mines is about £350,000. That in the last seven years the deep mines which produced about half the copper were wrought to a loss of £6690 beside above £2[illegible],000 claimed by Messrs. Boulton and Watt. That in the last six months (to the end of February 1799) the time when the price of copper is called unreasonable and exorbitant, the mines producing more than half of all the copper, were wrought to a loss of 1087l.; and that other mines suffered a loss of 17295l, under a standard of 113l. That owing to the increased price of labour and materials (above 50 per cent.) and the decreased richness of ores there is no reason to expect that the mines will in future be wrought to a greater advantage at the same standard. On those grounds the miners contend that any parliamentary restrictions which may tend to lower the price of copper would be impolitic, ruinous and unjust Impolitic inasmuch as their effect would be the very contrary to that which they have in view by stopping the deep mines, the quantity of copper produced would be lessened one half and the other half would consequently be sold dearer. Ruinous, forasmuch as they would deprive the owners of the deep mines of the chance which the times afford of recovering a part of the immense sum of 164,000l. which is sunk in them; and as they would do irreparable injury to the great concerns which depend on those mines. Unjust, because those sums have been expended on the faith of parliament in a full reliance that a free export would be always allowed, and the protecting import duty continued. On the part of the manufacturers it has been proved that their manufactories in general are much lessened; their export trade in particular, principally owing to the war, partly to the high price of copper and prohibiting duties in Germany, Russia&c. The trade to France, Spain, Italy and Holland is lost by the war, they cannot tell what quantity has been at any period, or is now exported That they are afraid if the copper should be cheaper on the continent than in England they shall be undersold, that they have been undersold in some articles, and that as far back as the year 1790. As to the markets of France, Spain, Italy, and Holland are lost by the war, it can be in the northern markets only that they are affected by the high price of copper. The returns from the custom-house afford that information which the maufacturers could not give.

An account of the export of brass and plated goods abstracted from the custom-house returns.

	1790, 1791, 1792. Tons.		1793, 1794, 1795, Tons.
France, Flanders, Holland, Spain, Cannaries, Italy, &c.	424		58
Germany, Poland, Russia, Sweden, Denmark Prussia and Norway.	84		96
	Tons 508	*Tons*	154
Say ⅔ copper, 236 Tons.		*Decrease*	354
			508

The average quantity of those goods exported in 1796, 1797, 1798 was	*Tons* 2652
Deduct in 1790, 1791, 1792,	2458
	Tons 194

This statement proves first, that the export to France &c. has been lost by the war, that the export to Germany &c. has increased notwithstanding the strict prohibition in Russia, Prussia, and Germany That the general export has increased notwithstanding the loss of the french and other markets by the war, which heretofore took one sixth of the whole export. That there is no danger of their being undersold in foreign markets in consequence of the low price of copper abroad is proved by showing that copper is at present much dearer in every market in Europe than in England."

Engraved by I. H. Meyer.

To Sir William Lemon Bart: M. P. for Cornwall:

This Plate of his Grand-Father

William Lemon Esq.r

is inscribed by R. POLWHELE.

These commodities are exported (with various others) from Looe, Polperro, Fawey, Charles-town, Mevagissey, Truro, Penryn, Falmouth,* Helford, Marazion, Penzance, St. Ives, Hayle, Portreath, Trevaunance, Porth, Padstow, Port-Isaac, and Bude.

In 1737, the officers of the customs &c. &c. were, for Looe, Nicholas Dyer, collector, his salary, £60 and five other officers, £185; for Fawey, William Tolley Treffry, £60 and twelve other officers, £160; for Falmouth, William Pye, collector, himself and clerk £70 and twenty-four other officers; for Penryn, Ambrose Thompson, collector, £40 and six inferior officers £150; for Truro, Zachariah Williams, collector, £40 and two tidesmen and a waiter, £80; for Gweek, Henry Tremenheere, collector, himself and clerk, £60 and two other officers, £50; for Penzance, Nathaniel Page, £60 and twenty other officers, £50; for St. Ives, Vivian Stevens, collector, £30 and six other officers, £124; and for Padstow, Richard Score, jun. collector, £40 and nine other officers, £78.† Our contraband trade was, ten or twelve years ago, of a very alarming magnitude. And, since the peace, the smugglers have reappeared in formidable bodies.[B]

III. Of the gentlemen who, in a mercantile character, live in the memory of a grateful country, or stand high in our estimation, were Robartes of Truro, through whom merchandize was dignified with an earldom, Hender Molesworth to whom Pencarrow owes its aggrandizement—Gregor of Truro, whence the house of Trewarthenic—Hearle of Penryn and Lemon of Truro—and Daniell, also of Truro; whose son Ralph Allen Daniell Esq. has enjoyed for several years that elegant retirement of Trelisick, leaving to the world many children to reflect honour on his name; among whom Thomas Daniell Esq. of Truro, has claims, not from birth only, to the priority.—Were I to memorize those who have not resided in Cornwall, I should mention as the most opulent, Hope Willyams Esq. and the Grenfells. But in recounting names of the first respectability, I must not omit the Foxes of Falmouth, Daubuz of Truro, and Oxenham of Penzance.—Looking back to the persons enumerated, we cannot but observe, that there is one, in particular, who merits much more at our hands than a transitory notice —I mean William Lemon Esq. Our "recollections" of such a man cannot but be interesting; since from his useful and comprehensive knowledge, the county derived incalculable advantages. He was born in the west of Cornwall (I have heard, Breage,) in 1697. A clerk (if I have not been misinformed, to Mr. Coster) he had the best opportunities of making his observations on the conduct of our mining adventurers and all their concerns, and of exercising his sagacity in detecting er-

* The exports from Falmouth are principally tin, copper, tin-plates, oil pilchards, and occasionally lead, and American cargoes warehoused for exportation. Some of the merchants in Falmouth do much business with Russia, Norway, Hamburgh, Italy, Turkey, and Portugal; and in time of peace with Holland, France, and Spain. A very considerable trade is carried on by some of the merchants at Falmouth in importing sundry supplies for the use of the mines and fishery, and also in importing salt from France, Spain, Portugal, and the Mediterranean for the use of the fishery Cargoes of wine have been frequently sent from Spain to Falmouth in order to pay the duties, and afterwards re-exported to Canada to comply with the navigation act.

† See Chamberlayne's Present State, &c. &c.

[B] "In 1803, there were twenty vessels of from nine to upwarde of one hundred tons burthen annually employed in smuggling spirituous liquors, wine, tobacco and salt from the island of Guernsey to the coast of Cornwall, viz. from Fowey round the Landsend to Port Isaac; the probable quantity yearly conveyed by those vessels was about 337,200 gallons of spirits and wine, and about 110 tons of tobacco and salt." From J. Beynon, late collector of the excise at Falmouth.—About this time a medical gentleman of my acquaintance informed me that the people of Cadgwith were all thrown into consternation by the story of a smuggler, who about midnight crossing Goonhilly-downs, saw in the great pool there, the vision of a lugger or king's ship!—"Not a Cadgwith-man (said he) will now venture upon Goonhilly."

rors, and his invention in planning improvements. In 1724, he married Isabella Vibert of Tolver in Gulval with whom he received a fortune sufficient to enable him to pursue his favourite speculations in mines: And so happily were they directed, that he shortly had the power of turning his whole attention to that object. He was the first who conceived the project of working the mines upon the grand scale on which they are at present carried on: and the success attending it, aided by the discovery of fire engines, caused him to enter largely into that commerce, (now divided amongst many) which became necessary for the supply of materials for so extended an undertaking.—He carried on his trade at Hayle, and at Truro; to which latter place he removed. His thorough knowlege in mining procured him a grant from Frederick Prince of Wales for 30 years of all minerals except tin in the duchy lands in Cornwall; where he made valuable discoveries. But his memorial produced to Sir R. Walpole, proving the policy of taking off the duty upon coals, was in its result most beneficial to himself and his countrymen. It was an admirable paper, stating in the clearest terms the advantage that must accrue to the trade from the discharge of that debenture. And it discovered such a mastery of the subject, as drew from the minister the most flattering compliments. In the last convocation of tinners, Mr. Lemon was one of the stannators; and in the regulation of the stannaries, his suggestions were, of course, of prime importance. In the framing of the militia act, government was indebted to him for several useful hints. There were few, in short, possessed talents equal to his own, and none who exerted them more to the advantage of his country. He served the office of sheriff, in 1742. With all this strength of mind, and all this commercial knowlege, he was conscious of deficiencies, and (what is rare in affluence) he owned and lamented them, though not with unavailing regret, but used every effort to supply them. Late in life, he put himself under the tuition of Mr. Conon, master of the Truro grammar-school, and (it is said) made some progress in the learned languages. I have given an instance of his humility—or rather of his resolution: And if, in proof of his liberal way of thinking, and his generous feeling, I produce a very trivial anecdote, let it be remembered that characters are best illustrated by little familiar occurrences. Mr. Lemon was as much attached to a Cornish chough, as an esquire of elder days ever was to "hawke high tow'ring or accoasting lowe." The favourite chough used at all times to obey his call. If he were walking on Truro-green, or through the streets, the chough mixing occasionally with other bids, or perched alone upon the housetop, would fly to him instantly at his whistle. This bird, therefore, was regarded at Truro with almost as much veneration as a stork at Athens. It happened, however, that Mr. Thomas, (our present vicewarden) then a schoolboy at Conon's, taking up his gun, contrary to the rules of the school, and proceeding to the back-quay where he had observed some birds, shot among them, and unluckily killed the sacred chough. His situation was indescribable. He was told by the by-standers that he would certainly be hanged. He had incurred the danger of a flogging for shooting, and of Mr. Lemon's displeasure for shooting his chough. But amidst despair, he at once took courage, went to Mr. Lemon's house, knocked at the door, was introduced to Mr. Lemon, and trembling and in tears, confessed the fact. Mr. Lemon paused a moment, and then said he was sorry for the poor bird—but freely forgave the little delinquent for so much candour in acknowledging his fault, and more than that, promised to keep it a profound secret, or, if it should come to Conon's ears, to intercede for him—a transaction apparently trifling, yet I think worth recording; as it discovered the mind and the heart—a transaction equally creditable to both parties. To amuse themselves with the chough, (a pleasant though most mischievous bird) was frequent with gentlemen in Mr. Lemon's days: and the recreation of ringing, was equally common. For her musical bells, Kenwyn had to thank Mr. Lemon, at whose expence chiefly they were erected, and who (with the Reverend Samuel Walker and other gentlemen of Truro) used often to pass the evening in an exercise, which the memory of Kennicott (a great ringer as well as a great Hebraist) must have rendered respectable in our eyes!—But notwithstanding his chough and his bells, Mr. Lemon had no familiarity in his deportment. To him all ages looked up, with a degree of awe. His approach occasioned a sensation. He owed much to a fine commanding person, but more to the opinion of his mental superiority. Such was Mr. Lemon (the founder of one of the first families* of Cornwall) whom I have endeavoured to delineate, though the sketch, I feel, is but too feeble and imperfect. For when I look down from this place on "the pride of Truro," though I could have known him only from report (since he died in the year of my birth) I cannot but imagine him there, giving to his "little senate laws," and (more happy than Cato) anticipating the future opulence which, through his wisdom and knowlege, should advance his favourite town to the first respectability, and which should emanate thence, as from a common centre, to the east and to the west, to be enjoyed through the years of many generations.

* He bought Carclew (now the seat of his grandson, Sir William Lemon) in 1749—His residence at Truro before the building of the great house, was in church-lane, now the property of Edward Collins, Esq.—Mr. Lemon died at Truro 25th March 1760, in the 63rd year of his age, and is buried there with the rest of the Lemon-family. He had one son named William; who resided in the house where Mr. Thomas John's house now stands. William died long before his father, leaving 3 children, William and John; and Anne, who married John Buller of Morval Esq. William, (who was created a baronet in 1774, and has from that time represented Cornwall in Parliament) married Jane, eldest daughter of James Buller of Morval, M. P. for Cornwall, by Jane the daughter of Allen first Lord Bathurst, by whom he has had eleven children. Sons; William, the eldest died unmarried; Charles, the second, married Charlotte Anne, sister to the present Earl of Ilchester, by whom he has issue. Daughters; Anne married Sir John Davey; Maria married Jodrell; Louisa married Lieut. Col. Dyke; Isabella married Anthony Buller; Caroline married J. H. Tremayne; and three are unmarried, and one dead.

END OF VOLUME THE FOURTH.

Michell and Co. Printers, Truro.